Justice and the Capabilities Appr

The International Library of Justice
Series Editor: Tom Campbell

Titles in the Series:

Global Justice
Christian Barry and Holly Lawford-Smith

Justice and the Capabilities Approach
Thom Brooks

Theories of Justice
Tom Campbell and Alejandra Mancilla

Distributive Justice
Julian Lamont

Procedural Justice
Larry May and Paul Morrow

Intergenerational Justice
Lukas H. Meyer

Justice and the Capabilities Approach

Edited by

Thom Brooks

Newcastle University, UK

Routledge
Taylor & Francis Group
LONDON AND NEW YORK

First published 2012 by Ashgate Publishing

Published 2016 by Routledge
2 Park Square, Milton Park, Abingdon, Oxon OX14 4RN
711 Third Avenue, New York, NY 10017, USA

First issued in paperback 2017

Routledge is an imprint of the Taylor & Francis Group, an informa business

British Library Cataloguing in Publication Data
Justice and the capabilities approach. – (The library of
essays on justice)
1. Justice. 2. Sociological jurisprudence.
I. Series II. Brooks, Thom.
340.1'15–dc22

Library of Congress Control Number: 2011935103

ISBN 13: 978-1-138-10773-1 (pbk)
ISBN 13: 978-1-4094-3042-1 (hbk)

Contents

PART V COSMOPOLITANISM AND GLOBAL JUSTICE

Acknowledgements

The editor and publishers wish to thank the following for permission to use copyright material.

Chicago Journal of International Law for the essay: Diane P. Wood (2010), 'Constitutions and Capabilities: A (Necessarily) Pragmatic Approach', *Chicago Journal of International Law*, **10**, pp. 415–29.

Columbia Journal of Gender and Law for the essay: Amrita Basu (2010), 'Who Secures Women's Capabilities in Martha Nussbaum's Quest for Social Justice?', *Columbia Journal of Gender and Law*, **19**, pp. 201–17.

Copyright Clearance Center for the essays: Martha C. Nussbaum (2007), 'The Supreme Court 2006 Term – Foreword: Constitutions and Capabilities: "Perception" against Lofty Formalism', *Harvard Law Review*, **121**, pp. 4–97. Copyright © 2007 Harvard Law Association; Noah Feldman (2007), 'Cosmopolitan Law?', *Yale Law Journal*, **116**, pp. 1024–70. Copyright © 2007 Yale Law Journal Company, Inc.

Fordham Law Review for the essay: Robin West (2001), 'Rights, Capabilities, and the Good Society', *Fordham Law Review*, **69**, pp. 1901–32.

John Wiley & Sons for the essays: Amartya Sen (2004), 'Elements of a Theory of Human Rights', *Philosophy and Public Affairs*, **32**, pp. 315–56; Ingrid Robeyns (2005), 'Assessing Global Poverty and Inequality: Income, Resources, and Capabilities', *Metaphilosophy*, **36**, pp. 30–49.

Journal of Philosophy for the essay: Amartya Sen (1985), 'Well-being, Agency, and Freedom: The Dewey Lectures 1984', *Journal of Philosophy*, **82**, pp. 169–221. Copyright © 1985 Amartya Sen.

Philosophical Topics for the eessay: Thom Brooks (2009), 'The Problem with Polygamy', *Philosophical Topics*, **37**, pp. 109–22.

Philosophy and Public Affairs for the essays: Ronald Dworkin (2000), 'Equality of Welfare', in *Sovereign Virtue*, Cambridge, MA: Harvard University Press, pp. 11–64. Copyright © 2000 Philosophy and Public Affairs; Ronald Dworkin (2000), 'Equality of Resources', in *Sovereign Virtue*, Cambridge, MA: Harvard University Press, pp. 65–119, 478–80. Copyright © 2000 Philosophy and Public Affairs.

Taylor & Francis for the essay: Martha C. Nussbaum (1997), 'Capabilities, Entitlements, Rights: Supplementation and Critique', *Journal of Human Development and Capabilities*, **12**, pp. 23–37.

Every effort has been made to trace all the copyright holders, but if any have been inadvertently overlooked the publishers will be pleased to make the necessary arrangement at the first opportunity.

Series Preface

Justice is one of the most enduring and central concepts within applied philosophy, and generates a vast and varied literature. This six-volume *International Library of Justice* series meets a number of distinct needs. The first volume, *Theories of Justice*, edited by Tom Campbell and Alejandra Mancilla, comprises a selection of some of the most important essays on the general theory of justice published over recent decades. One interesting aspect of this literature is the renewed attention that is being given to the notion of desert within theories of justice. Two further volumes, edited by Larry May and Paul Morrow, and Julian Lamont, respectively, deal with two traditional topics in justice that have undergone significant development in recent years – namely procedural justice, particularly with respect to constitutional law, and distributive justice, taking in important recent work on egalitarianism. Another two volumes, edited by Christian Barry and Holly Lawford-Smith, and Lukas H. Meyer, respectively, focus on the application of justice to less familiar areas, such as global institutions as they bear upon contemporary problems relating to extreme poverty and intergenerational justice. The sixth volume, *Justice and the Capabilities Approach*, edited by Thom Brooks, concentrates on the recent influential work by Amartya Sen and Martha Nussbaum on the relevance the concept of human capabilities in the formulation of policy on distributive justice, especially in developing countries.

Given the political priority that accrues to those matters that are categorized as having to do with justice, there is a tendency to extend the term beyond its distinctive uses and incorporate a very wide range of social values that relate to the proper ordering of social and political relationships. While the editors of each volume have striven to resist this inflation of the term 'justice' to cover all aspects of right human relationships, inevitably there is, in each volume, a substantial overlap with the bodies of literature concerned with the ideals of equality, reciprocity and humanity.

One such overlap arises with respect to rights, particularly human rights. Indeed, in some fields the discourse of justice has been largely overtaken by that of rights. The significance of this shift in emphasis within political rhetoric, which is one of the themes that features in *Theories of Justice*, recurs within the subsequent selections, raising interesting questions concerning contemporary political priorities and differing institutional approaches to social order.

The volumes in this series will assist those engaged in scholarly research by making available some of the most important contemporary essays on particular topics within the contemporary discourse of justice. The essays are reproduced in full, with the original pagination for ease of reference and citation.

The editors have been selected for their eminence in the study of law, politics and philosophy. Each volume represents each editor's selection of the most seminal recent essays in English on an aspect of justice. The Introductions present an overview of the issues in that particular volume, together with comments on the background and significance of the selected essays.

TOM CAMPBELL
Series Editor
Professorial Fellow, Centre for Applied Philosophy and Public Ethics (CAPPE),
Charles Sturt University, Canberra

Introduction

The capabilities approach is a widely influential alternative theory of justice, popularized by Amartya Sen, laureate of the Nobel Prize in Economics, and Martha C. Nussbaum. *Justice and the Capabilities Approach* is the first work of its kind to collect, in one volume, the most influential essays in the field, covering a number of topics, including distributive justice, human rights, constitutional law, the family and global justice. This book should help inform both scholars and students new to the study of the capabilities approach of the importance and complexity of the wider debate, as well as shed light on how the approach might be further improved and applied.

For this collection I have carefully selected essays that best explore key developments and central issues concerning the relationship between justice and the capabilities approach. This Introduction begins by providing a brief background to the capabilities approach before offering general remarks on the essays that are reproduced here. The aim is to help clarify the central issues and provide a helpful background.

The Capabilities Approach

A capability specifies an ability to do or be *x*. The ability to do or be *x* is distinct from whether we *choose* to do or be *x*. This difference is between our having a capability and actual functioning. Our actual functioning reflects our actual achievements. In contrast, capabilities capture the freedom of persons to achieve. This is a fundamental distinction that the capabilities approach is thought to capture best.

One central example of this distinction is as follows. What is the difference between starving and fasting? The two are relatively indistinguishable from the perspective of actual functioning because both the person starving and the person fasting possess the same achievement. The key difference is a difference of freedom. The person fasting may have the same actual functioning of a person starving, but only the person fasting possesses the freedom to choose to function in this way. His starvation is a product of choice. Capabilities mark out what we have the ability to do or achieve (Sen, 1999a). The person who fasts retains his capability to bodily health precisely because he has chosen to fast. Thus, the capabilities approach is grounded in a view about freedom: we have capabilities where we have the freedom to choose in certain conditions. It is not enough that I possess a particular good; I must possess sufficient opportunities for capability satisfaction. While certain goods may assist this pursuit, we must look much deeper into how goods relate to persons in terms of capability satisfaction.

So which capabilities do we have? Famously, Sen does not offer us any specific list. The task of drawing up a list of capabilities has fallen to many others, although the best known list is provided by Martha C. Nussbaum. Her theory of capabilities is a clear development of

Sen's approach with the addition of greater philosophical sophistication. Nussbaum argues that capabilities should mark out a threshold of a universal social minimum of 'a life that is worthy of the dignity of the human being' (2000, pp. 5–6). Although the capabilities approach is not itself a complete theory of justice, it does offer a standard that should be adopted by any just political society.

Nussbaum identifies the following ten capabilities:

1. *Life.* Being able to live to the end of a human life of normal length; not dying prematurely, or before one's life is so reduced as to be not worth living.
2. *Bodily health.* Being able to have good health, including reproductive health; to be adequately nourished; to have adequate shelter.
3. *Bodily integrity.* Being able to move freely from place to place; to be secure against violent assault, including sexual assault and domestic violence; having opportunities for sexual satisfaction and for choice in matters of reproduction.
4. *Senses, imagination, and thought.* Being able to use the senses, to imagine, think, and reason – and to do these things in a 'truly human' way, a way informed and cultivated by an adequate education, including, but by no means limited to, literacy and basic mathematical and scientific training. Being able to use imagination and thought in connection with experiencing and producing works and events of one's own choice, religious, literary, musical, and so forth. Being able to use one's mind in ways protected by guarantees of freedom of expression with respect to both political and artistic speech, and freedom of religious exercise. Being able to have pleasurable experiences and to avoid nonbeneficial pain.
5. *Emotions.* Being able to have attachments to things and people outside ourselves; to love those who love and care for us, to grieve at their absence; in general, to love, to grieve, to experience longing, gratitude, and justified anger. Not having one's emotional development blighted by fear and anxiety . . .
6. *Practical reason.* Being able to form a conception of the good and to engage in critical reflection about the planning of one's life . . .
7. *Affiliation.* (A) Being able to live with and toward others, to recognize and show concern for other human beings, to engage in various forms of social interaction; to be able to imagine the situation of another . . .(B) Having the social bases of self-respect and nonhumiliation; being able to be treated as a dignified being whose worth is equal to that of others. This entails provisions of non-discrimination on the basis of race, sex, sexual orientation, ethnicity, caste, religion, national origin.
8. *Other species.* Being able to live with concern for and in relation to animals, plants, and the world of nature.
9. *Play.* Being able to laugh, to play, to enjoy recreational activities.
10. *Control over one's environment.* (A) *Political.* Being able to participate effectively in political choices that govern one's life; having the right of political participation, protections of free speech and association. (B) *Material.* Being able to hold property (both land and movable goods), and having property rights on an equal basis with others; having the right to seek employment on an equal basis with others . . . (Nussbaum, 2011, pp. 33–34)

While others have produced different lists of capabilities, these lists have shared significant overlaps with Nussbaum's list (see Alkire, 2002; Qizilbash, 2002; Robeyns, 2003). Whereas Sen often refers to the approach as a *capability* approach, it is Nussbaum who emphasizes the approach as a *capabilities* approach. This is meant to highlight the approach's pluralism: it is not about any one capability, but a range of capabilities. This general characterization has been broadly accepted by other proponents of the approach. Crucially, the capabilities approach can respect pluralism, and these capabilities are thought to capture human freedom better than alternatives. For example, the utilitarian has the problem that utility measures may differ widely between persons, rendering it interpersonally incomparable. We each may perceive pleasure, pain and other concepts in different, perhaps contradictory, ways. The capabilities approach overcomes this problem through its inherent pluralism: the approach can account for interpersonal variability as it is 'intrinsically information-pluralist' (Sen, this volume, pp. 32–34 at p. 34).

Each capability is thought to hold central importance for us. If any single capability were closed off to us, then something of importance would be withheld from us. We do not always need to exercise capabilities whenever and wherever possible. Rather, it is crucial that we have the opportunities to do so whenever and wherever we choose. Capabilities are also non-competitive: there are no justifiable trade-offs between them. We should not be satisfied with being able to choose some capabilities, but not all. All capabilities should be available without trade-offs. The ability to exercise capabilities best secures our human dignity. Thus, we cannot forever close off any capability even if we would want to consent to it. While I may choose to act *as if* certain capabilities are closed off, I must always be free to choose all capabilities nonetheless. The capabilities approach is centred on the idea of freedom. Therefore, it is not *that* someone *has chosen* to do *x* that is of central importance, but rather *whether* someone *has the opportunity* to choose to do *x*.

We will now turn to a consideration of how the capabilities approach may be applied in the areas that concern this book – namely distributive justice, human rights, constitutional law, the family, and cosmopolitanism and global justice.

Distributive Justice

A crucial issue for theories of justice is distribution.[1] This is often referred to as distributive justice. One common view argues that distributive justice should be centred on resource allocations. Our concern should be on the distribution of resources in our search for justice. For example, considerations about justice should focus on levels of relative wealth. Thus, John Rawls (1971) defends the difference principle which states that a just political society should endorse a distribution whereby the least advantaged are best off. The focus is on the position of the least advantaged in terms of resource allocations.

In Chapter 1 of this volume Amartya Sen challenges this common view, arguing that it fails to satisfactorily account for the diversity of human beings (see also Sen, 1980). Our lives are diverse in a multitude of ways. We do not share the same needs with respect to climatic conditions, health, working conditions and many other factors. Since there is no 'one size fits

1 For an excellent discussion of justice more generally, see Campbell (2010).

all' model available, in response we must become more sensitive to this diversity as we find it. Therefore, although our understandings of need may overlap with others, we must ensure that we are suitably sensitive to important differences as these may become easily overlooked. The capabilities approach is Sen's alternative to do precisely this.

For example, we should consider economic development. One commonplace view is that we can measure improved development in terms of improvements to a country's gross domestic product (GDP). However, Sen (1999b) argues that development is best understood in terms of capabilities: we should focus on alleviating capability deprivations and not view development primarily in terms of resources. This is because greater resources do not entail that people will enjoy greater freedoms and capabilities. The Indian state of Kerala ranks comparatively low in terms of resources. However, it performs much better than many communities elsewhere, with far larger resources in terms of infant mortality, life expectancy and literacy. Sen concludes that development should focus on the ability of persons to freely exercise their capabilities as this best captures a more robust view of the human condition. Focusing only on resources makes us unable to appreciate development in terms of freedom. Thus, Kerala is, in fact, a better model for development than many more wealthy communities because it is better able to secure capabilities for its people.

Treating others equally might then mean that we should ensure that others enjoy capability satisfaction. But is this correct? In Chapters 2 and 3, taken from his book, *Sovereign Virtue* (2000), Ronald Dworkin argues that there are two different and important theories of distributional equality: equality of welfare and equality of resources. The first concerns distributing or transferring resources among persons until no further transfer leaves them more equal in terms of welfare. The second operates likewise until no further transfer leaves them more equal in terms of resources. Egalitarians must choose which they prefer.

Each theory runs up against potential objections. If equality of resources were our aim, would this be an attractive approach? One important objection is that an equality of resources would undermine equality in other respects. Consider someone with a physical disability. This person will require additional resources in terms of a wheelchair, ramps and so on in order to function in ways in which those without such a disability can function. In such circumstances, equality of welfare may appear more compelling. However, this approach encounters an important objection as well: the problem of expensive tastes. You and I may require very different resources to satisfy similar welfare needs. For example, you may prefer champagne and I may prefer beer. While the notion of equality of resources seems to run into problems, the problem of expensive tastes raises new concerns for equality of welfare.

The capabilities approach is thought to overcome these worries. It addresses the problem of equality of resources by claiming that we must ensure the capabilities of others to do or be *x*. Capability satisfaction for one person may require very different resources from another person. This is unproblematic. But what of expensive tastes? The capability approach is thought to overcome this worry as well because it focuses on the capabilities that mark out something essential and independent of individual taste. Although thresholds for capability satisfaction may differ from one community to the next, capabilities are thought to be sufficiently resilient and robust.

Human Rights

The capabilities approach has a close relationship with the idea of human rights. Both capabilities and human rights are thought to mark out important aspects of the protection of human dignity. Both serve as side-constraints on the ways in which we may pursue social goals: they signify a social minimum that any political society must secure (Nussbaum, 1997; also Chapter 4, this volume). Thus, states may pursue their conception of the social good in whatever way they like provided that they do not violate opportunities for their citizens to freely exercise their capabilities. Nussbaum says: 'I regard my list of basic capabilities in this way, as a list of very urgent items that should be secured to people no matter what else we pursue' (1997, p. 300).

There are a few notable differences. One difference concerns specificity. The language of rights is perhaps overly vague and unhelpful. The claim that 'I have a right to *x*' is sometimes too imprecise about what we may have rights to and any correlative duties. In addition, such rights-talk may be overly rigid and work against welfare (Posner, 2008). The capabilities approach aspires to provide more clarity: when we say that 'I have a capability to do or be *x*' we state something of substantive significance that is denser than most rights-talk – or so capabilities proponents often claim. A second important difference between capabilities and human rights is that the latter relate only to human beings. In contrast, capabilities are thought to more easily extend to include non-human animals (Nussbaum, 2006).

An important concern is whether capabilities should be conceived as rights. Rights are side-constraints on justifiable state action. The problem with demanding that states ensure capability satisfaction is that the effort to protect and promote capabilities may clash with individual rights. As Robin West states in Chapter 5, 'To secure the minimal preconditions of the good society for all of us, the state would have to violate the *rights* we hold as individuals – rights of liberty, property, contract, and privacy' (p. 194, emphasis in original). We might be best off with a theory of care rather than capabilities.

Capability proponents, such as Amartya Sen in Chapter 6 of this volume, would argue that there is no such conflict between theory and practice. In fact, if rights were more closely understood in terms of capabilities, then such talk would have greater acceptability and would be more realizable. This is because the capabilities approach has an inherent interpersonal pluralism, as already noted, and this overcomes the sometimes too rigid and stale conception of rights-talk.

Constitutional Law

Martha Nussbaum has more recently argued that the capabilities approach can help inform constitutional law.[2] In Chapter 7 she argues that the capabilities approach recommends an improved way of reasoning: it is a 'realistic, historically and imaginatively informed type of practical reasoning that focuses on the actual abilities of people to choose and act in their concrete social settings' (p. 269). Capability talk is also not inappropriate for American legal discourse. The reason is clear: American jurisprudence has been heavily influenced by

2 See also Nussbaum (2010a) on same-sex marriage.

numerous seventeenth- and eighteenth-century thinkers who articulated mixed Aristotelian and Stoic ideas of natural law through the then prevalent classical education. These influences are, in fact, also the philosophical inspiration behind the capabilities approach: indeed, the approach is perhaps best seen as a more philosophically complex and 'up-to-date' understanding of this past view.[3] Moreover, many of the capabilities in Nussbaum's list can be found in some related form within the US Bill of Rights (p. 303).

Diane P. Wood (Chapter 8) offers a powerful and constructive counter-reply. She agrees with Nussbaum that there are many intersections between the law and capabilities. She notes further that many constitutions, such as those found in India and South Africa, better exemplify provisions that appear to adapt, or at least reflect, the capabilities approach. Thus, the approach possesses genuine applicability in the case of the United States; however, it is not merely an American approach but, rather, one that is international in both spirit and fact.

Wood's critique is that Nussbaum's analysis concerns constitutional law. Moreover, Nussbaum must extend this analysis to a consideration of states. This is because

> [s]tates remain responsible for some of the most fundamental government tasks, such as the creation of relationships between people (marriage, adoption, inheritance), education, the definition and enforcement of property rights, and the law of contract. (Wood, this volume, p. 364)

While we have a view as to how capabilities may inform constitutional frameworks, we need more on how it may inform legal particulars. State law is one aspect, but another is how the capabilities approach might be dealt with in a court of law. There are any number of lines that must be drawn concerning liability and so on. Wood fears that judges are ill-placed to make such judgements with respect to the capabilities approach

Nussbaum has responded by arguing that her approach 'says what should be delivered to people, not through what set of institutions' (2010b, p. 432). This raises the problem of political structure for advocates of the approach – a problem that is highlighted well by Wood. This debate is particularly stimulating not simply because it emphasizes how the capabilities approach may be applied to law, but also because it helps frame the shape of future work yet to come. No doubt this will be an area of particular interest and exciting development for jurisprudential and institutional design scholars in considering how best to realize this view of justice.

The Family

The capabilities approach speaks to issues of the family and justice in important ways. One way concerns family structure. For example, would the capabilities approach endorse polygamy? While Nussbaum has argued that polygamy is 'a structurally unequal practice' (1999, p. 98), it is a practice that may be made acceptable. The problem is that there is an asymmetry of power between men and women. If we could identify 'a sex-equal polygamy' that respected

[3] It is worth noting that this intellectual heritage is substantively 'thick' and clearly includes the British Idealist philosopher Thomas Hill (T.H.) Green (see Nussbaum, this volume, pp. 316, 330). On Green, see Brooks (2003, 2008, 2011).

the consent of men and women equally, then polygamy would be justified (Nussbaum, 2008, p. 197). We do have a capability to form loving relationships, and polygamy may be such a relationship provided that it can respect the equality of men and women.

Thom Brooks (Chapter 9) argues that polygamy is objectionable on several grounds. First, he argues that it is a practice that is problematic in fact. Many studies have shown that women and children in polygamous relationships fare less well on many counts of well-being, such as education and family violence. Furthermore, men fare less well also, with some studies finding higher rates of alcoholism and poorer education. Second, Brooks argues that polygamy is also problematic in theory. Polygamy is structurally unequal all the way down. Polygamous marriages are heterosexual and take the form of either polygyny (one husband and multiple wives) or (far more rarely) polyandry (one wife and multiple husbands). In either form, one person has greater powers of consent than the others. Consider polygyny. The husband alone consents to each marriage; each wife only consents to her marriage with the husband. This is more vivid when we consider possibilities for exit. The husband alone can divorce each wife or all wives, but each wife can only divorce him. Who is a member of that wife's family in terms of other wives and children may not be a product of her consent. Although we may find polygamy acceptable on other grounds, it is structurally unequal and a violation of equal capability satisfaction.

Amrita Basu (Chapter 10) turns our attention to feminism and transnational institutions. Such groups include Women Living Under Muslim Laws (WLUML), for example. Transnational institutions can play an important role in promoting and protecting capabilities. This is partly because they can provide influence and leverage where democratic institutions are weak or lacking. The capabilities approach is uniquely situated for transnational solidarity, given the approach's universalism. This has particular significance for promoting the freedom of women, as they are often vulnerable in states that lack or have weak democratic institutions. The capabilities approach is not only a compelling view of freedom, but also an approach that has particular importance for women as well.

Cosmopolitanism and Global Justice

Basu's interest in feminism and transnational institutions leads us to consider the capabilities approach more broadly within the context of cosmopolitanism and global justice.

Noah Feldman (Chapter 12) considers our possible legal duties to others living beyond our borders. He explores the cosmopolitanism of Nussbaum's capabilities approach which holds the individual, rather than the state, as having most ethical significance. He argues that law contains 'the commands of a particular community and an aspiration to the universal' (p. 477) but is political at its core.

Ingrid Robeyns (Chapter 11) considers capabilities with reference to global poverty and issues concerning development. How can we best evaluate well-being, poverty, and inequality in the context of global justice? Robeyns argues that resource-based evaluations are not only deeply divided and conflicting, but also offer a poor option. The capabilities approach is a much improved perspective, partly because it considers a wider range of issues, including personal agency. The capabilities approach, thus, can capture more because it is more attentive to the particulars. Global justice is best understood from the perspective of the capabilities approach.

Conclusion

The capabilities approach has seen many developments since its initial formulation by Amartya Sen. Philosophers, led by Martha Nussbaum, have endowed the approach with greater philosophical sophistication and popularity to the extent that it has now become a powerful alternative to rival theories of justice. This collection brings together some of the best classic and contemporary work in this area. My hope is that the reader will enjoy these essays at least half as much as I enjoyed putting them together.

Acknowledgements

I must thank Tom Campbell for his warm encouragement from the outset of this project. Special thanks must also go to Valerie Saunders for her help and patience. Finally, my greatest thanks go to a wonderful friend, Martha Nussbaum. Her work has been truly inspirational, and I hope that, through engaging with this book, it will inspire others.

References

Alkire, Sabrina (2002), *Valuing Freedoms: Sen's Capability Approach and Poverty Reduction*, Oxford: Oxford University Press.

Brooks, Thom (2003), 'T. H. Green's Theory of Punishment', *History of Political Thought*, **24**, pp. 685–701.

Brooks, Thom (2008), 'Was Green a Utilitarian in Practice?', *Collingwood and British Idealism Studies*, **14**, pp. 5–15.

Brooks, Thom (2011), 'What Did the British Idealists Do for Us?' in Thom Brooks (ed.), *New Waves in Ethics*, Basingstoke: Palgrave Macmillan, pp. 28–47.

Campbell, Tom (2010), *Justice* (3rd edn), Basingstoke: Palgrave Macmillan.

Dworkin, Ronald (2000), *Sovereign Virtue*, Cambridge, MA: Harvard University Press.

Nussbaum, Martha C. (1997), 'Capabilities and Human Rights', *Fordham Law Review*, **66**, pp. 273–300.

Nussbaum, Martha C. (1999), *Sex and Social Justice*, Oxford: Oxford University Press.

Nussbaum, Martha C. (2000), *Women and Human Development: The Capabilities Approach*, Cambridge: Cambridge University Press.

Nussbaum, Martha C. (2006), *Frontiers of Justice: Disability, Nationality, Species Membership*, Cambridge, MA: Harvard University Press.

Nussbaum, Martha C. (2008), *Liberty of Conscience: In Defense of America's Tradition of Religious Equality*, New York: Basic Books.

Nussbaum, Martha C. (2010a), *From Disgust to Humanity: Sexual Orientation and Constitutional Law*, Oxford: Oxford University Press.

Nussbaum, Martha C. (2010b), 'Reply to Diane Wood, Constitutions and Capabilities: A (Necessarily) Pragmatic Approach', *Chicago Journal of International Law*, **10**, pp. 431–36.

Nussbaum, Martha C. (2011), *Creating Capabilities: The Human Development Approach*, Cambridge, MA: Harvard University Press.

Posner, Eric A. (2008), 'Human Welfare, Not Human Rights', *Columbia Law Review*, **108**, pp. 1758–801.

Qizilbash, Mozaffar (2002), 'Development, Common Foes and Shared Values', *Review of Political Economy*, **14**, pp. 463–80.

Rawls, John (1971), *A Theory of Justice*, Cambridge, MA: Harvard University Press.

Robeyns, Ingrid (2003), 'Sen's Capability Approach and Gender Inequality: Selecting Relevant Capabilities', *Feminist Economics*, **9**, pp. 61–92.

Sen, Amartya (1980), 'Equality of What?', in Sterling M. McMurrin (ed.), *Tanner Lectures on Human Values*, Vol. I, Cambridge: Cambridge University Press, pp. 197–220.

Sen, Amartya (1999a), *Commodities and Capabilities*, New Delhi: Oxford University Press.

Sen, Amartya (1999b), *Development as Freedom*, Oxford: Oxford University Press.

Sen, Amartya (2004), 'Elements of a Theory of Human Rights', *Philosophy and Public Affairs*, **32**, pp. 315–56.

Part I
Distributive Justice

[1]

WELL-BEING, AGENCY AND FREEDOM
THE DEWEY LECTURES 1984*

MORAL INFORMATION

Amartya Sen

THE main aim of these lectures is to explore a moral approach that sees persons from two different perspectives: *well-being* and *agency*. Both the "well-being aspect" and the "agency aspect" of persons have their own relevance in the assessment of states and actions. Each aspect also yields a corresponding notion of freedom.

A second objective is to examine a set of metaethical issues, making use of an "informational" approach to moral analysis which focuses on the admissibility and use of different types of information in moral valuation (by imposing a set of "invariance restrictions" on moral judgments). The two objectives are closely related in the sense that the substantive moral analysis draws on the metaethical arguments.

The first lecture is concerned primarily with metaethical issues, the second with well-being, and the third with agency.

I. INFORMATION AND INVARIANCE

Informational analysis can be used to bring out the content, scope, and limitations of different moral principles. Each moral principle needs some types of information for its use, and—no less impor-

* These John Dewey Lectures were presented at Columbia University on September 17, 18, and 19 of 1984. They constitute the fifth series of John Dewey Lectures, which were established in 1967 to honor the late John Dewey, who had been from 1905 to 1930 a professor of philosophy at Columbia.

In preparing these lectures for publication, I have benefited greatly from extensive comments of John Bennett, G. A. Cohen, Ronald Dworkin, Richard Hare, Isaac Levi, Tom Nagel, T. M. Scanlon, Ian White, and Bernard Williams. I have also had helpful suggestions from Bruce Ackerman, Kenneth Arrow, John Broome, Partha Dasgupta, James Griffin, Peter Hammond, Ted Honderich, Susan Hurley, Hidé Ishiguro, Stig Kanger, John Mackie, Sidney Morgenbesser, Derek Parfit, and John Rawls.

tantly—"rules out" direct use of other types of information. In their latter role, moral principles impose "informational constraints," demanding that certain types of information should not be allowed to influence the moral judgments to be made.

Informational constraints are typically imposed implicitly—entailed by other conditions—rather than stated explicitly.[1] But some principles do take the explicit form of informational constraints. For example, typical requirements of "universalizability" of moral judgments are direct informational constraints. The necessity to make "similar" judgments in "similar" circumstances rules out the use of all types of information not included in the notion of "similarity" of circumstances.

The basic form of an informational constraint is that of an invariance requirement: if two objects x and y belong to the same *isoinformation set* I, then they must be treated in the same way J. For all x, y: $x, y \in I \Rightarrow J(x,y)$. Such an invariance requirement is specified in a particular context, involving (among other things) the characterization of "objects" (x,y, etc.) and that of being treated "in the same way" (J). The invariance requirement takes the form of specifying, in that context, a class of isoinformation sets of objects, and any two objects in a given isoinformation set I must be treated in the same way.[2] An invariance restriction is based on a reading—explicit or implicit—of some types of information as being relevant for the moral judgment in question, and others not so. It asserts that any difference between two objects x and y belonging to the same isoinformation set is *irrelevant* in the current context.

A few examples may help to illustrate the diversity of ways in which informational constraints may be used through the specification of invariance requirements. When Henry Sidgwick claimed that "if a kind of conduct that is right (or wrong) for me is not right (or wrong) for some one else, it must be on the ground of some difference between the two cases, other than the fact that I and he are dif-

[1] Implicit uses of informational conditions are examined and illustrated in my "Informational Analysis of Moral Principles," in Ross Harrison, ed., *Rational Action* (New York: Cambridge, 1979).

[2] The role of informational constraints in the form of invariance restrictions in social choice theory is examined in my *Collective Choice and Social Welfare* (San Francisco: Holden-Day, 1970; republished, Amsterdam: North-Holland, 1979), hereafter, CCSW, and "On Weights and Measures: Informational Constraints in Social Welfare Analysis," *Econometrica*, XLV (1977): 1539–1572, reprinted in *Choice, Welfare and Measurement* (Oxford: Blackwell, and Cambridge, Mass.: MIT Press, 1982), hereafter, CWM. See also Claude d'Aspremont and Louis Gevers, "Equity and the Informational Basis of Collective Choice," *Review of Economic Studies*, XLIV (1977): 199–209, and Kevin Roberts, "Interpersonal Comparability and Social Choice Theory," *Review of Economic Studies*, XLVII (1980): 421–439.

ferent persons,"[3] he used a powerful informational constraint to rule out taking note of personal identity, as such, in making these judgments of conduct. Other requirements of "universalization" of moral judgments take the form of similarly general informational constraints.[4]

Another example—rather more specialized than Kantian and other requirements of universalization—is Kenneth Arrow's condition of "the independence of irrelevant alternatives" in social choice.[5] Here the "objects" x and y stand respectively for alternative n-tuples of individual preference orderings $\{R_i\}$ and $\{R_i^*\}$. The two are seen as belonging to the same isoinformation set, in the context of choice from a given subset S of social states, if and only if each individual's preference ordering of the states in S is the same in the first case as in the second (no matter how the two preferences differ regarding states *not* in S). The interpretation of $J(x,y)$, i.e., of x and y being treated in the same way, is that the *same* social choice is made from S in the two cases.[6] The *independence condition* demands that, in the context of choice from the set S, all information *other than* the individual rankings of the elements of S by each person must be regarded as irrelevant and such information must not influence social choice over S.

Another interesting example is that of the Pareto principle, which is widely used in welfare economics. This can be defined in rather different forms, each imposing some informational constraint. One particular form—that of the *Pareto indifference rule*—is *purely* informational, and this demands that, if everyone is indifferent between two states x and y, then x and y are socially exactly as good as each other. Here the objects are states; the interpretation of $J(x,y)$ is that state x and state y are socially equally good; and the isoinformation sets are based on the congruence of x and y in individual preference rankings. The informational constraint imposed by this invariance restriction rules out the use of any information other than the placing of the respective states in individual preference orderings in the special case in which everyone happens

[3] *The Method of Ethics* (London: Macmillan, 7th ed., 1907), Book III, ch. XII, p. 379.

[4] Different types of universalization requirements are carefully distinguished by John Mackie, *Ethics: Inventing Right and Wrong* (Harmondsworth: Penguin Books, 1977), ch. 4. See also Richard Hare, *Moral Thinking: Its Levels, Method and Point* (New York: Oxford, 1981), ch. 6.

[5] *Social Choice and Individual Values* (New York: Wiley, 1951; 2nd ed., 1963).

[6] There can, however, be different interpretations of what "social choice" stands for. Some alternative ones have been explored and distinguished from one another in my "Liberty and Social Choice," this JOURNAL, LXXX, 1 (January 1983): 5–28. The independence condition can be correspondingly defined for each of the distinct interpretations.

to be indifferent between x and y. Given the congruence of two states in individual preference rankings, no *other* information can have any influence on the ranking of the two states in terms of social goodness, according to the Pareto indifference rule. Indeed, we do not have to know anything else at all about the two states to be able to make this judgment, and any other information would, in this context, be redundant and useless.[7]

II. UNIVERSALIZABILITY AND INVARIANCE

The informational constraints imposed by requirements of universalizability used in the literature have been justified in several different ways. They can be taken to be substantive moral principles, on which we have to exercise judgment, or as being necessitated by the very nature of ethics.[8] In his *Language of Morals*,[9] Richard Hare has powerfully argued that universalizability in the form of the need to make identical judgments in identical circumstances is entailed by the meaning of moral language. It can, however, be argued that if this claim is accepted, then it would follow that the so-called "Hume's law" (to wit: the impossibility of deriving moral propositions from factual premises), endorsed by Hare, among others, must be, strictly speaking, false.[10] If two actions are factually identical, then universalizability (seen by Hare as a necessity due to the meaning of moral language) will require that they be *morally* equivalent.

In fact, this can also be seen as an aspect of the theory of identity, whereby if $x = y$, then $f(x) = f(y)$. If the "theory of valuation," to use John Dewey's term,[11] indicates that moral values must be seen as a function f of factual information, then factual identity ($x = y$) must entail moral equivalence: $f(x) = f(y)$.[12] This does not depend on the nature of the function $f(.)$, except that it *is* a function.

The relevance of this line of reasoning does, however, depend on

[7] Though the Pareto principle is usually taken to be "mild" and "innocuous," its cutting power is indeed quite severe, because of the power of the informational constraint in excluding the use of nonpreference information in judging the social goodness of states of affairs. It is a demanding condition on its own and becomes remarkably exacting when combined with other conditions (such as Arrow's independence condition and "unrestricted domain," or a condition of personal liberty). These issues are discussed in my "Personal Utilities and Public Judgments: Or What's Wrong with Welfare Economics?" *Economic Journal*, LXXXIX (1979): 537-558, reprinted in CWM; and in "Utilitarianism and Welfarism," this JOURNAL, LXXVI, 9 (September, 1979): 479-487.

[8] Sidgwick took "the Kantian maxim" to be "certainly fundamental, certainly true, and not without practical importance" (*op. cit.*, p. xvii).

[9] New York: Oxford, 1952; rev. ed., 1961.

[10] This proposition was stated and defended in my "Hume's Law and Hare's Rule," *Philosophy*, XLI (January 1966): 75-79. Richard Hare's response to this point can be found in *Moral Thinking* (1981), pp. 233/4.

[11] *Theory of Valuation* (Chicago: University Press, 1939).

[12] It is sometimes argued that to say that two actions (or two states) are morally

the interpretation of the idea of "identity" in dealing with universalizability of moral judgments. There is an exacting sense in which it can be said that two factual circumstances are never exactly identical. The notion of identity used in the application of universalizability is based on some informational constraint, ruling out some differences as irrelevant. Richard Hare, in fact, concentrates on different cases being "identical in their *universal properties*".[13] There is an important problem in deciding whether the informational constraints that rule out the relevance of what are seen as *non*universal properties must not themselves be substantive moral requirements—not necessitated by the language of morals itself. What is at issue is the *scope* of the principle of universalizability (seen as a necessity due to the nature of moral language).[14] I shall not pursue this question further here. The theses presented in these lectures do not depend on taking a particular position on this question.

The possible conflict between the demands of Hume's law and the thesis that universalizability is necessitated by the nature of moral language, may well be a rather esoteric question. But in focusing on the need to relate moral valuation functionally to factual circumstances, the issue of universalizability does relate to the more general question of the "objectivity" of moral beliefs.[15] The question of ob-

equally good is not in itself a moral judgment. According to this view, "*x* is morally good" *is* a moral judgment, but "*x* and *y* are morally equally good" is not, since it does not specify whether either of them is "morally good." (I am grateful to Ted Honderich for forcefully raising this eminently discussable question, when responding to a version of this paper at a meeting of the Philosophical Society in Oxford.) I believe that such a view is hard to defend, since moral equivalence must be saying *something* about moral matters. In fact, there is a strong case for taking the relation "at least as good as" as the primitive concept in goodness judgments (as, say, in Arrow's framework, *op. cit.*, ch. 2). From this relation, that of being "equally good" can follow through conjunction. It can even be argued that a statement such as "This action is *good*" can be fully understood only in terms of some comparison (usually implicit) with *other possible actions*. The idea of being "equally good" belongs solidly to that inescapably comparative framework of moral judgment.

[13] *Moral Thinking* (1981), p. 108; italics added.

[14] The exact proposition put forward in my "Hume's Law and Hare's Rule" (1966) was, in fact: "*Either* Hare's principle of universalizability is empty of content, *or* it conflicts with Hume's Law" (79).

[15] See Thomas Nagel, *Mortal Questions* (New York: Cambridge, 1979), Essay 14, and "The Limits of Objectivity," in S. McMurrin, ed., *Tanner Lectures on Human Values*, vol. I (Salt Lake City: Utah UP, 1980). See also Simon Blackburn, "Moral Realism," in J. Casey, ed., *Morality and Moral Reasoning* (London: Methuen, 1971); David Wiggins, "Truth, Invention, and the Meaning of Life," *Proceedings of the British Academy*, LXII (1976); Donald Davidson, "Psychology as Philosophy," in *Essays on Action and Events* (New York: Oxford, 1980); John McDowell, "Noncognitivism and Rule-following," in S. H. Holtzman and C. M. Leich, eds., *Wittgenstein: To Follow a Rule* (London: Routledge & Kegan Paul, 1981); Susan Hurley, "Objectivity and Disagreement," Honderich, ed., *Ethics and Objectivity* (London: Routledge & Kegan Paul, forthcoming).

jectivity will be taken up later on in this lecture (in section VII), but what is important to stress here is the need, in this context, to examine the invariance requirements that must be imposed on moral beliefs. Objectivity of moral beliefs must require some types of invariance, but the necessity to make identical moral judgments in *exactly* identical circumstances is perhaps too "minimal" to take us very far into that question. It will be argued later that what may be called *authorship invariance* is indeed required by objectivity of moral beliefs, but this can coexist with the possibility that moral valuations of different persons (sharing exactly the *same* moral system) may vary with the different positions that they respectively occupy in the given states of affairs. Invariance conditions involving informational constraints will have to be formulated differently in that context (section VII).

III. UTILITARIANISM AND INFORMATION

It is manifest that the actual availability of information can affect the possibility of using specific moral approaches. For example, Lionel Robbins's celebrated attack on utilitarian welfare economics—an attack which had a profound influence on the direction of welfare economics for several decades—centered mostly on the unavailability of information regarding interpersonal comparison of utility, making utilitarianism allegedly unworkable.[16] That attack was rather wrong-headed, and it was based on a failure to grasp the nature and the evidential basis of utility comparisons.[17] But certainly the more difficult it is to get utility information, the more limited is the scope of application of utilitarianism. Other moral approaches are similarly constrained by the availability of information.

The dependence of the usability of moral principles on the availability of information is obvious enough. What is perhaps less obvious is the dependence of the usability of information on the particular moral principles adopted. This question of *implicit* informational constraints was briefly discussed earlier (in section I). A substantive moral system can indeed be substantially—though not

[16] *An Essay on the Nature and Significance of Economic Science* (London: Macmillan, 1932), and "Interpersonal Comparisons of Utility," *Economic Journal*, XLVIII (1938).

[17] See particularly I. M. D. Little, *A Critique of Welfare Economics* (New York: Oxford, 2nd ed., 1957); Richard C. Jeffrey, "On Interpersonal Utility Theory," this JOURNAL, LXVIII, 20 (Oct. 21, 1971): 647-656; Ilmar Waldner, "The Empirical Meaningfulness of Interpersonal Utility Comparisons," *ibid.*, LXIX, 4 (Feb. 24, 1972): 87-103; and my "Interpersonal Comparisons of Welfare," in M. Boskin, ed., *Economics and Human Welfare* (New York: Academic Press, 1979), reprinted in my CWM. See also the papers of Donald Davidson and Allan Gibbard to be included in a volume of essays edited by J. Elster and A. Hylland, provisionally called *Foundations of Social Choice Theory*, to be published by Cambridge University Press, and an unpublished paper by Robert Nozick, "Interpersonal Comparisons of Utility."

completely—characterized by specifying the informational constraints it imposes.[18]

Take simple act utilitarianism, which can be factored into: (1) *act consequentialism* (the goodness of an act is given by the goodness of its consequent states of affairs), (2) *welfarism* (the goodness of a state of affairs is given by the goodness of the utility information regarding that state), and (3) *sum ranking* (the goodness of utility information is given by the sum total of the utilities in question).[19] Other types of utilitarianism, such as rule utilitarianism, motive utilitarianism, etc., would require the replacement of act consequentialism by different consequentialist requirements such as rule consequentialism, motive consequentialism, etc. The common building block of different types of utilitarian consequentialism is given by the combination of some consequentialist form with *outcome utilitarianism,* which is produced by the union of welfarism and sum ranking, making the goodness of states of affairs be given by the utility sum total in that state.

These requirements impose a set of informational constraints, in the form of invariance restrictions linked to specific information types. The isoinformation sets are given by the factored conditions individually or jointly. For example, in judging states of affairs, *welfarism* would put two states in the same isoinformation set if they are identical in terms of utility (i.e., if they are mapped onto the same point in the n-dimensional utility space, in an n-person society). If *sum ranking* is also imposed, this requires further that two states must belong to the same isoinformation set whenever they have the same utility *total* (even if they are mapped onto different points in the n-dimensional utility space). Finally, additionally imposing a minimal (direction-neutral) version of *act consequentialism* will put two acts (even though they *are* different acts) in the same isoinformation set if the two states of affairs they respectively yield have the same utility total. And that, of course, takes us more or less all the way to act utilitarianism (all we need further is a "directional" axiom that says the more the better). In assessing act utilitarianism (and any other moral system), it is important to examine both what information it regards as appropriate *and* what information it constrains out as irrelevant and unusable.

IV. PLURALISM: PRINCIPLES AND INFORMATION

The informational parsimony of utilitarianism reflects its apparently "monist" rather than "pluralist" informational format. This

[18] This is discussed in my "Informational Analysis of Moral Principles" (1979).

[19] The rationale of this factorization is discussed in my "Utilitarianism and Welfarism" (1979). See also the "Introduction" to Sen and Williams, eds., *Utilitarianism and Beyond* (New York: Cambridge, 1982).

appearance of monism is somewhat deceptive because utility can be sensibly seen as a "plural" notion itself,[20] and I shall have more to say on this in the second lecture.

The issue of pluralism has been discussed a fair amount, and more specifically, the question has been seen as important in examining alternatives to utilitarianism. Is it necessary that a plausible alternative to utilitarianism be itself monist?

The idea of pluralism vis-à-vis monism not only is ambiguous, but also is sometimes viewed in a way that has no essential relation to the feature of plurality. A common approach seems to take the form of identifying the use of plurality of principles with *intuitionism.*[21] Pluralism is a claim about the *form* of moral structures, whereas intuitionism—unless radically redefined—is a claim about how the moral structure may be *derived and supported* (i.e., whether by intuition only). The two things are not essentially related. The suggestion that if there are many ultimate principles (and they are not in a hierarchy), then the balance among them *must be* struck by intuition, is, of course, completely baseless. John Rawls, who does restrict the term 'intuitionism' to pluralist moral theories, does at least make clear that "a conception of justice can be pluralist without requiring us to weigh its principles by intuition."[22]

Even when the confusing identification of pluralism with intuitionism has been rejected, there remain at least two different ways of defining pluralism. One is in terms of plurality of principles (I shall call this *principle pluralism*), and the other in terms of plurality of informational variables (to be called *information pluralism*).

It is probably not particularly worth while to try to define a metric on the space of principles (including "combining" principles) to be able to count them precisely and to be "really" sure how many principles there are in a particular moral structure. The genuine worry that seems to motivate concern about principle pluralism lies elsewhere and is easy to see; to wit, that a nonintegrated moral structure could leave many moral issues unresolved. In an often-quoted passage, John Stuart Mill put the problem thus:

> There must be some standard by which to determine the goodness or badness, absolute and comparative, of ends or objects of desire. And

[20] I have tried to discuss different aspects of this plurality of utility in "Plural Utility," *Proceedings of the Aristotelian Society,* LXXXI (1980/81): 193-215. See also Martha C. Nussbaum, "Plato on Commensurability and Desire," *Proceedings of the Aristotelian Society,* LXXXIII (1984): 50-80.

[21] See J. D. Urmson, "A Defence of Intuitionism," *Proceedings of the Aristotelian Society,* LXXV (1974/75): 111-119, where Urmson contrasts: (i) "mononomic," (ii) "hierarchical," and (iii) "intuitionist" moral structures.

[22] *A Theory of Justice* (1971), p. 34.

whatever that standard is, there can be but one: for if there were several ultimate principles of conduct, the same conduct might be approved by one of those principles and condemned by another; and there would be need for some more general principle as umpire between them.[23]

The argument clearly has some force.[24] It is, however, interesting to note that here Mill is not disputing the case for having a principle-pluralist structure with a combining principle (what he calls an "umpire"), but rather asserting only the need for such a principle for a principle-pluralist structure. He is concerned to show that if that is how pluralism is to be dealt with, then it would again be true that there is "but one" ultimate standard. One could dispute this—the role of the "umpire" does not obliterate the continuing role of the plural principles in the final ranking of actions, states, etc. But not much really hangs on how such a system is described.

V. PLURALISM AND INCOMPLETENESS

The really important questions regarding pluralism seem to be the following. First, the scope of combining principles may be limited;[25] the "diversity of goods" may be too deep.[26] The conflicting values may be unreconcilable and may be hard to integrate, as Karl Marx argued in his well-known *Critique of the Gotha Programme,* referring to the German Workers Party's simultaneous loyalty to the principles of "equal distribution" and the worker's right to get "the undiminished proceeds of labor."[27] On a different type of problem, it has been argued, by Isaiah Berlin in particular, that elimination of value conflicts inevitably implies some loss of value, and perhaps even that "we cannot conceive of a situation in which it was true both that all value-conflict had been eliminated, and that there had been no loss of value on the way."[28]

[23] *A System of Logic,* Book VI, ch. XII, s. 7. See also Hillel Steiner, "Reason and Intuition in Ethics," *Ratio,* XXV, 1 (June 1983); 59-68.

[24] One point to note, though, is that it cannot be assumed that the existence of "several ultimate principles of conduct" *must* necessarily lead to conflict. Whether it would or not would depend inter alia on the overlap of the domains of the respective ultimate principles. Conditions of compatibility of principles are discussed in my "Informational Analysis of Moral Principles" (1979).

[25] See Bernard Williams, *Moral Luck* (New York: Cambridge, 1981), especially Essay 5 ("Conflicts of Values").

[26] See Charles Taylor, "The Diversity of Goods," in Sen and Williams, *op. cit.,* in which see also Stuart Hampshire, "Morality and Convention." For a different aspect of the issue of diversity and commensurability, see Nussbaum, *op cit.*

[27] *Critique of the Gotha Programme* (1875; New York: International Publishers, 1966).

[28] The quoted sentence is Bernard Williams' statement of one of Berlin's arguments; *Moral Luck,* p. 71. See Berlin, *Concepts and Categories* (New York: Oxford, 1980).

If value conflicts do remain unresolved and if conflicting principles are not "umpired" together (to use Mill's phrase) by some balancing principle, then the over-all ranking may well be incomplete (if such a combined ranking is sought).[29] The "intersection" of the different criteria will, of course, yield a partial order, and although that "intersection partial order" may be extendable by weights that are not fully determined (and could vary over a wide range), the "maximal" partial order, given everything, may still be quite seriously incomplete. Then there may not, quite possibly, exist any "best" action (or "best state"). Is that incompleteness an embarrassment for a principle-pluralist moral approach? That is, indeed an important question, to be faced.

Second, if we do happen to resolve the problem of incompleteness by some combining principle, leading to what Mill takes to be a unique "standard," would that integrated system be *informationally* monist, in the sense of taking only one type of information (like utility) to be intrinsically valuable?

I take up the second question first. The answer is straightforward: informational monism is a completely different issue and is not required for an integrated, complete structure. Indeed, if integration is brought about by a combining principle "umpiring" together various demands based on various informational bases, it would *have to be* information-pluralist. Even if we are entirely persuaded by the quoted argument from Mill, there would still be no particular reason for us to look for some single informational base of the kind that, say, utility allegedly provides. There is no argument in all this for expecting that moral goodness must be ultimately decidable by counting the units of some homogeneous nonmoral quantity (as utility is taken to be), rather than having to balance the relative importance of different considerations that conflict.[30] It is not so much that information pluralism can be defended, as that there is no special need for a defense.

I turn now to the first question—the alleged need for completeness. In a recent paper, "Moral Struggle,"[31] Isaac Levi has followed the lead of John Dewey in discussing the importance of conflicts of principles that may or may not get resolved, and has addressed the

[29] On the "disparity between the fragmentation of value and the singleness of decision," see T. Nagel, "The Fragmentation of Value," in *Mortal Questions*. See also R. Dworkin, "No Right Answer?" in P. M. S. Hacker and J. Raz, eds., *Law, Morality and Society: Essays in Honour of H. L. A. Hart* (New York: Oxford, 1977).

[30] See also Sen and Williams, "Introduction," pp. 16–18.

[31] Mimeographed, Philosophy Department, Columbia University, 1984; this is in fact the first chapter of a forthcoming book.

problem of decision making under those circumstances. To quote Dewey and Tufts:

> The struggle is not between a good which is clear to him and something else which attracts him but which he knows to be wrong. It is between values each of which is an undoubted good in its place but which now get in each other's way. He is forced to reflect in order to come to a decision. Moral theory is a generalized extension of the kind of thinking in which he now engages.[32]

Decision making with unresolved conflicts is part of a more general problem, viz., decision making with *incomplete* rankings.[33] We may begin by noting that incomplete rankings may have to be faced even with *one* ultimate principle of valuation. The most obvious reason for this is the limitation of informational availability. For example, partial comparability of utilities—in *interpersonal* correspondences—will make the utilitarian ranking a partial ordering.[34] It can also be argued that partial comparability of utilities may be caused not only by the actual limitation of factual knowledge, but also by the intrinsic nature of interpersonal utility comparisons. Utilities may not, in this view, be things that can, even in principle, be fully compared between persons, leading to an exact one-to-one correspondence of the utility measures (levels, units, etc.) of different persons.[35] The incompleteness of the utilitarian ranking would, on this view, be unremovable through richer factual knowledge. In these circumstances, a pure utilitarian would have to *assert* the incompleteness of moral ranking as the correct moral position.

In fact, depending on the status of the incompleteness, it is possible to distinguish between (1) open incompleteness, and (2) closed incompleteness. The former is exemplified by a partial ordering that can still be extended, e.g., by more information (as in the case of utilitarianism with contingent partial comparability), or by the use of some other supplementary principle (e.g., extending the in-

[32] J. Dewey and J. H. Tufts, *Ethics* (New York: Holt, 1932), p. 175.

[33] More generally, decision making with incomplete *valuation structures*, which may or may not be binary.

[34] See my "Interpersonal Aggregation and Partial Comparability," *Econometrica*, XXXVIII (1970), reprinted in CWM; and *Collective Choice and Social Welfare* (1970), ch. 7*. See also C. Blackorby, "Degrees of Cardinality and Aggregate Partial Orderings," *Econometrica*, XLIII (1975); B. J. Fine, "A Note on 'Interpersonal Aggregation and Partial Comparability'," *ibid.*; and K. Basu, *Revealed Preference of Governments* (New York: Cambridge, 1979).

[35] See my *Collective Choice and Social Welfare* (1970), ch. 7, and CWM, Essays 9 and 12.

complete ranking given by the Pareto criterion by some supplementary "distributional" judgment), or by moving toward the resolution of "moral struggles" (as in the case of conflicts of principles). The partial ordering stays, as it were, "ready" to be extended.

In contrast, for "closed" incompleteness, the absence of completeness is *assertive,* and there is no room for extending the partial order. In stating that x and y "cannot" be ranked vis-à-vis each other in terms of moral goodness, a substantive and definite moral assertion is being made. Though the demands of practical choice may force us to choose one or the other, there is—on this view—no additional moral criterion that can be used to rank the unranked pairs *in terms of moral goodness.*

Assertive incompleteness, like assertive completeness, has the effect of closing a substantive issue, declaring further search to be pointless. There is obviously an important problem here of decidability. It is also arguable that assertive incompleteness should never be "accepted," because that may discourage moral inquiry.[36] This methodological point (regarding search and research) might well be supportable, but it does not, of course, rule out the real possibility of assertive incompleteness.

When an incomplete ranking refers not to moral goodness as such but to some specific moral quality, e.g., justice, then the completion of that partial ranking by some *other* criterion may give a combined, complete view of moral goodness, but this would do nothing to complete the ranking of justice itself, which would continue to remain assertively incomplete. It could then be the case that while, say, state x is more just than y, states x and z simply cannot be compared in terms of justice (i.e., neither is more just than the other, nor can they be seen as equally just; they are simply noncomparable as far as justice is concerned). And that would continue to be so even if the incompleteness could be removed in the over-all ranking, or in decision making, by the supplementary use of some *other* criterion.

Yielding complete orders cannot be an a priori requirement of the legitimacy of a moral principle, or even of an entire moral approach with its full structure of principles. It is not a matter of getting metamoral passmarks. It does not determine a substantive moral approach, but rather *gets determined* by such an approach, which could yield completeness of valuations or not (possibly even *asser-*

[36] The strategic role of openness in this sense is discussed in my note, "The Nature and Classes of Prescriptive Judgments," *Philosophical Quarterly,* XVII, 66 (January 1967): 46-62.

tively not). If the appropriate moral approach produces the result that *x* and *y* are morally noncomparable, then decision making has to reckon with that.

It is often pointed out that in real life we have to choose something or other—we must decide, we must act. This is certainly so, and we must end up doing something or other, if only nothing, by default. If our actions are to be morally guided, then our incomplete moral valuations must be used to eliminate some alternatives, while permitting others.[37] We must not act like a moral counterpart of Buridan's ass—needlessly starving by default, unable to figure out which of the nonstarving alternatives happened to be the best.[38] Intelligent moral choice demands that we not choose—explicitly or by default—an alternative that we can see is morally inferior to another feasible alternative. But this does not require that the chosen alternative be seen to be "best" in that set of feasible alternatives, since there may be no best alternative at all, given the incompleteness of our moral ranking.

VI. STATES, ACTIONS, WELFARISM, AND CONSEQUENTIALISM

One source of informational pluralism is the possibility that acts themselves may have value or disvalue, distinct from the valuation of states resulting from such acts. This is an important issue in assessing consequentialism and in examining agent-relative moral approaches.

In examining states of affairs, we have to be sure of what they "contain." That actions are part of the respective states of affairs is sometimes denied, especially to draw a sharp contract between consequentialist and deontological theories. It is hard to defend this exclusion. A state of affairs in which Brutus kills Caesar is not just one in which Caesar has expired. It is one in which the killing of Caesar by Brutus (and others) figures. There is, of course, also the question as to how we choose to *describe* the state.[39] But what the

[37] The specification of "permissibility" based on an incomplete ranking of moral goodness may, of course, be used to generate a complete binary relation of its own, but the *derived* binary relation of being "equally permissible" will typically lack some of the standard properties of a preference relation, such as transitivity (see my CCSW, pp. 48/9).

[38] I interpret Buridan's ass's problem as the inability to rank the two haystacks, rather than—as in the more standard version—viewing them as equally good, in which case *both* haystacks would have been "best" (and either could have been unproblematically chosen in terms of binary optimality). See my "Behaviour and the Concept of Preference," *Economica,* XL (1973); reprinted in CWM, pp. 61/2.

[39] See Frederic Schick, "Under Which Description?" in Sen and Williams. See also Davidson, "Logical Form of Action Sentences," in *Essays on Actions and Events* (1980). I have tried to discuss some of the issues involved in description in "Description as Choice," *Oxford Economic Papers,* XXXII (1980); reprinted in CWM.

state of affairs includes is really a matter of what *in fact* happened. Caesar could have expired in many different ways, and the fact that he got knifed by Brutus must be a *part* of that state, no matter how we *choose* to describe it in one particular context or another. If we choose to leave out this fact in the description of the state of affairs, that is just a decision to be silent about one part of that state.[40]

It is, of course, true that utilitarianism *values* states of affairs in an informationally limited way, attaching no intrinsic importance to nonutility information about states, and thus inter alia ignoring actions too—except as variables for causal analysis (in linking utility to objects that yield utility), or perhaps as surrogates for utility (when utility information is hard to get). This feature of utilitarianism is welfarism, and it is a feature that is shared by some other approaches, such as utility-based "maximin" (seeing the goodness of a state as the utility level of the worst-off individual in that state.)[41]

It is important to distinguish between the respective roles of welfarism and consequentialism in making the evaluation of *actions* informationally restricted. Welfarism filters out all information other than utility information in the evaluation of *states of affairs,* and it is precisely because of that informational constraint that consequentialism has, in this compound system, the effect of ignoring everything other than utilities (in the consequent states) in *evaluating actions.* Had welfarism not been additionally imposed, consequentialism could have coexisted with taking note of such things as the values and disvalues of actions *through* the valuation of the states, which include these actions.

VII. AGENCY, POSITION, AND OBJECTIVITY

If the action information is not blocked out by welfarism or some other informational constraint) in evaluating states of affairs, the relation of the evaluator and his or her *agency* role in the state has to be considered in the moral assessment of states. It is often thought that although, in deliberating on the correctness of one's own *actions,* one must take ample note of one's responsibility for

[40] See Charles Taylor's argument for taking out actions from the assessment of consequent states ("The Diversity of Goods," 1982). On this, see my "Evaluator Relativity and Consequential Evaluation," *Philosophy and Public Affairs,* XII, 2 (Spring 1983): pp. 128–130.

[41] Inspired by Rawls's Difference Principle, this "maximin" criterion—and its lexicographic variant ("leximin")—have been much used in welfare economics; see, for example, E. S. Phelps, ed., *Economic Justice* (Harmondsworth: Penguin, 1973); Sen, *On Economic Inequality* (New York: Oxford, 1973); James Meade, *The Just Economy* (London: Allen & Unwin, 1976); A. B. Atkinson, *Social Justice and Public Policy* (Brighton: Wheatsheaf, 1983). Rawls's own Difference Principle is defined, however, not in terms of utility, but in terms of an index of "primary goods."

these actions, that issue does not arise in the evaluation of states. But since states do include one's own actions (albeit inter alia), that contrast is not sharp. One is responsible for, as it were, a part of the state, and as far as one's own actions in that state are concerned, one is responsible for them in a straightforward way. If some act—such as knifing a friend—is a bad thing to do and if the agent who did the knifing was responsible for that act, then that special badness must be a part of the over-all evaluation, *made by the knifer*, of that state. It could, of course, still be the case that, despite the badness of that action, everything considered, knifing Caesar produced a better state of affairs even from the evaluative position of Brutus ("Not that I loved Caesar less, but that I loved Rome more"). However, Brutus cannot evaluate the state, of which his killing Caesar is a part, without taking note of his own responsibility for that act.

A consistent moral approach may, therefore, require that the moral valuation function be *position-relative*. Given Brutus's role in the knifing of Caesar, Brutus cannot view the resulting state—of which that knifing was also a part—in the same way as, say, Appian, the historian, completely uninvolved in the matter, can. The difference can exist even when Appian and Brutus share exactly the same moral approach, and it arises because of the objective differences in their positions vis-à-vis the state in question. A position-relative valuation function builds in the parameter of the assessor's position *within* the valuation function itself.[42] Consider the following imaginary remark of Appian to Brutus: "If I were you, Brutus, I should have evaluated the state to be even worse than I do now, not having been involved in the knifing of Caesar myself." The statement is of the form $f(x,a,b) < f(x,a,a)$, in which $f(x,a,b)$ is the valuation of the state x by a (Appian) in the position of b (Brutus), and $f(x,a,a)$, the valuation made by Appian from his own position. Notice that the relativity in question links not to the *authorship* (the second variable), but to the position from which the evaluation is being made (the third variable), i.e., whether a's position or b's. The authorship is immaterial for "position relativity" of a moral system.

Indeed, that the approach is not subject-relative (and does not include "subjectivism" *within* the system) can be guaranteed by insisting on an invariance requirement regarding authorship. "Authorship invariance" requires that the moral valuations of a

[42] See my "Rights and Agency," *Philosophy and Public Affairs*, XI, 1 (Winter 1982): 3–39, and the exchange with Donald Regan in the same journal next year: Regan, "Against Evaluator Relativity: A Response to Sen," *ibid.*, XII, 2 (Spring 1983); 93–112.

state in a given moral system must not vary with the person making the judgment, even though it can vary with the *position from which* the valuation is to be made. Despite Appian's assertion (stated earlier) that $f(x,a,b) < f(x,a,a)$, which shows position-relativity, Appian would be bound by the requirements of authorship invariance to assert $f(x,a,b) = f(x,b,b)$.[43] "You, Brutus, should evaluate the state in the same unfavorable way as I should if I were in your position."

The possibility of combining position relativity with authorship invariance is also the reason why positionality of moral valuation is perfectly consistent with objectivity of moral values. Moral valuation can be position-relative in the same way as such statements as "The sun is setting." The truth of that statement varies with the position of the person, but it cannot vary from person to person among those standing in the same position. The aspect of objectivity related to authorship invariance, i.e., to $f(x,a,b) = f(x,b,b)$, for all x, a, and b, has to be, I believe, a part of what Thomas Nagel calls objectivity in "the primary sense"—that of "beliefs and knowledge."[44]

VIII. CONCLUDING REMARKS

This lecture has been concerned entirely with general—primarily methodological—issues. The use of informational constraints in the form of invariance requirements has been examined, both in an explicit form (e.g., in the requirement of universalizability) and in implicit ways (e.g., in utilitarianism, through the features of welfarism, sum ranking, and consequentialism). I have also argued against ruling out principle pluralism, information pluralism, and incompleteness in valuations (such as partial orderings of acts, states, or rules). The case for position relativity in moral valuation has been outlined, and it has been argued that position relativity is consistent with authorship invariance, and indeed with the corresponding aspect of objectivity in moral beliefs. The importance of the informational perspective suggests the need for improving the standard informational accounts of states of affairs. These issues will figure rather prominently in the substantive moral discussion to be presented in the next two lectures.

[43] A "subjectivist" ethical approach can deny this invariance condition. Indeed, it can even insist that *everyone* must accept the possibility of this denial. This involves authorship invariance of a different type altogether, operating at a "meta" level (invariably denying the requirement of authorship invariance of moral valuation). I am grateful to Thomas Nagel for raising this question.

[44] "The Limits of Objectivity" (1980), p. 77.

WELL-BEING AND FREEDOM

THOMAS M. SCANLON argues that "utilitarianism derives much of its appeal from alleged difficulties about the foundations of rival views."[1] He also suggests that "the wide-spread influence of utilitarian principles" derives from the "attractiveness" of what he calls "philosophical utilitarianism," which is "a particular philosophical thesis about the subject matter of morality, namely the thesis that the only fundamental moral facts are facts about individual well-being" (108). This "philosophical utilitarianism" can be taken to provide a "foundation" for utilitarianism in a rather limited sense.[2] It specifies an "informational" basis that is indeed highly attractive, but this does not, of course, indicate that there is no further need for justification of this informational basis. However, it does provide an interesting and important way of looking at utilitarianism, and provides a focus for critical assessment. That will indeed be the point of departure of this lecture. But since the term 'philosophical utilitarianism' is a little misleading (even nonutilitarian approaches can be consistent with "the thesis that the only fundamental moral facts are facts about individual well-being"), I shall call the use of this informational foundation by the more descriptive (though much less elegant) name 'well-being as informational foundation', or WAIF for short.[3]

Defending utilitarianism with the help of WAIF raises some immediate questions. (1) Is the thesis of this informational foundation really believable? Does it survive critical examination? (2) Do utilitarian principles really follow from WAIF? In fact, I shall split up the last question into two parts: (2a) Is well-being best seen as utility? (2b) Do utilitarian principles follow from WAIF if well-being is seen as utility?

I. WELL-BEING AND AGENCY

I start with the first question: Is the well-being foundation believable? It would, of course, be altogether amazing if moral goodness had nothing to do with well-being. It is easy to argue that well-being is fundamentally important. If we were tied to informational

[1] "Contractualism and Utilitarianism," in Sen and Williams, *op. cit.*, p. 103.

[2] Scanlon himself goes on to propose a rival foundational structure, of a procedural variety (involving a "contractual account"), motivated by his diagnosis that "what a successful alternative to utilitarianism must do, first and foremost, is to sap this source of strength [of utilitarianism] by providing a clear account of the foundations of nonutilitarian moral reasoning" (103).

[3] This acronym is not, I fear, very helpful (though the association of loneliness may not be altogether inappropriate for the information monism of WAIF).

monism, that elementary thought would have already pushed us much of the way to WAIF, since there would be "room" for only one thing at the top. But, as was argued in the last lecture, insisting on informational monism is a crude prejudice. By recognizing the importance of well-being, we do not close the door on the possible importance—intrinsic importance—of other things. So the question is not whether well-being is an intrinsically important variable for moral analysis, but whether it is uniquely so.

People have aspects other than well-being. Not all their activities are aimed at maximizing well-being (nor do their activities always contribute to it), no matter how broadly we define well-being within the limits of that general concept. There are goals other than well-being, and values other than goals. "Human beings," as John Dewey said in *Theory of Valuation,* "are continuously engaged in valuations" (58). It can be argued that something so central to human life—indeed to our being persons—cannot fail to be intrinsically relevant to moral analysis.

Indeed it is useful to distinguish clearly between the "well-being aspect" and the "agency aspect" of a person. John Rawls's "Kantian constructivism," in his Dewey lectures,[4] started at the agency end—with "persons characterized as rational agents of construction." Persons were seen as "having the moral power to have a conception of the good"; the agency role—broadly construed—came first, and other things followed. Although I shall not follow Rawls's route of Kantian constructivism, I would argue that the conception of "persons" in moral analysis cannot be so reduced as to attach no intrinsic importance to this agency role, seeing them ultimately only in terms of their well-being.

There is a particular sphere in which such an agency role may be especially important, and that is the person's own life. Various concepts of "autonomy,"[5] and "personal liberty,"[6] relate to this special role of agency in personal life, going well beyond considerations of well-being. The moral foundation of well-being is informationally extremely restrictive, and the agency aspect is much too crucial to leading a life for it to be intrinsically of no moral importance.

It is important to emphasize that in pointing to the informa-

[4] "Kantian Constructivism in Moral Theory: The Dewey Lectures 1980," this JOURNAL, LXXVII, 9 (September 1980): 515-572.

[5] See Jonathan Glover, *Causing Death and Saving Lives* (Harmondsworth: Penguin Books, 1977) for some interesting—and important—conflicts involving autonomy and other values, including well-being.

[6] Discussed in my CCSW (1970) and in "Liberty and Social Choice," this JOURNAL, LXXX, 1 (January 1983): 5-28.

tional limitation of WAIF, in that it gives no fundamental place to the agency aspect of a person, the assumption is *not* being made that the agency and well-being aspects of a person are unrelated. For an integrated person it is likely—possibly even inevitable—that the person's well-being will be influenced by his or her agency role. This does not, however, imply that the well-being information itself could capture the important features of agency, or act as its informational surrogate. In fact, some types of agency roles, e.g., those related to fulfilling obligations, can quite possibly have a negative impact on the person's well-being. Even when the impact is positive, the importance of the *agency aspect* has to be distinguished from the importance of the *impact of agency on well-being*.

II. WELL-BEING AND UTILITY

Is well-being best seen as utility? This is not an easy question to answer, for various reasons. The most immediate reason is that there are different interpretations of utility, in particular (1) happiness, (2) desire fulfillment, (3) choice.[7]

The *choice* view of utility, it is fair to say, is more popular among economists than among philosophers. In this view utility is seen as a real-valued (that is, numerical) representation of a person's choice behavior, i.e., what the person chooses from each subset of the set of alternatives (or would choose if such choices were to arise). This view of utility is, of course, purely "ordinal." Attempts to get "cardinal" utility from the choice approach are deeply hampered by the necessity of having to assume a much more elaborate framework, with much stronger requirements of consistency *and* the willingness to accept the influence of arbitrary elements in the numbering system (e.g., that of one's attitude to risk if cardinality is constructed from choices over lotteries). The extension to interpersonal comparisons is also very problematic, since we do not actually face the choice of becoming someone else, and it is hard to decide what importance to attach to answers that may be given when such choices are posed hypothetically. The natural domain of the choice interpretation of utility is in providing non-interpersonally-comparable ordinal valuations, as under Paul Samuelson's "revealed preference" approach.[8]

[7] See James Griffin, "Modern Utilitarianism," *Revue Internationale de Philosophie*, XXXVI.3, 141 (1982): 331–375, for an illuminating survey of different notions of utility and their use in utilitarian theory and for a critical assessment of some anti-utilitarian arguments, from a firm (but undogmatic) utilitarian perspective. See also J. C. B. Gosling, *Pleasure and Desire* (New York: Oxford, 1969).

[8] See *Foundations of Economic Analysis* (Cambridge, Mass.: Harvard, 1947). Some of these issues are discussed in my CWM (1982).

Even in this limited form, a serious problem with this approach arises from the fact that a person's choice behavior may fail to have any binary representation, or it may be representable by a binary relation that is not transitive (as the utility relation is required to be).[9] But perhaps a more basic problem with this approach comes from the fact that a person's choice may be guided by a number of motives of which the pursuit of personal well-being is only one. The well-being motivation may well be dominant in some choices, but not in others. Moral considerations may, inter alia, influence a person's "commitment."[10] The mixture of motivations makes it hard to form a good idea of a person's well-being on the basis of choice information only.[11]

The other two views of utility—happiness and desire fulfillment—undoubtedly have some plausibility. However, happiness has two basic problems in its claim to stand for well-being. First, as it is interpreted in the utilitarian tradition, happiness is basically a mental state, and it ignores other aspects of a person's well-being. If a starving wreck, ravished by famine, buffeted by disease, is made happy through some mental conditioning (say, via the "opium" of religion), the person will be seen as doing well on this mental-state perspective, but that would be quite scandalous. Second, as a mental-state concept, the perspective of happiness may give a very limited view of other mental activities. There are mental states

[9] The respective conditions for binary representability and transitive binariness (and other—intermediate—structures), are identified and analyzed in Arrow, "Rational Choice and Orderings," *Economica,* XXVI (1959): 121-127; my "Choice Functions and Revealed Preference," *Review of Economic Studies,* XXXVIII (1971): 307-317, reprinted in CWM; Hans Herzberger, "Ordinal Preference and Rational Choice," *Econometrica,* XLI (1973): 187-237; K. Suzumura, *Rational Choice, Collective Decisions, and Social Welfare* (New York: Cambridge, 1983).

[10] This issue, among others, is discussed in my "Choice, Orderings and Morality," in S. Körner, ed., *Practical Reason* (Oxford: Blackwell, 1974), and "Rational Fools: A Critique of the Behavioural Foundations of Economic Theory," *Philosophy and Public Affairs,* VI (1977): 317-344, both reprinted in CWM.

[11] See Thomas Nagel, *The Possibility of Altruism* (New York: Oxford, 1970); my "Behaviour and the Concept of Preference," *Economica,* XL (1973): 241-259, reprinted in CWM; Stephan Körner, *Experience and Conduct* (New York: Cambridge, 1974); Harvey Leibenstein, *Beyond Economic Man* (Cambridge, Mass.: Harvard, 1976); Tibor Scitovsky, *The Joyless Economy* (New York: Oxford, 1976); Kurt Baier, "Rationality and Morality," *Erkenntnis,* XI, 2 (August 1977): 197-223; Thomas Schelling, *Micromotives and Macrobehavior* (New York: Norton, 1978); Jon Elster, *Ulysses and the Sirens* (New York: Cambridge, 1979); Albert Hirschman, *Shifting Involvements* (Princeton, N.J.: University Press, 1982); Howard Margolis, *Selfishness, Altruism and Rationality* (New York: Cambridge, 1982); George Akerlof, "Loyalty Filters," *American Economic Review,* LXXIII (1983); Michael McPherson, "Economics: On Hirschman, Schelling, and Sen," *Partisan Review,* LI (1984): 236-247; Derek Parfit, *Reasons and Persons* (New York: Oxford, 1984).

other than being just happy, such as stimulation, excitement, etc., which are of direct relevance to a person's well-being.[12] Furthermore, mental activities involve *valuation* of one's life—a reflective exercise—and the role of valuation in the identification of the person's well-being obviously cannot be seen in terms merely of the happiness that such reflection itself creates. It is hard to avoid the conclusion that although happiness is of obvious and direct relevance to well-being, it is inadequate as a representation of well-being.

Consider, now, the *desire* approach. There is some possibility of doubt about whether this is also a mental-state view of well-being. There can be, of course, hardly anything more "mental" than desires. But as James Griffin has recently argued in his important survey of "modern utilitarianism," "the desire account does not require that satisfaction of desire translates itself in every case into experience" (338, *op. cit.*). Griffin sees the desire approach as one in which welfare lies in "the state of the world," rather than in "the state of mind."

I believe that Griffin underestimates the extent to which a desire account has to be concerned with "the state of mind." An account of well-being that is to serve as a basis for a utilitarian calculus must be able to present a cardinal and interpersonally comparable view of utility. Neither of these types of information can be obtained just by checking whether the person's desires have been realized in the state of the world. The metric that will be needed for an informationally adequate view of utility cannot be obtained from the observation of objects of desire. The strength of desire must come into the picture, and the desires of different people have to be compared. Thus, the desire account of well-being is also, in an important sense, a mental-state account, though it is not a *purely* mental-state account (given the need to observe the objects of desire *as well*).

Is the importance of desire mainly *evidential,* viz., that it gives evidence—*possible* evidence—of value, or does desire have a "value-giving" role? That is, is it the case that the activity of desiring *makes* the objects of desire have value? This question can be posed in the general context of value as such, and also in the context of the value of well-being in particular.

I begin with the general context. I would argue that the primary

[12] See Scitovsky, *op. cit.*, and "The Desire for Excitement in Modern Society," *Kyklos,* XXXIV (1981).

role of desire is evidential and that the immediate linkage is with what the person regards as valuable. Compare the two following statements:

(I) I desire *x* because *x* is valuable for me.
(II) *x* is valuable for me because I desire *x*.

The former statement is intelligible and cogent in a way the latter clearly is not. Valuing something is a good reason for desiring it, but desiring something is not an obvious reason for valuing it. Of course the latter can still make sense in some special way, which can be explained, e.g., "Having first formed the desire for *x*, I have come to value *x*, because being frustrated in my desire will be disappointing and disvaluable."[13] Though such—and other possible—special considerations do give desiring something more than a *purely* "evidential" role, it is hard to escape the conclusion that the main connection between desire and value is the evidential connection articulated in (I).[14]

If this line of reasoning is accepted, then the next step is to investigate the connection between what a person regards as valuable and the value of the person's well-being. That connection will be weakened precisely by the fact that a person may well value things other than personal well-being. Indeed, the agency aspect of a person and the power to form and pursue a conception of the good may well take a person's desires in a direction different from personal well-being, and the evidence for the person's valuation may not fully translate into evidence for his or her well-being. Nevertheless, there is a serious connection here, and the evidential importance of desires in reflecting a person's well-being may well be quite substantial.

III. INTERPERSONAL COMPARISONS OF DESIRES

The evidential role of desires is, however, deeply problematic in the context of *interpersonal* comparisons. Comparative intensities of desire may be a very dubious guide indeed to well-being intensities in comparing one person with another, since these intensities are influenced by many contingent circumstances that are arbitrary for

[13] Cf. "Well-being and distress are to be understood as two kinds of human experience, those in which desires are satisfied and those in which desires are frustrated" [Ted Honderich, "The Question of Well-being and the Principle of Equality," *Mind*, XC, 360 (October 1981): 481-504, p. 481].

[14] In third-person contexts, desire fulfillment may plausibly be seen as having much strategic importance. The fact that you desire something may be a good reason for me to value it. But this too may have an evidential base. In treating your desire as evidence of what you value, I may value your desire fulfillment *as a consequence* of my valuing your success in getting what you yourself value.

well-being comparisons. Our reading of what is feasible in our situation and station may be crucial to the intensities of our desires, and may even affect what we dare to desire. Desires reflect compromises with reality, and reality is harsher to some than to others. The hopeless destitute desiring merely to survive, the landless laborer concentrating his efforts on securing the next meal, the round-the-clock domestic servant seeking a few hours of respite, the subjugated housewife struggling for a little individuality, may all have learned to keep their desires in line with their respective predicaments. Their deprivations are gagged and muffled in the interpersonal metric of desire fulfillment. In some lives small mercies have to count big.

It may be asked whether this problem cannot be dealt with in the same way as some utilitarians have proposed in "purifying" desires of "imperfection." Hare demands "perfectly prudent" preferences—"fully informed and unconfused." Harsanyi wants that, and *more;* to wit, to "exclude all antisocial preferences, such as sadism, envy, resentment, and malice."[15] These devices raise questions about how we may decide on what "purifications" are appropriate and justifiable within the general logic of utilitarianism, but they may well be able to deal sensibly with some problems, particularly those associated with factual ignorance and thoughtless decisions.

Can such purification procedures eliminate the problem under discussion, viz., the *circumstantial* contingency of desires? It is not clear how they could. Desiring is a part of living; it plays a strategic role in making our wants credible, our aspirations viable. To ask what one would desire in unspecified circumstances—abstracting from the concreteness of *everyone's* life—is to misunderstand the nature of desire and its place in human life. Of course, we can *pretend* to answer this question. Since all this is imaginary anyway, we need not live in the fear of being proved wrong. This can be done by making—explicitly or by implication—some simple assumption, e.g., that our desires would be in line with what Scanlon[16] has called "an objective criterion" of well-being, appealing to a certain "consensus" of values about the content of well-being. But if that is

[15] "Ethical Theory and Utilitarianism," in Sen and Williams, *op. cit.*, p. 28; Harsanyi, "Morality and the Theory of Rational Behaviour," in Sen and Williams, p. 56. See also James Mirrlees, "The Economic Uses of Utilitarianism," and Peter Hammond, "Utilitarianism, Uncertainty and Information," both in Sen and Williams, *op. cit.*

[16] "Preference and Urgency," this JOURNAL, LXXIII, 19 (Nov. 6, 1975): 655–669. Scanlon is, however, primarily concerned with *moral* urgency rather than with getting a concept of well-being that may be used for other purposes as well.

what we are going to do, we could just as easily have started from the objective criterion itself, and "founded" it on the consensus of values on well-being, rather than having the imaginary exercise of *counterfactual desiring*. Since, according to the arguments presented earlier in this lecture, the importance of desiring is primarily "evidential" anyway, that imaginary exercise is particularly pointless. There is little merit in justifying interest in desire information on the ground that it gives evidence of valuation and then going on to "obtain" the "purified" desire information through the knowledge (or assumption) of a consensus of valuations.

IV. EQUALITY AND MORAL VALUATION

I turn now to question (2b): Do utilitarian principles follow from WAIF if well-being is taken as utility? It was argued in the first lecture that utilitarianism is really a combination of welfarism, sum ranking, and some—direct or indirect—version of consequentialism. Therefore, the question can be seen as being about the derivability of these different *factors* from the union of (1) WAIF and (2) the identification of utility with well-being.

Deriving welfarism, obviously, poses no challenge to this task. Nor, in fact, does welfarist consequentialism in general. If nothing other than well-being can count as a morally fundamental fact and if well-being is just utility, then it will be necessary to evaluate actions and other choice variables in terms of utility consequences only.

The factor that remains unmarshalled even in this demanding framework is sum ranking, viz., the view that the utilities are best valued aggregatively by summing them and by ignoring every other aspect of utility distributions, including the extent of inequality. Nothing in WAIF *or* in the identifiction of well-being with utility can make sum ranking follow automatically without invoking some consideration that makes us unconcerned with equality of well-being. It is, therefore, a matter of considerable interest that arguments have been presented by some utilitarians that make sum ranking allegedly inescapable simply on grounds of logic, mathematics, or rationality.[17] How is this unusual feat performed?

Consider the Vickrey-Harsanyi model[18] of "ethical preferences"

[17] See, for example, John Harsanyi, "Nonlinear Social Welfare Functions: Or Do Welfare Economists Have a Special Exemption from Bayesian Rationality?" *Theory and Decision*, VI, 3 (August 1975): 311-332; M. McDermott, "Utility and Distribution," *Mind*, 91, 364 (October 1982): 572-578.

[18] W. S. Vickrey, "Measuring Marginal Utility by Reactions to Risk," *Econometrica*, XIII (1945): 691-707; Harsanyi, "Cardinal Welfare, Individualistic Ethics, and Interpersonal Comparisons of Utility," *Journal of Political Economy*, LXIII (1955): 309-321.

based on choosing between different states of affairs in a state of primordial equiprobability in which the chooser has an equal chance of being anyone.[19] If the *as if* behavior of this chooser satisfies certain "rationality" conditions (such as the von Neumann-Morgenstern axioms[20]), then the position of being any persion i in any state x can be given a value $W_i(x)$ such that the chooser's behavior can be represented as maximizing the mathematical expectation of these individual W_i values, i.e., maximizing $\Sigma_i\, p_i W_i$, when p_i is the probability of being person i. With the assumption of equiprobability of being anyone, this is no different from maximizing $\Sigma_i\, W_i$. If W_i is seen as person i's utility, then it looks as if sum ranking has somehow been deduced simply from rational behavior. Rationality must, it would seem, preclude any concern for equality of well-being in aggregating different persons' well-being![21]

But what are these W_i values? They are simply accounting values for predicting choice under uncertainty. They need not coincide with any concept of utility that has independent meaning, such as happiness, or satisfaction, or desire fulfillment. Not only may the values of W_i differ from the utilities U_i as perceived by persion i himself (his happiness, his desire fulfillment, etc.), but they may also differ from what the *chooser* expects to enjoy in the counterfactual position of becoming person i. The fact that W is the sum

[19] I abstain in the present context from questioning the acceptability of this general approach to moral valuation, since I am concerned here only with the specific question of how it deals with the issue of inequality. For discussions of different types of problems raised by this moral approach, see P. A. Diamond, "Cardinal Welfare, Individualistic Ethics, and Interpersonal Comparisons of Utility: A Comment," *Journal of Political Economy,* LXXV (1967): 765/6; my CCSW, ch. 9; Rawls, *A Theory of Justice* (1971); P. K. Pattanaik, *Voting and Collective Choice* (New York: Cambridge, 1971); Levi, "Four Types of Ignorance," *Social Research,* XLIV (1977): 745-756; E. F. McClennen, "The Minimax Theory and Expected Utility Reasoning," in C. A. Hooker, J. J. Leach, and McClennen, eds., *Foundations and Applications of Decision Theory,* vol. I (Boston: Reidel, 1978); C. Blackorby, D. Donaldson, and J. A. Weymark, "On John Harsanyi's Defences of Utilitarianism," Discussion Paper, University of British Columbia, 1980; M. Machina, "'Expected Utility' Analysis without the Independence Axiom," *Econometrica,* L (1982): 277-324; J. Broome, "Uncertainty and Fairness," *Economic Journal,* XCIV (1984): 624-632. Harsanyi's own assessment is to be found in his *Essays on Ethics, Social Behavior, and Scientific Explanation* (Boston: Reidel, 1976).

[20] J. von Neumann and O. Morgenstern, *Theory of Games and Economic Behavior* (Princeton, N.J.: University Press, 1944). For an excellent discussion of the contents, interpretation and implications of the axioms, see R. D. Luce and H. Raiffa, *Games and Decision* (New York: Wiley, 1957).

[21] See also Harsanyi, "Non-linear Social Welfare Functions: A Rejoinder to Professor Sen," and my "A Reply to Professor Harsanyi," in Robert E. Butts and Jaakko Hintikka, eds., *Foundational Problems in the Special Sciences* (Boston: Reidel, 1977).

of the W_i values does not tell us anything at all about what the relationship is between W and the independently characterized utilities U_i of the respective persons. In terms of the language of the von Neumann-Morgenstern model of choice, we might employ the term 'utility' for W_i, but W_i has no necessary role other than yielding accounting values in terms of which the chooser's behavior can be predicted.

In fact, the numbering system of W_i works the way it does precisely by *incorporating* attitudes toward risk in the W_i values themselves. And, in this framework, these attitudes toward risk correspond neatly to attitudes toward inequality.[22] If the chooser's attitude toward inequality changes (but "consistency" of choice is retained in the form of continuing to satisfy the von Neumann-Morgenstern axioms), then the W_i functions will change correspondingly, even though the utilities U_i of the persons in the form of happiness or desire fulfillment may remain completely unaltered. The fact that W is the *sum* of the W_i values does not imply sum ranking of the utility values U_i, and it presents an additive accounting procedure only through the *devised* values of W_i. No *substantive* sum ranking result is entailed by the accounting procedure.

It is, in fact, not surprising that the relevance of equality in moral valuation cannot be settled without assessing equality itself. The informational foundation of well-being yielded by WAIF leaves it open how the well-being of different people are to be combined in assessing states and actions. And this issue is not obliterated even when "rational" behavior under uncertainty with primordial equiprobability is taken to be the basis of moral valuation. Rationality—even in the limited sense of satisfying von Neumann-Morgenstern axioms—is no enemy of valuing equality of well-being.

While the issue of equality has to be faced, the fact that there are many different notions of equality implies that conflicts among these different egalitarian views have to be faced as well. In an important study called *Equalities,* Douglas Rae has argued that the "one idea that is more powerful than order or efficiency or freedom in resisting equality" is "equality itself."[23] Peter Westen has gone further and has suggested that equality is "an empty form having no substantive content of its own."[24] It may be tempting to dismiss

[22] See A. B. Atkinson, "On the Measurement of Inequality," *Journal of Economic Theory,* II (1970): 244-263; P. Dasgupta, A. Sen, and D. Starrett, "Notes on the Measurement of Inequality," *Journal of Economic Theory,* VI (1973): 180-187; M. Rothschild and J. E. Stiglitz, "Some Further Results in the Measurement of Inequality," *Journal of Economic Theory,* VI (1973): 188-204.

[23] Cambridge, Mass.: Harvard, 1981; p. 150.

[24] "The Empty Idea of Equality," *Harvard Law Review,* VC (1982): 537-596, p. 596.

concern with equality in moral evaluation on grounds of this alleged "emptiness."

However, the multiplicity of notions of equality arises from various sources, and often enough these sources do not appear to be peculiar to equality at all. A person's advantage can be judged in many different ways, and corresponding to these different ways, there are various characterizations of equality. Utility, income, opulence, need-fulfillment, etc., provide different ways of seeing a person's success, and each of them would lead to a corresponding approach to equality. But this plurality is not special to equality. Any derivative notion for which individual advantage provides the informational base, would have this plurality. For example, the notion of "efficiency" in terms of achievements (that the situation is such that no one can be made more advantaged without reducing someone else's advantage) will have exactly the same variability. If advantage is seen in absolute terms *and* identified with utility, then the notion of efficiency immediately becomes the concept—much used in economics—of "Pareto optimality." But related to the other notions of advantage—income, opulence, need fulfillment, etc.—there will be the corresponding notions of efficiency.

In rejecting the claims of utility to represent well-being, we have outlined the need for an alternative approach. The issue of equality will again arise in whatever alternative concept of well-being we accept. I return now to the characterization of well-being.

V. FUNCTIONINGS AND WELL-BEING

It is useful to contrast two closely related ideas, which are quite clearly different. One is the idea of being "well off" and the other of being "well," or having "well-being." The former is really a concept of opulence—how rich is she? what goods and services can she buy? what offices are open to her? and so on. This refers to a person's command over things outside—including what Rawls calls "primary goods." Having "well-being," on the other hand, is not something outside her that she commands, but something in her that she achieves. What kind of a life is she leading? What does she succeed in doing and in being? Being "well off" may help, other things given, to have "well-being," but there is a distinctly personal quality in the latter absent in the former.

In looking for an appropriate approach to well-being, there are two different dangers to avoid, coming from two different directions. One problem lies in taking a basically subjectivist view in terms of one of the mental-state metrics of utility. The difficulties of this approach have already been discussed (sections II and III). Being happy may be a valuable thing to be, and not having one's desires frustrated may also have value, but there are clearly other things that are also valuable to do or be. We have to value the different types of doings and beings, but "desiring" is not a valuational activity in itself, though it may be the consequence of one. The linkage may give desiring an "evidential" value, which was discussed, but the limitations of which, especially in interpersonal comparison, also emerged clearly enough. We are, thus, pulled in the objectivist (and, in one sense, "impersonal") direction, looking for a criterion that does not get messed up by circumstantial contingencies (as the "evidential" value of desire information clearly can).

What form would an "objective" criterion of well-being take? "By an *objective criterion* I mean a criterion that provides a basis for appraisal of a person's well-being which is independent of the person's tastes and interests," says Scanlon.[25] But why should an objective criterion not take note of the objective basis of differences of different people's "tastes and interests"? As discussed in the first lecture (in the context of the quite different problem of position-relativity of moral judgments of actions and states, 183/4), the personal features that make a *relevant* objective difference (and which others too can see) can be built *parametrically* into an evaluation function without losing objectivity.

One reason why "being well off" is quite different from "being well," despite the fact that the former is causally related to the latter, is the variability of personal characteristics which makes the causal relations *person-specific*. The Charybdis of overrigidity threatens us as much as the Scylla of subjectivist variability, and we must not lose sight of the important personal parameters in developing an approach to well-being.

Consider a disabled person, who, with the same level of real income and opulence, cannot do many things that a normal person can. His tastes in commodities will be different (and typically more expensive), and his interests will make very different demands on others. In what way does this disabled person differ in terms of this issue from the person with "expensive tastes," who has received such a lot of attention recently (and, to indulge in an aside, whose taste for having expensive and exquisite attention must by now be well satisfied by what he has got from Kenneth Arrow, Ronald Dworkin, John Rawls, and Tim Scanlon, among others)?[26]

[25] "Preference and Urgency" (1975), p. 658. Scanlon qualifies the statement in several different ways (pp. 658/9). Also, his concern is primarily with what is morally significant and not with developing a notion of well-being relevant in other contexts as well.

[26] Arrow, "Some Ordinalist-Utilitarian Notes on Rawls's Theory of Justice," this

One important difference between the two cases relates to the likely fact that the expensive-taste person may be able to *do* most things a normal person can and be handicapped only in the context of achieving contentment or satisfaction, whereas the disabled person may be handicapped in terms of a much wider range of activities.[27] As Scanlon describes the refined being, he could not be raised to a "normal level of satisfaction" without very high expenditure (659). The Arrow-Dworkin creature hooked on "plovers' eggs and pre-phylloxera claret" is unhappy unless he gets these extraordinary provisions, even though there is nothing to suggest that he cannot do the usual things that other people can, except that of being happy. In contrast, the deprivation of the handicapped person relates also to his inability to do many entirely normal things (unless, of course, we are considering some exotic type of handicap). The disadvantages that he suffers in his "being" do not have to be seen in terms of utilities at all.

In fact, handicapped people are often cheerful enough, and do not lead a life of frustrated desires, since their desires adapt to the reality of their handicap (a point that relates to the issue of circumstantial contingency of desires, which was discussed earlier, 190/1). The primary disability certainly would be in matters of leading a normal life—being able to get around, being able to hear or see, or something like that. That it is reflected in a lowered utility level is secondary, if true, and it may not even be true. There is no real comparison with the "plover's egg" fan.

The primary feature of well-being can be seen in terms of how a person can "function," taking that term in a very broad sense. I shall refer to various doings and beings that come into this assessment as *functionings*. These could be activities (like eating or reading or seeing), or states of existence or being, e.g., being well nourished, being free from malaria, not being ashamed by the poverty of

JOURNAL, LXX (1973): 245–288; R. Dworkin, "What Is Equality? Part I: Equality and Welfare," *Philosophy and Public Affairs*, X, 3 (Summer 1981): 185–246; Rawls, "Social Unity and Primary Goods," in Sen and Williams; Scanlon, "Preference and Urgency" (1975).

[27] Another difference emphasized particularly by Dworkin, Rawls, and Scanlon relates to the "responsibility" of the person with expensive taste in the genesis of his disadvantage. However, although that consideration is of obvious interest in judging a person's *moral claim* for support, it may not be of direct relevance in judging a person's *actual well-being*. In terms of the categorization used in these lectures, the issue of responsibility relates immediately to the agency aspect of a person, rather than to the well-being aspect. There is a further problem arising from the fact that the responsibility may have to be traced over a long period of time, and this is made more complicated by issues of personal identity; see Derek Parfit, *Reasons and Persons* (New York: Oxford, 1984), and Michael Slote, *Goods and Virtues* (New York: Oxford, 1983).

one's clothing or shoes (to go back to a question that Adam Smith discussed in his *Wealth of Nations*[28]). I shall refer to the set of functionings a person actually achieves as the *functioning vector* (though it would have been more accurate to describe it as an *n-tuple,* since some of the functionings may not be numerically representable).

The primary feature of a person's well-being is the functioning vector that he or she achieves. The functioning vectors can be ranked and partially ordered in line with some common valuations, or in the light of what Scanlon calls "urgency," or some other acceptable criterion. This, then, is the secondary representation, in the form of the place of a functioning vector in a partial order of such vectors. If the ordering is complete, we should be able to get even a real-numbered "index" of well-being (in the absence of some technical peculiarities in that ordering[29]). In fact, even a partial order will typically have numerical representation with some "transparency" properties.[30] The "natural" form of well-being ranking is indeed that of a partial, incomplete order. It would be just as extraordinary if every possible pair of functioning vectors could be compared in terms of over-all well-being, as it would be if none of them could be. There will, of course, be many agreed valuations, and many decisive judgments, and the clarity of these cases is not compromised by the muddiness of others.

VI. OPULENCE, FUNCTIONINGS, AND UTILITY

The contrast between opulence and functioning achievements is simple enough, but its significance in the context of well-being may be worth spelling out. The example of the crippled (or otherwise handicapped person) is, in some respects, particularly misleading. It may suggest that personal variations are uncommon and unusual things. In fact, however, interpersonal variations in "transforming" goods into functionings is extremely common. Take, for example, the consumption of *food,* on the one hand, and the functioning of *being well nourished,* on the other. The relationship between them

[28] *An Inquiry into the Nature and Causes of the Wealth of Nations* (1776; Everyman's Library, London: Dent, 1954), vol. II, p. 352.

[29] An example of a non-numerically-representable complete order is a "lexicographic" order over the unit square: see Gerard Debreu, *Theory of Value* (New York: Wiley, 1959), ch. 4. Since lexicographic orderings have some interest in moral philosophy, as with the "lexicographic maximim" version of Rawls's difference principle [see my *Collective Choice and Social Welfare* (1970), p. 138; Rawls, *A Theory of Justice* (1971), pp. 42–45], it is perhaps just worth recording the elementary fact that a lexicographic order—or indeed any other order—over any *finite* set (no matter how large) will never have such a representation problem.

[30] See Mukul Majumdar and Amartya Sen, "On Representing Partial Orderings," *Review of Economic Studies,* XLIII (1976): 543–545. The real problem arises with guaranteeing the continuity of such a numerical function.

varies with (1) metabolic rates, (2) body size, (3) age, (4) sex (and if a woman, whether pregnant or lactating), (5) activity levels, (6) climatic conditions, (7) presence of parasitic diseases, (8) access to medical services, (9) nutritional knowledge, and other influences.

Interpersonal variability of the relation between goods and functionings turns out to be quite central to many important policy issues. For example, the comparison between the positions of men and women in terms of nutritional achievements in the poorer countries is often distorted by the use of food intake figures, which are not only unreliable, but also difficult to relate to well-being. The comparisons are usually made with some arbitrarily assumed sex-specific nutritional requirements, and there is some evidence that the most widely used requirements norms (the so-called "FAO-WHO standards") not only are inappropriate in a great majority of cases, but also involve a systematic sex bias, helping to conceal the extent of the relative deprivation of women in many of these countries. In contrast, direct information on the actual *functionings* achieved by men and women (in this case, avoiding undernourishment, escaping avoidable morbidity, etc.) are both easier to use and more sensibly interpreted in terms of well-being.[31]

Interpersonal variations are not, of course, confined to such elementary functionings as being well nourished, or escaping avoidable morbidity. Personal and social influences on the conversion of opulence into functioning achievements can be powerful in many other fields as well. The resource requirements of such functionings as "appearing in public without shame" (emphasized by Adam Smith), taking part in the life of the community, being able to visit and entertain friends, being acceptably well informed, and so on, vary a good deal with the nature of the community in which one lives and with other contingent circumstances.[32]

Opulence does, of course, *contribute* to functioning, and the command that it gives can indeed be important for a person's well-being and advantage. Rawlsian analysis of "primary goods" has forcefully demonstrated the usefulness of that perspective compared with reliance on the mental metric of utility.[33] But an index of opu-

[31] Some of these issues are discussed, along with presenting some empirical results, in Jocelyn Kynch and Amartya Sen, "Indian Women: Well-being and Survival," *Cambridge Journal of Economics*, VII (1983): 363-380, and in Essays 13, 15, and 16 in my *Resources, Values and Development* (Oxford: Blackwell, and Cambridge, Mass.: Harvard, 1984), hereafter, RVD.

[32] Some of these issues are discussed in my "Poor, Relatively Speaking," *Oxford Economic Papers*, XXXV (1983): 153-169, reprinted in RVD; and "The Living Standard," *Oxford Economic Papers*, XXXVI (1984): 74-90.

[33] Rawls, *A Theory of Justice* (1971), and "Social Unity and Primary Goods" in Sen and Williams. Rawls is concerned with agency as well, not just well-being, in his analysis of primary goods.

lence, or of primary goods, cannot be seen as an index of well-being as such. Nor can the "advantage" of different persons (or groups) be ranked on the basis of the primary goods index, because of interpersonal variations in what people can *do* with primary goods, depending on biological, social, and other parameters.

Nor, of course, is it a matter of utility, as we have already seen. Happiness may be a valuable part of well-being, and being happy is certainly a momentous functioning, but there are other important functionings that are not congruent with happiness and for which happiness cannot serve as a surrogate, especially in interpersonal comparisons. Desire intensities may also be relevant to the valuation of functionings for evidential reasons, but—as was discussed earlier—the problem of valuation of functionings cannot be avoided by concentrating instead on the observation of desires and their intensities. The central feature of well-being is the ability to achieve valuable functionings.[34] The need for identification and valuation of the important functionings cannot be avoided by looking at something else, such as happiness, desire fulfillment, opulence, or command over primary goods.

It is, of course, clear that the functioning approach is intrinsically information-pluralist.[35] Although some consensus of valuations and the usability of various objective criteria may take us a great distance in establishing an extensive partial ordering in the comparison of well-being, it would be quite wrong to expect anything like the kind of complete ordering that utilitarians have made us prone to demand. As was discussed in the first lecture, such a completeness requirement is neither methodologically sensible nor substantively plausible (nor in fact actually met by the utilitarian calculus itself, except under the artificial assumption of complete and unproblematic interpersonal comparability). Incompleteness is *not* an embarrassment.

VII. CAPABILITY AND FREEDOM

The information pluralism of the functioning approach to well-being has to be further extended if we shift attention from the person's actual functionings to his or her *capability* to function. A

[34] The problem of evaluation of functioning vectors has been discussed in my *Commodities and Capabilities* (Amsterdam: North-Holland, 1985).

[35] The feature of plurality can, however, be reduced by the use of "invariance restrictions" in the analysis of well-being, e.g., "being well nourished" defining an isoinformation set (ignoring differences between being well-nourished through eating bread *or* rice, etc.), and "being entertained" as another such category (ignoring differences between entertainment from the cinema or the theatre, etc.). There will, of course, be gradations in being well-nourished, being entertained, etc., with corresponding layers of isoinformation sets.

person's *capability set* can be defined as the set of functioning vectors within his or her reach. In examining the well-being aspect of a person, attention can legitimately be paid to the capability set of the person and not just to the chosen functioning vector. This has the effect of taking note of the positive freedoms in a general sense (the freedom "to do this," or "to be that") that a person has.

Importance may well be attached to checking whether one person did have the opportunity of achieving the functioning vector that another actually achieved. This involves comparison of actual opportunities that different persons have. If one person could have achieved all the relevant functioning vectors that the other could, then in some important sense the first person had at least as much freedom to live well. The general idea of the freedom to achieve well-being can be called *well-being freedom.*

To illustrate, consider two persons with identical actual functioning vectors, including—as it happens—both of them starving. Person *A* is starving because she is very poor and lacks the means to command food. Person *B* is starving out of choice, because of his religious beliefs, which have made him decide to starve and undergo the consequent suffering. In terms of the misery caused by the starvation, we learn that there is no difference between *A*'s experience and *B*'s. Even if it were plausible to say that *A* and *B* both have the same level of well-being, in terms of being undernourished, miserable, etc. (that complex issue will be examined presently), there would nevertheless remain an important difference between the two cases, viz., *B could have* in a straightforward sense, chosen an alternative life style which *A* could not have chosen. This is a difference that is relevant to assessing the well-being aspect of the two persons respectively, though it is not necessarily a difference between the *actual* well-being levels achieved by the two. In judging a person's advantage (and the kind of "deal" that he or she has got), the importance of well-being freedom must be recognized.[36]

A second reason for being interested in the capability set arises from a different type of consideration altogether. The existence of genuine choice may actually affect the nature and significance of the functionings achieved. The first—and primitive—characterization of functionings in terms of doing this or being that may have to be modified and made more sophisticated by taking note of more

[36] The problem of ranking capability sets involves many difficulties; on this see my *Commodities and Capabilities* (1985). Cases of dominance (*either* in the form of one set being a proper subset of another, *or* in the sense of one set being *element-by-element* dominated by the other in terms of the partial ordering of functioning vectors) would of course induce a *minimal* partial ordering on the space of capability sets.

complexly characterized doings, e.g., choosing to do *x* rather than *y*. *Fasting* involves an abstention from eating that goes beyond just starving, and it can be argued that in the example being considered, rich and religious *B* could choose to fast, whereas poverty-stricken *A* could not. The possibility of starving was open to both, but *fasting* by choice was open only to *B*.[37] Examining capability sets of primitive functionings may permit us to move to a richer analysis of functionings, taking note of the choices exercised.

It can be argued that the well-being that a person actually enjoys is often more closely related to such *refined* functioning achievements. This view relates to the idea that the good life is inter alia also a life of freedom.[38] It is a view that has found rather eloquent expression in the writings of many social and political philosophers.[39]

On this line of reasoning, the extent of the capability set is relevant to the significance and value of the respective functionings. This might look like introducing a circularity in the relationship between functionings and capabilities, and between well-being and well-being freedom. But what it, in fact, does is to force us to see these concepts as mutually dependent, taking note of the simultaneity of the relationships involved. The refined characterization of functionings has to take note of the capability set of the "primitive" functionings, but the refined functionings, in their turn, yield a (corresponding) refined capability set.[40]

VIII. CONCLUDING REMARKS

In this lecture I have argued (1) *against* accepting the adequacy of WAIF (well-being as informational foundation), (2) *against* the

[37] I am grateful to Ian White for helpful discussions on these issues.

[38] On related matters, see Jon Elster, "Sour Grapes," in Sen and Williams, pp. 227/8, and *Sour Grapes* (New York: Cambridge, pp. 128/9.

[39] One of them is, of course, Karl Marx, whose political philosophy gives a special role to bringing "the conditions for the free development and activity of individuals under their own control" and who outlines a vision of a liberated future society which "makes it possible for me to do one thing to-day and another tomorrow, to hunt in the morning, fish in the afternoon, rear cattle in the evening, criticize after dinner, just as I have in mind, without ever becoming hunter, fisherman, shepherd or critic" [K. Marx and F. Engels, *The German Ideology* (1845/46; republished New York: International Publishers, 1947), p. 22]. This perspective of freedom has a strong bearing also on other aspects of the Marxian tradition. Examples of different types of connections can be found in G. A. Cohen, *Karl Marx's Theory of History: A Defence* (New York: Oxford, 1978); J. E. Roemer, *A General Theory of Exploitation and Class* (Cambridge, Mass.: Harvard, 1982); G. G. Brenkert, *Marx's Ethics of Freedom* (London: Routledge & Kegan Paul, 1983); J. Elster, *Making Sense of Marx* (Cambridge: Cambridge, 1985); S. Lukes, *Marxism and Morality* (Oxford: Oxford, 1985).

[40] It is, of course, possible to do more than one round of refining, though the advantages of such extended refinement might be rather limited.

identification of well-being with utility (in any of its forms: happiness, desire fulfillment, choice), and (3) *against* treating sum ranking as trivial and equality as having no independent force. More positively, I have argued *for* seeing well-being in terms of functioning vectors and the capability to achieve them. The well-being aspect of a person leads to a particular concept of freedom, which has been called *well-being freedom.*

FREEDOM AND AGENCY

IN the last lecture it was argued that the well-being aspect of a person calls for dual accounting—in terms, respectively, of freedom and achievement. The significance of the distinction relates particularly to the agency aspect of a person. Values other than the pursuit of well-being may figure prominently in a person's assessment of choices. Not making maximal use of the freedom to pursue well-being may not reflect any failure of evaluation or action. In judging what kind of a deal a person has in terms of the opportunity to pursue his or her own well-being, the concept of *well-being freedom* is, therefore, necessary, and its role cannot be subsumed by the observation of actual *achievements* of well-being. The autonomy of the agency aspect of a person, which has the effect of making WAIF an inadequate basis for substantive moral reasoning, also has the result that the well-being aspect of a person must be seen in terms of freedom as well as actual achievement.

I. AGENCY FREEDOM

Well-being freedom is freedom of a rather particular type. It concentrates on a person's capability to have various functioning vectors and to enjoy the corresponding well-being achievements. This concept of freedom, based on the well-being aspect of a person, has to be clearly distinguished from a broader concept of freedom, related to the agency aspect of a person. A person's "agency freedom" refers to what the person is free to do and achieve in pursuit of whatever goals or values he or she regards as important. A person's agency aspect cannot be understood without taking note of his or her aims, objectives, allegiances, obligations, and—in a broad sense—the person's conception of the good. Whereas well-being freedom is freedom to achieve something in particular, viz., well-being, the idea of agency freedom is more general, since it is not tied to any one type of aim. Agency freedom is freedom to achieve whatever the person, as a responsible agent, decides he or she should achieve. That *open conditionality* makes the nature of agency freedom quite different from that of well-being freedom, which concentrates on a particular type of objective and judges opportunities correspondingly.[1]

This open conditionality does not imply that the person's view of his agency has no need for discipline, and that anything that appeals to him must, for that reason, come into the accounting of his agency freedom. The need for careful assessment of aims, objectives, allegiances, etc., and of the conception of the good, may be important and exacting. But despite this need for discipline, the use of one's agency is, in an important sense, a matter for oneself to judge. When the requirement of careful assessment cannot be fulfilled (e.g., in the case of young children, or with persons mentally ill in ways that rule out such assessment), the agency aspect will be, obviously, less important. This does not indicate that the demands of the agency aspect for such a person would have to be assessed by *others* on his or her behalf, but only that no such demands would then be made. This would not, of course, in any way compromise the importance of their *well-being aspect.* Indeed in the absence of the relevance of their agency aspect, it is their *well-being achievement* that would uniquely command attention.

The importance of the agency aspect, in general, relates to the view of persons as responsible agents. Persons must enter the moral accounting by others not only as people whose well-being demands concern, but also as people whose responsible agency must be recognized. Although well-being achievement is geared to a specific objective, and well-being freedom is seen in terms of the freedom to achieve that objective through the choice of functioning vectors, agency freedom cannot be examined in terms of any prespecified objective. The open conditionality referred to above is central to that concept.

II. PLURALITY, WELL-BEING, AND AGENCY

In terms of the analysis presented so far, we have a plural informational base for substantive moral analysis, which has to take note of several distinct considerations involving well-being and agency. These different considerations may quite possibly pull in different directions.

A person's actual well-being has intrinsic importance. This tends to give WAIF some apparent plausibility, and is reflected more

[1] Agency freedom has claims to being taken as freedom *tout court,* which well-being freedom clearly does not have.

generally in the hold of "well-being" on moral thinking (including utilitarian moral thinking, though—as was argued in the last lecture—utility provides rather limited ways of seeing well-being). For responsible adults, the concept of "well-being freedom" has a clear relevance in judging the opportunities a person has for pursuing his or her own advantage. The supplementation of well-being by well-being freedom, in the case of responsible adults, involves a refinement in the assessment of the well-being aspect of a person. But well-being freedom is only a specific type of freedom, and it cannot reflect the person's over-all freedom as an agent; we have to turn to the notion of agency freedom in that context. It is hard to see how any part of this plurality (involving both the well-being aspect and the agency aspect of persons) can fail to have some intrinsic importance.

This plurality would have been a matter of considerable embarrassment if for methodological reasons we were obliged to reject any information-pluralist framework, with "monism" as the only acceptable approach. But, as was discussed in the first lecture, there is no good reason for that monist presumption, and none for imposing monism as an a priori requirement.

Furthermore, as was also discussed in the first lecture, it is not a matter of embarrassment that there might be scope for variation in the assessment of the relative importance of the different elements in a pluralist structure. Although "dominance" reasoning will, as was discussed, be able to provide a minimal partial ordering in a pluralist structure, and variable valuations within given *ranges* of weights will extend that partial ordering further, nevertheless even such enhanced partial orderings may well remain incomplete. The need to consider both the agency aspect and the well-being aspect of persons is not compromised by the possibility that the combined structure may leave a large subset of unordered pairs. Those who see substantive moral reasoning as worthless unless it completely orders the space of all actions and states will, of course, find much to complain about in this incompleteness. But, as was seen in the first lecture, there is no good reason why we should have to yield to this external pressure for completeness.

It can, however, be argued that while plurality and incompleteness are not themselves objectionable, nevertheless in this particular case there happen to be redundant elements in the proposed plural structure. I have already discussed, in the second lecture, why well-being is inadequate as an informational basis of moral judgments, given the intrinsic importance of agency. But I have not yet explicitly provided any reason why agency information may not be adequate for moral judgment (thereby making it redundant to incorporate well-being information—in the form of achievement *or* freedom— in the basic structure). Agency information includes each person's pursuits and choices. The hypothesis of the adequacy of agency information might appear to have considerable plausibility,[2] especially since agency freedom can be seen as incorporating well-being freedom, inter alia. "Open conditionality" indicates that if a person were to pursue well-being, then assessment of the agency freedom of that person would have to include his or her well-being freedom as well. And if the person were unconcerned about pursuing his or her own well-being, then why should it matter whether the person had well-being freedom or not?

In responding to this issue, the important thing to recognize is that the well-being aspect and the agency aspect of persons have dissimilar roles in moral accounting. They invite attention in *disparate* ways. At the risk of oversimplification it can be said that the well-being aspect of a person is important in assessing a person's *advantage,* whereas the agency aspect is important in assessing what a person can do in line with his or her conception of *the good.* The ability to do more good need not be to the person's advantage.

Perhaps an illustration may help to bring out the distinction a little more clearly. You are enjoying eating a sandwich on a nice spring day, sitting on the bank of the river Avon. Meanwhile, far away, a man who cannot swim is drowning. You cannot do anything to save him—he is hundreds of miles away. Consider now a *counterfactual* situation in which that man, instead of drowning at that lonely, distant spot, is about to drown right in front of you. How are *you* affected by this counterfactual change? Your agency freedom is, in an important way, increased. You can now very likely save the man. You will, let us assume, value this opportunity highly and decide to save him, and, further, you will even succeed. You will chuck your sandwich, jump into the cold river, and haul the man out. Your agency freedom would have been well used, and the state of affairs would have been better, as you would yourself judge it.

But your *well-being* is, quite possibly, reduced. You may, of course, enjoy saving a life, and a part of your well-being may certainly be positively influenced by the opportunity to do good. But it is possible that, everything considered, your own well-being is no

[2] I am grateful to Bruce Ackerman for providing good arguments in favor of this possibility and for insisting that *either* agency freedom be regarded as adequate *or* its inadequacy be explicitly established.

higher, and let us assume (to pursue our contrasts) that it is actually lower—with the quiet lunch being replaced by a ducking in the chilling river, risking your own life in undertaking the life-saving operation. An expansion of agency freedom can go with a reduction in actual well-being, through your own choice, even though you are not, by any means, indifferent to your own well-being.

What about your "well-being freedom?" That was certainly not enhanced by the counterfactual change. The additional opportunity of saving the drowning person did not give you a better (or even as good a) way of pursuing your own well-being. In fact, in an important way, the counterfactual change actually *reduced* your well-being freedom. You were no longer free to eat your sandwich *without anxiety*, and, in terms of the "refined" functionings discussed in the last lecture (pp. 201/2), there was a genuine loss of opportunity to pursue your own well-being.

Since agency freedom includes inter alia the freedom to pursue your own well-being, it can, of course, also be said that *in that respect* your agency freedom too would have been adversely affected. But if it is the case (as it is here assumed to be) that, given the choice, you would rather have the opportunity of saving the drowning person than eat your sandwich without anxiety, and that your valuations as an agent confirm the correctness of this choice, then there is clearly a *net* gain in terms of your *agency freedom*. As an agent you value the new opportunity (saving the person) more than the lost opportunity (eating the sandwich without anxiety). But in terms of your *well-being freedom*, there *is* a net loss, since the lost opportunity is more valuable from the narrow perspective of your own well-being than the new opportunity. It is, in this sense, arguable that even though agency freedom does "include" well-being freedom, the latter can quite possibly go down when the former goes up (and, of course, vice versa). The ranking of alternative opportunities from the point of view of agency need not be the same as the ranking in terms of well-being, and thus the judgments of agency freedom and well-being freedom can move in contrary directions.[3] So, even though agency freedom is "broader" than well-being freedom, the former *cannot* subsume the latter.

Insofar as each person's advantage commands attention and respect in moral accounting, the well-being aspect of the person has to be directly considered. This role cannot be taken over by agency

[3] The relationship between the ranking of *elements* and the ranking of *sets* of elements is discussed in my *Commodities and Capabilities* (1985), ch. 7, in the specific context of judging "capability sets" and the corresponding "freedoms."

information. Although the agency aspect and the well-being aspect both are important, they are important for quite different reasons. In one perspective, a person is seen as a doer and a judge, whereas in the other the same person is seen as a beneficiary whose interests and advantages have to be considered.[4] There is no way of reducing this plural-information base into a monist one without losing something of importance.[5]

The well-being aspect may be particularly important in some specific contexts, e.g., in making public provisions for social security, or in planning for the fulfillment of basic needs.[6] In judging what a person may expect from social arrangements, the demands of well-being (and, in the case of responsible adults, also of well-being freedom) may loom rather large. On the other hand, in many issues of personal morality, the agency aspect, and one's responsibility to others, may be central. The well-being aspect and the agency aspect both demand attention, but they do so in different ways, and with varying relevance to different problems.

III. FREEDOM: POWER OR CONTROL?

Within the idea of freedom itself, there tends to be an internal plurality. There are, in fact, two distinct elements in the idea of freedom (they may be called, respectively, "power" and "control"), and the assessment of freedom has to deal with this internal plurality as well.[7] The distinction is of special relevance to particular issues of freedom, such as liberty and autonomy.

A person's freedom may well be assessed in terms of the power to achieve chosen results: whether the person is free to achieve one outcome or another; whether his or her choices will be respected and the corresponding things will happen. This element of freedom, which I shall call *effective power,* or *power* (for short), is not really concerned with the mechanism and procedures of control. It does not matter for effective power precisely *how* the choices are

[4] This dichotomy has a close connection with the contrast between "interest aggregation" and "judgment aggregation" in social choice theory, discussed in my "Social Choice Theory: A Reexamination," *Econometrica,* XLV (1977): 53–89; reprinted in my CWM (1982).

[5] However, while the agency and well-being aspects are quite distinct from each other, they are *not* independent of each other. The dependence arises from at least two obvious facts: that a person's agency may affect his or her well-being, and that being well may help a person's ability to act in pursuit of other objectives as well.

[6] This applies both to formal modeling of plan priorities [see, for example, G. Chichilnisky, "Basic Needs and Global Models: Resources, Trade and Distribution," *Alternatives,* VI (1980)] and to broader planning "strategies" [see, for example, P. Streeten, *et al., First Things First* (New York: Oxford, 1981)].

[7] The contrast is discussed in my "Liberty as Control: An Appraisal," *Midwest Studies in Philosophy,* VII (1982): 207–221.

"executed." Indeed the choices may not even be directly addressed. Effective power can take note of *counterfactual choice:* things might be done because of knowledge of what the person would choose *if* he actually had control over the outcome.

In contrast, a person's freedom may also be assessed in terms of whether the person is himself exercising *control* over the process of choice. Is he actively doing the choosing in the procedure of decision and execution? This element of freedom may be called *procedural control,* or *control* (for short). It does not matter for freedom as control whether the person succeeds at all in achieving what he would choose.[8]

It is fair to say that, in the literature on liberty and freedom in political philosophy, it is the control element that has tended to receive the lion's share of attention. There is, of course, the related but distinct question of whether freedom should be seen in positive or negative terms, and whether one's obligations should take the form of not interfering with other people's control over spheres of their lives rather than the form of duties to help positively. I shall take up these questions later, but the distinction between effective power and procedural control is, in a sense, more elementary. While the control view is often combined with a constraint-based approach (to wit: *do not interfere* with other people's control over some specific matters), there is a general issue of whether the control view is *itself* an adequate approach to freedom, even when its use is not restricted to the negative perspective. I would argue that this concentration on control tends to produce an unacceptably narrow conceptualization of liberty and freedom.

To illustrate the contrast, I begin with a shortened version of an example I have used elsewhere.[9] Your friend is injured in an accident and is unconscious. The doctor says that either treatment *A* or treatment *B* can be used and one would be just as effective as the other, but that your friend would suffer less from *A* because of its

[8] In commenting on an earlier version of this text (and on the paper cited in fn 7), G. A. Cohen has argued that the terms 'power' and 'control' may be misleading. When a person has "effective power" in the sense specified, even if he does not have control over the process of selection, it *could be said* (Cohen points out) that he *had,* in fact, exercised control. This point might well be correct, but, if the basic distinction is accepted, it may not matter much whether we see it as a contrast between "procedural control" and "control" in some suitably broad sense, or between "procedural control" and "effective power", as it is presented here. The important issue relates to the fact that in modern society many powers are indirectly exercised, and, in that context, concentration on the levers of control provides an inadequate approach to freedom.

[9] "Liberty and Social Choice," (1983), pp. 18–20.

smaller side effects. However, you happen to know that your friend would have chosen treatment *B*, since treatment *A* is associated with some experiments on live animals of which your friend disapproves totally. He would, in fact, agree that treatment *A* would have been better for his well-being, but as a free agent he would have nevertheless chosen treatment *B*, if he were given the choice. If you now decide to ask the doctor to give your friend treatment *B*, you are giving your friend effective power even though he is not exercising the control himself. And your ground for choosing treatment *B* for him is surely not his well-being (he too agrees that *A* would be better for that), but his freedom (in the general form of *agency freedom*). It is also worth noting that your decision regarding what treatment your friend gets is *dependent* on what your friend would himself have chosen. It is not only that he happens to be getting what he would have chosen; he is getting it *because* he would have chosen it.

The contrast between effective power and procedural control is important in practice. It is often not possible to organize society in such a way that people can directly exercise the levers that control all the important aspects of their personal lives. To try to see freedom exclusively in terms of control is to miss out on the demands of freedom when control cannot feasibly be exercised by the persons themselves.

If, for example, we want the freedom not to be mugged in the streets and the liberty to move about without being so treated, we are looking for effective power. Precisely who exercises the control may be less important than the ability to achieve what we would have chosen. If the streets are cleared of the muggers *because* we would choose not to be mugged,[10] our freedom is being well served, even though we have not been given control over the choice of whether to be mugged or not.

To avoid possible misunderstandings, it may be useful to clarify what is being asserted here, and what is not. First, it is, of course, typically the case that not being mugged also serves our well-being. But in asserting that our freedom—even *agency freedom*—is well served by the streets being cleared of the muggers, something more is being asserted. It is that we would have *chosen* not to be mugged, and the streets are being cleared precisely because that is what we would have chosen.

Second, with the streets cleared of the muggers, we have, of

[10] While the dependence of the choice of antimugging policy on what we would choose is important for the "power" view of freedom, it is not necessary for that approach that this be achieved though some formal *procedure* of referendum-based execution.

course, the opportunity to walk as we please. This reflects the positive freedom, in most cases, to walk or not. But in that part of the story there is *no* contrast between control and power. We have the power to walk and also control over *that* decision. The contrast arises in considering the alternatives of being mugged and not being mugged. We do not control *this* choice ourselves, and we do not have the option of "being mugged" once the streets are cleared. But though that control is not ours, it was exercised in line with what we would have chosen and because of it.[11] It is in this sense that we have effective power, though no procedural control.

Third, in the example of mugging, the power is enjoyed not by each individual separately, but by the individuals taken together. There are other examples in which the individual on his own has effective power without control, e.g., in the example of your friend getting the treatment he would have chosen. Given the interdependences of social living, many liberties are not separately exercisable,[12] and effective power may have to be seen in terms of what all, or nearly all, members of the group would have chosen, e.g., in this case *not* to be mugged. What Isaiah Berlin calls "a man's, or a people's, liberty to choose to live as they desire"[13] has implications for effective power of individuals taken together *as well as* separately.

Concentrating on the control view of freedom and liberty has a long history. But in recent years it has tended to be particularly emphasized in the context of criticizing the practice in social choice theory of seeing freedom and liberty in terms of effective power only.[14] Robert Nozick, Peter Bernholz, Peter Gärdenfors, Robert

[11] There can, however, be *directional asymmetries* in effective power. For example, although the choice of "not being mugged" may be respected and executed, that of "being mugged" may not be similarly guaranteed. The real way to check whether we are getting *x because* we would have chosen *x*, is not so much to examine whether we would invariably have got "*not x*" if that is what we would have chosen, but to ascertain whether *x* is guaranteed in the first case but not in the second. Many standard liberties do, of course, have directional asymmetries; e.g., Miss *A* has the liberty *not to marry* Mr. *B* no matter what he wants, but not the liberty *to marry* Mr. *B* irrespective of his decisions.

[12] The issue of interdependence is well discussed by Christian Seidl, "On Liberal Values," *Zeitschrift für Nationalökonomie*, XXXV (1975): 257–292, and Jonathan Barnes, "Freedom, Rationality and Paradox," *Canadian Journal of Philosophy*, X (1980): 545–565.

[13] Isaiah Berlin, *Four Essays on Liberty* (New York: Oxford, 1969), p. 170.

[14] See my CCSW, ch. 6; and Allan Gibbard, "A Pareto-consistent Libertarian Claim," *Journal of Economic Theory*, VII (1974): 388–410. The "social choice" literature on this subject is now quite vast. For references, see the bibliographies in W. Gaertner and L. Krüger, "Self-supporting Preferences and Individual Rights: The Possibility of Paretian Libertarianism," *Economica*, XLVII (1981): 241–252; Sen, "Liberty and Social Choice" (1983); K. Suzumura, *Rational Choice, Collective Decisions and Social Welfare* (New York: Cambridge, 1983); and J. Wrigglesworth, *Libertarian Conflicts in Social Choice* (New York: Cambridge, forthcoming).

Sugden, Brian Barry, and others have pursued the control view, and though their formulations have differed from one another, there seems to have been solid agreement on the folly of seeing liberty in terms of power rather than procedural control.[15] It is not my intention to deny that the control element of freedom is indeed important in many contexts. But it is not the only important element in freedom. The power element cannot be neglected in any adequate formulation of freedom or liberty.

One may, of course, attach importance to having control over certain mechanisms of decision making and procedures of choice. In matters of what to eat, what to drink, what to wear, etc., it may not be adequate just to get what one would have chosen; one must actually do the choosing oneself. However, it is, in fact, also possible to argue that if achievements are characterized in a more articulate and apposite way than they are in the conventional formulations, then the motivation underlying any intrinsic concern with the control element of freedom can be *subsumed* within the notion of the power to achieve results. This question relates to the issue of the contents of states of affairs, which was discussed in the first lecture (181-183). Since states of affairs include actions and since agency information is part of the information regarding the states, the power to achieve particular states of affairs may have to include the power to use specific controls as well. Thus, the power view can be broadened to make room for attaching importance to control in the assessment of outcomes. The evaluation of the power to achieve different states of affairs may be control-sensitive, and the power view of freedom can, inter alia, accommodate whatever is important in the control view.

IV. AGENCY AND CONSEQUENTIALISM

Taking note of actions, agency, and control in the valuation of states of affairs raises an important question regarding the status of

[15] Nozick, *Anarchy, State and Utopia* (1974); Peter Bernholz, "Is a Paretian Liberal Really Impossible?" *Public Choice,* XIX (1974): 99-107; Peter Gärdenfors, "Rights, Games and Social Choice," *Nous,* XV (1981): 341-356; Robert Sugden, *The Political Economy of Public Choice* (Oxford: Martin Robertson, 1981); Brian Barry, "Lady Chatterley's Lover and Doctor Fischer's Bomb Party: Liberalism, Pareto Optimality and the Problem of Objectionable Preferences," mimeographed, 1982, to be published in J. Elster and A. Hylland, eds., *op. cit.,* forthcoming. A somewhat similar view is taken by Allan Gibbard, "Rights and the Theory of Social Choice," in *Logic, Methodology and Philosophy of Science,* VI (Amsterdam: North-Holland, 1982), in which volume contrast the analysis of Peter Hammond, "Liberalism, Independent Rights and the Pareto Principle." See also Isaac Levi, "Liberty and Welfare," and Peter Hammond, "Utilitarianism, Uncertainty and Information," in Sen and Williams, and Peter Bernholz, "A General Social Dilemma: Profitable Exchange and Intransitive Group Preferences," *Zeitschrift für Nationalökonomie,* XL (1980): 1-23.

that influence. If the moral approach in question incorporates "welfarism" (as the standard versions of utilitarianism do), then the value that can be attached to actions, agency, and such, must be entirely derivative. They must be based on their influence on utilities, since welfarism insists that the valuation of states must be a function of the utility information regarding the respective states. In the first lecture, this derivative view was disputed (sections VI and VII). In particular, arguments were presented against the "invariance restriction" which insists on *positional invariance,* i.e., the requirement that within a given moral approach the valuation of a state must be independent of the evaluator's position vis-à-vis the state, including his agency.

Positional invariance raises some difficult issues. It may look superficially like a condition of elementary consistency. How can two persons, sharing exactly the same moral approach, value the same state differently? The issue of consistency can be dealt with in formal terms easily enough. The valuation of the state may take note of such positional information as the agency of persons involved in bringing about that state, and the influence of that agency can vary *parametrically* depending on whether the evaluator is one of the agents involved (and if so, what has been his specific role). The real issue is not formal consistency, but cogency.[16] *Why* should the evaluator's own agency make a difference to the valuation made by him?

The issue of cogency relates to the recognition (discussed in the first lecture) that action and agency are integral parts of the state, and furthermore, that agency can be an important aspect of the person (a question also discussed in the second lecture). It would be extraordinary to require that a person himself must take no more note of his own agency in evaluating a state of affairs than others should and that a morally relevant assessment of the state can be made in this oddly detached way. When the evaluator happens to be also the agent whose action helped to bring about the state in question and when the action for which the person is peculiarly responsible is an integral part of that state, it is not at all clear why the evaluator must ignore this important connection in assessing the state, for moral reasoning. Lady Macbeth may well have got a little carried away in the state of affairs resulting from the murder

[16] I have argued elsewhere that "consistency conditions" used in the literature of rational choice and decision theory often make it difficult to see the real issues involved; and that there are no "natural" conditions—universal in scope—of "internal consistency of choice" ("Consistency," Presidential Address to the Econometric Society, 1984; to be published in *Econometrica*).

she committed when she asked, "Will these hands ne'er be clean?", but on the other hand we might mislead her a little if we were to inform her that, in the post-murder state, the perfumes of Arabia *would* sweeten her "little hand" as easily as any other hand. The responsibility of agency surely extends to evaluating states including the evaluator's own role, and that responsibility cannot suddenly disappear in the morally relevant evaluation of the state.

One reason why agency invariance may appeal, is a tendency to confuse this type of invariance with "authorship invariance," which was discussed in the first lecture. Authorship invariance does have some claims to being a reasonable requirement of moral evaluation (and, as was argued in the first lecture, can also be seen as a requirement of objectivity of moral beliefs). This is because the authorship of a statement is a very contingent fact. *A* can easily consider what he should say if he were in fact in *B*'s position rather than in his own. But the *positions* themselves are not without significance in evaluating the states, and this position relativity can be combined with authorship invariance and indeed objectivity of the corresponding type. The general thesis was presented in a broad way in the first lecture, but the gravity of the agency aspect of a person (further pursued later) has the implication of underlining the substantive importance of the position of being an agent, without in any way affecting the case for authorship invariance. The agency position has to be parameterized in the evaluation of states in a way that authorship need not be.

There is an interesting question whether these considerations require that the much-discussed condition of "consequentialism" should also be rejected. I don't believe that the outlined considerations entail either a rejection or an endorsement of consequentialism. The introduction of position relativity does have the effect of relaxing the overtight informational constraints imposed by the traditional combination of welfarism and consequentialism, and in this sense, it does make room for less blind judgments under consequentialist evaluation. But it does not require either the acceptance or the rejection of consequentialism as such.

Take Bernard Williams's famous example of Jim having to consider killing one person himself to save nine lives; the one to be killed by him would be killed anyway.[17] Whereas others have a straightforward reason to rejoice if Jim goes ahead, Jim has no option but to take serious note of his own responsibility in that state

[17] "A Critique of Utilitarianism," in J. J. C. Smart and B. Williams, *Utilitarianism: For and Against* (New York: Cambridge, 1973).

and his agency in killing someone himself. Position relativity will certainly be adequate to bring in a deep asymmetry between Jim's position and those of others even in consequential evaluation.

Nevertheless, even with this modification, Jim's decision may be ultimately straightforward in a consequentialist framework. In the state that will result from his killing one person, nine people are saved, and the one who is killed would have been killed anyway. Jim would have to attach an extraordinary degree of importance to the position of not being a killer himself to come to the conclusion that the value difference between one person being killed by Jim rather than by someone else is enough to outweigh the gain of nine people being saved from sure death. Even with position relativity, the decision is fairly straightforward. If, in fact, Jim's decision problem is *not* straightforward, as Williams argues it is not, then the difference must rest somewhere else.

It is possible to argue that there *is* a difference between an *action* being right and *the state resulting from that action* being the best feasible state, after taking note of the value or disvalue of the action itself (including agency). The first judgment concerns an *action*, and the second a *state* (*including* inter alia that action). There is no *necessity* that the two must correspond to each other in the rigid way that consequentialism would demand.[18] Whether they should, in fact, be linked in this way or not is a matter for further moral analysis, and the need to examine this link remains even after position relativity has been incorporated in the evaluation of states of affairs. Jim could still ask: "Can it be right for me to kill this man, just because the state of affairs resulting from that would be better (even after taking note of the disvalue of my action, judged as a *part* of the state of affairs)?"

The question of consequentialism will have to be settled by other arguments, since this one leaves that issue open. It is certainly true (as can easily be shown[19]) that agent relativity of every kind that has been proposed in the literature (by such authors as Bernard Williams, Thomas Nagel, and Derek Parfit[20]) can be accommodated *within* a consequentialist structure, once position relativity in the evaluation of states is admitted and used. But the *force* of the deontological considerations may not be fully captured in this way,

[18] See my "Evaluator Relativity and Consequential Evaluation," *Philosophy and Public Affairs*, XII (1983): 113–132.

[19] Discussed in my "Rights and Agency," *Philosophy and Public Affairs*, XI (1982): 3–39.

[20] Williams, "A Critique of Utilitarianism" (1973), and *Moral Luck* (1981); Nagel, "Limits of Objectivity" (1980); Parfit, *Reasons and Persons* (1984).

since part of that argument rests on distinguishing between the nature of action judgments and that of state judgments, no matter how inclusively (and position-relatively) the states are judged. The approach to moral reasoning utilized in these lectures does not force us to take a position one way or the other on this question. The welfarist part of utilitarianism (scrutinized in this lecture and the last) and the requirement of sum ranking (examined in the last lecture) stand rejected in a way that consequentialism is not; but neither is it positively endorsed.

However, the exacting demands of consequentialism must be distinguished from the requirement of "consequence sensitivity," and a firmer view can be taken about the latter. The analysis presented in these lectures would certainly be hard to reconcile with moral approaches that try to judge actions in a consequence-*independent* way. Given the intrinsic importance of well-being, and indeed of agency, it is not credible that a person can morally evaluate his or her actions without taking note of their effects on the well-being and agency aspects of others (including their well-being freedom and agency freedom).

Even the attempt to get a limited sphere of consequence-independent evaluation of actions by declaring some particular types of action to be invariably rejectable, no matter how good their consequences are, leads to problems. This "openness" is relevant even in assessing acts that are terrible judged on their own, e.g., killing. In fact, even in Williams's example involving Jim's problem, the dilemma would amount to nothing at all if some unexceptionable deontological constraint were definitively to rule out Jim's killing anyone. Whereas a nonconsequentialist Jim is *not* obliged to go ahead and shoot, simply because the resulting state of affairs (including his having killed someone) would be better, the dilemma with which Williams is concerned arises also because Jim cannot decide, in an equally straightforward way, that he *must not* shoot under any circumstances. The decision is difficult because there *is* a case for doing *either* alternative, and no unexceptionable constraint. That indeed is precisely the problem. Consequences *are* relevant even if consequence judgments do not enjoy a hegemony over action judgments.

V. RIGHTS AND NEGATIVE FREEDOM

This issue becomes particularly relevant in examining the possibility of having a substantive moral system that gives absolute priority to certain constraints related to rights, as, for example, in the system explored by Robert Nozick in *Anarchy, State and Utopia*. In such a system rights impose unrelaxable constraints, which have the effect of excluding certain alternatives. People must obey these constraints, no matter what else they may or may not do.

I have discussed elsewhere[21] why we may have good grounds for violating someone's rights if that prevents even worse consequences, e.g., a worse violation of the rights of others, arguing that this type of consideration is inescapable given the problems of interdependence that moral analysis has to face. For example, the violation of the property rights of some can prevent a developing famine and decimation.[22] Or, to take a different type of example, the violation of the rights of privacy of someone may yield the necessary information to prevent someone else from being battered, kidnapped, raped, or murdered. It is not at all clear why violating property rights, privacy, etc., must still remain rejectable, everything considered, in the cases specified. This necessity of considering, as it were, "everything" makes the proposals of consequence-independent absolute rights hard to defend. And the considerations of well-being and agency discussed in these lectures are impossible to reconcile with any proposal of consequence independence.

The nature of the rights considered by Nozick raises two different types of question. One concerns their *force,* in particular, their irresistibility; and the other relates to their *form,* namely their focus on "control" and more specifically their concentration on the "negative" perspective—imposing constraints on what others are permitted to do. The question of force, which has already been briefly addressed, must be distinguished from the issue of the appropriate form.

Considerations of well-being freedom and agency freedom need not, of course, have this negative concentration. Concern for well-being, well-being freedom, and agency freedom can all figure in a system in which conflicting positive contributions have to be weighed against each other when we are faced with a choice. Some of the relevant freedoms can also yield straightforward notions of rights. For example, minimal demands of well-being (in the form of basic functionings, e.g., not to be hungry), and of well-being freedom (in the form of minimal capabilities, e.g., having the means of avoiding hunger), can well be seen as rights that command attention and call for support. This perspective, which is close to the traditional format of the pursuit of positive freedoms, emerges naturally from the analysis that I have tried to present in these lectures.

[21] "Rights and Agency" (1982).

[22] Discussed, and empirically illustrated, in my *Poverty and Famines: An Essay on Entitlement and Deprivation* (New York: Oxford, 1981).

Some demands of *agency* freedom can also be seen as rights. The importance of self-agency has easily recognized urgency, and the force of such considerations as autonomy and liberty relate to the capability to take decisions in certain personal spheres in one's own life and to choose for oneself certain basic features of one's personal existence.[23] Although, as has been argued earlier in this lecture, the formulation of these freedoms requires us to look beyond control at effective power, this reformulation does not change the reasons for which such rights are taken to be important. One's ability to decide on certain matters in one's own personal life is given general support, and this support is not confined only to valuing procedural control or merely to wanting others not to violate these controls.

It is, in this general context, legitimate to ask: Where does *negative* freedom fit into this picture? Or does it not at all? The identification of the *source* of negative freedom has to be distinguished from that of its relative *strength* and its comparative force in a pluralist approach. In particular, the possibility that the source may be entirely *instrumental* is not ruled out by the general recognition that considerations of negative freedom may limit other people's actions very forcefully. Giving people powerful rights of, say, immunity from interference by others may help in furthering various intrinsic goals, including that of enhancing well-being freedom and agency freedom. Focusing on instrumentality (vis-à-vis utility) is, of course, precisely the way Jeremy Bentham reconciled attaching importance, on the one hand, to negative freedom (and to institutionalized rights) and, on the other hand, also regarding "natural rights" as "simple nonsense" and "bawling upon paper," and "natural and imprescriptible rights" as "rhetorical nonsense, nonsense upon stilts".[24]

It is, in fact, quite possible that much of the actual force of negative freedom and the rationale of institutional rights come from instrumental considerations of one kind or another. But without trying to rival the "instrumental" approaches through an alternative ("intrinsic") view that would yield these rights with *comparable force,* it is possible to argue that there are other—more intrinsic—sources of value in negative freedom. A violation of negative

[23] I have discussed some of these issues in "Liberty and Social Choice" (1983).

[24] For an interesting and useful analysis of Bentham's treatment of moral and natural rights, see Ross Harrison, *Bentham* (London: Routledge & Kegan Paul, 1983), ch. IV. The instrumental approach need not, of course, be utilitarian. On this see Scanlon, "Rights, Goals and Fairness," in S. Hampshire, ed., *Public and Private Morality* (New York: Cambridge, 1978), pp. 104/5.

freedom involves a direct failure on the part of the violator as a moral agent. And this failure of agency can be seen as having some significance of its own.

Consider a case in which person *A* pushes person *B*, who does not swim, into the river. *B* in fact drowns, and *A* cannot justify his action, we assume, in terms of some greater good that would follow from this drowning. It is possible to distinguish between two bad things that have happened. First, *B* is drowned and his positive freedom to live on and not to die prematurely has been violated. Second, *A* has failed rather badly as a responsible moral agent. So something worse than *B*'s drowning has occurred, especially as it should be viewed from the position of *A*.

This way of seeing the problem can appear to be erroneous, involving double-counting. Everything follows, it can be argued, from the bad thing happening to *B*. But is such an objection really sustainable? *A*'s failure is, of course, not unrelated to the bad thing happening to *B*, but there is a source of badness in *A* as well, in terms of his agency aspect, since he has failed so badly as an agent. Indeed, *A*'s failure as a responsible agent could have taken place even without the same bad thing happening to bedraggled *B*. For example, *A* pushes *B* with all his might, but unexpectedly *B* somehow does manage to stay on land; *or B* does fall, but is saved by the accidental presence nearby of a good swimmer. *B*'s positive freedom is, thus, very little affected, but *A*'s agency failure remains serious, if the saving happened to be unexpected and accidental.

In evaluating the states and actions, agent *A* cannot but take note of his own agency in the attempted drowning. His moral assessment must take note of both *B*'s loss, if any, and his own failure as a moral agent (if he were to take the step of pushing *B* into the river). Once the agency aspect of a person is given a central place in moral accounting, there is no escape from including this type of consideration in evaluating states and actions, and what looks like double-counting is, in fact, the union of two different, though not independent, bad things. The state in which *B* drowns accidentally—not pushed by anyone—cannot be as bad, especially as it should be seen by agent *A*, as the state in which *B* drowns after being deliberately pushed by *A* himself into the river. Thus, negative freedom does have some intrinsic importance of its own, *in addition to* its instrumental role in the pursuit of positive freedom.

There are many ambiguities in analyzing responsibility, and it is not my intention to suggest that this way of seeing negative freedom is unproblematic. But the coupling of agency considerations with well-being considerations does provide a much wider basis for analyzing the moral value of various traditional concepts—negative freedom among them.

To prevent a possible misunderstanding, I should also say that this type of agency-based consideration is not specifically confined to negative freedom only. The agency failure may well take a different form. For a variant of this case, consider one in which *B* falls accidentally into the river, with swimming champion *A* standing close to the spot, doing absolutely nothing to save *B*. Though *A* has not violated *B*'s negative freedom, it can be argued that this is also a case of agency failure on the part of *A* and that the state of affairs is, in a morally relevant way, worse for agent *A* than it would have been had *B* drowned without *A* standing nearby, or had *A* tried to save *B* unsuccessfully (with, of course, exactly the same result, so far as *B*'s life is concerned). Agency failure is a more general consideration than failure to respect negative freedom, which does not stand, by any means, alone in supplementing considerations of positive freedoms. But the relevance of agency failure provides some reason for intrinsic interest, inter alia, in negative freedom, in addition to whatever instrumental relevance negative freedom may have.

VI. CONCLUDING REMARKS

In these lectures I have tried to explore some of the implications of seeing persons from two different perspectives, viz., well-being and agency, neither of which can subsume the other. The substantive moral discussions drew on the examination of methodological issues in the first lecture, using an informational approach to ethical questions, and dealing with such matters as pluralism, incompleteness, positionality, agent relativity, and objectivity.

The adequacy of the foundational structure that Scanlon calls "philosophical utilitarianism" (more descriptively renamed here as "well-being as informational foundation"—WAIF for short) was examined and rejected. But that informational foundation provided one of the two major bases of moral reasoning used in the second and the third lectures. While the attractiveness of well-being as a foundation accounts for a good deal of the appeal of utilitarian moral approaches, it was argued in the second lecture that the identification of well-being with utility fails for each of the three main interpretations of utility (in the form of choice, happiness, and desire fulfillment). It was further argued that even if such an identification were, for the sake of argument, to be accepted, utilitarianism still could not be derived substantially from WAIF. Contrary to some claims, the issue of sum ranking is not trivial nor unproblematic.

More positively, it was argued that a more plausible view of well-being is provided by the accounting of functioning vectors, refined by considerations of capabilities to function. This approach yields partial orderings which are typically incomplete but eminently usable.

The third lecture has been largely concerned with examining the relevance of agency and the nature of freedom. Each of the two basic aspects of persons, viz., well-being and agency, leads to a particular concept of freedom. Using this dual base, I have tried to comment on a number of related issues concerning control, power, rights, consequences, agency, and positive and negative freedoms. Both well-being freedom and agency freedom have important—though disparate—relevance to the assessment of states of affairs and actions. And the informational base of the moral approach explored in these lectures cannot, in general, dispense with either agency information or well-being information, each of which has intrinsic interest—in the form of freedom as well as that of achievement. These lectures have been much concerned with examining these plural informational elements and their respective roles in moral valuation and judgment.

AMARTYA SEN

All Souls College, Oxford

[2]

Equality of Welfare

Ronald Dworkin

I. Two Theories of Equality

Equality is a popular but mysterious political ideal. People can become equal (or at least more equal) in one way with the consequence that they become unequal (or more unequal) in others. If people have equal income, for example, they will almost certainly differ in the amount of satisfaction they find in their lives. It does not follow, of course, that equality is worthless as an ideal. But it is necessary to state, more exactly than is commonly done, what form of equality is finally important.

This is not a linguistic or even conceptual question. It does not call for a definition of the word "equal" or an analysis of how that word is used in ordinary language. It requires that we distinguish various conceptions of equality, in order to decide which of these conceptions (or which combination) states an attractive political ideal, if any does. That exercise may be described, somewhat differently, using a distinction I have drawn in other contexts. There is a difference between treating people equally, with respect to one or another commodity or opportunity, and treating them as equals. Someone who argues that people should be more equal in income claims that a community that achieves equality of income is one that really treats people as equals. Someone who urges that people should instead be equally happy offers a different and competing theory about what society deserves that title. The question is then: which of the many different theories of that sort is the best theory?

In this chapter and the next I discuss one aspect of that question, which might be called the problem of distributional equality. Suppose some community must choose between alternative schemes for distributing money and other resources to individuals. Which of the possible schemes treats people as equals? This is only one aspect of the more general problem of equality, because it sets aside a variety of issues that might be called, by way of contrast, issues about political equality. Distributional equality, as I describe it, is not concerned with the distribution of political power, for example, or with individual rights other than rights to some amount or share of resources. It is obvious, I think, that these questions I throw together under the label of political equality are not so independent from issues of distributional equality as the distinction might suggest. Someone who can play no role in determining, for example, whether an environment he cherishes should be preserved from pollution is poorer than someone who can play an important role in that decision. But it nevertheless seems likely that a full theory of equality, embracing a range of issues including political and distributional equality, is best approached by accepting initial, even though somewhat arbitrary, distinctions among these issues.

I shall consider two general theories of distributional equality. The first (which I shall call equality of welfare) holds that a distributional scheme treats people as equals when it distributes or transfers resources among them until no further transfer would leave them more equal in welfare. The second (equality of resources) holds that it treats them as equals when it distributes or transfers so that no further transfer would leave their shares of the total resources more equal. Each of these two theories, as I have just stated them, is very abstract, because, as we shall see, there are many different interpretations of what welfare is, and also different theories about what would count as equality of resources. Nevertheless, even in this abstract form, it should be plain that the two theories will offer different advice in many concrete cases.

Suppose, for example, that a man of some wealth has several children, one of whom is blind, another a playboy with expensive tastes, a third a prospective politician with expensive ambitions, another a poet with humble needs, another a sculptor who works in expensive material, and so forth. How shall he draw his will? If he takes equality of welfare as his goal, then he will take these differences among his children into account, so that he will not leave them equal shares. Of course he will have to decide on some interpretation of welfare and whether, for example, expensive tastes should figure in his calculations in the same way as handicaps or expensive ambitions. But if, on the contrary, he takes equality of resources as his goal, then, assuming his children have roughly equal wealth already, he may well decide that his goal requires an equal division of his wealth. In any case the questions he will put to himself will then be very different.

It is true that the distinction between the two abstract theories will be less clear-cut in an ordinary political context, particularly when officials have very little information about the actual tastes and ambitions of particular citizens. If a welfare-egalitarian knows nothing of this sort about a large group of citizens, he may sensibly decide that his best strategy for securing equality of welfare would be to establish equality of income. But the theoretical difference between the two abstract theories of equality nevertheless remains important in politics, for a variety of reasons. Officials often do have sufficient general information about the distribution of tastes and handicaps to justify general adjustments to equality of resources (for example by special tax allowances) if their goal is equality of welfare. Even when they do not, some economic structures they might devise would be antecedently better calculated to reduce inequality of welfare under conditions of uncertainty, and others to reduce inequality of resources. But the main importance of the issue I now raise is theoretical. Egalitarians must decide whether the equality they seek is equality of resources or welfare, or some combination or something very different, in order plausibly to argue that equality is worth having at all.

I do not mean that only pure egalitarians need take any interest in this question. For even those who do not think that equality is the whole story in political morality usually concede that it is part of the story, so that it is at least a point in favor of some political arrangement, even if not decisive or even central, that it reduces inequality. People who assign equality even this modest weight must nevertheless identify what counts as equality. I must emphasize, however, that the two abstract conceptions of equality I shall consider do not exhaust the possible theories of equality, even in combination. There are other important theories that can be captured only artificially by either of these. Several philosophers, for example, hold meritocratic theories of distributional equality, some of which appeal to what is often called equality of opportunity. This claim takes different forms; but one prominent form holds that people are denied equality when their superior position in either welfare or resources is counted against them in the competition for university places or jobs, for example.

Nevertheless the claims of both equality of welfare and equality of resources are both familiar and apparent, and it is these that I shall consider. In this chapter I examine, and on the whole reject, various versions of the former claim. In Chapter 2 I shall develop and endorse a particular version of the latter. I might perhaps add two more caveats. It is widely believed that certain people (for example criminals) do not deserve distributional equality. I do not consider that question, though I do raise some questions about merit or desert in considering what distributional equality is. John Rawls (among others) has questioned whether distributional equality might not require deviations from an equal base when this is in the interests of the then worst-off group, so that, for example, equality of welfare is best served when the worst-off have less welfare than others but more than they would otherwise have. I discuss this claim in the next chapter, with respect to equality of resources, but not in this one, where I propose that equality in welfare is not a desirable political goal even when inequality in welfare would not improve the position of the worst-off.

II. A First Look

There is an immediate appeal in the idea that insofar as equality is important, it must ultimately be equality of welfare that counts. For the concept of welfare was invented or at least adopted by economists precisely to describe what is fundamental in life rather than what is merely instrumental. It was adopted, in fact, to provide a metric for assigning a proper value to resources: resources are valuable so far as they produce welfare. If we decide on equality, but then define equality in terms of resources unconnected with the welfare they bring, then we seem to be mistaking means for ends and indulging a fetishistic fascination for what we ought to treat only as instrumental. If we want genuinely to treat people as equals (or so it may seem), then we must contrive to make their lives equally desirable to them or give them the means to do so, not simply to make the figures in their bank accounts the same.

This immediate attraction of equality of welfare is supported by one aspect of the domestic example I described. When the question arises how wealth should be distributed among children, for example, those who are seriously physically or mentally handicapped do seem to have, in all fairness, a claim to more than others. The ideal of equality of welfare may seem a plausible explanation of why this is so. Because they are handicapped, the blind need more resources to achieve equal welfare. But the same domestic example also provides at least an initially troublesome problem for that ideal. For most people would resist the conclusion that those who have expensive tastes are, for that reason, entitled to a larger share than others. Someone with champagne tastes (as we might describe his condition) also needs more resources to achieve welfare equal to those who prefer beer. But it does not seem fair that he should have more resources on that account. The case of the prospective politician, who needs a great deal of money to achieve his ambitions to do good, or the ambitious sculptor, who needs more expensive materials than the poet, perhaps falls in between. Their case for a larger share of their parent's resources seems stronger than the case of the child with expensive tastes, but weaker than the case of the child who is blind.

The question therefore arises whether the ideal of equality in welfare can be accepted in part, as an ideal that has a place, but not the only place, in a general theory of equality. The theory as a whole might then provide that the handicapped must have more resources, because their welfare will otherwise be lower than it could be, but not the man of champagne tastes. There are a number of ways in which that compromise within the idea of equality might be constructed. We might, for example, accept that in principle social resources should be distributed so that people are as equal in welfare as possible, but provide, by way of exception, that no account should be taken of differences in welfare traceable to certain sources, such as differences in tastes for drink. That gives equality of welfare the dominant place, but it prunes the ideal of certain distinct and unappealing consequences. Or we might, at the other extreme, accept only that differences in welfare from certain specified sources, such as handicaps, should be minimized. On this account equality of welfare would play only a part—perhaps a very minor part—in any general theory of equality, whose main political force must then come from a very different direction.

I shall postpone, until later in this chapter, the question of how far such compromises or combinations or qualifications are in fact available and attractive, and also postpone until then consideration of the particular problems of expensive tastes and handicaps. But I want to single out and set aside in advance one form of objection to the feasibility of compromises of equality of welfare. It might be objected, against any such compromise, that the concept of welfare is insufficiently clear to permit the necessary distinctions. We cannot tell (it might be said) how much any welfare differences between two people who have equal wealth are in fact traceable to differences in the cost of their tastes or in the adequacy of their physical or mental powers, for example. So any theory that embraces equality of welfare must pay attention to people's welfare as a whole rather than welfare derived or lost through any particular source. Obviously, there is much in this sort of objection, though how strong the objection is must depend on the form of compromise proposed. I want, however, to set aside all objections about the feasibility of distinguishing welfare sources.

I also want to set aside the more general objection, that the concept of welfare is itself, even apart from distinctions as to source, too vague or impractical to provide the basis for any theory of equality. I said earlier that there are many different interpretations or conceptions of welfare, and that a theory of equality of welfare that uses one of these will have very different consequences, and will require a very different theoretical support, from a theory that uses another. Some philosophers think of welfare as a matter of pleasure or enjoyment or some other conscious state, for example, while others think of it as success in achieving one's plans. We shall later have to identify the leading conceptions of welfare and look at the different conceptions of equality of welfare they supply. But we may notice, in advance, that each of the familiar conceptions of welfare raises obvious conceptual and practical problems about testing and comparing the welfare levels of different people. Each of them has the consequence that comparisons of welfare will often be indeterminate: it will often be the case that of two people neither will have less welfare, but that their welfare will not be equal. It does not follow, however, that the ideal of equality of welfare, on any interpretation, is either incoherent or useless. For that ideal states the political principle that, so far as is possible, no one should have less welfare than anyone else. If that principle is sound, then the ideal of equality of welfare may sensibly leave open the practical problem of how decisions should be made when the comparison of welfare makes sense but its result is unclear. It may also sensibly concede that there will be several cases in which the comparison is even theoretically pointless. Provided these cases are not too numerous, the ideal remains both practically and theoretically important.

III. Conceptions of Equality of Welfare

There are several theories in the field about what welfare is, and therefore several conceptions of equality of welfare. I shall divide what I consider the most prominent and plausible such theories into two main groups, without, however, supposing that all the theories in the literature can fit comfortably into one or the other. The first group I shall call success theories of welfare.

These suppose that a person's welfare is a matter of his success in fulfilling his preferences, goals, and ambitions, and so equality of success, as a conception of equality of welfare, recommends distribution and transfer of resources until no further transfer can decrease the extent to which people differ in such success. But since people have different sorts of preferences, different versions of equality of success are in principle available.

People have, first, what I shall call political preferences, though I use that term in a way that is both narrower and more extended than the way it is often used. I mean preferences about how the goods, resources, and opportunities of the community should be distributed to others. These preferences may be either formal political theories of the familiar sort, such as the theory that goods should be distributed in accordance with merit or desert, or more informal preferences that are not theories at all, such as the preference many people have that those they like or feel special sympathy for should have more than others. Second, people have what I shall call impersonal preferences, which are preferences about things other than their own or other people's lives or situations. Some people care very much about the advance of scientific knowledge, for example, even though it will not be they (or any person they know) who will make the advance, while others care equally deeply about the conservation of certain kinds of beauty they will never see. Third, people have what I shall call personal preferences, by which I mean their preferences about their own experiences or situation. (I do not deny that these types of preferences might overlap, or that some preferences will resist classification into any of the three categories. Fortunately my arguments will not require the contrary assumption.)

The most unrestricted form of equality of success that I shall consider holds that redistribution should continue until, so far as this is possible, people are equal in the degree to which all their various preferences are fulfilled. I shall then consider the more restricted version that only nonpolitical preferences should be counted in this calculation, and then the still more restricted version that only personal preferences should count. More complex versions of equality of success, which combine the satisfaction of some but not all preferences from the different groups, are of course available, though I hope that the arguments I make will not require me to identify and consider such combinations.

The second class of theories of welfare I shall call conscious-state theories. Equality of welfare linked to that sort of theory holds that distribution should attempt to leave people as equal as possible in some aspect or quality of their conscious life. Different conceptions of that ideal are constructed by choosing different accounts or descriptions of the state in question. Bentham and other early utilitarians took welfare to consist in pleasure and the avoidance of pain; equality of welfare, so conceived, would require distribution that tended to make people equal in their balance of pleasure over pain. But most utilitarians and other partisans of the conscious-state conception of welfare believe that "pleasure" and "pain" are much too narrow to represent the full range of conscious states that should be included. For example, "pleasure," which suggests a specific kind of sensuous glow, poorly describes the experience produced by a harrowing piece of drama or poetry, an experience people nevertheless sometimes aim to have, and "pain" does not easily capture boredom or unease or depression.

I do not wish to discuss the issues this dispute raises. Instead I shall use the words "enjoyment" and "dissatisfaction" indiscriminately to name the full range of desirable and undesirable conscious states or emotions that any version of a conscious-state conception of equality of welfare might suppose to matter. This usage gives those words, of course, a broader sense than they have in ordinary language, but I intend that broad sense, provided only that they must name conscious states that people might aim to have or avoid for their own sakes, and states that are introspectively identifiable.

People often gain enjoyment or suffer dissatisfaction directly, from sensuous stimulation through sex or food or sun or cold or steel. But they also gain enjoyment or suffer dissatisfaction through the fulfillment or defeat of their preferences of different sorts. So there are unrestricted and restricted versions of the conscious-state conception of equality of welfare parallel to the versions I distinguished of conceptions of equality of success. One version aims to make people more equal in enjoyment without restriction as to source, another only in the enjoyment they take directly and from nonpolitical preferences, and another in the enjoyment they take directly and from personal preferences only. As in the case of equality of success, more discriminating versions that combine enjoyment from subdivisions of these different sorts of preferences are also available.

I shall also consider, though only very briefly, a third class of conceptions of equality of welfare, which I shall call objective conceptions. Many subdivisions and further classifications among these three classes of conceptions, beyond those I have just noticed, would have to be considered in any full account of possible theories of welfare, and there are theories of welfare not represented in this list at all. But these seem the most plausible candidates for constructing theories of distribution. I shall just mention, however, two sorts of complexities that we should at least bear in mind. First, many of the conceptions and versions I have distinguished raise the question of whether equality in that conception is reached when people are in fact equal in welfare so conceived, or rather when they would be equal if they were fully informed of the relevant facts. Does someone attain a given level of success, for purposes of equality of success, when he believes that his preferences have been fulfilled to a given degree, or rather when he would believe that if he knew the facts? I shall try, when questions of that sort might affect the argument, either to discuss both possibilities or to assume the version that seems to me in context more plausible. Second, many of the conceptions I shall discuss raise problems about time. People's preferences change, for example, so that the question of how far someone's preferences for his life have been fulfilled overall will depend on which set of his preferences is chosen as relevant, or which function of the different preferences he has at different times. I do not believe that any of these temporal problems affects the various points that I shall make, but readers who do should consider whether my arguments hold against alternate versions.

There is, however, a further preliminary question that must detain us longer. We can distinguish two different questions. (1) Is someone's overall welfare—his essential well-being—really just a matter of the amount of his success in fulfilling his preferences (or just a matter of his enjoyment)? (2) Does distributional equality really require aiming to leave people equal in that success (or enjoyment)? The first of these questions takes a certain view of the connection between theories of welfare, such as those I described, and the concept of welfare itself. It supposes that this connection is rather like the connection between theories or conceptions of justice and the concept of justice itself. We agree that justice is an important moral and political ideal, and we ask ourselves which of the different theories about what justice actually consists in is the best such theory. So we might suppose that (for one or another purpose) the welfare of persons, conceived as their essential well-being, is an important moral and political concept, and then ask ourselves which of the traditional theories (or new theories we might deploy) is the best theory of what welfare, so conceived, actually is.

But the second question does not, in itself, require that we confront—or even acknowledge the sense of—that last question. We may believe that genuine equality requires that people be made equal in their success (or enjoyment) without believing that essential well-being, properly understood, is just a matter of success (or enjoyment). We may, indeed, believe that equality requires equality in success even if we are skeptical about the whole idea of essential well-being, considered to be a deep or further fact about people conceptually independent from their success or enjoyment. That is, we may accept equality of success as an attractive political ideal even if we reject the very sense of the question whether two people who are equal in success are equal in essential well-being. And we may do so even if we deny that this question is analogous to the question whether producing the highest possible average utility makes an institution just.

I make these remarks because it is important to distinguish between two strategies that someone anxious to defend a particular conception of equality of welfare might use. He might begin, first, by accepting the idea of welfare as essential well-being, and then take, as at least the tentative premise of his argument, the proposition that genuine equality requires people to be equal in essential well-being. He might then argue for a particular theory of welfare (success, for example) as the best theory of what essential well-being consists in, and so conclude that equality requires that people be made equal in success. Or, second, he might argue for some conception of equality of welfare, such as equality of success, in a more direct way. He might take no position on the question whether essential well-being consists in success, or even on the prior question whether that question makes sense. He might argue that, in any case, equality of success is required for reasons of fairness, or for some other reasons having to do with the analysis of equality that are independent of any theory about the sense or content of essential well-being.

Is it therefore necessary to consider both of these strategies in assessing the case for any particular conception of equality of welfare? I think not, because the defeat of the second strategy (at least in a certain way) must count as a defeat of the first as well. I do not mean myself to claim that the idea of essential well-being, as a concept admitting of different conceptions, is nonsense, so that the first strategy, shorn of nonsense, is just the second. On the contrary, I think that idea, at least as defined by certain contexts, is an important one, and the question of where a person's essential well-being lies, when properly conceived, is sometimes, in those contexts, a question of profound importance. Nor do I think it follows from the conclusion that people should not be made equal in some particular conception of welfare, that this is a poor conception of welfare (conceived as essential well-being). I mean rather to deny something like the opposite claim: that if some conception is a good conception of welfare, it follows that people should be made equal in welfare so conceived. This does not follow. I might accept, for example, that people are equal in essential well-being when each is roughly equally successful in achieving a certain set of his preferences, without thereby conceding that an advance toward that situation is even pro tanto an advance toward genuine distributional equality. Even if I initially accept both propositions, I should abandon the latter if I am then persuaded that there are good reasons of political morality for not making people equal in that sort of success, and that these reasons hold whether or not the former proposition is sound. So any arguments capable of defeating the second strategy, by showing that there are strong reasons of political morality why distribution should not aim to make people equal in success, must also count as strong arguments against the first strategy, though not, of course, as arguments defeating the interim conclusion of that strategy: that essential well-being consists in success. In what follows I shall try to oppose the second strategy in this manner.

IV. Success Theories

I want now to examine equality of welfare conceived in the various ways I have described, beginning with the group of theories I called success theories. As I said, I do not intend to make much of the practical difficulties (as such) of applying these or any other conceptions of equality of welfare. If any society dedicated itself to achieving any version of equality of success (or of enjoyment), it could do at best only a rough job, and could have only a rough idea of how well it was doing. Some differences in success would be beyond the reach of political action, and some could be eliminated only by procedures too expensive of other values. Equality of welfare so conceived could be taken only as the ideal of equality, to be used as a standard for deciding which of different practical political arrangements seemed most or least likely to advance that ideal on the whole as a matter of antecedent tendency. But precisely for that reason it is important to test the different conceptions of equality of welfare as ideals. Our question is: If (impossibly) we could achieve equality of welfare in some one of these conceptions, would it be desirable, in the name of equality, to do so?

Political Preferences

I shall begin by considering equality of success in the widest and most unrestricted sense I distinguished, that is, equality in the fulfillment of people's preferences when these include political as well as other forms of preferences. We should notice a threshold difficulty in applying this conception of equality in a community in which some people themselves hold, as a matter of their own political preferences, exactly the same theory. Officials could not know whether such a person's political preferences were fulfilled until they knew whether their distribution fulfilled everyone's preferences equally, including his political preferences, and there is danger of a circle here. But I shall assume that equality of welfare, so conceived, might be reached in such a society by trial and error. Resources might be distributed and redistributed until everyone pronounced himself satisfied that equality of success on the widest conception had been achieved.

We should also notice, however, a further threshold difficulty: that it would probably prove impossible to reach a reasonable degree of equality in this conception even by trial-and-error methods in a community whose members held very different and very deeply felt political theories about justice in distribution. For any distribution of goods we might arrange, some group, passionately committed to a different distribution for reasons of political theory, might be profoundly dissatisfied no matter how well they fared personally, while others might be very pleased because they held political theories that approved the result. But because I propose to ignore practical or contingent difficulties, I shall assume a society in which it is possible to achieve rough equality in the amount by which people's unrestricted preferences were fulfilled, that is roughly equal success on this wide conception, either because people all hold roughly the same political theories, or because, though they disagree, anyone's dissatisfaction with a solution on political grounds could be made up by favoritism in his personal situation, without arousing so much antagonism in others as to defeat equality so conceived for that reason.

This latter possibility—that people who lose out because their political theories are rejected could be given more goods for themselves by way of compensation—makes this conception of equality of welfare immediately unattractive, however. Even people otherwise attracted to the idea of equality of welfare, on any conception, would presumably not wish to count gains or losses in welfare traceable to, for example, racial prejudice. So I assume that almost everyone would wish to qualify equality of success at least by stipulating that a bigot should not have more goods than others in virtue of the fact that he would disapprove a situation in which blacks have as much as whites unless his own position were sufficiently favored to make up the difference.

But it is unclear why this stipulation should not apply to all political theories that are in conflict with the general ideal of equality of success, and not just to racial bigotry. It should apply equally to people who think that aristocrats should have more than plebs, or to meritocrats who think that, as a matter of political morality, those who are more talented should have more. Indeed, it should apply even to egalitarians who think that people should be equal in resources or enjoyment or in the success each has in his personal life rather than in the fulfillment of all his preferences, including his political preferences. These "wrong" egalitarian theories will of course seem more respectable to officials who have accepted the latter conception of equality than will bigoted or meritocratic theories. But it still seems odd that even wrong egalitarians should have extra resources credited to their personal account just to make up for the fact that their overall approval of the situation would otherwise be lower than those who hold the political theory assumed to be correct, and on which any claims the former might make to extra resources must in some sense rely. It seems odd (among other reasons) because a good society is one that treats the conception of equality that society endorses, not simply as a preference some people might have, and therefore as a source of fulfillment others might be denied who should then be compensated in other ways, but as a matter of justice that should be accepted by everyone because it is right. Such a society will not compensate people for having preferences that its fundamental political institutions declare it is wrong for them to have.

The reason why racial bigotry should not count, as a justification for giving the bigot more in personal goods, is that this political theory or attitude is condemned by the proper conception of equality, not that the bigot is necessarily insincere or unreflective or personally wicked. But then other forms of nonegalitarian political theory, and even misconceived forms of egalitarian theory, should be discounted in the same way. Suppose, moreover, that no one has a nonegalitarian or wrong-egalitarian political theory of any formal sort, but that some people are merely selfish and have no political convictions even in the extended sense, so that their overall approval of the state of affairs after any distribution is just a matter of their own private situation, while others are benevolent, so that their overall approval is increased by, say, the elimination of poverty in the society. Unless we refuse to take that benevolence into account, as a positive source of success in meeting the preferences overall of those who are benevolent, we shall end once again by giving those who are selfish more for themselves, to compensate for the success others have from that benevolence. But it is surely a mark against any conception of equality that it recommends a distribution in which people have more for themselves the more they disapprove or are unmoved by equality.

Consider, finally, a different situation. Suppose no one holds, in any case very deeply, any formal political theory, but each is generally benevolent. Many people, however, by way of what I called a political theory in the extended sense, sympathize especially with the situation of one group of those less fortunate than themselves—say, orphans—and have special preferences that these be looked after well. If these preferences are allowed to count, this must have one or the other of two results. Either orphans will, just for this reason, receive somewhat better treatment than equality would itself have required in the absence of these special preferences, at the inevitable expense of other groups—including those disadvantaged in other ways, such as, say, cripples; or, if this is ruled out on egalitarian grounds, those who care more about orphans than about cripples will be given extra resources to make up for the failure to fulfill this discrete preference (which extra resources they then may or may not contribute to orphans). Neither of these results does credit to an egalitarian theory.

So we have good reason to reject the unrestricted conception of equality of success, by eliminating from the calculation of comparative success both formal and informal political preferences, at least for communities whose members differ in these political preferences, which is to say for almost all actual communities with which we might be concerned. We might just pause to consider, however, whether we must reject that conception for all other communities as well. Imagine a community in which people by and large hold the same political preferences. If these common preferences endorse equality of success, including success in political preferences, then that theory for all practical purposes collapses into the more restricted theory that people should succeed equally in their nonpolitical preferences. For if a distribution is reached that everyone regards with roughly equal overall approval, and the force of individual political convictions, in each person's judgment of how well he regards it, is simply to approve the result because everyone else does regard it equally, then the distribution must be one in which each person regards his own impersonal and personal preferences as equally fulfilled as well. Suppose Arthur is less satisfied with his impersonal and personal situation than Betsy. Arthur can have, by hypothesis, no political theory or attitude that could justify or require a distribution in which he is less satisfied in this way than Betsy is, so Arthur can have no reason to regard the distribution with as much general or overall approval, combining political, impersonal, and personal assessments, as Betsy does.

But suppose the shared political theory is not the ideal of equality of overall approval, but some other, nonegalitarian theory that could provide such a reason. Suppose everyone accepts a caste theory, so that though Amartya is somewhat poorer than others, the distribution leaves his preferences as a whole equally fulfilled because he believes that he, as a member of a lower caste, should have less, so that his preferences as a whole would be worse fulfilled if he had more. Bimal, from a higher caste, would also be less satisfied overall if Amartya had any more. In this situation, unrestricted equality of success does recommend a distribution that no other conception of equality of welfare would. But it is unacceptable for that very reason. An inegalitarian political system does not become just simply because everyone wrongly believes it to be.

Unrestricted equality of success is acceptable only when the political preferences that people happen to have are sound rather than simply popular, which means, of course, that it is in the end an empty ideal, useful only when it rubber-stamps a distribution already and independently shown to be just through some more restricted conception of equality of success or through some other political ideal altogether. Suppose someone denies this and argues that it is good, in and of itself, when everyone approves of a political system highly and equally no matter what that system is. This seems so arbitrary, and so far removed from ordinary political values, as to call into question whether he understands what a political theory is or is for. In any case he does not state an interpretation of equality, let alone an attractive one.

Impersonal Preferences

We must surely restrict equality of success still further by eliminating, from the calculation it proposes, at least some of what I called people's impersonal preferences. For it is plainly not required by equality that people should be equal, even insofar as distribution can achieve this, in the degree to which all their nonpolitical hopes are realized. Suppose Charles very much and very deeply hoped that life would be discovered on Mars, or that the Great American Novel would be written within his lifetime, or that the coast of Martha's Vineyard would not be eroded by the ocean as it inevitably continues to be. Equality does not require that funds be taken from others, who have more easily fulfilled hopes about how the world will go, and transferred to Charles so that he can, by satisfying other preferences he has, decrease the overall inequality in the degree to which his and their nonpolitical preferences are fulfilled.

Should any impersonal preferences be salvaged from the further restriction this suggests? It might be said that the various impersonal preferences I just took as examples are all impossible dreams or, in any case, all dreams that the government can do nothing to fulfill. But I cannot see why that matters. If it is right to aim to decrease inequality in disappointment in all genuine nonpolitical aims or preferences, then the government should do what it can in that direction, and though it cannot bring it about that there is life on Mars, it can at least partially compensate Charles for his failed hopes by allowing him to be more successful otherwise. In any case, I might have easily taken as examples hopes people have that are not impossible, or even particularly difficult, for government to realize. Suppose Charles hopes that no distinctive species will ever become extinct, not because he enjoys looking at a variety of plants and animals, or even because he thinks others do, but just because he believes that the world goes worse when any such species is lost. He would overwhelmingly prefer that a very useful dam not be built at the cost of losing the snail darter. (He has not set out deliberately to cultivate his views about the importance of species. If he had, then this might be thought to raise the special issues about deliberate cultivation of expensive tastes that I shall consider later. He just finds he has these views.) But after the political process has considered the issue and reached its decision, the dam is built. Charles's disappointment is now so great (and he cares so little about everything else) that only the payment of a vast sum of public money, which he could use to lobby against further crimes against species, could bring his welfare, conceived as the fulfillment of all nonpolitical preferences, back to the general level of the community as a whole. I do not think that equality requires that transfer, nor do I believe that many, even of those who find appeal in the general ideal of equality of welfare, will think so either.

Of course equality does require that Charles have a certain place in the political process I described. He must have an equal vote in selecting the officials who will make the decision, and an equal opportunity to express his opinions about the decision these officials should take. It is at least arguable, moreover, that the officials should take his disappointment into account, perhaps even weighted for its intensity, in the general cost-benefit balancing they undertake in deciding whether the dam should be built all things considered, that his dissatisfaction should count in a Benthamite calculation and be weighted against the gains to others that the dam would bring. We might wish to go beyond this, perhaps, and say that if the community faces a continuing series of decisions that pit economic efficiency against species preservation, it should not take these decisions discretely, through separate cost-benefit calculations each of which Charles would lose, but as a series in which the community should defer to his opinion at least once. But none of this comes near arguing that the community treats Charles as an equal only if it recognizes his eccentric position in a different way, by undertaking to insure, so far as it can, that his success in finding all his nonpolitical preferences fulfilled remains as high as everyone else's when the series of decisions is completed, no matter how singular his impersonal preferences are. Indeed this proposition contradicts rather than enforces what conventional ideals of political equality recommend, because if the community acknowledged that responsibility, Charles' opinions would very probably play a role far beyond what these traditional ideas provide for them.

But someone might still protest that my arguments depend on assigning to people impersonal preferences that are in the circumstances unreasonable, or, rather, unreasonable to expect the community to honor by compensating for their failure. My arguments do not, it might be said, suggest that reasonable impersonal preferences should not be honored in that way. But this introduces a very different idea into the discussion. For we now need an independent theory about when an impersonal preference is reasonable or when it is reasonable to compensate for one. It seems likely that such a theory will assume that a certain fair share of social resources should be devoted to the concerns of each individual, so that a claim for compensation might be appropriate when this fair share is not in fact put at his disposal, but not if deciding as he wishes or compensating him for his disappointment would invade the fair share of others. We shall consider, later in this section, the consequences of using the idea of fair shares in this way within a theory of equality of success. It is enough to notice now that some such major refinement would be necessary before any impersonal preferences would qualify for the calculation of equality of success.

Nor does it seem implausible to restrict a conception of equality of welfare to success in achieving personal, as distinct from both all political and all impersonal, ambitions. For that distinction is appealing in other ways. Of course people do care, and often care very deeply, about their political and impersonal preferences. But it does not seem callous to say that insofar as government has either the right or the duty to make people equal, it has the right or the duty to make them equal in their personal situation or circumstances, including their political power, rather than in the degree to which their differing political convictions are accepted by the community, or in the degree to which their differing visions of an ideal world are realized. On the contrary, that more limited aim of equality seems the proper aim for a liberal state, though it remains to see what making people equal in their personal circumstances could mean.

Equality of Personal Success

Relative success. We should therefore consider the most restricted form of equality of success that I shall discuss, which requires that distribution be arranged so that people are as nearly equal as distribution can make them in the degree to which each person's preferences about his own life and circumstances are fulfilled. This conception of equality of welfare presupposes a particular but plausible theory of philosophical psychology. It supposes that people are active agents who distinguish between success or failure in making the choices and decisions open to them personally, on the one hand, and their overall approval or disapproval of the world in general, on the other, and seek to make their own lives as valuable as possible according to their own conception of what makes a life better or worse, while recognizing, perhaps, moral constraints on the pursuit of that goal and competing goals taken from their impersonal preferences. There is no doubt a measure of idealization in this picture; it may never be a fully accurate description of any person's behavior, and it may require significant qualification in many cases. But it seems a better model against which to describe and interpret what people are than the leading and perhaps more familiar alternatives.

So I shall not quarrel with this psychological theory. But we must notice at once a difficulty in the suggestion that the resources of a community should be distributed, so far as possible, to make people equal in the success they have in making their lives valuable in their own eyes. People make their choices, about what sort of a life to lead, against a background of assumptions about the rough type and quantity of resources they will have available with which to lead different sorts of lives. They take that background into account in deciding how much of what kind of experience or personal relationship or achievement of one sort must be sacrificed for experiences or relationships or achievements of another. They therefore need some sense of what resources will be at their disposal under various alternatives before they can fashion anything like the plan for their lives of the sort that this restricted conception of equality of success assumes that they have, at least roughly, already created. Some of these resources are natural: people need to make assumptions about their expected life span, health, talents, and capacities, and how these compare with those of others. But they also need to make assumptions about the resources they will have of just the sort society would allocate under any scheme of equality of welfare: wealth, opportunities, and so on. But if someone needs a sense of what wealth and opportunities will be available to him under a certain life before he chooses it, then a scheme for distribution of wealth cannot simply measure what a person should receive by figuring the expense of the life he has chosen.

There is therefore again danger of a fatal circle here. But I propose to set that problem aside, as another instance of the kind of technical problem that I promised not to labor. So I shall suppose, once again, that the problem can be solved in a trial-and-error way. Suppose a society in which people in fact have equal resources. It is discovered that some are much more satisfied than others with the way their lives are going. So resources are taken from some and given to others, on a trial-and-error basis, until it is true that, if people were fully informed about all the facts of their situation, and each was asked how successful he believed himself to be at fulfilling the plans he had formed given the level of resources he now has, each person would indicate roughly the same level or degree of success.

But this "solution" of the practical difficulty I describe brings to the surface a theoretical problem to which the practical difficulty points. People put different values on personal success and failure, not only as contrasted with their political and moral convictions and their impersonal goals, but just as part of their personal circumstances or situation. At least they do in one sense of success and failure. For we must now notice an important distinction I have so far neglected. People (at least as conceived in the way just described) choose plans or schemes for their lives against a background of natural and physical resources they have available, in virtue of which they have discrete goals and make discrete choices. They choose one occupation or job over another, live in one community rather than another, seek out one sort of lover or friend, identify with one group or set of groups, develop one set of skills, take up one set of hobbies or interests, and so forth. Of course, even those people who come closest to the ideal of that model do not make all these choices deliberately in the light of some overall scheme, and perhaps make none of them entirely deliberately. Luck and occasion and habit will play important roles. But once the choices they do make have been made, these choices define a set of preferences, and we can ask how far someone has succeeded or failed at fulfilling whatever preferences he has fixed in that way. That (I shall say) is the question of his relative success—his success at meeting the discrete goals he has set for himself.

But people make these choices, form these preferences, in the light of a different and more comprehensive ambition, the ambition to make something valuable of the only life they have to lead. It is, I think, misleading to describe this comprehensive ambition as itself only another preference people have. It is too fundamental to fit comfortably under that name; and it is also too lacking in content. Preferences represent the result of a decision, of a process of making what one wants more concrete. But the ambition to find value in life is not chosen as against alternatives, for there is no alternative in the ordinary sense. Ambition does not make plans more concrete; it is simply the condition of having any plans at all. Once someone has settled on even a tentative or partial scheme for his own life, once his discrete preferences have been fixed in that way, then he can measure his own relative success in a fairly mechanical way, by matching his situation to that scheme. But he cannot tell whether his life has succeeded or failed in finding value simply by matching his achievements to any set target in that way. He must evaluate his life as a whole to discover the value that it has, and this is a judgment that must bring to bear convictions that, however inarticulate these are, and however reluctant he might be to call them this, are best described as philosophical convictions about what can give meaning or value to any particular human life. I shall call the value that someone in this way attributes to his life his judgment of that life's overall success.

People disagree about how important relative success is in achieving overall success. One person might think that the fact that he is likely to be very successful at a particular career (or love affair or sport or other activity) counts strongly in favor of his choosing or pursuing it. If he is uncertain whether to be an artist or lawyer, but believes he would be a brilliant lawyer and only a good artist, he might regard that consideration as decisive for the law. Someone else might weigh relative success much less. He might, in the same circumstances, prefer to be a good artist to being a brilliant lawyer, because he thinks art so much more important than anything lawyers do.

This fact—that people value relative success differently in this way—is relevant here for the following reason. The basic, immediate appeal of equality of welfare, in the abstract form in which I first set it out, lies in the idea that welfare is what really matters to people, as distinct from money and goods, which matter to them only instrumentally, so far as these are useful in producing welfare. Equality of welfare proposes, that is, to make people equal in what is really and fundamentally important to them all. Our earlier conclusion, that in any event the fulfillment of political and impersonal preferences should not figure in any calculation aimed at making people equal in welfare through distribution, might well be thought to damage that appeal. For it restricts the preferences that people are meant to fulfill in equal degree to what I have called personal preferences, and people do not care equally about the fulfillment of their personal preferences as opposed to their political convictions and impersonal goals. Some care more about their personal preferences, as opposed to their other preferences, than others do. But a substantial part of the immediate appeal I describe remains, though the point would now be put slightly differently. Equality of welfare (it might now be said) makes people equal in what they all value equally and fundamentally so far as their own personal situations or circumstances are concerned.

But even that remaining claim is forfeit if equality of welfare is construed as making people equal, so far as distribution can achieve this, in their relative success, that is, in the degree to which they achieve the goals they fix for themselves. On this conception, money is given to one rather than another, or taken from one for another, in order to achieve equality in a respect some value more than others and some value very little indeed, at the cost of inequality in what some value more. A person of very limited talents might choose a very limited life in which his prospects of success are high because it is so important to be successful at something. Another person will choose almost impossible goals because for him the meaning is the challenge. Equality of relative success proposes to distribute resources—presumably much fewer to the first of these two and much more to the second—so that each has an equal chance of success in meeting these very different kinds of goals.

Suppose someone now replies that the appeal of equality of welfare does not lie where I located it. Its purpose is not to make people equal in what they do value fundamentally, even for their own lives, but rather in what they should value fundamentally. But this change in the claims for equality of welfare achieves nothing. For it is absurd to suppose that people should find value only in relative success without regard to the intrinsic value or importance of the life at which they are relatively successful. Perhaps some people—those with grave handicaps—are so restricted in what they can do that they must choose just so as to be able to be minimally successful at something. But most people should aim to do more than what they would be, relatively, most successful in doing.

Overall success. This discussion might be thought to suggest a better interpretation of equality of welfare, namely equality of overall rather than relative success. But if we are to explore equality of welfare in that conception we must make a distinction not necessary (or in any case not so plainly necessary) in comparing relative success. We must distinguish a person's own judgment of his overall success (or, if we prefer, the judgment he would make if fully informed of the pertinent ordinary sorts of facts) from the objective judgment of how much overall success in fact he has. A person's own judgment (even if fully informed of the facts) will reflect his own philosophical convictions about what gives value to life, and these might be, from the standpoint of the objective judgment, confused or inaccurate or just wrong. I shall suppose, here, that equality of overall success means equality in people's overall success as judged by themselves, from the standpoint of their own perhaps differing philosophical beliefs. I shall later consider, under the title of objective theories of welfare, the different conception that requires equality in the success of their lives judged in some more objective way.

So let us now alter the exercise we have imagined. Now we rearrange resources, as far as we are able, so that when we have finished, each person would, at least if fully informed, offer the same assessment, not of his relative success in achieving the goals he selected for himself, but of his overall success in leading a valuable life. But we must take care in describing just what we take that latter opinion to be. For there are many different beliefs each of which might possibly be thought to count as an assessment of one's own overall success, and it is of crucial importance to decide which of these, if any, should play a role in rearranging resources in the name of equality. Nor can we find much guidance in the literature either of welfare economics or of utilitarianism, which are the natural places to look. For most of those writers who argue or assume that welfare consists in the fulfillment of preferences seem to have had relative rather than overall success in mind, and in any case have not discussed the problems raised by the latter idea when the two ideas are separated. The language they use—the language of preferences (or wants or desires)—seems too crude to express the special, comprehensive judgment of the value of a life as a whole.

We might begin by distinguishing the question of how valuable someone believes his life has been, taken as a whole, from the question of how much he wants his life to continue. These are certainly different matters. Some people, to be sure, wish their life to end, or are in any case almost indifferent whether it continues, because they regard it as a failure. But others wish to die just because they think their life has been too brilliant to tarnish with a slow decline. And others think that a successful life can be made more successful by the timely use of suicide as a creative act. People can want to end, that is, a life they are proud to have led. Can we say at least that if someone wishes to die he must regard the future life he would otherwise lead as having no or little value? This will certainly be so in most cases, but the connection is nevertheless, I think, contingent. He may only think that though his future life would be quite successful, his life as a whole would be more successful if it ended now. Nor does it follow from the fact that someone very much wishes to continue living, for as long as he can imagine, that he thinks that his life is a successful life, or even that his future life will be especially successful. He may, on the contrary, want to live longer because he thinks his life has been unsuccessful, because he needs more time to do anything worth doing, though it is more likely that he simply fears death. The distinction I want to make can be summarized, perhaps, this way. Someone's preferences about the length of his life are just that, preferences that are like his choices of jobs and lovers, fixed as part of the dominating exercise of deciding what life, given background assumptions about resources, would be the most valuable life all things considered. They are not in themselves judgments of overall success or failure.

Can we make a further distinction between the value someone finds in his own life and the value he believes it has *for* him? I am not sure what that latter phrase would mean as part of this contrast. We sometimes say that a person puts a low value on his own life when we mean, not that he is not proud of the life he has or will lead, but rather that he counts the value of that life low compared with the value he puts on his duty or the lives of others. But we are now considering something different, not the value someone puts on his own life as compared with his moral or impersonal values, but the value he puts on that life as part of the assessment of his own situation.

Perhaps "the value of someone's life for him" means only the intensity of his preference that his life continue. If so, the distinction between the value someone finds in his life and its value for him is the distinction we have already discussed. But someone who uses that phrase may have in mind something more complex and more elusive than that. He may mean to distinguish someone's judgment about the value of any single human life (or indeed human life in general) to the universe as a whole from that person's judgment from the inside, from the standpoint of someone charged with making something valuable of his own life. If so, then it is the latter judgment with which we are now concerned. Or he may mean to distinguish someone's judgment of his own success in that assignment, given his talents and opportunities, from his judgment of whether it was good for him to have had the talents and opportunities and convictions that made him the person whose life would have most value lived that way. It is not hard to imagine lives that illustrate the distinction so understood. It is in fact a cliché that great artists often work, not out of enjoyment (even in the widest sense of enjoyment), but rather in constant misery simply because it is not possible for them not to write poetry or music or paint. A poet who says this may well think that a life he spent in any other way would be, in the most fundamental sense, a failure. But he might well think that the conspiracy of talents and beliefs that made this true was bad for him, meaning only that his life would be more enjoyable if he lacked these talents or did not have the belief, which he could not however shake, that a life of creating poetry in misery and despair was all things considered the most valuable life for him to lead. Suppose we then ask him the dark question only philosophers and sentimental novelists ask: Would it have been better for you if you had never been born? If he says yes, as he might in some moods, we would know what he meant, and it would not be that he has done nothing valuable with his life. If the distinction between someone's judgment of the value of his life and his judgment of the value it has for him is taken in this way, then it is the former judgment I mean by his judgment of his overall success. But if the distinction cannot be taken in this way, or in any of the other ways I have considered, then I do not understand it, and suspect that it is no distinction at all.

These scrappy remarks are intended to clarify the comparison we must intend when we propose that people should be equal in their overall success. We cannot carry out this comparison simply by discovering two people's own fixed preferences and then matching their situations to these preferences. That is only a comparison of their relative success. We must invite them to make (or ourselves make from their point of view) an overall rather than a relative judgment that takes fixed preferences as part of what is judged rather than the standard of assessment. If we ask them to make that assessment themselves, however, and then try to compare the assessments each makes, we may discover the following difficulty. Suppose we ask Jack and Jill each to evaluate the overall success of his or her own life, and we make plain, by a variety of distinctions, what we mean by overall success as distinct from relative success, enjoyment, how much they wish their lives to continue, and so forth. And we provide them with a set of labels, from "total failure" to "very great success" with several stops in between, from which to choose. We have no guarantee that each will use any of these labels to make the same judgment that the other makes in using the same label. Jack may use one or more of the labels with a different meaning from the meaning Jill uses, and they may be using different scales in judging the intervals between these labels. Jack might suppose, for example, that there is a vast difference between "great success" and "very great success," while Jill understands these terms to enforce only a marginal difference; so that both might use the latter label to report judgments that we, on the basis of further conversation with them, would come to believe were in fact very different judgments. This difficulty, so described, is a difficulty in translation, and I shall suppose that we could in principle conquer it, at least for speakers of our own language, by the further conversations just mentioned.

But of course all this assumes that there is indeed a single kind of overall judgment that we are asking Jack and Jill each to make (or that we propose to make from their standpoint, on their behalf) and that this judgment is in fact a judgment about the inherent value of their life and therefore different from a judgment of relative success or a judgment about how much a person wants his life to continue or how much enjoyment he finds in it. Many people are, of course, skeptical about such judgments so interpreted. If they are right, then the judgments we ask Jack and Jill to make are meaningless judgments. But then equality of overall success is itself meaningless for that reason. (Though someone might still propose, for reasons we need not explore, that people should nevertheless be equal in the character of each's illusion.) If we assume that the skeptics are wrong, however (or even that equality of illusion is the true aim), then equality of overall success must suddenly seem a peculiar goal indeed, at least in the following circumstances.

Suppose that Jack and Jill have equal resources and that they are otherwise roughly similar in every way except in respect of the beliefs I am about to mention. They are both healthy, neither handicapped, both reasonably successful in their chosen occupations, neither outstandingly accomplished or creative. They take roughly the same enjoyment from their day-to-day life. But Jack (who has been much influenced by genre painting) thinks that any ordinary life fully engaged in projects is a life of value, while Jill (perhaps because she has taken Nietzsche to heart) is much more demanding. Jack thinks, for example, that the life of a busy peasant who achieves very little and leaves nothing behind is full of value, while Jill thinks that such a life is only full of failure. If each is asked to assess the overall value of his or her own life, Jack would rate his high and Jill hers low. But there is surely no reason in that fact for transferring resources from Jack to Jill provided only that Jill would then rate her life, while still of little overall success, a bit higher.

It might seem that the difficulty this example exposes arises only from the fact that our procedures attempt to compare judgments of value reached on the basis of very different theories about what gives value to life, which is like comparing apples and oranges. Someone might object that we would do better if we asked Jack and Jill each to make comparative judgments using their own standards for each comparison, and then compared these comparative judgments in some way that would neutralize the difference in their philosophical convictions. This is, I think, a mistake, but we should explore the suggestion nevertheless. We might ask Jack, for example, to compare the value, in his eyes, of his present life with the value of the life he would have under whatever conditions of physical and mental power and whatever collection of material resources and opportunities at his disposal he would take to be ideal. Or we might ask him to compare in this way his present life with the life he would have under what he would take to be the worst conditions. We might ask him how far his life is better than the life he would have if he had no or very few resources or opportunities. We would then put the same questions to Jill. Or we might ask each a rather different sort of question, not asking them to imagine different material circumstances, but rather to compare their present lives with lives in which each would find no value at all.[1] We might ask each how far his or her life exceeded, in its value, that life. And so on. Once some one of these questions (or perhaps some weighted group of them) had been selected as for some reason especially appropriate for the purpose, equality of overall success, as a political ideal, would recommend redistribution until either the proportion or the flat amount hypothetically reported by way of answer was as close to the same in all cases as could be achieved in that way.

I should say at once that there is room for doubt, at least, whether all or possibly even any of these various questions could actually be answered, or be answered by any but the most philosophically inclined respondents. I shall set the doubts aside, however, and assume that people generally have a sufficient grasp of theories of value to be able intelligently to answer them. But of course the different comparisons the different questions prompted might, if each was harnessed to the ideal of equality of overall success, yield different recommendations for redistribution. Suppose, for example, that Jack thought his present life much better than the worst life he could imagine, but also much worse than the best life, while Jill thought her life not much better than the worst and not much worse than the best. Then the direction of redistribution would depend on which of these two comparisons was thought more important for comparing levels of overall success. Even if all the answers to all the questions we could invent pointed in the same direction for redistribution, we should still have to show that at least one of these questions was the right question to ask.

When we look more closely at the questions I listed, however, they turn out to be very much the wrong questions. Suppose Jack and Jill (who, as I imagined, are now roughly equal in resources and enjoyment and relative success in their chosen lives) do disagree radically in judgments about how much more valuable their lives would be if they had everything they could have, for example. Jack believes that with all these resources he could solve the riddle of the origin of the universe, which would be the greatest imaginable achievement for human beings, while Jill believes that riddle unsolvable and has no comparable dream in hand. So Jack believes his present life is only a small fraction as good as what it could ideally be, but Jill believes her life is not that much worse than what it could possibly be. Surely we have no reason of equality here for transferring resources from Jill to Jack (destroying their assumed equality of resources and enjoyment and relative success) even if such a transfer would cause Jack to rank his new life as having come somewhat closer to his ideal solving-the-riddle life.

Suppose that Jack considers his present life much more valuable than any life he would consider to have no value at all, while Jill thinks her life just barely better, on any flat scale of value in life, than a life she would think had absolutely no value, but that this is for the reason already suggested. Jack considers any life fully engaged and active, with as much day-to-day enjoyment as his has, of enormous value, something to be treasured and protected and pursued. He can imagine a life about which he would be indifferent, but it is a life so impoverished that he has no trouble reporting that his life is better than that by a very long chalk. Jill has roughly as much day-to-day pleasure or enjoyment. She is not depressive, but rather very demanding in her idea of what life could be deemed a really successful life. She cannot say, when asked seriously to consider this grave question in a philosophical mood, that she thinks her life, for all its apparent richness, is in fact a life of much real value; she can easily imagine a life that she would believe had absolutely no value and cannot say that she honestly thinks her life is really, all things considered, much more valuable than that one. Once again it seems implausible that equality demands that resources be transferred from Jack to Jill.

Why are all these comparative questions so plainly the wrong questions to ask? Because we have not in fact escaped, in switching from flat questions to comparative ones, the difficulty we found in the former. Because the differences between Jack and Jill we have noticed are still differences in their beliefs but not differences in their lives. They are differences in their speculative fantasies about how good or bad their lives would be under very different and bizarre circumstances, or differences in their philosophical convictions about what could give great value to any life; but not, for that reason, a difference in what their lives now are. Each of the judgments Jack or Jill makes, in responding to the different questions we put to them, can be considered a judgment about the value or overall success of their lives. But they are not all the *same* judgment, and none of the judgments we have so far described seems appropriate for a theory of equality of overall success.

I want now to suggest a comparison of the overall success in people's lives, very different from the comparisons suggested in all these questions, that does seem to be connected, at least, to problems of distributional equality. Differences in people's judgments about how well their lives are going overall are differences in their lives, rather than simply differences in their beliefs, only when they are differences not in fantasy or conviction but in fulfillment, which is, I take it, a matter of measuring personal success or failure against some standard of what *should* have been, not merely of what conceivably *might* have been. The important, and presently pertinent, comparison seems to me this. The more that people can reasonably regret not having done something with their lives, the less overall success their lives have had.

"Reasonably," of course, carries much weight here. But it is all necessary. No one can reasonably regret that he has not had the life that someone with supernatural physical or mental powers, or the life span of Methuselah, would have had. So no one has a less successful life, all things considered, just because he thinks that such a life would be infinitely more valuable, in the philosophical way, than the life he has. But people can reasonably regret that they have not had the normal powers or the normal span of life that most people have. No one can reasonably regret that he has not had the life that someone with an unfairly large share of the world's resources would have led, so no one person's life is less successful than another's because the first thinks his life would be much more valuable in those circumstances while the other does not. But people can reasonably regret not having whatever share of material resources they are entitled to have.

Perhaps the point is now clear. Any proposed account of equality of overall success that does not make the idea of reasonable regret (or some similar idea) pivotal in this way is irrelevant to a sensible theory of equality in distribution. It may develop a concept of overall success useful for some purpose, but not for this purpose. But any proposed account that does make this idea pivotal must include, in its description of equality of overall success, assumptions about what a fair distribution would be, and that means that equality of overall success cannot be used to justify or constitute a theory of fair distribution. I do not mean simply that equality of success could not be applied in some cases without having an independent theory of fair distribution as a supplement for such cases. If the point were only that, then it would show only that equality of overall success could not be the whole story in a theory of distribution. The point is more striking. Equality of overall success cannot be stated as an attractive ideal at all without making the idea of reasonable regret central. But that idea requires an independent theory of fair shares of social resources (this might, for example, be the theory that everyone is entitled to an equal share of resources) which would contradict equality of overall success not in some cases only, but altogether.

Suppose someone contests this important conclusion in the following way. He concedes that the aim of equality of success, properly conceived, is to make people equal in what they have reasonably to regret. But he believes that the idea of reasonable regret can be elucidated in some way that does not require any theory of fair share of resources *other than* some version or refinement of the equal-success theory itself. He might propose the following. People cannot reasonably regret that they are not leading the life of someone with supernatural powers, or the life of a successful sadist, or a life in which they have resources such that, with those resources, they could achieve a life with less reasonably to regret than others can have with the resources then left for them. This will not do, however. We aim to make people equal in what they have reasonably to regret. Suppose (as before) that Jack and Jill have equal resources. Jack has (as we saw) grand ambitions and, though he does not believe himself entitled to anything in particular, will always regret not having more than he does. We want to know whether Jack and Jill are nevertheless equal in what they have *reasonably* to regret. On the proposed test, we must ask Jack (or ask ourselves from his point of view) how far the life he can now lead falls short of the life he would lead if he had (among other things) the amount of resources such that if he had those resources he would have the same amount reasonably to regret as others would then have. Jack cannot answer that question (nor can we). He can pick some different distribution at random—say, a distribution in which he has a million dollars more and others in the aggregate a million less. But he cannot tell whether his new-distribution life is the proper baseline against which to measure his present life without knowing whether the reasonable regret he would feel with one more million is no more than others would reasonably regret with what they could then have, and he cannot tell this without picking some *further* new distribution at random (in which, perhaps, he has two million more) against which to compute his regret at the one-million-more life. And so on into infinite regress. We cannot, of course, repair this failure (as we tried to repair other failures) by some trial-and-error device. For the problem is not that we can offer no noncircular algorithm for reaching an initial distribution to test, but rather that we can offer no method for testing any distribution however reached.[2]

I conclude that reasonable regret cannot itself figure in the distributional assumptions against which the decision whether some regret is reasonable is to be made. Nor can I think of any other conception or refinement of equality of overall success that can fill that role. If so, then the goal of making people equal in what they have reasonably to regret is self-contradictory in the way I described. I do not mean that comparisons of fulfillment—of how far different people have been able to make a success of their lives in their own eyes—have no place in discussions of equality. Many differences in overall regret—many occasions that people have properly to regret what they have not done—flow from handicaps or bad luck or weakness of will or sudden changes, too late for anything but regret, in people's perceptions of what they really take to be valuable. But it is perhaps the final evil of a genuinely unequal distribution of resources that some people have reason for regret just in the fact that they have been cheated of the chance others have had to make something valuable of their lives. The ideas of fulfillment and of reason for regret are competent to express this final argument against inequality only because they are ideas that reflect, in their assumptions, what inequality independently is.

I cannot, of course, prove that no one will invent a test or metric for overall success that will be both pertinent to equality and independent of prior assumptions about equality in distribution. For that reason I considered a fairly wide variety of suggested tests of this sort, hoping to show why I think it unlikely that one can be found. Certainly nothing that I am aware of in the present literature will do. But now suppose someone defending equality of overall success concedes that no such distribution-independent test can be found. I have been assuming that he must then concede that equality of overall success is useless as a distinct political goal because, insofar as it recommends changes from the independent distribution it assumes to be fair, it must recommend distributions it condemns as unfair. But is this too quick a conclusion?

Suppose he argues that we must distinguish between the measure and the means of achieving equality of overall success. He might suggest, for example, that a fair distribution for purposes of computing some person's present overall success is an equal distribution of resources. We compute Jack's and Jill's overall success by asking how far each regards his or her life as less successful than the best life he or she could have if resources were shared equally in society. If Jack's overall success, so measured, is greater than Jill's, we transfer resources from Jack to Jill so far as we can thus reduce the difference. It is true that Jack and Jill will not then have equal resources. Jill will have more resources than Jack. But they will be (more) equal in overall success as measured in the proper, reasonable-regret-oriented, way. There is no contradiction in using the idea of equal resources internally, within the metric for determining overall success, and then actually distributing so as to achieve equality of overall success rather than equality of resources.

But this reply misses the point. The reasonable-regret metric for determining overall success makes assumptions about what distribution is fair, about the distribution to which people are *entitled*. If that metric assumes that a fair distribution is an equal distribution of resources, and Jill is then given more than an equal share, she is given more than the theoretical argument supposedly justifying the transfer says is her fair share. Of course Jill might not complain about having more than the share of resources to which she is, by hypothesis, entitled. But Jack will complain about having less than the justification assumes he is entitled to have, and the only way to give Jill more than that share is to give Jack (or someone else) less.

V. Equality of Enjoyment

I now propose to discuss the second group of conceptions of equality of welfare that I distinguished at the outset, which take equality of welfare to consist in equal amounts or degrees of a conscious state. I shall simplify this discussion, as I said there, by taking the concept of enjoyment to stand for a particularly broad version of the conscious state or states in question. Fortunately, this discussion can be simplified in another way as well, for much of the argument I used in considering unrestricted versions of equality of success apply to unrestricted versions of equality of enjoyment as well.

People gain enjoyment, as I said, from the satisfaction of their political and impersonal preferences as well as directly and from their personal preferences, and they suffer dissatisfaction when these political and impersonal preferences are defeated. But the same considerations that argue for a restricted form of equality of success, which does not count success or failure in achieving these preferences in the calculations that theory recommends, argue for similar restrictions in equality of enjoyment. So I shall assume that equality of enjoyment, as a theory of equality in distribution, holds that resources should be distributed, so far as possible, so that people are equal in the enjoyment they take directly and from their beliefs that their personal preferences are achieved.

My first argument against this restricted version of equality of enjoyment is also modeled on the argument I used against equality of relative success. The main appeal of a restricted form of equality of enjoyment lies in the claim that it makes people equal in what they all value equally and fundamentally so far as their personal position is concerned. But that appeal cannot be sustained, because in fact people differ in the importance each attaches to enjoyment even in the widest sense that leaves that term a description of conscious states. When they are made equal in that one respect, they become unequal in other respects many value much more.

For almost everyone, pain or dissatisfaction is an evil and makes life less desirable and valuable. For almost everyone, pleasure or enjoyment of some other form is of value, and contributes to the desirability of life. Conscious states of some such form, positive and negative, figure as components of everyone's conception of the good life, but *only* as components, because almost no one pursues only enjoyment or will make any large sacrifice of something else he values to avoid a small amount of pain. And different people give even these conscious states very different weight. Two scholars, for example, may both value creative work, but one may be willing to give up more, by way of social pleasure or the enjoyments of reputation or the satisfaction that comes from completing a piece of research well done, to do work that is in fact more original.

Someone might now object that the first scholar does not value enjoyment less but rather finds it in a different source—not in the delights of society or the glow of fame but in the deeper satisfactions of the pursuit of genuine discovery. But this is plainly not necessarily or even usually so. Some of the most ambitious scholars (and artists and statesmen and athletes) set off in a direction that they predict will bring them only failure, and they know that they will find no delight or satisfaction just in the fact that they are aiming high, but only misery in how far they have fallen short. They may truly say (in the spirit of the poet whose views I described earlier) that they wish that some goal or project had not occurred to them or fallen in their path, or that they did not have the talents that made it necessary for them to pursue it, because then their lives would have been more satisfactory, more enjoyable all things considered. It perverts their report, misunderstands their complex situation, to say that they have actually found more enjoyment in the life they have led. For it is exactly their point that they have led that life in spite of, rather than for, the quality of the conscious life it has brought them.

Now of course not many people are dedicated to some ambition in that particularly strenuous way. But most of us, I think, are dedicated to something whose value to us is not exhausted or captured in the enjoyment its realization will bring, and some are dedicated to more things in that way, or more strongly dedicated, than others. Even when we do enjoy what we have or have done, we often enjoy it because we think it valuable, not vice versa. And we sometimes choose, in the same manner, though not to the same dramatic degree as the most ambitious scholar, a life that we believe will bring less enjoyment because it is in other ways a better life to lead. This is evident, I think, in a psychological fact that in some ways illustrates a different point, but is nevertheless relevant. Suppose you had a genuine choice (which, once made, you would forget) between a life in which you in fact achieved some goal important to you, though you did not realize that you had, and a different life in which you falsely believed that you had achieved that goal and therefore had the enjoyment or satisfaction flowing from that belief.[3] If you make the former choice, as many would, then you rank enjoyment, however described, as less important than something else.

Suppose someone now says, however, that equality of enjoyment is an attractive political goal, not because people all do value that state equally and fundamentally, when they decide what is important for themselves, but rather because they ought to do so. He says, not that the ambitious scholar I described really values enjoyment, but rather that he is mistaken, perhaps even irrational, because he does not. Someone making this objection, that is, abandons what I said is the immediate appeal of any conception of equality of welfare, which is that it claims to make people equal in what they value equally and fundamentally. He argues that the appeal of that political ideal is rather that it makes people equal in what they ought to value equally and fundamentally.

We have, I think, two answers. First, he is wrong in his view about what people ought to value. He is wrong in supposing either that the most valuable life is a life of maximum enjoyment, no matter how generously that conscious state is described, or that everyone ought to hold that view of what is the best life. Second, even if that theory about what people ought to value is more plausible than I think, even if it is in fact true, a political theory of equality based on that conception of the good life is an unattractive theory for a society in which many if not most people reject that conception, and some reject it as alien to their most profound beliefs about the goodness of their own lives.

We may, moreover, find a second argument against the restricted form of equality of enjoyment in the arguments we considered against equality of overall success. Though I have emphasized the error in supposing that ambitious people all take enjoyment in their strenuous lives, or pursue those lives for the sake of the enjoyment they will bring, it is nevertheless true that people of ambition often find dissatisfaction in the failure of their grand aims, and in their regret that they do not have the additional resources of talent and means that would make success more likely, whether or not they hold political theories that suppose that they are entitled to more than they have. Though this was not part of my story of Jack and Jill, we might vary that story to suppose, for example, that Jack found keen disappointment and day-to-day dissatisfaction in the fact that he did not have solving-the-riddle talents and means. But it would seem as wrong to transfer resources to him on account of that greater dissatisfaction as on account of his lower success ratio measured in that way. No one, I think, would want to aim at counting more than the dissatisfaction he found in reasonable regret. But if the arguments I offered earlier are sound, introducing the idea of reasonable regret for the sake of that limitation would introduce a different and inconsistent theory of distribution into the very statement of and justification for equality of enjoyment.

VI. Objective Theories of Welfare

The conceptions of equality of welfare thus far considered are all subjective in the following sense. They may each be enforced without asking whether a person's own consistent and informed evaluation of how far he meets the deployed standard of welfare is correct. Of course the arguments in favor of choosing one or another conception of equality of welfare may assume that people are wrong in what they take to be important, or even in what they would take to be important if fully informed of the pertinent facts. We considered, for example, the argument in favor of equality of enjoyment that people ought to value enjoyment as fundamentally important to their lives, in spite of the fact that many do not. But even if the conscious-state conception is defended in that way, it may be applied without any evaluation of the enjoyment in question. It directs officials to produce the distribution such that each person takes equal enjoyment in the life he leads, without asking whether people are right to take enjoyment in what they then would.

Equality of overall success in the form we considered it is also subjective in that way. It aims to make people equal in (as we should now say) the amount or degree by which each person could reasonably regret that he was not leading a life he would deem to be a life of greater value. That judgment is in certain ways, it is true, nonsubjective. It imposes constraints on reasonable regret that the person in question might himself reject, for example. If that person's assessment of what gives value to life changes over the course of his life, the judgment requires some amalgamation or selection among his different judgments. But the judgment does not allow the computation of someone's reasonable regret to be based on assessments of value in life that are wholly foreign to him, that he would reject even if fully informed of the ordinary facts.

I should now mention a version of equality of overall success that is more objective in just that way, however. Someone might propose that people be made equal in the amount of regret they should have about their present lives. On this revised test officials would have to ask whether someone who in fact does not value friendship, for example, and believes his life good though it is solitary and without love, and believes this in spite of the fact that he is aware of the comforts and joy that others find in friendship, is wrong. If so, then resources might be transferred to him, either directly or through special education for him about the values of friendship, on the ground that his overall success is low even though he would count it high, at least before the special education takes hold.

Now we may well object that officials have no business relying on their own judgments about what gives value to life in redistributing wealth. We might believe that such a scheme for redistribution invades autonomy or is in some other way foreign to the correct liberal principles. But we need not consider these objections, because this more objective version of equality of overall success meets the same argument we used against the more subjective version. Any pertinent test of what someone should regret about the life he is in fact leading, even on the best rather than his own theory about what gives value to life, must rely on assumptions about what resources an individual is entitled to have at his disposal in leading any life at all. So the objective version, like the subjective version, must assume an independent theory of fair distribution, and has no more power to justify giving some people more and others less than what they are entitled to have under that theory. Both versions are self-defeating insofar as they recommend any changes in a distribution independently, under some other theory of distribution, shown to be fair.

I should just mention, though very briefly, another putative conception of equality of welfare that might also be considered an objective conception. This supposes that a person's welfare consists in the resources available to him, broadly conceived, so as to include physical and mental competence, education, and opportunities as well as material resources; or, on some versions, more narrowly conceived so as to include only those that are in fact, whatever people think, most important. It holds that two people occupy the same welfare level if they are both healthy, mentally sound, well educated, and equally wealthy even though one is for some reason malcontent and even though one makes much less of these resources than the other. This is an objective theory in the sense that it refuses to accept a person's own judgment about his welfare, but rather insists that his welfare is established by at least certain kinds of basic resources at his command.

Equality of welfare, so interpreted, requires only that people be equal in the designated resources. This version of equality of welfare is therefore not different from equality of resources or at least equality in some resources. It is rather a statement of equality of resources in the (misleading) language of welfare. The abstract statement of equality of resources, of course, as I said, leaves open the question of what counts as a resource and how equality of resources is to be measured. These are the complex questions left for Chapter 2. But there is no reason to think that these questions will be easier to answer if we tack on to the ideal of equality of resources the rider that if people are equal in resources, on the correct conception of that ideal they will also be equal in some objective concept of welfare.

VII. An Ecumenical Suggestion

I must now consider what might seem a wise and ecumenical suggestion. Perhaps an attractive conception of equality of welfare can be found, not exclusively in one or another of the different conceptions we have now inspected and dismissed, but in some judicious and complex mix of these. In that case the strategy I followed in the last three sections might be the misleading and fallacious strategy of divide and conquer, rejecting each conception of equality of welfare by supposing that unless that conception tells the whole story it may be wholly ignored. Perhaps the ideal of equality of welfare may be considered fairly only by treating the different unrestricted and restricted versions of equality of success and equality of enjoyment each as strands to be considered in a complex package rather than as isolated theories.

It would be foolish to say, in advance, that no new conception of equality of welfare could be described that would make that ideal attractive. We must wait to see what new conceptions are presented. But it is perhaps not foolish to suppose that no successful conception could be formed using the conceptions we considered as components in some larger package. In any case my arguments were intended to reduce confidence in that project. I did not argue simply that no one of the versions I discussed is satisfactory on its own, or that each leads to unappealing consequences if unchecked by some other. If my arguments had been of that character, they would indeed invite the suggestion that these conceptions might be combined so as to supplement or check the shortcomings of each alone. But I meant to support a more radical criticism: that we have no reason to accept any of these versions of equality of welfare as a theory of distributional equality, even pro tanto.

It is of course desirable, in some sense at least, that people's overall success be improved, though philosophers and politicians might disagree whether the subjective or objective versions of that goal should be controlling when the two conflict. But, for reasons explained, neither version can provide other than an idle or self-defeating principle of equality in distribution. Nor, for the same reasons, can either figure as useful components in some complex package of conceptions of equality of welfare. Insofar as equality of overall success figured, even as one component among many, it would figure because some independent test of fair distribution was assumed, and it could not recommend, nor could the package overall, any deviation from that independent test.

The other conceptions of equality of welfare we considered we rejected for different reasons. We found no reason to support the idea that a community should accept the goal of making people more equal in any one of these different ways even when it could do so without damage to any of the others. If that is so then it is unlikely that it should accept the goal of making people more equal in some way that is a composite or compromise among these different ways. Combinations and trade-offs are appropriate when a set of competing goals or principles, each of which has independent appeal, cannot all be satisfied at once. They are not appropriate when no goal or principle has been shown to have independent appeal, at least as a theory of equality, at all.

VIII. Expensive Tastes

I said at the outset that equality of welfare, even as stated simply in the abstract, without specifying any of the conceptions we later distinguished, seems to produce initially troubling counterexamples. The most prominent of these is the problem of expensive tastes (a term I shall use, most often, to include expensive ambitions as well). Equality of welfare seems to recommend that those with champagne tastes, who need more income simply to achieve the same level of welfare as those with less expensive tastes, should have more income on that account. But this seems counterintuitive, and I said that someone generally attracted to the ideal would nevertheless wish to limit or qualify it so that his theory did not have that consequence. I want to return to that suggestion now, not because the problem of expensive tastes is of practical importance in politics, but for two different reasons. First, many readers initially attracted to some conception of equality of welfare may suspect that the arguments I directed against their favorite conception, in the last several sections, would have less force if a limitation or qualification suitable to exclude the expensive-tastes consequence had been built into my description of that conception. I think that this suspicion, if indeed it exists, is mistaken, but it is nevertheless worthwhile to consider, for this reason alone, whether such a limitation is in fact possible. Second, there will be readers who are left unpersuaded by my earlier arguments, but would nevertheless abandon their favorite conception of equality of welfare if they believed that it could not in fact be qualified so as to avoid that consequence.

We must be careful to distinguish, when we consider possible qualifications of any such conception, the compromise of a principle from its contradiction. A compromise reflects the weight of some independent and competing principle; a contradiction is a qualification that reflects instead the denial of the original principle itself. The question I want to press is this: Can the principle of equality of welfare be compromised (under any interpretation of what equality of welfare is) in such a way as to block the initially counterintuitive results of that principle, like the proposition that people with champagne tastes should have more resources? Or is any qualification capable of barring those results rather a contradiction that concedes the final irrelevance of the principle?

Imagine that a particular society has managed to achieve equality of welfare in some chosen conception of that ideal. Suppose also that it has achieved this through a distribution that in fact (perhaps just by coincidence) gives everyone equal wealth. Now suppose that someone (Louis) sets out deliberately to cultivate some taste or ambition he does not now have, but which will be expensive in the sense that once it has been cultivated he will not have as much welfare on the chosen conception as he had before unless he acquires more wealth. These new tastes may be tastes in food and drink: Arrow's well-known example of tastes for plovers' eggs and pre-phylloxera claret.[4] Or they may (more plausibly) be tastes for sports, such as skiing, from which one derives pleasure only after acquiring some skill; or, in the same vein, for opera; or for a life dedicated to creative art or exploring or politics. Can Louis be denied extra wealth, taken from those who acquire less expensive tastes (or simply keep those they already have), without contradicting the ideal of equality of welfare that his community has embraced?

Let us first consider how we might explain what Louis has done. No doubt people often put themselves in the way of new tastes carelessly or on whim, without considering whether they will really be better off if they acquire these tastes, or even perversely, knowing that they will be worse off. Even when they think they would be better off, they might be mistaken. But I want to suppose that Louis is not only acting deliberately rather than inadvertently, but is also acting on the basis of the kind of judgment I said people often make when they form and change their preferences. He is trying to make his life a better life in some way. This does not make his claim for extra resources any more appealing or less counterintuitive, I think. On the contrary, the fact that he is acting so deliberately in his own interests seems to make his claim, if anything, less appealing than the claim of someone who tries an expensive experience on a whim, for the pleasure of the moment, and then finds that he is hooked.

Louis will, of course, have his own ideas of what makes a life better, of where his own essential well-being lies. If his society has chosen one of the discrete conceptions of welfare, such as enjoyment or relative success, however, as the welfare in which people should be equal, then Louis cannot think that his own well-being consists in the maximum amount of welfare in that conception. If he did, his behavior would make no sense. This means that one possibly appealing description of what he has done must be wrong. Many people, first hearing this story, might assume that Louis cultivates expensive tastes in order to steal a march on others, so that it would "reward" improper efforts if he were to receive more income. But if stealing a march means acquiring more welfare than others in the chosen conception, then this is impossible. Of course someone might pretend to like plovers' eggs, though he hates them in fact, in order to gain more income, and then spend that income secretly buying more hens' eggs and thus more enjoyment than others can afford. But the problem of expensive tastes is not the problem of fraud—that problem must be handled separately in any society based on equality of welfare because someone could, after all, pretend to be crippled. If Louis sets out to acquire a taste for plovers' eggs so that, if successful, he will in fact have less welfare on the chosen conception if he does not have them, then he cannot purpose to gain some advantage in that form of welfare over others by this decision. He may of course think that he will in the end get more welfare in that conception from a dollar's worth of plovers' eggs than from a dollar's worth of hens' eggs, costly though the former are. In that case he knows that his income will be reduced if he is successful. Or he may think that he will not gain more welfare per dollar by cultivating a taste for plovers' eggs, but rather less. In that case he knows that his welfare (as always, on the chosen conception) will decline overall (though not by much in a very large community) because the total welfare that can then be produced (of which in the end he can expect only *1/n*th) will decrease. It would be absurd to think that he sets out to reduce his own welfare in order to have a larger income, either absolutely or relative to others. After all, though he may have a larger income than others, they are, by hypothesis, no worse off in the chosen conception of welfare than he is, and he is at least by some degree worse off than he would otherwise have been.

Louis does, as I said, suppose that if he cultivates his new taste his life will be better. But this is because he does not accept that the value of his life is measured just by the welfare in which his society has, for some reason, undertaken to make people equal. It is hard to see how the fact that he has this opinion can justify either the suggestion that he has acted improperly or the decision not to give him more resources but rather to leave him unequal to others in the chosen conception. The choice of that conception was society's choice, not his, and society chose that people be equal in it, not the other conception that Louis values more. After all there is no reason to think that people were equal in welfare on Louis's conception even before he developed his new taste, and he may still have less than others have of that even if he is brought back to equality in the chosen conception.

Louis thinks, as I said, that his life would be a more successful life overall—would provide less reason for regret—if he had the expensive taste or ambition even at the small cost in welfare in the chosen conception he would lose if society reestablished equality in that conception for him. Indeed he might think that his life would be more successful overall even if society did not reestablish equality for him. (People develop expensive tastes even in our own society, when they must bear the increased costs themselves.) Suppose the chosen conception is enjoyment. If Louis develops a taste for plovers' eggs, he must believe that a life of satisfying expensive tastes is a better life overall in spite of the fact that it will provide less enjoyment, and might believe it better even if it would provide much less enjoyment. These may, in fact, be plausible beliefs. Or at least they may be plausible if we substitute, for the contrived examples of plovers' eggs, the sorts of expensive tastes that people do seem to cultivate deliberately and in their own interests, such as a taste for sports that follows from developing skill, or a desire for practical power that follows taking an interest in the public weal. It is plausible to suppose that beliefs of that sort figure even in the best accounts of why people in our own economy develop the less admirable expensive tastes—champagne tastes—that figure in the usual examples. For if someone like Louis wishes to lead the life of people in *New York* magazine ads, this must be because he supposes that a life in which rare and costly goods are savored is a life better because it knows a greater variety of pleasure, or more sophisticated pleasures, or, indeed, simply pleasures that others do not know, in spite of containing less pleasure overall.

This explanation of Louis's behavior challenges the importance of the distinction we have thus far been assuming between expensive tastes that are deliberately cultivated and other aspects of personality or person, such as native desires or socially imposed tastes, that affect people's welfare. For the explanation suggests that such tastes are often cultivated in response to beliefs—beliefs about what sort of life is overall more successful—and such beliefs are not themselves cultivated or chosen. Not, that is, in any sense that provides a reason for ignoring differences in welfare caused by these beliefs in a community otherwise committed to evening out differences in welfare. I do not mean that beliefs are afflictions, like blindness, that people find that they have and are stuck with. People reason about their theories of what gives value to life in something of the same way in which they reason about other sorts of beliefs. But they do not choose that a life of service to others, for example, or a life of creative art or scholarship, or a life of exquisite flavors, be the most valuable sort of life for them to lead, and therefore do not choose that they shall believe that it is. We may still distinguish between the voluntary decision someone makes to become a person with certain tastes, or to lead the sort of life likely to have that consequence, and his discovery of tastes and ambitions that he just has. But the distinction is less important than is sometimes thought, because that decision is rarely if ever voluntary all the way down.

If Louis's society aimed to make people equal, not in one of the discrete conceptions of welfare we have thus far been assuming in his story, such as enjoyment or relative success, but in subjective overall success, then we would need a somewhat different account of why he would develop expensive tastes, and of whether it would be fair to deny him extra resources. I argued earlier that any attractive version of equality of overall success must provide a place for the idea of reasonable regret, and that this idea in turn presupposes some independent nonwelfare theory defining a fair distribution of resources. If this is right, then no one could claim extra resources for expensive tastes in a community ostensibly governed by equality of overall success. If his share of resources is fair before he cultivates his new taste, his share remains fair after he has done so. But since I want to offer independent arguments in this section, I shall assume that my earlier arguments are unsound, and that an attractive subjective version of equality of overall success can be developed that is not self-defeating in that way.

But then, since the chosen conception is now overall success, we can no longer say that Louis acts as he does because he believes his life would be more successful overall though less successful on the chosen conception. Suppose that before Louis conceived his expensive taste he was satisfied that his life was roughly as successful overall as everyone else's. He then came to believe that his life would be more valuable if he cultivated some expensive hobby, for example. We must ask what he now thinks about the value of the life he had before he formed that belief. He may think that, though his earlier life was just as good as he thought it was, and would remain so if he could not pursue his new hobby, it would be much better if he could. In that case the problem of expensive tastes does not arise. For Louis is claiming additional resources in order to have more welfare than others on the chosen conception, and he does not have even a prima facie claim to that. But he may instead have changed his beliefs about how valuable his life was. He may have read more widely, or reflected more deeply, and come to the conclusion that his former life, for all its former appeal to him, was in fact a worthless and insipid life. He wants to cultivate new and more challenging tastes to repair the defects in his life, as he now understands them. He asks only the resources necessary to make his life as valuable, in his eyes after they have been opened, as other people find their lives. How can a society committed to equality in this respect deny him these resources? It cannot say that he was wrong to continue to reflect on how best to live. An unexamined life is for that very reason a poor life. If Louis had reached his present opinions about value in life before the initial distribution, he would have received then the resources he now seeks. Why should he be refused them now, and be condemned to a life he finds less valuable than everyone else finds his?[5]

We might summarize the position we have reached in this way. If the chosen conception is one of the discrete conceptions we considered, other than overall success, then Louis is attempting to improve his welfare on some other conception he values more, while retaining equality in the chosen conception. But if the chosen conception is what really matters for equality, and if in any case others may already have more welfare in the conception Louis prefers, what ground does society have for now refusing him equality in the chosen conception? If the chosen conception is overall success (which is assumed, arguendo, not to be self-defeating), then if a claim for extra resources arises at all, it arises because Louis now believes that the earlier distribution was based on a mistake. He asks no special advantage, but only that society reach the distribution it would have reached if he had been able to see more clearly then. What ground could society have for refusing him that?

One ground perhaps suggests itself, which is the ordinary utilitarian principle that average welfare in society (which we should understand to mean welfare in the chosen conception) should be as high as possible. If society "rewards" people who develop expensive tastes by giving them extra resources with which to satisfy these tastes, then people will not be discouraged from doing so. But expensive tastes (by definition) decrease the total welfare that can be produced from a given stock of resources. So the independent principle of utility justifies a compromise with the principle of equality of welfare by recommending that people not be brought to parity of welfare if they develop expensive tastes, in order to discourage them from doing so. If the chosen conception is a discrete conception, this means that people are to be discouraged, for the sake of average utility, from bringing it about that they will need more resources to achieve the same welfare, even though they may think that their lives would be more successful if they did bring that about. If the chosen conception is overall success, judged subjectively, then people are to be discouraged from reexamining their lives in a way that might leave them dissatisfied with the value of the lives they have.

But in fact the principle of utility does not explain what needs explaining here. I can at best explain why compensating those who develop expensive tastes is inefficient. It cannot explain why the ideal of equality does not recommend doing so. It is, after all, a familiar idea in political theory that a just society will make some compromise between efficiency and distribution. It will sometimes tolerate less than perfect equality in order to improve average utility. But the compromise intuitively demanded by the problem of expensive tastes is not such a compromise between efficiency and equality. It is rather a compromise within the idea of equality. Our difficulty is not that, though we believe that equality requires us to pay Louis more because he has forced himself to like champagne, we must deny him equality in order to protect the overall stock of utility. Expensive tastes are embarrassing for the theory that equality means equality of welfare precisely because we believe that equality, considered in itself and apart from questions of efficiency, condemns rather than recommends compensating for deliberately cultivated expensive tastes.

I should also point out, parenthetically, that it is far from plain that the utilitarian principle, by itself, can even provide an explanation of what it does purport to explain, which is why a society that does wish to compromise equality for efficiency would select expensive tastes as the point of sacrifice for equality. Refusing to compensate people who develop expensive tastes will protest average utility only if it succeeds in discouraging at least some people from developing such tastes who would otherwise do so. It is impossible to predict how much of such experimentation would take place in a society dedicated to equality of welfare even without this kind of deterrence, or how effective the deterrence would be. (After all, people develop expensive tastes even in our own society when they do not receive extra resources when they do.) It is also impossible to predict the long-term consequences for utility under any particular assumptions about the success of the deterrence. Any society bent on using noncompensation as a deterrent must set a fairly articulate policy that stipulates reasonably clearly when people whose tastes and ambitions change will be compensated and when they will not be. How would the policy distinguish, for example, between tastes that are deliberately cultivated and those that simply steal up on people? What level of expense—what level of efficiency in producing enjoyment, for example, per dollar cost—would be stipulated as making a taste expensive rather than inexpensive? Beer may very well be less expensive, in this sense, than champagne, but it is also more expensive than water. Suppose the community responds to these difficulties by refusing to compensate for new tastes if people take any positive steps to acquire them or even act in a way that they should know makes their acquisition more likely, whenever these tastes are any more expensive than the tastes, if any, that they replace. If this policy succeeds in discouraging experimentation in tastes to any marked degree, then it might well end, for all we know, in a dull, conformist, unimaginative, and otherwise unattractive community, and a community with a less long-term utility as well. There are many reasons for predicting that latter consequence, but I shall mention only the two most obvious. First, some tastes that are expensive when taken up only by a few people become inexpensive—produce more utility per dollar than present tastes—when they become very popular through the example of those few. Second, a society that does become dull and conformist is a society in which no one takes much pleasure in anything, or cares very deeply about achieving the goals that have been taken mechanically from others rather than developed for himself. It is of course not plain that this policy of noncompensation tacked to a general principle of compensation for tastes acquired in a less voluntary way would have these consequences. But that is because no hypothesis about what levels of utility would be achieved by such a society, so different from our own, is worth much, which hardly recommends this explanation of why an equality of welfare society that is also utilitarian would refuse compensation.

So the supposed utilitarian justification of our intuitive conviction, that equality does not require that those who deliberately cultivate expensive tastes have equal welfare after they have done so, fails on two grounds. We still lack a justification for that conviction. But suppose someone now argues in the following way. It is true that people do not choose their beliefs about what would make their lives overall more successful. But they do choose whether and how far to act on these beliefs. Louis knows, or at least ought to know, that if he cultivates some expensive taste in a society dedicated to equality of enjoyment, for example, and is compensated, then that will decrease the enjoyment available for others. If, knowing this, he chooses the more expensive life, then he does not *deserve* compensation. He is no longer a member of the company of those who deserve equal enjoyment in their lives.

Louis has a choice. He may choose to keep the presently equal resources I said he had, and settle for a life with the enjoyment he now has but without the tastes or ambitions he proposes to cultivate. Or he may keep his present resources and settle for a life that *he* deems more successful overall than his present life, but one that contains less enjoyment. It is quite unfair that he should have a third choice, that he should be able, at the expense of others, to lead a life that is more expensive than theirs at no sacrifice of enjoyment to himself just because he would, quite naturally, consider *that* life a more successful life overall than either of the other two. The reason why Louis does not deserve compensation is not that the more expensive life he might choose is necessarily a worse life. He might be right in thinking that enjoyment is not all that matters, and that a life poorer in enjoyment may be, just from the personal standpoint, a more successful life overall. We say only that the first two choices are rightly his, but that the third is not.

I myself find this argument both powerful and appealing. It is also an important argument for the following reason. The objection to allowing Louis the third choice described is most naturally put this way. Louis should be free (at least within the limits allowed by a defensible form of paternalism) to make the best sort of life he can with his fair share of social resources. But he should not be free to trespass on the fair shares of others, because that would be unfair to them. But of course once the point is put that way it cannot stand simply as an argument for a compromise to equality of welfare tailored to the problem of expensive tastes. For the idea of fair shares cannot then mean simply shares that give people equal welfare on the chosen conception, because that is exactly the conception to which Louis appeals in asking for extra resources. If fair shares are shares fixed independently of that conception, however, then any compromise using the idea of fair shares becomes a contradiction.

Can the idea of fair shares be defined for this purpose in some way that does not make the shares that produce equal welfare in the chosen conception automatically fair shares, but nevertheless uses that conception in some way that avoids contradicting it? Suppose someone's fair share is taken to be the share that produces equal welfare in that conception, or would produce it if the person in question had not deliberately cultivated an expensive taste. This will not help, as we saw, if the chosen conception is overall success, and if Louis believes that the life he would lead if he did not cultivate new tastes would be a life of less overall success than others believe their lives to be. Even if the chosen conception is one of the discrete conceptions, such as enjoyment, defining fair shares in this way will not help. The argument I said I found powerful uses the idea of fair shares not simply to describe the limitation on equality of welfare it recommends, but also to justify that limitation. It proposes to explain why, in spite of the various objections I made earlier in this section, independent and noncontradictory considerations of fairness justify a compromise of equality of welfare. But if the definition of fair shares just assumes that the compromise in question is for some unspecified reason fair, then the appeal to fair shares can itself provide no justification that is not immediately circular. If the idea of fair shares is to do any work, then it must appeal to some independent account of fairness in distribution, and any independent account contradicts the conception to which it is attached, as I said, because it occupies all the space that conception claims for itself. I might add that I think that the most plausible independent account, which I myself had in mind when I said that the argument against Louis's third choice was powerful, is some conception of equality of resources (though of course there are others available, including, for example, the principle that resources are fairly distributed when those with more merit have more).

Perhaps ingenuity could produce some explanation or interpretation of the argument in question—that Louis does not deserve more resources just because he has chosen a more expensive life—which does not use this idea of fair shares or any similar ideas. But any such account would, I suspect, fall before the following further example. Imagine now a society newly dedicated to equality of enjoyment in which, when resources are redistributed in order to achieve equality of enjoyment, Jude has far less money than anyone else because his wants are so simple and so inexpensively satisfied. But one day (perhaps after reading Hemingway) he decides that his life, for all its richness in enjoyment, is a life of less overall success than it might be, and proposes to cultivate a new taste for some challenging sport, such as bullfighting. Suppose that after he does so he finds himself seriously frustrated by his lack of funds with which, for example, to travel to Spain, and asks for more funds through a further redistribution after which he would still, as things fall out, have less than anyone else. Do we now have any grounds for saying that he is undeserving of the increase, when we know that if it is denied he will have both fewer funds and less enjoyment than anyone else? I doubt anyone will want to say this. But if so then we cannot say that the reason Louis is undeserving of an increase is simply that the taste he has cultivated is expensive. Jude's new taste may be just as expensive. The difference is that Louis asks that more than an equal share of social resources be put at the disposal of his life while Jude asks only that something closer to an equal share be put at the disposal of his. We need the idea of fair shares (in this particular case the idea of an equal share of resources) in order to express the force of this difference.

Suppose that if Jude is given more funds and can travel to Spain he will have not merely as much as but *more* welfare than anyone else, in whatever conception has been chosen, including overall success, though he will still have much less money than anyone else. Does equality now require that he be denied the additional money? If not, then Jude's case makes an even stronger point. Not only may Jude reestablish equality of welfare in spite of the expensive taste he has deliberately cultivated. He may even succeed, by developing such a taste, in having more welfare than others. In both cases it is the idea of equality of resources that is doing the work.

I hope the moral of this long section is clear. If someone begins anxious to defend some version or conception of equality of welfare, but also wishes to resist the consequence that those who develop expensive tastes should have more, he will come, in the end, to a very different theory of equality. He will find that he must presuppose some other theory that makes his conception of equality of welfare either idle or self-defeating. That is, of course, exactly the conclusion that we reached in studying certain of these conceptions separately. It remains to consider, in the next section, whether there are strong reasons for nevertheless trying to find some small room for equality of welfare within a general and different theory of equality.

IX. Handicaps

I conceded, at the beginning, the immediate appeal of the idea that genuine equality is equality of welfare. One aspect of that immediate appeal may easily have survived the various doubts I have raised, which is apparent power of equality of welfare to explain why people with physical or mental handicaps (or with other special needs) should have extra resources. Surely (it might still be said) this is because they are able to achieve less of something that falls within the general ambit of "welfare" than others are on the same share of resources. Perhaps we care about the handicapped because they are able to achieve less enjoyment or relative or overall success, or perhaps it is some discrete combination of these, or all of them. But some tug toward equality of welfare under some interpretation must be part of our intuitions about the handicapped. If so, then this fact might be thought to show that any final theory of equality must provide at least some space for equality of welfare, though perhaps only as a supplement to or qualification of another theory of equality, if only to capture the provisions we insist on making for those who are unfortunate in this particular way.

But it is far from clear that some welfare concept is needed to explain why the handicapped should sometimes have more material resources than the healthy. In the next chapter I shall describe a different approach to the problem of handicaps which does not rely on welfare comparisons but which might explain this equally as well. There is no reason to assume, in advance of considering this and other suggestions, that only a welfare-based theory of equality can provide the account that is necessary. In fact (and moreover) a welfare-based theory can provide only a less satisfactory account than might at first appear. The argument we are now considering is that equality of welfare deserves a place, at least, in any general theory of equality, because it so accurately captures our intuitions about how the handicapped should be treated in the name of equality. But is this true? It does seem plausible to say, on any conception of welfare, that people with severe handicaps are likely, as a class, to have less welfare than others. But this is of course true only statistically. In many cases those with handicaps have in consequence less income, and therefore do not have even equal material resources with others. And some people with appalling handicaps need extra income just to survive. But many people with serious handicaps have high levels of welfare on any conception—higher than many others who are not handicapped. That is true, for example, of Tiny Tim and Scrooge. Tim is happier than Scrooge, approves the way the world is going more, is more successful in his own eyes, and so forth.

The intuition I spoke of, however, that those with handicaps should have extra resources, is not limited to those among the handicapped who do in fact have lower-than-average welfare on some conception. If Tim had as much money as Scrooge (when perhaps Tim's welfare would be greater than Scrooge's by an even larger margin) but Tim nevertheless did not have enough money to afford physiotherapy, many of us would think him entitled to extra resources for that purpose. Now of course we might believe this only because our intuitions have been schooled by the statistical fact. On this hypothesis, we feel that the handicapped as a group should have more because their welfare is as a group lower, and we then apply the general intuition to individual cases without checking to see whether the general rule holds. But I do not find that a persuasive account of why we feel as we do. If, when we know that someone handicapped is not particularly low in welfare, we still believe that he is entitled to extra resources in virtue of that handicap, then this belief is poorly explained by supposing that we have lost the power to discriminate.

So our beliefs about the handicapped are not in fact justified so accurately or powerfully by the idea of equality of welfare as to suggest that any general theory must on that account include some measure of that ideal. The lower-welfare explanation of these beliefs has further shortcomings as well. Suppose that the welfare (on any interpretation) of an entirely paralyzed but conscious person is vastly less than the welfare of anyone else in the community, that putting more and more money at his disposal would steadily increase his welfare but only by very small amounts, and that if he had at his disposal all the resources beyond those needed simply to keep the others alive he would still have vastly less welfare than they. Equality of welfare would recommend this radical transfer, that is, until the latter situation was reached. But it is not plain to me (or, I think, to others) that equality, considered just on its own, and without regard to the kinds of considerations that sometimes might be thought to override it, really does require or even recommend that radical transfer under these circumstances.

I do not claim (as this last observation recognizes) that any community that embraced equality of welfare in principle would then be committed to the radical transfer. Some other principle the community also accepted (for example the principle of utility) might recommend some compromise with equality here. But where should the line be drawn? It might, perhaps, be left to the practical politics of intuition to draw such a line. But then the victim of total paralysis might well receive nothing at all. The equality principle would in itself offer no reason for the community's accepting an initial utility loss to do him some good that would not also apply to doing him more good, at least in the circumstances I describe in which the marginal utility to him of further transfers does not much decline. The principle would offer almost no guidance to the community here, beyond a call for help equally strident over the whole range of possible transfers to this victim, a call too impractical to honor in full and too unstructured for principled compromise.

Now suppose different facts. There is an expensive piece of equipment that would enable a paraplegic to lead a much more normal life, and the community can afford that equipment at great but not crippling sacrifice to its other needs and projects. The community votes to levy a special tax to provide this machine for him. But he is an excellent and dedicated violinist, and he replies that he would rather have a superb Stradivarius, which he could purchase with the same funds. Can the community properly refuse to honor that choice?[6] On any of the conceptions of welfare we might choose, the paraplegic's welfare might in fact be increased more by owning the violin than by having the machine. Even if he knew all the facts he would prefer to have it, it would bring him more enjoyment, make his life both relatively and overall more successful in his own eyes and objectively. The independent principle of utility would recommend the same choice, of course.

But these facts would be embarrassing to a scheme that was not committed generally to equality of welfare, and allowed that ideal only a limited place in order to handle the special problem of handicaps. For consider someone else, not handicapped, who has a low level of welfare on all the same conceptions. He takes little enjoyment from his life, counts it a failure, and so forth, just because, though he has the same amount of wealth as everyone else not handicapped, that is not enough to buy the Stradivarius he covets above all else. If the paraplegic is allowed to use his extra funds to buy the violin, that other person might properly complain. The paraplegic treats the transfer, not as the occasion to remove or mitigate his handicap, but simply as an opportunity to increase his welfare in other ways, and the other violin-lover would seem to have, in his low state of welfare, as much claim to do that as the paraplegic has. But if the community denies the handicapped person that use of his extra funds, and requires him to buy the machine instead, its position seems perverse. It grants extra funds to him just on the ground that this will increase his lower-than-average welfare, and yet denies him the right to increase his welfare, with those funds, as much as he can.

X. Welfarism

If I am right in the various arguments I have made here, then equality of welfare is not so coherent or attractive an ideal as it is often taken to be. We therefore have reason to consider with some care the alternative ideal of equality of resources. But it is worth stopping now to consider very briefly whether the arguments I have made against equality of welfare might be effective against other forms of welfarism and, in particular, how far they might be effective against utilitarianism. (I am using Amartya Sen's account of welfarism as the general theory that the justice of distributions must be defined exclusively by stipulating some function of individual welfare.)[7]

The different versions of equality of welfare that we have been studying are varieties of welfarism. Utilitarianism, which calls for some maximizing function over some conception of welfare, is another, or rather, another group. Two kinds of justification are in principle available for any form of welfarism. A welfarist theory can be defended on the teleological ground that the stipulated function of the stipulated conception of welfare is something good in itself that ought to be produced for its own sake. Or it can be defended as a particular conception of equality, as a particular theory about when people are being treated as equals. The distinction between these two types of grounds is reasonably clear, I think, in the case of utilitarianism.

That theory can be supported in a direct teleological way: not only is pain bad in itself but pleasure (or some other conception of positive welfare) is good in itself, and the more there is of it, the better. Or it can be supported as a conception of equality. It is then understood as the theory that people are treated as equals when and only when their pleasures and pains (or components of some other conception of welfare) are taken into account quantitatively only, each in that sense to count as one and only one. Of course this egalitarian version of utilitarianism cannot, as the teleological version can, purport to supply all of a plausible general political or moral theory. The egalitarian utilitarian would have to explain why it is not as good to aim at maximum average misery as maximum average happiness, for example, or why there is anything to regret in a natural disaster that kills thousands though it improves the situation of a few. But he might find this explanation either in a further political principle, which holds that those who aim at others' misery or failure do not show these others the concern to which human beings, at least, are entitled, or in a distinct morality of outcomes which holds that death or pain or some other kind of suffering is bad in itself, but which uses neither the same conception nor the same metric of welfare as his egalitarian utilitarianism deploys.

The arguments we considered against equality of welfare would seem, at least on a first look, equally effective against utilitarianism when it is understood in that second way, that is, as a conception of equality. Once again we should proceed by stating different interpretations of utilitarianism composed by taking different conceptions of welfare as the maximands for a given community. And once again it will seem implausible only to take gains and losses in enjoyment, for example, or in relative success, as the measure of when people are being treated as equals, because people value welfare in these particular conceptions differently. Nor will it be helpful to take gains and losses in overall success, interpreted either subjectively or objectively, as the measure, because, as we saw, these conceptions of welfare depend on already having accepted a different, independent test of when people are being treated as equals.

These various arguments are plainly beside the point, however, when utilitarianism is supported in the first way, that is, as the teleological theory that welfare on some conception is inherently good in itself. Against that argument my claim, that people cannot be treated as equals by making them equal in some dimension they value unequally, is irrelevant, because what is then in question is only whether welfare on that conception is good in itself.

I might add that I think that the teleological ground of utilitarianism, which my arguments do not touch, is much less appealing than the egalitarian ground, which they do. It is the egalitarian ground, I think, rather than the teleological ground, that accounts for whatever appeal utilitarian arguments still have for modern politicians and lawyers.

The distinction between these two types of grounds for welfarist theories might seem less plausible when applied to forms of welfarism other than utilitarianism. But it is available at least in principle, I think, and we can construct a teleological defense of at least some conceptions of equality of welfare. Someone might say that it is simply a good thing when people have the same amount of enjoyment, for example, whether or not everyone agrees that enjoyment is fundamentally important in their own lives, or even, perhaps, whether they ought to agree that it is important in that way. The arguments I have offered do not reach equality of welfare taken to be a theory about treating people as equals. Equality of welfare, so conceived, is weaker than we might initially have thought. Is equality of resources stronger?

Notes

1. I owe this last suggestion to Derek Parfit, and through him, I understand, to J. P. Griffin and J. McMahon.
2. In the case of some people, but not Jack, we might be able to find an amount of resources such that their actual regret at not having more is so weak that we do not need to compute their reasonable regret at that amount to say that the latter must be less than the actual regret that others would have if the former had that amount. But many questions arise even then. Is it not necessary still to compute the reasonable regret, as distinguished from the actual regret, of the latter group, before deciding that the former group may not have more than that amount? Can this be done without regress? In any case, the total of amounts fixed as maxima for particular people, in this way, would undoubtedly exceed the total available for distribution. I shall not pursue these complexities further.
3. See Bernard Williams, "Egoism and Altruism," in *Problems of the Self* (Cambridge: Cambridge University Press, 1973), p. 262.
4. Kenneth J. Arrow, "Some Ordinalist-Utilitarian Notes on Rawls's Theory of Justice," *Journal of Philosophy* 70, no. 9 (10 May 1973): 254.
5. If the chosen conception is some objective version of equality of success, rather than the subjective version discussed in this paragraph, the situation is different still. If the change in Louis's tastes has the consequence that his life is now objectively more successful, then he should have fewer rather than more resources. If (because Louis's convictions are mistaken) the change makes his life objectively worse, then the claim that someone might make on his behalf, for still further resources for reeducation, seems especially strong. But I am assuming that the objective version of equality of overall success has little appeal for a liberal society, so I shall not pursue this line.
6. See T. M. Scanlon's discussion of this problem in "Preference and Urgency," *Journal of Philosophy* 72, no. 19 (6 November 1975): 659–661.
7. A. K. Sen, "Utilitarianism and Welfarism," *Journal of Philosophy* 76, no. 9 (September 1979): 463–489.

[3]

Equality of Resources

Ronald Dworkin

I. The Auction

In Chapter 1 we considered the claims of equality of welfare as an interpretation of treating people as equals. Here we shall consider the competing claims of equality of resources. But we shall be occupied, for the most part, simply in defining a suitable conception of equality of resources, and not in defending it except as such definition provides a defense. I shall assume, for this purpose, that equality of resources is a matter of equality in whatever resources are owned privately by individuals. Equality of political power, including equality of power over publicly or commonly owned resources, is therefore treated as a different issue, reserved for discussion on another occasion. This distinction is, of course, arbitrary on any number of grounds. From the standpoint of any sophisticated economic theory, an individual's command over public resources forms part of his private resources. Someone who has power to influence public decisions about the quality of the air he or she breathes, for example, is richer than someone who does not. So an overall theory of equality must find a means of integrating private resources and political power.

Private ownership, moreover, is not a single, unique relationship between a person and a material resource, but an open-textured relationship many aspects of which must be fixed politically. So the question of what division of resources is an equal division must to some degree include the question of what powers someone who is assigned a resource thereby gains, and that in turn must include the further question of his right to veto whatever changes in those powers might be threatened through politics. Here, however, I shall for the most part assume that the general dimensions of ownership are sufficiently well understood that the question of what pattern of private ownership constitutes an equal division of private resources can be discussed independently of these complications.

I argue that an equal division of resources presupposes an economic market of some form, mainly as an analytical device but also, to a certain extent, as an actual political institution. That claim may seem sufficiently paradoxical to justify the following preliminary comments. The idea of a market for goods has figured in political and economic theory, since the eighteenth century, in two rather different ways. It has been celebrated, first, as a device for both defining and achieving certain communitywide goals variously described as prosperity, efficiency, and overall utility. It has been hailed, second, as a necessary condition of individual liberty, the condition under which free men and women may exercise individual initiative and choice so that their fates lie in their own hands. The market, that is, has been defended both through arguments of policy, which appeal to the overall, communitywide gains it produces, and through arguments of principle, which appeal instead to some supposed right to liberty.

But the economic market, whether defended in either or both of these ways, has during this same period come to be regarded as the enemy of equality, largely because the forms of economic market systems developed and enforced in industrial countries have permitted and indeed encouraged vast inequality in property. Both political philosophers and ordinary citizens have therefore pictured equality as the antagonist or victim of the values of efficiency and liberty supposedly served by the market, so that wise and moderate politics consists in striking some balance or trade-off between equality and these other values, either by imposing constraints on the market as an economic environment, or by replacing it, in part or altogether, with a different economic system.

I shall try to suggest, on the contrary, that the idea of an economic market, as a device for setting prices for a vast variety of goods and services, must be at the center of any attractive theoretical development of equality of resources. The main point can be shown most quickly by constructing a reasonably simple exercise in equality of resources, deliberately artificial so as to abstract from problems we shall have to face later. Suppose a number of shipwreck survivors are washed up on a desert island that has abundant resources and no native population, and any likely rescue is many years away. These immigrants accept the principle that no one is antecedently entitled to any of these resources, but that they shall instead be divided equally among them. (They do not yet realize, let us say, that it might be wise to keep some resources as owned in common by any state they might create.) They also accept (at least provisionally) the following test of an equal division of resources, which I shall call the envy test. No division of resources is an equal division if, once the division is complete, any immigrant would prefer someone else's bundle of resources to his own bundle.[1]

Now suppose some one immigrant is elected to achieve the division according to that principle. It is unlikely that he can succeed simply by physically dividing the resources of the island into *n* identical bundles of resources. The number of each kind of the nondivisible resources, like milking cows, might not be an exact multiple of *n,* and even in the case of divisible resources, like arable land, some parcels of land would be better than others, and some better for one use than for another. Suppose, however, that by a great deal of trial and error and care the divider could create *n* bundles of resources, each of which was somewhat different from the others but was nevertheless such that he could assign one to each immigrant and no one would in fact envy anyone else's bundle.

The distribution might still fail to satisfy the immigrants as an equal distribution, for a reason that is not caught by the envy test. Suppose (to put the point in a dramatic way) the divider achieved his result by transforming all the available resources into a very large stock of plovers' eggs and pre-phylloxera claret (either by magic or by trade with a neighboring island that enters the story only for that reason) and divides this glut into identical bundles of baskets and bottles. Many of the immigrants—let us say all but one—are delighted. But if that one hates plovers' eggs and pre-phylloxera claret he will feel that he has not been treated as an equal in the division of resources. The envy test is met—he does not prefer any one's bundle to his own—but he prefers what he would have had under some fairer treatment of the initially available resources.

A similar, though less dramatic, piece of unfairness might be produced even without magic or bizarre trades. For the combination of resources which composes each bundle the divider creates will favor some tastes over others, compared with different combinations he might have composed. That is, different sets of *n* bundles might be created by trial and error, each of which would pass the envy test, so that for any such set that the divider chooses, someone will prefer that he had chosen a different set, even though that person would not prefer a different bundle within that set. Trades after the initial distribution may, of course, improve that person's position. But they will be unlikely to bring him to the position he would have had under the set of bundles he would have preferred, because some others will begin with a bundle they prefer to the bundle they would have had in that set, and so will have no reason to trade to that bundle.

So the divider needs a device that will attack two distinct foci of arbitrariness and possible unfairness. The envy test cannot be satisfied by any simple mechanical division of resources. If any more complex division can be found that will satisfy it, many such might be found, so that the choice among these would be arbitrary. The same solution will by now have occurred to all readers. The divider needs some form of auction or other market procedure in order to respond to these problems. I shall describe a reasonably straightforward procedure that would seem acceptable if it could be made to work, though as I shall describe it would be impossibly expensive of time. Suppose the divider hands each of the immigrants an equal and large number of clamshells, which are sufficiently numerous and in themselves valued by no one, to use as counters in a market of the following sort. Each distinct item on the island (not including the immigrants themselves) is listed as a lot to be sold, unless someone notifies the auctioneer (as the divider has now become) of his or her desire to bid for some part of an item, including part, for example, of some piece of land, in which case that part becomes itself a distinct lot. The auctioneer then proposes a set of prices for each lot and discovers whether that set of prices clears all markets, that is, whether there is only one purchaser at that price and all lots are sold. If not, then the auctioneer adjusts his prices until he reaches a set that does clear the markets.[2] But the process does not stop then, because each of the immigrants remains free to change his bids even when an initially market-clearing set of prices is reached, or even to propose different lots. But let us suppose that in time even this leisurely process comes to an end, everyone declares himself satisfied, and goods are distributed accordingly.[3]

Now the envy test will have been met. No one will envy another's set of purchases because, by hypothesis, he could have purchased that bundle with his clamshells instead of his own bundle. Nor is the choice of sets of bundles arbitrary. Many people will be able to imagine a different set of bundles meeting the no-envy test that might have been established, but the actual set of bundles has the merit that each person played, through his purchases against an initially equal stock of counters, an equal role in determining the set of bundles actually chosen. No one is in the position of the person in our earlier example who found himself with nothing but what he hated. Of course, luck plays a certain role in determining how satisfied anyone is with the outcome, against other possibilities he might envision. If plovers' eggs and old claret were the only resources to auction, then the person who hated these would be as badly off as in our earlier example. He would be unlucky that the immigrants had not washed up on an island with more of what he wanted (though lucky, of course, that it did not have even less). But he could not complain that the division of the actual resources they found was unequal.

He might think himself lucky or unlucky in other ways as well. It would be a matter of luck, for example, how many others shared various of his tastes. If his tastes or ambitions proved relatively popular, this circumstance might work in his favor in the auction, if there were economies of scale in the production of what he wanted; or against him, if what he wanted was scarce. If the immigrants had decided to establish a regime of equality of welfare instead of equality of resources, then these various pieces of good or bad luck would be shared with others, because distribution would be based, not on any auction of the sort I described, in which luck plays this role, but on a strategy of evening out differences in whatever concept of welfare had been chosen. Equality of resources, however, offers no similar reason for correcting for the contingencies that determine how expensive or frustrating someone's preferences turn out to be.[4]

Under equality of welfare, people are meant to decide what sorts of lives they want independently of information relevant to determining how much their choices will reduce or enhance the ability of others to have what they want. That sort of information becomes relevant only at a second, political level at which administrators then gather all the choices made at the first level to see what distribution will give each of these choices equal success under some concept of welfare taken as the correct dimension of success. Under equality of resources, however, people decide what sorts of lives to pursue against a background of information about the actual cost their choices impose on other people and hence on the total stock of resources that may fairly be used by them. The information left to an independent political level under equality of welfare is therefore brought to the initial level of individual choice under equality of resources. The elements of luck in the auction just described are in fact pieces of information of a crucial sort; information that is acquired and used in that process of choice.

So the contingent facts of raw material and the distribution of tastes are not grounds on which someone might challenge a distribution as unequal.

They are rather background facts that determine what equality of resources, in these circumstances, is. Under equality of resources, no test for calculating what equality requires can be abstracted from these background facts and used to test them. The market character of the auction is not simply a convenient or ad hoc device for resolving technical problems that arise for equality of resources in very simple exercises like our desert island case. It is an institutionalized form of the process of discovery and adaptation that is at the center of the ethics of that ideal. Equality of resources supposes that the resources devoted to each person's life should be equal. That goal needs a metric. The auction proposes what the envy test in fact assumes, that the true measure of the social resources devoted to the life of one person is fixed by asking how important, in fact, that resource is for others. It insists that the cost, measured in that way, figures in each person's sense of what is rightly his and in each person's judgment of what life he should lead, given that command of justice. Anyone who insists that equality is violated by any particular profile of initial tastes, therefore, must reject equality of resources and fall back on equality of welfare.

Of course it is sovereign in this argument, and in this connection between the market and equality of resources, that people enter the market on equal terms. The desert island auction would not have avoided envy, and would have no appeal as a solution to the problem of dividing the resources equally, if the immigrants had struggled ashore with different amounts of money in their pockets, which they were free to use in the auction, or if some had stolen clamshells from others. We must not lose sight of that fact, either in the argument that follows or in any reflections on the application of that argument to contemporary economic systems. But neither should we lose sight, in our dismay over the inequities of those systems, of the important theoretical connection between the market and the concept of equality of resources.

There are, of course, other and very different sorts of objections that might be made to the use of an auction, even an equal auction of the sort I described. It might be said, for example, that the fairness of an auction supposes that the preferences people bring to the auction, or form in its course, are authentic—the true preferences of the agent rather than preferences imposed upon him by the economic system itself. Perhaps an auction of any sort, in which one person bids against another, imposes an illegitimate assumption that what is valuable in life is individual ownership of something rather than more cooperative enterprises of the community or some group within it as a whole. Insofar as this (in part mysterious) objection is pertinent here, however, it is an objection against the idea of private ownership over an extensive domain of resources, which is better considered under the title of political equality, not an objection to the claim that a market of some sort must figure in any satisfactory account of what equality in private ownership is.

II. The Project

Since the device of an equal auction seems promising as a technique for achieving an attractive interpretation of equality of resources in a simple context, like the desert island, the question arises whether it will prove useful in developing a more general account of that ideal. We should ask whether the device could be elaborated to provide a scheme for developing or testing equality of resources in a community that has a dynamic economy, with labor, investment, and trade. What structure must an auction take in such an economy—what adjustments or supplements must be made to the production and trade that would follow such an auction—in order that the results continue to satisfy our initial requirement that an equal share of the resources be available to each citizen?

Our interest in this question is threefold. First, the project provides an important test of the coherence and completeness of the idea of equality of resources. Suppose no auction or pattern of post-auction trade could be described whose results could be accepted as equality in any society much more complex or less artificial than a simple economy of consumption; or that no auction could produce equality without constraints and restrictions that violate independent principles of justice. This would tend to suggest, at least, that there is no coherent ideal of equality of resources or that the ideal is not politically attractive after all.

We might discover, on the contrary, less comprehensive gaps or defects in the idea. Suppose, for example, that the design for the auction we develop does not uniquely determine a particular distribution, even given a stipulated set of initial resources and a stipulated population with fixed interests and ambitions, but is instead capable of producing significantly different outcomes depending on the order of decisions, arbitrary choices about the composition of the initial list of options, or other contingencies. We might conclude that the ideal of equality of resources embraces a variety of distributions, each of which satisfies the ideal, and that the ideal is therefore partially indeterminate. This would show limitations on the power of the ideal to discriminate between certain distributions, but it would not for that reason show that the ideal is either incoherent or practically impotent. So it is worth trying to develop the idea of an equal auction as a test of the theoretical standing and power of the political ideal.

Second, a fully developed description of an equal auction, adequate for a more complex society, might provide a standard for judging institutions and distributions in the real world. Of course no complex, organic society would have, in its history, anything remotely comparable to an equal auction. But we can nevertheless ask, for any actual distribution, whether it falls within the class of distributions that might have been produced by such an auction over a defensible description of initial resources, or, if it does not, how far it differs from or falls short of the closest distribution within this class. The device of the auction might provide, in other words, a standard for judging how far an actual distribution, however it has been achieved, approaches equality of resources at any particular time.

Third, the device might be useful in the design of actual political institutions. Under certain (perhaps very limited) circumstances, when the conditions for an equal auction are at least roughly met, then an actual auction might be the best means of reaching or preserving equality of resources in the real world. This will be true, particularly, when the results of such an auction are antecedently indeterminate in the way just described, so that any result the auction reaches will respect equality of resources even though it is not known, in advance, which result would be reached. In such a case it may be fairer to conduct an actual auction than to choose, through some other political means, one rather than another of the results that an auction might produce. Even in such a case it will rarely be possible or desirable to conduct an actual auction in the design our theoretical investigations recommend. But it may be possible to design an auction surrogate—an economic or political institution having sufficient of the characteristics of a theoretical equal auction that the arguments of fairness recommending an actual auction were it feasible also recommend the surrogate. The economic markets of many countries can be interpreted, even as they stand, as forms of auctions. (So, too, can many forms of democratic political process.) Once we have developed a satisfactory model of an actual auction (to the extent we can) we can use that model to test these institutions, and reform them to bring them closer to the model.

Nevertheless our project is in the main, in the discussion here, entirely theoretical. Our interest is primarily in the design of an ideal, and of a device to picture that ideal and test its coherence, completeness, and appeal. We shall therefore ignore practical difficulties, like problems of gathering information, that do not impeach these theoretical goals, and also make simplifying counterfactual assumptions that do not subvert them. But we should try to notice which simplifications we are making, because they will be of importance, particularly as to the third and most practical application of our projects, at any later stage, at which we consider second-best compromises of our ideal in the real world.

III. Luck and Insurance

If the auction is successful as described, then equality of resources holds for the moment among the immigrants. But perhaps only for the moment, because if they are left alone, once the auction is completed, to produce and trade as they wish, then the envy test will shortly fail. Some may be more skillful than others at producing what others want and will trade to get. Some may like to work, or to work in a way that will produce more to trade, while others may like not to work or prefer to work at what will bring them less. Some will stay healthy while others fall sick, or lightning will strike the farms of others but avoid theirs. For any of these and dozens of other reasons some people will prefer the bundle others have in, say, five years, to their own.

We must ask whether (or rather how far) such developments are consistent with equality of resources, and I shall begin by considering the character and impact of luck on the immigrants' post-auction fortunes. I shall distinguish, at least for the moment, between two kinds of luck. Option luck is a matter of how deliberate and calculated gambles turn out—whether someone gains or loses through accepting an isolated risk he or she should have anticipated and might have declined. Brute luck is a matter of how risks fall out that are not in that sense deliberate gambles. If I buy a stock on the exchange that rises, then my option luck is good. If I am hit by a falling meteorite whose course could not have been predicted, then my bad luck is brute (even though I could have moved just before it struck if I had had any reason to know where it would strike). Obviously the difference between these two forms of luck can be represented as a matter of degree, and we may be uncertain how to describe a particular piece of bad luck. If someone develops cancer in the course of a normal life, and there is no particular decision to which we can point as a gamble risking the disease, then we will say that he has suffered brute bad luck. But if he smoked cigarettes heavily then we may prefer to say that he took an unsuccessful gamble.

Insurance, so far as it is available, provides a link between brute and option luck, because the decision to buy or reject catastrophe insurance is a calculated gamble. Of course, insurance does not erase the distinction. Someone who buys medical insurance and is hit by an unexpected meteorite still suffers brute bad luck, because he is worse off than if he had bought insurance and not needed it. But he has had better option luck than if he had not bought the insurance, because his situation is better in virtue of his not having run the gamble of refusing to insure.

Is it consistent with equality of resources that people should have different income or wealth in virtue of differing option luck? Suppose some of the immigrants plant valuable but risky crops while others play it safer, and that some of the former buy insurance against uncongenial weather while others do not. Skill will play a part in determining which of these various programs succeed, of course, and we shall consider the problems this raises later. But option luck will also play a part. Does its role threaten or invade equality of resources?

Consider, first, the differences in wealth between those who play it safe and those who gamble and succeed. Some people enjoy, while others hate, risks; but this particular difference in personality is comprehended in a more general difference between the kinds of lives that different people wish to lead. The life chosen by someone who gambles contains, as an element, the factor of risk; someone who chooses not to gamble has decided that he prefers a safer life. We have already decided that people should pay the price of the life they have decided to lead, measured in what others give up in order that they can do so. That was the point of the auction as a device to establish initial equality of resources. But the price of a safer life, measured in this way, is precisely forgoing any chance of the gains whose prospect induces others to gamble. So we have no reason to object, against the background of our earlier decisions, to a result in which those who decline to gamble have less than some of those who do not.

But we must also compare the situation of those who gamble and win with that of those who gamble and lose. We cannot say that the latter have chosen a different life and must sacrifice gains accordingly; for they have chosen the same lives as those who won. But we can say that the possibility of loss was part of the life they chose—that it was the fair price of the possibility of gain. For we might have designed our initial auction so that people could purchase (for example) lottery tickets with their clamshells. But the price of those tickets would have been some amount of other resources (fixed by the odds and the gambling preferences of others) that the shells would otherwise have bought, and which will be wholly forgone if the ticket does not win.

The same point can be made by considering the arguments for redistribution from winners to losers after the event. If winners were made to share their winnings with losers, then no one would gamble, as individuals, and the kind of life preferred by both those who in the end win and those who lose would be unavailable. Of course, it is not a good argument, against someone who urges redistribution in order to achieve equality of resources, that redistribution would make some forms of life less attractive or even impossible. For the demands of equality (we assume in this chapter) are prior to other desiderata, including variety in the kinds of life available to people. (Equality will in any case make certain kinds of lives—a life of economic and political domination of others, for example—impossible.) In the present case, however, the difference is apparent. For the effect of redistribution from winners to losers in gambles would be to deprive both of lives they prefer, which indicates, not simply that this would produce an unwanted curtailment of available forms of life, but that it would deprive them of an equal voice in the construction of lots to be auctioned, like the man who hated both plovers' eggs and claret but was confronted only with bundles of both. Winners and losers all wanted gambles to be in the mix, either originally or as represented by resources with which they can take risks later, and the chance of losing is the correct price, measured on the metric we have been using, of a life that includes gambles with a chance of gain.

We may, of course, have special reasons for forbidding certain forms of gambles. We may have paternalistic reasons for limiting how much any individual may risk, for example. We may also have reasons based in a theory of political equality for forbidding someone to gamble with his freedom or his religious or political rights. The present point is more limited. We have no general reason for forbidding gambles altogether in the bare fact that in the event winners will control more resources than losers, any more than in the fact that winners will have more than those who do not gamble. Our initial principle, that equality of resources requires that people pay the true cost of the lives they lead, warrants rather than condemns these differences.

We may (if we wish) adjust our envy test to record that conclusion. We may say that in computing the extent of someone's resources over his life, for the purpose of asking whether anyone else envies those resources, any resources gained through a successful gamble should be represented by the opportunity to take the gamble at the odds in force, and comparable adjustments made to the resources of those who have lost through gambles. The main point of this artificial construction of the envy test, however, would be to remind us that the argument in favor of allowing differences in option luck to affect income and wealth assumes that everyone has in principle the same gambles available to him. Someone who never had the opportunity to run a similar risk, and would have taken the opportunity had it been available, will still envy some of those who did have it.

Nor does the argument yet confront the case of brute bad luck. If two people lead roughly the same lives, but one goes suddenly blind, then we cannot explain the resulting differences in their incomes either by saying that one took risks that the other chose not to take, or that we could not redistribute without denying both the lives they prefer. For the accident has (we assume) nothing to do with choices in the pertinent sense. It is not necessary to the life either has chosen that he run the risk of going blind without redistribution of funds from the other. This is a fortiori so if one is born blind and the other sighted.

But the possibility of insurance provides, as I suggested, a link between the two kinds of luck. For suppose insurance against blindness is available, in the initial auction, at whatever level of coverage the policyholder chooses to buy. And also suppose that two sighted people have, at the time of the auction, equal chance of suffering an accident that will blind them, and know that they have. Now if one chooses to spend part of his initial resources for such insurance and the other does not, or if one buys more coverage than the other, then this difference will reflect their different opinions about the relative value of different forms or components of their prospective lives. It may reflect the fact that one puts more value on sight than the other; or, differently, that one would count monetary compensation for the loss of his sight as worthless in the face of such a tragedy while the other, more practical, would fix his mind on the aids and special training that such money might buy; or simply that one minds or values risk differently from the other, and would, for example, rather try for a brilliant life that would collapse under catastrophe than a life guarded at the cost of resources necessary to make it brilliant.

But in any case the bare idea of equality of resources, apart from any paternalistic additions, would not argue for redistribution from the person who had insured to the person who had not if, horribly, they were both blinded in the same accident. For the availability of insurance would mean that, though both had had brute bad luck, the difference between them was a matter of option luck, and the arguments we entertained against disturbing the results of option luck under conditions of equal antecedent risk hold here as well. But then the situation cannot be different if the person who decided not to insure is the only one to be blinded. For once again the difference is a difference in option luck against a background of equal opportunity to insure or not. If neither had been blinded, the man who had insured against blindness would have been the loser. His option luck would have been bad—though it seems bizarre to put it this way—because he spent resources that, as things turned out, would have been better spent otherwise. But he would have no claim, in that event, from the man who did not insure and also survived unhurt.

So if the condition just stated were met—if everyone had an equal risk of suffering some catastrophe that would leave him or her handicapped, and everyone knew roughly what the odds were and had ample opportunity to insure—then handicaps would pose no special problem for equality of resources. But of course that condition is not met. Some people are born with handicaps, or develop them before they have either sufficient knowledge or funds to insure on their own behalf. They cannot buy insurance after the event. Even handicaps that develop later in life, against which people do have the opportunity to insure, are not randomly distributed through the population, but follow genetic tracks, so that sophisticated insurers would charge some people higher premiums for the same coverage before the event. Nevertheless the idea of a market in insurance provides a counterfactual guide through which equality of resources might face the problem of handicaps in the real world.

Suppose we can make sense of and even give a rough answer to the following question. If (contrary to fact) everyone had at the appropriate age the same risk of developing physical or mental handicaps in the future (which assumes that no one has developed these yet) but the total number of handicaps remained what it is, how much insurance coverage against these handicaps would the average member of the community purchase? We might then say that but for (uninsurable) brute luck that has altered these equal odds, the average person would have purchased insurance at that level, and compensate those who do develop handicaps accordingly, out of some fund collected by taxation or other compulsory process but designed to match the fund that would have been provided through premiums if the odds had been equal. Those who develop handicaps will then have more resources at their command than others, but the extent of their extra resources will be fixed by the market decisions that people would supposedly have made if circumstances had been more equal than they are. Of course, this argument does involve the fictitious assumption that everyone who suffers handicaps would have bought the average amount of insurance, and we may wish to refine the argument and the strategy so that no longer holds.[5] But it does not seem an unreasonable assumption for this purpose as it stands.

Can we answer the counterfactual question with sufficient confidence to develop a program of compensation of that sort? We face a threshold difficulty of some importance. People can decide how much of their resources to devote to insurance against a particular catastrophe only with some idea of the life they hope to lead, because only then can they decide how serious a particular catastrophe would be, how far additional resources would alleviate the tragedy, and so forth. But people who are born with a particular handicap or who develop one in childhood will of course take that circumstance into account in the plans they make. So in order to decide how much insurance such a person would have bought without the handicap we must decide what sort of life he would have planned in that case. But there may be no answer, even in principle, to that question.

We do not need, however, to make counterfactual judgments that are so personalized as to embarrass us for that reason. Even if people did all have equal risk of all catastrophes, and evaluated the value and importance of insurance differently entirely as a result of their different ambitions and plans, the insurance market would nevertheless be structured through categories designating the risks against which most people would insure in a general way. After all, risks of most catastrophes are now regarded by the actual insurance market as randomly distributed, and so we might follow actual insurance practice, modified to remove the discriminations insurers make when they know that one group is more likely, perhaps for genetic reasons, to suffer a particular kind of brute bad luck. It would make sense to suppose, for example, that most people would make roughly the same assessment of the value of insurance against general handicaps, such as blindness or the loss of a limb, that affect a wide spectrum of different sorts of lives. (We might look to the actual market to discover the likelihood and the contours of more specialized insurance we might decide to use in more complex schemes, like the insurance of musicians against damage to their hands.)

We would, in any case, pay great attention to matters of technology, and be ready to adjust our sums as technology changed. People purchase insurance against catastrophes, for example, against a background of assumptions about the remedial medical technology, or special training, or mechanical aids that are in fact available, and about the cost of these remedies. People would seek insurance at a higher level against blindness, for example, if the increased recovery would enable them to purchase a newly discovered sight-substitute technology, than they would if that increased recovery simply swelled a bank account they could not, in any case, use with much satisfaction.

Of course, any judgments that the officials of a community might make about the structure of the hypothetical insurance market would be speculative and open to a variety of objections. But there is no reason to think, certainly in advance, that a practice of compensating the handicapped on the basis of such speculation would be worse, in principle, than the alternatives, and it would have the merit of aiming in the direction of the theoretical solution most congenial to equality of resources.

We might now remind ourselves of what these alternatives are. I said in Chapter 1 that the regime of equality of welfare, contrary to initial impressions, does a poor job of either explaining or guiding our impulse to compensate the severely handicapped with extra resources. It provides, in particular, no upper bound to compensation so long as any further payment would improve the welfare of the wretched; but this is not, as it might seem, generous, because it leaves the standard for actual compensation to the politics of selfishness broken by sympathy, politics that we know will supply less than any defensible hypothetical insurance market would offer.

Consider another approach to the problem of handicaps under equality of resources. Suppose we say that any person's physical and mental powers must count as part of his resources, so that someone who is born handicapped starts with less by way of resources than others have, and should be allowed to catch up, by way of transfer payments, before what remains is auctioned off in any equal market. People's powers are indeed resources, because these are used, together with material resources, in making something valuable out of one's life. Physical powers are resources for that purpose in the way that aspects of one's personality, like one's conception of what is valuable in life, are not. Nevertheless the suggestion, that a design of equality of resources should provide for an initial compensation to alleviate differences in physical or mental resources, is troublesome in a variety of ways. It requires, for example, some standard of "normal" powers to serve as the benchmark for compensation.[6] But whose powers should be taken as normal for this purpose? It suffers, moreover, from the same defect as the parallel recommendation under equality of welfare. In fact, no amount of initial compensation could make someone born blind or mentally incompetent equal in physical or mental resources with someone taken to be "normal" in these ways. So the argument provides no upper bound to initial compensation, but must leave this to a political compromise likely to be less generous, again, than what the hypothetical insurance market would command.

Quite apart from these practical and theoretical inadequacies, the suggestion is troublesome for another reason. Though powers are resources, they should not be considered resources whose ownership is to be determined through politics in accordance with some interpretation of equality of resources. They are not, that is, resources for the theory of equality in exactly the sense in which ordinary material resources are. They cannot be manipulated or transferred, even so far as technology might permit. So in this way it misdescribes the problem of handicaps to say that equality of resources must strive to make people equal in physical and mental constitution so far as this is possible. The problem is, rather, one of determining how far the ownership of independent material resources should be affected by differences that exist in physical and mental powers, and the response of our theory should speak in that vocabulary.

It might be wise (if for no other reason than as a convenient summary of the argument from time to time) to bring our story of the immigrants up to date. By way of supplement to the auction, they now establish a hypothetical insurance market that they effectuate through compulsory insurance at a fixed premium for everyone on the basis of speculations about what the average immigrant would have purchased by way of insurance had antecedent risk of various handicaps been equal. (We choose for them, that is, one of the simpler possible forms of instituting the hypothetical insurance market. We shall see, when we discuss the problem of skills, that they might well choose a more complex scheme of the sort discussed there.)

But now a question arises. Does this decision place too much weight on the distinction between handicaps, which the immigrants treat in this compensatory way, and on accidents touching preferences and ambitions (like the accidents of what material resources are in fact available and of how many other people share a particular person's taste)? The latter will also affect welfare, but they are not matters for compensation under our scheme. Would it not now be fair to treat as handicaps eccentric tastes, or tastes that are expensive or impossible to satisfy because of scarcity of some good that might have been common? We might compensate those who have these tastes by supposing that everyone had an equal chance of being in that position and then establishing a hypothetical insurance market against that possibility.

A short answer is available. Someone who is born with a serious handicap faces his life with what we concede to be fewer resources, just on that account, than others do. This circumstance justifies compensation, under a scheme devoted to equality of resources, and though the hypothetical insurance market does not right the balance—nothing can—it seeks to remedy one aspect of the resulting unfairness. But we cannot say that the person whose tastes are expensive, for whatever reason, therefore has fewer resources at his command. For we cannot state (without falling back on some version of equality of welfare) what equality in the distribution of tastes and preferences would be. Why is there less equality of resources when someone has an eccentric taste that makes goods cheaper for others, than when he shares a popular taste and so makes goods more expensive for them? The auction, bringing to bear information about the resources that actually exist and the competing preferences actually in play, is the only true measure of whether any particular person commands equal resources. If the auction has in fact been an equal auction, then the man of eccentric tastes has no less than equal material resources, and the argument that justifies a compensatory hypothetical auction in the case of handicaps has no occasion even to begin. It is true that this argument produces a certain view of the distinction between a person and his circumstances, and assigns his tastes and ambitions to his person, and his physical and mental powers to his circumstances. That is the view of a person I sketched in the introductory section, of someone who forms his ambitions with a sense of their cost to others against some presumed initial equality of economic power, and though this is different from the picture assumed by equality of welfare, it is a picture at the center of equality of resources.

In one way, however, my argument might well be thought to overstate the distinction between handicaps and at least certain sorts of what are often considered preferences. Suppose someone finds he has a craving (or obsession or lust or, in the words of an earlier psychology, a "drive") that he wishes he did not have, because it interferes with what he wants to do with his life and offers him frustration or even pain if it is not satisfied. This might indeed be some feature of his physical needs that other people would not consider a handicap at all: for example, a generous appetite for sex. But it is a "preference" (if that is the right word) that he does not want, and it makes perfect sense to say that he would be better off without it. For some people these unwanted tastes include tastes they have (perhaps unwittingly) themselves cultivated, such as a taste for a particular sport or for music of a sort difficult to obtain. They regret that they have these tastes, and believe they would be better off without them, but nevertheless find it painful to ignore them. These tastes are handicaps; though for other people they are rather an essential part of what gives value to their lives.

Now these cases do not present, for particular people, borderline cases between ambitions and handicaps (though no doubt other sorts of borderline cases could be found). The distinction required by equality of resources is the distinction between those beliefs and attitudes that define what a successful life would be like, which the ideal assigns to the person, and those features of body or mind or personality which provide means or impediments to that success, which the ideal assigns to the person's circumstances. Those who see their sexual desires or their taste for opera as unwanted disadvantages will class these features of their body or mind or personality firmly as the latter. These are, for them, handicaps, and are therefore suitable for the regime proposed for handicaps generally. We may imagine that everyone has an equal chance of acquiring such a craving by accident. (Of course, for each person the content of a craving that would have that consequence would be different. We are supposing here, not the risk of any particular craving, but the risk of whatever craving would interfere with set goals in that way.) We may then ask—with as much or as little intelligibility as in the case of blindness—whether people generally would purchase insurance against that risk, and if so at what premium and what level of coverage. It seems unlikely that many people would purchase such insurance, at the rates of premium likely to govern if they sought it, except in the case of cravings so severe and disabling as to fall under the category of mental disease. But that is a different matter. The important point, presently, is that the idea of an insurance market is available here, because we can imagine people who have such a craving not having it, without thereby imagining them to have a different conception of what they want from life than what in fact they do want. So the idea of the imaginary insurance auction provides at once a device for identifying cravings and distinguishing them from positive features of personality, and also for bringing these cravings within the general regime designed for handicaps.

IV. Labor and Wages

Equality of resources, once established by the auction, and corrected to provide for handicaps, would be disturbed by production and trade. If one of the immigrants, for example, was specially proficient at producing tomatoes, he might trade his surplus for more than anyone else could acquire, in which case others would begin to envy his bundle of resources. Suppose we wished to create a society in which the division of resources would be continuously equal, in spite of different kinds and degrees of production and trade. Can we adapt our auction so as to produce such a society?

We should begin by considering a different sequence after which people would envy each other's resources, and the division might be thought no longer to be equal. Suppose all the immigrants are in fact sufficiently equal in talent at the few modes of production that the resources allow each to produce roughly the same goods from the same set of resources. Nevertheless they wish to lead their lives in different ways, and they in fact acquire different bundles of resources in the initial auction and use them differently thereafter. Adrian chooses resources and works them with the single-minded ambition of producing as much of what others value as possible; and so, at the end of a year, his total stock of goods is larger than anyone else's. Each of the other immigrants would now prefer Adrian's stock to his own; but by hypothesis none of them would have been willing to lead his life so as to produce them. If we look for envy at particular points in time, then each envies Adrian's resources at the end of the year, and the division is therefore not equal. But if we look at envy differently, as a matter of resources over an entire life, and we include a person's occupation as part of the bundle of his goods, then no one envies Adrian's bundle, and the distribution cannot be said to be unequal on that account.

Surely we should take the second, synoptic, point of view. Our final aim is that an equal share of resources be devoted to the lives of each person, and we have chosen the auction as the right way to measure the value of what is made available to a person, through his decision, for that purpose. If Bruce chooses to acquire land for use as a tennis court, then the question is raised how much his account should be charged, in the reckoning whether an equal share has been put to his use, in virtue of that choice, and it is right that his account should be charged the amount that others would have been willing to pay had the land been devoted to their purposes instead. The appeal of the auction, as a device for picturing equality of resources, is precisely that it enforces that metric. But this scheme will fail, and the device disappoint us, unless Adrian is able to bid a price for the same land that reflects his intention to work rather than play on it and so to acquire whatever gain would prompt him to make that decision. Otherwise those who want tomatoes and would pay Adrian his price for them will not be able to bid indirectly, through Adrian's decision, against Bruce, who will then secure his tennis court at a price that, because it is too low, defeats equality of resources. This is not, I should add, an argument from efficiency as distinct from fairness, but rather an argument that in the circumstances described, in which talents are equal, efficiency simply is fairness, at least as fairness is conceived under equality of resources. If Adrian is willing to spend his life at drudgery, in return for the profit he will make at prices that others will pay for what he produces, then the land on which he would drudge should not be used for a tennis court instead, unless its value as a tennis court is greater as measured by someone's willingness to invade an initially equal stock of abstract resources.

Now this is to look at the matter entirely from the standpoint of those who want Adrian's tomatoes, a standpoint that treats Adrian only as a means. But we reach the same conclusion if we look at the matter from his point of view as well. If someone chooses to have something inexpensive in his life, under a regime of equality of resources, then he will have more left over for the rest of what he wants. Someone who accepts Algerian wine may use it to wash down plovers' eggs. But a decision to produce one thing rather than another with land, or to use the land for leisure rather than production, is also the choice of something for one's life, and this may be inexpensive as well. Suppose Adrian is desperate for plovers' eggs but would rather work hard at tilling his land than settle for less than champagne. The total may be no more expensive, measured in terms of what his decisions cost others, than a life of leisure and grape juice. If he earns enough by working hard, or by working at work that no one else wants to do, to satisfy all his expensive tastes, then his choice for his own life costs the rest of the community no more than if his tastes were simpler and his industry less. So we have no more reason to deny him hard work and high consumption than to deny him less work and frugality. The choice should be indifferent under equality of resources, so long as no one envies the total package of work plus consumption that he chooses—so long as no one envies, that is, his life as a whole. Of course, Adrian might actually enjoy his hard work, so that he makes no sacrifice. He prefers working hard to anything else. But his preference cannot provide any argument, under equality of resources, that he should gain less in money or other goods by his work than if he hated every minute of it, any more than it argues against charging someone a low price for lettuce, which he actually prefers to truffles.

So we must apply the envy test diachronically: it requires that no one envy the bundle of occupation and resources at the disposal of anyone else over time, though someone may envy another's bundle at any particular time. It would therefore violate equality of resources if the community were to redistribute Adrian's wealth, say, at the end of each year. If everyone had equal talents (as we have been assuming just now), the initial auction would produce continuing equality of resources even though bank-account wealth became more and more unequal as years passed.

Is that unlikely condition—that everyone has equal talent—absolutely necessary to that conclusion? Would the auction produce continuing equality of resources if (as in the real world) talents for producing differed sharply from person to person? Now the envy test would fail, even interpreted diachronically. Claude (who likes farming but has a black thumb) would not bid enough for farming land to take that land from Adrian; or, if he did, he would have to settle for less in the rest of his life. But he would then envy the package of Adrian's occupation and wealth. If we interpret occupation in a manner sensitive to the joys of craft, then Adrian's occupation, which must then be described as skillful, craftsmanlike farming, is simply unavailable to Claude. If we interpret occupation in a more censuslike fashion, then Claude may undertake Adrian's occupation, but he cannot have the further resources that Adrian has along with it. So if we continue to insist that the envy test is a necessary condition of equality of resources, then our initial auction will not insure continuing equality, in the real world of unequal talents for production.

But it may now be objected that we should not insist on the envy test at this point, even in principle, for the following reason. We are moving too close to the goal that people must not envy each other, which is different from the requirement that they must not envy one another's bundles of resources. People may envy each other for a variety of reasons: some are physically more attractive, some more easily satisfied with their condition, some better liked by others, some more intelligent or able in different ways, and so on. Of course, under a regime of equality of welfare each of these differences would be taken into account, and transfers made to erase their welfare consequences so far as possible or feasible. But the point of equality of resources is fundamentally different: it is that people should have the same external resources at their command to make of them what, given these various features and talents, they can. That point is satisfied by an initial auction, but since people are different it is neither necessary nor desirable that resources should remain equal thereafter, and quite impossible that all envy should be eliminated by political distribution. If one person, by dint of superior effort or talent, uses his equal share to create more than another, he is entitled to profit thereby, because his gain is not made at the expense of someone else who does less with his share. We recognized that, just now, when we conceded that superior industry should be rewarded, so that Adrian, who worked hard, should be allowed to keep the rewards of his effort.

Now this objection harbors many mistakes, but they all come to this: it confuses equality of resources with the fundamentally different idea sometimes called equality of opportunity. It is not true, in the first place, that someone who does more with his initial share does not, in so doing, lessen the value of what others have. If Adrian were not so successful at agriculture, then Claude's own efforts would be rewarded more, because people would buy his inferior produce having no better alternative. If Adrian were not so successful and hence so rich he would not be able to pay so much for wine, and Claude, with his smaller fortune, would be able to buy more at a lower price. These are simply the most obvious consequences of the fact that the immigrants form one economy, after the initial auction, rather than a set of distinct economies. Of course these consequences also follow from the situation we discussed a moment ago. If Adrian and Bruce have the same talents, but Adrian chooses to work harder or differently and acquires more money, then this circumstance may also decrease the value of Claude's share to him. The difference between these two circumstances, if there is one, lies elsewhere; but it is important to reject the claim, instinct in some arguments for equality of opportunity, that if people start with equal shares the prosperity of one does no damage to the other.

Nor is it true that if we aim at a result in which those with less talent do not envy the circumstances of those with more talent we have destroyed the distinction between envying others and envying what they have. For Adrian has two things that Claude would prefer to have which belong to Adrian's circumstances rather than his person. The desires and needs of other people provide Adrian but not Claude with a satisfying occupation, and Adrian has more money than Claude can have. Perhaps nothing that can be done, by way of political structure or distribution, to erase these differences and remove the envy entirely. We cannot, for example, alter the tastes of other people by electrical means so as to make them value more what Claude can produce and value less what Adrian can produce. But the fact that we could not and should not do this provides no argument against other schemes, such as schemes of education that would allow Claude to find satisfaction in his work or of taxation that would redistribute some of Adrian's wealth to him, and we could fairly describe these schemes as aiming to remove Claude's envy of what Adrian has rather than his envy of what Adrian is.

Important as these points are, it is more important still to identify and correct another mistake that the present objection makes. It misunderstands our earlier conclusion, that when talents are roughly equal the auction provides continuing equality of resources, and so misses the important distinction between that case and the present argument. The objection supposes that we reached that conclusion because we accept, as the basis of equality of resources, what we might call the starting-gate theory of fairness: that if people start in the same circumstances and do not cheat or steal from one another, then it is fair that people keep what they gain through their own skill. But the starting-gate theory of fairness is very far from equality of resources. Indeed it is hardly a coherent political theory at all.

The starting-gate theory holds that justice requires equal initial resources. But it also holds that justice requires laissez-faire thereafter, in accordance, presumably, with some version of the Lockean theory that people acquire property by mixing their labor with goods or something of that sort. But these two principles cannot live comfortably together. Equality can have no greater force in justifying initial equal holdings when the immigrants land—against the competing view that all property should be available for Lockean acquisition at that time—than later in justifying redistributions when wealth becomes unequal because people's productive talents are different. The same point may be put the other way around. The theory of Lockean acquisition (or whatever other theory of justice in acquisition is supposed to justify the laissez-faire component in a starting-gate theory) can have no less force in governing the initial distribution than it has in justifying title through talent and effort later. If the theory is sound later, then why does it not command a Lockean process of acquisition in the first instance, rather than an equal distribution of all there is? The moment when the immigrants first land is, after all, an arbitrary point in their lives at which to locate any one-shot requirement that they each have an equal share of any available resources. If that requirement holds then, it must also hold on the tenth anniversary of that date, which is, in the words of the banal and important cliché, the first day in the rest of their lives. So if justice requires an equal auction when they land, it must require a fresh, equal auction from time to time thereafter; and if justice requires laissez-faire thereafter, it must require it when they land.

Suppose someone replies that there is an important difference between the initial distribution of resources and any later redistribution. When the immigrants land, no one owns any of the resources, and the principle of equality therefore dictates equal initial shares. But later, after the initial resources have been auctioned, they are each owned in some way by someone, so that the principle of equality is superseded by respect for people's rights in property or something of that sort. This reply begs the question straightway. For we are considering precisely whether a system of ownership should be established in the first instance that has that consequence, or whether a different system of ownership should be chosen that explicitly makes any acquisition subject to schemes of redistribution later. If the latter sort of system is chosen at the outset, then no one can later complain that redistribution is ruled out by his property rights alone. I do not mean that no theory of justice can consistently distinguish between justice in initial acquisition and justice in transfer on the ground that anyone may do what he wants with property that is already his. Robert Nozick's theory, for example, does just that.[7] This is consistent, because his theory of justice in initial acquisition purports to justify a system of property rights which have that consequence: justice in transfer, that is, flows from the rights that the theory of acquisition claims are acquired in acquiring property. But the theory of initial acquisition on which the starting-gate theory relies, which is equality of resources, does not even purport to justify a characterization of property that necessarily includes absolute control without limit of time thereafter.

So the starting-gate theory, that the immigrants should start off equal in resources but grow prosperous or lean through their own efforts thereafter, is an indefensible combination of very different theories of justice. Something like that combination makes sense in games, such as Monopoly, whose point is to allow luck and skill to play a highly circumscribed and, in the last analysis, arbitrary role; but it cannot hold together a political theory. Our own principle, that if people of equal talent choose different lives it is unfair to redistribute halfway through those lives, makes no appeal to the starting-gate theory. It is based on the very different idea that the equality in question is equality of resources devoted to whole lives. This principle offers a clear answer to the question that embarrasses the present objection. Our theory does not suppose that an equal division of resources is appropriate at one moment in someone's life but not at any other. It argues only that resources available to him at any moment must be a function of resources available or consumed by him at others, so that the explanation of why someone has less money now may be that he has consumed expensive leisure earlier. Nothing like that explanation is available to explain why Claude, who has worked as hard and in the same way as Adrian, should have less in virtue of the fact that he is less skillful.

So we must reject the starting-gate theory and recognize that the requirements of equality (in the real world at least) pull in opposite directions. On the one hand we must, on pain of violating equality, allow the distribution of resources at any particular moment to be (as we might say) ambition-sensitive. It must, that is, reflect the cost or benefit to others of the choices people make so that, for example, those who choose to invest rather than consume, or to consume less expensively rather than more, or to work in more rather than less profitable ways must be permitted to retain the gains that flow from these decisions in an equal auction followed by free trade. But on the other hand, we must not allow the distribution of resources at any moment to be endowment-sensitive, that is, to be affected by differences in ability of the sort that produce income differences in a laissez-faire economy among people with the same ambitions. Can we devise some formula that offers a practical, or even a theoretical, compromise between these two apparently competing requirements?

We might mention, but only to dismiss, one possible response. Suppose we allow our initial auction to include, as resources to be auctioned, the labor of the immigrants themselves, so that each immigrant can bid for the right to control part or all of his own or other people's labor. Special skills would accrue to the benefit, not of the laborer himself, but of the community as a whole, like any other valuable resource the immigrants found when they landed. Except in unusual cases, since people begin with equal resources for bidding, each agent would bid enough to secure his own labor. But the result would be that each would have to spend his life in close to the commercially most profitable manner he could or, at least if he is talented, suffer some very serious deprivation if he did not. For since Adrian, for example, is able to produce prodigious income from farming, others would be willing to bid a large amount to have the right to his labor and the vegetables thereof, and if he outbids them, but chooses to write indifferent poetry instead of farming full-time, he will have spent a large part of his initial endowment on a right that will bring him little financial benefit. That is indeed the slavery of the talented.

We cannot permit this, but it is worth pausing to ask what grounds we have for barring it. Shall we say that since a person owns his own mind and body, he owns the talents that are only capacities thereof, and therefore owns the fruit of those talents? This is, of course, a series of non sequiturs. It is also a familiar argument in favor of the laissez-faire labor market we have decided is a violation of equality of resources when people are unequal in talent. But we could not accept it in any case, because it uses the idea of prepolitical entitlement based on something other than equality, and that is inconsistent with the premise of the scheme of equality of resources we have developed.

So we must look elsewhere for the ground of our objection to taking people's labor as a resource for the auction. We need not, in fact, look very far; for the principle that people should not be penalized for talent is simply part of the same principle we relied on in rejecting the apparently opposite idea, that people should be allowed to retain the benefits of superior talent. The envy test forbids both of these results. If Adrian is treated as owning whatever his talents enable him to produce, then Claude envies the package of resources, including occupation, that Adrian has over his life considered as a whole. But if Adrian is required to purchase leisure time or the right to a less productive occupation at the cost of other resources, then Adrian will envy Claude's package. If equality of resources is understood to include some plausible version of the envy test as a necessary condition of an equal distribution, then the role of talent must be neutralized in a way that no simple addition to the stock of goods to be auctioned can accomplish.

We should turn, therefore, to a more familiar idea: the periodic redistribution of resources through some form of income tax.[8] We want to develop a scheme of redistribution, so far as we are able, that will neutralize the effects of differential talents, yet preserve the consequences of one person's choosing an occupation, in response to his sense of what he wants to do with his life, that is more expensive for the community than the choice another makes. An income tax is a plausible device for this purpose because it leaves intact the possibility of choosing a life in which sacrifices are constantly made and discipline steadily imposed for the sake of financial success and the further resources it brings, though of course it neither endorses nor condemns that choice. But it also acknowledges the role of genetic luck in such a life. The accommodation it makes is a compromise; but it is a compromise of two requirements of equality, in the face of both practical and conceptual uncertainty how to satisfy these requirements, not a compromise of equality for the sake of some independent value such as efficiency.

But of course the appeal of a tax depends on our ability to fix rates of taxation that will make that compromise accurately. It might be helpful, in that aim, if we were able to find some way of identifying, in any person's wealth at any particular time, the component traceable to differential talents as distinguished from differential ambitions. We might then try to devise a tax that would recapture, for redistribution, just this component. But we cannot hope to identify such a component, even given perfect information about people's personalities. For we will be thwarted by the reciprocal influence that talents and ambitions exercise on each other. Talents are nurtured and developed, not discovered full-blown, and people choose which talents to develop in response to their beliefs about what sort of person it is best to be. But people also wish to develop and use the talents they have, not simply because they prefer a life of relative success, but because the exercise of talent is enjoyable and perhaps also out of a sense that an unused talent is a waste. Someone with a good eye or a skilled hand conceives a picture of what would make his life valuable that someone more clumsy would not.

So we cannot hope to fix the rates of our income tax so as to redistribute exactly that part of each person's income that is attributable to his talent as distinguished from his ambitions. Talents and ambitions are too closely intertwined. Can we do better by proceeding on a slightly different tack? Can we aim to fix rates so as to leave each person with the income he would have had if, counterfactually, all talents for production had been equal? No, because it is impossible to say, in any relevant way, what sort of world that would be. We should have to decide what sort and level of talent everyone would have equally, and then what income people exploiting those talents to different degrees of effort would reach. Should we stipulate that in that world everyone would have the talents that the most talented people in the real world now have? Do we mean, by "the most talented people," the people who are able to earn the most money in the actual world if they work single-mindedly for money? But in a world in which everyone could hit a high inside pitch or play sexy roles in films with equal authority, there would probably be no baseball or films; in any case no one would be paid much for exercising such talents. Nor would any other description of the talents everyone would be supposed to have in equal degree be any more help.

But though this crude counterfactual exercise must fail, it suggests a more promising exercise. Let us review our situation. We want to find some way to distinguish fair from unfair differences in wealth generated by differences in occupation. Unfair differences are those traceable to genetic luck, to talents that make some people prosperous but are denied to others who would exploit them to the full if they had them. But if this is right, then the problem of differential talents is in certain ways like the problem of handicaps we have already considered.

V. Underemployment Insurance

Though skills are different from handicaps, the difference can be understood as one of degree: we may say that someone who cannot play basketball like Wilt Chamberlain, paint like Piero, or make money like Geneen, suffers from an (especially common) handicap. This description emphasizes one aspect of skills, which is their genetic and, hence, luck component, at the expense of hiding the more intimate and reciprocal play we noticed between skills and ambitions. But it also points to one theoretical solution to the problem of identifying at least the minimum requirements of a fair redistribution policy responding to differences in skill. We may capitalize on the similarities between handicaps and relative lack of skill to propose that the level of compensation for the latter be fixed, in principle, by asking how much insurance someone would have bought, in an insurance subauction with initially equal resources, against the possibility of not having a particular level of some skill.

Of course, there is no actual insurance market against lack of what we ordinarily take to be skill, as there is an insurance market against catastrophes that result in handicap. For one thing, a person's level of skills is sufficiently fixed and known, at least roughly, before that person enters the insurance market, so that lack of skill is primarily a matter of history rather than one of future contingency. (There are other reasons as well, which we shall have to identify in a moment.) But let us nevertheless try to frame a hypothetical question something like the questions we asked in the case of handicaps. Suppose an imaginary world in which, though the distribution of skills over the community were in the aggregate what it actually is, people for some reason all had the same antecedent chance of suffering the consequences of lacking any particular set of these skills, and were all in a position to buy insurance against these consequences at the same premium structure. How much insurance would each buy at what cost? If we can make sense of that question, and answer it even by fixing rough lower limits on average, then we shall have a device for fixing at least the lower bounds of a tax-and-redistribution program satisfying the demands of equality of resources.

There are several ways in which we might construct a hypothetical or imaginary insurance market of that sort. We might try to imagine, for example, that people are ignorant of the skills they actually have, though they know how many people will turn out to have each skill, and therefore what their own chances are. People might then be supposed to insure against turning out to lack some particular skill at some particular level, either a very precise skill like the ability to capture September light at dusk in oil, or a more general skill, like a very good memory or a quick way with numbers. This model would be very like the model we constructed for handicaps, and would therefore provide theoretical continuity for our theory as a whole. We might even propose to integrate the two hypothetical insurance markets by taking seriously the suggestion that the lack of some skill is just another handicap, and simply asking how many so-called skills would find their way into a general market for catastrophe insurance.

But this model for the hypothetical insurance market for skills is subject to a certain objection. We noticed, in considering the hypothetical insurance market for handicaps, the following difficulty. There is a certain indeterminacy in the issue of what ambitions and tastes someone who is handicapped would have if he were not, and this indeterminacy infects the question of how much of what insurance he would then buy. The indeterminacy is manageable in the case of ordinary handicaps, because generalizations are nevertheless possible. But it would not be manageable in the case of skills, because if we suppose that no one has any idea what talents he has, we have stipulated away too much of his personality to leave any intelligible base for speculation about his ambitions, even in a general or average way. The connection between talents and ambitions, which I described much earlier, is much closer than that between ambitions and handicaps—it is, for one thing, reciprocal—and much too close to permit that sort of counterfactual speculation.

So let us suppose, not that people are wholly ignorant of what talents they have, but rather that for some other reason they do not have any sound basis for predicting their economic rent—what income the talents they do have can produce, or even whether the economic situation will be such that these talents will find any employment. There are, of course, many different ways of imagining such a state of affairs, and it does not much matter, for present purposes, which we select. So let us fall back on our immigrants once again. Suppose that before the initial auction has begun, information about the tastes, ambitions, talents, and attitudes toward risk of each of the immigrants, as well as information about the raw materials and technology available, is delivered to a computer. It then predicts not only the results of the auction but also the projected income structure—the number of people earning each level of income—that will follow the auction once production and trade begin, on the assumption that there will be no income tax.

Now the computer is asked a further hypothetical question. Assume each immigrant knows the projected income structure but is ignorant of the computer's data base, except for its information about himself, and is therefore radically uncertain what income level his own talents would permit him to occupy. He supposes, in fact, that he has the same chance as anyone else of occupying any particular level of income in the economy, though he takes the number projected for that level into account. Assume that there is no monopoly in insurance, and insurance firms offer policies of the following sort. Insurance is provided against failing to have an opportunity to earn whatever level of income, within the projected structure, the policyholder names, in which case the insurance company will pay the policyholder the difference between that coverage level and the income he does in fact have an opportunity to earn.[9] Premiums will vary with the level of coverage chosen, must be the same for everyone at any particular coverage level, and will be paid, not out of the policyholder's initial stock of resources (or clamshells), but rather from future earnings after the auction at fixed periods. How much of such insurance would the immigrants, on average, buy, at what specified level of income coverage, and at what cost?

That problem seems amenable, at least in principle, to the various types of analysis that economists devote to problems of decision making under uncertainty, and there is no reason to doubt that the computer could furnish an answer. Even without the computer's information and powers, we can make some general observations about what it is likely to predict. Economists make a rough distinction between two kinds of decisions under uncertainty. An insurance problem is posed when a small cost purchases reimbursement for an unlikely but serious loss. A gambling problem is posed when a small cost purchases a small chance of a large gain. Let us define a financially advantageous bet of either of these types as a bet such that the cost of the bet is less than the amount of the return if "successful"—if the covered risk eventuates or if the bet is won—discounted by the improbability of success. Insurance for a dollar premium that pays ten dollars in the event of a loss that is as likely as not to occur, or a ten-to-one bet that a fair coin flip will come up heads, are financially advantageous bets. A bet is financially disadvantageous if the cost of the bet exceeds the expected return so calculated. Let us say that someone is risk-neutral if he will accept any financially advantageous bet and reject any financially disadvantageous bet, no matter what the size or other character of the bet.

Commercial insurance companies and commercial bookmakers will offer only financially disadvantageous bets, of course, because their income must equal not only the expected return to the policyholders and bettors but also their costs, including opportunity costs. So if everyone were risk-neutral no one would buy insurance or bet on the numbers or pools. But almost no one is risk-neutral over the full range of his utility curve: for almost everyone the marginal utility of more money declines over at least part of the graph that pictures how his welfare behaves as a function of his income. It is fairly easy to see how this explains the phenomenon of commercial insurance (though of course any explanation of why rates for particular policies are what they are would require more detailed information about these utility functions and would be much more complex). Suppose there is a one-in-ten chance that my \$50,000 house will burn down in the next year, and I am offered full insurance at a cost of \$6,000. I am offered the choice, that is, between a certainty of \$44,000 (if I purchase insurance) and a gamble with an expected return of \$45,000 (if I do not). If the loss of my house would be more than nine times as serious as the loss of \$6,000 (because, for example, I could not find or borrow enough money to build a suitable house, my marriage would dissolve, and my children become delinquent) then it is worth my while to buy the insurance, though it is a financially disadvantageous bet. It is much harder to explain gambles. (Kenneth Arrow, discussing gambling, quoted the preacher who reached a sticky point in theology and said that the problem was a very difficult one which the congregation should face firmly and then pass on.) It is perhaps necessary to suppose that gamblers either mistake the actual odds (because they think that luck is a lady) or attach value to uncertainty for its own sake; and though both these assumptions hold sometimes, it seems doubtful that they hold sufficiently often to explain how popular gambling is.

What can be said, against this background, about the two hypothetical insurance markets we have described? Our insurance market for handicaps is sufficiently like ordinary insurance markets and requires no special comment. But the hypothetical insurance market we just described for talents is different, in part because it seems, at first blush, to allow for decisions that look much more like gambles than insurance. For it might seem that many immigrants would leap at the chance to buy a policy that would protect them against not having the very highest income projected for the economy, and would pay them, if they do not, the difference between the great income and what they can actually earn. But in fact that policy would be a very poor wager indeed.[10] We take it as given that insurance at that level would be a financially disadvantageous bet. Otherwise it would not be offered by the insurance firm. So if it is a good bet, it is good on grounds of expected welfare rather than financial grounds, as is my insurance policy on my house. But the bet is much more likely to be silly than sound in welfare terms.

Since (unlike lottery tickets generally) the chances of "winning" are extremely high—very few immigrants will turn out to have that maximum earning power—the cost of the premium will be extremely high as well.[11] It will approach the value of the projected return if the risk eventuates. So someone who buys this insurance faces an extremely high chance of gaining very little. Suppose he loses, however; suppose he is one of those who does have the maximum earning power. He is now in much worse position than if he had never insured, because he must now work at close to his top earning capacity just to pay the high premium for his insurance on which he collected nothing—just, that is, to break even. He will be a slave to his maximum earning power.[12]

Now just how bad a bargain this is will depend upon facts not specified, including the question of how many people can be expected to have the talents necessary to earn at the highest level. But it is likely to be a very bad bargain in any case. It is very different from the situation that apparently tempts large numbers of people to make financially disadvantageous bets on vast lotteries, which is the prospect of a small chance of a large fortune in return for a very small certain cost. This insurance decision would be the very different financially disadvantageous bet of a very small chance of a very great loss in return for the very large chance of a very small gain, and nothing in the literature of the psychology of gambling (except perhaps the literature of Russian roulette) supports the idea that bets of that character would be popular.

Nor does the explanation of why people purchase ordinary financially disadvantageous insurance policies offer any support. I buy insurance on my house because the marginal utility loss of an uncompensated fire is so much greater than the utility cost of the premium. But considerations of marginal utility would if anything condemn rather than support any immigrant's bet that he would not have the skills necessary to earn the highest income. For that bet pits the almost certain prospect of a tiny and probably unnoticeable welfare gain against the tiny chance of an enormous welfare loss on financially disadvantageous terms. Of course, we make assumptions in presuming that almost no one would have a utility curve that would make that bet sensible in welfare terms. But it does seem plausible that almost no one would.

Does this argument prove too much? Does it prove that insurance against lacking skills, on the model we described, would almost always be a bad buy for almost everyone? If so, it would seem to follow that the hypothetical insurance device could not, after all, provide reasonable guides for redistribution through income tax. Or, perhaps worse, it might suggest that no such redistribution would ever be justified. But in fact the argument does not have this consequence, because the lower the income level chosen as the covered risk, the better the argument becomes that most people given the chance to buy insurance on equal terms would in fact buy at that level. The argument becomes compelling, I think, well above the level of income presently used to trigger transfer payments for unemployment or minimum wage levels in either Britain or the United States.

The argument becomes stronger, as the chosen income level declines, for the following reasons. First, as the level declines, the odds that any particular person will have the talents necessary to earn that income at full stretch improve and, for a substantial section of income levels in normal economies, improve faster than the rate of that decline. Many more than twice as many people have the abilities necessary to earn the amount earned in the fiftieth percentile than in the ninety-ninth percentile of a normal income distribution. So the premium falls, and falls, at least over a considerable range, at a rate faster than the rate of the coverage. So, correspondingly, do the odds against "winning," of course, but the situation grows steadily closer to the normal case of insurance, in which people incur a small certain loss to prevent an unlikely great loss whose marginal utility costs are serious enough to justify a financially disadvantageous transaction. For even though the financial loss in falling from, say, the seventieth to the sixtieth percentile in income is vastly greater than the loss in falling from the fortieth to the thirtieth, the welfare consequences will probably, on average, be much worse for the latter drop.

As the income level covered drops, moreover, so the penalties of "losing" the insurance bet, by turning out to have the abilities to earn at least that income, diminish in importance and, once again, at what seems likely to be a faster rate. Someone who "loses" in this sense must work hard enough to cover his premium before he is free to make the trade-offs between work and consumption he would have been free to make if he had not insured. If the level of coverage is high, then this will enslave the insured, not simply because the premium is high, but because it is extremely unlikely that his talents will much surpass the level that he has chosen, which means that he must indeed work at full stretch, and that he will not have much choice about what kind of work to do. Only one form of work, and that full-time, will be likely to produce the income needed to pay the premium that is now his albatross. So his penalty has special welfare disadvantages not measurable in ordinary financial terms. It is these that make it appropriate to speak of his enslavement.

But as the level of coverage and hence the premium drop, these special welfare disadvantages are not simply mitigated, but entirely fall away. For it becomes likely that anyone who has the qualifications needed to earn at, say, the thirtieth percentile level will also have the talents to earn at a higher level, and so would retain a considerable freedom of choice about the character of work, and the mix of work and labor and additional consumption, that he prefers. Even if he just barely "loses" the insurance bet, and has exactly the talents needed to earn the level of income he covered, but no more, he will still probably retain a great freedom of choice. The premium will be small enough to sustain even if he works at a lower level of income than he could, particularly if he is willing to sacrifice consumer goods. There are, moreover, a greater variety of types of jobs that will produce a lower level of income than a higher (at least in most complex economies at least over a range of income levels), so that someone committed to earning as much as he can will nevertheless have more choice of work at that lower level. Even if he must work flat out and has no choice in his work, his situation is very little worse than if he had taken no insurance. For if the coverage level is so low that almost everyone must earn it to have a decent life, he would have worked that way and practically that hard anyway, and if the premium is very low, as it then would be, he would not have to work much harder to cover it. He is not much differently enslaved by his talent if he insures than he would be enslaved by his lack of talent if he did not.

The hypothetical insurance market might nevertheless produce apparent anomalies. Suppose Deborah and Ernest both purchase insurance at the sixtieth percentile level. Deborah is beautiful and could in fact earn at the ninetieth percentile as a movie star. Otherwise they have the same talents and interests, and these other talents would not earn at the sixtieth level. Ernest recovers under his policy, but Deborah does not. She is faced with the choice of a movie career, which she detests, or trying to pay the premium and the other expenses of her life from whatever salary she could earn at jobs both she and Ernest would prefer. Ernest can have both such a job and compensation under his policy, and is therefore much better off.[13] Is this advantage unfair? Deborah is, as it turns out, enslaved by her singular talent. But this is because she ran the risk described by purchasing insurance at a coverage level commanding a high premium and such that few jobs could produce income approaching that level. Ernest ran the same risk but had better option luck. The anomaly is therefore only a further (and more complex) example of the undesirable welfare risks of insurance at a high level. If Deborah and Ernest had purchased insurance at a lower level, the premium would have been lower and Deborah would have had a much better choice of jobs other than a film career. They would still fare differently, but the difference would be much less, and would (arguably) then be an appropriate mark of the fact that Deborah had an option Ernest did not. In any case, this unfairness, if it is unfairness, would disappear in any plausible translation of the hypothetical insurance market into an actual tax scheme of the sort described in the next section.

VI. Tax as Premium

Now let us assume that the computer fixes the average coverage level that would be reached in the hypothetical insurance market, and declares some premium to be the premium that level would command. The premiums would be a sufficiently small proportion of the coverage that (for the average person) the expected welfare of insuring would be higher than the expected welfare of not doing so. Can we translate that hypothetical insurance structure into a tax scheme? Can we base tax rates on the assumed premium, and then redistribute by paying those who do not have the ability to earn at the assumed coverage level the difference between that level and what they can earn?

We might assume that any tax system constructed to model the hypothetical insurance market in that way would suffer from serious defects. First, it seems unfair that everyone, rich and poor alike, should pay the same tax, but this would seem to be the consequence of modeling tax rates on hypothetical premiums. Second, the requirement that both the incidence and amount of payments from the fund depend on what the recipient could earn if willing seems inefficient and troublesome in a variety of ways. It might be very expensive to enforce that requirement, and in practice the requirement will tempt some people to cheat by hiding their abilities under a bushel. In any case, even honest people cannot know what they might earn at a given occupation without trying, and in the case of some professions, trying is impossible without half a lifetime of preparation. So a battery of new tests to discover latent talent would be necessary, and these would be vulnerable to many sorts of mistakes.

But these objections make certain assumptions about what the hypothetical insurance market would be like, and these assumptions are both unjustified and probably false. For suppose the insurance firms had offered, in place of the flat-rate premium for a given coverage that the objections assume, a premium fixed as an increasing percentage of the income the policy owner turns out to earn. The premium of someone who barely earns the average coverage amount would be less than the premium the insurance market would have fixed on a flat-rate basis, though the premium of someone who earns much more would be much greater. The insurance firms would have reason to offer this different scheme if the total premiums paid would be more, and the immigrants buying insurance would also have reason to accept it if the change increased their expected welfare under the conditions of equal risk we have stipulated. Since we assume declining marginal utility of money over the range in question, as part of the assumptions on which we speculate that insurance would be bought at all, these conditions will be met. Immigrants would prefer a "bet" under which the cost of the bet will be an increasing function of their income, and will prefer it by enough to provide profit for the insurance firms even counting the increased administrative costs of a progressive premium scheme.

The firms would also have reason to reduce what insurers call the "moral hazard" of such insurance—the risk that insurance will make the covered risk even more likely to occur or the level of recovery higher if it does—and to pass on part of their savings to policyholders as inducements to accept the necessary constraints. One technique insurers now use for that purpose is co-insurance. First-person automobile policies provide, for example, that the owner must assume the first several hundred dollars of damage before the insurer makes up the balance. Co-insurance in our story means that if one of the immigrants is unable to earn the average coverage amount, he will receive somewhat less than that amount as compensation. Of course people will buy insurance at a higher coverage level with co-insurance than without, though at a lower premium than the higher amount would otherwise attract, which means that the average coverage level would be higher than under a scheme with no co-insurance. But if substantial savings for the insurance firm would result from reducing the moral hazard (and popular resentment about welfare cheats under present welfare schemes in the United States, for example, supposes that they would), then the savings in premium along the range should also be substantial; if so, then the presumed coverage would indeed be higher under a co-insurance regime. How much co-insurance would obtain—by how much the payment to those who fail to earn the covered amount would fall short of that amount and what the effect on the premium structure and the presumed coverage level would be—depends only on information that has already been given to the computer.

The problem and the cost of accuracy in determining people's actual abilities to earn are made less pressing for the insurer by co-insurance. It sharply reduces the motives people have for not earning at least the covered amount in order to claim that they cannot earn it. But the insurer has another device for reducing the cost of accuracy enough to lower premiums and so make the device attractive to policyholders. Since policyholders will almost always have more information about their abilities and opportunities than the insurer will, there is room for joint savings by assigning the burden of proof to the policyholders. This burden will be more severe for coverage at the higher levels, I expect, than at the lower, because it is often difficult to prove that one could not have had a career for which special training or education or experience is necessary unless one has undertaken these. But if

I am right that the average coverage level would be relatively low, we need not pursue that problem. At the lower levels the proof will be easily provided by failed attempts to find employment or by evidence of less than average general physical and mental abilities, and so forth.

So the actual insurance profile the computer would predict is likely to be much more complex than the simple structure our defective tax system copied. If the immigrants translate this more complex insurance profile into a tax scheme they reach a more recognizable pattern of tax. They might establish a graduated income tax financing transfer payments in the amount of the difference between the average coverage level less the co-insurance factor and what an applicant can plausibly argue is the highest income he can in fact command. This exercise, of course, neither need nor should stop at this point. Further reflection about the hypothetical insurance market might develop further refinements or adjustments to the corresponding tax scheme. And we might decide that a tax scheme should differ from the best approximation of that hypothetical market for other reasons. We might decide that a tax scheme so closely modeled on that market is offensive to privacy, or too expensive in administrative costs, or too inefficient in other ways. We might decide, for these or other reasons, that a scheme that tied redistribution to actual earnings rather than to ability to earn, for example, was a better second-best approximation to the ideal of mimicking the insurance market than any other scheme we could develop.

But I want to put aside for now any further study of these issues, because we have carried them far enough, I think, to justify turning instead to the question waiting in the wings. Is the general approach sensible? Is a tax scheme constructed as a practical translation of a hypothetical insurance market, which assumes equal initial assets and equal risk, a proper response to the problem of differential talents under equality of resources?

It might be criticized from two standpoints: either that it does not justify enough redistribution, or that it justifies too much. The latter objection seems the weaker of the two. Recall the competing constraints we discovered. Equality requires that those who choose more expensive ways to live—which includes choosing less productive occupations measured by what others want—have less residual income in consequence. But it also requires that no one have less income simply in consequence of less native talent. Any objection that the transfer payments guided by the hypothetical insurance market are too great must show a lively danger that the first of these requirements has been given insufficient weight. But if the hypothetical insurance market justifies the selection of a particular level as the average assumed coverage, this argues strongly for the probability that any particular immigrant is ready to work at one of the occupations that could produce income at that level rather than have a lesser income, if the choice were available. Otherwise he would have run too great a risk by taking on a premium that makes sense only for someone ready to earn the income needed to support it, particularly if the average level is sufficiently low that the odds were great that he would have to do exactly that. He may be ready to do so because a wide range of occupations, suiting very different personalities, would produce that level of income, or because that level is necessary to lead what popular culture considers an acceptable style of life, or, more probably, both together. Of course, this favorable counterfactual would not, in fact, hold in the case of everyone who lacks appropriate talents, or does not find a job in the employment market for some other reason. Some such immigrants would not have taken insurance at the average coverage level even if it were available. But this presents a question of valuing the relative importance of the two constraints on a theory of redistribution for differential talents. Taking the average coverage level as decisive, which we have done, is an appropriate way of weighting them equally.[14] It supposes that it is at least no worse to err on the side of redistributing to someone who would not have insured than to deny redistribution to one who would have. Someone may be able to show that this is wrong, and thereby justify taking, as the standard for redistribution through taxation, a lower figure such that the odds are very strong, possibly even overwhelming, that any particular person would have insured at that level. But I do not know of any arguments for that view. Perhaps the difference between the average coverage level and some lower level of that sort would not be very great. Perhaps, that is, the utility curves of most people would look very much alike for the lower percentiles of possible coverage. But this is one of the legion of quasi-technical questions that I make no attempt to discuss here.

The opposite objection, that transfer payments based on the average coverage level are not enough, is more difficult to answer. It might be supported in two different ways. It might be said that the hypothetical insurance approach is the wrong approach through which to attempt to compromise the two requirements we discovered; or that the hypothetical insurance approach is the right approach but requires transfer payments at a higher level. The second argument presumably agrees with the objection just described, that the two requirements of equality in wage structure are not of equal weight, but insists that it is much worse to deny payments to someone who would have insured than to award them to someone who would not have done so. It insists, in other words, that the level of assumed coverage chosen should be some level such that it is very unlikely that anyone would have insured above that level. Once again, it is worth noticing that this level might not be much above the average coverage level. We saw, earlier, reasons why almost no one would insure at a very high income level in any case. Once again, however, I shall not explore the technical issue raised, but simply set the suggestion aside until the substantive argument, in favor of special deference to one requirement of equality in wage structure over the other, has been made.

But we must now state and consider the important argument that the hypothetical insurance market is altogether the wrong approach to the problem of reconciling these two requirements, because it undervalues the transfer payments that those whose talents are not in great demand should receive. The hypothetical insurance market approach aims to put such people in the position they would have been in had the risk of their fate been subjectively equally shared. But it does not make them as well-off in the end as those whose talents are in more demand, or as those with similar talents lucky enough to find more profitable employment. Some people (movie stars and captains of industry and first basemen) in fact earn at a rate far beyond the rate of coverage any reasonable person would choose in an insurance market, as our inspection showed. The hypothetical insurance market approach is beside the point (it might be said) exactly because it provides no answer to someone who is unable to find a job, points to the movie star, and declares, perfectly accurately, that he would do that work for that pay if asked. The fact that no one would buy coverage at a movie-star level in an equal insurance market simply underscores the injustice. The movie star had no need to buy that insurance. He won his life of luxury and glamor without it. The brute fact remains that some people have much more than others of what both desire, through no reason connected with choice. The envy test we once seemed to respect has been decisively defeated, and no defensible conception of equality can argue that equality recommends that result.

This is a powerful complaint, and there is no answer, I think, but to summarize and restate our earlier arguments to see if they can still persuade with that complaint ringing in our ears. Let us return to the immigrants. Claude cannot argue, on grounds of equality, for a world in which he has the movie star's income. The immigrants cannot create a world in which everyone who would be willing to work movie-star hours can have movie-star pay. If Claude is unhappy with his situation, even after the tax scheme is put into play, he must propose a world in which no one will have such an income and his income will be relatively (and perhaps absolutely) higher in consequence. But whichever such world he proposes will be changed not only for those who under our scheme would have more than he does, but for everyone else as well, including those who for one reason or another, including their preferences for work, leisure, and consumption, will have less. If, for example, no one can earn movie-star wages, people who wish to watch movies may perhaps find very different fare available which, rightly or wrongly, they will not regard as highly as what they now have. It is, of course, impossible to say in advance just what the consequences of any profound change in an economic system would be, and who would gain or lose in the long run. These changes could not be properly charted along any one simple dimension. They could not be measured simply in the funds or other "primary goods" available to one or another economic class, for example. For they also affect the prices and scarcity of different goods and opportunities that members of any particular class, even economic class, will value very differently from one another. That is exactly why the immigrants chose an auction, sensitive to what people in fact wanted for their lives, as their primary engine for achieving equality.

So though Claude may truly say that the difference between him and the movie star does not reflect any differences in tastes or ambitions or theories of the good, and so does not in itself implicate our first, ambition-sensitive requirement of equality in wage structure, he could not recommend any general change in relative economic positions that would not wreak wholesale and dramatic changes in the positions of others, changes which do implicate that requirement. Of course, this fact does not in itself rule out any changes that Claude might propose. On the contrary, the status quo achieved by laissez-faire production and trade from an equal start has no natural or privileged status, as I have been at pains to emphasize, particularly my argument against the starting-gate theory of equality. If Claude can show that a proper conception of equality of resources recommends some change, the fact that many people from all ranks would then be worse-off, given their particular tastes and ambitions, provides no objection, any more than the fact that Claude is worse-off without some change in itself provides an argument in favor of that change. I mean to emphasize only that Claude needs some argument in favor of the change he recommends which is independent of his own relative position. It is not enough for him to point to people, even those of the same ambitions and tastes as himself, who do better as things are.

The argument from the hypothetical insurance market is such an argument. It contrasts two worlds. In the first those who are relatively disadvantaged by the tastes and ambitions of others, vis-à-vis their own talents to produce, are known in advance and bear the full consequences of that disadvantage. In the second the same pattern of relative disadvantage holds, but everyone has subjectively an equal antecedent chance of suffering it, and so everyone has an equal opportunity of mitigating the disadvantage by insuring against it. The argument assumes that equality prefers the second world, because it is a world in which the resources of talent are in one important sense more evenly divided. The hypothetical insurance argument aims to reproduce the consequences of the second world, as nearly as it can, in an actual world. It answers those who would do better in the first world (who include many of those who would have more money at their disposal in the second) by the simple proposition that the second is a world that, on grounds independent of how things happen to work out for them given their tastes and ambitions, is more nearly equal in resources.

The availability of that argument is no bar to the production of other arguments showing how some further change would improve equality of resources still further. However, it is hard to anticipate how great a motive we should have to search for further arguments if the hypothetical insurance argument were in fact accepted and enforced in, for example, our immigrant case. That would depend, among other things, on how high a level of income could be shown to be the average coverage level in that society. It might be that wealth disparities would be so greatly reduced by the features of the economy we have already described that we would be much less troubled than we might suspect in advance by the wealth inequalities that would remain. Indeed it might be that the costs in overall efficiency of even those features would be so great that those who are prepared to compromise equality of resources either for general utility or in service of some strategy of making the worst-off as well-off as possible, would argue that even that much equality would be condemned by their more embracing conception of justice.

Of course, many of the political philosophers and theorists who object to inequality are concerned not simply with how poor those at the bottom are in absolute terms, but with what might be called the moral costs of a society with substantial wealth inequality, costs that remain, and indeed are sometimes exacerbated, when the position of the least well-off is sharply improved but the inequality remains. It would be a mistake, however, to suppose that the bizarre and mutually dependent attitudes about wealth that mark our own society—the ideas that the accumulation of wealth is a mark of a successful life and that someone who has arranged his life to acquire it is a proper object for envy rather than sympathy or concern—would find any footing in an economic system that is free of genuine poverty and that encourages people, as the initial auction encourages them, to see bank-account wealth as simply one ingredient among others of what might make a life worth living. For in our world, these attitudes are sustained and nourished by the assumption that a life dedicated to the accumulation of wealth or to the consumption of luxuries—a major part of whose appeal lies just in the fact that they are reserved for the very rich—is a valuable life for people given only one chance to live. That proposition comes as close as any theory of the good life can to naked absurdity.

It is no doubt an important question for social psychology and intellectual history how that proposition finds a footing in any society. It has, after all, been condemned in all literature or any other form of art taken seriously for very long in even deeply capitalistic communities, and though I understand the possibility that its rejection in art might be parasitic upon its unthinking acceptance in life, the protests of even the most popular forms of art nevertheless deepen the mystery. My present point is much more banal than any attempt to solve that mystery. It is simply this: that we are so ignorant about the complex genealogy of the implausible attitudes about wealth that we find among us, which those who point to the moral costs of the market system deplore, that we would do wrong to assume in advance that these same attitudes will rise in a market system whose very point is to encourage the kind of reflective examination about costs and gains under which these attitudes would seem most likely to shrivel and disappear.

But it is nevertheless important to try to discover arguments showing that equality of resources, as a distinct ideal, would recommend erasing even those wealth differentials that the hypothetical insurance argument would permit, and this project is not threatened by my uncertainty whether we should feel dismayed, or find our intuitions undermined, if we did not in fact discover any. I do not doubt that such arguments can be found, and it is part of my purpose to provoke them. But it is worth mentioning certain arguments that do not seem promising. It might be said, for example, that equality of resources would approve a different world still, in which people had in fact equal talents for production, more than either of the other two I described, so that we ought to strive to create a system in which wealth differences traceable to occupation were no greater than they would be in that world. There is an important point locked in that claim, which is that an egalitarian society ought, just in the name of equality, to devote special resources to training those whose talents, as things fall out, place them lower on the income scale. That is part of the larger question of an egalitarian theory of education, which I have not even attempted to take up here. But the more general point suffers from the fact that we could not even begin to replicate the wealth distribution that would hold in that different world without making assumptions about the mix of talents that everyone in that world would share in equal abundance, and no specification of the mix could be neutral among the various ambitions and tastes in the real world in which we attempt that replication.

Suppose someone says simply (and with creditable impatience) that equality of resources just *must* prefer a world in which people have more nearly equal wealth than they are likely to have in a world of free trade, even against a background of equal initial wealth and even as corrected by the hypothetical insurance market. To deny that (it might be said) is simply to prefer other values to equality, not to state an acceptable conception of equality itself. That is, of course, exactly what my arguments have been meant to challenge. Once we understand the importance, under equality of resources, of the requirement that any theory of distribution must be ambition-sensitive, and understand the wholesale effects of any scheme of distribution or redistribution on the lives that almost everyone in the community will want and be permitted to lead, we must regard with suspicion any flat statement that equality of resources just must be defined in a way that ignores these facts. Equality of resources is a complex ideal. It is probably (as the various arguments we have canvassed here suggest) an indeterminate ideal that accepts, within a certain range, a variety of distributions. But this much seems clear: any defensible conception of that ideal must attend to its different dimensions, and not reject out of hand the requirement that it be sensitive to the cost of one person's life to other people. The present suggestion, that genuine theories of equality must be concerned only with the quantity of disposable goods or liquid assets people command at a particular time, is a piece of preanalytic dogma that does not, in fact, protect the boundaries of the concept of equality from confusion with other concepts, but rather thwarts the attempt to picture equality as an independent and powerful political ideal.

VII. Other Theories of Justice

It is hardly worth repeating how far the remarks here fall short of a full theory of equality of resources even under simple and artificial conditions like those of the immigrant society. I have said nothing, for example, about how far equality, properly understood, constrains people from giving to others what they are entitled to keep and use for themselves. That question includes, of course, the troublesome issue whether those who have amassed wealth through sacrifices in their own lives should be allowed to pass this on as extra wealth for their children. Nor have I said anything about what accommodation an equal distribution of resources should make for radical changes in people's minds about how they wish to spend their lives. Is someone entitled to a fresh stock of resources when he rejects his former life and wants a fresh start? Suppose he is a profligate who has wasted his initial endowment and now finds himself with less than he needs to provide even for basic needs in later life.

These questions are of great theoretical interest, and of central practical importance when we come to ask what the requirement of an equal start, which in our immigrant world could be satisfied by an equal initial auction, would mean for the real world. I have also set aside for another occasion the entire issue of equality of political power, though as I noticed at the beginning it is quite illegitimate to regard political equality as an issue entirely distinct from economic equality. Nevertheless we have covered enough ground here that it might be useful to contrast the direction in which we are traveling with those taken by certain prominent theories of justice now in the field.

It should be reasonably plain how the conception of equality defended here contrasts with equality of welfare, the theory considered in Chapter 1. There is nothing in the idea of an equal initial auction, followed by trade and production constrained by taxation mimicking hypothetical insurance markets, that either aims at equality in any concept of welfare or makes convergence toward such equality likely. Indeed, there is no place in the theory, as developed so far, even for comparisons of the welfare levels of different people. The theory does make use of the idea of individual utility levels, for example in the calculations it recommends about how people would behave in certain hypothetical markets. But these calculations use only the rather antiseptic concept of utility proposed by John von Neumann and Oskar Morgenstern,[15] among others, rather than any of the more complex and judgmental conceptions of welfare that are necessary for interpersonal comparisons, whose shortcomings I discussed in Chapter 1.

There might well be interesting connections between the theory described here and some form of utilitarianism, which commands the maximization of some concept of welfare overall rather than equality in its distribution. Of course our theory as a whole could not be expected to maximize any concept of welfare across society, except under special and quite extravagant assumptions about individual utility functions. The assumption that people should enter economic activity with equal initial resources, for example, would count as a dubious theorem for a utilitarian, rather than as a cardinal axiom. Nevertheless the idea of an equal auction for goods and services, from the base of an equal abstract distribution of economic power, might seem to suggest a utilitarian strain in the theory, because an auction would promote overall utility better than a more mechanical division of available goods into equal lots. I do not think that this mild similarity, insofar as it does exist, is entirely accidental. On the contrary, utilitarianism owes part of its appeal, I think, to the fact that in certain circumstances a distribution that maximizes overall marginal utility from an intuitively fair basic distribution would also be recommended by the present conception of equality. This is even more plainly true of the wealth-maximization theory of justice, which is a cousin of utilitarianism and is presently popular among academic lawyers. This theory argues that, at least in certain circumstances, a distribution that maximizes marginal wealth is fair. The circumstances in which the wealth-maximization theory seems intuitively plausible[16] are in fact just the circumstances in which our conception of equality would probably recommend the decision that in fact maximizes wealth. The overall fit between our conception of equality and the wealth-maximization theory, indeed, is likely to be closer than the fit of our conception of equality with utilitarianism.[17] But in both cases, so far as the present argument holds, the connection is one-way only. A distribution that fits the two theories is fair because equality, and not the maximization of either utility or wealth, recommends it.

There are also at least superficial connections between the theory of equality of resources suggested here and various forms of the Lockean theory of justice in private property, particularly in Robert Nozick's distinguished and influential version. Of course the differences, even on the surface, are more striking. There is no place in a theory such as Nozick's for anything like the idea of an equal distribution of abstract economic power over all the goods under social control. But both Nozick's theory and equality of resources as described here give a prominent place to the idea of a market, and recommend the distribution that is achieved by a market suitably defined and constrained. It may be that those parts of Nozick's arguments that seem intuitively most persuasive are based on examples in which the present theory would reach very similar results.

The famous Wilt Chamberlain example is a case in point. Nozick supposes an equal distribution of wealth, followed by uncoerced trades to mutual advantage in which each of many people pays a small sum to watch Chamberlain play basketball, after which he grows rich and wealth is no longer equal. Equality of resources would not denounce that result, considered in itself. Chamberlain's wealth reflects the value to others of his leading his life as he does. His greater wealth, at the end of the process, is of course traceable mainly to his greater talent, and only in small part, we may assume, to the fact that he is willing to lead a life that others would not be willing to lead. But almost no one would have purchased, in the hypothetical insurance market we described, insurance against not having talents that would provide such wealth. That insurance would be, for almost everyone, a strikingly irrational investment. So our discussion would not justify taxing any of Chamberlain's wealth for redistribution to others not so fortunate, if we attend only to the fact, as Nozick does, that others have much less wealth than he does.

But our discussion left open, as Nozick's did not, that arguments justifying such redistribution might be found in a more thorough study of the actual circumstances in which wealth like Chamberlain's is accumulated. Suppose Chamberlain plays his game, not in a community whose only wealth disparity lies in his enormous wealth against the equal wealth of all others, each of whom has only slightly less than the most equal distribution we can imagine, but in Philadelphia in the early 1970s. Now a great many people earn less than the average presumed coverage of a plausible hypothetical insurance market for that society, so even if we assume that the complex wealth differences we find are all traceable to lack of talent rather than to lack of equal start (which is absurd), we are still required to put in place a tax system for redistribution to them, and Chamberlain will be required to contribute to that system. Indeed, since our argument justified the conclusion that premiums in the hypothetical insurance market would lie at progressive rates, based on income realized, Chamberlain would be required to contribute more than anyone else, both absolutely and as a percentage of his income. When the discussion is broadened in this way, equality of resources travels very far from the boundaries of the nightwatchman state.

The difference between the use the two theories make of the market is therefore clear enough. For Nozick the role of the market in justifying distributions is both negative and contingent. If someone has justly acquired something, and chooses to exchange it with someone else in return for the latter's goods or services, then no objection can be taken, in the name of justice, to the distribution that results. The history of the transaction insulates it from attack and, in this negative way, certifies its moral pedigree. There is no room, in this theory, for hypothetical markets of any form, except in the special case of restitution for demonstrated injustice in the past. For Nozick does not use the market (as, for example, some wealth-maximizers do) simply to define another of what he calls "patterned" theories of justice. Justice consists, not in the distribution that a fair market of rational persons would reach, but in the distribution that has actually, as a matter of historical contingency, been reached by a process that might, but need not, include any market transactions at all.

Under equality of resources the market, when it enters, enters in a more positive but also more servile way. It enters because it is endorsed by the concept of equality, as the best means of enforcing, at least up to a point, the fundamental requirement that only an equal share of social resources be devoted to the lives of each of its members, as measured by the opportunity cost of such resources to others. But the value of actual market transactions ends at just that point, and the market must be abandoned or constrained when analysis shows, from any direction, that it has failed in this task, or that an entirely different theoretical or institutional device would do better. Hypothetical markets are plainly of comparable theoretical importance to actual markets for this purpose. We are less certain about their results, but have a great deal more flexibility in their design, and the objection that they have no historical validity is simply beside the point.

I shall try to say something, finally, about the connections and differences between our conception of equality of resources and John Rawls's theory of justice. That theory is sufficiently rich to provide a question of connection at two different levels. First, how far do the arguments in favor of equality of resources, as described, follow the structure of argument Rawls deploys? How far do they depend, that is, on the hypothesis that people in the original position Rawls described would choose the principles of equality of resources behind the veil? Second—and independently—how far are the requirements of equality of resources different from the two principles of justice that Rawls suggests people in that position would in fact choose?

It is obviously better to start with the second of these questions. The comparison in point is that between equality of resources and Rawls's second principle of justice, whose main component is the "difference" principle, which requires no variation from absolute equality in "primary goods" save as works to the benefit of the worst-off economic class. (Rawls's first principle, which establishes what he calls the priority of liberty, has more to do with the topics I have set aside as belonging to political equality, discussed in Chapter 4.) The difference principle, like our conception of equality of resources, works only contingently in the direction of equality of welfare on any conception of welfare. If we distinguish broadly between theories of equality of welfare and of resources, the difference principle is an interpretation of equality of resources.

But it is nevertheless a rather different interpretation from our conception. From the standpoint of our conception, the difference principle is not sufficiently fine-tuned in a variety of ways. There is a conceded degree of arbitrariness in the choice of any description of the worst-off group, which is, in any case, a group whose fortunes can be charted only through some mythical average or representative member of that group. In particular, the structure seems insufficiently sensitive to the position of those with natural handicaps, physical or mental, who do not themselves constitute a worst-off group, because this is defined economically, and would not count as the representative or average member of any such group. Rawls calls attention to what he calls the principle of redress, which argues that compensation should be made to people so handicapped, as indeed it is, in the way I described, under our conception of equality. But he notes that the difference principle does not include the principle of redress, though it would tend in the same direction insofar as special training for the handicapped, for example, would work to the benefit of the economically worst-off class. But there is no reason to think that it would, at least in normal circumstances.

It has often been pointed out, moreover, that the difference principle is insufficiently sensitive to variations in distribution above the worst-off economic class. This complaint is sometimes illustrated with bizarre hypothetical questions. Suppose an existing economic system is in fact just. It meets the conditions of the difference principle because no further transfers of wealth to the worst-off class would in fact improve its position. Then some impending catastrophe (for example) presents officials with a choice. They can act so that the position of the representative member of the small worst-off class is worsened by a just noticeable amount or so that the position of everyone else is dramatically worsened and they become almost as poor as the worst-off. Does justice really require the much greater loss to everyone but the poorest in order to prevent a very small loss by them?

It may be a sufficient reply to such questions that circumstances of that sort are very unlikely to arise, and that in fact the fates of the various economic orders are or can easily be "chained" together so that improvements in the worst-off class will in fact be accompanied by improvement in at least the other classes just above them. But this reply does not remove the theoretical question whether, in all circumstances, it is really and exclusively the situation of the worst-off group that determines what is just.

Equality of resources, as described here, does not single out any group whose status has that position. It aims to provide a description of (or rather a set of devices for aiming at) equality of resources person by person, and the considerations of each person's history that affect what he should have, in the name of equality, do not include his membership in any economic or social class. I do not mean that our theory, even as so far detailed, claims any impressive degree of accuracy for those devices. On the contrary, even in the artificially simple case we treated, we several times had to concede speculation and compromise, and sometimes even indeterminacy, in the statement of what equality would require in particular circumstances. But the theory nevertheless proposes that equality is in principle a matter of individual right rather than one of group position. Not, of course, in the sense that each has a predetermined share at his disposal regardless of what he does or what happens to others. On the contrary, the theory ties the fates of people together in the way that the dominant devices of actual and hypothetical markets are meant to describe, but in the different sense that the theory supposes that equality defines a relation among citizens that is individualized for each, and therefore can be seen to set entitlements as much from the point of view of each person as from that of anyone else in the community. Even when our theory helps itself to the idea of an average utility curve, as it does in the construction of hypothetical insurance markets, it does so as a matter of probability judgments about particular people's particular tastes and ambitions, in the interests of giving them what they are, as individuals, entitled to have, rather than as part of any premise that equality is a matter of equality between groups. Rawls, on the other hand, assumes that the difference principle ties justice to a class, not as a matter of second-best practical accommodation to some deeper version of equality which is in principle more individualized, but because the choice in the original position, which defines what justice even at bottom is, would for practical reasons be framed in class terms from the start.[18]

It is impossible to say, a priori, whether the difference principle or equality of resources will work to achieve greater absolute equality in what Rawls calls primary goods. That would depend upon circumstances. Suppose, for example, that the tax necessary to provide the right coverage for handicaps and the unemployed has the long-term effect of discouraging investment and in this way reducing the primary-goods prospects of the representative member of the worst-off class. Certain individual members of the worst-off group who are handicapped or who are and will remain unemployed would be better off under the tax scheme (as would certain members of other classes as well), but the average or representative member of the worst-off class would be worse off. The difference principle, which looks to the worst-off group as a whole, would condemn the tax, but equality of resources would recommend it nevertheless.

In the circumstances of the familiar bizarre questions just described, when a just-noticeable loss to the representative member of the worst-off class, from a just base, could be prevented only by very substantial losses to those better off, the difference principle is committed to preventing that small loss even at that cost. Equality of resources, on the contrary, would be sensitive to quantitative differences of just the sort that those who object to Rawls's theory on that account believe should matter. If the base is an equal division of resources, this means, not that any transfer to the worst-off group would work to the long-run loss of that group, which it might or might not, but that any such transfer would be unfair to others. The fact that those at the bottom do not have more would not indicate that it is impossible to give them more, but rather that they have all that they are entitled to have. If some economic catastrophe is now threatened, a government that allows a much greater loss to fall on one citizen, in order to avert a much smaller loss to a second, would not be treating the former as an equal, because, since equality in itself requires no further special attention to the second, that government must have more concern with his fate than it has for the fate of others. So if the loss threatened to the financially worst-off is indeed really inconsequential to him, as the bizarre question assumes, then that is an end of the matter.

But it does not follow that equality of resources turns into utilitarianism in the face of examples like these. It is, in fact, sensitive to more, or at least different, quantitative information than either the difference principle or utilitarianism is. For suppose the impending catastrophe threatens the worst-off group, not with a trivial loss as in the original question, but with a substantial loss, though not as great, in aggregate, as the loss threatened to those better-off. Equality of resources must ask whether the calculations of the hypothetical insurance market, and of the tax scheme in force, took adequate account of the risk of the threat now about to materialize. It might not have. The possibility of a substantial loss from the unexpected quarter, if it had been anticipated, might have led the average buyer in that market to purchase either catastrophe or unemployment insurance at a higher level of coverage, and this fact might affect an official's present decision about how to distribute the coming loss. He might be persuaded, for example, that allowing the loss to fall on those better-off, in spite of the overall welfare loss, would reach a situation closer to the situation all would have been in had the tax scheme better reflected what people would have done in the hypothetical market with that additional information.

Such contrasts in the practical advice that the difference principle and equality of resources offer in particular circumstances are in fact myriad, and these examples are meant only to be suggestive of others. These contrasts are organized around the theoretical distinction I have already noticed. The difference principle is tuned to only one of the dimensions of equality that equality of resources recognizes. The former supposes that flat equality in primary goods, without regard to differences in ambition, taste, occupation, or consumption, let alone differences in physical condition or handicap, is basic or true equality. Since (once the priority of liberty is satisfied) justice consists in equality, and since true equality is just this flat equality, any compromise or deviation can be justified only on the grounds that it is in the interests of the only people who might properly complain of the deviation.

This unidimensional analysis of equality would plainly be unsatisfactory if applied person by person. It would fall before the argument that it is not an equal division of social resources when someone who consumes more of what others want nevertheless has as much left over as someone who consumes less; nor that someone who chooses to work at a more productive occupation, measured by what others want, should have no more resources in consequence than someone who prefers leisure. (It would fall before such arguments, that is, unless it were converted into a form of equality of welfare through the doubtful proposition that equality in primary goods, in spite of different consumption or occupational histories, is the best guarantee of equality of welfare.)

So (as Rawls makes plain) the difference principle does not tie itself to groups rather than individuals as a second-best accommodation to some deeper vision of equality that is individualistic. Any such deeper vision would condemn the difference principle as inadequate. It ties itself to groups in principle, because the idea of equality among social groups, defined in economic terms, is especially congenial to the flat interpretation of equality. Indeed, the idea of equality as equality among economic groups permits no other interpretation. Since the members of any economic group will be widely diverse in tastes, ambitions, and conceptions of the good life, these must drop away from any principle stating what true equality among groups requires, and we are left with only the requirement that they be equal on the only dimension on which they can, as groups, possibly differ. The tie between the difference principle and the group taken as its unit of social measure is close to definitional.

We must be wary in rushing from this fact to conclusions about Rawls's theory of justice as a whole. The first of his principles of justice is plainly meant to be individualistic in a way that the difference principle is not, and any evaluation of the role of the individual in the theory as a whole would require a careful analysis of that principle and of the manner in which the two principles might work in harness. But insofar as the difference principle is meant to express a theory of equality of resources, it expresses a theory different in its basic vocabulary and design from the theory sketched here. It might well be worthwhile to pursue that difference further, perhaps by elaborating and working out in more detail the differences between the consequences of the two theories in practical circumstances. But I shall turn instead to the first of the two issues of comparison I distinguished.

I have tried to show the appeal of equality of resources, as interpreted here, only by making plainer its motivation and defending its coherence and practical force. I have not tried to defend it in what might be considered a more direct way, by deducing it from more general and abstract political principles. So the question arises whether that sort of defense could be provided and, in particular, whether it could be found in Rawls's general method. The fact that equality of resources differs in various ways, some of them fundamental, from Rawls's own difference principle is not decisive against this possibility. For perhaps we might show that the people who inhabit Rawls's original position would choose, behind the veil of their ignorance, not his difference principle, but either equality of resources or some intermediate constitutional principles such that, when the veil was lifted, it would be discovered that equality of resources satisfied these principles better than the difference principle could.

I hope it is clear that I have not presented any such argument here. It is true that I have argued that an equal distribution is a distribution that would result from people's choices under certain circumstances, some of which, as in the case of the hypothetical insurance markets, require the counterfactual assumption that people are ignorant of what in fact they are very likely to know. But this argument is different from an argument from the original position in two ways. First, my arguments have been designed to permit people as much knowledge as it is possible to allow them without defeating the point of the exercise entirely. In particular, they allow people enough self-knowledge, as individuals, to keep relatively intact their sense of their own personality, and especially their theory of what is valuable in life, whereas it is central to the original position that this is exactly the knowledge people lack. Second, and more important, my arguments are constructed against the background of assumptions about what equality requires in principle. It is not intended, as Rawls's argument is intended, to establish that background. My arguments enforce rather than construct a basic design of justice, and that design must find support, if at all, elsewhere than in those arguments.

I do not mean to suggest, however, that I am simply agnostic about the project of supporting equality of resources as a political ideal by showing that people in the original position would choose it. I think that any such project must fail, or rather, that it is misconceived, because some theory of equality, like equality of resources, is necessary to explain why the original position is a useful device—or one among a number of useful devices—for considering what justice is. The project, as just described, would therefore be too self-sustaining. The device of an original position (as I have argued at length elsewhere)[19] cannot plausibly be taken as the starting point for political philosophy. It requires a deeper theory beneath it, a theory that explains why the original position has the features that it does and why the fact that people would choose particular principles in that position, if they would, certifies those principles as principles of justice. The force of the original position as a device for arguments for justice, or of any particular design of the original position for that purpose, depends, in my view, on the adequacy of an interpretation of equality of resources that supports it, not vice versa.

Dworkin discusses the differences and similarities between equality of resources and the capabilities approach to justice at pages 209-303 of his book, *Sovereign Virtue*.

Notes

1. D. Foley, "Resource Allocation and the Public Sector," *Yale Economic Essays* 7 (Spring 1967); H. Varian, "Equity, Energy and Efficiency," *Journal of Economic Theory*, September 1974, pp. 63–91.
2. I mean to describe a Walrasian auction in which all productive resources are sold. I do not assume that the immigrants enter into complete forward contingent claims contracts, but only that markets will remain open and will clear in a Walrasian fashion once the auction of productive resources is completed. I make all the assumptions about production and preferences made in G. Debreu, *Theory of Value* (New Haven: Yale University Press, 1959). In fact the auction I describe here will become more complex in virtue of a tax scheme discussed later.
3. The process does not guarantee that the auction will come to an end in this way, because there may be various equilibria. I am supposing that people will come to understand that they cannot do better by further runs of the auction, and will for practical reasons settle on one equilibrium. If I am wrong, then this fact provides one of the aspects of incompleteness I describe in the next section.
4. See, however, the discussion of handicaps below, which recognizes that certain kinds of preferences, which people wish they did not have, may call for compensation as handicaps.
5. The averaging assumption is a simplifying assumption only, made to provide a result in the absence of the detailed (and perhaps, for reasons described in the text, indeterminate) information that would enable us to decide how much each handicapped person would have purchased in the hypothetical market. If we had such full information, so that we could tailor compensation to what a particular individual in fact would have bought, the accuracy of the program would be improved. But in the absence of such information, averaging is second best, or in any case better than nothing.
6. The hypothetical insurance approach does not require any stipulation of "normal" powers, because it allows the hypothetical market to determine which infirmities are compensable.
7. Robert Nozick, *Anarchy, State, and Utopia* (New York: Basic Books, 1974).
8. Notice that our analysis of the problem that differential talents presents to equality

of resources calls for an income tax, rather than either a wealth or a consumption tax. If people begin with equal resources, then we wish to tax to adjust for different skills so far as these produce different income, because it is only in that way that they threaten equality of resources. Someone's decision to spend rather than save what he has earned is precisely the kind of decision whose impact should be determined by the market uncorrected for tax under this analysis. Of course, there might be technical or other reasons why a society dedicated to equality of welfare would introduce taxes other than income taxes. Such a society might want to encourage savings, for example. But these taxes would not be responses to the problem now under consideration. Should unearned (investment) income be taxed under the present argument? I assume that unearned income reflects skill in investment as well as preferences for later consumption, in which case that argument would extend to taxing such income. Since I am not considering here the problem of later generations, I do not consider inheritance or estate taxes.

9. Other forms for the insurance market we are imagining are possible, but those I have considered seem to produce roughly the same results. Amartya Sen has suggested to me, for example, that the insurer might offer a policy guaranteeing the named level of coverage to every policyholder, but making the premium depend on the economic rent people turn out to have. This would not, I think, produce different results from the arrangement I describe in the next section, and I think it useful to consider, as I do there, why these elaborations would be necessary.
10. If I am wrong in this, the hypothetical insurance argument would insist on radical redistribution and substantial wealth equality. So the scheme would offer an argument for that consequence, on that assumption.
11. I have neglected the question of the technology that will be available for the insurance firms to decide and prove who has what level of talent, and the cost of that technology. I assume that the computer will have that information, as part of its technological data base, and will use it to predict the premium structure and other incidents of the contract of insurance. When I speak of "winning" or "losing" the insurance bet, I mean qualifying for compensation or failing to qualify under the incidents the computer predicts.
12. He may also run the even graver risk of losing under the tests specified in the policy and yet not, in fact, having the ability to earn the covered level. I do not emphasize this risk, because it assumes failures of technology about which it is impossible to speculate. I therefore assume, arguendo, that no one will be in that perilous position.
13. Thomas Scanlon provided this example.
14. As in the case of handicaps, I have chosen to make premiums and therefore tax payments turn on the average coverage level as a simplifying device. I might, of course, have chosen either the median or the mode of coverage selected in the hypothetical market instead of the average or mean. It is an interesting question whether either of these would be better. I chose the average on the assumption that our assessment of the chance of error in particular cases (the chance that the "pre-

mium" extracted differs from what the individual in question actually would have paid in the hypothetical market) should reflect the amount as well as the fact of that difference.

15. John von Neumann and Oskar Morgenstern, *The Theory of Games and Economic Behavior,* 3d ed. (Princeton: Princeton University Press, 1980).
16. As it often does, I think, in hard cases at common law when those who would benefit and those who would lose by the introduction of any new rule of law are or must be assumed to be classes roughly equal in their command over resources. See R. Posner, "The Ethical and Political Basis of the Efficiency Norm in Common Law Adjudication," *Hofstra Law Review* 8 (1980): 487.
17. Ronald Dworkin, "Why Efficiency?" *Hofstra Law Review* 8 (1980): 563.
18. John Rawls, *A Theory of Justice* (Cambridge, Mass.: The Belknap Press of Harvard University Press, 1971), p. 98.
19. Ronald Dworkin, *Taking Rights Seriously* (Cambridge, Mass.: Harvard University Press, 1977), chap. 6.

Part II
Human Rights

[4]

Capabilities, Entitlements, Rights: Supplementation and Critique

MARTHA C. NUSSBAUM

Martha C. Nussbaum is Ernst Freund Distinguished Service Professor of Law and Ethics at the University of Chicago, USA

Abstract Capabilities are closely related to human rights. Capabilities are important human entitlements, inherent in the idea of basic social justice, and can be viewed as one species of a human rights approach. This paper explores this relationship, expanding on earlier publications, notably *Capabilities and Human Rights* (1997), *Women and Human Development* (2000), *Capabilities as Fundamental Entitlements* (2003), and *Frontiers of Justice* (2005). Capabilities are complementary to and augment, rather than competing with, human rights. Capabilities can supplement the language of rights in clarifying the basic concept of human rights, by emphasizing the material and social aspect of all rights and the need for government action to protect and secure all rights. They also ground entitlements in the lives of ordinary people, without tying them down to a specific cultural context. Human rights can also supplement the language of capabilities. Human rights makes clear that the idea of capabilities is not an optional entitlement, but an urgent demand that should not be ignored nor compromised in pursuit of other objectives such as expansion of aggregate wealth. Human rights have gained support and endorsement the world over, and the idea of rights has the capacity to mobilize political action.

Key words: Human rights, Capabilities, Justice

Capabilities and the language of human rights

Ten 'central capabilities,' I have argued, are important human entitlements, inherent in the idea of basic social justice (Nussbaum, 2000, 2003, 2005). My capabilities list includes many of the entitlements that are also stressed in the human rights movement: political liberties, the freedom of association, the free choice of occupation, and a variety of economic and social rights. And a list of capabilities, like a list of human rights, supplies a moral and humanly rich set of goals for development, in place of the focus on Gross Domestic Product per capita as the single important development goal.

Capabilities, as I understand them, clearly have a very close relationship to human rights, as understood in contemporary international discussions. In effect, the capabilities on my list cover the terrain covered by both the so-called 'first-generation rights' (political and civil liberties) and the so-called second-generation rights (economic and social rights). And they play a similar role, providing both a basis for cross-cultural comparison and the theoretical underpinning for basic constitutional principles.

Both Sen and I connect the capabilities approach (CA) closely to the idea of human rights (see Sen, 2004). In both *Women and Human Development* and *Frontiers of Justice*, I have described the relationship between the two ideas at some length (Nussbaum, 2000, ch. 1; 2005, see also Nussbaum, 1997), and I have tried to show how my version of the CA responds to some criticisms frequently made of human rights approaches. For example, the human rights approach had frequently been criticized by feminists for being male-centered, and for not including as fundamental entitlements some abilities and opportunities that are fundamental to women in their struggle for sex equality. They proposed adding to international rights documents such rights as the right to bodily integrity, the right to be free from violence in the home and from sexual harassment in the workplace.[1] My list of capabilities explicitly incorporates that proposal. (Sen's more informal discussion of specific capabilities does so implicitly.) More needs to be done, however, to explain the theoretical reasons for supplementing the language of human rights with the language of capabilities. The aim of the present paper is to clarify the relationship further, in ways that go beyond the analysis offered in my earlier article on the topic (Nussbaum, 1997).

I view (my version of) the CA as one species of a human rights approach. It supplements those approaches in several useful ways. It also differs from some (other) versions of such an approach, and offers a useful critique of those versions. In some ways, I shall argue, it thus offers significant advantages over all (other) versions. The relationship between capabilities and human rights is, then, one of inclusion—the CA is a type of human rights approach—but also one of both supplementation and critique.

Supplementation: clarity about the basic notions

The idea of human rights is by no means a crystal clear idea (see also Sen, 2004). Rights have been understood in many different ways, and difficult theoretical questions are frequently obscured by the use of rights language, which can give the illusion of agreement where there is deep philosophical disagreement. People differ about what the *basis* of a rights claim is: rationality, sentience, and mere life have all had their defenders. They differ, too, about whether rights are prepolitical or artifacts of laws and institutions. The CA, in my version, has the advantage of taking clear positions on these disputed issues, while stating clearly what the motivating concerns are and what the goal is.

In my two books about the CA, I argue that the ten central capabilities are fundamental entitlements inherent in the very idea of minimum social justice, or a life worthy of human dignity (Nussbaum, 2000, 2005: see also Nussbaum, 2003). Where humans are concerned, the basis of these entitlements lies not in rationality, nor in any other specific human property, but, rather, in the bare fact of being a living human being: being born from human parents, and having a minimal level of agency or capacity for activity. That is enough to give a human being a dignity that is equal to that of every other human being (Nussbaum, 2008). Thus a person in a persistent vegetative state does not have these entitlements, nor an anencephalic child. But human beings with high levels of mental retardation, unable to use language, unable to move, and so forth, do have them, provided they have some degree of active functioning or striving. In this way, my approach differs from most human rights approaches, which, historically, have grounded entitlements in the possession of rationality and have excluded human beings with severe mental disabilities (Nussbaum, 2005, 2008).

Nor are human beings the only creatures with fundamental entitlements, according to me: I argue that all sentient beings, at least, have entitlements to the basic conditions of a life according to the dignity of their species (Nussbaum, 2005). So human rights are just one species of rights, and all animals have rights of some sort. Here the CA departs radically from almost all human rights approaches, where the accent is firmly on *human*.

The capabilities on my list are what I call *combined capabilities*, by which I mean the internal preparation for action and choice, plus circumstances that make it possible to exercise that function. For example, the capability of free speech requires not only the ability to speak (that would be an *internal capability*, cultivated through development and education), but also the actual political and material circumstances in which that ability can be used. Governments do not support the capability of free speech, in the sense required by my list, if they educate people to be eloquent speakers but then deny them the political right to speak freely in public.

Of course human beings have all sorts of capabilities, meaning abilities or opportunities to act and choose. The items on my list, however, are the result of an evaluative argument that asks the question: 'What opportunities are entailed by the idea of a life worthy of human dignity?' The approach, then, does not read capabilities off from a factual observation of human nature as it is. Many capacities inherent in our nature are bad (e.g. the capacity for cruelty); and many are too trivial to be inherent in the idea of a life worthy of human dignity. My approach, then, does not value capabilities as such, or freedom as such. Some freedoms or opportunities to act are good and some bad, some important and some trivial (Nussbaum, 2003).[2]

In my view, these central entitlements are prepolitical, belonging to people independently of and prior to membership in a state; and they generate constraints that political institutions must meet, if they are to be even minimally just. In other words, they belong to humans just on account of their human dignity, and would be there even if there were no political organization at all, although no doubt they would not be secured to people. The CA in this way takes issue with those human rights approaches that consider rights to be an artifact of laws and institutions (see also Sen, 2004). In the absence of a world state (a goal that I do not support), we can speak of duties to secure the capabilities to everyone in the world only if we do think of them as prepolitical in this way. Approaches that make all entitlements the artifact of political organization have a very difficult time justifying redistribution from richer to poorer nations. The CA, then, is like a type of human rights approach that sees human rights as prepolitical, inherent in people's very humanity. This has been overwhelmingly the most common type of human rights theory.

Entitlements, in my view, are correlative with duties: if people have entitlements, then there is a duty to secure them, even if it is difficult to say to whom the duty belongs (see also Sen, 2004, pp. 340–341). In *Frontiers of Justice* I argue that the whole world is under a collective obligation to secure the capabilities to all world citizens, even if there is no worldwide political organization. How to assign the duties to specific groups and individuals is a difficult matter, and I attempt to take that on, at least in a preliminary way (Nussbaum, 2005, ch. 5). The difficulty is greatest in the global context, where there is no state, and no good reasons to think that we ought to have a single overarching state. Even here, many of the duties to secure human capabilities are assigned to states (Nussbaum, 2005); but some belong, as well, to non-governmental organizations, to corporations, to international organizations, and to individuals. In that sense the duties are ethical rather than political: they do not require a state enforcement mechanism to be morally binding (Nussbaum, 2005; cf. Sen, 2004).

Nonetheless, I do not agree with Sen that rights (or the central capabilities) have no conceptual connection to state action (see Sen, 2004, pp. 320 and 345–348). I agree with my American revolutionary ancestors: one key purpose of the state is to secure to people their most central entitlements. As the US Declaration of Independence puts it, recapitulating a long tradition of argument, '[T]o secure these rights, Governments are instituted among Men, deriving their just powers from the consent of the governed'—and any government that fails to secure basic entitlements has failed in its most essential task.[3] If a capability really belongs on the list (or, if a given human right really belongs in a list of human rights), then governments have the obligation to protect and secure it, using law and public policy to achieve this end. The world context is unique, because there is no overarching state, and thus none that can be shown unjust because it flunks this task. When we are thinking of a specific nation-state, however, we are entitled to ask whether it has secured the ten capabilities (the central human rights) to people. If it has not, it is not even minimally just.

Sen attempts to avoid granting a conceptual connection between capabilities and government by citing examples of capabilities (rights) that should not be legally enforced, such as the right of a family member to be consulted in all family decisions (2004, p. 345). Of this example I would say: either such conduct is required by a notion of a life worthy of human dignity, or it is not. If it is, then it ought to be legally enforced (just as we legally enforce prohibitions on child abuse and domestic violence). If it is not, then it will not belong on a list of central capabilities or human rights. If we do put something on that list, we connect it, both practically and conceptually, to the idea of the purposes for which 'governments were instituted among men.' My own view is that such matters of consultation are matters concerning which citizens may reasonably disagree, given differences in their comprehensive doctrines, religious and ethical. They should not be coercively enforced, but by the same token they should not be on the capabilities list, which is said to be the potential object of an overlapping consensus among all the reasonable comprehensive doctrines.

The ten capabilities then, are *goals* that fulfill or correspond to people's prepolitical entitlements: thus, we say of people that they are entitled to the ten capabilities on the list. In the context of a nation, it then becomes the job of government to secure them, if that government is to be even minimally just. In effect, then, the presence of entitlements gives governments a job to do, and a central job of government will be to secure the capabilities to people. The existence of human and animal lives gives a reason for governments to exist and generates obligations of a distinctly political kind. When, in the case of the whole world, we decide that an overarching single government might not be the best way of solving problems of capability failure in poorer nations, government still plays a major role in securing them: the government of the poorer nations, in the first place, and, in the second place, the governments of richer nations, who have obligations to assist the poorer (Nussbaum, 2005, ch. 5). Giving people what they are entitled to have, in virtue of their humanity, is a major reason for governments to exist in the first place, and a major job they have once they exist.

The capability goal ought to be set in a way that is realistic for each capability singly, and a way that promises reasonably coherent deliverance of the whole interlocking set of capabilities. Where we face the need to make trade-offs, promoting one capability at the expense of another, we ought to say that this is a tragic situation in which minimal justice cannot be done, and we should get to work to produce a future in which all citizens can enjoy all the capabilities. It is reasonable to set the level of each capability quite high, aspirationally; nonetheless, it would be wrong to set the level in a utopian manner, precluding all possibilities of realization. Thus, I basically agree with Sen that human rights, and capabilities so understood, should not be thought to be absent because they are at present unrealizable (Sen, 2004, p. 326). I would add, however, that the specification has to be responsive to the conditions of human life as it is, and not one that would require a total transformation of the world in order to permit realization. The right way to set the level is a job for judgment and discussion.

When we talk about capabilities as fundamental entitlements, what is the motivating concern? Human rights approaches sometimes leave a blank here, although at times they invoke a notion of human dignity. The dominant intuitive idea, in my view, is that of waste or starvation. Some lives that people are given are pinched and cramped; they are unable to unfold themselves, to choose, to act, to use key human powers. Their lives are thus not worthy of human dignity. The intuition underlying my version of the approach is that idea of waste or tragedy, coupled with the idea of the inherent dignity of the life of the being in question, which demands better than that. (From now on, putting other animals to one side, I shall speak of human dignity: but it must never be forgotten that this is just one type of dignity that laws and institutions should recognize.)

Why does the task of securing capabilities belong (apart from the global context) to government? I am operating, here, with a very widespread and basic notion of the purpose of government, one that many nations share all over the world: governments are instituted to secure things to people that they could not secure without government, and governments must be measured by the extent to which they fulfill that task (Nussbaum, 2007a). There are many ways in which governments can secure human capabilities, but I have focused on their role in generating accounts of fundamental constitutional entitlements and then securing those entitlements (Nussbaum, 2007a). Thus I would agree with Sen (2004) that capabilities need not always be secured by legislation, but I would remark that almost all modern democracies divide these functions among the executive, the judiciary, and the legislature; if I focus on the part that involves constitutional law and its judicial interpretation, this is not to neglect the role of these other branches. There is much more to be written about the relationship between capabilities and political structure, and I hope to attempt this task in the future.

What is the scope of capabilities? Sen holds that the idea of human rights is broader than the idea of capabilities, because both processes and opportunities figure in the idea of human rights, whereas capabilities are concerned with opportunities and not with process (Sen, 2004, pp. 330–337). I am not convinced; indeed, I just do not understand the reasons for this alleged bifurcation. One of the many things that people need to be able to do, if their life is to be worthy of human dignity, is to have access to the legal system on terms of equality with other people; one way this right is often impeded is to have asymmetrical procedural hurdles put before one. The due process rights that all modern constitutions guarantee, in a way closely bound up with guarantees of equal protection, are procedural rights, but they are also fundamental opportunities to act and be treated as a fully equal citizen. Again, one procedural right that most modern democracies treat as salient is the right to privacy, understood as a type of control over one's intimate decisions. That right (fundamental to women's control over their reproductive capacities) is a procedural right, but it is also an individual capability or opportunity. Sen says procedural rights differ from others because they involve governmental structure: but so do all the capabilities.

All the central capabilities, like all human rights, are best seen as occasions for choice, areas of freedom: thus a person can have all ten capabilities on my list without using all of them, and this is true of rights as well. A person may have the right to religious freedom, for example, in a secure form, and care nothing about religion (see also Sen, 2004, p. 335). The central reason why capabilities and not the associated functions are held to be central goals of government is that it would be wrong for government to push people into functioning in these areas, since citizens reasonably differ over which functions they will choose and which they will not. In this way the CA, like human rights approaches, avoids being 'imperialistic,' or imposing a single lifestyle on all. Instead, it asks governments to create and protect contexts of choice.

In this section I have gone over some of the ways in which the CA *supplements* human rights approaches: by taking clear positions on these disputed and sometimes ignored questions.

Supplementation: capabilities on the ground

There is another way in which the CA usefully supplements the language of human rights: by simply being highly concrete and close to the ground. The language of rights often strikes people as abstract. The daily question 'What am I able to do and be?' is, by contrast, down-to-earth and practical. It is a question that people in all walks of life ask themselves every day, even when they do not have any education. It does not require any philosophical grounding to ask and answer this question, nor does it require a formation that is peculiar to one culture rather than another.

Thus when development practitioners or activists discuss with people what they think they need and should have, the language of capabilities seems like a natural extension of their demands, not like a foreign imposition. The important cross-cultural study of Wolff and de-Shalit shows that new immigrant groups, discussing their disadvantages, gravitate naturally to capabilities language and understand the approach very quickly. They are able to use it to add items that my list does not include, and to add general concepts, such as that of 'capability security,' which my approach did not foreground (Wolff and de Shalit, 2007). I have heard similar reports from activists in many places.

Throughout my own work on the CA, I have always emphasize this specificity, saying that what is universal in the approach is only a starting point: each nation must and should describe the capabilities it pursues more concretely, using their own history and traditions as a guide (Nussbaum, 2000, 2005; compare Sen, 2004, p. 323). And of course even a constitution is likely to be pretty general: the capabilities then have to be further specified through both legislation and judicial interpretation, together with the work of administrative agencies (Nussbaum, 2007a). Human rights documents do not typically comment on this interpretive process, or perform the further specification of the rights they include (although human rights practitioners do typically perform this further work).

One further advantage of using such a down-to-earth language, a language people in nations all over the world use in their daily activities, is that we do not even appear to be imposing a western construct upon formerly colonized peoples. I do not believe that the idea of human rights is especially western: it has roots in many traditions (Sen, 1997; 2004, pp. 351–355). Moreover, the experience of colonial subjects did not show them that any idea of human rights was central to western culture: for what they saw every day was a blatant disregard of human rights (of freedoms of speech and assembly, of economic entitlements, and many others). When Nehru and Gandhi put rights into the Indian constitution, they did not see themselves as aping western powers, but rather as constructing bulwarks against what, in their experience, the West had stood for. In recent years, the work of human rights activists in many nations has grounded rights talk in local realities. Nonetheless: if we do not want to waste time responding to the postcolonial critique of rights, which is very widespread in places where people do not know much history, we will get some advantage from focusing on the neutral and international language of what people are actually able to do and be.

Because capabilities language is determinate and down-to-earth, when we are operating within a legal or constitutional framework that uses the language of rights, we still need capabilities language to make clear what it is really to secure the entitlement in question. The right to political participation, the right to religious free exercise, the right of free speech—these and others are all best thought of as secured to people only when the relevant capabilities to function are present. In other words, to secure a right to citizens in these areas is to put them in a position of capability to function in that area. To the extent that rights are used in defining social justice, we should not grant that the society is just unless the capabilities have been effectively achieved. This understanding of rights helps us understand what questions judges should be asking when they pose questions about constitutional rights (Nussbaum, 2007a).

Of course people may have a prepolitical right to good treatment in this area that has not yet been recognized or implemented; or it may be recognized formally and yet not implemented. But by defining the securing of rights in terms of capabilities, we make it clear that a people in country C do not really have an effective right to political participation—for example, a right in the sense that matters for judging that the society is a just one—simply because this language exists on paper: they really have been given right only if there are effective measures to make people truly capable of political exercise. Women in many nations have a nominal right of political participation without having this right in the sense of capability: for example, they may be threatened with violence should they leave the home. In short, thinking in terms of capability gives us a benchmark as we think about what it is really to secure a right to someone.

Here we are dealing above all with *supplementation*, but it will be seen that supplementing rights language with that understanding of what it is to secure a right to someone leads directly to a *critique* of some versions of the human rights approach.

Critique: positive and negative, action and inaction

Securing the central human capabilities, as I describe them in the CA, clearly involves affirmative material and institutional support, not simply a failure to impede. 'Combined capabilities' are the goal: and these require the preparation of the material and institutional environment (and the education of the person) so that the function in question can actually be selected.

We see here a major advantage of the CA over understandings of rights—very influential and widespread—that derive from the tradition within liberalism that is now called 'neoliberal,' for which a key idea is that of 'negative liberty.' The idea of 'negative liberty' is frequently traced back to the work of Isaiah Berlin, but his subtle categories are often ill-understood, and I do not want to digress in order to pursue the correct interpretation of his work, since I am interested in contesting the Libertarian or 'neoliberal' understanding of rights that borrows this term.

Often fundamental entitlements have been understood as nothing more than prohibitions against interfering state action. If the state keeps its hands off, those rights are taken to have been secured; the state has no further affirmative task. Indeed, if one reads the US Constitution, one sees this conception directly: for negative phrasing concerning state action predominates, as in the First Amendment:

> Congress shall make no law respecting an establishment of religion, or prohibiting the free exercise thereof; or abridging the freedom of speech, or of the press; or the right of the people peaceably to assemble, and petition the Government for a redress of grievances.

Similarly, the Fourteenth Amendment's all-important guarantees are also stated in terms of what the state may not do:

> No State shall make or enforce any law which shall abridge the privileges or immunities of citizens of the United States; nor shall any State deprive any person of life, liberty, or property, without due process of law; nor deny to any person within its jurisdiction the equal protection of the laws.

This phraseology, deriving from the Enlightenment tradition of negative liberty, leaves things notoriously indeterminate as to whether impediments supplied by the market, or private actors, are to be considered violations of fundamental rights of citizens. By now, as interpreted, our tradition has recognized that the state must in some cases act to prevent private discrimination, but the whole terrain is contested, and the language of rights certainly does not resolve the difficulty.

Of course even libertarians believe that the state must act to secure rights—maintaining a system of contract, property rights, and so forth. Their list is a lot shorter than the list I favor, but they too believe that state action is required: not even their state is purely negative. However, the libertarian position on the justifiability of state action and positive intervention is fluctuating and, frequently, unclear, whereas the CA makes it clear from the start that the state has an affirmative task of securing capabilities.

The Indian Constitution, by contrast to the US Constitution, typically specifies rights affirmatively.[4] Thus for example: 'All citizens shall have the right to freedom of speech and expression; to assemble peaceably and without arms; to form associations or unions; ... [etc.]' (Indian Constitution, Article 19). These locutions have usually been understood to imply that impediments supplied by non-state actors may also be deemed violative of constitutional rights. Moreover, the Constitution is quite explicit that affirmative action programs to aid the lower castes and women are not only not incompatible with constitutional guarantees, but are actually in their spirit. Such an approach seems very important for gender justice: the state needs to take action if traditionally marginalized groups are to achieve full equality. Whether a nation has a written constitution or not, it should understand fundamental entitlements in this way.

The CA, we may now say, sides with the Indian Constitution, and against the neoliberal interpretation of the US Constitution. It makes it clear that securing a right to someone requires more than the absence of negative state action. Measures such as the recent constitutional amendments in India that guarantee women one-third representation in the local *panchayats*, or village councils, are strongly suggested by the CA, which directs government to think from the start about what obstacles there are to full and effective empowerment for all citizens, and to devise measures that address these obstacles.

One place where Enlightenment notions of state inaction and negative liberty have been especially pernicious is in the state's relation to the household or family. The classic liberal distinction between the public and the private spheres aids the natural stand-offishness that many liberal thinkers have about state action: even if it is fine for the state to act to secure people's rights, there is one privileged sphere in which they should not do this, the sphere of the family. Some liberal thinkers, for example John Stuart Mill, have pointed out that non-intervention in the family allows egregious rights-violations to go unaddressed: marital rape, domestic violence, child abuse. The notion of the 'private domain' simply shields such abuses from scrutiny and correction (see Nussbaum, 2000, ch. 4).

The language of capabilities does not automatically guarantee a critique of this baneful distinction. It all depends how one frames the capability list. If, however, one is in the habit of asking what each person is actually able to do and be, one will be very likely to notice that vulnerability to violence within the home stops women and children from doing and being many things they want to do and be, *and* have a right to do and be. More generally, asking about capabilities leads us to notice all sorts of inequalities women and girls suffer inside the family: inequalities in resources and opportunities, educational deprivations, the failure of work to be recognized as work, insults to bodily integrity. Feminists in the human rights domain have long been insisting that the notion of rights must be expanded to include women's rights to be free from abuse within the family, and they have achieved public recognition of women's rights against abuse in documents such as the Convention on the Elimination of All Forms of Discrimination Against Women (CEDAW). Furthermore, the Declaration on Violence Against Women, the appointment of the Special Rapporteur on Violence Against Women, and the General Recommendations of the Committee on the Elimination of All Discriminations Against Women have clarified that CEDAW does cover abuses that take place within the family. Nonetheless, the history and philosophical background of the notion of rights has made this a difficult struggle, given the traditional association of rights talk with the public–private distinction. Traditional rights talk neglected these issues, prior to the feminist critique of the past 30 years, and, even after CEDAW (which the USA, a nation with one of the highest rates of domestic violence, has never ratified), the feminist critique of rights continues to be contested. This is no accident, I would argue: for rights language is strongly linked, historically at least, with the traditional distinction between a public sphere, which the state regulates, and a private sphere, which it must leave alone.

Critique: first and second generations

Commonly, the human rights tradition has divided rights into two groups: the political and civil rights, which are often called 'first-generation' rights, and the economic and social rights, which are called 'second-generation.' This way of carving things up suggests that the political and civil rights have no economic and social preconditions. The CA has always insisted that they do. When we keep our eyes focused on what people are actually able to do and be, we quickly see that they do not have the ability to participate in political debate, to vote, to run for office, and so forth, if they are inhibited by extreme poverty, lack of education, and ill health—at least they do not have these entitlements securely, or on a basis of equality.

Thus the CA has insisted from the start that we refuse to make this misleading separation. All entitlements have material and institutional necessary conditions. Education, for example, is a distinct entitlement on its own, but it is also a precondition of the adequate exercise of a group of political rights. Domestic violence is bad *per se*, a violation of women's entitlement to bodily integrity. But it also impedes women from the exercise of many other capabilities, including the political capabilities.

By now some versions of the human rights approach would appear to grant the centrality of economic factors in securing the 'first-generation rights.' But then the whole distinction ought to be dropped, and we should look at each entitlement separately, asking what its material and institutional preconditions are.

M. C. Nussbaum

Consequentialism and deontology

The family of human rights approaches looks distinctly deontological: it says that overall good social consequences may not be pursued in ways that violate the items on the list of rights. Sen, however, has long argued convincingly that rights may be incorporated into an approach that focuses on producing overall good social consequences (Sen, 1984). I agree with that analysis, although I would add the stipulation that the rights play a special role: they are entitlements for each and every person, and if they are violated, or not secured, there is a failure of basic justice, which cannot be adequately captured in the language of cost-benefit analysis (Nussbaum, 2001). There is thus a tragic aspect to a rights violation (to the failure to secure a central human capability) that distinguishes it from other failures to secure some social benefit.

Thus my version of the CA can be seen as a cousin of consequentialism, in the sense that it is what I call 'outcome-oriented': whether the society is just is determined by looking at the outcomes it produces, importantly including whether it secures the central capabilities to all citizens. It is in that way distinct from procedural approaches to justice that determine whether a situation is just by looking at the procedures that generated it (see Nussbaum, 2005). It is, then, an outcome-oriented approach in which the securing of central capabilities plays a central role. Many human rights approaches have a similar structure, if they are developed as an overall account of political justice. Here, then, the CA seems to march in harmony with human rights approaches, even though it seems to be closer to consequentialism. As Sen has insisted, consequentialism need not be insensitive to the special importance of rights (Sen, 1984; see also Sen, 2004).

There is one way, however, in which my CA, albeit a cousin of consequentialism, is not a form of consequentialism. Consequentialism is an overall view of the good and right: it says that the rightness of any choice is measure by whether it maximizes good consequences. I have argued, however, following John Rawls, that in a pluralistic society, containing many different religious and secular comprehensive views of the good, it is undesirable and disrespectful to base political choice on any comprehensive doctrine (see Rawls, 1996; Nussbaum, 2000, 2005). Instead, political principles should be only a *partial* view of the social good, and one that can, we hope, become the object of an *overlapping consensus* among the major religious and secular comprehensive doctrines. I have argued that my CA, and the capabilities list, can become the object of such a consensus (Nussbaum, 2005).

The reason why I use the term 'outcome-oriented' rather than the term 'consequentialist' to describe my approach is that I view consequentialism as a comprehensive ethical theory and thus not (I hold) an acceptable source of political principles in a pluralistic society.

While we are on the topic of political liberalism, it may be time to clear up (again) a common misreading: *the CA is not a form of 'cosmopolitanism'* (Nussbaum, 2007b). Although the approach includes an account of global as well as domestic justice, it would be just mistaken to identify it with the comprehensive ethical theory known as 'cosmopolitanism,' which is usually defined as the view that one's first loyalty should be to humanity as a whole, rather than to one's nation, region, religion, or family. Cosmopolitans can probably accept most of what I recommend, but one does not have to be a cosmopolitan to accept the idea that all citizens (in one's nation, and then, in a second step, in all nations) should have a threshold amount of the ten capabilities. Most of the major comprehensive doctrines, religious and secular, can, I argue, accept that idea, and few of them could accept a comprehensive cosmopolitanism. Whether my own comprehensive ethical doctrine is cosmopolitan or not is a separate questions (it is not, but it is close). The point that is relevant here is that the CA is a political doctrine. As such, it should not recommend any comprehensive ethical doctrine or be built upon one. Thus calling the CA a form of cosmopolitanism is tantamount to saying that it does not respect the diversity of religious and secular doctrines that all modern nations contain. But respecting that plurality is a central aim of my theoretical approach.

There is one criticism of the human rights idea that I wish to resist: this was the claim once made by Sen that we should think of rights as part of a system of goals but not as having any power to 'trump' the pursuit of social welfare (Sen, 1984). I argued against this claim in detail in Nussbaum (1997), and I will not repeat my arguments here. Suffice it to say that the central capabilities on my list, like human rights, are 'trumps' in the sense that they have a very strong priority over the pursuit of welfare generally: if any one of them is not fulfilled, the nation is not even minimally just. Sen was arguing against Robert Nozick's account of property rights as 'trumps' stopping redistribution of wealth and income in society. I agree with Sen that Nozick's position is wrong, but I disagree about what is wrong with it. In my view, Nozick has the wrong account of property rights and ownership. We should not grant that people own what they happen to be holding on to: we should agree with Mill that, if some property is needed for the support of other people's basic entitlements, it is fine to take that property through taxation, and the person from whom it is allegedly taken did not even have just title to that property (see Nussbaum, 1997). Both capabilities and rights, then, are 'trumps,' and I reject Sen's claim that capabilities are more soft or negotiable than rights—at any rate, not the central capabilities on my list.

What role for rights language?

If we have the language of capabilities, do we also need the language of rights? The argument of this paper so far has defended the ongoing relevance and importance of the central concepts involved in the human rights tradition, since the CA, as I have defended it, is a species of the human rights approach. At this point, however, we still need to ask what the language of rights adds to the language of capabilities: why should we continue to employ both, if we are convinced, as I am, that a version of the CA preserves what is best in the human rights tradition and avoids some deficiencies that some versions of that approach at times slip into.

We might want to be pragmatists here: the language of human rights has such wide currency and resonance in global politics that it would be rather unwise to try to do away with it—all the more since the CA is just a species of that approach, not a rival. But it would be good if we could say something more about why the language of rights is independently useful and illuminating. I believe that we can.

The word 'capability' does not by itself suggest the idea of an urgently important entitlement grounded in an idea of basic justice. The rest of my theoretical approach makes this point, by invoking ideas of human dignity, basic justice, a threshold amount of opportunity, and so forth. But the idea that capabilities are not just optional needs to be hammered home in any way we can, since people are all too inclined to think that we may deny people this or that important thing in order to pursue aggregate wealth. Indeed, when we note that the dominant approach in development economics still measures quality of life in terms of Gross Domestic Product per capita, without asking whether these central individual entitlements have been secured, we can see why we should continue hammering.

Human rights language helps us perform that task (see also Sen, 2004). When used as in the sentence 'A has a right to have the basic political liberties secured to her by her government', the language of rights reminds us that people have justified and urgent claims to certain types of treatment, treatment that secures their central capabilities—no matter what the world around them has done about that. This is a key idea in my CA (although less clear in the more open-ended approach to entitlements mapped out in Sen, 1999). So I can welcome the focus and intensification given to these key ideas by the language of human (and animal) rights.

By now, too, the human rights tradition has built up a wide array of valuable documents that describe central human entitlements in ways that have gained the support of the world community. Political action has mobilized around these documents, national constitutions have been written under their influence, and so forth (see Sen, 2004). We should not junk that tradition, we should instead make sure that it is connected to an analysis of what rights are; the CA supplies that analysis. When coupled with the idea of capabilities, as in the *Human Development Reports* of the United Nations Development Programme, the idea of rights provides a valuable intensification, connecting the idea of capabilities to the idea of social and political urgency and human centrality. I would argue, then, that the capabilities theorist or practitioner should not be skeptical of the language of rights, but should employ it in close connection to the language of capabilities, thus making clear what analysis of rights is being offered.

The human rights tradition is a heroic struggle for basic justice. It would be foolhardy to turn away from that tradition. Nonetheless, the tradition has points of vagueness and unclarity: here the CA can supplement it usefully.

And it also has versions or offshoots that lead the mind away from important issues of justice. Here the CA supplies a valuable critique. The two approaches (one being a species of the other) should march forward as allies in the combat against an exclusive focus on economic growth, and for an approach to development that focuses on people's real needs and urgent entitlements.

Notes

1 As I discuss at the end of the 'Critique: Positive and Negative, Action and Inaction' section, this situation evolved dramatically in the late 1980s and early 1990s, although the feminist expansion of the terrain of rights remains contested, not least in the USA.
2 Sen (2004) seems to grant this point (see pp. 319 and 321); however, I argue in Nussbaum (2003) that in Sen (1999) he treats freedom as an all-purpose good, even something that ought to be maximized.
3 Declaration of Independence, 4 July 1776.
4 Not invariably: Article 14, closely modeled on the equal protection clause of the US Fourteenth Amendment, reads: 'The State shall not deny to any person equality before the law or the equal protection of the laws within the territory of India.'

References

Nussbaum, M. C. (1997) 'Capabilities and human rights', *Fordham Law Review,* 66, pp. 273–300.

Nussbaum, M. C. (2000) *Women and Human Development: The Capabilities Approach,* Cambridge University Press, Cambridge.

Nussbaum, M. C. (2001) 'The costs of tragedy: some moral limits of cost-benefit analysis', in M. D. Adler and E. A. Posner (Eds), *Cost-Benefit Analysis: Legal, Economic, and Philosophical Perspectives,* University of Chicago Press, Chicago, pp. 169–200.

Nussbaum, M. C. (2003) 'Capabilities as fundamental entitlements', *Feminist Economics,* 9, pp. 33–59.

Nussbaum, M. C. (2005) *Frontiers of Justice: Disability, Nationality, Species Membership,* Harvard University Press, Cambridge, MA.

Nussbaum, M. C. (2007a) 'Constitutions and capabilities: "perception" against lofty formalism', *Harvard Law Review,* 121, pp. 4–97.

Nussbaum, M. C. (2007b) 'The capabilities approach and ethical cosmopolitanism: a response to Noah Feldman', *The Pocket Part,* online supplement to *Yale Law Journal,* 30 October, [http://yalelawjournal.org/the-yale-law-journal-pocket-part/international-law/the-capabilities-approach-and-ethical-cosmopolitanism:-a-response-to-noah-feldman/], accessed 4 January 2011.

Nussbaum, M. C. (2008) 'Human dignity and political entitlements', in *Human Dignity and Bioethics: Essays Commissioned by the President's Council on Bioethics,* US government Printing Office, Washington, D.C, pp. 351–380.

Rawls, J. (1996) *Political Liberalism,* expanded paperback edition, Columbia University Press, New York.

Sen, A. (1984) 'Rights and capabilities', in *Resources, Values, and Development,* Blackwell, Oxford, pp. 307–324.

Sen, A. (1997) 'Human rights and Asian values', *The New Republic,* 14/21 July, pp. 33–40.

Sen, A. (1999) *Development as Freedom,* Knopf, New York.

Sen, A. (2004) 'Elements of a theory of human rights', *Philosophy and Public Affairs,* 32, pp. 315–356.

Wolff, J. and de-Shalit, A. (2007) *Disadvantage,* Oxford University Press, New York.

[5]

RIGHTS, CAPABILITIES, AND THE GOOD SOCIETY

*Robin West**

INTRODUCTION

What is a "good society," as opposed to a just one, and what is demanded of the state by the demand of "goodness" in a good society? Must a state in a good society ensure for its citizens the minimal material preconditions of a decent life? Is it obligated to do so? Many of course, think not, but of those who think there is such an obligation, there are a variety of reasons, or arguments proffered, as to why. One "civic republican" argument, revitalized over the last fifteen years by Michael Sandel,[1] is basically instrumental. A state, in a good society, might be obligated to ensure for its citizens some minimal level of material goods, but if so, it is required to do so in order to instill some threshold level of civic virtue: in a good society, citizens must be able to be free and equal participants in the collective project of self rule, and if some threshold level of material well-being is necessary for that participation, then the state is obligated to provide it.[2]

A quite different and perhaps more basic sort of response, held by scores of liberal, progressive, and radical legal theorists over the last century, as well as innumerable political activists and state actors, might be called a "welfarist" conception—the state, in a good society, is directly, not just instrumentally, obligated to ensure that all citizens enjoy some minimal threshold level of material well-being, or welfare, or met needs, or access to primary goods.[3] They must enjoy this minimal threshold, furthermore, *not* because such a threshold is necessary to the exercise of the various civic virtues required of them

---

* Professor of Law, Georgetown University Law Center.

1. *See* Michael J. Sandel, Democracy's Discontent: America in Search of a Public Philosophy (1996) [hereinafter Sandel, Democracy's Discontent].

2. *Id.* at 124-28, 329-38.

3. *See, e.g.*, Frank I. Michelman, *Constitutional Welfare Rights: One View of Rawls' Theory of Justice*, 121 U. Pa. L. Rev. 962 (1973) [hereinafter, Michelman, *Constitutional Welfare Rights*]; Frank I. Michelman, *The Supreme Court 1968 Term–Forward: On Protecting the Poor Through the Fourteenth Amendment*, 83 Harv. L. Rev. 7 (1969) [hereinafter Michelman, *On Protecting the Poor*]. The welfarist conception is heavily indebted to John Rawls' early work, particularly *A Theory of Justice* (1971).

if they are to participate as free and equals in a liberal state, nor for any other instrumental reason.[4] More basically, the state must ensure some minimal level of well-being because such a threshold is necessary if citizens are to live fully human lives and have the dignity to which their humanity entitles them.[5] Many citizens of even prosperous democratic states cannot possibly enjoy such a minimal threshold, furthermore, without some state involvement in the distribution of resources, particularly with the inequalities that persist and threaten to worsen today.[6] States are required, by justice and goodness both, to treat citizens with dignity, and with equal dignity at that. Therefore, welfarists conclude, the state is obligated to do whatever it takes to provide that minimal level of well-being to each of its citizens.[7]

In a number of books and articles over the last ten years, Martha Nussbaum and Amartya Sen have carved out a third position, which, they argue, is in greater accord with liberal commitments to individual autonomy, and particularly the autonomous right of individuals to determine their own conceptions of the good.[8] The state, Nussbaum and Sen argue, as a matter of goodness and justice both, must not ensure minimal welfare directly—that would indeed be unduly paternalistic, illiberal, and in important respects, impossible: a state cannot ensure, say, a healthy, long life for each citizen.[9] Rather, a decent and liberal state in a good society must ensure that citizens achieve and enjoy certain fundamental human *capabilities* (thereby leaving to the citizens the choice whether or not to avail themselves of those capabilities)—including the capability to live a safe, well-nourished, productive, educated, social, and politically and culturally participatory life of normal length.[10] Thus, to be "fully human," Nussbaum argues, and to be possessed of the full dignity that one's humanity implies, just *is* to enjoy this minimal threshold level of capability.[11] If they are to have fully human lives, citizens must have access to, and the capability to attain, non-alienating, non-discriminatory and non-humiliating work.[12] They must have, or have the capability to acquire, various welfare goods such as decent health

4. *See e.g.*, Sandel, Democracy's Discontent, *supra* note 1, at 330-32.

5. *See e.g.*, Michelman, *On Protecting the Poor*, *supra* note 3, at 13-14.

6. *Id.* at 13-15.

7. *Id.*

8. *See* Martha Nussbaum, Women and Human Development 11-15, 111-61 (2000) [hereinafter Nussbaum, Women and Human Development]; Amartya Sen, Rights as Goals, *in* Equality and Discrimination: Essays in Freedom and Justice 14-19 (Stephen Guest & Alan Milne eds., 1985).

9. Nussbaum, Women and Human Development, *supra* note 8, at 51-60, 81; Sen, *supra* note 8, at 15-16.

10. Nussbaum, Women and Human Development, *supra* note 8, at 75-83; Sen, *supra* note 8, at 16.

11. Nussbaum, Women and Human Development, *supra* note 8, at 75-83.

12. *Id.*

care, adequate food, shelter, and clothing.[13] They must have a good and liberal education, a safe upbringing, protection against physical and sexual assault, and security in their intimate and affiliative associations. Citizens must have access to the material preconditions of these capabilities, if they are to have the ability to live fully human lives.[14]

Furthermore, Nussbaum argues, for many or even all of us, these preconditions cannot be met without considerable state and community assistance, or more pointedly, without considerable state-run redistribution and regulation.[15] These are not preconditions readily satisfied in either a state of nature or a minimally regulated social order. A good society, therefore, Nussbaum concludes, *and* a liberal, just society, is one in which the state is not just permitted, but is obligated to ensure, on behalf of its citizens, that these material preconditions of our fundamental human capabilities are met.[16] All states, particularly liberal states, ought to regard their obligation to secure the preconditions of basic human capabilities as fundamental and as required by justice.[17] Liberal states should regard their obligation to secure the minimal material preconditions of the basic human capabilities to be a basic *constitutional* duty.[18]

I do not want to take issue with the basic welfarist version of the good society thesis, or with Nussbaum's more liberal, antipaternalist, "capabilities-based" (rather than primary goods-based) approach. Rather, I assume the welfarist thesis, and for reasons that I think will become clear, I take Nussbaum's "capabilities" approach to be its best account. In this essay, I want instead to re-open what some might regard as a stale question: whether individual, constitutional rights, as they have been understood by liberal theorists, and as they have been employed and are now employed in various constitutional liberal democracies, might be a vehicle for securing those state obligations. Briefly, if justice and goodness require that liberal states have an obligation to secure the minimal preconditions of our fundamentally human capabilities, as Nussbaum argues, and also require that states respect citizens' rights, as countless liberals assert, then doesn't it follow that citizens in liberal states have a right to enjoy those capabilities, and a right to a state obligated to commit itself to ensuring them? More to the point, does it not follow that welfare or capabilities advocates should be arguing as much?

In the last twenty-five years, a sort of conventional wisdom has emerged, at least in the legal academy, that the answer to both of

13. *Id.*; Sen, *supra* note 8, at 15-16.
14. Nussbaum, Women and Human Development, *supra* note 8, at 86-87.
15. *Id.* at 54-55, 91.
16. *Id.* at 74-75, 89-90.
17. *Id.*
18. *Id.* at 74.

these questions must be "no." According to Amartya Sen himself,[19] some liberal rights theorists,[20] scores of "rights critics" from the critical legal studies movement,[21] and a handful of Sandelian critics of liberal proceduralism who are committed to some version of a welfarist conception of the good society,[22] liberal rights, for better or for worse, but virtually by definition, are all obstacles to, rather than a possible vehicle for, any welfarist effort—even Nussbaum's liberalized, capabilities-based version. There is good reason for this remarkably widespread consensus. Liberal-constitutional rights, as they are now conventionally understood and authoritatively interpreted, at least in the United States, do not obligate the state to ensure anything resembling what welfarist "good society" advocates envision, whether put in terms of primary goods, civic virtue, or fundamental human capabilities—or at least, they have never been construed that way.

Worse, liberal constitutional rights, as they are sometimes authoritatively interpreted in this country and others, actually *limit* the state's authority to take action to secure the material preconditions of the good society. According to some strands of liberal rights theory as construed by at least some United States constitutional and legal theorists, individual rights on the one hand, and the state's obligation to ensure the minimal material preconditions of either well-being, civic virtue, or capabilities on the other, do not support one another but rather inevitably collide. And individual rights trump state's obligations. Essentially and inevitably then, liberal rights undercut, rather than support, efforts to even conceive, much less achieve, an obligatory state role to secure general well-being. As liberal rights expand, any state role, including any

19. *See* Sen, *supra* note 8, at 11, 19. Nussbaum is more ambivalent. Although she has addressed the relationship between capabilities approaches to liberalism and human rights, and has elsewhere described the obligation of states to provide for minimal capabilities as "constitutional," she does not directly argue that citizens in liberal states have a constitutional right to the minimal material conditions of fundamental human capabilities. *See* Martha C. Nussbaum, *Capabilities and Human Rights*, 66 Fordham L. Rev. 273, 287-88 (1997); *see also* Nussbaum, Women and Human Development, *supra* note 8, at 97-101.

20. *See, e.g.*, Richard A. Epstein, Takings: Private Property and the Power of Eminent Domain 295 (1985).

21. For a sampling of the voluminous literature criticizing rights on these and related grounds, see, e.g., Mary E. Becker, *The Politics of Women's Wrongs and the Bill of "Rights": A Bicentennial Perspective*, 59 U. Chi. L. Rev. 453, 454 (1992); Peter Gabel, *The Phenomenology of Rights-Consciousness and the Pact of the Withdrawn Selves*, 62 Tex. L. Rev. 1563, 1595-97 (1984); Morton J. Horwitz, *Rights*, 23 Harv. C.R.-C.L. L. Rev. 393, 402-04 (1988); Mark Tushnet, *An Essay on Rights*, 62 Tex. L. Rev. 1363, 1386-92 (1984).

22. William A. Galston, *Political Economy and the Politics of Virtue: U.S. Public Philosophy at Century's End*, *in* Debating Democracy's Discontent: Essays on American Politics, Law, and Public Philosophy 63, 74-77 (Anita L. Allen & Milton C. Regan, Jr. eds., 1998).

obligatory role, contracts. This result would hold were well-being defined in terms of capabilities rather than basic human goods or civic virtue. The good society, and the state's obligation to ensure that citizens have access to the minimal capabilities necessary to participate in it, must then be both conceived and achieved by recourse to some means other than rights.

In Part I this essay explores and then criticizes the two major arguments behind the conventional wisdom that rights undermine efforts to secure a state role in ensuring the material preconditions for a good society, and therefore, the material preconditions for the development of those human capabilities essential to a fully human life. I conclude in this part that this understanding of rights is mistaken.

In Part II, I urge that the pragmatic argument put forward by rights critics and some welfare advocates for forgoing rights-talk and rights-rhetoric also fails: there are very real costs, both in theory and in law, in deciding to forgo putting the case for the state's obligation to provide minimal material goods in terms of rights.

In Part III, I briefly describe two core rights that a refashioned liberal state, understood as a vehicle for protecting not just the liberty but also the capabilities of citizens, should recognize: first, a right to be protected against private violence, and second, a right of caregivers to give care to dependents without incurring the risk of severe impoverishment or subordination—a right, to use the provocative phrase coined by the philosopher Eva Kittay, to *doulia*.[23] Both rights, I think, are directly entailed by the state's obligation to provide the minimal preconditions for the development of those fundamental human capabilities that are themselves essential to a fully human life. Both rights however, could be and should be conceived in the most traditionally liberal terms. The first such right—the right to protection against private violence—although now disfavored in United States rights discourse, seems fully authorized by both the liberal tradition and the American Constitution itself. The second right for which I will argue—the right to provide care to dependents—has no similar basis of support in either liberal theory or American constitutionalism. It is not incompatible with either, however, and is at least arguably required by the deepest commitments of both. The right to protection and the right to care are rights that can be framed in liberal terms, and both rights would go a long way toward securing for individual citizens the minimal preconditions of a good society.

23. Eva Feder Kittay, Love's Labor: Essays on Women, Equality, and Dependency 70 (1999).

I. NEGATIVE RIGHTS AND THE GOOD SOCIETY

A. *Liberal Rights*

Liberal, constitutional rights, according to their legions of critics and numerous rights theorists, undercut any state obligation to secure the preconditions for the fundamental human capabilities for two basic and interconnected reasons. The first is political. The good society, as envisioned by virtually all "good society" theorists, requires substantial state intervention into various "private" spheres, and substantial redistribution of the goods, resources, and power found in those spheres.[24] Liberal rights, as defended and constructed by contemporary constitutional theorists and jurists both, limit the power of states to do precisely that.[25] Were a state to go about the task of ensuring the material preconditions of a good life for all, or, in the Nussbaumian version of the same idea, ensuring the preconditions for the capabilities which are themselves requisite to a "fully human life," it would have to break down the walls of insularity that liberal rights, both in theory and to a considerable degree in practice, protect. To secure the minimal preconditions of the good society for all of us, the state would have to violate the *rights* we hold as individuals—rights of liberty, property, contract, and privacy. Indeed, not only do we lack a "right" to a state obligated to ensure minimal preconditions of a good society—whether the "good society" is as envisioned by Karl Marx, John Dewey, Michael Sandel, Frank Michelman, William Forbath, or Martha Nussbaum—but if anything, we have a right to a state that does not *attempt* to ensure that the material preconditions of a good society are met. Rights protect us against the paternalistic state that might otherwise regard the "good society" as its business.

Furthermore, rights deter the creation of a state interested in good society ambitions by structural design, not because they are misused by Machiavellian political actors. In many liberal states, and virtually by definition in the United States, rights are overwhelmingly negative. We have whatever rights we have, against the state, and against the

24. Most famously, of course, Rawls argued that liberal states are obligated to redistribute toward equality up to the point where remaining inequalities benefit the least well off. John Rawls, A Theory of Justice 100-02 (1971); *see also* Nussbaum, Women and Human Development, *supra* note 8, at 55, 91-95, 105 (comparing redistributive measures in India and the United States); Sandel, Democracy's Discontent, *supra* note 1, at 255-56 (discussing Franklin D. Rooselvelt's tax proposals of 1935); William E. Forbath, *Caste, Class, and Equal Citizenship*, 98 Mich. L. Rev. 1, 8 (1999) (reviewing the legal arguments regarding redistributive rights and remedies); Michelman, *Constitutional Welfare Rights*, *supra* note 3, at 966 (discussing "specific welfare guaranty"); Michelman, *On Protecting the Poor*, *supra* note 3, at 9 (discussing "minimum welfare").

25. *See, e.g.*, Epstein, *supra* note 20, at 337-38; Robert Nozick, Anarchy, State, and Utopia 26-53 (1974). *See generally*, Horwitz, *supra* note 21 (discussing the concept of constitutional rights as developed by the courts since the 1930s).

state's actions, and against the state's actors; we do not have rights that positively obligate the state to do something. We do not have rights that require, rather than forbid, the state to take some action. It is, of course, because we have rights against the state (and only against the state) rather than rights to some particular sort of state action or state intervention, that rights protect the individual against an overreaching state in the manner celebrated by rights advocates. But it is also because of their negativity that rights preclude the state from taking any role in securing to citizens the material preconditions of the good society.

Negative rights thus disempower the state from pernicious, intermeddling, paternalistic, or malign intervention into the private affairs of individual citizens. By virtue of so doing, however, negative rights also disempower the state from intervening into the private sphere for the democratically progressive purpose of redistributing power or resources within it. Negative rights elevate or empower the citizen relative to an overreaching, paternalistic state. Yet by staying the paternalist's intervening hand, negative rights both subordinate that citizen to his stronger brother—thereby entrenching private inequalities—and disable the state from securing, on behalf of weaker citizens, the material preconditions to developing the capabilities necessary to a fully human life. Good society theorists, rights critics, and a number of liberal rights theorists, have all concluded from this argument that rights, as conceived and employed in at least United States liberal and constitutional jurisprudence, are fundamentally at odds with any purported state obligation to ensure the material preconditions of a good society. If this conclusion is correct, then it obviously holds for a capabilities approach to welfarism as well. If so, the state's obligation to promote conditions that secure the minimal capabilities essential to a fully human life, even if such an obligation exists, would have to be secured by some means other than individual rights.

But is this analysis correct? Perhaps not: the conclusion seems overbroad on three counts. First, there is nothing about a right that *logically* requires that it be understood as a constraint on state action, forbidding interference with individual spheres of privacy or liberty, rather than as a state obligation entitling the individual to state intervention in the name of welfare, capabilities, or basic goods. The notion of a positive right may be disfavored in contemporary liberal discourse, but it is by no means oxymoronic. Ronald Dworkin, in his seminal, mid-seventies writings on liberal constitutional rights, did focus—indeed overwhelmingly—upon rights that follow from the moral constraints on liberal states.[26] But he suggested no reason to

26. Ronald Dworkin, Taking Rights Seriously vii-xv, 184-205 (1977) [hereinafter Dworkin, Taking Rights Seriously].

define rights in such a way, and at any rate, nothing in the remainder of his powerful jurisprudential treatment of rights depends on it. A right could readily be defined as including *both* the individual entitlement that follows from the moral *obligations* of liberal states and the entitlement that follows from constraints upon the states. In other words, rights could be defined as the individual entitlements that follow from what states are morally required to do *and* what liberal states are morally prohibited from doing.[27] Doing so, furthermore, would seem to be consistent with the robust Kantian moral imperative that, according to both Dworkin and Nussbaum, underlies liberalism: that every individual must be accorded equal dignity, equal concern, and equal respect.[28] To accord all individuals dignity, concern, and respect, sometimes requires the state to refrain from acting, and sometimes requires it to act.

The connection, in other words, between the liberal idea of rights and the constraint of negativity is contingent, not inherently logical. Thus, rights have at different times and for different subcultures in American history, been widely understood as positive rather than negative in character. To conceive of rights as either positive or negative, depending upon contingent political necessity, would be consistent with those perhaps forgotten parts of our histories.[29] It would also be consistent with common usage in much of the rest of the world. Any number of liberal states, as Mary Ann Glendon and others have amply demonstrated, recognize positive rights, although not always in conjunction with the entailment of judicial enforcement and remedies for their breach.[30] Nevertheless, the rights so recognized have political meaning and impact, and more to the point, the societies that recognize them do not noticeably sacrifice their liberality by doing so. Again, the connection between rights and negativity inheres in American history. It does not follow from the nature of a right itself.

Second, a recognition that rights might sometimes be positive entitlements to state action, as well as, at other times, negative entitlements to be free of state action, is *truer* to the philosophical liberal classics that animate the liberal tradition than the insistence of liberal constitutional rights theorists on the essential negativity of rights. Let me start with Thomas Hobbes. Hobbes regarded the positive *obligation* of the state to protect individuals against private

27. Dworkin suggests as much. *See id.* at 193.

28. *See id.* at 180-83, 272-78; Nussbaum, Women and Human Development, *supra* note 8, at 73.

29. *See, e.g.*, Akhil Reed Amar, *Forty Acres and a Mule: A Republican Theory of Minimal Entitlements*, 13 Harv. J.L. & Pub. Pol'y 37, 39 (1990); Elizabeth B. Clark, *Religion, Rights, and Difference in the Early Woman's Rights Movement*, 3 Wis. Women's L.J. 29, 46-53 (1987); Forbath, *supra* note 24, at 4-5.

30. *See* Mary Ann Glendon, *Rights in Twentieth-Century Constitutions*, 59 U. Chi. L. Rev. 519, 521, 523-30 (1992).

violence as being at the heart of the social contract. The individual's right to that protection was the only "right" created by the transition from nature into civil society. Otherwise, the Hobbesian Leviathan can do what it wishes and the individual citizen must submit—the Hobbesian citizen does indeed lack negative rights. This is *not so*, however, with respect to the state's duty to protect the individual against private violence: there, the state is bound to act affirmatively, and the individual is fully entitled to a positive right. This positive right of the citizen to the state's affirmative action was by no means a peripheral feature of Hobbes' jurisprudence. Rather, the bargain struck—the individual relinquishes self help, *in exchange for* the state's obligation to protect him from violence—was, for Hobbes, the raison d'être of the state's existence. The Leviathan's protection of the individual against the private violence of others is the quid pro quo for the individual's relinquishment of his right to self-help available to him in the state of nature.[31] The individual, in other words, is just as contractually entitled to receive that protection as the state is obligated to provide it—in short, the citizen has a right to it. The state's obligation to protect the citizen against private violence and the citizen's continuing right to receive it, in Hobbes' view, was foundational and inalienable. If we take Hobbes seriously, the individual has a right to the state's protection against the violence or aggression of other private parties—for Hobbes, this was, to borrow a phrase from Steven Heyman's important article on this point, the "first duty of government."[32]

If we again take Hobbes seriously, the right to that protection is positive in character. The state is required to do something—to protect the individual—not just to refrain from doing something. If Hobbes was right about this, which I think he was, and if this very positive right to protection against private violence is central, rather than peripheral, to the metaphoric "social contract" so fundamental to liberalism, then the distinctively modern claim that liberal rights are *essentially* negative—whether insisted by rights proponents, rights critics, Fourth Circuit or Seventh Circuit Judges, or Supreme Court Justices—is mistaken, and even perverse. At least according to Thomas Hobbes, the core, foundational right to which the liberal state owes its existence is indisputably positive in character.

And what of Locke? As Epstein and other property rights advocates rightly insist,[33] Locke substantially modified the Hobbesian picture. For Locke, but not for Hobbes, the individual brings to the civil state rights of property bestowed by nature, which have the effect

31. Thomas Hobbes, Leviathan 165 (J.M. Dent & Sons Ltd. 1928) (1651).

32. Steven J. Heyman, *The First Duty of Government: Protection, Liberty and the Fourteenth Amendment*, 41 Duke L.J. 507, 508 (1991).

33. Epstein, *supra* note 20, at 7-10.

of significantly limiting state sovereignty.[34] The tying of modern liberalism to these "negative rights" that bar the state from acting in various impermissible ways stems from Locke's writings, roughly in the way Epstein describes.[35] But Locke at no point *repudiated* the Hobbesian positive right of the citizen to state protection against private violence. In fact, he expressly endorsed and expanded it. For Locke, the citizen has the right to expect and demand more from the state than just protection against violence, he also has the right to expect governance in accordance with rules, and indifferent and impartial adjudication.[36] At no point, though, does Locke urge that the core, Hobbesian, positive right to the protection of the state should be displaced with a set of negative rights limiting state power. He urged, rather, that the relation of state and citizen be construed as constituted by both. The individual gives up natural powers of dominion, punishment, and adjudication, while the state acquires the power to administer these functions, but only toward proper ends.[37] The citizen, from a Lockean perspective and a Hobbesian perspective, has rights, logically positive in character, to a state that acts in ways conducive to his safety, not just negative rights to insist on restraints.

Other prominent liberal theorists have also quite explicitly embraced the joint claims that the state has positive obligations and the individual has positive rights, and have expanded the list well beyond the Hobbesian positive right to protection against private violence. John Stuart Mill and John Dewey both insisted upon what we would today recognize as liberal welfare rights to the minimal preconditions of a good life, broadly construed. According to Mill and Dewey, the individual has rights the liberal state must recognize and act on, not only to safety and food and shelter, but also to meaningful work, a decent and liberal education, and participation in society's political, civic, and cultural life.[38] Even Isaiah Berlin, perhaps the harshest twentieth century critic of positive rights, stated in his celebrated essay on the topic that his fears of overintrusive states did not go so far as to obliterate the state's positive obligation to ensure, and the individual's positive right to receive, a threshold level of minimal well-being.[39] Indeed, there may be *no* important *classical* liberal theorist either of "rights" or of states, prior to the libertarian interventions of Robert Nozick and his followers that insists on the tie

34. *Id.* at 7-15.
35. *See id.*
36. John Locke, An Essay Concerning the True Original, Extent and End of Civil Government §§ 128-31 (Henry Regnery Co. 1949) (1690).
37. *Id.*
38. *See* John Dewey, Liberalism and Social Action (Capricorn Books 1963) (1935); John Stuart Mill, *Utilitarianism*, *in* Utilitarianism, Liberty and Representative Government 66-67 (E.P. Dutton & Co. 1950) (1863).
39. Isaiah Berlin, *Two Concepts of Liberty*, *in* Four Essays on Liberty 123-24, 164-65, 169 (1969).

between rights and negativity that has become such an entrenched part of the contemporary American constitutional mindset.

Third, the negativity of rights is neither required nor justified by the American Constitution, as a number of constitutional theorists and historians have now shown.[40] This is a large debate beyond the scope of this symposium, but two points are worth quickly noting here. The first is logical. The widely shared conviction that "the American Constitution is one of negative rights only" seems to rest largely on the mistaken assumption that because the Constitution's Bill of Rights addresses States, and not private actors, it therefore only consists of negative rights.[41] The state action requirement, in other words, is said to preclude not only the possibility that the Constitution reaches private actors as well as state actors, but also that the Constitution cannot reach state *in*action as well as state action. But this inference is unwarranted. Regardless of whether the Constitution contains a "state action" requirement that limits the Constitution's reach to state actors, it does not follow from such a requirement that the rights contained are necessarily negative in character. A positive right, no less than a negative right, would be directed at states and not private actors. The difference between them is that a positive right would condemn as unconstitutional state *in*action rather than state action, not that it would extend the Constitution's reach to private actors. The difference between positive and negative rights, in other words, is *not* that the former would impose constitutional constraints on private actors.

And finally, both the history and the plain language support rather than undercut the existence—even the prominence—of positive rights in the Constitution. The plain language of the text of the Fourteenth Amendment contemplates state *in*action rather than action as its main target. The first sentence of Section 1 declares that "No State shall *deny*" various entitlements. It may be unfortunate that the drafters chose to use a double negative, but the meaning is not obscure. If *no* state is allowed to deny, then all states must provide. And what states must provide, again according to the clause's plain text, is protection of the law—and equal protection at that. Historically, the Amendment's insistence that states must provide protection of the law was the result, in part, of the inaction of the states to protect both the safety and civil rights of freed slaves.[42] The Fourteenth Amendment,

40. Susan Bandes, *The Negative Constitution: A Critique*, 88 Mich. L. Rev. 2271, 2308-27 (1990); Heyman, *supra* note 32, at 526.

41. The clearest explication of this mistaken conception is found in Judge Posner's decision in *Bowers v. DeVito*, 686 F.2d 616, 618 (7th Cir. 1982). The opinion states, "The Constitution is a charter of negative liberties; it tells the state to let people alone." *Id.* Tribe makes the same criticism of this view as is found in this essay. Laurence H. Tribe, Constitutional Choices 247 (1985).

42. *See* Jacobus TenBroek, Equal Under Law 57-58 (First Collier Books 1965) (1951).

in short, plainly provides for positive individual rights and explicit state obligations both.

B. *Rights' Atomism*

The second major way in which rights undercut efforts to secure a state obligation to ensure the minimal material preconditions of those human capabilities themselves requisite to the enjoyment of a fully human life, according to our major rights critics and good society theorists, is *existential*: it goes to how rights envision and then construct our self-identity. Rights and rights-consciousness render us unduly atomized. In liberal societies that take rights seriously, individuals are described as, and then tragically become, isolated from each other in individualized rights-spun cocoons, increasingly incapable of even approaching each other, much less achieving any meaningful moral or political empathic connections with fellow citizens.[43] No less than their negativity, rights' atomism also undercuts attempts to secure the material preconditions for the basic human capabilities in three ways.

First, for there to be a state obligation to provide for minimal capabilities requisite to a fully human life, at least in a democratic state in which state actors, and hence the "state" itself, are some subset of citizens, there must exist the political *will* for it. That will, in turn, requires some degree of communal solidarity among citizens. Rights, however, disincline us to even regard each other, much less assume responsibility for each others' welfare. Rights erode rather than enhance our feelings of obligation toward our neighbors, co-citizens, and arguably even our intimates and family members. Rights leave us identified with our possessions, rather than with each other. For that reason alone, they seriously undercut the empathic solidarity necessary to sustain a democratic case for a state obligation to provide for the well-being of others.

Second, at least some of the material preconditions of human capabilities which a good state is obligated to provide are those preconditions for our capability for social affiliation or connection with others, and mutual and moral responsibility for each others' well being.[44] To live a fully human life, according to Nussbaum and others, *means* in part to have the capability to live responsibly and safely with

43. *See* Sandel, Democracy's Discontent, *supra* note 1, at 16-17; Gabel, *supra* note 21, at 1572-76; Glendon, *supra* note 30, at 520-23; Michael J. Sandel, *The Constitution of the Procedural Republic: Liberal Rights and Civic Virtues*, 66 Fordham L. Rev. 1, 4-6 (1997) [hereinafter, Sandel, *Constitution of the Procedural Republic*]; Michael J. Sandel, *Moral Argument and Liberal Toleration: Abortion and Homosexuality*, 77 Cal. L. Rev. 521, 523-25 (1989) [hereinafter Sandel, *Moral Argument and Liberal Toleration*].

44. Nussbaum, Women and Human Development, *supra* note 8, at 79.

and for others, at work, at home, and in the community.[45] The capability for doing just that, then, is part of what a just state is obligated to ensure, if the state is obligated to ensure the minimal material preconditions of a good society. The atomism that is at the core of liberal understandings of rights, however, implies at most an atomistic individual in need of rights of isolation, of privacy, and of individuation; not rights that might stem from a frank recognition of our social or relational nature. In terms of capabilities, current rights rhetoric implies that the capability for autonomy is the core capability in need of protection through rights, to the virtual exclusion of relational capabilities. Because of the power of modern individualistic rights rhetoric, we not only lack "relational rights" that might bolster our social capabilities, but we become disinclined to even envision or argue for them. In an atomistic rights culture, we come to view ourselves, and then increasingly come to be, possessors of individual rights against each other and the state. We are not only without any responsibilities toward others, but also without any rights to ensure that we have the capabilities to safely exercise those responsibilities toward others. As a result, we come to identify our "rights"—our most precious political entitlements, and hence our political identity—as rights to individuate and distance or sever ourselves from, rather than rights to safely connect or relate to, our families, intimates, communities, or co-citizens.

Third, for the state to have an obligation to ensure the minimal preconditions for the development of fundamental human capabilities themselves essential to a fully human life, the state obviously cannot be entirely "neutral" toward competing conceptions of the good life. It must, rather, be committed to a vision of the good as defined by those human capabilities, and obligated to achieve it. But the same atomistic understanding of individual nature that drives liberalism's commitment to individualistic rights also is behind its signature insistence on state neutrality toward competing conceptions of the good life. Because we each individually and idiosyncratically author our own understanding of the good—the state, or the community, or the collective, is obviously incapacitated from doing so on our behalf.[46] The resulting insistence on state neutrality toward competing conceptions of the good renders liberalism, as a politics, peculiarly moot on issues regarding the nature of the good society and incapacitated in the task of bringing it to fruition. The result is not only alienated individuals, but also a sterile reluctance on the part of

45. *Id.*

46. Sandel draws out the implications of this connection most clearly. *See* Sandel, Democracy's Discontent, *supra* note 1, at 25-54; Michael Sandel, *A Reply to Critics*, *in* Debating Democracy's Discontent: Essays on American Politics, Law, and Public Philosophy 319, 319-23 (Anita L. Allen & Milton C. Regan, Jr. eds., 1998) [hereinafter Sandel, *A Reply to Critics*].

liberal states to endorse some conceptions of the good over others, even where such a commitment seems warranted and in the national interest. More fundamentally, it leaves the liberal state with no role to play, even in theory, in the creation of a good society. The individual has a "right" not to the material preconditions of a good life, but to a state fundamentally disinterested in committing itself to that project. For this existential, identity-based reason as well, then, rights critics and welfarists have concluded that "rights-talk" is a part of the problem rather than part of the solution. Rights construct us in such a way as to guarantee our disinterest or hostility toward any state obligation to ensure the good society, and the "we" that is disinterested or hostile to such a project is the "we" that would have to be charged with the duty to carry it out. If this conclusion is right, then it surely holds for welfarist approaches that center capabilities, rather than primary goods or virtue, as that which triggers and defines the state's obligation.

But is it right? This existential argument also seems overbroad. There is even less reason to think that rights, in order to be liberal rights, must be based on a falsely atomistic account of our nature than to think that rights, in order to be liberal rights, must be invariably negative. Rights, in the liberal tradition, are justified by and emanate from some conception of our human nature,[47] but there is nothing in the rights tradition per se that obligates it to honor a *false* conception of our nature. Indeed, although classical liberals undoubtedly highlighted our autonomy and our individuality, the centrality of the "right to be left alone" to the rights tradition, and the neurotic understanding of our atomistic nature on which such a right rests, is a late nineteenth and early twentieth century invention. Such a view is not "central" to liberalism and not required by the logic of rights; it is

47. *See generally* Dworkin, Taking Rights Seriously, *supra* note 26 (arguing that rights derive from membership in the human community and the concept of political equality). A serious regard for rights, Dworkin argues, rests on "the vague but powerful idea of human dignity... [which] supposes that there are ways of treating a man that are inconsistent with recognizing him as a full member of the human community, and holds that such treatment is profoundly unjust." *Id.* at 198. H.L.A. Hart and others have noted that Dworkin does not specify a sufficiently thick view of human nature to sustain a strong case for any particular set of rights, thus distinguishing him from classical liberal rights theorists such as Mill. *See* H.L.A. Hart, *Between Utility and Rights, in* Ronald Dworkin and Contemporary Jurisprudence 214, 218 (Marshall Cohen ed., 1983). Nevertheless, Dworkin directly rests his defense of the idea of rights itself on an appeal to a conception of human life, which he himself labels "Kantian," and from which the basic rights to equal concern and respect are directly derived. *Dworkin*, Taking Rights Seriously, *supra* note 26, at 198-99. For further examples of rights arguments that rely to varying degrees on specified accounts of human nature, see, e.g., Laurence H. Tribe, American Constitutional Law 1302-08 (2d ed. 1988); Thomas C. Grey, *Eros, Civilization and the Burger Court*, 43 Law & Contemp. Probs., 83 Summer 1980; David A. J. Richards, *Sexual Autonomy and the Constitutional Right to Privacy: A Case Study in Human Rights and the Unwritten Constitution*, 30 Hastings L.J. 957, 964-72 (1979).

central to liberal states, only to the extent that the state, the Constitution, or the tradition that defines the content of the rights we actually have, designate it as such. Rights could as readily be grounded in a view of our nature that respects our individuality and also gives full recognition to our social nature: our extended periods of biological dependence on caregivers, the resulting dependence of those caregivers on the support of others, our obligations to our communities and neighborhoods, our civic and charitable duties, and our responsibilities to engage in civic life. In short, neither negativity nor atomism are necessary features of the rights tradition.

II. THE COSTS OF ABANDONING RIGHTS

So—why insist that they are? And what are the costs of doing so? Some of the earliest and harshest critics of rights, particularly from the critical legal studies movement, at various points conceded or insisted upon the possibility of precisely the reformulation that I am suggesting above.[48] Nevertheless, those same rights critics have urged abandonment, not a reformulation, of rights and rights discourse. The reason given for that urged abandonment, for the most part, has been largely strategic or pragmatic, rather than theoretical or visionary. It has also had quite an impact. Welfarist theorists have seemingly turned their backs on rights as a possible vehicle for achieving (or even articulating) the state obligations that they think are owed.

The argument roughly is this: rights, according to the most far-reaching critics, are (almost) invariably negative,[49] and (almost) inevitably tied to a falsely insular conception of individual nature.[50] They are also (almost) infinitely malleable, or indeterminate, and accordingly easily co-opted, or subject to capture.[51] For both reasons, while they may from time to time guarantee a measure of individual freedom, they also—and (almost) inexorably—are co-opted by larger forces and reformulated, so as to frustrate rather than promote the good society. However they are initially conceived, and with whatever good intentions and progressive motivations, rights end up insulating inequalities, disabling the state from redistributive regulatory governance, benefitting the privileged, giving false hope and a false sense of security to the subordinated, teaching complicity in one's own disempowerment, and holding out the possibility of small progressive steps forward only toward the end of co-opting their beneficiaries, and ultimately securing large steps back. There is nothing to gain and quite a bit to lose by even envisioning a

48. Gabel, Tushnet, and Horwitz all insisted on the contingency rather than the necessity of rights' negativity and atomism. *See* Gabel, *supra* note 21, at 1586-90; Horwitz, *supra* note 21, at 404-06; Tushnet, *supra* note 21, at 1379-80.

49. *See* Horwitz, *supra* note 21, at 399-400; Tushnet, *supra* note 21, at 1386-94.

50. Gabel, *supra* note 21, at 1566-71.

51. Horwitz, *supra* note 21, at 396-99; Tushnet, *supra* note 21, at 1371-84.

progressive or positive alternative rights agenda, much less striving to put one in place. The idea that we might profit from a reformulation of rights as positive and honoring our social rather than asocial nature, is worse than a harmless utopian chimera; it is a dangerous delusion. If put in practice, it promises at most a pointless diversion of resources. At worst, it promises continuing liberal complicity in the work of injustice. It will leave us farther from, not closer to, a good society, and farther from, not closer to, a state obligated to commit itself to that end.

This is not a groundless worry. There is plenty in our recent and not so recent history that explains the rights critics' most extreme forms of rights skepticism. The rhetoric from the last great American rights revolution—the civil rights movements of the fifties and sixties—has indeed become the shell of the reactionary anti-affirmative action movement of the eighties, nineties and aughts. The reproductive rights movement of the mid and late twentieth century has similarly become nothing but a bare commodificationist right to purchase an abortion, rather than a positive entitlement to exercise meaningful autonomy or choice in one's reproductive life.[52] Negative rights of free speech—fervently sought after by dissenters as a way to protect the interests and liberties of persecuted pacifists, anarchists, and communists at mid-century—have become, at the turn of the century, the vehicle by which advertisers manipulate public desire with impunity, and corporate wealth maintains its headlock on the levers of political decision-making.[53] The peculiarly American so-called "right to bear arms," intended to protect the rights of colonial citizens against a centralized, distant military force, has become instead the means by which citizens terrorize each other, reducing the state to such cartoonish sub-minimalism that the right threatens to return us all to the very Hobbesian state of nature from which the Leviathan promised deliverance. The rights critics have, in essence, urged us to internalize the moral of these examples, and innoculate ourselves against future delusions. This is the way of all rights movements, hopes, and ambitions. There is no articulable right that will not eventually, and sooner more likely than later, become the vehicle for reactionary politics. The entrenchment of the status quo achieved by such a discourse is never worth whatever momentary gain might be had through an expansion of rights.

52. Others have criticized *Roe* on these grounds. *See* Catharine MacKinnon, Feminism Unmodified: Discourses on Life and the Law 99-101 (1987); Eileen L. McDonagh, Breaking the Abortion Deadlock: From Choice to Consent 46-48 (1996); Catharine A. MacKinnon, *Reflections on Sex Equality Under Law*, 100 Yale L.J. 1281, 1308-24 (1991).

53. *See generally*, Cass R. Sunstein, Democracy and the Problem of Free Speech (1993) (suggesting a reassessment of the guarantee of free speech in light of current trends and developments).

There are, however, costs in abandoning rights, rather than joining the debate regarding their substance. The first is rhetorical. It concerns the nature of moral, aspirational discourse, and the relative power or impoverishment of the rhetoric with which such discourse is articulated. When architects of the good society disown rights, they distance themselves from a tradition that has been unduly attentive to individualistic needs for property, contract, and privacy, and insufficiently attentive to human and social needs for safe intimacy, civic participation, meaningful work, or basic welfare goods. But they also distance themselves from a discourse that whatever its historic shortcomings is *also* explicitly utopian, moralistic, and imperativist. The rights tradition directs states and state actors to attend to what we might universally share, and to focus on the utopian aspirations we might universally hold, and then to bring that vision to earth. Rights are morally grounded imperatives, not a list of suggestions for good governance. It is a language that requires lawmakers to think in terms of what we morally ought to do and be. Good society advocates should not loosely turn their backs on a discourse which has historically been the means by which we marry our moral beliefs about governance to ethical imperativism. There aren't all that many ways by which critics, citizens, or even legislators can make the point that moral judgment rather than realpolitik ought to—and must—guide the business of politics. It is not so clear that the abandonment, rather than reform, of one such language—whatever may be its flaws—is a wise strategy for good society advocates, or will prove to be a benefit for the party of humanity.

The second cost of abandoning rights is borne by the state of normative legal scholarship. When good society theorists who are also lawyers heed the critics' call to abandon rights talk, the development, through scholarship, of alternative directions legal doctrine could take toward the realization of that good society, bears the mark of that abandonment. To a considerable degree we can already trace the effects of that retreat. We still lack a credible, broad-based, coherent jurisprudence of welfare rights, Frank Michelman's herculean efforts of twenty-five years ago notwithstanding.[54] We might lack this jurisprudence, in part, because those who might otherwise have been inclined to contribute to that jurisprudence have been convinced not only of the futility of the project, but also of its counterproductivity. We lack a credible jurisprudence of education rights, and it is at least possible that we lack it, in part, due to that same skepticism. We lack a jurisprudence of dignitary rights, labor rights, and environmental rights—and, as I will discuss in a little more detail, *doulia* rights, or rights to provide

54. Michelman, *Constitutional Welfare Rights*, *supra* note 3; Michelman, *On Protecting the Poor*, *supra* note 3.

care. We lack them in part because those who might produce the scholarship have become convinced that rights and rights talk cannot be productively turned to the work of achieving or even conceiving a good society, and might even undercut it. Obviously, other factors as well have played a role—a hostile Supreme Court is only the most obvious. Additionally, the turn among some leftist scholars to an explicitly antinormative, skeptical postmodernism has also fueled a late-century retreat from visionary, utopian scholarship, including rights scholarship that might aim to carve out a constitutional argument for a state obligation to secure the minimal preconditions of a good society. Nevertheless, the explicit disavowal of rights by both rights critics and good society advocates is a part of that story, as well as reflective of it.

Third, there is a doctrinal cost paid when lawyers, and not just social theorists, abandon rather than seek to reform rights and rights talk. The abandonment of rights discourse by those committed to constructing a good society through law, goes some way toward rendering the rights critique a self-fulfilling prophecy. When lawyers forgo the task of creating a positive rights jurisprudence, they also forgo the opportunity to assert a credible counterweight, *within* doctrine and within rights-structured doctrinal discourse, to the assertion of negative rights which do indeed undercut the good society, and in precisely the ways urged by the critics. With no credible counterweight, when a negative right of the sort the rights critics lament *is* asserted, it is typically met not with a positive right that might counter it, but instead with a claimed "policy" to be weighed against it. But rights, as both their proponents and critics know, trump policy; that is their function. If we had what we currently do not have—a developed jurisprudence of positive and relational rights, constructed around the ideal of the good society—then a negative, individualist right might alternatively, or additionally, be met in the courts of law and in the courts of public opinion, with the claim that it conflicts with a positive one. Conflicting rights, as Dworkin reminds us, do not "trump" each other; rather, conflicting rights must be read in such a way as to reduce the conflict. Proponents of the good society have been dissuaded, in part by the rights critique itself, from developing the jurisprudence that might counter the rights decried by that critique.

Let me illustrate with one example. In Texas two years ago, a federal district court held that a man's constitutional right to bear arms was unconstitutionally abridged by a federal law that forbade domestic violence offenders from owning firearms.[55] The judge accordingly struck down the law as unconstitutional. In that case, the state attempted, unsuccessfully, to meet the defendant's claimed

55. United States v. Emerson, 46 F. Supp. 2d 598, 610-11 (N.D. Tex. 1999).

assertion of the negative right to bear arms by arguing that the Second Amendment right on which the defendant rested his case does not exist.[56] The court rejected the argument that if the right does exist, it should be balanced, weighed against, or limited by, a policy favoring public safety.[57] But policy arguments do not win against asserted rights. They are not supposed to. The very logic of a right—that it must be protected even in the face of sound policies that conflict with it—virtually assures as much. Again, rights, by definition, trump policy. It is inherent in rights that they do so. In this case, once the court accepted the dubious premise that there exists an individual right to bear arms, there could be no effective rejoinder.

Alternatively, if there had existed a developed understanding of positive rights to which the state might have turned, the negative right to bear arms asserted in the Texas case could have been met not simply with a policy favoring disarmament of violent domestic abusers, but with a claimed *right*. After making the sound and central claim that no such Second Amendment right exists, the state could have proceeded to urge that even if the right to bear arms exists, it must be understood in such a way as not to conflict with our more fundamental positive right to a liberal state that is obligated to protect us against private violence. Such a right, had it been asserted, could not be trumped by a conflicting right. The judge would have been forced to reconcile, in a principled way, the asserted right to bear arms with the civil right to be protected by the state against private violence. How the court would have achieved that reconciliation is an open question; the claim that the negative right to bear arms would have to be limited so as to accommodate the positive right to be protected against a known threat of violence from an identified offender with a history of abuse, may or may not have proven persuasive. It likely would not have proven persuasive to the judge that wrote the majority opinion—although it may have captured the legal imagination of a judge writing in dissent. My point here is only that the rights critique—along with a host of other factors—dissuades us from the need to build the case for the constitutional rejoinder. That alone is a cost.

It is not hard to imagine other examples. Property owners and, increasingly, courts argue that environmental regulations that impact the value of privately held property unconstitutionally restrict the property owners' various negative rights of property. Such a claim, one might think, ought ideally to be met with a robust argument that we have a positive right to a state that protects our wilderness, air, water, and public health. Instead, it is typically met by a plea that the property owner's multiple and conceded negative rights to own

56. *Id.* at 600.
57. *Id.* at 609-10.

property free of state regulation ought to be balanced against environmental policy. But again, in a rights versus policy debate, the right will trump. The consequence, for environmentalism, of abandoning the attempt to construct a positive jurisprudence of environmental *rights*, is clearly not good. In a similar vein, the claim that a landlord's contract and property rights are infringed by laws requiring him to rent to couples regardless of sexual orientation, is met only by the hope that the court will in its discretion come to view such non-discrimination laws as protecting compelling state interests, rather than by a strongly asserted positive right to shelter, unburdened by litmus tests of moral propriety. The claim that a propagandist's hate speech is unconstitutionally infringed by a speech regulation, or that broadcasters' news coverage is unconstitutionally infringed by broadcast regulations, is met by asserted policies protecting interests in freedom from harm or fairness, rather than with the claim that liberalism ought properly honor not only our negative rights to be free of censorship, but also our positive rights to a political dialogue unpolluted by hate or profit. In short, without a tradition of positive rights on which to draw, we meet constitutional claims of negative speech rights, property rights, contract rights, and gun rights with exhortations of policy—exhortations which sometimes are but more often aren't heard, and when they are heard, are then readily trumped. But that these cases are all posed as, and understood as, asserted rights on the one hand, and policies on the other, does not bode well for the regulatory state. Again—rights, by definition, trump policy. Negative rights, unchecked by positive rights that might counter them, threaten to reduce that regulatory state to the vanishing point. Such a reduction would hardly be a victory for the party of humanity. More pointedly, a regulatory state reduced to the vanishing point is clearly not one that is obligated to secure minimal preconditions of a fully human life.

Lastly, the failure to articulate a positive rights jurisprudence that includes a state's obligation to ensure the minimal preconditions of the good society has resulted in the lack of a meaningful counterweight, not only within rights discourse, but also to counter the balancing of costs and benefits that now dominates ordinary, or non-rights-based, legal analysis. As a result, legal analysis, across the map, is now driven in toto *either* by the logic of negative rights, or in the absence of rights, by an economic calculus that funnels all values into monetary equivalents, assigning some to the cost and some to the benefit side of the ledger, and then balancing the one against the other, according victory to whichever comes out on top. The failure to enrich the rights tradition with a positive rights jurisprudence and a defensible conception of our social nature has thus facilitated the ascendency of an economic method of legal analysis that relentlessly asserts the comparability, fungibility, and commensurability of all values, translates values into dollar terms, and leads to the ease of trading off one against the other. The cost of health is balanced against lost profits, the value of future life is measured against present dollars, the cost of suffering against the cost of prevention, the monetary benefits of speech against the cost of permitting it, the cost of sexual harassment against the benefits of non-intervention. This cost-benefit analysis has widely recognized and well-known pitfalls: it relies on real or shadow market values that are themselves reflective of little but the forces of profit; it ferociously solidifies and legitimates the status quo by ignoring the effects of given distributions on felt entitlements; it discriminates between us by valuing our lives differently on the basis of our projected or actual incomes; it creates a wealth-based mentality that measures all, including goodness, truth and justice, by reference to profit. But for all of its problems—for all of its well-known absurdities—cost-benefit analysis now dominates legal analysis. It does so primarily for the absence of credible normative alternatives.

Here again, this is a loss felt not only in theory but in doctrine as well. As Lisa Heinzerling demonstrates, costs of environmental protection to individuals and corporations, for example, are balanced against the benefits to individuals, where these benefits of health and well-being are then measured by projected incomes, and then discounted by various factors, such as the proximity to us of the lives in question, in terms of either time or distance. Rather than present a rights-based challenge to this entire normative apparatus, advocates of environmental regulation instead debate the amounts, challenge the discount rates, or question various economic assumptions behind the economic models. What we do not hear, even from committed environmentalists, is a principled moral and legal argument that we are entitled by right—meaning *regardless of cost*—to some degree of state-protected environmental health. Accident victims and their advocates similarly tally their costs in lottery-styled torts cases, rather than assert a right to health care to which we are entitled, as a matter of right. Sexually harassed workers or their advocates debate the subtleties of the value of a harassment free environment as implied by their employment contracts, rather than assert a right to dignified labor. Our legal system, as well as our discourse, has been thoroughly transformed by cost-benefit econometrics, and without a rights discourse to offset, trump, or challenge it, there is little relief in sight. By eschewing rights and rights talk, we have arguably engendered a more efficient state. But we have not noticeably moved any closer to achieving, or conceiving, the good society.

III. TOWARD A JURISPRUDENCE OF POSITIVE AND RELATIONAL RIGHTS

What might be worth considering, in light of the costs of the rights critique, is the possibility of revitalizing the rights tradition, rather than abandoning it altogether. Doing so may advance the end of constructing liberal rights that protect and guarantee, not just individual autonomy, but also fundamental capabilities. What might a liberal state look like, if it employed positive and relational rights, as well as negative and individualist rights, and conceived of those rights as directed toward the protection of both capabilities and autonomy?

There would no doubt be many similarities. As Nussbaum and others have argued, a state committed to ensuring material preconditions of the good society would also be committed to ensuring many of the negative rights now understood as essential to a liberal state.[58] The major difference would lie in what additional rights would be regarded as being in the "core," and in the nature of the penumbral rights that might be inferred from that core. Our current liberal state, structured by negative and atomistic rights, and committed to securing the minimal preconditions of participation not in a good society, but in a free society, has in its core, rights of autonomy, contract and property. These are all now interpreted, variously, so as to ward off the danger of an overly zealous state. By contrast, a liberal state similarly structured by rights, but committed to securing the minimal preconditions of capabilities as well as autonomy, would explicitly recognize additional fundamental rights, including welfare rights and rights to work, currently unrecognized or underrecognized by liberal states overly committed to the atomism and negativity of rights. It would also recognize two rights currently underrecognized by liberal states and undertheorized by welfare advocates. Both of these core rights are highlighted rather than marginalized by the "fundamental capabilities" approach of Nussbaum and Sen.

The first right, I would call a right to security against private violence. The rationale of this right is essentially Hobbesian, and laid out above. As Hobbes claimed, our nature is such that the state must monopolize the tools and instruments of violence if our lives are to be relatively secure. Security against private violence is the core, material precondition of our capability for living safely and free of fear, and hence of meaningfully participating in a good life or good society. In terms of modern utopianists, we cannot lead "fully human lives" without such a right. In Hobbesian terms, we would not have a

58. Nussbaum, Women and Human Development, *supra* note 8, at 111-66.

state without it—it is the right for which we relinquish natural freedoms. The state therefore has an obligation—a first duty—to protect citizens against private violence and aggression, including private sexual violence and aggression. It has that obligation, or first duty, because such an obligation is necessary to the creation of a good society. Again, we cannot lead "fully human" lives otherwise.

A liberal state that fails to provide such protection violates the individual's right to that protection, as well as the state's "first duty" to provide it.[59] What might follow from the existence of such a right? A state that failed to criminalize, or failed to enforce existing laws that criminalize, domestic violence, for example, or marital rape, or violence against lesbians and gay men, or people of color, would violate those citizens' right to protection, and not just equal protection, of the law. Likewise, a state that turned its police force on its citizenry, rather than employed it in their protection, would violate positive rights to protection as well as a negative right to be free from unwarranted state intrusion. These would be clear, unequivocal violations of the citizen's most fundamental right and the state's most fundamental duty. Less blatant, and even unintentional or neglectful failures to protect citizens from violence, however, might also violate such a right. A failure, for example, to enact adequate gun control legislation so as to ensure the safety of school children, women, or urban residents, might constitute a failure to provide for the safety of citizens, and hence violate their rights to protection of the law. A consistent pattern of punishing violence against a group of citizens more leniently than the same crimes committed against another more favored group might also constitute such a violation, as Randall Kennedy argued some time ago.[60]

What might be the penumbral rights implied by the recognition of a core positive right to protection against private violence? It would depend on the rationale of the core right itself. Three possibilities come to mind. First, if we have a positive right to protection against private violence because of our natural vulnerability to the violent propensities of others, and the calamitous consequences of that vulnerability, then we might also want to recognize that we have a positive right to the state's protection against other sorts of natural "violence" with equally calamitous results. We might, for example, have a positive right to be protected against natural disaster, misfortune, or even disfavor and bad luck, if the consequences of that disfavor are brutal. This might sensibly be regarded as the "welfarist" interpretation of the right to security.

59. *See* Heyman, *supra* note 32, at 530-45.

60. *See* Randall L. Kennedy, McClesky v. Kemp: *Race, Capital Punishment, and the Supreme Court*, 101 Harv. L. Rev. 1388, 1421-29 (1988).

Alternatively, we might reason that we recognize a positive right to security, or protection against the violence of others, not because of the calamitous potential consequences of our vulnerability to that violence, but because of the potentially subordinating, and hence inegalitarian, consequences of that vulnerability. Unchecked private violence leads to unchecked private political hierarchies and also leads to domination and acquiescence in those spheres in which the violence goes unchecked by the state. A security right against unchecked private violence, then, might imply not just a right to assistance in the event of natural disaster, but a different set of "penumbral rights" to be protected against extreme forms of private aggression, whether or not that aggression takes the form of physical violence. We may, for example, have a positive right to be protected against the harmful effects of a polluted environment, or an unregulated and dangerous product, or exploitative employers. We might think of this as the "antisubordinationist" interpretation of the security right.

And third, we might reason that we have a positive right to security against private violence because of a yet more fundamental right to security against extreme deprivation or impoverishment that threatens fundamental human capabilities, regardless of whether that vulnerability can be attributed to either undue private aggression or natural disaster. If we have a right to protection against violence not because we have egalitarian rights not to be subordinated, and not because we have a natural right to community assistance in the event of natural disaster, but because we have a right to a fully human life free of fear and anxiety brought on by conditions of deprivation, then we might impliedly also have a right to be freed of these non-subordinating but no less damaging sorts of vulnerabilities. This would be the most far-reaching penumbral interpretation of the right to security, and might be called the "capabilities-based" interpretation. We have a right to security, in this view, because we have a right to live the "fully human" life such security in part ensures. A liberalism grounded in a "first right" to protection against private violence, so understood, in other words, might support the existence of penumbral rights to protection against other sorts of vulnerabilities—and hence, at the outer reaches, rights to whatever is minimally necessary to attain those capabilities in turn essential to a fully human life. Obviously, such rights would entail state obligations to act, rather than simply refrain from acting.

The second core right that might be recognized in a liberal tradition unwedded to atomism can be called a "right to provide care," or as the philosopher Eva Kittay refers to it, a right to *doulia*.[61] This right is currently undertheorized in the welfarist literature. We do not, contrary to Hobbesian myth, spring upon this earth mushroom style,

61. *See* Kittay, *supra* note 23, at 132.

as fully formed, autonomous adults. Rather, all of us enjoy or suffer an extended period of absolute dependency upon caregivers, and most of us, as adults, enjoy or suffer (or both) an even longer period during which we bestow care upon infants and children dependent upon us, and eventually upon aging parents in similar need. The ability to give care to dependent others, and the ability to receive such care as a dependent other, is at least as fundamental to a "fully human life" as is the ability to rest secure against threats of private violence or subordination. As a species, we are not just interdependent creatures, we are also, for substantial periods, fully dependent upon others, and others are, for substantial periods, fully dependent upon us. Those simple facts of our human existence, to a considerable degree, mark our species, define and constitute our moral sense, and form the basis for our social nature.

As a consequence, when we are infants and children, and likewise when we are sick or aged, we desperately need, not the rights of autonomy and independence so central to classical liberalism, but a regime that protects us in our dependent state, and protects those upon whom we are dependent as well. And, when we are acting as caregivers, we need not rights that falsely presuppose our autonomy and independence, but rights that frankly acknowledge our relational reality. When infants, children, or aging parents are dependent upon us, we are dependent upon others for support and sustenance.[62] People who are providing care to dependents are themselves in need of assistance from others, and caregivers will eventually become, again, dependents in need of care themselves. That circle of mutual need, caregiving, dependency, and assistance is as much a part of our social contract as is the individual's relinquishment of rights to self-defense in exchange for a right to protection against violence. A rights tradition that forthrightly acknowledged the natural reality of our inescapable dependence on each other—to say nothing of our social nature—would give pride of place to "relational rights" that would protect the caregiver, and hence the care bestowed in dependency relationships.

Needless to say, perhaps, such relational rights are nowhere mentioned in various constitutional documents, nor are they well-grounded in liberal theory. But they ought to be. We have the rights we have in liberal, democratic societies, at least according to widely shared conventional wisdom, for essentially one (or more) of three basic reasons. First, we construct or recognize rights when, for some reason, the sphere of life, service, freedom, activity, or identity that is protected by the right, and so necessary to flourishing, might nevertheless be systematically undervalued, underappreciated, or underprotected by standard political or economic processes, even in a

62. For a sustained argument to this effect, see generally *id.*, at 132-46.

liberal democracy. Second, at least sometimes in the United States and elsewhere, we construct rights when we have reason to believe that a particular practice or activity, if unchecked, will have a severe and adverse effect on a subgroup that has historically been subordinated. And lastly, here and elsewhere, at least on occasion, we construct rights to underscore our most fundamental and most shared intergenerational values. The panoply of rights we protect expresses our self understanding, and more specifically, it expresses a self-understanding meant to endure even in times of the value's political neglect.

Does this widely shared, and I think, uncontroversial understanding of the various rationales for rights suggest a basis for a right to give care, and a right to the *doulia* needed to support it? I think so. First, we have very good reason to think that standard political and economic tools will not generate market or political protections for this labor, or for those who provide it. Caregivers do not, as a rule, willy-nilly abandon infants or dependents, take a better opportunity as it arises, or go on strike, even under very harsh conditions. Caregivers, virtually by definition, are emotionally and ethically committed to perform the work without interruption once it is undertaken. That emotional and ethical attachment of caregiver and cared-for that results from caregiving labor strongly suggests that the work will be less supported than it should be in both democratic political systems and market economies. Caregivers have all of the vulnerability, but none of the autonomy, which comes from the "at will" employment status they share with other vulnerable employees. There is no political will or need to support caregiving labor and no organizational ability to confront that lack of will with some set of non-negotiable "caregivers' demands," so long as caregivers continue to provide the services regardless, enduring either impoverishment or dependency as the cost of doing so. We therefore have good reason to believe that familial and economic institutions, if unchecked, will continue to undercompensate caregiving labor, and that women will be adversely impacted, as a group, by that practice. For this unexceptional reason, familiar to liberal theorists, we need rights of care to protect caregivers against the pendulum swings of public support and neglect of their work.

Likewise, we need rights of care to protect women from the inegalitarian consequences of that neglect, just as we need rights of nondiscrimination to protect potential employees from the adverse consequences of irrational racism. It is increasingly clear that some such panoply of relational rights is necessary if women, who have traditionally assumed the work of unassisted caregiving with no correlative state obligation to protect them in that work, and who have suffered either the risk of impoverishment or subordination by virtue of doing so, are to enjoy any measure of equality in an otherwise liberal and autonomy-protecting society. In a related point, such rights are necessary if caregivers, whether men or women, are to enjoy the rights of autonomy promised them by conventional liberalism.

Lastly, we need a right of care and a right to supported caregiving labor to better express our self-understanding as a species for whom caregiving is a central life activity. Clearly, our nature is such that we thrive when cared for. As a species, our period of infantile need is extended over time, as is our period of caregiving labor. We flourish both individually and communally when decent care is provided, and we suffer when it is not. The better the care, the more the cared-for will thrive, and the more likely they will mature to become liberal and equal citizens who can themselves provide care as well as fulfill responsibilities of citizenship in a liberal society. And, the more demanding and consuming is the care, the harder it is to provide without support.

But most fundamentally, liberalism ought to recognize such rights because such rights are necessary to a good and liberal society, virtually regardless of how that society is defined. Those who give care to dependents over extended periods of time need material security against need, if that care is to be of high quality. One cannot see to the needs of an infant or an elderly parent and engage in wage-earning labor at the same time; caregiving labor, by its nature, renders the caregiver less autonomous. Falsely assuming that we can, is ultimately as disastrous and self-destructive as falsely assuming that grown people will naturally and peacefully cohabit in the state of nature. An artificial, socially constructed, civil Leviathan has proven necessary to protect us against the second false illusion—the illusion of our own invulnerability and natural sociability. A similarly artificial, socially constructed, civil network of support ought to be created to protect us against the first—the illusion of our natural independence. A right to give care without risking severe impoverishment or subordination, grounded in our nature, and protective of the caregiver's security, safety and material well-being when she relinquishes her independence so as to care for the needs of dependent others, should be a part of that social construction.

Thus, all three rationales for rights—the dysfunction of political and economic processes for protecting caregiving labor; the inegalitarian consequences for an historically subordinated group of not doing so; and our self-understanding that caregiving is important work—point in the direction of care and *doulia* rights. Whether we are presently in a "constitutional moment" which might support the creation of such a right is of course an open question. We may now be in a period when the jurisprudential will to support caregiving labor in any way other than through traditional family structures is at an all time low. But we are also in a political period when the need for such a right has become clear to many people who historically have had no sense of it whatsoever: men, who are actually *doing* caregiving labor, and are consequently experiencing some of the risks of that work. Women and men who are caring for dependents know they need support, and they also know that complete economic dependency upon a marital partner in an unequal economic relationship is not a viable long term solution to the problem. A right to support for caregiving labor might then express that quite fundamental shift in our collective and social self-understanding.

What might be the practical consequences of such a right? Mothers or fathers caring for infants, and adult children caring for aging parents, protected by rights to care, might be possessed both of penumbral negative rights, recognized "inside the courts," against unwise state action that endangers caregiving, caregivers, and the cared-for, such as the Personal Responsibility and Work Opportunity Reconciliation Act of 1996,[63] and positive rights, "outside the courts," to state action that supports care-giving labor, such as an expanded version of the Family and Medical Leave Act.[64] Of course, such a right would be subject to interpretation, change, and re-interpretation in light of changing politics and circumstances, no less than are rights of privacy or speech. And, such a right, or rights, would share in the risks and pitfalls of rights generally, as exposed by rights critics. A "right to care" could be subject to capture in ways both imaginable and unimaginable. Or it may be subject (I think) more importantly, to trivialization—the right could well become, and in short order, nothing but a commodificationist right to hire a nanny of one's free choosing, or a right to be a nanny and set one's own low wage and bad working conditions unimpeded by meddlesome and paternalistic labor regulations.

Nevertheless, we shouldn't dismiss the upside potential out of hand. A "right to care" would share in the rhetorical power of rights discourse. Acknowledgment or insistence upon the existence of such a right would honor the centrality of caregiving labor to social life. Neither would it require a herculean effort to locate such a right in our constitutional history. The substantive due process clause, before it became, post-*Eisenstadt v. Baird*,[65] the source of individual, negative rights to contraception and abortion, did prominently include "a right to parent"[66]—a right which, particularly if modernized and coupled with our current recognition of the constitutional status of norms of

63. Personal Responsibility and Work Opportunity Reconciliation Act of 1996, Pub. L. No. 104-193, 110 Stat. 2105 (codified as amended in scattered sections of 7 U.S.C., 8 U.S.C., 21 U.S.C., 25 U.S.C. and 42 U.S.C.).

64. 29 U.S.C. § 2601 (1994).

65. 405 U.S. 438 (1972).

66. Prince v. Massachusetts, 321 U.S. 158, 166 (1944); Skinner v. Oklahoma, 316 U.S. 535, 541 (1942); Pierce v. Soc'y of Sisters, 268 U.S. 510, 535 (1925); Meyer v. Nebraska, 262 U.S. 390, 399 (1923).

gender equality—could easily be viewed as "penumbral" to a more fundamental right to give care. As a practical matter, as mentioned, such a right casts doubt on not just the wisdom but also the constitutionality of legislation like the mid 1990s welfare reform act,[67] and such a right, were we to recognize it, gives needed dimensions of both universality and moral imperative to political demands for greater support of vulnerable caregivers. Just as important, a "right to care," if recognized, would go a long way toward aligning the idea of rights with a conception of our nature that acknowledges our natural dependencies as well as our social responsibilities toward others, rather than a conception of our nature that insists falsely and dangerously on our self-sufficiency.

CONCLUSION: RIGHTS, CAPABILITIES, LIBERALISM AND THE MATERIAL PRECONDITIONS OF THE GOOD SOCIETY

Even if successful, of course, this imaginative reconstruction of rights from negative to positive and from atomistic to relational does not establish that any of these welfarist rights to enjoy basic capabilities actually *exist*. A right—whether to anti-subordination, to give care, to dignified labor, to a living wage, to welfare—must also be found in the language, logic or history of a state or a nation's constitution. Rights we actually have, rather than rights we could have, must, to use Dworkin's suggestive phrase, confront the brute facts of our legal history.[68] Constitutions may or may not explicitly provide for positive rights, and constitutions that do not do so may or may not be read so as to implicitly endorse them. There is, of course, a great deal of scholarship in constitutional democracies debating the interpretive limits and possibilities of particular constitutional provisions. Much of that debate, furthermore, goes to the possibility of locating either positive or relational rights or both within a document that seemingly only provides for negative and atomistic rights.

Nevertheless, one obstacle to the recognition of positive and relational rights within both liberal constitutional discourse and welfarist theory, stems not from brute fact of constitutional law and history, but rather from the widely held conviction that the notion of a positive right or a relational right is somehow oxymoronic—that rights *by definition* constrain states from certain acts, rather than requiring *of* them certain acts, and that rights by definition valorize individualism and denigrate dependency. These are circular claims that ought to be laid to rest, both for the sake of liberalism, and its

67. Personal Responsibility and Work Opportunity Reconciliation Act of 1996, 110 Stat. 2105.

68. Ronald Dworkin, Law's Empire 255-56 (1986); *see also* Dworkin, Taking Rights Seriously, *supra* note 26, at 81-149 (arguing that although a judge may not invent rights, existing rights should be interpreted from an activist perspective).

apparently forsaken humanistic core, and for welfarism, at least a welfarism that has any legal bite.

Let me start with liberalism. If rights exist, and if as liberals generally contend, they are justified by reference to our human nature, then they surely direct as well as constrain states: states must act as well as refrain from acting if they are to provide for civic liberty, equality, well-being, and the "full human lives" of citizens.[69] The liberal tradition, generously read, requires states to protect our individualistic capacity for free thought and our desire to master our own fate, and it requires states to do so by refraining from paternalistic intrusion. It also, however, generously read, as Nussbaum has argued, requires states to protect our capabilities: our capability for self rule, for safe intimacy, for a healthy and long life, and for productive work, and it requires states to do so because these capabilities, among others, are essential for us to lead fully human lives. The rights needed to provide that protection are distinctively positive. If they are at the heart of liberalism, then the widely held belief that liberalism can at most embrace a negative understanding of rights is mistaken.

Second, if committed to a full and true conception of our social as well as autonomous nature, rather than a truncated one that denies the former and valorizes the latter, liberal rights and hence liberalism itself could be aligned with the work of fashioning a social fabric that protects us in our cross-generational web of dependencies, rather than one that blithely ignores them. Our capacity for caring over extended periods of time for those who are dependent upon us is at least as central to our human identity as our capacity for free thought, our propensity to bargain through contracts, or the security we gain through our possessions. The nature and quality of the care we bestow upon those who are dependent upon us mark our species, and as a set of practices, generates an ethical way of being in the world that is at least as integral both to a well-led individual life and to the well-being of our communities, as is our individualized capacity for autonomous conviction or independent action.[70] A liberalism that embraced at its core a right to give care without incurring unjustified vulnerability—a liberalism that would marry, so to speak, a recognition of the importance of caregiving labor to the well-being of the species with the robustness of the liberal rights tradition—would thereby acknowledge a relational and communitarian world substantially different from the overly atomized individualistic hell currently decried by liberalism's critics. A liberal society defined in part by its recognition of rights to care, and a liberal culture that took

69. *See also* Cass R. Sunstein & Stephen Holmes, The Cost of Rights: Why Liberty Depends on Taxes 54-58 (1999) ("Protection 'against' government is therefore unthinkable without protection 'by' government.").

70. Carol Gilligan, In a Different Voice 64-105 (1982).

the care to embellish its assumptions, would enrich, not undermine, the egalitarianism and individualism of citizens that the liberal rights tradition, to its credit, has always sought to foster. It would also further, rather than hinder, attempts to construct a good society, and it would do so by obligating the state to fulfill the material preconditions of at least this one quite basic human capability.

And finally, what do good society advocates have to gain by articulating the basis for the state's obligation to ensure the minimal preconditions of the good society in the liberal terms of citizens' rights? Most important, if proponents of a welfarist version of the good society were to revitalize and refashion rights rather than abandon them, they won't risk losing either the utopian universalism, or the imperativism, that the liberal rights tradition has long lent to political and legal practices. The language of rights connects politics with not just the hope, but the demand, that law both can and should structure a decent social world: rights are justified demands against a state, not just a catalog of ideas of good governance. How we conceive of that "decent social world" is clearly a political question, and in a conservative and libertarian time, the language of rights will reflect those politics—the rights we have or recognize will always reflect the dominant political discourse, and our dominant political discourse now is both conservative and libertarian. But it does not follow that rights have a necessary connection to those or any other set of political ideals; nor does it mean that those who envision a different political ideal than the reigning one should abandon it. Rights, whatever their content, are premised on the grandly egalitarian assumption that we have a shared nature, from which universal norms follow. If proponents of the good society give up on rights, they will have given up on one way of envisioning our fate in a way that honors that humanity.

There are, of course, many ways to think of and envision ideals, and it is true that political actors, no less than legal actors, can articulate visions, and urge political action on behalf of them, in language that makes no reference to our rights. It is not the case that without rights talk, good society theorists—whether welfarists or civic virtueists or capabilities advocates—are automatically reduced to the realpolitik of costs, benefits, preferences, markets, and sites of power and influence. There are other ways—alternatives to rights and efficiency both—to think about what a good society ought to be and what the state in a good society ought to do. Nevertheless, rights are and have been one way of asserting claims about what society ought to be, and what the state ought to do, and what the state must do, with respect to our laws, on behalf of all humanity.[71] When proponents of the good society

71. *See* Hendrik Hartog, *The Constitution of Aspiration and "The Rights That Belong to Us All"*, 74 J. Am. His. 1017, 1024-25 (1987).

turn their backs on rights, they relinquish one way of insisting that moral judgment, moral choice, and moral vision—and not just interests, preferences, votes, power, and money—guide political and legal action. They turn their backs on a path—not the only path, but a path—for transforming those universalistic utopian ideals of the good society into political realities.

[6]

Elements of a Theory of Human Rights

AMARTYA SEN

I. The Need for a Theory

Few concepts are as frequently invoked in contemporary political discussions as human rights. There is something deeply attractive in the idea that every person anywhere in the world, irrespective of citizenship or territorial legislation, has some basic rights, which others should respect. The moral appeal of human rights has been used for a variety of purposes, from resisting torture and arbitrary incarceration to demanding the end of hunger and of medical neglect.[1]

At the same time, the central idea of human rights as something that people have, and have even without any specific legislation, is seen by many as foundationally dubious and lacking in cogency. A recurrent question is, Where do these rights come from? It is not usually disputed that the invoking of human rights can be politically powerful. Rather, the worries relate to what is taken to be the "softness" (some would say "mushiness") of the conceptual grounding of human rights. Many philosophers and legal theorists see the rhetoric of human rights as just

An earlier version of this article served as my Gilbert Murray Lecture ("Why Invent Human Rights?") given in Oxford on 14 November 2002. For helpful suggestions, I am particularly grateful to the Editors of *Philosophy & Public Affairs*, and also to Catherine Barnard, Rosanne Flynn, Sakiko Fukuda Parr, Ivan Hare, Will Kymlicka, Jo Miles, Martha Nussbaum, Onora O'Neill, Siddiq Osmani, Mary Robinson, Emma Rothschild, Thomas Scanlon, Arjun Sengupta, Frances Stewart, Rosemary Thorpe, and Rosie Vaughan.

1. See *International Human Rights in Context: Law, Politics and Morals*, ed. Henry J. Steiner and Philip Alston (New York: Oxford University Press, 2000); Richard Falk, *Human Rights Horizons: The Pursuit of Justice in a Globalizing World* (New York: Routledge, 2000); Jack Donnelly, *Universal Human Rights in Theory and Practice*, 2nd ed. (Ithaca: Cornell University Press, 2003). See also Micheline R. Ishay, *The Human Rights Reader: Major Political Writings, Essays, Speeches, and Documents from the Bible to the Present* (New York: Routledge, 1997).

loose talk—perhaps kindly and well meaning forms of locution—but loose talk nevertheless.

The contrast between the widespread use of the idea of human rights and the intellectual skepticism about its conceptual soundness is not new. The U.S. Declaration of Independence, in 1776, took it to be "self-evident" that everyone is "endowed by their Creator with certain inalienable rights," and thirteen years later, the French declaration of "the rights of man" asserted that "men are born and remain free and equal in rights." But it did not take Jeremy Bentham long, in his *Anarchical Fallacies* written during 1791 and 1792 (aimed against the French "rights of man"), to propose the total dismissal of all such claims. Bentham insisted that "natural rights is simple nonsense: natural and imprescriptible rights (an American phrase), rhetorical nonsense, nonsense upon stilts."[2] That suspicion remains very alive today, and despite persistent use of the idea of human rights in practical affairs, there are many who see the idea of human rights as no more than "bawling upon paper," to use another of Bentham's barbed portrayals of natural right claims.

The dismissal of human rights is often comprehensive and is aimed against any belief in the existence of rights that people can have unconditionally, simply by virtue of their humanity (rather than having them contingently, on the basis of specific qualifications, such as citizenship or legal entitlements). Some critics, however, propose a discriminating rejection: they accept the general idea of human rights but exclude, from the acceptable list, specific classes of proposed rights, in particular the so-called economic and social rights, or welfare rights. These rights, which are sometimes referred to as second generation rights, such as a common entitlement to subsistence or to medical care, have mostly been added relatively recently to earlier enunciations of human rights, thereby vastly expanding the claimed domain of human rights.[3] These

2. Jeremy Bentham, *Anarchical Fallacies; Being an Examination of the Declaration of Rights Issued during the French Revolution* (1792); republished in *The Works of Jeremy Bentham*, vol. II, ed. J. Bowring (Edinburgh: William Tait, 1843), p. 501.

3. See Ivan Hare, "Social Rights as Foundational Human Rights," in *Social and Labour Rights in Global Context*, ed. Bob Hepple (Cambridge: Cambridge University Press, 2002), and William F. Felice, *The Global New Deal: Economic and Social Human Rights in World Politics* (Lanham: Rowman & Littlefield, 2003). See also Cass R. Sunstein, *After the Rights Revolution: Reconceiving the Regulatory State* (Cambridge, Mass.: Harvard University Press, 1990), and Thomas W. Pogge, *World Poverty and Human Rights: Cosmopolitan Responsibilities and Reforms* (London: Polity Press, 2002).

additions have certainly taken the contemporary literature on human rights well beyond the eighteenth-century declarations that concentrated on a narrower class of "rights of man," including such demands as personal liberty and political freedom. These newer inclusions have been subjected to more specialized skepticism, with the critics focusing on their feasibility problems and their dependence on specific social institutions that may or may not exist.[4]

Human rights activists are often quite impatient with such critiques. The invoking of human rights tends to come mostly from those who are concerned with changing the world rather than interpreting it (to use a classic distinction made famous, oddly enough, by that overarching theorist, Karl Marx). It is not hard to understand their unwillingness to spend time trying to provide conceptual justification, given the great urgency to respond to terrible deprivations around the world. This proactive stance has had its practical rewards, since it has allowed immediate use of the colossal appeal of the idea of human rights to confront intense oppression or great misery, without having to wait for the theoretical air to clear. However, the conceptual doubts must also be satisfactorily addressed, if the idea of human rights is to command reasoned loyalty and to establish a secure intellectual standing. It is critically important to see the relationship between the force and appeal of human rights, on the one hand, and their reasoned justification and scrutinized use, on the other.

There is, thus, need for some theory and also for some defense of any proposed theory. The object of this article is to do just that, and to consider, in that context, the justification of the general idea of human rights and also of the includability of economic and social rights within the broad class of human rights. For such a theory to be viable it is necessary to clarify what kind of a claim is made by a declaration of human rights, and how such a claim can be defended, and furthermore how the diverse criticisms of the coherence, cogency and legitimacy of human

4. The reasoning behind such rejection has been powerfully presented by Maurice Cranston, "Are There Any Human Rights?" *Daedalus* (1983): 1–17, and Onora O'Neill, *Towards Justice and Virtue* (Cambridge: Cambridge University Press, 1996). See also the critique of Michael Ignatieff, supporting some claims to human rights while strongly disputing others, in *Human Rights as Politics and Idolatry* (Princeton: Princeton University Press, 2001).

rights (including economic and social rights) can be adequately addressed. That is the aim of this article.

However, before going into this investigation, I should make a clarificatory point. The rhetoric of human rights is sometimes applied to particular legislations inspired by the idea of human rights. There is clearly no great difficulty in seeing the obvious judicial status of these already legalized entitlements. No matter what they are called ("human rights laws" or any other appellation), they stand shoulder to shoulder with other established legislations. The present inquiry on the foundations and cogency of human rights does not have any direct bearing on the obvious *legal* status of these "human rights laws," once they have been properly legislated. As far as these laws are concerned, the relevance, if any, of this study would lie, rather, in the *motivation* that leads to the enacting of such laws, which builds on the pre-legislative standing of these claims.

Indeed, a great many acts of legislation and legal conventions (such as the "European Convention for the Protection of Human Rights and Fundamental Freedoms") have been clearly inspired by a belief in some pre-existing rights of all human beings. This applies even to the adoption of the U.S. Constitution, including the Bill of Rights, linked to the normative vision of the U.S. Declaration of Independence (as was noted earlier). The difficult questions regarding the status and standing of human rights arise in the domain of ideas, before such legalization occurs. We also have to examine whether legislation is the pre-eminent, or even a necessary, route through which human rights can be pursued.

II. Questions to Be Answered

A theory of human rights must address the following questions in particular:

(1) What kind of a statement does a declaration of human rights make?

(2) What makes human rights important?

(3) What duties and obligations do human rights generate?

(4) Through what forms of actions can human rights be promoted, and in particular whether legislation must be the principal, or even a necessary, means of implementation of human rights?

(5) Can economic and social rights (the so-called second generation rights) be reasonably included among human rights?

(6) Last but not least, how can proposals of human rights be defended or challenged, and how should their claim to a universal status be assessed, especially in a world with much cultural variation and widely diverse practice?

These questions are addressed sequentially in what follows. However, since this is not a detective story, I am perhaps allowed to give away a sketch of the proposed answers, with the hope that this might help in following this long and not entirely uncomplicated article (even though there is some risk of oversimplification involved in any summary formulation).

(1) Human rights can be seen as primarily ethical demands. They are not principally "legal," "proto-legal" or "ideal-legal" commands. Even though human rights can, and often do, inspire legislation, this is a further fact, rather than a constitutive characteristic of human rights.

(2) The importance of human rights relates to the significance of the freedoms that form the subject matter of these rights. Both the opportunity aspect and the process aspect of freedoms can figure in human rights. To qualify as the basis of human rights, the freedoms to be defended or advanced must satisfy some "threshold conditions" of (i) special importance and (ii) social influenceability.

(3) Human rights generate reasons for action for agents who are in a position to help in the promoting or safeguarding of the underlying freedoms. The induced obligations primarily involve the duty to give reasonable consideration to the reasons for action and their practical implications, taking into account the relevant parameters of the individual case. The reasons for action can support both "perfect" obligations as well as "imperfect" ones, which are less precisely characterized. Even though they differ in content, imperfect obligations are correlative with human rights in much the same way as perfect obligations are. In particular, the acceptance of imperfect obligations goes beyond volunteered charity or elective virtues.

(4) The implementation of human rights can go well beyond legislation, and a theory of human rights cannot be sensibly confined within the juridical model in which it is frequently incarcerated. For example, public recognition and agitation (including the monitoring of violations)

can be part of the obligations—often imperfect—generated by the acknowledgment of human rights. Also, some recognized human rights are not ideally legislated, but are better promoted through other means, including public discussion, appraisal and advocacy (a basic point that would have come as no surprise to Mary Wollstonecraft, whose *A Vindication of the Rights of Woman: with Strictures on Political and Moral Subjects* was published in 1792).

(5) Human rights can include significant and influenceable economic and social freedoms. If they cannot be realized because of inadequate institutionalization, then, to work for institutional expansion or reform can be a part of the obligations generated by the recognition of these rights. The current unrealizability of any accepted human right, which can be promoted through institutional or political change, does not, by itself, convert that claim into a *non*-right.

(6) The universality of human rights relates to the idea of survivability in unobstructed discussion—open to participation by persons across national boundaries. Partisanship is avoided not so much by taking either a *conjunction*, or an *intersection*, of the views respectively held by dominant voices in different societies across the world (including very repressive ones), but through an *interactive* process, in particular by examining what would survive in public discussion, given a reasonably free flow of information and uncurbed opportunity to discuss differing points of view. Adam Smith's insistence that ethical scrutiny requires examining moral beliefs from, inter alia, "a certain distance" has a direct bearing on the connection of human rights to global public reasoning.

III. Human Rights: Ethics and Law

What kind of an assertion does a declaration of human rights make? I would submit that proclamations of human rights are to be seen as articulations of ethical demands. They are, in this respect, comparable with pronouncements in utilitarian ethics, even though their respective substantive contents are, obviously, very different. Like other ethical claims that demand acceptance, there is an implicit presumption in making pronouncements on human rights that the underlying ethical claims will survive open and informed scrutiny. Indeed, the invoking of such an interactive process of critical scrutiny, open to information (including that about other societies) as well as to arguments coming from far as well as near, is a central feature of the theory of human rights proposed here. It differs both (i) from trying to justify the ethics of human rights in terms of shared—and already established—universal values (the uncomplicated "non-partisan" view), and (ii) from abdicating any claim of adherence to universal values (and in this sense, eschewing any claim to being "non-partisan") in favor of a particular political conception that is suitable to the contemporary world.[5]

These issues, which relate to the foundational discipline of ethical critique, will be examined later, in Section IX, in response to question (6). But the point to note for the moment, in answer to the first question, is that pronouncements of human rights are quintessentially ethical articulations, and they are *not,* in particular, putative legal claims, despite considerable confusion on this point, generated not least by Jeremy Bentham, the obsessive slayer of what he took to be legal pretensions. (I shall return later in this section to the nature of the misapprehension involved.)

A pronouncement of human rights includes an assertion of the importance of the corresponding freedoms—the freedoms that are identified and privileged in the formulation of the rights in question—and is indeed motivated by that importance. For example, the human right of not being tortured springs from the importance of freedom from torture for all. But it includes, furthermore, an affirmation of the need for others to consider what they can reasonably do to secure the freedom from torture for any person. For a would-be torturer, the demand is obviously quite straightforward, to wit, to refrain and desist. The demand takes the clear form of what Immanuel Kant called a perfect obligation.[6] However, for others too (that is, those other than the would-be torturers) there are responsibilities, even though they are less specific and come in the general form of "imperfect obligations" (to invoke another Kantian

5. There are different variants of these two contrasting positions, and also other alternatives that differ from both, which are helpfully discussed and distinguished in Charles Beitz, "Human Rights as a Common Concern," *American Political Science Review* 95 (June 2001): 269–82.

6. Immanuel Kant, *Critique of Practical Reason* (1788), trans. L. W. Beck (New York: Bobbs-Merrill, 1956).

concept).[7] The perfectly specified demand not to torture anyone is supplemented by the more general, and less exactly specified, requirement to consider the ways and means through which torture can be prevented and then to decide what one should, thus, reasonably do. The relations between human rights, freedoms, and obligations will be further investigated in Sections IV through VI.

Even though recognitions of human rights (with their associated claims and obligations) are ethical affirmations, they need not, by themselves, deliver a complete blueprint for evaluative assessment. An agreement on human rights does involve a firm commitment, to wit, to give reasonable consideration to the duties that follow from that ethical endorsement. But even with agreement on these affirmations, there can still be serious debates, particularly in the case of imperfect obligations, on (i) the ways in which the attention that is owed to human rights should be best paid, (ii) how the different types of human rights should be weighed against each other and their respective demands integrated together, (iii) how the claims of human rights should be consolidated with other evaluative concerns that may also deserve ethical attention, and so on.[8] A theory of human rights can leave room for further discussions, disputations and arguments. The approach of open public reasoning, which is central to the understanding of human rights as proposed here, can definitively settle some disputes about coverage and content (including the identification of some clearly sustainable rights and others that would be hard to sustain), but may have to leave others, at least tentatively, unsettled.[9] The admissibility of a

7. I have discussed, in an earlier paper, the relevance of the Kantian distinction between "perfect" and "imperfect" obligations even for a largely consequentialist framework. "Consequential Evaluation and Practical Reason," *Journal of Philosophy* 97 (2000): 477–502.

8. Some of the central issues are discussed by John Mackie, "Can There Be a Rights-based Moral Theory?" *Studies in Ethical Theory: Midwest Studies in Philosophy* 3, ed. Peter A. French, et al. (Morris : University of Minnesota, 1978). Reprinted in *Theories of Rights*, ed. Jeremy Waldron (Oxford: Oxford University Press, 1984), pp. 168–81.

9. This applies not only to the persistence of interpersonal disagreements, but also to specific areas of unresolved disputes within one person's own reasoned assessment. An adequate theory of rationality has to make room for such "incompleteness" of assessment. The general issue of admissibility of incompleteness is discussed in my *Collective Choice and Social Welfare* (San Francisco: Holden-Day, 1970; republished, Amsterdam: North-Holland, 1979); "Maximization and the Act of Choice," *Econometrica* 65 (1997): 745–80,

domain of continued dispute is no embarrassment to a theory of human rights.[10]

In practical applications of human rights, such debates are, of course, quite common and entirely customary, particularly among human rights activists. What is being argued here is that the possibility of such debates—without losing the basic recognition of the importance of human rights—is not just a feature of what can be called human rights *practice*, they are actually part of the general *discipline* of human rights including the underlying theory (rather than being an embarrassment to that discipline). An acknowledgment of the necessity to pay ethical attention to human rights, far from obliterating the need for such deliberation, actually invites it. A theory of human rights can, therefore, allow considerable internal variations, without losing the commonality of the agreed principle of attaching substantial importance to human rights (and to the corresponding freedoms and obligations) and of being committed to considering seriously how that importance should be appropriately reflected.

Variability of this kind is not only not an embarrassment, it tends to be standardly present in all general theories of substantive ethics. Indeed, a similar diversity can be found within utility-centered ethics, even though this feature of that large ethical discipline often receives little or no recognition. In the case of utility-based reasoning, variations can arise not only from the different ways in which utilities can be interpreted (as *pleasures*, fulfillment of *desires*, or realization of *choices*),[11] nor only from the acknowledged heterogeneity of utilities themselves (well

---

reprinted in *Rationality and Freedom* (Cambridge, Mass.: Harvard University Press, 2002); and also "Incompleteness and Reasoned Choice," *Synthese* (forthcoming 2004). See also Isaac Levi, *Hard Choices: Decision Making under Unresolved Conflict* (Cambridge: Cambridge University Press, 1986), and Hilary Putnam, "Über die Rationalität von Präferenzen," *Allgemeine Zeitschrift für Philosophie* 21 (1996): 204–28, English version, "On the Rationality of Preferences," in his *The Collapse of the Fact / Value Dichotomy and Other Essays* (Cambridge, Mass.: Harvard University Press, 2002).

10. Also, as Jeremy Waldron has argued, disagreement about rights "is a sign—the best possible sign in modern circumstances—that people *take rights seriously*." See *Law and Disagreement* (Oxford: Oxford University Press, 2001), p. 311.

11. See Jeremy Bentham, *An Introduction to the Principles of Morals and Legislation* (London: Payne, 1789; republished, Oxford: Clarendon Press); Henry Sidgwick, *The Method of Ethics* (London: Macmillan, 1874); A. C. Pigou, *The Economics of Welfare* (London: MacMillan, 1920); Frank P. Ramsey, *Foundations: Essays in Philosophy, Logic, Mathematics*

recognized by both Aristotle and John Stuart Mill).[12] They can also arise from the diversity of ways in which utilities can be used, whether by mere *addition*, or by *multiplication* (after suitable normalization), or through the *addition of concave transformations* of utility functions, all of which have been proposed and pursued, within the discipline of utility-based evaluation.[13] Further, the discipline of interpersonal comparison of utilities may itself allow alternative procedures of quantification of utilities and go comfortably with accommodating permissible variations within specified classes of "partial comparability."[14] The existence of different ways of making use of utility-based reasoning and alternative utilitarian procedures does not invalidate or even undermine the general approach of utility-centered ethics. And, similarly, the ethics of human rights is not nullified or thwarted by internal variations that it allows and incorporates.

Thus, the analogy between articulations of human rights and utilitarian pronouncements has considerable perspicacity, even though the great founder of modern utilitarianism, Jeremy Bentham, managed to miss that connection altogether in his classic hatchet job on natural rights in general and on the "rights of man" in particular. Bentham took

and Economics (London: Routledge, 1978); Richard M. Hare, *Freedom and Reason* (Oxford: Clarendon Press, 1963); J.C.B. Gosling, *Pleasure and Desire* (Oxford: Clarendon Press, 1969); Derek Parfit, *Reasons and Persons* (Oxford: Clarendon Press, 1984); R. E. Goodin, "Laundering Preferences," in *The Foundations of Social Choice Theory*, ed. Jon Elster and Aanund Hylland (Cambridge: Cambridge University Press, 1986), pp. 75–101; James Griffin, *Well-being* (Oxford: Clarendon Press, 1986); John Broome, *Weighing Goods* (Oxford: Blackwell, 1991); among many other contributions.

12. See Aristotle, *The Nicomachean Ethics*, trans. David Ross, rev. ed. (Oxford: Clarendon Press, 1980), and John Stuart Mill, *Utilitarianism* (London, 1861; republished London: Collins/Fontana, 1962). I have discussed the issues involved in "Plural Utility," *Proceedings of the Aristotelian Society* 81 (1980–81): 193–215.

13. See John F. Nash, "The Bargaining Problem," *Econometrica* 18 (1950): 155–62; John C. Harsanyi, "Cardinal Welfare, Individualistic Ethics, and Interpersonal Comparisons of Utility," *Journal of Political Economy* 63 (1955): 309–21; James A. Mirrlees, "An Exploration of the Theory of Optimum Income Taxation," *Review of Economic Studies* 38 (1971): 175–208.

14. These issues are discussed in Amartya Sen, "Interpersonal Aggregation and Partial Comparability," *Econometrica* 38 (1970): 393–409, and *Choice, Welfare and Measurement* (Oxford: Blackwell, 1982; republished, Cambridge, Mass.: Harvard University Press, 1997); Charles Blackorby, "Degrees of Cardinality and Aggregate Partial Orderings," *Econometrica* 43 (1975): 845–52; Ben J. Fine, "A Note on 'Interpersonal Aggregation and Partial Comparability'," *Econometrica* 43 (1975): 169–72; *Interpersonal Comparisons of Well-beings*, ed. Jon Elster and John Roemer (Cambridge: Cambridge University Press, 1991).

the appropriate comparison to be that between the legal significance, respectively of: (1) declarations of human rights, and (2) actually legislated rights. Not surprisingly, he found the former to be essentially lacking in legal status in the way the latter, obviously enough, would have. Bentham's dismissal of human rights came, thus, with amazingly swiftness.

> *Right,* the substantive *right,* is the child of law; from *real* laws come *real* rights; but from *imaginary* laws, from "law of nature" [can come only] "*imaginary* rights."[15]

It is easy to see that Bentham's rejection of the idea of natural "rights of man" depends substantially on the rhetoric of privileged use of the term of "rights," seeing it in its specifically legal interpretation. However, insofar as human rights are meant to be significant ethical claims, the pointer to the fact that they do not by themselves have legal or institutional force is obvious enough, but also quite irrelevant to the discipline of human rights.[16] The appropriate comparison is, surely, between:

(1) a utility-based ethics (championed by Bentham himself), which sees intrinsic ethical importance in utilities but none in human rights or human freedoms (any role that the latter can have in the utilitarian system is, thus, entirely instrumental), and

(2) an ethics that makes room for the fundamental significance of human rights (as the advocates of "rights of man" did), linked with a diagnosis of the basic importance of human freedoms and the obligations generated by that diagnosis.[17]

15. Jeremy Bentham, *Anarchical Fallacies*, in *Collected Works*, vol. II, p. 523.

16. Accepting a general contrast between the respective categories of ethical assertions and legal pronouncements does not, of course, deny the possibility that ethical views may contribute to the interpretation and, thus, the substantive content of laws. The recognition of that possibility may go against a strictly positivist theory of law (on which see Ronald Dworkin, *A Matter of Principle* [Cambridge, Mass.: Harvard University Press, 1985]). This understanding does not, however, obliterate the motivational and substantive distinction between primarily ethical claims and principally legal proclamations.

17. The importance of rights and freedoms can, of course, be combined with incorporating the significance of utility or well-being in ethical reasoning, but if such a "combined" system is to be pursued, some consistency problems will have to be faced in devising a coherent and integrated social choice procedure; on this see Amartya Sen, "The

Just as utilitarian ethical reasoning takes the form of insisting that the utilities of the relevant persons must be taken into account in deciding on what should be done, the human rights approach demands that the acknowledged human rights must be given ethical recognition (the form and the informational basis of that recognition will be discussed further in the next two sections). The relevant comparison lies in this contrast, *not* in differentiating the legal force of legislated rights (for which Bentham's phrase "the child of law" is an appropriate description) from the absence of any legal standing generated by an ethical recognition of rights (without any legislation or legal reinterpretation). Indeed, even as Bentham was busy in 1791 and 1792 writing down his dismissal of "rights of man," the reach and range of ethical interpretations of rights were being powerfully explored by Thomas Paine's *Rights of Man*, and by Mary Wollstonecraft's *A Vindication of the Rights of Woman: with Strictures on Political and Moral Subjects*, both published during the period 1791 to 1792 (though neither seemed to arouse Bentham's curiosity).[18]

An ethical understanding of human rights goes not only against seeing them as legal demands (and against taking them to be, as in Bentham's view, legal *pretensions*), but also differs from a law-centered approach to human rights that sees them as if they are basically *grounds* for law, almost "laws in waiting." Ethical and legal rights do, of course, have motivational connections. In a rightly celebrated article "Are There Any Natural Rights?" Herbert Hart has argued that people "speak of their moral rights mainly when advocating their incorporation in a legal system." He added that the concept of a right "belongs to that branch of morality which is specifically concerned to determine when one person's freedom may be limited by another's and so to determine what actions may appropriately be made the subject of coercive legal

Impossibility of a Paretian Liberal," *Journal of Political Economy* 78 (1970): 152–57, and *Rationality and Freedom* (Cambridge, Mass.: Harvard University Press, 2002), essays 12–14 and 20–22. See also Robert Nozick, *Anarchy, State and Utopia* (New York: Basic Books, 1974), and the special number of *Analyse & Kritik* 18 (1996) on "the Liberal Paradox," particularly Kotaro Suzumura, "Welfare, Rights and Social Choice Procedures," pp. 20–37.

18. Thomas Paine, *The Rights of Man: Being an Answer to Mr. Burke's Attack on the French Revolution* (1791); second part, *Combining Principle and Practice* (1792); republished, *The Rights of Man* (London: Dent, and New York: Dutton, 1906). Mary Wollstonecraft, *A Vindication of the Rights of Woman* (1792); republished, *The Rights of Woman* (London: Dent, and New York: Dutton, 1929).

rules."[19] Whereas Bentham saw rights as a "child of law," Hart's view takes the form, in effect, of seeing some natural rights as *parents* of law: they motivate and inspire specific legislations. Although Hart does not make any reference whatever to human rights in his article, the reasoning about the role of natural rights as inspiration for legislation can be seen to apply to the concept of human rights as well.[20]

There can, in fact, be little doubt that the idea of moral rights can serve, and has often served in practice, as the basis of new legislation. It has frequently been utilized in this way, and this is indeed an important *use* of human rights. That, for example, is precisely the way the diagnosis of inalienable rights was invoked in the U.S. Declaration of Independence and reflected subsequently in the Bill of Rights, a route that has been well-trodden in the legislative history of many countries in the world.[21] Providing inspiration for legislation is certainly one way in which the ethical force of human rights has been constructively deployed.

However, to acknowledge that such a connection exists is not the same as taking the relevance of human rights to lie *exclusively* in determining what should "appropriately be made the subject of coercive legal rules." It is important to see that the idea of human rights can be, and is, actually used in several other ways as well. Indeed, if human rights are seen as powerful moral claims, indeed as "moral rights" (to use Hart's phrase), then surely we have reason for some catholicity in considering different avenues for promoting these claims. (This question will be pursued in Section VII.) The ways and means of advancing and implementing human rights need not, thus, be confined only to making new laws (even though sometimes legislation may indeed turn out to be the right way to proceed). For example, monitoring and other activist support, provided by such organizations as Human Rights Watch or

19. H. L. A. Hart, "Are There Any Natural Rights?" *The Philosophical Review* 64 (1955), reprinted in *Theories of Rights*, ed. Jeremy Waldron (Oxford: Oxford University Press, 1984), p. 79.

20. On this see Maurice Cranston, "Are There Any Human Rights?"

21. The framers of the Universal Declaration of Human Rights in 1948 hoped, in fact, that this declaration would serve as a template for bills of rights in different nations, with national courts taking a lead in their enforcement. See Mary Ann Glendon's wonderful account of that remarkable history, *A World Made New: Eleanor Roosevelt and the Universal Declaration of Human Rights* (New York: Random House, 2001).

Amnesty International or OXFAM or Médicins Sans Frontièrs, can themselves help to advance the effective reach of acknowledged human rights.[22] In many contexts, legislation may not, in fact, be involved.

IV. Rights, Freedoms and Social Influence

Why are human rights important? Since declarations of human rights are ethical affirmations of the need to pay appropriate attention to the significance of freedoms incorporated in the formulation of human rights (as was discussed in the last section), an appropriate starting point must be the importance of freedoms of human beings to be so recognized. Note that while rights involve claims (specifically, claims on others who are in a position to make a difference), freedoms, in contrast, are primarily descriptive characteristics of the conditions of persons.[23]

By starting from the importance of freedoms as the appropriate human condition on which to concentrate, rather than on utilities (as Bentham did), we get a motivating reason not only for celebrating our own rights and liberties, but also for our taking an interest in the significant freedoms of others, not just in their pleasures and desire-fulfillment (as under utilitarianism). Bentham's insistence on choosing utility as the basis of ethical evaluation can be contrasted with the reasons for focusing instead on freedoms. I have discussed elsewhere why those reasons are weighty and how the focus on freedoms can avoid some of the major pitfalls of concentrating only on utility in the form of pleasure or desire fulfillment. For example, the utilitarian calculus can suffer from valuational distortions resulting from the neglect of substantive deprivation of those who are chronically disadvantaged but who learn, by force of circumstances, to take pleasure in small mercies and

22. Since the Gilbert Murray Lecture given at Oxford in November 2002, in which this article originated, was arranged by OXFAM (Gilbert Murray was one of OXFAM's founders), it was also a suitable occasion to discuss this broader connection of human rights with a plurality of ways of pursuing them.

23. However, the ethical force of freedoms can help to generate claims on others. On different aspects of the "entanglements" between descriptive and evaluative concerns, see Hilary Putnam, *The Collapse of the Fact / Value Dichotomy and Other Essays* (Cambridge, Mass.: Harvard University Press, 2002). See also William Van Orman Quine, "Two Dogmas, Of Empiricism," in his *From a Logical Point of View* (Cambridge, Mass.: Harvard University Press, 1961), pp. 20–46, and Vivian Walsh, "Philosophy and Economics," in *The New Palgrave: A Dictionary of Economics*, ed. John Eatwell, Murray Milgate and Peter Newman (London: Macmillan, 1987), pp. 861–69.

get reconciled to cutting down their desires to "realistic proportions" (thereby appearing to be not particularly deprived in the special metric of pleasures or desire-fulfillment).[24]

Before going into the difficult issue of duties related to rights, which will be examined in Section VI, some exploration of the connection between rights and freedoms is necessary, to which I devote the rest of this section as well as Section V. Freedoms can vary in importance and also in terms of the extent to which they can be influenced by social help. For a freedom to count as a part of the evaluative system of human rights, it clearly must be important enough to justify requiring that others should be ready to pay substantial attention to decide what they can reasonably do to advance it. It also has to satisfy a condition of plausibility that others could make a material difference through taking such an interest.

There have to be some "threshold conditions" of (i) importance and (ii) social influenceability for a freedom to figure within the interpersonal and interactive spectrum of human rights. Insofar as the idea of human rights demands public discussion and engagement, which I noted earlier and will further discuss in Section IX, the agreement that would be sought is not only on whether some specific freedom of a particular person has any ethical importance whatsoever (that condition can be easy to satisfy), but also whether its significance and its influenceability meet the threshold conditions for inclusion among the human rights on which the society should focus.

The threshold conditions may prevent, for a variety of reasons, particular freedoms from being an appropriate subject matter of human rights. To illustrate, it is not hard to argue that some importance should be attached to all four of the following freedoms:

(1) a person's freedom not to be assaulted;
(2) her freedom to receive medical care for a serious health problem;
(3) her freedom not to be called up regularly by her neighbors whom she detests;
(4) her freedom to achieve tranquillity.

24. The evaluative framework of substantive freedoms can provide a more robust appreciation of a person's inability to achieve what they have reason to value. On this see my "Well-being, Agency and Freedom: The Dewey Lectures 1984," *Journal of Philosophy* 82 (1985): 169–220; *Inequality Reexamined*; and *Development as Freedom* (New York: Knopf, 1999).

However, even though all four may be important in one way or another, it is not altogether implausible to argue that the first (freedom not to be assaulted) is a good subject matter for a human right, and so is the second (freedom to receive necessary medical care),[25] but the third (freedom not to be called up by detested neighbors) is not, in general, important enough to cross the threshold of social significance to qualify as a human right. Also, the fourth, while quite possibly extremely important for the person, is too inward-looking—and too hard to be influenced by others—to be a good subject matter for human rights. The exclusion of a "right to tranquillity" relates not to any skepticism about the possible importance of tranquillity and the significance of a person's being free to achieve it, but to the difficulty of guaranteeing it through social help.

There can be fruitful debates on the thresholds and their use, and in particular on whether a specific case of freedom meets the threshold conditions or not. As was briefly discussed in Sections II and III (and will be further examined in Section IX), such discussions are part of the discipline of human rights. The analyses of thresholds, related both to the seriousness and to the social influenceability of particular freedoms, cannot but have a significant place in the discipline of human rights.

V. Processes, Opportunities and Capabilities

I turn now to a closer scrutiny of the contents of freedom and its multiple features. I have argued elsewhere that "opportunity" and "process" are two aspects of freedom that require distinction, with the importance of each deserving specific acknowledgment.[26] An example can help to bring out the *separate* (though not necessarily independent) relevance of both *substantive opportunities* and *freedom of processes.*

Consider an adult person, let us call her Rima, who decides that she would like to go out in the evening. To take care of some considerations

25. However, in the second case (that is, the entitlement to necessary medical care), we shall have to discuss whether this type of a "welfare right," or more generally, economic and social rights, can be seen as human rights, and this examination will be taken up in Section VIII.

26. See *Rationality and Freedom* (Cambridge, Mass.: Harvard University Press, 2002), particularly my Arrow Lectures ("Freedom and Social Choice") included there: essays 20 through 22.

that are not central to the issues involved here (but which could make the discussion more complex), it is assumed that there are no particular safety risks involved in her going out, and that she has critically reflected on this decision and judged that going out would be the sensible, indeed the ideal, thing to do. Now consider the threat of a violation of this freedom if some authoritarian guardians of society decide that she must not go out in the evening ("it is most unseemly"), and if they force her, in one way or another, to stay indoors. To see that there are two distinct issues involved in this one violation, consider an alternative case in which the authoritarian bosses decide that she must—absolutely *must*—go out ("you are expelled for the evening: just obey"). There is clearly a violation of freedom here even though Rima is being forced to do exactly what she would have chosen to do anyway, and this is readily seen when we compare the two alternatives "choosing freely to go out" and "being forced to go out." The latter involves an immediate violation of the *process aspect* of Rima's freedom, since an action is being forced on her (even though it is an action she would have freely chosen also).

The opportunity aspect may also be affected, since a plausible accounting of opportunities can include having options and it can inter alia include valuing free choice. However, the violation of the opportunity aspect would be more substantial and manifest if she were not only forced to do something chosen by another, but in fact, forced to do something she herself would not otherwise choose to do. The comparison between "being forced to go out" (when she would have gone out anyway, if free) and, say, "being forced to polish the shoes of others at home" (not her favorite activity) brings out this contrast, which is primarily one of the opportunity aspect, rather than the process aspect. In being forced to stay home and polish the shoes of others, Rima loses freedom in two different ways, related respectively to (1) being forced with no freedom of choice, and (2) being obliged in particular to do something she would not choose to do.[27]

Both processes and opportunities can figure in human rights. A denial of "due process" in being, say, imprisoned without a proper trial can be the subject matter of human rights (no matter what the outcome of the

27. More complex features of the opportunity aspect and the process aspect of freedoms are also discussed in my Arrow Lectures ("Freedom and Social Choice") in *Rationality and Freedom*, essays 20 through 22.

fair trial might be), and so can be the denial of the opportunity of medical treatment, or the opportunity of living without the danger of being assaulted (going beyond the exact process through which these opportunities are made real).

For the opportunity aspect of freedom, the idea of "capability" (that is, the opportunity to achieve valuable combinations of human functionings: what a person is able to do or be) can typically provide a helpful approach.[28] It allows us to distinguish appropriately between (1) what she values *doing or being,* and (2) the *means* she has to achieve what she values. By shifting attention, in particular, towards the former, the capability-based approach resists an overconcentration on means (such as incomes and primary goods) that can be found in some theories of justice (for example, in the Rawlsian Difference Principle). The capability approach can capture the fact that two persons can have very different substantial opportunities even when they have exactly the same set of means: for example, a disabled person can do far less than an able-bodied person can, with exactly the same income and other "primary goods." The disabled person cannot, thus, be judged to be equally advantaged—with the same substantive opportunities—as the person without any physical handicap but with the same set of means (such as income and wealth and other primary goods). The capability perspective concentrates on what actual opportunities a person has, not the means over which she has command. More particularly, the capability perspective allows us to take into account the parametric variability in the relation between the means, on the one hand, and the actual opportunities, on the other.[29]

28. On the concept of capability, see my "Equality of What?" in *Tanner Lectures on Human Values,* vol. I, ed. Sterling M. McMurrin (Cambridge: Cambridge University Press, and Salt Lake City: University of Utah Press, 1980), pp. 197–220, and *Commodities and Capabilities* (Amsterdam: North-Holland, 1985), and also, jointly edited with Martha Nussbaum, *The Quality of Life* (Oxford: Clarendon Press, 1993). The approach is powerfully developed and applied by Martha Nussbaum, *Women and Human Development: The Capabilities Approach* (Cambridge: Cambridge University Press, 2000). See also the related theories of substantial opportunities developed by Richard Arneson, "Equality and Equality of Opportunity for Welfare," *Philosophical Studies* 56 (1989): 77–112; G. A. Cohen, "On the Currency of Egalitarian Justice," *Ethics* 99 (1989): 906–44; and John E. Roemer, *Theories of Distributive Justice* (Cambridge, Mass.: Harvard University Press, 1996), among others contributors.

29. The importance of this variability for a theory of justice is discussed in my "Justice: Means versus Freedoms," *Philosophy & Public Affairs* 19 (1990): 111–21. Differences in the capability to function can arise even with the same set of personal means (such as primary

The capability perspective can also help in bringing out the need for transparent valuational scrutiny of individual advantages and adversities, since the different *functionings* have to be assessed and weighted in relation to each other, and the opportunities of having different *combinations* of functionings also have to be evaluated.[30] The richness of the capability perspective broadly interpreted, thus, includes its insistence on the need for open valuational scrutiny for making social judgments, and in this sense, it fits in well with the importance of public reasoning.[31] This openness of transparent valuation contrasts with burying the evaluative exercise in some mechanical, and valuationally opaque, convention (for example, by taking market-evaluated income to be the invariable standard of individual advantage, thereby giving implicit normative priority to institutionally determined market prices).

goods) for a variety of reasons, such as (1) *personal heterogeneities* (related, for example, to disability, or proneness to illness), (2) *environmental diversities* (such as climatic conditions, or varying threats from epidemic diseases or from local crime), (3) *variations in non-personal resources* (such as the nature of public health care, or social cohesion), or (4) *different relative positions vis-à-vis others* (well illustrated by Adam Smith's discussion, in the *Wealth of Nations*, of the fact that the clothing and other resources one needs "to appear in public without shame" depends on what other people standardly wear and how they typically live in that society).

30. The need for an explicit valuational exercise is, thus, seen as an advantage, rather than a limitation of the capability approach. For arguments in different directions on this issue, see Charles R. Beitz, "Amartya Sen's Resources, Values and Development," *Economics and Philosophy* 2 (1986): 282–90; Bernard Williams, "The Standard of Living: Interests and Capabilities," in Amartya Sen et al., *The Standard of Living*, ed. Geoffrey Hawthorn (Cambridge: Cambridge University Press, 1987), pp. 94–102; Amartya Sen, *Inequality Reexamined*, and "Capability and Well-being," in *The Quality of Life*, ed. Nussbaum and Sen, pp. 31–53.

31. The capability approach can allow considerable difference in application. For a somewhat different perspective, see Martha Nussbaum, "Nature, Function, and Capability: Aristotle on Political Distribution," *Oxford Studies in Ancient Philosophy*, Supplementary Volume (1988), pp. 145–54, and *Women and Human Development: The Capabilities Approach*. Nussbaum has discussed the importance of identifying an overarching "list of capabilities," with given priorities, in a more Aristotelian way. My own reluctance to join the search for such a canonical list arises partly from my difficulty in seeing how the exact lists and weights would be chosen without appropriate specification of the context of their use (which could vary), but also from a disinclination to accept any substantive diminution of the domain of public reasoning. The framework of capabilities, as I see it, helps to clarify and illuminate the *subject matter* of public reasoning, which can involve epistemic issues (including claims of objective importance) as well as ethical and political ones. It does not—and cannot—displace the need for public reasoning.

There has, however, been some serious criticism of describing these substantive opportunities—to live one kind of a life or another—as "freedoms," and it has been argued that this makes the idea of freedom too inclusive. For example, in her illuminating and sympathetic critique of my *Development as Freedom*, Susan Okin has presented arguments to suggest that I tend "to overextend the concept of freedom."[32] She argues: "It is hard to conceive of some human functionings, or the fulfillment of some needs and wants, such as good health and nourishment, as freedoms without stretching the term until it seems to refer to everything that is of central value to human beings" (p. 292).

There is indeed scope for argument on how broadly the concept of freedom should be used. But the particular example considered in Okin's counterargument is, I think, based on a misinterpretation of the idea of freedom underlying the concept of capability. It has not been suggested at all that a functioning (for example, being in good health or being well-nourished) should be seen as freedom of any kind. Rather, freedom, in the form of capability, concentrates on the *opportunity* to achieve combinations of functionings (including, inter alia, the opportunity to be well-nourished or in good health, as in this particular case): the person is *free to use* this opportunity or not. A capability reflects the alternative combinations of functionings over which the person has freedom of effective choice.

It is, therefore, not being suggested at all that *being* well-nourished or in good health is to be seen as a freedom in itself.[33] Capability, as a kind of freedom, refers to the extent to which the person is *able to choose* particular combinations of functionings (including, inter alia, such things as being well-nourished), no matter what the person actually decides to choose. Mahatma Gandhi famously did not use that opportunity to be well-fed when he chose to fast, as a protest against the

32. Susan Okin, "Poverty, Well-being and Gender: What Counts, Who's Heard?" *Philosophy & Public Affairs* 31 (2003): 280–316. On related issues see also Joshua Cohen, "Review of Sen's *Inequality Reexamined*," *Journal of Philosophy* 92 (1994): 275–88, esp. 278–80, and G. A. Cohen, "Review: Amartya Sen's Unequal World," *The New Left Review* (1995): 117–29, esp. 120–25.

33. I have discussed this issue in "Well-being, Agency and Freedom: The Dewey Lectures 1984." It is also important to examine how the concept of "freedom" links with a broadly defined idea of "interest," which underlies Joseph Raz's reasoned diagnosis: "Rights ground requirement for action in the interest of other beings." See *The Morality of Freedom* (Oxford: Clarendon Press, 1986), p. 180.

policies of the British Raj in India. In terms of the actual functioning of being well-nourished, the fasting Gandhi did not differ from a starving famine victim, but the freedoms and opportunities they respectively had were quite different. The *freedom to have* any particular thing can be distinguished from actually *having* that thing. What a person is free to have, not just what he or she actually has, is relevant, I have argued, to a theory of justice.[34] A similar point can be made about the relevance of substantive freedoms in a theory of human rights.

The fact that many of the terrible deprivations in the world seem to arise from a lack of freedom to avoid those deprivations (rather than from choice, including choosing to be "indolent": a classic issue in the historical literature on poverty) is an important motivational reason to emphasize the role of freedom. This led Marx to argue passionately for the need to replace "the domination of circumstances and chance over individuals by the domination of individuals over chance and circumstances."[35] The general idea of freedom, with its many distinct components, seems particularly relevant to normative social choice theory, in general, and to the theory of justice, in particular. The argument here is that it can also figure powerfully in the normative foundations of human rights.

To take a different type of example, consider the freedom of new immigrants to West Europe or North America to conserve the ancestral cultural customs and life-styles from their countries of origin. This complex subject cannot be adequately assessed without distinguishing between *doing* something and being *free* to do that thing. A strong argument can be constructed in favor of an immigrant's having the freedom to retain at least parts of her ancestral life-style, but this must not be seen as an argument in favor of her pursuing her ancestral life-style whether she chooses to do this or not. The central issue, in this argument, is the *freedom* to choose how she should live, including the *opportunity* to

34. G. A. Cohen has presented arguments in favor of focusing on achieved functionings—related to his concept of "midfare"—rather than on capability; see his "On the Currency of Egalitarian Justice," and "Equality of What? On Welfare, Resources and Capabilities," in *The Quality of Life*, ed. Nussbaum and Sen, pp. 125–41. See also Richard Arneson, "Equality and Equality of Opportunity for Welfare," *Philosophical Studies* 56 (1989): 77–112.

35. Karl Marx, *The German Ideology*, with Friedrich Engels, in *Karl Marx: Selected Writings*, ed. David McLellan (Oxford: Oxford University Press, 1977), p. 190.

pursue ancestral customs, and it cannot be turned into an argument for her specifically pursuing those customs in particular, irrespective of the alternatives she has and the choices she would make.[36] The importance of capability, reflecting opportunities, is central to this distinction.[37]

I have been concentrating on what the capability perspective can do for a theory of justice or of human rights in the immediately preceding discussion, but I now to turn to what it *cannot* do. Although the idea of capability has considerable merit in the assessment of the opportunity aspect of freedom, it cannot possibly deal adequately with the process aspect of freedom, since capabilities are characteristics of individual advantages, and they fall short of telling us enough about the fairness or equity of the processes involved, or about the freedom of citizens to invoke and utilize procedures that are equitable.

Let me illustrate the contrast of perspectives with a somewhat harsh example. It is now fairly well established that given symmetric care, women tend to live longer than men. If one were concerned only with capabilities (and nothing else), and in particular with equality of the capability to live long, it would have been possible to construct an argument for giving men more medical attention than women to counteract the natural masculine handicap. But giving women less medical attention than men for the same health problems would clearly violate an important requirement of process equity, and it seems reasonable to argue, in cases of this kind, that demands of equity in process freedom could sensibly override a single-minded concentration on the opportunity aspect of freedom (and the requirements of capability equality in particular). While it is important to emphasize the relevance of the capability perspective in judging people's substantive opportunities (particu-

36. Though this is not the occasion to provide a critical assessment of "multiculturalism" as a social policy, it is perhaps worth noting here that there is a big difference between (1) valuing multiculturalism because of the way, and to the extent that, it enhances the freedoms of the people involved to choose to live as they would like (and have reason to like); and (2) valuing cultural diversity *per se*, which focuses on the descriptive characteristics of a societal pattern, rather than on the freedoms of the people involved.

37. Capability is also central to the relationship between multiculturalism and gender equity. The important question that Susan Okin asks in her joint book, *Is Multiculturalism Bad for Women?*, ed. J. Cohen, M. Howard and M. C. Nussbaum (Princeton, N.J.: Princeton University Press, 1999), turns, to a great extent, on possible tensions between multiculturalism and the freedom of individual persons (in this case, women) within a community to freely consider and choose how they would live.

larly in comparison with alternative approaches that focus on incomes, or primary goods, or resources), that point does not, in any way, go against seeing the simultaneous relevance also of the process aspect of freedom in a theory of human rights, or, for that matter, in a theory of justice.

Related to this issue, I should perhaps take the opportunity here to correct a misinterpretation of the place of the capability perspective in a theory of justice. A theory of justice, or more generally an adequate theory of normative collective choice, has to be alive both to the fairness of the processes involved and to the equity and efficiency of the substantive opportunities that people can enjoy.[38] In dealing with the latter, capability can indeed provide a very helpful perspective, in comparison with, say, the Rawlsian concentration on "primary goods." But capability can hardly serve as the sole informational basis for the other considerations, related to processes, that must also be accommodated in normative collective choice theory.

Perhaps the point can be seen most easily by considering the different components of Rawls's theory of justice. His "first principle" of justice involves the priority of liberty, and the first part of the "second principle" involves process fairness, through demanding that "positions and offices be open to all." Even though the concerns that lead Rawls to these particular formulations can be dealt with in different ways, not only in the way that Rawls himself addresses them, the force and cogency of these Rawlsian concerns can neither be ignored nor be adequately addressed through relying only the informational base of capabilities.[39]

In contrast, capability comes into its own in dealing with the *remainder* of the second principle, viz. "the Difference Principle" (with its con-

38. The plurality of concerns, involving processes as well as opportunities, which is inescapably involved in normative collective choice (including theories of justice), is discussed in my *Collective Choice and Social Welfare* (1970) and "Well-being, Agency and Freedom: The Dewey Lectures 1984," *Journal of Philosophy* 82 (1985). Since I have seen it asserted that I propound a "capability-based theory of justice," I should make it absolutely clear that this could be true only in the rather limited sense of naming something according to a *principal* part of it (comparable with, say, using England for Great Britain, or Holland for the Netherlands).

39. See my *Collective Choice and Social Welfare*, particularly chapters 5 through 9, and "Well-being, Agency and Freedom: The Dewey Lectures 1984." The issues involved are more fully addressed in my forthcoming book *Freedom and Justice*, to be published by Harvard University Press.

centration on "primary goods").[40] The territory that Rawls reserved for the accounting of primary goods, as used in his Difference Principle, would indeed be, I argue, better served by the capability perspective. That does not, however, obliterate in any way the relevance of the rest of the territory of justice, in which process considerations, including liberty and procedural equity, figure. The same plurality of informational base links with the multiplicity of considerations that can be invoked in a theory of human rights. Capabilities and the opportunity aspect of freedom, important as they are, have to be supplemented by considerations of fair processes and the lack of violation of the individual's right to invoke and utilize them.

VI. Duties, Reasonable Consideration and Imperfect Obligations

I turn now from rights to correlative duties. We can, again, proceed from the importance of freedoms and their different aspects. Since freedoms are important, people have reason to ask what they should do to help each other in defending or promoting their respective freedoms. Since violation, or non-realization, of the freedoms underlying significant rights are, in this evaluative system, bad things to happen, even others who are not themselves responsible for causing the violation have a good reason to consider what they should do to help.[41] Nevertheless, the move from a *reason* for action to help another person, which is easy to see in a consequence-sensitive ethical system, to an actual *duty* to give

40. It was indeed in the context of identifying an inadequacy in the Rawlsian focus on primary goods in the Difference Principle, for judging distributional equity, that the use of the capability perspective was proposed in my 1979 Tanner Lectures, published as "Equality of What?" (1980). In judging distributional equity, the capability perspective also has, I believe, advantages over the concentration on what Ronald Dworkin calls "resources" in "What Is Equality? Part 2: Equality of Resources," *Philosophy & Public Affairs* 10 (1981): 185–243. Dworkin has recently argued that on one interpretation, there is no substantial difference between my focus on capability and his focus on resources, while on another interpretation, he is just right and I am plain wrong (*Sovereign Virtue: The Theory and Practice of Equality* [Cambridge, Mass.: Harvard University Press, 2000]). I resist the temptation, which I must confess is fairly strong, to join that debate in this article.

41. The rationale and reach of a consequence-sensitive framework for this type of ethical reasoning have been investigated in my essays "Rights and Agency," *Philosophy & Public Affairs* 11 (1982): 3–39, "Positional Objectivity," *Philosophy & Public Affairs* 22 (1993): 126–45, and "Consequential Evaluation and Practical Reason," *Journal of Philosophy* 97 (2000).

reasonable consideration to undertaking such an action might appear, at least at first sight, to be a rather gigantic jump.

However, that sense of distance is largely illusory. The difference would indeed involve an immense escalation if the duty in question were not one of giving reasonable consideration to a possible action, but an absolute obligation to undertake that action, no matter what other values one has and what other commitments one has reason to consider. But that way of seeing one's duties—as compulsory action—is not only at some distance from the acknowledgment of reasons for action, but it also lacks cogency, and even internal coherence. There are many fine deeds for each of which a reason for action exists, but it would typically be impossible to carry out the totality of all those deeds. There is a need for the assessment of priorities and for discrimination in the way the obligation to give reasonable consideration may be followed up by sensible choices of action.

To accept that one has a duty to give reasonable consideration to many different types of actions is not an agreement to tie oneself up in hopeless knots. And it is particularly important in the present context to emphasize the converse: the determination not to get into a pandemonium of practical reasoning is not a ground for denying that one does have a duty to give reasonable consideration to what one can sensibly do for the rights, and the underlying significant and influenceable freedoms, of others. The demands of reasonable consideration would vary with a great many parameters that may be relevant to a person's practical reasoning.[42] Even though the acknowledgment that certain freedoms qualify as human rights already reflects an assessment of their general importance and their possible influenceability (discussed in Section IV), a person has to go beyond these pervasive features into more specific circumstances in giving reasonable consideration to what he or she, in particular, should do in a specific case.

The person has to judge, for example, how important the freedoms and rights are in the case in question compared with other claims on the person's possible actions (involving other rights and freedoms, but also

42. Making adequate room for parametric variations is a general feature of rational assessment, and not a characteristic only of ethical reasoning in particular. I have discussed this issue in *Rationality and Freedom* (Cambridge, Mass.: Harvard University Press, 2002), essays 1 through 5.

altogether different concerns that a person may, inter alia, sensibly have). Furthermore, the person has to judge the extent to which he or she can make a difference in this case, either acting alone or in conjunction with others. It will be relevant also to consider what others can be expected to do, and the appropriateness of how the required supportive actions may be shared among possible agents. A great many parametric considerations of these and other kinds will inescapably figure in the reasoned evaluation of what a person should do, even after the need to undertake such an evaluation has been fully accepted. Also, since detailed reflection on what one should do is itself time consuming (and cannot even be actually undertaken for all the ills of the world), the duty of reasonable consideration will not, in a great many cases, translate into an obligation to take on an elaborate scrutiny—only a willingness to do just that, when it seems relevant and appropriate.

The recognition of obligations in relation to the rights and freedoms of all human beings need not, thus, be translated into preposterously demanding commands. And yet, despite the parametric variability of the reach and force of reasonable consideration, the requirement to give such consideration is not by any means vacuous. The basic general obligation is that one must be willing to *consider* seriously what one should reasonably do, taking note of the relevant parameters of the cases involved. The necessity to ask that question (rather than proceeding on the assumption that we owe nothing to others, unless we have actually harmed them) can be the beginning of a more comprehensive line of ethical reasoning.[43] The territory of human rights firmly belongs there. The reasoning cannot, however, end there. Given one's limited abilities and reach, and the need for priorities involving different types of obligations as well as the demands of other moral concerns, there are serious exercises of practical reasoning to be undertaken, in which one's various obligations (including "imperfect obligations") must figure, in an explicit or implicit form.

The recognition of human rights is not an insistence that everyone everywhere rises to help prevent every violation of every human right no matter where it occurs. It is, rather, an acknowledgment that if one is in a plausible position to do something effective in preventing the violation

43. The centrality of that general question is powerfully discussed by Thomas Scanlon, *What We Owe to Each Other* (Cambridge, Mass.: Harvard University Press, 1998).

of such a right, then one does have an obligation to consider doing just that. It is still possible that other obligations or non-obligational concerns may overwhelm the reason for the particular action in question, but that reason cannot be simply brushed away as being "none of one's business." Loosely specified obligations must not be confused with no obligations at all. Rather, they belong, as was mentioned earlier, to the important category of duties that Immanuel Kant called "imperfect obligations" (and to which he attached great importance).

It is to be noted that, in this understanding, imperfect obligations are ethical requirements that stretch beyond the fully delineated duties, "the perfect obligations," that specific persons may have to perform particular acts. They involve the demand that serious consideration be given by anyone in a position to provide reasonable help to the person whose human right is threatened. These "imperfect obligations" firmly correlate, in the same way as fully specified "perfect obligations" do, with the recognition of rights. The difference lies in the nature and form of the obligations, not in the general correspondence between rights and obligations, which apply in the same way to imperfect as well as perfect obligations.

It may be useful to illustrate, with a concrete example, the distinction between different kinds of obligations that, despite their differences in content, relate in a similar way to human rights. Consider a real-life case that occurred in Queens, New York, in 1964, when a woman, Kitty Genovese, was fatally assaulted in full view of many others watching the event from their apartments, who did nothing to help her. It is plausible to argue that three terrible things happened here, which are distinct but interrelated:

(1) the woman's freedom—and right—not to be assaulted and killed was violated (this is clearly the principal nastiness in this case);

(2) the murderer violated the immunity that anyone should have against assault and killing (a violation of a "perfect obligation"); and

(3) the others who did nothing whatever to help the victim also transgressed their general—and "imperfect"—obligation to seriously consider providing the help which they could reasonably be expected to provide.

These distinct failings bring out a complex pattern of rights–duties correspondence in a structured ethics, which can help to explicate the evaluative framework of human rights, which yields imperfect as well as perfect obligations.[44]

The presumed precision of legal rights is often contrasted with inescapable ambiguities in the ethical claims of human rights. This contrast, however, is not in itself a great embarrassment for ethical claims, including those of imperfect obligations, since a framework of normative reasoning can sensibly allow variations that cannot be easily accommodated in fully specified legal requirements. As Aristotle remarked in the *Nicomachean Ethics*, we have "to look for precision in each class of things just so far as the nature of the subject admits."[45]

As it happens, however, in the laws of some countries, there is even a legal demand, which can hardly have extreme precision, for providing reasonable help to third parties. For example, in France there is provision for "criminal liability of omissions" in the failure to provide reasonable help to others suffering from particular types of transgressions. Not surprisingly, ambiguities in the application of such laws have proved to be quite large and have been the subject of considerable legal discussion in recent years.[46] The ambiguity of duties of this type, whether in ethics or in law, would be difficult to escape if third-party obligations of others in general are given some room, and this cannot be avoided for an adequate theory of human rights.

VII. Recognition, Agitation and Legislation

While the preceding analysis has been concerned with giving reasonable consideration to actions in general that people can undertake in defending or advancing the human rights of others, it is the legislation of human rights, along with their institutionalization, that has tended to

44. In this analysis I do not go into the distinction between *agent-specific* and *agent-neutral* moral evaluations. The present line of characterization can be further extended through making room for "position specific" assessments, in ways that I have tried to investigate in "Rights and Agency," and "Positional Objectivity."

45. The admissibility of inescapable ambiguities within a framework of rational assessment is discussed in my "Internal Consistency of Choice," *Econometrica* 61 (1993): 495–521, and "Maximization and the Act of Choice," *Econometrica* 65 (1997): 745–79, both reprinted in *Rationality and Freedom*. See also *Inequality Reexamined*, pp. 46–49, 131–35.

46. See, for example, Andrew Ashworth and Eva Steiner, "Criminal Omissions and Public Duties: The French Experience," *Legal Studies* 10 (1990): 153–64; Glanville Williams, "Criminal Omissions: The Conventional View," *Law Quarterly Review* 107 (1991): 86–98.

receive the lion's share of attention in the theoretical literature in this field. It is this legislative outlook that has also been firmly incorporated in much of the institutional understanding of human rights. However, while legislation is an important domain of public action, there are other ways and means which are also important and often effective in advancing the cause of recognized human rights.

First, under what can be called the "recognition route" (to be distinguished from the "legislative route"), there is acknowledgment but not necessarily any legalization or institutional enforcement of a class of claims that are seen as fundamental human rights.[47] The Universal Declaration of Human Rights, sponsored by the United Nations in 1948, which was perhaps the most important move that promoted global activities on human rights in the last century, falls solidly into this category (even though, as was discussed earlier, the framers of the Declaration had also hoped that it would lead to specific bills of rights in different countries). Subsequently, there has been a sequence of other international declarations, often through the United Nations, giving recognition, rather than a legal and coercive status, to various general demands, for example the "Declaration on the Right to Development," signed in 1986.[48] This approach is motivated by the idea that the ethical force of human rights is made more powerful in practice through giving it social recognition and an acknowledged status, even when no enforcement is instituted.

A second line of advance goes beyond recognition to active agitation. There can be organized advocacy urging compliance with certain basic claims of all human beings that are seen as human rights, and there can

47. As Charles Beitz has pointed out, human rights play "the role of a moral touchstone—a standard of assessment and criticism for domestic institutions, a standard of aspiration for their reform, and increasingly a standard of evaluation for the policies and practices of international economic and political organizations." See "Human Rights as a Common Concern," p. 269.

48. Analyses of the content of the right to development have been presented in United Nations Development Programme, *Human Development Report 2000* (New York: United Nations, 2000); S. R. Osmani, "Human Rights to Food, Health, and Education," mimeographed, UNDP and the University of Ulster, 2000; Arjun Sengupta, "Development Policy and the Right to Development," *Frontline*, February 7–March 2, 2001; Arjun Sengupta, Asborn Eide, Stephen Marks, and Bård Anders Andreassen, "The Right to Development and Human Rights in Development," presented at the Nobel Symposium in Oslo on Right to Development, October 2003.

also be monitoring of violations of these rights and attempts to generate effective social pressure. The global NGOs have increasingly been involved in advancing human rights, through public discussion and support, on the one hand, and publicizing and criticizing violations, on the other. These efforts have come not only from dedicated human rights organizations, such as Human Rights Watch and Amnesty International, but also from broader organizations, such as OXFAM, Médicins Sans Frontièrs, the Red Cross, Save the Children, and Action Aid. The rights invoked in this "agitation route" may or may not have any legal status in the country in question, but advocacy and support are not necessarily rendered useless by the absence of legal backing.[49] Furthermore, even when some identified human rights have legal status, good *enforcement* of the relevant legislation may also call for public activism, which is to be distinguished from the process of *legislation* itself.

The third approach is, of course, that of "legislation." As was discussed in Section III, even though the ethics of human rights must not be seen merely as "parents" of "human rights laws," it is certainly the case that many such legislations have been encouraged or inspired by considerations of human rights. Many actual laws have been enacted by individual states, or by associations of states, which gave legal force to certain rights seen as basic human rights. For example, the European Court of Human Rights, established in 1950 following the European Convention, can consider cases brought by individuals from the signatory states against violations of human rights. This has been supplemented by the Human Rights Act of 1998, aimed at incorporating the main provisions of the European Convention into domestic law, with an overseeing role of the European Court to see "just satisfaction" of these provisions in

49. It is also worth noting that even when the agents involved in activist promotion of human rights do not have any special legal status, they can still make a difference to political, social and administrative practice through the use of existing laws, combined with seeking public disclosures and critical debates. For example, unlike the Indian and South African Human Rights Commissions, which are recognized in the respective national laws, the Pakistan Human Rights Commission is basically just an NGO, and yet under the visionary and courageous leadership of Asma Jahangir, I. A. Rehman, and others, it has been remarkably effective in identifying and resisting violations of human rights, and in defending vulnerable persons, including religious minorities and ill-treated women. For a good discussion of some of these supportive activities, see *The State of Human Rights, 2001* (Lahore: Human Rights Commission of Pakistan, 2002).

domestic judgments. Many other examples can be given from different parts of the world. The "legislative route" has had much active use.

There is an interesting question about the appropriate *domain* of the legislative route. It would be a mistake, I would argue, to presume in general that if a human right is important, then it must be ideal to legislate it into a precisely specified legal right. For example, recognizing and defending a wife's moral right to be consulted in family decisions, even in a traditionally sexist society, may well be extremely important, and can plausibly satisfy the threshold conditions needed to qualify as a human right.[50] And yet the advocates of this human right, who emphasize, correctly, its far-reaching ethical and political relevance, can quite possibly agree that it is not sensible to make this human right into, in Herbert Hart's language, a "coercive legal rule" (perhaps with the result that a husband would be taken in custody if he were to fail to consult his wife). The necessary change would have to be brought about in other ways. Because of the importance of communication, advocacy, exposure and informed public discussion, human rights can have influence *without* necessarily depending on coercive legislation.

Similarly, the moral or political entitlement, which can easily be seen as a human right, of a somewhat slow speaker not to be snubbed in an open public meeting by a rudely articulate sprinter may well be important both for the self-respect of the leisurely speaker and for public good, but it is not likely to be a good subject for punitive legislation. The protection of that human right would have to be sought elsewhere. The effectiveness of the human rights perspective does not rest on seeing them invariably as putative proposals for legislation.[51]

VIII. Economic and Social Rights

I turn now to criticisms that have been particularly aimed against extending the idea of human rights to include economic and social rights, such as the right not to be hungry, or the right to basic education or to medical attention. Even though these rights did not figure in the

50. The importance and social reach of woman's participation in family decisions is discussed in my *Development as Freedom*, ch. 8, "Women's Agency and Social Change."

51. For an early advocacy of a much broader approach, see Mary Wollstonecraft, *A Vindication of the Rights of Woman: with Strictures on Political and Moral Subjects* (1792).

classic presentations of rights of human beings in, say, the U.S. Declaration of Independence, or French "rights of man," they are very much a part of the contemporary domain of what Cass Sunstein calls the "rights revolution."[52] The legitimacy of including these claims within the general class of human rights has been challenged through two specific lines of reproach, which I shall call, respectively, the *institutionalization critique* and the *feasibility critique.*

The institutionalization critique, which is aimed particularly at economic and social rights, relates to the general issue of the exact correspondence between authentic rights and precisely formulated correlate duties. Such a correspondence, it is argued, would exist only when a right is institutionalized. Onora O'Neill has presented this line of criticism with force:

> Unfortunately much writing and rhetoric on rights heedlessly proclaims universal rights to goods and services, and in particular "welfare rights," as well as to other social, economic and cultural rights that are prominent in international Charters and Declarations, without showing what connects each presumed right-holder to some specific obligation-bearer(s), which leaves the content of these supposed rights wholly obscure.... Some advocates of universal economic, social and cultural rights go no further than to emphasize that they *can* be institutionalized, which is true. But the point of difference is that they *must* be institutionalized: if they are not there is no right.[53]

In responding to this significant criticism, we have to invoke the understanding, already discussed, that obligations can be both perfect and imperfect. Even the classical "first generational" rights, like freedom from assault, can be seen as yielding imperfect obligations on others, as was illustrated with the example of the case of assault on Kitty Genovese in public view in New York. Depending on institutional possibilities, economic and social rights may similarly call for both perfect and imperfect obligations. There is a large area of fruitful public discussion and possibly effective pressure, concerning what the society and the state, even

52. Sunstein, *After the Rights Revolution: Reconceiving the Regulatory State.*

53. Onora O'Neill, *Towards Justice and Virtue,* pp. 131–32. See also her *Bounds of Justice* (Cambridge: Cambridge University Press, 2000).

an impoverished one, can do to prevent violations of certain basic economic or social rights (associated with, say, the prevalence of famines, or chronic undernourishment, or absence of medical care).

Indeed, the supportive activities of social organizations are often aimed precisely at institutional change, and these activities can be seen as part of imperfect obligations that individuals and groups have in a society where basic human rights are violated. Onora O'Neill is right to emphasize the importance of institutions for the realization of "welfare rights" (and even for economic and social rights in general), but the ethical significance of these rights provide good grounds for seeking realization through institutional expansion and reform. This can be helped through a variety of approaches, including demanding and agitating for appropriate legislation, and the supplementation of legal demands by political recognition and social monitoring. To deny the ethical status of these claims would be to ignore the reasoning that motivates these constructive activities.

The *feasibility critique* proceeds from the argument that even with the best of efforts, it may not be feasible to arrange the realization of many of the alleged economic and social rights for all. This would have been only an empirical observation (of some interest of its own), but it is made into an allegedly powerful criticism of the acceptance of these claimed rights on the basis of the presumption, largely undefended, that recognized human rights must, of necessity, be wholly accomplishable. If this presumption were accepted that would have the effect of immediately putting many so-called economic and social rights outside the domain of possible human rights, especially in the poorer societies.

Maurice Cranston puts the argument thus:

> The traditional political and civil rights are not difficult to institute. For the most part, they require governments, and other people generally, to leave a man alone. . . . The problems posed by claims to economic and social rights, however, are of another order altogether. How can governments of those parts of Asia, Africa, and South America, where industrialization has hardly begun, be reasonably called upon to provide social security and holidays with pay for millions of people who inhabit those places and multiply so swiftly?[54]

54. Cranston, "Are There Any Human Rights?" p. 13.

In assessing this line of rejection, we have to ask: why should complete feasibility be a condition of cogency of human rights when the objective is to work towards enhancing their actual realization, if necessary through expanding their feasibility? The understanding that some rights are not fully realized, and may not even be fully *realizable* under present circumstances, does not, in itself, entail anything like the conclusion that these are, therefore, not rights at all.[55] Rather, that understanding suggests the need to work towards changing the prevailing circumstances to make the unrealized rights realizable, and ultimately, realized.[56]

It is also worth noting in this context that the question of feasibility is not confined to economic and social rights only; it is a much more widespread problem. Even for liberties and autonomies, to guarantee that a person is "left alone," which Cranston seems to think is simple to guarantee, has never been particularly easy. That elementary fact, easily seen always, cannot but be rather clearly recognized now, at least since September 11, 2001 (and more recent events). If the current feasibility of guaranteeing complete and comprehensive fulfillment were made into a necessary condition for the cogency of every right, then not only economic and social rights, but also liberties, autonomies and even political rights may well fall far short of cogency.

IX. The Reach of Public Reasoning

How can we judge the acceptability of claims to human rights and assess the challenges they may face? How would such a disputation—or a defense—proceed? I would argue that like the assessment of other ethical claims, there must be some test of open and informed scrutiny,

55. For this reason, I would argue, it would be a misapplication to invoke the familiar principle "ought implies can" to suggest that claims that are not yet fully realizable cannot be taken to be rights at all. To see the ethical force of some claims is also a demand to consider what one should do to make them realizable, for example through working for the development of new institutions.

56. This corresponds to what Charles Beitz calls the "practical conception" of human rights: "To say something is a human right is to say that social institutions that fail to protect the right are defective" with the implication that "international efforts to aid or promote reform are legitimate and in some cases may be morally required." ("Human Rights and the Law of Peoples," in *The Ethics of Assistance: Morality and the Distant Needy* ed. Deen Chatterjee [Cambridge: Cambridge University Press, 2004], p. 210. See also Henry Shue, *Basic Rights: Subsistence, Affluence, and U.S. Foreign Policy* [Princeton: Princeton University Press, 1980; 2nd ed., 1996].)

and it is to such a scrutiny that we have to look in order to proceed to a disavowal or an affirmation. The status of these ethical claims must be dependent ultimately on their survivability in unobstructed discussion.[57] In this sense, the viability of human rights is linked with what John Rawls has called "public reasoning" and its role in "ethical objectivity."[58]

Indeed, the connection between public reasoning and the formulation and use of human rights is extremely important to understand. Any general plausibility that these ethical claims, or their denials, have is dependent, on this theory, on their survival and flourishing when they encounter unobstructed discussion and scrutiny, along with adequately wide informational availability. The force of a claim for a human right would be seriously undermined if it were possible to show that they are unlikely to survive open public scrutiny. But contrary to a commonly offered reason for skepticism and rejection, the case for human rights cannot be discarded simply by pointing to the fact (even when that is the case) that in politically and socially repressive regimes, which do not allow open public discussion, many of these human rights are not taken seriously at all. Uncurbed critical scrutiny is essential for dismissal as well as for defense. Even as far as use is concerned, the fact that monitoring of violations of human rights and the procedure of "naming and shaming" can be so effective (at least in putting the violators on the defensive) is some indication of the reach of public reasoning when information becomes available and ethical arguments are allowed rather than suppressed.

However, it is important not to confine the domain of public reasoning to a given society only, especially in the case of human rights, in view of the inescapably non-parochial nature of these rights, which are meant to apply to all human beings. This is in contrast with Rawls's inclination,

57. Even though this requirement has a largely procedural form, the very insistence on open public discussion from which no one is excluded involves an acceptance of equality, which has substantive implications also for the content of the deliberation. On the substantive aspects of deliberative democracy, see Joshua Cohen, "Procedure and Substance in Deliberative Democracy," in *Democracy and Difference: Contesting the Boundaries of the Political*, ed. Seyla Benhabib (Princeton: Princeton University Press, 1996), pp. 95–119.

58. John Rawls, *A Theory of Justice* (Cambridge, Mass.: Harvard University Press, 1971), and *Political Liberalism* (New York: Columbia University Press, 1993), esp. pp. 110–13. On related matters, see also Amy Guttman and Dennis Thompson, *Democracy and Disagreement* (Cambridge, Mass.: Harvard University Press, 1996), and *Democracy and Difference*, ed. Seyla Benhabib.

particularly in his later works, to limit such public confrontation within the boundaries of each particular nation (or each "people," as Rawls calls this regional collectivity), for determining what would be just, at least in domestic affairs.[59] We can demand, on the contrary, that the discussion include, even for domestic justice (if only to avoid parochial prejudices and also to examine a broader range of counterarguments), views also from "a certain distance." The necessity of this was powerfully identified by Adam Smith:

> We can never survey our own sentiments and motives, we can never form any judgment concerning them; unless we remove ourselves, as it were, from our own natural station, and endeavour to view them as at a certain distance from us. But we can do this in no other way than by endeavouring to view them with the eyes of other people, or as other people are likely to view them.[60]

The universalist nature of Adam Smith's approach raises the question whether distant people can, in fact, provide useful scrutiny of local issues, given what are taken to be "uncrossable" barriers of culture. One of Edmund Burke's criticisms of the French declaration of the "rights of man" and its universalist spirit was concerned with disputing the acceptability of that notion in other cultures. Burke argued that "the liberties and the restrictions vary with times and circumstances, and admit of infinite modifications, that cannot be settled upon any abstract rule."[61] The argument that, for this, or some similar, reason, the universality that underlies the notion of human rights is profoundly mistaken can be found in many other writings as well.

59. See particularly John Rawls, *The Law of Peoples* (Cambridge, Mass.: Harvard University Press, 1999). See also Rawls's formulation of the original position in *Political Liberalism*, p. 12: "I assume that the basic structure is that of a closed society: that is, we are to regard it as self-contained and as having no relations with other societies. . . . That a society is closed is a considerable abstraction, justified only because it enables us to focus on certain main questions free from distracting details." If my reasoning is right, the Rawlsian restrictions eliminate much more than the influence of "distracting details."

60. Adam Smith, *The Theory of Moral Sentiments* (1759; rev. ed., 1790; republished, Oxford: Clarendon Press, 1976), III, 1, 2, p. 110. The Smithian perspective on moral reasoning is pursued in my "Open and Closed Impartiality," *The Journal of Philosophy* 99 (2002): 445–69.

61. Quoted in Steven Lukes, "Five Fables about Human Rights," in *The Human Rights Reader*, ed. Micheline R. Ishay (London: Routledge, 1997), p. 238.

For example, Rosa Luxemburg, a leading Marxist thinker and political leader in the early twentieth century, invoked a similar line of criticism of what she called the "metaphysical cliché of the type of 'rights of man' and 'rights of the citizen'."[62] However, a scrutiny of Rosa Luxemburg's real concerns brings out the remarkable fact that she persistently invoked universalist principles herself, as is quite standard in the Marxist tradition (consider: "from each according to his ability, to each according to his needs"). Rather, Luxemburg was keen on emphasizing that the *substantiation* of these principles must depend on specific circumstances that obtain. Shorn of the rhetoric, there is, in fact, no particular difficulty in using basic universalist principles in general, while taking note of Luxemburg's pointer to the relevance of local circumstances and regional conditions in appropriately contingent, or parametric, specification of the exact demands of human rights.

However, a belief in uncrossable barriers between the values of different cultures has surfaced and resurfaced repeatedly over the centuries, and they are forcefully articulated today. The claim of magnificent uniqueness, and often of superiority, has sometimes come from critics of "Western values," varying from champions of regional ethics (well illustrated by the fuss in the 1990s about the peerless excellence of "Asian values"), or religious or cultural separatists (with or without being accompanied by fundamentalism of one kind or another). Sometimes, however, the claim of uniqueness has come from Western particularists. A good example is Samuel Huntington's insistence that the "West was West long before it was modern," and his claim that "a sense of individualism and a tradition of individual rights and liberties" are "unique among civilized societies."[63] Similarly, no less a historian of ideas than Gertrude Himmelfarb has argued that ideas of "justice," "right," "reason" and "love of humanity" are "predominantly, perhaps even uniquely, Western values."[64]

62. Rosa Luxemburg, "The National Question and Autonomy," *The Human Rights Reader*, p. 291.

63. Samuel P. Huntington, *The Clash of Civilizations and the Remaking of World Order* (New York: Simon and Schuster, 1996).

64. Gertrude Himmelfarb, "The Illusions of Cosmopolitanism," in *For Love of Country: Debating the Limits of Patriotism / Martha Nussbaum with Respondents*, ed. Joshua Cohen (Boston: Beacon Press, 1996), pp. 74–75.

I have discussed these diagnoses elsewhere.[65] Contrary to cultural stereotypes, the histories of different countries in the world have shown considerable variations over time as well as between different traditions within the same country. The championing of open public discussion, tolerating and encouraging different points of view, has a long history in many countries in the world. Indeed, some of the earliest open general meetings aimed specifically at settling disputes between different points of view took place in India in the so-called Buddhist councils, the first of which was held shortly after Gautama Buddha's death twenty-five hundred years ago. The grandest of these councils, the third, occurred under the patronage of Emperor Ashoka in the third century BCE. Ashoka also tried to codify and propagate what must have been among the earliest formulations of rules for public discussion, a kind of ancient version of the nineteenth-century *Robert's Rules of Order*. He demanded, for example, "restraint in regard to speech, so that there should be no extolment of one's own sect or disparagement of other sects on inappropriate occasions, and it should be moderate even in appropriate occasions." Even when engaged in arguing, "other sects should be duly honoured in every way on all occasions."

To consider another historical example, in early seventh-century Japan, the Buddhist Prince Shotoku, who was regent to his mother, Empress Suiko, produced the so-called constitution of seventeen articles, in 604 AD. The constitution insisted, much in the spirit of the *Magna Carta* to be signed six centuries later in 1215 AD: "Decisions on important matters should not be made by one person alone. They should be discussed with many."

When, in the twelfth century, the Jewish philosopher Maimonedes had to flee an intolerant Europe to try to safeguard his human right to stick to his own religious beliefs and practice, he sought shelter in Emperor Saladin's Egypt (via Fez and Palestine), and found an honored position in the court of this Muslim emperor. Several hundred years later, when, in Agra, the Moghul emperor of India, Akbar, was arguing, and legislating, on the government's duty to uphold the right to religious

65. See my *Development as Freedom*, ch. 10. Also "Human Rights and Asian Values," *The New Republic*, July 14 and 21, 1997, pp. 33–40; "The Reach of Reason: East and West," *The New York Review of Books*, July 20, 2000, pp. 33–38; "Democracy and Its Global Roots," *The New Republic*, October, 2003, pp. 28–35.

freedom of all citizens, the European Inquisitions were still going on, and Giardino Bruno was burnt at the stake in Rome, in 1600.

In his autobiography, *Long Walk to Freedom*, Nelson Mandela describes how he learned about democracy and individual rights, as a young boy, by seeing the proceedings of the local meetings held in the regent's house in Mqhekezweni:

> Everyone who wanted to speak did so. It was democracy in its purest form. There may have been a hierarchy of importance among the speakers, but everyone was heard, chief and subject, warrior and medicine man, shopkeeper and farmer, landowner and laborer.[66]

Not only are the differences on the subject of freedoms and rights that actually exist between different societies often much exaggerated, but also there is, typically, little note taken of substantial variations *within* each local culture—over time and even at a point of time (in particular, right now). What are taken to be "foreign" criticisms often correspond to internal criticisms from non-mainstream groups. If, say, Iranian dissidents are imprisoned by an authoritarian regime precisely because of their heterodoxy, any suggestion that they should be seen as "ambassadors of Western values" rather than as "Iranian dissidents" would only add serious insult to manifest injury.

This issue is particularly important in determining what may be taken to be culturally "partisan" in a world of many cultural differences. Charles Beitz rejects, rightly, the plausibility of seeing the use of human rights as emanating from a "supposedly symmetrical relationship to the conception of political justice or legitimacy to be found in the world's cultures," and he goes on to seek their justification in terms of "the role they play in international relations."[67] But how should this "role" be judged in terms of its acceptability, and in what sense should such an evaluation be culturally "partisan"? If the reasoning presented here is right, then we must distinguish between (1) the values that are dominantly favored in a society (no matter how repressive it is), and (2) the values that could be expected to gain wider adherence and support when open discussion is allowed, when information about other

66. Nelson Mandela, *Long Walk to Freedom* (Boston: Little, Brown & Co, 1994), p. 21.
67. Beitz, "Human Rights as a Common Concern," pp. 279–80.

societies becomes more freely available, and when disagreements with the established views can be expressed and defended without suppression and fear.

Being "non-partisan" requires respecting the participation of people from any corner of the earth, which is not the same thing as accepting the prevailing priorities in existing societies when information is extremely restricted and discussions and disagreements are not permitted. Widespread *acceptability,* which must be distinguished from pre-existing ubiquitous *acceptance,* is an important issue in any social evaluation, even in dealing with the role that human rights play in international relations.

There does, of course, exist considerable variation in the balance of manifest opinions and observed preconceptions in different countries and different societies. These opinions and beliefs often reflect, as Adam Smith noted in a powerfully illuminating analysis, strong influence of existing *practices* in different parts of the world, along with a lack of broader intellectual engagement. The need for open scrutiny, with unrestrained access to information (including that about practices elsewhere in the world and the experiences there), is particularly great because of these connections. Which is precisely why Adam Smith's insistence on the necessity of viewing actions and practices from a "certain distance" is so important for substantive ethics in general and the understanding of human rights in particular.

In a chapter entitled "On the Influence of Custom and Fashion upon the Sentiments of Moral Approbation and Disapprobation," Smith illustrated his contention:

> . . . the murder of new-born infants was a practice allowed of in almost all the states of Greece, even among the polite and civilized Athenians; and whenever the circumstances of the parent rendered it inconvenient to bring up the child, to abandon it to hunger, or to wild beasts, was regarded without blame or censure. . . . Uninterrupted custom had by this time so thoroughly authorized the practice, that not only the loose maxims of the world tolerated this barbarous prerogative, but even the doctrine of philosophers, which ought to have been more just and accurate, was led away by the established custom, and upon this, as upon many other occasions, instead of censuring, supported the horrible abuse, by far-fetched considerations of public utility. Aristotle talks of it as of what the magistrates ought upon many

occasions to encourage. Plato is of the same opinion, and, with all that love of mankind which seems to animate all his writings, no where marks this practice with disapprobation.[68]

What are taken to be perfectly "normal" and "sensible" in an insulated society may not be able to survive a broad-based and less limited examination once the parochial gut reactions are replaced by critical scrutiny, including an awareness of variations of practices and norms across the world.[69]

Scrutiny from a distance may have something to offer in the assessment of practices as different from each other as the stoning of adulterous women in Taliban's Afghanistan and the abounding use of capital punishment (sometimes with mass jubilation) in parts of the United States. This is the kind of issue that made Smith insist that "the eyes of the rest of mankind" must be invoked to understand whether "a punishment appears equitable."[70] Ultimately, the discipline of critical moral scrutiny requires, among other things, "endeavouring to view [our sentiments and beliefs] with the eyes of other people, or as other people are likely to view them."[71]

The need for interactions across the borders can be as important in rich societies as they are in poorer ones.[72] The point to note here is not so much whether we are *permitted* to make cross-boundary scrutiny, but that the discipline of critical assessment of moral sentiments, no matter how locally established they are, *demands* that such scrutiny be undertaken.

X. A Concluding Remark

I have tried to present, in this article, the elements of a theory of human rights, which sees them as pronouncements in social ethics, sustainable

68. Adam Smith, *The Theory of Moral Sentiments* (rev. ed., 1790, V.2.15; republished, Oxford: Clarendon Press, 1976), p. 210.

69. I have discussed this issue in "Open and Closed Impartiality," *Journal of Philosophy* 99 (2002): 445–69.

70. Adam Smith, *Lectures on Jurisprudence*, ed. R. L. Meek, D. D. Raphael and P. G. Stein (Oxford: Clarendon Press, 1978; reprinted, Indianapolis: Liberty Press, 1982), p. 104.

71. Smith, *The Theory of Moral Sentiments*, III, 1, 2, p. 110.

72. The treatment of prisoners held by the United States in the so-called war against terrorism raises important issues of human rights, and the analysis of the prevailing practice can be helped by more wide-ranging public discussion and a fuller understanding of the nature of global concerns on this issue.

by open public reasoning. They may or may not be reflected in a legal framework through, say, specific "human rights legislation," but there are also other ways of implementing human rights (including public recognition, agitation and monitoring).

Since the main themes developed in this article were specifically noted in Section II, I shall not try to provide a further summary in this concluding section. I should, however, emphasize that the understanding and viability of human rights are, in this perspective, intimately linked with the reach of public discussion, between persons and across borders. The viability and universality of human rights are dependent on their ability to survive open critical scrutiny in public reasoning. The methodology of public scrutiny draws on Rawlsian understanding of "objectivity" in ethics, but the impartiality that is needed cannot be confined within the borders of a nation.

The fact that authoritarian orders are typically quite afraid of uncensored news media and of uncurbed public discussion, which make them resort often enough to suppression (including censorship, intimidation, incarceration, and even execution), provides some indirect evidence that the influence of public reasoning can indeed be quite large. That influence also lies behind the effectiveness of the interactive ways and means, including social recognition, informational monitoring and public agitation, which human rights activists tend to use. There is certainly a need for a fuller understanding of the associative nature of the acceptability of values, and this requires us to go well beyond lazy reliance on the given mores of the dominant social groups in the respective societies.

To conclude, despite their practical preoccupations, human rights activists have reason enough to pay attention to the skepticism that the idea of human rights generates among many legal and political theorists. These doubts have to be—and can be—addressed. But it is also important to note that the conceptual understanding of human rights, in turn, can benefit substantially from considering the reasoning that moves the activists and the range and effectiveness of practical actions they undertake, including recognition, monitoring and agitation, in addition to legislation. Not only is conceptual clarity important for practice, the richness of practice, I have argued, is also critically relevant for understanding the concept and reach of human rights. There is, I must conclude, no great deficit in the balance of trade between theory and practice.

Part III
Constitutional Law

[7]

THE SUPREME COURT
2006 TERM

FOREWORD:
CONSTITUTIONS AND CAPABILITIES: "PERCEPTION" AGAINST LOFTY FORMALISM

Martha C. Nussbaum

TABLE OF CONTENTS

THE SUPREME COURT 2006 TERM

FOREWORD: CONSTITUTIONS AND CAPABILITIES: "PERCEPTION" AGAINST LOFTY FORMALISM

*Martha C. Nussbaum**

> A man, without the proper use of the intellectual faculties of a man, . . . seems to be mutilated and deformed in a[n] . . . essential part of the character of human nature. Though the state was to derive no advantage from the instruction of the inferior ranks of people, it would still deserve its attention that they should not be altogether uninstructed.
>
> — Adam Smith[1]

> Excellence grows like a young vine tree
> Fed by the green dew,
> Raised up among wise and just people
> To the liquid sky.
>
> — Pindar[2]

> It is evident that the best political order is that arrangement in accordance with which anyone whatsoever might do very well and live a flourishing life.
>
> — Aristotle[3]

What are people able to do and to be? And are they *really* able to do or be these things, or are there impediments, evident or hidden, to their real and substantial freedom? Are they able to unfold themselves or are their lives, in significant respects, pinched and starved?

---

* Ernst Freund Distinguished Service Professor of Law and Ethics, The University of Chicago (Law, Philosophy, and Divinity). I am grateful to Ryan Long and Nick Nassim for research assistance, and to Scott Anderson, Douglas Baird, John Deigh, Chad Flanders, Andrew Koppelman, Charles Larmore, Gabriel Richardson Lear, Jonathan Lear, Brian Leiter, Eric Posner, Richard Posner, Adam Samaha, Geoffrey Stone, David Strauss, and Cass Sunstein for valuable comments on earlier drafts.

1 2 ADAM SMITH, AN INQUIRY INTO THE NATURE AND CAUSES OF THE WEALTH OF NATIONS 788 (R.H. Campbell et al. eds., Liberty Classics 1981) (1776) [hereinafter SMITH, THE WEALTH OF NATIONS].

2 PINDAR, *Nemea VIII*, ll. 39–42, *in* CARMINA (C.M. Bowra ed., 2d ed. 1947) (author's translation).

3 ARISTOTLE, POLITICA 1324a23–25 (W.D. Ross ed., 1957) (author's translation).

What about their environment — material, social, and political? Has it helped them to develop their capacities to be active in important areas of life? If people are like Pindar's vine tree, is their environment more like a rich soil tended by wise and just gardeners, or more like an arid soil tended by indifferent gardeners, or gardeners with a restricted conception of their task?

More specifically, to focus on just one part of our larger question that touches on constitutional law: How have the basic constitutional principles of a nation, and their interpretation, promoted or impeded people's abilities to function in some central areas of human life? Does the interpretation of constitutional entitlements yield real abilities to choose and act, or are the constitution's promises more like hollow verbal gestures?

The idea that all citizens in a nation are equally entitled to a set of substantial preconditions for a dignified human life has had a lasting appeal over the centuries in Western political and legal thought — less because intellectuals have favored it than because it has great resonance in the lives of real people.

Appealing though the idea is, however, many things can go wrong when a nation sets up and interprets political principles that define citizens' basic entitlements.

Often, in one way or another, citizens are less like substantially free people, who can choose to act in the ways most pertinent to human dignity, than like prisoners, unable to select modes of activity that are central to a life worthy of human dignity. This happens most obviously when a regime represses choice across the board, curtailing many of the entitlements that are traditionally thought central to such a life.

Sometimes, however, imprisonment is only partial. It does not extend across the entire range of central entitlements, and yet citizens are like prisoners in at least some areas of life — as, for example, when a regime that supports some central opportunities curtails the freedom of religion or the freedom of speech.

Sometimes, imprisonment is partial in a different way: only certain groups are affected. Some (privileged) people are free to select the core set of valuable functions, while other people are not — as, for example, when a hierarchical constitution accords basic entitlements to men and not to women, to whites and not to blacks, to the rich and not to the poor.

Sometimes, these two types of partial imprisonment intersect, as when a regime treats blacks and whites, women and men, equally with respect to voting rights, but denies them equal educational or employment opportunities.

Sometimes, imprisonment is subtle, almost hidden: the words in a nation's constitution may be promising, extending basic entitlements to all citizens on a basis of equality, but the interpretation of these entitlements is so narrow that groups of citizens are not *really able* to select some crucial activities. In name, they are equally free, but not in actuality.

For example, a group of citizens might have rights to free speech and political participation, but be deprived of educational opportunities that are necessary to exercise those rights on a basis of equality with others. Or they might have the freedom of religion in name, but be unprotected against some common assaults against their equal dignity as citizens with diverse religious (and non-religious) views of the good life. Or they might be guaranteed protection against discrimination on the basis of sex, but discover that their legal entitlements have been interpreted in such a way as to render the meaningful exercise of that right extremely difficult.

For several centuries, an approach to the foundation of basic political principles that draws its key insights from Aristotle and the ancient Greek and Roman Stoics has played a role in shaping European and American conceptions of the proper role of government, the purpose of constitution-making, and the nature of basic constitutional entitlements.[4] This normative approach, the "Capabilities Approach" (CA), holds that a key task of a nation's constitution, and the legal tradition that interprets it, is to secure for all citizens the prerequisites of a life worthy of human dignity — a core group of "capabilities" — in areas of central importance to human life.

The purpose of this Foreword is to study the CA as a framework for understanding the foundations of political entitlements and constitutional law, to sketch its history, and to measure against this norm some salient aspects of our tradition of constitutional interpretation, both formerly and in the 2006 Term. My contention is that the United States has had an inconstant relation to the CA, protecting some entitlements very effectively, but shying away from the protection of entitlements in the area of what are usually called social and economic rights — that is, welfare rights. This reluctance (which distinguishes the United States from most of the nations of Europe and the developing world[5]) is made more complicated by disputes over institutional competence and the proper scope of judicial action. Sometimes, when courts refuse to protect a given entitlement (refusing, for example, to give education the status of a fundamental right), the reason may be that judges do not believe that the existing constitution is plausibly interpreted to protect a certain entitlement. At other times, judges may simply oppose the recognition of such a right.

---

[4] The approach has been creatively extended in recent years by developing nations such as India and South Africa.

[5] *See* CASS R. SUNSTEIN, THE SECOND BILL OF RIGHTS 127–38 (2004).

At present, some aspects of the CA are deeply entrenched in our legal traditions and well protected by the courts; in such cases, the CA can provide a useful template against which to assess our achievements. In other areas, the CA provides a norm against which to assess what we have neglected and failed to protect.

The 2006 Term provides examples of different kinds: examples that illustrate our success in protecting central human capabilities and other examples (perhaps more striking because of the shift in thinking that they would appear to embody) that show an ominous failure to protect the capabilities of citizens. These latter cases also show a failure to use the sort of reasoning recommended by the CA — a realistic, historically and imaginatively informed type of practical reasoning that focuses on the actual abilities of people to choose and act in their concrete social settings. Although it is too soon to judge the achievements of the Roberts Court in any overall way, the 2006 Term, in its most divisive and controversial cases, seems to show a marked turn away from the CA's understanding of constitutional principles toward a much weaker understanding of the protections such principles offer. In some cases, this turn spells a reversion to selective imprisonment.

This is a new Court, and many people are thinking about its nature and identity. At such a time it would be easy to be drawn to specifics and to the study of emerging judicial styles, particularly of the Court's new members. But it is precisely at such a time that we do best to turn, instead, to first principles, pausing to ask about the deeper goals and ideals embodied (and sometimes not embodied) in our constitutional tradition. This approach gives us a deeper understanding of judicial styles and their relation to larger goals; it also gives us a benchmark for assessing how our legal and constitutional system performs when held up against persuasive norms of justice.

Although this Foreword outlines a theoretical normative approach to the law, it is important to notice from the start that this theoretical approach has deep ties to the common law tradition of legal reasoning.

The CA was an important element in the work of numerous thinkers of the seventeenth and eighteenth centuries, who articulated a mixed Aristotelian and Stoic idea of "natural law" that they derived from their classical education. It was highly influential in the American founding, expressing the ideas of several leading American intellectuals, particularly Thomas Paine and James Madison. It played an active role in our constitutional tradition from the beginning.

In nineteenth-century Britain, the CA was developed by politically influential philosophers John Stuart Mill and T.H. Green, who were both strongly influenced by Aristotelian ideas, in connection with controversies over the provision of public education, sex equality, and the protection of liberty. Meanwhile, in the United States, it began to figure in judicial interpretation. Its influence in this area reached its apogee in the mid- to late twentieth century, when some key constitutional and statutory provisions were explicitly interpreted along lines suggested by the CA, rather than by its most influential rivals. Other aspects of the approach were enacted through legislation, during the New Deal and, later, during the Great Society. In the aftermath of the Reagan Revolution, legislative support for key aspects of the approach has proven fragile; judicial support in areas once agreed to be the legitimate domain of judicial action appears to be on the wane.

Currently, in the world of international development policy, the CA is becoming increasingly influential as an alternative to utilitarian approaches.[6] In short, the world is embracing the CA in preference to its major alternatives, while our own nation — to judge, at least, from the 2006 Term — is becoming increasingly indifferent to it.

This Foreword describes the CA, shows what makes it attractive as a normative approach to constitutional law, and describes the type of judicial reasoning that it invites. I argue that it is deeply embedded in many aspects of our history and our constitutional tradition — but also consistently opposed by what I shall call "lofty formalism," an approach to judicial reasoning that is strikingly present in a group of cases from the 2006 Term.

In Part I, I examine the CA as a normative account of political principles. In Part II, I clarify the approach by contrasting it with two rival normative approaches, utilitarian welfarism and libertarian minimalism. I then turn to a procedural contrast and argue that the approach is committed to a definite mode of reasoning about complicated practical situations, and that it is opposed to lofty formalism. In Part III, I examine some of the historical antecedents of the CA, particularly those that influenced our own tradition: the ideas of Aristotle and the Stoics, early American reflections about liberty of conscience, the eighteenth-century ideas of Adam Smith and Thomas Paine, and nineteenth- and twentieth-century neo-Aristotelian liberalism. In Part IV, I identify the CA as one prominent (though never unopposed) strand in U.S. traditions of constitutional reasoning, focusing on the freedom of religion, equal protection arguments against "separate but equal" facilities, procedural protections for welfare opportunities, and access to education. In Part V, turning to the present, I argue that, from the normative vantage point of the CA and its associated model of good reasoning, the 2006 Term contains some markedly positive developments in the areas of environmental protection and disability education, but also a manifest trend in the direction of lofty formalism

---

[6] Through the influential *Human Development Reports* of the United Nations Development Programme and their domestic analogues in many nations the CA now has a widespread influence on the ways in which nations around the world measure their own success and think of their political goals. *See, e.g.*, UNITED NATIONS DEVELOPMENT PROGRAMME, HUMAN DEVELOPMENT REPORT 1990, *available at* http://hdr.undp.org/reports/global/1990/en.

in the areas of women's rights (employment discrimination and abortion), affirmative action, and, finally, religious equality.

I. PHILOSOPHICAL ELEMENTS

At the heart of the CA[7] is an idea that it borrows from and shares with most of the world's great religious traditions: the idea that all human beings are precious, deserving of respect and support, and that the worth of all human beings is equal. What respect centrally involves, the CA holds, is supporting human beings in the development and exercise of some central human abilities, especially prominent among which is the faculty of selection and choice.

One might agree with all of this and yet believe that law and government have only a restricted function in human life — *if* one also believed that human beings have all they need in order to live lives worthy of their dignity, or could easily get what they need by personal effort alone, without law and political organization. One might, for example, believe that the world is benign and usually gives everyone what they need, and that other people are benign, supplying to the needy whatever the world of nature does not. But who could believe this, in a world marred by violence, hunger, persecution, and humiliation? The tradition from which the U.S. Constitution emerged placed large constraints on government, to be sure, but the tradition was hardly willing to deny a substantial role for government, or even to minimize its presence.

One might believe, instead, that people usually have what they need, not because the world is benign, but because a life worthy of human dignity does not need anything from the material and social world. The Greek and Roman Stoics, for example, thought that people only needed their inner resources to live complete lives. Malnutrition, rape, humiliation, lack of education, slavery: none of these makes life worse, they thought; none is an insult to human dignity. A slave who is humiliated, beaten, and used as a sexual tool every day has a life fully worthy of human dignity, so long as he or she has the power of moral choice within.[8]

---

[7] For discussions of my version of the CA, see MARTHA C. NUSSBAUM, WOMEN AND HUMAN DEVELOPMENT: THE CAPABILITIES APPROACH (2000) [hereinafter NUSSBAUM, WOMEN AND HUMAN DEVELOPMENT]; and MARTHA C. NUSSBAUM, FRONTIERS OF JUSTICE: DISABILITY, NATIONALITY, SPECIES MEMBERSHIP (2006) [hereinafter NUSSBAUM, FRONTIERS OF JUSTICE]. For Amartya Sen's approach, and the differences between that and my approach, see AMARTYA SEN, DEVELOPMENT AS FREEDOM (1999); and Martha C. Nussbaum, *Capabilities as Fundamental Entitlements: Sen and Social Justice*, 9 FEMINIST ECONOMICS 33 (2003) [hereinafter Nussbaum, *Capabilities as Fundamental Entitlements*].

[8] *See* Martha C. Nussbaum, *The Worth of Human Dignity: Two Tensions in Stoic Cosmopolitanism* [hereinafter Nussbaum, *The Worth of Human Dignity*], *in* PHILOSOPHY AND POWER IN THE GRAECO-ROMAN WORLD 31 (Gillian Clark & Tessa Rajak eds., 2002).

The Stoic view is not obviously false, the way the "benign world" view is, because it is a normative and not a descriptive view. It asks us, in effect, not to value the body's satisfactions, the character of social interactions, or, in short, any of the "gifts of fortune" as elements in a life worthy of human dignity. Many people have found the Stoic view attractive as a source of steadiness in an uncertain world. Yet, on the whole, it is difficult to accept it for two reasons. First, the human powers that the Stoics valued are more dependent on the world than the Stoics maintained. The capacities of thought, ethical selection, and will are undermined by malnutrition, humiliation, and lack of education. Second, things outside a person's rational and ethical faculties also matter: health, bodily integrity, the chance to have relationships with friends, family, and children, the conditions of political action, the freedom to worship in one's own way, and the ability to live on terms of respect and equality with others. The Stoic view has both an idealized view of the things it values and an excessively narrow view of what has value.

The CA rejects this Stoic doctrine, combining the idea of equal dignity with the idea of human vulnerability. It holds that the most important human powers, including the power of choice itself, are vulnerable and not rock-hard. It also holds that elements outside the control of a person's rational will have worth and rightly play a part in our assessment of whether that person has access to a life in accordance with human dignity. For these reasons, the CA ascribes an important role to government in human life: government is charged with securing for citizens a comprehensive set of necessary conditions for a life worthy of human dignity.

People come into the world with rudimentary abilities to lead a dignified life. These abilities, however, need support from the world, especially the political world, if they are to develop and become effective. First, they need internal cultivation, usually supplied above all by a nation's system of education — together with whatever support people receive from their families and other voluntary institutions. I call the developed form of innate abilities "internal capabilities."[9]

People may be well educated, well fed, and healthy, however, and yet lack meaningful opportunities to use their powers in action. Many people who are capable of speaking freely, in the sense that they have been educated and cultivated, lack the meaningful opportunity to speak freely in public, because their nation has not protected their freedom of speech, or has not protected it equally for all. For women in many parts of the world, it has been a common experience to find oneself full of internal capabilities that one never gets a chance to use,

[9] *See* NUSSBAUM, WOMEN AND HUMAN DEVELOPMENT, *supra* note 7, at 84–86.

because many nations have not given women political rights, property rights, rights over their own bodies, and so forth, or have not given these rights to women and men on a basis of equality. So the job of government, as the CA sees it, is not just to produce internal capabilities, but, instead, to produce what I call "combined capabilities": internal capabilities combined with suitable external circumstances to select the function in question.

Notice that the political goal is capability, not actual functioning. Government ought to give people a full and meaningful choice; at that point, the decision whether to take up a given opportunity must be their own. Respect for a person requires not dragooning that person into a particular mode of activity, however desirable it might seem.[10] Thus, having meaningful political rights (and *really* having them, not just as words on paper) does not require one to participate in politics. Members of the Old Order Amish have the right to vote, and they choose not to use it. That is just fine. To compel them to vote would be insufficiently respectful of their freedom. Similarly, people who have adequate nutrition available may always choose to fast — for example, for religious reasons. There is, however, a large difference between fasting and starving, and it is that difference that the CA wishes to capture.

There is also a large difference between *really being* in a position to acquire adequate nourishment (but choosing to fast) and being a jobless person in a nation without basic welfare support. This difference, too, the CA wishes to capture. Such a person *might* get adequate nutrition, but only by good luck, or by some humiliating performance (begging, sex work), and not because the government of her nation has, like Pindar's just gardener, taken cognizance of her situation and accorded her the combined capability to be adequately nourished. A woman who is beaten by her husband in a nation that looks the other way when domestic violence is afoot *might* protect her bodily integrity, but, again, only by some kind of rare luck, or by killing the perpetrator, or by eluding him and taking to the streets.[11] In this case, again, we would not say that the nation in question has protected the woman's capability to protect her bodily integrity. It is not enough for the law not to block her; it must actively support her.

On the whole, the CA holds that the question we need to ask is what is *adequate* — what basic minimum justice requires. Thus, it employs the notion of a threshold, and does not comment on what justice requires us to do about inequalities over the threshold. It is in

[10] Compulsory education of children is an exception to this rule, because children are not yet fully capable of meaningful choice.

[11] Many sex workers in developing countries are escapees from abusive marriages who lack employable skills and the education necessary to acquire them.

that sense a partial account of justice. But there is also a fundamental role for equality in the theory. Because the CA holds that people are fundamentally equal in dignity, it will sometimes require that entitlements be secured to people on a basis of full equality, reasoning that only this equality is compatible with their equal dignity as citizens. Thus, the right to vote, the freedom of religion, the freedom of speech, and quite a few other entitlements, have not been *adequately* distributed unless they have been *equally* distributed. Any other mode of distribution would set up ranks and orders of citizens, failing to treat citizens with equal respect. It is important to notice that the CA is not just about welfare rights: it is centrally concerned with the distribution of entitlements that are almost universally recognized in modern societies.

The CA, however, does not apply this constraint mechanically across the board. In many cases, citizens may have *adequate* capabilities without having fully *equal* capabilities. This will often be the case in areas dealing with property and material welfare. In a nation that recognizes a right to adequate housing, it would seem that such a right could be secured without making certain that everyone has a house of equal value; to attach too much emphasis to the precise cost of every house would be unrealistic; it would probably also show an excessive focus on material goods. To decide whether a given entitlement, such as a right to education or a right to health care, falls in one group or the other will require wise practical reasoning. The question that must be pressed is whether inequality in that area affects the equal dignity of citizens in the public realm.[12] Inequalities that track traditional sources of discrimination, such as race and sex, will be impermissible for that reason. Thus equality in the sense of nondiscrimination and nonhierarchy is always central to the CA. Even if the *content* of an entitlement is that all should have a threshold level of a given good thing, it will not be permissible to implement that entitlement in a way that subordinates one group of citizens.

Several key features of the CA help us distinguish it from rival approaches to constitutional law:

(1) *Entitlement, not Charity.* Support for the specified list of opportunities is not just a kind of handout, or *de haut en bas* charity. It is the right of each and every citizen, and all citizens have equal rights in the specified areas.

(2) *Combined Capability, not Notional Freedom.* The political goal is understood in a rather exigent way: the person has to be *really able* to select the activity in question. All capabilities, then, may require state action for their support; benign neglect is not enough.

---

12 *See* NUSSBAUM, FRONTIERS OF JUSTICE, *supra* note 7, at 291–95.

(3) *Capability, not Satisfaction of Desire.* The CA focuses on what people are actually able to do and be, not on whether their desires are satisfied. Desire is a malleable and inconstant element of people's lives. Desires are often artifacts of what people expect for themselves. Women who are told for centuries that a good woman does not get very much schooling may not demand more education, but that is hardly the end of the question of justice. In general, the absence of rebellion against a deprivation does not justify ignoring it. People may also become accustomed to having more than others, and they may protest if those unequal privileges are curtailed; but their great dissatisfaction does not dispose of the question of equal justice.

(4) *Each Person an End.* Government should not promote the overall good in a way that violates the entitlement of each citizen to a decent life. The idea of "general welfare" must be understood to mean the welfare of *all* individual citizens, not the welfare of some fused organic entity in which distinctions among persons have vanished.

(5) *Plural and Noncommensurable Opportunities.* The opportunities protected by the CA are not simply quantities of some single homogeneous value: they are distinct, plural, and different in quality. Because they are distinct, one cannot satisfy one entitlement by giving people a very large amount of another. For example, one cannot atone for an absence of religious liberty by giving people a very comprehensive health care scheme. The plurality and distinctness of the ends does not mean, however, that they do not often support one another. For example, education supports political activity, the freedom of speech, *and* the ability to protect one's bodily integrity from abuse (because education gives employment options and thus exit options from an abusive marriage).

(6) *Centrality of Choice.* The goal of the CA is capability, because respect for people's power of choice is at the center of the entire approach.[13]

(7) *Special Role of Education.* Because the approach aims at making people *really able* to choose in certain areas of importance, the

[13] There is a subtle difference between Aristotle's reasons for making choice central and the reasons I endorse. For Aristotle, choice is central because no action can count as virtuous unless it is chosen, and the best life is a life in accordance with virtue. *See* ARISTOTLE, ETHICA NICOMACHEA 1106a3–4, 1098a16–17 (Ingram Bywater ed., 1890). For me, choice is central because respect for human dignity is central, and respect requires us to give people room to live lives that are not merely dictated by someone else. This difference is closely connected to the difference about pluralism that I discuss *infra* in section II.A. In my view, the group of central capabilities should be understood as specifically political goals, and not as embodying a comprehensive view of the good life; that more comprehensive view will be supplied in different ways by citizens' religious and secular views of life's meaning. People who differ about ultimate meaning, however, can agree (or so I argue) on a group of capabilities as worthy of being promoted for all citizens in a pluralistic society.

formation of powers of perception, thought, and choice plays a special role. If we were aiming to produce pliant tools of an ideology, we might not care very much what education people had, so long as they were docile. The CA, by contrast, aims at a nation of free choosers, and so it matters greatly that they have had the opportunity to learn and develop in ways that open a meaningful world of choice to them. Choice is seen as crucial for citizenship and for options in life generally.[14] Nor is the CA interested in a narrow form of education that produces skilled robots: critical thinking and imagining are central to its aims.

(8) *Need for Imagination.* What the wise decisionmaker must see is how people are really placed, what obstacles stand between them and the substantive, not merely nominal, exercise of their powers. Seeing this requires keen scrutiny of a wide range of social positions. This scrutiny, in turn, requires experience, the study of history, and imagination. Imagination is necessary because no decisionmaker has first-hand experience of the lives of all the different groups in society (women, racial minorities, immigrants) who may need to be considered.[15]

---

[14] Note, however, that the CA does not insist that the only worthwhile lives are those that actually use the power of choice. In this sense the CA diverges from John Stuart Mill's comprehensive doctrine of autonomy. *See* JOHN STUART MILL, ON LIBERTY 56–74 (Stefan Collini ed., Cambridge Univ. Press 1995) (1859). Lives lived in a rule-bound traditional society, or in an authoritarian profession such as the military, are fully respected by the approach, *so long as* people have enough education first to opt for such lives in a meaningful way.

[15] I have also defended a more specific list of capabilities as necessary conditions of a life worthy of human dignity. This list, which is closely linked to the Universal Declaration of Human Rights, is a template for persuasion in the international community, not a recommendation for any single nation's constitution:

Central Human Functional Capabilities

(1) *Life.* Being able to live to the end of a human life of normal length; not dying prematurely, or before one's life is so reduced as to be not worth living.

(2) *Bodily Health.* Being able to have good health, including reproductive health; to be adequately nourished; to have adequate shelter.

(3) *Bodily Integrity.* Being able to move freely from place to place; to be secure against violent assault, including sexual assault and domestic violence; having opportunities for sexual satisfaction and for choice in matters of reproduction.

(4) *Senses, Imagination, and Thought.* Being able to use the senses, to imagine, think, and reason — and to do these things in a "truly human" way, a way informed and cultivated by an adequate education, including, but by no means limited to, literacy and basic mathematical and scientific training. Being able to use imagination and thought in connection with experiencing and producing works and events of one's own choice, religious, literary, musical, and so forth. Being able to use one's mind in ways protected by guarantees of freedom of expression with respect to both political and artistic speech, and freedom of religious exercise. Being able to have pleasurable experiences and to avoid nonbeneficial pain.

(5) *Emotions.* Being able to have attachments to things and people outside ourselves; to love those who love and care for us, to grieve at their absence; in general, to love, to grieve, to experience longing, gratitude, and justified anger. Not having one's emotional

That is the approach in an abstract outline. Each nation, of course, makes its own list of core entitlements and sets a threshold to establish an adequate level of support. Nations make different decisions about which capabilities will get constitutional protection and which will be left to the majoritarian democratic process. What judges must interpret is the list validated by their own nation, together with the tradition of precedent that interprets it.

II. THREE CONTRASTS

We can understand the CA more precisely by contrast, holding it up against two rival normative views of the function of government and one rival conception of how one should reason about basic entitlements.

The first normative rival view, which I shall call "utilitarian welfarism," originated in the classical utilitarianism of Jeremy Bentham. Bentham's primary interest was in providing the philosophical basis for law,[16] and the ideas he developed eventually had great influence in legal scholarship, particularly through the law and economics move-

---

development blighted by fear and anxiety. (Supporting this capability means supporting forms of human association that can be shown to be crucial in their development.)

(6) *Practical Reason.* Being able to form a conception of the good and to engage in critical reflection about the planning of one's life. (This entails protection for the liberty of conscience and religious observance.)

(7) *Affiliation.*

A. Being able to live with and toward others, to recognize and show concern for other human beings, to engage in various forms of social interaction; to be able to imagine the situation of another. (Protecting this capability means protecting institutions that constitute and nourish such forms of affiliation, and also protecting the freedom of assembly and political speech.)

B. Having the social bases of self-respect and non-humiliation; being able to be treated as a dignified being whose worth is equal to that of others. This entails provisions of nondiscrimination on the basis of race, sex, sexual orientation, ethnicity, caste, religion, national origin.

(8) *Other Species.* Being able to live with concern for and in relation to animals, plants, and the world of nature.

(9) *Play.* Being able to laugh, to play, to enjoy recreational activities.

(10) *Control over One's Environment.*

A. Political. Being able to participate effectively in political choices that govern one's life; having the right of political participation, protections of free speech and association.

B. Material. Being able to hold property (both land and movable goods), and having property rights on an equal basis with others; having the right to seek employment on an equal basis with others; having the freedom from unwarranted search and seizure. In work, being able to work as a human being, exercising practical reason and entering into meaningful relationships of mutual recognition with other workers.

NUSSBAUM, FRONTIERS OF JUSTICE, *supra* note 7, at 76–78; *see also* NUSSBAUM, WOMEN AND HUMAN DEVELOPMENT, *supra* note 7, at 78–80.

16 *See* Alan Ryan, *Introduction* to UTILITARIANISM AND OTHER ESSAYS 7, 31 (Alan Ryan ed., 1987); *see also* John Stuart Mill, *Bentham*, *in* UTILITARIANISM AND OTHER ESSAYS, *supra*, at 132, 136–37 (assessing Bentham's contribution to law).

ment.[17] The other, which I shall call "libertarian minimalism," has had a steady influence for several centuries and is currently championed by numerous American thinkers. As we shall see, a form of libertarianism seems to be gaining influence within the current Supreme Court. The third rival conception, lofty formalism, is an approach to judgment that has often been found in constitutional interpretation. Although it can be combined with a variety of normative approaches, it is distinctly hostile to the CA.

A. *Utilitarian Welfarism*

Utilitarianism began as a radically democratic view, expressing the basic idea that social decisionmaking should pay attention to everyone and should count the satisfactions of each person the same (rather than weighting them by class and education).[18] Thus, although I argue that utilitarianism actually fails to give the right sort of respectful attention to each person, it is important to bear in mind its underlying commitment to equality. (In that sense, many of my criticisms are internal

---

17 *See* RICHARD A. POSNER, ECONOMIC ANALYSIS OF LAW (6th ed. 2003) (setting forth the basic theory of utilitarianism as applied to law); RICHARD A. POSNER, THE ECONOMICS OF JUSTICE (1981) (discussing the theory's applicability to constitutional law); *see also* GARY S. BECKER, THE ECONOMIC APPROACH TO HUMAN BEHAVIOR (1976) (applying utilitarian economic analysis to nonmarket behavior). For the most part, law and economics is a positive, predictive discipline: it assumes that people are rational maximizers of satisfactions, *see* POSNER, THE ECONOMICS OF JUSTICE, *supra*, at 1–2, and advances the hypothesis "that the common law is best explained as if the judges were trying to maximize economic welfare," *id.* at 4. Generally, the view does not say that the maximization of satisfactions ought to be a social goal. However, Richard Posner does often venture into normative territory: he announces that "efficiency as I define the term is an adequate concept of justice," *id.* at 6, and remains critical of the privacy jurisprudence of the Supreme Court because it "has no systematic relationship to the economics of the problem," *id.* at 8. Here, Posner moves very close to the normative theorizing of the classical utilitarians.

18 The slogan, "each to count for one, and none for more than one," nicely expresses this underlying commitment to equality. This famous and oft-cited quote is attributed to Bentham by Mill, who quotes it in the form, "everybody to count for one, nobody for more than one." John Stuart Mill, *Utilitarianism*, *in* UTILITARIANISM AND OTHER ESSAYS, *supra* note 16, at 272, 336 (internal quotation marks omitted); *see also* DON A. HABIBI, JOHN STUART MILL AND THE ETHIC OF HUMAN GROWTH 84 (2001) (suggesting that Mill simply paraphrases Bentham's "egalitarian statements on hedonism"); *cf.* JEREMY BENTHAM, AN INTRODUCTION TO THE PRINCIPLES OF MORALS AND LEGISLATION 31 (Hafner Publ'ns Co. 1948) (1789) [hereinafter BENTHAM, PRINCIPLES OF MORALS AND LEGISLATION]. Bentham *does* write: "[E]very individual in the country tells for one; no individual for more than one." JEREMY BENTHAM, *Rationale of Judicial Evidence*, *in* 7 THE WORKS OF JEREMY BENTHAM 1, 334 (John Bowring ed., 1962). He also writes:

> The happiness of the most helpless pauper constitutes as large a portion of the universal happiness, as does that of the most powerful, the most opulent member of the community. Therefore the happiness of the most helpless and indigent has as much title to regard at the hands of the legislator, as that of the most powerful and opulent.

JEREMY BENTHAM, *Constitutional Code*, *in* 9 THE WORKS OF JEREMY BENTHAM, *supra*, at 1, 107.

criticisms, arguing that the view does not fully realize its admirable goal.) Another similarity between the CA and utilitarianism should also be mentioned: like utilitarianism, the CA is an *outcome-oriented* view of justice, rather than a strictly *procedural* view. Under the CA, whether or not a society is just is to be decided by looking at the result of its decisions, namely, what people are really able to do and be, rather than simply looking at whether procedural rules have been correctly applied.[19] In that sense, the CA shares the worldliness and the commitment to an illusion-free confrontation with reality that are among the best features of utilitarianism.[20]

According to utilitarianism, the proper function of government (and of correct choice more generally) is to maximize society's total (or, in some versions, average) utility.[21] As Amartya Sen and Bernard Williams helpfully analyze it, utilitarianism has three parts[22]:

(1) *Consequentialism.* The right choice is the one that produces the best overall consequences (rather than, for example, the one that secures a core group of basic entitlements or rights).

(2) *Sum-Ranking.* The utilities of all people are combined by simply adding them together (rather than, for example, by focusing on the provision of a minimum threshold of utility for all, or on raising the utility level of the least well-off).

(3) *A Definite View of Utility.* Bentham and Henry Sidgwick preferred pleasure; more recent utilitarians prefer satisfaction of desires or preferences.[23] Whatever their specific content, however, all these views see utility as a single homogeneous entity, varying only in quantity.[24] Thus utilitarian welfarism contains a deep commitment to the

---

[19] *See* NUSSBAUM, FRONTIERS OF JUSTICE, *supra* note 7, at 82–85 (using the example of a criminal trial, where the proceduralist will assess the result by asking whether fair procedures are followed, whereas the outcome-oriented theorist will assess the procedure by asking whether it results, by and large, in convicting the guilty and exonerating the innocent).

[20] Mill, indeed, liked to say that Aristotle was a utilitarian (and Jesus too!). *See* Ryan, *supra* note 16, at 20. For the truth in this claim, see Martha C. Nussbaum, *Mill Between Aristotle and Bentham*, DAEDALUS, Spring 2004, at 60.

[21] *See* BENTHAM, PRINCIPLES OF MORALS AND LEGISLATION, *supra* note 18; HENRY SIDGWICK, THE METHODS OF ETHICS 411 (7th ed. 1907).

[22] *See* Amartya Sen & Bernard Williams, *Introduction* to UTILITARIANISM AND BEYOND 1, 4–5 (Amartya Sen & Bernard Williams eds., 1982). Sen and Williams are both critics of utilitarianism, but this analysis of its elements is accurate, and is independent of the critical points they raise.

[23] *See* BENTHAM, PRINCIPLES OF MORALS AND LEGISLATION, *supra* note 18, at 11 (arguing that pleasure and pain are the standards of right and wrong); *see also* SIDGWICK, *supra* note 21, at 413 (making clear that he is using the word "happiness" to mean "pleasure"). For an example of the modern preference-satisfaction view, see generally PETER SINGER, PRACTICAL ETHICS (2d ed. 1993).

[24] Bentham mentions four dimensions of quantitative variation: intensity, duration, certainty, and propinquity. *See* BENTHAM, PRINCIPLES OF MORALS AND LEGISLATION, *supra* note 18, at 38.

commensurability of all the salient goods in a human life: all are seen as sources of this one homogeneous thing.[25]

The CA takes issue with utilitarianism in several ways.[26] Most centrally, it takes issue with the idea of commensurability: the important goods that it is the business of government to protect or secure are plural and distinct. One cannot promote one good, the CA holds, by giving people a very large amount of another.[27]

At this point, utilitarians will surely say that the satisfaction of desire is a good proxy for all these diverse goods. Moreover, they will claim that desire-satisfaction is a way of thinking about the good that is democratic and respectful of persons: it lets them decide what is worth pursuing. In response, the defender of the CA will say that desire is an unreliable proxy for the good. Desires can be created and extinguished by social manipulation.[28] As for the utilitarians' claim about respecting people, the CA accomplishes that in a more satisfactory way: both by focusing on creating conditions in which genuine choice is possible and by giving people a rich set of opportunities and then letting them choose whether and how to use them.

The CA also takes issue with sum-ranking: individual citizens' lives are not merely inputs into a glorious social total or average. It matters how *each* is placed. Notoriously, utilitarian views approve results that augment the social total or average, even when they give some people extremely miserable lives.[29] (Even slavery, in utilitarianism, is ruled out, to the extent that it is, only by fragile empirical claims to the effect that it does not in fact augment the total or average welfare.) The CA,

---

25 Sidgwick admits that to some extent utilitarianism departs from common sense, but he argues that this departure is necessary for scientific precision. *See* SIDGWICK, *supra* note 21, at 424–25; *see also Mill, Utilitarianism*, *supra* note 18, at 278–79 (famously rejecting the thesis of commensurability in favor of the idea that pleasures differ in quality as well as quantity).

26 *See* NUSSBAUM, WOMEN AND HUMAN DEVELOPMENT, *supra* note 7, at 111–66.

27 *See* MARTHA C. NUSSBAUM, THE FRAGILITY OF GOODNESS 290–317 (rev. ed. 2001); *see also* MARTHA C. NUSSBAUM, *The Discernment of Perception: An Aristotelian Conception of Private and Public Rationality* [hereinafter NUSSBAUM, *The Discernment of Perception*], *in* LOVE'S KNOWLEDGE 54 (1990).

28 Many utilitarians reject a simple view of desire-satisfaction, preferring the idea of "informed desire." Such corrections, however, are insufficient: informational corrections do not weed out "adaptive preferences," preferences shaped by background social conditions that govern people's likely expectations, nor do they weed out preferences of a malicious sort. One may introduce separate corrections for these problems, but at this point the view ceases to be utilitarian in any genuine sense, since it will be informed by a complex account of noncommensurable goods. *See* NUSSBAUM, WOMEN AND HUMAN DEVELOPMENT, *supra* note 7, at 122–42 (discussing the literature on adaptive preferences and corrections proposed by John Harsanyi and Richard Brandt).

29 *See* JOHN RAWLS, A THEORY OF JUSTICE 75–83 (1971) (arguing that we should prefer principles of justice that devote special attention to the situation of the least well-off, and refuse to accept inequalities that do not improve that person's overall situation); *see also id.* at 150–61 (discussing classical utilitarianism).

by contrast, focuses on the provision to *each* of a basic minimum set of opportunities and freedoms — it sees people's lives as *separate and distinct*. The opportunities and possibilities of one person's life are not made richer by giving opportunities to someone else, or even to quite a few other people.

Finally, the CA takes issue with consequentialism. Good consequences can be produced by strategies that subordinate people, give them very miserable lives, or violate their basic rights. Insisting, again, on the separateness and worth of each citizen's life, the CA refuses to go after good consequences in this way.

A more subtle point about consequentialism concerns its sweeping invasiveness. A government truly dedicated to pursuing the best overall consequences must have some overall view of what is good, and it must impose this view on everyone in order to maximize this good, despite the fact that in every society citizens differ about the good life.[30]

The CA, by contrast, is quite abstemious: it identifies a very short list of core entitlements that should be secured to all citizens as the basic entitlements of a just society. Beyond that short list, the CA does not make sweeping claims about the overall good. It allows people to make their own choices based on their different views of the good life. Moreover, since the core entitlements are understood as *capabilities*, rather than as actual functions or actions, giving one of them to a person does not require him or her to use it.[31]

---

[30] People have different religions and secular views of the meaning and purpose of life. A thoroughgoing consequentialist has to opt for one of these views, and the view usually chosen is one that equates the good with pleasure or the satisfaction of desire. Needless to say, this is not an overall view of the good that all citizens in a religiously and ethically diverse society can share. There consequently seems to be something dictatorial and disrespectful about imposing it on everyone, by suggesting that all major decisions should be made in accordance with the utilitarian principle.

Sen has proposed a version of consequentialism in which rights-violations count as bad elements of the consequence, and thus count against a course that involves them. *See* Amartya Sen, *Rights and Agency*, 11 PHIL. & PUB. AFF. 3 (1982). This form of consequentialism is so nonstandard as to be more or less sui generis, however. Furthermore, it does not contain any special protection for rights when other consequences (wealth, desire-satisfaction) tell against protecting them.

We can imagine that, on due reflection, a utilitarian might come to accept the idea that respect for one's fellow citizens requires not making the principle of utility an overall doctrine of good choice. Such a utilitarian could then become a "political liberal," endorsing a utilitarian set of political principles as the basis for common life and not as a comprehensive doctrine. However, this distinction between the political and the comprehensive is not made by either classical or modern utilitarian philosophers. *See generally* JOHN RAWLS, POLITICAL LIBERALISM (expanded ed. 2005).

[31] *See* NUSSBAUM, WOMEN AND HUMAN DEVELOPMENT, *supra* note 7, at 105 (stating that capabilities should function as a goal and that one should "leave to citizens the choice whether to pursue the relevant function or not to pursue it"); *see also* NUSSBAUM, FRONTIERS OF JUSTICE, *supra* note 7, at 297–98.

B. Libertarian Minimalism

Libertarian minimalism[32] is another normative view that has had considerable influence in law; in constitutional law it has been more influential than utilitarianism.[33] Like utilitarianism, libertarianism begins from some attractive ideas: that people ought to have large areas of free choice around them, rather than being programmed by an intrusive government; that once people have state protection of a very basic type, they can be trusted to set goals for themselves and find the means to those goals. As in the case of utilitarianism, then, the CA applauds some of the deeper ideas behind libertarianism, particularly its defense of the freedom of choice, while parting company with its more detailed understanding of what that freedom is and how it is best promoted.

Libertarians hold that the proper role of government is simply to protect citizens from violation of some very basic rights — above all rights of personal security and property. Beyond this, government governs best when it governs least. Defenders of libertarianism may say that they favor "negative rights," or "negative liberty," that is, liberty from state interference, and oppose "positive liberty," that is, liberty produced by affirmative state action.[34]

The idea of negative rights, however, is confused and confusing. All rights and liberties are liberties *to* do something (they are positive), and they all require something negative as well, namely, the prevention

---

32 Libertarianism is not the only view that could be described as a form of minimalism; the view I am criticizing here is distinct from a minimalism pertaining to the judicial role (the view that judges should not make ambitious decisions, or should decide incrementally). For a presentation of the latter view, see generally CASS R. SUNSTEIN, LEGAL REASONING AND POLITICAL CONFLICT (1996).

33 *See generally* CRAIG DUNCAN & TIBOR R. MACHAN, LIBERTARIANISM (2005); RICHARD EPSTEIN, FORBIDDEN GROUNDS: THE CASE AGAINST EMPLOYMENT DISCRIMINATION LAWS (1992); BARRY GOLDWATER, THE CONSCIENCE OF A CONSERVATIVE (1960); ROBERT NOZICK, ANARCHY, STATE, AND UTOPIA (1974). Since libertarianism was, in effect, the creed of the Reagan administration, its influence on the political process, in rolling back the programs of the Great Society, has been vast. Such views are aggressively put forward by the Cato Institute today. The legal developments that I address in Part IV, such as denial that education has the status of a fundamental right and the narrow interpretation of welfare rights, are at least plausible examples of the influence of this pervasive American way of thinking. *See* SUNSTEIN, THE SECOND BILL OF RIGHTS, *supra* note 5, at 149–71 (analyzing the political developments behind the Supreme Court's failure to recognize social and economic rights as inherent in the Constitution).

34 These terms are often traced to Isaiah Berlin, but I am not contending that this loose talk of "negative" and "positive" represents a correct interpretation of Berlin's distinction. For Berlin, "negative liberty" is the liberty of noninterference, while "positive liberty" is the liberty of self-command — the ability to take charge of one's life and realize one's projects. *See* ISAIAH BERLIN, *Two Concepts of Liberty*, *in* THE PROPER STUDY OF MANKIND 191, 203–06 (1997). The libertarians I am talking about do not focus on the latter ability.

of interference by others.[35] I am not free to use my property unless you are prevented, by the state, from stealing or destroying it. Moreover, as proponents of libertarianism themselves soon concede, all valuable liberties require affirmative state action, not just a retreat on the part of the state. There is no system of property rights without laws regulating ownership or without enforceable laws against theft and fraud. There is no bodily security unless people are restrained by law (and effective law enforcement) from crimes against the person — as women suffering from domestic battery have long realized. So libertarians cannot really be saying that the state should keep its hands off of citizens' lives; they see clearly (or they should) that there could be no liberty without state action — and, indeed, without state expenditure. What they are really saying is that these protections and expenditures should focus on a small and specific range of rights — property, contract, bodily security — and that other things should be left to the market and to the personal choices of citizens.[36]

Libertarians therefore need to offer an argument about why some things and not others should be the focus of state action and expenditure; they also need to show that the items on their favored list do not require other items not on their list for their full attainment. Often, the language of negative rights papers over the failure to offer such arguments.

Libertarianism, then, is not a view diametrically opposed to the CA. Unlike utilitarianism, it does not insist on the commensurability of all the valuable things in citizens' lives, nor does it adopt a view of aggregation that allows some people's lives to be used as means to enhance the happiness of other people's lives. In keeping with the individualism of its proponents, it insists firmly that each and every citizen has certain rights, and it is happy enough to assert, at least, that those rights are equal. So, libertarianism looks like not an opponent of the CA but a sliver of it.

What, then, is the difference between the two approaches? Is it only that the CA has a somewhat longer list of the functions that are the proper role of government? That is surely one part of the difference: the CA sees an important role for the state in ensuring citizens adequate education, health care, nondiscrimination, equal employment

---

35 Even liberties whose most prominent aspect is negative, for example, the freedom from arbitrary imprisonment, cannot be fully analyzed without speaking of their positive element, the freedoms of movement and speech that are curtailed by imprisonment. We do not begin to have a concept of imprisonment, or of what might be problematic about it, unless we think, at the same time, of the entitlements that citizens have in areas such as movement and choice.

36 *See generally* STEPHEN HOLMES & CASS R. SUNSTEIN, THE COST OF RIGHTS (1999).

opportunities, and a threshold level of basic welfare, while libertarians deny that the state properly has a role in these areas.[37]

We can, however, find a deeper difference, by focusing on the idea of capability. The CA asks what position people are *really* in, what people are actually able to do and to be; it does not assume that if there is no obvious state interference with liberty, then all is well. The capabilities valued by the CA typically require both internal preparation and preparation of the external environment, both *internal* and *combined* capability. Libertarian minimalists are typically not very much concerned with internal capability: they do not see education, for example, as integral to the rights of free speech and political participation. They are also not very exigent in looking into the material and institutional circumstances that affect whether a combined capability is present. If there is a system of contract in place, they do not ask whether people are equally able to use that system. If there is a system of criminal law in place, they do not ask whether women face unequal obstacles to their bodily integrity through the reluctance of law enforcement to intervene in domestic violence. So they will often conclude that a liberty has been protected in a situation where an advocate of the CA would conclude that people were not really free to choose or to act in the relevant ways.

In general, libertarians are unwilling to acknowledge the fact that most, if not all, of the liberties they cherish have social and economic necessary conditions. It is very difficult to participate in political life on a basis of equality with others, or to enjoy the freedom of speech, if one has not had access to basic health care, or the opportunity for a decent education. The libertarian operates not only with a shorter list of basic entitlements but also with a thinner account of all of them, ignoring material and institutional conditions that turn mere words on paper into a working reality.

The CA, however, does not grant that two citizens have fully equal liberty if one of them is unable to take advantage of his or her entitlements because of poverty or other social obstacles; understanding liberty as capability, it denies that a liberty is equally present if the "worth of liberty" is dramatically different.[38]

---

[37] Though most libertarians by now concede the value of state provision of education, at one time they did not do so, and they do so somewhat uneasily today. See the discussion of T.H. Green *infra* Part III.D; Green's political opponents in the education debate were the nineteenth-century equivalents of modern libertarians.

[38] The distinction between a merely nominal liberty and a full-fledged capability lies close to a distinction proposed by John Rawls between "liberty" and the "worth of liberty." RAWLS, A THEORY OF JUSTICE, *supra* note 29, at 179. Rawls holds that two people may have equal liberties and yet be very unequal in their ability to take advantage of these liberties and opportunities, "as a result of poverty and ignorance, and a lack of means generally." *Id.*

Libertarians may, and often do, favor ample support for the capabilities of poorer citizens, in the sense that they think poor people should get support from some generous source.[39] So, they believe that poor people ought to have a wide range of central capabilities — it is just that they think this should be a matter of private charity, not a matter of public entitlement. Libertarians frequently also make the shaky[40] empirical claim that leaving things to the market and to private actors will actually work out better than trusting government action, and they often thus feel confident that their minimalism does not leave real people in the lurch. Meanwhile, to make things even more complicated, a supporter of the CA may use the private sector to secure citizens' entitlements, if that seems the best way to do things in a difficult situation.

The difference between libertarianism and the CA, however, is not merely a matter of differing about means to agreed-upon ends. Unlike libertarianism, the CA holds that the purpose of government is to promote a set of core necessary conditions for reasonably flourishing lives, lives worthy of human dignity. If that purpose has not been fulfilled, government is ultimately to blame, and minimal justice has not been achieved. The buck stops there. If government tries a voucher program, or sells a public highway to a private developer, or privatizes the control of a prison system, it is ultimately government that is responsible for the result, and the issue is one of basic justice. Support for citizens' capabilities is not mere charity, it is their right — what they are entitled to expect from the nation in which they live, as a matter of basic justice, and out of respect for their equal worth.

C. *Lofty Formalism (Versus "Perception")*

Our first two contrasts delineate the CA against rival normative views.[41] But the CA does not simply lay out a normative blueprint for

---

[39] Barry Goldwater always emphasized that his own personal choices were decent ones: for example, while opposing antidiscrimination laws for race (he voted against the Civil Rights Act of 1964 and often criticized the Supreme Court's decision in *Brown v. Board of Education*, 347 U. S. 483 (1954)), he strongly supported integration in his personal choices and was even a member of the NAACP. *See* Louis Menand, *He Knew He Was Right: The Tragedy of Barry Goldwater*, NEW YORKER, Mar. 26, 2001, at 92 (book review).

[40] *See, e.g.*, INDIAN DEVELOPMENT (Jean Drèze & Amartya Sen eds., 1997). The Indian states provide a handy laboratory for testing the empirical claim, since some have pursued economic growth without direct state action to support the entitlements of citizens, whereas others have pursued direct state action. The field studies conclude that in the areas of health and education, direct state action is essential; on the other hand, too much state control over the economy has bad effects on economic growth.

[41] I have omitted Kantian views, which are both important in themselves and important in law. *See, e.g.*, RAWLS, POLITICAL LIBERALISM, *supra* note 30, at 99–106; RAWLS, A THEORY OF JUSTICE, *supra* note 29, at 221–27. My omission does not indicate a lack of respect for such views: entirely the contrary. Indeed, I have drawn on Kant in developing my own version of the

basic justice; it also recommends a distinctive way of reasoning about entitlements: here, too, it has an influential rival.

The CA asks us to figure out what human beings are actually able to do and to be, in the totality of their circumstances: material, political, and social. It therefore cannot be implemented without the ability to understand the manifold ways in which context bears on individual striving. Libertarian minimalists ask only whether some very basic freedoms are legally protected. The CA goes deeper, asking searching questions about whether, and to what extent, people are really in a position to avail themselves of these freedoms; and it directs attention to other areas of choice and opportunity as well, such as education and health. Nations sometimes have attractive political conceptions on paper, without delivering opportunities to their people in the sense of capability, so the partisan of the CA needs to be able to imagine in detail how circumstances of many different sorts bear on the abilities of human beings of various sorts to choose and to act.

Aristotle spoke of an ability that he called "perception," which he made central to the account of the good political actor and the good judge.[42] Perception is experienced contextual understanding. Aristotle emphasizes that it cannot be delivered by abstract rules: only long experience will yield it. That is why, in his view, a young person cannot be a "person of practical wisdom."[43] But mere age is not enough either: the person must really be able to see into the details of a case, with what Aristotle calls a "sympathetic understanding" of human matters.[44] Advanced, in part, as an account of what the reasoning of a competent judge is like, Aristotle's view has great resonance with ideals of judging inherent in the common law tradition.[45]

At this point, the CA encounters another very formidable opponent, lofty formalism. This opponent is not, like the other two, a rival normative view. It is an approach to judgment that has frequently appeared, in both ethics and law, in connection with normative views of

---

CA. *See, e.g.*, NUSSBAUM, WOMEN AND HUMAN DEVELOPMENT, *supra* note 7, at 73. *See generally* NUSSBAUM, FRONTIERS OF JUSTICE, *supra* note 7 (arguing that Rawls's particular Kantian theory does not give adequate guidance on several specific issues, but making those critical points in the spirit of fine-tuning, not rejection).

42 *See, e.g.*, ARISTOTLE, ETHICA NICOMACHEA, *supra* note 13, at 1126b4–5 ("The discrimination is in the particulars and in perception." (author's translation)). In the secondary literature, particularly important studies of "perception" in Aristotle are JOHN MCDOWELL, *Virtue and Reason*, *in* MIND, VALUE, AND REALITY 50 (1998); and David Wiggins, *Deliberation and Practical Reason*, *in* ESSAYS ON ARISTOTLE'S ETHICS 221 (Amélie Oksenberg Rorty ed., 1980).

43 *See* ARISTOTLE, ETHICA NICOMACHEA, *supra* note 13, at 1142a11–30 (contrasting practical wisdom with mathematics, in which a young person can excel).

44 *See id.* at 1137b17–33.

45 On the judge, see *id.*, further discussed in NUSSBAUM, *The Discernment of Perception*, *supra* note 27, at 69–70.

different types. Lofty formalism has often been found, and even defended, in constitutional interpretation.

Lofty formalism is the view that good judgment requires standing at a considerable distance from the facts of the case and the history of struggle that they frequently reveal. There are several different reasons why one might consider this distanced judging a good thing. One might believe that a more contextual or situational judgment is bound to be ad hoc or biased, influenced by one's own political sympathies. Or one might think that consistency over time is best served by a distanced procedure, rather than by immersed contextual judgment. Or, more narrowly, one might simply believe that courts are good at judging in this distanced formal way, and not so good at reasoning contextually and historically. In general, lofty formalism is seen by its proponents as ensuring neutrality or absence of bias.[46]

In ethics, formalism often takes the shape of claiming that good ethical judgment applies principles that have been defended in a general way and that have their place in a hierarchy of rules.[47] Often the appeal to rules is defended by arguing that human beings have a strong tendency to make personally biased judgments, and, once again, this contention is plausible in some cases, where no device exists to eliminate bias.[48] Similarly, judicial formalism sometimes takes the form of an appeal to rules: consider, for example, Benjamin Cardozo's description of his longing, early in his judicial career, for "the solid land of fixed and settled rules, the paradise of a justice that would declare itself by tokens plainer and more commanding than its pale and glimmering reflections in my own vacillating mind and conscience."[49] Christopher Columbus Langdell, similarly, thought of the job of a true lawyer or judge as that of applying fixed principles "with constant facility and certainty to the ever-tangled skein of human af-

---

46 Thus formalism might be connected with utilitarianism, or with minimalism, or with yet other views, such as an excessively rule-oriented type of Kantianism. I do not contrast the CA with Kant's own views, since I believe that those are not excessively rule-oriented, and in most instances close to the analyses suggested by the CA. For the role of "perception" in Kant, see BARBARA HERMAN, THE PRACTICE OF MORAL JUDGMENT 79–83 (1993).

47 *See generally* NUSSBAUM, *The Discernment of Perception*, *supra* note 27.

48 Such a device might involve cutting the person off from information that would make a biased judgment possible, as in the practice of blind review in academic journals. Rawls's famous veil of ignorance is a similar device: parties choosing political principles behind this "veil" will be unable to favor their own social class, race, or gender. *See* RAWLS, A THEORY OF JUSTICE, *supra* note 29, at 118–23. In a related way, Adam Smith urges the ethical chooser to think from the viewpoint of a "judicious spectator" who is concerned with the case, attentive to all of its features, but personally uninvolved. *See* ADAM SMITH, THE THEORY OF MORAL SENTIMENTS 1–43 (D.D. Raphael & A.L. Macfie eds., Oxford Univ. Press 1976) (1759). Smith's ideal is closely related to norms of the good judge in the common law tradition. *See* MARTHA C. NUSSBAUM, POETIC JUSTICE: THE LITERARY IMAGINATION AND PUBLIC LIFE 72–77 (1995) [hereinafter NUSSBAUM, POETIC JUSTICE].

49 BENJAMIN N. CARDOZO, THE NATURE OF THE JUDICIAL PROCESS 166 (1921).

fairs."[50] Often, however, the judicial search for fixity takes a different form: sometimes fixity is sought in textualism, sometimes in a simple refusal to consider certain aspects of the cases (historical, contextual, or experiential).

There is nothing wrong with using rules and principles when they are good ones, embodying all the pertinent features of a complex situation; such principles are likely to be themselves very complex and close to the ground, since the world is complex and many historical features need to be taken into account in a good principle.[51] Kant seems right that a good decision should be *universalizable*, in the sense that, if all the relevant features were to reappear, the same decision would, once again, be correct.[52] The CA, however, insists that many historical features (for example, the history of discrimination suffered by a group) are highly relevant to judgment; one will, in consequence, rarely find principles that are highly *abstract* and *general*, covering a large number of cases without distinction.[53] Aristotle compares people who rely on such principles to builders who would try to measure a complex curved structure using a straight-edge; he points out that real builders use, instead, a flexible strip of metal that "bends to the shape of the stone, and is not fixed."[54] The CA does not repudiate universalizability, or the judicious use of rules; it does insist on the relevance of context and history, and thus makes the prediction that useful principles will usually not be highly general or abstract.[55] One reason for study-

---

[50] C.C. LANGDELL, A SELECTION OF CASES ON THE LAW OF CONTRACTS, at viii (2d ed. 1879).

[51] *See* R.M. HARE, MORAL THINKING (1981) (defending a type of universal principle that is highly concrete).

[52] *See* IMMANUEL KANT, *Grounding for the Metaphysics of Morals*, *in* ETHICAL PHILOSOPHY 1, 30–34 (James W. Ellington trans., Hackett Publ'g Co. 1983) (1785).

[53] On the distinction between the universal and the general, see MARTHA C. NUSSBAUM, *Introduction* to LOVE'S KNOWLEDGE, *supra* note 27, at 3, 38–39; NUSSBAUM, *The Discernment of Perception*, *supra* note 27, at 67–68; and MARTHA C. NUSSBAUM, *"Finely Aware and Richly Responsible": Literature and the Moral Imagination* [hereinafter NUSSBAUM, *Finely Aware and Richly Responsible*], *in* LOVE'S KNOWLEDGE, *supra* note 27, at 148, 165–66. I make an exception to universalizability for the case of personal love: we should not grant that a clone of the person one loves, even one that is formally indistinguishable from the actual person and that has all the "same" memories, is an adequate substitute for the real person. NUSSBAUM, *Introduction*, *supra*, at 39.

[54] ARISTOTLE, ETHICA NICOMACHEA, *supra* note 13, at 1137b29–33 (author's translation); *see also* NUSSBAUM, *The Discernment of Perception*, *supra* note 27, at 69–70.

[55] Thus, my own version of the CA is very friendly to many of Kant's ethical insights, and I have distanced myself from the more anti-principle versions of Neo-Aristotelian ethics. *See* Martha C. Nussbaum, *Why Practice Needs Ethical Theory: Particularism, Principle, and Bad Behavior*, *in* THE PATH OF THE LAW AND ITS INFLUENCE: THE LEGACY OF OLIVER WENDELL HOLMES, JR. 50 (Steven J. Burton ed., 2000).

ing history is that, suitably sifted, it can reveal certain types of principles, those of a type congenial to Aristotle.[56]

What I am calling lofty formalism is, then, not the bare determination to seek rules and principles, which, with suitable qualification, the proponent of the CA applauds; it is the determination to seek principles at a high level of abstraction and distance from history, whether or not that level is the one that best captures the complexity of the case at hand. Throughout the history of human life, people of intelligence and good will have sought such lofty abstractions, perhaps preferring, as Cardozo insightfully sees, a clear, schematic ideal to the sometimes messy and complicated realities of life.[57]

A classic example of the kind of lofty formalism that I reject here is given by Herbert Wechsler in his famous article, *Toward Neutral Principles of Constitutional Law*.[58] Wechsler begins his argument with an unexceptionable contention: courts should not function as a "naked power organ."[59] Instead, he argues, they should seek criteria that can be publicly articulated, that "transcend any immediate result that is involved."[60] As his argument continues, however, he makes it clear that he believes that this search for articulable reasons demands that one stand so far away from present circumstances and their history that one will ignore many specific social and historical facts. He insists at one point that his conception of principle does not entail disregarding history.[61] In his reading of the school desegregation cases, he nonetheless makes it clear that good judgment precludes close historical and social understanding: the relevant criteria must be sought at a level of abstraction far above the concrete situation.[62] Above all, judges deciding cases relating to "separate but equal" facilities should refuse themselves concrete empathetic understanding of the special disadvantages faced by minorities, and the asymmetrical meaning of segregation for blacks and whites, in order to ensure that their principles are applied without political bias.[63] The reasoning in *Brown v.*

---

[56] Hare pointed out that novels have similar properties. He suggested that they are "universal prescriptions" of the sort he favored: fine-grained, historically sensitive, detailed, and therefore neither abstract nor highly general. *See* NUSSBAUM, *Finely Aware and Richly Responsible*, *supra* note 53, at 166.

[57] *See* CARDOZO, *supra* note 49, at 166.

[58] Herbert Wechsler, *Toward Neutral Principles of Constitutional Law*, 73 HARV. L. REV. 1 (1959).

[59] *Id.* at 19.

[60] *Id.*

[61] *See id.* at 17.

[62] *See id.* at 33–34.

[63] *See id.* at 31–33 (arguing that the reference to the asymmetrical experience of minority children is a defect in the reasoning of the case). Notice that the concrete understanding of this asymmetrical meaning could itself generate an articulable principle, of a more historically situated and more pertinent sort.

Board of Education[64] was defective to the extent that it involved considering the experience of minority children in their separate schools. From the correct vantage point, he argues, the central legal issue raised by segregation is not one of discrimination at all: it is the denial of freedom of association, "a denial that impinges in the same way on any groups or races that may be involved."[65] To say otherwise is mere (illicit) politics.[66]

Wechsler now offers a revealing aside: "In the days when I was joined with Charles H. Houston in a litigation in the Supreme Court . . . he did not suffer more than I in knowing that we had to go to Union Station to lunch together during the recess."[67] Wechsler suggests, then, that the fact that a white man and a black man cannot eat together in a white restaurant involves a symmetrical burden for both, a simple denial of associational freedom.[68] Besides his strange omission of the fact that whites were always perfectly free to visit black restaurants (a fact that the history of jazz clubs in Harlem would have made famous), his account of the example is oddly obtuse, given his passionate opposition to segregation. Had Wechsler asked with imagination what people are able to do and to be, he would quickly have seen that the meaning of that denial is very different for Houston and for himself: for Wechsler, an inconvenience and, possibly, a source of guilt;[69] for Houston, a public brand of inferiority.

Wechsler claims to state not only the constitutional but also the human meaning of the laws in question. He is wrong on both counts. There is such a lofty distance from the human experience of segregation that the facts, and, hence, the principles, are distorted. The meaning of the denial of associational freedom is not symmetrical. Wechsler's claim that the issue of segregation is not one of discrimination at all has a bizarre Martian quality, as if he were standing so far above the world that the most salient facts cannot be seen. From this vantage point, furthermore, he fails to notice or to articulate perfectly rational and generalizable constitutional principles that would include the asymmetrical meaning of segregation and its history. Nonsubordination is one such principle.

---

64 347 U.S. 483 (1954).

65 Wechsler, *supra* note 58, at 34.

66 *See* NUSSBAUM, POETIC JUSTICE, *supra* note 48, at 87–89 (giving a similar account of Wechsler); *see also* MARTHA C. NUSSBAUM, *Equity and Mercy*, *in* SEX AND SOCIAL JUSTICE 154 (1999) (making related observations about narrative and judgment).

67 Wechsler, *supra* note 58, at 34.

68 *Id.*

69 Before the Houston anecdote, Wechsler says that segregation is a source of guilt for the Southern white. *Id.* He was not of Southern origin himself, but when the incident took place both he and Houston were working in the South, so it is not clear whether he intends to apply this reference to himself.

Wechsler's obtuseness extends, however, beyond *Brown*. His paragraph on the case ends with two rhetorical questions: "Does enforced separation of the sexes discriminate against females merely because it may be the females who resent it and it is imposed by judgments predominantly male? Is a prohibition of miscegenation a discrimination against the colored member of the couple who would like to marry?"[70] These questions are supposed to receive a quick answer in the negative, and thus to serve as a reductio ad absurdum of the mode of reasoning in *Brown*. Therefore, he implies, if following that mode of reasoning (thinking of separation as discriminatory), one is led to treat gender separation and laws against miscegenation as discriminatory (and we all can see how absurd that would be). Once again, his refusal of perception dooms his argument: there are perfectly good reasons for considering enforced separation of the sexes to be, in some cases, discriminatory, and the Court would soon find antimiscegenation laws to be so.[71]

As I argue in Part V, the lofty formalism exhibited in Wechsler's analysis is prominent in the opinions of the 2006 Term. One aspect of Wechsler's argument, however, proves absent: the sense of inner struggle and "deepest conflict"[72] with which Wechsler, vigorously opposed to segregation, comes to the conclusion that *Brown* is defective.

The case of Wechsler shows how lofty formalism can prove an ally of libertarian minimalism: a simple guarantee of freedom of association is said to be all that the law may require, and this guarantee must suffice to resolve the problem presented by the case. Both lofty formalism and libertarian minimalism, in turn, favor existing power interests: the close scrutiny of history and context is more important for the powerless, who face unequal obstacles to opportunity. Wechsler is basically asking us to look at everyone as if they were placed as are the powerful. That perspective naturally discourages the thought that equal protection requires special ameliorative efforts.[73]

---

70 *Id.* at 33–34.

71 *See* Loving v. Virginia, 388 U.S. 1, 11–12 (1967).

72 Wechsler, *supra* note 58, at 31 (comparing himself to Hamlet!).

73 Is there a connection between lofty formalism and utilitarianism? In a sense there should not be: utilitarianism focuses intently on suffering, and so it ought to adopt a mode of reasoning that is able to imagine and assess the sufferings of people in many different situations. In practice, however, utilitarianism's commitment to quantitative commensuration of all the pleasures and pains in a given choice situation makes it adopt a mode of reasoning that, like lofty formalism, lies rather far from the experiences of real people. Real people typically do not see their difficulties as quantities of some single homogeneous feeling: they make distinctions between (for example) the pain of a toothache and the pain caused by segregation. Nor do real people typically view their own lives as simply one input into an overall calculus of total utility. They generally consider lives one by one, and they tend not to feel that the pleasure of a dominant group atones for the pain of a minority. According to the utilitarian calculus, it is difficult to find fault with segregation, since it caused pleasure to a larger number of people than it pained. The utilitarian

The proponent of the CA does not deny that a type of formalism is sometimes useful — for example, when one does not have time to consider all the facts of the case fully, when one has little experience of history or life, or when one feels that one's own judgment is especially likely to be biased.[74] The good judge, however, will rarely if ever be in such a position, since judges (as the proponent of the CA sees it) should be selected in part for their wide experience of life and knowledge of history. Good judicial structures will both allow plenty of time to consider the case and mandate recusal in cases of personal bias.

In general, proponents of the CA have seen as a key advantage of the approach its ability to offer a pertinent, context-sensitive account of the disadvantages faced by women, racial and ethnic minorities, and people with disabilities.

The sort of understanding the CA requires is like the understanding a reader derives from reading a social novel (with, of course, attention to historical truth).[75] Aristotle's vocabulary on this point suggests a link to his understanding of the social role of tragedies, which inspire compassion by their depiction of human predicaments.[76] For the Greeks, such literary works were seen as essential formations of citizenship and public debate.[77] Similarly, in the modern era, the reader of Charles Dickens or George Eliot sees how human striving is consis-

---

calculator, then, is required by the theory to adopt a mode of valuation that is lofty, in the sense of being very far from the perceptions of people in their daily lives. Sidgwick acknowledges this gap frankly, saying that this discrepancy between the ordinary person's view and the expert's view is a ubiquitous characteristic of science. *See* SIDGWICK, *supra* note 21, at 425. Mill, indeed, criticizes Bentham for his lack of sympathetic imagination, calling his view "the empiricism of one who has had little experience." Mill, *Bentham*, *supra* note 16, at 149; *see also id.* at 148 ("[T]he faculty by which one mind understands a mind different from itself, and throws itself into the feelings of that other mind, was denied him by his deficiency of Imagination.").

74 *See* NUSSBAUM, THE FRAGILITY OF GOODNESS, *supra* note 27, at 304.

75 *See generally* NUSSBAUM, POETIC JUSTICE, *supra* note 48, at 79–121 (discussing the interaction of literature, poetry, and judging).

76 *See, e.g.*, ARISTOTLE, ARS RHETORICA 1374b2–10 (W.D. Ross ed., 1959) (author's translation) (using *suggnômê*, "sympathetic understanding"); *see also* ARISTOTLE, ETHICA NICOMACHEA, *supra* note 13, at 1143a19–20 (connecting *suggnômê* with equity, and both with perception of the particular); *id.* at 1110a24–25, 1111a1–2 (discussing *suggnômê* in tragic situations). These passages do not establish clearly that Aristotle is interested in cultivating the imagination; he relies primarily upon experience to produce understanding. However, he argues elsewhere that tragedy is "philosophical" because it brings its spectator into contact with events "such as might happen" in a human life. ARISTOTLE, POETICS 1451a36–b11 (D.W. Lucas ed., 1968). For two accounts of Aristotle's views about the role of the imaginative experience of tragedy in ethical learning, see STEPHEN HALLIWELL, THE AESTHETICS OF MIMESIS 177–206 (2002); and Martha C. Nussbaum, *Tragedy and Self-Sufficiency: Plato and Aristotle on Fear and Pity*, *in* ESSAYS ON ARISTOTLE'S POETICS 261 (Amélie Oksenberg Rorty ed., 1992).

77 There is a huge historical literature on this point (which, in a sense, is obvious, given that tragedies were staged at major civic festivals attended by all citizens, and often addressed issues central to the politics of the day). For recent discussions, see generally J. PETER EUBEN, CORRUPTING YOUTH: POLITICAL EDUCATION, DEMOCRATIC CULTURE, AND POLITICAL THEORY (1997); and GREEK TRAGEDY AND POLITICAL THEORY (J. Peter Euben ed., 1986).

tently hedged in by a variety of social obstacles deriving from class, gender, and social norms, and how unequal access to law is often the result of unequal social placement. When we see, for example, how difficult it is for David Copperfield to get even a minimal education, when we see how Stephen Blackpool's access to divorce and to employment rights is blocked by poverty, when we see how Dorothea is unable to use all her talents because of expectations connected to her gender, we have begun to see how societies form the capabilities of their members, often in unfair ways.

The good judge, as the CA imagines that role, will read a case the way an attentive reader reads such a novel, asking what the people are actually able to do and to be, what the history of their efforts is, and whether the freedoms and rights at issue are real for them, or distant and unavailable abstractions.[78] Because, as Aristotle emphasizes, such understanding is not conveyed by rules of the highly general and abstract type, the jurisprudence of the CA may sometimes look piecemeal, rather than elegant.[79] Nothing less, however, is required if the judgment is to present an accurate picture of people's substantive freedoms.

---

78 During his Supreme Court confirmation hearings before the Senate Judiciary Committee, Justice Breyer alluded to the understanding a judge might derive from reading novels (his example was Charlotte Brontë's *Jane Eyre*). *See* NUSSBAUM, POETIC JUSTICE, *supra* note 48, at 79. When you see a city, he said, you might think that all the people are the same, but a novel shows you that they are not:

> Each one of those persons in each one of those houses and each one of those families is different, and they each have a story to tell. Each of those stories involves something about human passion. Each of those stories involves a man, a woman, children, family, work, lives — and you get that sense out of the book. And so sometimes I've found literature very helpful as a way out of the tower.

Id. More than two centuries earlier, Adam Smith — whose economic views are discussed in section III.C, *infra* pp. 46–53 — published one of the great works on this topic in the Western philosophical tradition. *See* SMITH, THE THEORY OF MORAL SENTIMENTS, *supra* note 48. Throughout his work, Smith emphasizes the idea that the good judge, in ethical matters, ought to be a "judicious spectator" of the predicaments of which he writes: not unfairly partisan, but close enough to the parties and their sufferings to see what their problems are and what they are able to do. Frequently he compares the stance of the judicious spectator to that of someone who reads a narrative or watches a play: a person who follows with keen interest the plights of the characters, who feels a wide range of emotions about their fate, but who does not permit himself to judge their plight with personal spite or favor. *See* MARTHA C. NUSSBAUM, *Steerforth's Arm: Love and the Moral Point of View*, *in* LOVE'S KNOWLEDGE, *supra* note 27, at 335, 338–46 (analyzing the pertinent passages from Smith's *Theory of Moral Sentiments*). The contrast between lofty formalism and the CA might be summarized as a contrast between the view of life from "the tower" and the experienced perception characteristic of the experienced (literary) reader.

79 Thus, some of the best writers on Aristotle speak of his view as insisting that ethics is not "codifiable," in contrast with views that hold that ethical rules and principles can be fixed in advance of the particular case. *See, e.g.*, MCDOWELL, *supra* note 42, at 72–73. McDowell is difficult to interpret, but I believe that he does not reject Kantian universalizability here, but insists that highly general and abstract rules given before the fact are rarely adequate guides to choice.

Good judgment, so described, has deep links with practices of analogical reasoning embedded in the common law tradition. Good analogical reasoning requires perceiving what features of a case are salient, and this ability, in turn, requires an ability to grapple with the manifold features of a concrete case in all their historical and contextual complexity. The Aristotelian mode of reasoning requires experienced judgment, and is utterly opposed to a formalistic imposition of some abstract algorithm on the material of life. Therefore, the Aristotelian judge would be likely to take the part of the experienced common law judge, rather than the more mechanical decision procedures characteristic of libertarian minimalism, utilitarianism, and formalisms of yet other types.

III. HISTORICAL SOURCES

The CA is a modern view, but it has a long history. This history, fascinating in itself, is also pertinent to the CA's role in constitutional law, since it shows that the CA had a distinct presence on the American scene from an early date — never uncontested, but a force to reckon with. The following highly selective sketch singles out themes that turn out to be prominent in the cases of the 2006 Term.

A. Aristotle and the Stoics

To talk about Greek and Roman thought in the context of modern American law might seem oddly remote, and yet the historical sources of the modern ideas I discuss continue to be highly salient. Until very recently, around the mid-twentieth century, more or less all future judges and politicians had a lengthy classical education. This Foreward, then, studies the early conversation partners of a host of later thinkers — prominently including the Framers of our Constitution.

The political and ethical thought of Aristotle is the primary source for the CA. Aristotle believes that political planners need to understand what human beings require for a flourishing life,[80] and sees his writings as guides for politicians.[81]

Because choice is all-important for Aristotle — no action is counted as virtuous in any way, unless it is mediated by a person's own thought and selection[82] — he does not instruct politicians to make everyone perform desirable activities. Instead, they are to aim at producing capabilities or opportunities.[83] Aristotle is no liberal, but he does

---

[80] ARISTOTLE, POLITICA, *supra* note 3, at 1323a15–22, 1325a7–15.

[81] *See* ARISTOTLE, ETHICA NICOMACHEA, *supra* note 13, at 1179a33–b2.

[82] *See id.* at 1106a3–4, 1098a16–17.

[83] For a discussion of the evidence bearing on this contention (including arguments about the correct textual readings and translations of disputed passages), see Martha Nussbaum, *Nature,*

think that satisfaction achieved without choice is unworthy of the humanity of human beings.[84] And he understands that, even where no prohibitions exist, impediments to meaningful choice might be supplied by lack of education, or conditions of labor that make it impossible to inform oneself or to reflect.[85] Aristotle claims that political planning should focus "above all" on the education of the young, since the neglect of education does great harm to political life.[86] Repeatedly in his writings he identifies different levels of human capability (or *dunamis*), roughly corresponding to the distinctions I have introduced (innate capabilities, developed internal capabilities, and, finally, combined capabilities).[87]

Aristotle is particularly adamant that the pursuit of wealth is not an appropriate overall goal for a decent society.[88] Wealth is but a means to an end, and the human values that should guide political planning would be utterly debased and deformed were wealth to be understood as an end in itself.[89] Nor does he favor any account of the overall end of political planning that posits some single homogeneous goal varying only in quantity.[90] Although utilitarianism as such is un-

---

Function, and Capability: Aristotle on Political Distribution, *in* OXFORD STUDIES IN ANCIENT PHILOSOPHY 145 (Julia Annas & Robert H. Grimm eds., supp. vol. 1988).

84 ARISTOTLE, ETHICA NICOMACHEA, *supra* note 13, at 1145b8–20.

85 Thus, Aristotle excludes manual laborers from citizenship on the grounds that the conditions of their labor preclude education. ARISTOTLE, POLITICA, *supra* note 3, at 1328a23–35, 1328b38–1329a2, 1278a15–38.

86 *Id.* at 1337a10–11 (author's translation). Aristotle's conception of education's contribution is shaped by his univocal conception of the constituents of the best human life, and is thus subtly different from the one that I would favor.

87 Aristotle's use of the vocabulary of *dunamis* is unusually complex and requires clarification. A typical example of the first meaning ("innate") is found at ARISTOTLE, ETHICA NICOMACHEA, *supra* note 13, at 1105b20–28, which contrasts *dunamis* with a developed capacity. But in other passages, *dunamis* is clearly used in the sense of a developed capacity. *Id.* at 1094b2, 1101b13, 1143a28. Finally, the term is sometimes used when the capacity is already active, and thus the conditions for its activation must be present. *See* ARISTOTLE, DE ANIMA 412a1–413a10 (W.D. Ross ed., 1956) (defining *psuchê* as the active organization of a body that has life, potentially, or *dunamei*). Of course, as Aristotle immediately points out, one is alive only when the body is *actually* alive, thus meeting all the "external" conditions for the presence of *psuchê*. *See id.*; *see also* Martha C. Nussbaum, *Commentary* on ARISTOTLE, DE MOTU ANIMALIUM 271, 363–64 (Martha Craven Nussbaum trans., 1978) (discussing ARISTOTLE, DE MOTU ANIMALIUM 702a30–31, 703b29–32).

88 *See* ARISTOTLE, POLITICA, *supra* note 3, 1256a1–1258b8.

89 *See id.*

90 *See generally* NUSSBAUM, THE FRAGILITY OF GOODNESS, *supra* note 27 (describing Aristotle's approach of favoring practical perception over scientific reasoning as an aid to complex public and personal decisionmaking); NUSSBAUM, *The Discernment of Perception*, *supra* note 27; HENRY S. RICHARDSON, PRACTICAL REASONING ABOUT FINAL ENDS (1994) (providing a fine account of the nonutilitarian aspects of Aristotle's conception, which contrasts Aristotle's view explicitly with that of the British utilitarians). Key passages are found in ARISTOTLE, ETHICA NICOMACHEA, *supra* note 13, at 1096b23–5 (insisting on the nonhomogeneity of our

known to him, he is aware of hedonist views that identify the good with the greatest net balance of pleasure over pain, and he makes a range of arguments against hedonism that remain valid today against Benthamite forms of utilitarianism.[91] With Mill, Aristotle holds that pleasures differ in quality as well as quantity;[92] he also argues that some pleasures are bad and should not count at all in favor of a project; that some choiceworthy human activities, such as risking one's life for one's country, are not pleasant;[93] that there are other activities, such as seeing, remembering, and knowing, that we would choose even if they brought no pleasure.[94] In general, he argues that pleasure and the satisfaction of desire are utterly unreliable as guides to what is to be promoted in society, since people learn to derive pleasure from all sorts of things, good and bad, depending on the type of education they have had.[95]

Any decent political plan, then, would seek to promote a range of diverse and incommensurable goods, involving the unfolding and development of distinct human abilities. Moreover, such a plan must seek to promote these goods not just for some overall aggregate group, but for each and every citizen. Aware of Plato's corporate state, where the overall good of society was allegedly promoted in ways that permanently subordinated one class of citizens, Aristotle rejects the idea of corporate flourishing as mistaken: "A city is by nature a plurality. . . . The good of each is what preserves each."[96] Elsewhere he observes that there are some concepts that can apply to a whole without applying to its parts: "even number" is such a concept. Human flourishing or *eudaimonia*, however, he argues, is not like "even number": it applies to a whole (like a city-state) only if it applies to "all or most" of its members individually.[97]

Many political thinkers in the much later liberal tradition have had similar insights. Aristotle's contributions are of continuing importance in political thought because he couples an understanding of choice and its importance with an understanding of human vulnerability. A great biologist, and the son of a doctor, Aristotle is never tempted to view

ends). *See also id.* at 1095b16–17 (condemning as crude or base the idea that pleasure is the end of life); *id.* at 1174a1–4 (arguing that we would not choose the life of contented children).

91 *See* NUSSBAUM, *The Discernment of Perception*, *supra* note 27 (discussing the contemporary relevance of Aristotle's arguments).

92 *See* ARISTOTLE, ETHICA NICOMACHEA, *supra* note 13, at 1173b28–31, 1175a23–1176a3 (arguing that each pleasure is bound up with the activity that it completes).

93 *Id.* at 1117b10–16.

94 *Id.* at 1174a4–8; *cf. id.* at 1097b1–4 (arguing that we choose virtue, reason, and some other valuable things for their intrinsic value, as well as for the sake of happiness).

95 *Id.* at 1173b28–30, 1175b24–29, 1176a21–29.

96 ARISTOTLE, POLITICA, *supra* note 3, at 1261a17–b10 (author's translation).

97 *Id.* at 1264b15–22.

the human being as a disembodied creature. He advises his students not to view with disgust the animal body and the unattractive parts from which it is made.[98] He understands, and he tells his students, that a human being is a kind of animal.[99] Human beings, like all animals, move from birth through infancy, childhood, maturity, and, if they live long enough, old age, with all its infirmities.[100] Thus the human life cycle brings with it periods of heightened vulnerability. Discussing occasions for compassion, Aristotle offers a remarkable list of such vulnerabilities: deaths, bodily violations, bodily infirmities, old age, illnesses, lack of food, friendlessness, having few friends, being separated from one's friends and relations, ugliness, weakness, deformity, getting something bad from a source from which you were expecting something good, having something good happen only after the worst has happened, having no good fortune at all, or, finally, not being able to enjoy good fortune when it does come.[101] So Aristotle clearly knew human life and its vulnerabilities.

Aristotle's understanding of human vulnerability led him to believe that government needs to address it by thinking about things like the purity of a water supply and the quality of air, as well as education.[102] Vulnerability cannot be removed altogether, of course, but Aristotle does lay emphasis on the way in which some cities support human weakness better than others. A scheme he particularly likes is the provision of nutrition by government, in the form of communal meals that promote fellowship and friendship as well as health. Richer people would pay for the costs of their own meals, but the participation of poor people would be supported by the city.[103] Therefore, fully half of the city's land should be publicly owned in order to subsidize both public meals and civic festivals.[104] These are some of the consequences Aristotle derives from his idea that the job of government is to

---

[98] ARISTOTLE, PARTS OF ANIMALS 644b21–645b1 (A.L. Peck trans., 1961).

[99] *Id.* at 639a25.

[100] Aristotle devoted an entire treatise to the topic of old age, another to the topic of sleep, another to memory and failures of memory. These treatises are typically gathered under *Parva Naturalia*, a title added long after the pieces were originally published. *See, e.g.*, ARISTOTLE, PARVA NATURALIA (W.D. Ross ed., 1955) (includes Greek text and commentary in English).

[101] *See* ARISTOTLE, ARS RHETORICA, *supra* note 76, at 1385b11–1386b7.

[102] *See* ARISTOTLE, POLITICA, *supra* note 3, at 1330b11–17 ("The things that we use most of and most frequently where our bodies are concerned, these have the biggest impact on health . . . . Water and air are things of that sort. So good political planning should make some decisions about these things." (author's translation)); *see also* Martha Nussbaum, *Aristotelian Social Democracy*, *in* LIBERALISM AND THE GOOD 203 (R. Bruce Douglass, Gerald M. Mara & Henry S. Richardson eds., 1990) (discussing this and related passages).

[103] ARISTOTLE, POLITICA, *supra* note 3, at 1330a3–9.

[104] Even land that is privately owned is to be available for use by people in need. Elsewhere he mentions using produce one needs from farms that are privately owned in one's area. *Id.* at 1263a30–38; *see also id.* at 1330a1–2.

make all citizens capable of leading a flourishing life in accordance with their choice.

I have mentioned citizens. One of the great defects of Aristotle's thought lies here. Aristotle is happy with a system like that of the Athens of his day, in which only free adult nonimmigrant males were citizens and in which slavery was practiced. Indeed, he criticizes Athens for being too inclusive, since it admitted to full citizenship people who perform manual labor and who therefore, he thinks, cannot get an education.[105] What Aristotle seems to lack is the basic idea of human equality, of a worth all humans share across differences of gender, class, and ethnicity.

Stoicism remedied this deficiency. The most influential school of ethical and political thought in Greco-Roman antiquity, and perhaps the most influential philosophical school at any time in the Western tradition, Stoicism exercised such a widespread sway, particularly in Rome, that every educated person, and many who were not educated, were at some level guided by it.[106] Roman Stoic authors such as Cicero, Seneca, Epictetus, and Marcus Aurelius were more influential in the seventeenth and eighteenth centuries than Plato or even Aristotle.[107]

---

[105] Aristotle's lack of concern with questions of inclusion and exclusion is all the odder in that he was himself a nonresident alien in Athens, lacking civil rights, even the right to own property. (A student of his had to handle the financial arrangements for his school.) *See* David Whitehead, *Aristotle the Metic*, 21 PROC. CAMBRIDGE PHILOLOGICAL ASS'N 94 (1975) (arguing that Aristotle did not have special privileges of ownership distinguishing him from ordinary metics).

[106] For a study of the philosophical learning of average Romans, arguing that even quite nonintellectual people are expected to be able to understand jokes and references based on philosophical allusions, see Miriam T. Griffin, *Philosophical Badinage in Cicero's Letters to his Friends*, *in* CICERO THE PHILOSOPHER 325, 327–30 (J.G.F. Powell ed., 1995). *Cf.* Miriam Griffin, *Philosophy, Cato, and Roman Suicide* (pts. 1 & 2), 33 GREECE & ROME 64, 191 (1986) (discussing the profound influence of Stoicism in shaping Roman attitudes toward death and suicide). Even when Christianity replaced Stoicism as the daily creed of the Roman Empire, it was a Christianity profoundly influenced by Stoicism, and the whole history of subsequent Western thought in the European Christian tradition bears the impress of Stoic philosophical ideas. *See generally* 1 & 2 MARCIA L. COLISH, THE STOIC TRADITION FROM ANTIQUITY TO THE EARLY MIDDLE AGES (1985). Both major Greek Christian authors such as Clement of Alexandria and Latin authors such as Augustine are steeped in Stoicism. For a discussion of Clement's familiarity with Stoicism, see Mark Julian Edwards, *Clement of Alexandria*, *in* THE OXFORD CLASSICAL DICTIONARY 344, 344 (Simon Hornblower & Antony Spawforth eds., 3d ed. 1996). Augustine quarrels with the Stoics, showing a detailed knowledge of their doctrines, in many places, not least in Book XIV of *The City of God*. *See* 4 SAINT AUGUSTINE, THE CITY OF GOD AGAINST THE PAGANS 258–407 (Philip Levine trans., 1966). For discussion of early Christian writers, see 1 COLISH, *supra*, at 7–224. Augustine is reviewed in *id.* at 142–238; his use of the Stoic doctrine of natural law is covered in *id.* at 159–165.

[107] *See* Martha C. Nussbaum, *Duties of Justice, Duties of Material Aid: Cicero's Problematic Legacy*, 8 J. POL. PHIL. 176, 179 (2000) [hereinafter Nussbaum, *Duties of Justice*] (discussing Cicero's influence on Grotius, Pufendorf, and Adam Smith); *see also infra* section III.C, pp. 46–53 (discussing the influence of the Stoics on the American Founders). On Kant's debt to the Roman Stoics, see Martha Nussbaum, *Kant and Stoic Cosmopolitanism*, *in* PERPETUAL PEACE: ESSAYS

The Stoics taught that every human being, just by virtue of being human, has dignity and is worthy of reverence.[108] The human ability to perceive ethical distinctions and to make ethical judgments is held to be the "god within" and is worthy of boundless reverence.[109] Ethical capacity is found in all human beings, male and female, slave and free, high-born and low-born, rich and poor. Wherever this basic human capacity is found, then, it must be respected, and that respect should be equal, treating the artificial distinctions created by society as trivial and insignificant.[110] This idea of equal respect for humanity lies at the heart of what the Stoics called "natural law," the moral law that should provide guidance even when people are outside the realm of positive law.[111]

Because their thinking was not bounded by the walls of the city-state, the Stoics developed elaborate doctrines of duties to humanity, including proper conduct during wartime.[112] These ideas had a forma-

---

ON KANT'S COSMOPOLITAN IDEAL 25, 36–47 (James Bohmann & Matthias Lutz-Bachmann eds., 1997). On Kant's reading (which includes a single dialogue of Plato's that has been translated into German and partially rewritten as an original work by Moses Mendelssohn, but, otherwise, focused on Roman works), see Klaus Reich, *Kant and Greek Ethics* (pts. 1 & 2), 48 MIND 338, 446, at 338–39, 345–46, 447–60 (W.H. Walsh trans., 1939). As Ernst Cassirer puts it, "[Kant] seems to have been affected hardly at all by the spirit of Greek, which was taught exclusively by use of the New Testament." ERNST CASSIRER, KANT'S LIFE AND THOUGHT 15 (James Haden trans., 1981). Needless to say, these are but a few examples of my point.

108 The texts of the ancient Greek Stoics survive only in fragments, unlike the later Roman texts. For discussion of the major texts on these ideas, see Nussbaum, *Kant and Stoic Cosmopolitanism*, *supra* note 107. Particularly central is Seneca's *Moral Epistle 41*. *See* SENECA, AD LUCILIUM EPISTULAE MORALES 108–10 (L.D. Reynolds ed., 1965). Two typical works arguing for the equal entitlement of a previously excluded group are Musonius Rufus, *Should Daughters Get the Same Education as Sons?*, *reprinted in* THE SLEEP OF REASON 314 (Martha C. Nussbaum & Juha Sihvola eds., Martha C. Nussbaum trans., 2002); and Musonius Rufus, *That Women Too Should Do Philosophy*, *reprinted in* THE SLEEP OF REASON, *supra*, at 316.

109 SENECA, *supra* note 108, at 108–10. Christian authors influenced by Stoicism often call this power "conscience." *See* discussion of Roger Williams, *infra* section III.B, pp. 41–45.

110 For one eloquent and typical expression of this idea, see MARCUS AURELIUS, MEDITATIONS 10 (C.R. Haines trans., 1916). Marcus, a Roman emperor who was also a Stoic philosopher, says that even the distinction between oneself and one's enemies ought to be overcome by the thought that we all possess a similar "morsel of the divine." *Id.* at 27. On the artificiality of distinctions of rank, see, for a typical utterance, SENECA, *supra* note 108, at 114–15 (urging Lucilius not to define himself in terms of social class, "[w]e should look not at where people come from, but at where they are going" (author's translation)). *See also id.* at 93–96 (noting the importance of not deferring to intellectual authority: each person should strive for truth within him or herself).

111 For one typical use of the phrase natural law, see CICERO, ON DUTIES 109–10 (M.T. Griffin & E.M. Atkins eds. & trans., 1991); *cf. id.* at 21–22 (arguing that the law of nature gives all human beings moral duties to all other human beings).

112 *See id.* at 14–18. More than most, the Stoics meant what they said: they campaigned for the equal education of women, *see* Rufus, *Should Daughters Get the Same Education as Sons?*, *supra* note 108, and their ranks included a former slave (Epictetus), a foreigner from the far reaches of the Empire (Seneca, born in Spain), and various women, not to mention Cicero himself, whose non-aristocratic origins are a constant theme in his writings. Rufus's ideas appear to be based on

tive influence on modern founders of international law such as Grotius, Pufendorf, and Kant.[113]

The idea of human dignity, and of its boundless and equal worth, is the primary contribution of Stoicism to the CA. What political principles and actions does this idea suggest? Cicero and the Stoics hold that human dignity should never be abused by making it subject to the arbitrary will of another. Because human beings have dignity, one must not treat them like objects, pushing them around without their consent.[114] And because human dignity is equal, it is abhorrent to set up ranks and orders of human beings, allowing some to dominate others.[115]

The Romans themselves derived a range of different political lessons from these ideas. Cicero, a passionate defender of the Roman Republic in its waning days, believed that human dignity required republican institutions through which people could govern themselves without arbitrary tyranny. He defended the assassination of Julius Caesar in those terms, and he risked (and ultimately lost) his life in defense of the Republic. Many of Cicero's friends fully agreed with him about the Republic, whether they were Stoics or not,[116] and two anti-imperial movements during the early years of the Empire had Stoic roots.[117]

---

lost works by earlier Greek Stoics. *See* Martha C. Nussbaum, *The Incomplete Feminism of Musonius Rufus, Platonist, Stoic, and Roman*, *in* THE SLEEP OF REASON, *supra* note 108, at 283.

113 This influence is traced in Nussbaum, *Duties of Justice*, *supra* note 107; and Nussbaum, *Kant and Stoic Cosmopolitanism*, *supra* note 107. *See also* MARTHA C. NUSSBAUM, THE COSMOPOLITAN TRADITION (forthcoming) (on file with the Harvard Law School Library).

114 *See* CICERO, *supra* note 111, at 108.

115 *See* Nussbaum, *Duties of Justice*, *supra* note 107, at 184–85 (summarizing Cicero's theory of duties of justice); Nussbaum, *The Worth of Human Dignity*, *supra* note 8, at 36–40 (referring to relevant passages in CICERO, *supra* note 111, and other Stoic authors). For a very good account of the role of Stoicism in the formation of the Republicanism of the Founders, see PHILIP PETTIT, REPUBLICANISM (1997). Cicero, it should be said, is not a thoroughgoing Stoic. He rejects their positions on metaphysics and epistemology; in ethics he defends a distinct, albeit very similar, view. In political thought, however, the differences between Cicero and the Stoics become insignificant.

116 Brutus himself was a Platonist, and Cassius was an Epicurean. *See* David Sedley, *The Ethics of Brutus and Cassius*, 87 J. ROMAN STUD. 41, 41–42 (1997).

117 Seneca and the poet Lucan lost their lives in the conspiracy of Piso during Nero's reign. *See* TACITUS, THE ANNALS OF TACITUS 400–01 (Henry Furneaux ed., 1907) (discussing Seneca's death). A later alleged conspiracy led to the death of the Stoic philosopher Thrasea Paetus. *See id.* at 453–72. Some later Stoics thought, or at least said — since freedom of speech was compromised under the Empire — that a decently accountable monarchy might be acceptable. Some wrote praises of "good" emperors, such as Trajan. *E.g.*, PLINY, *Panegyricus*, *in* 2 LETTERS AND PANEGYRICUS 317 (Betty Radice trans., 1969). One Stoic, Marcus Aurelius, was himself the emperor. The experience of empire showed, however, that Cicero was correct: once a monarchy is in place, nothing prevents it from turning in an arbitrary and oppressive direction. So, as time went on, it came to seem more and more reasonable for Stoic thought to ally itself firmly to the idea of accountable republican institutions: only within these can human beings live lives worthy of human dignity.

Stoicism also contained, however, the seeds of a more quietistic response, suggested by their anti-Aristotelian ideas about human invulnerability. Because the Stoics taught that dignity was all-important and material conditions utterly unimportant, it was possible to maintain that the soul was always free within, whether or not institutions enslaved it on the outside.[118] In one striking example of this general point, Seneca's famous letter on slavery asks masters to show respect to their slaves, and to treat them like full-fledged and equal human beings, but it does not attack the institution of slavery, which Seneca holds to be compatible with a dignified free life within.[119] These disturbing conclusions were reached not by compromising the Stoic commitment to equal worth, but, instead, by denying the Aristotelian thought of human vulnerability: external conditions are not really important to a person's attempt to live well, so it is not very important for law and government to supply those conditions.[120]

The early modern thinkers who shaped the American founding were, thus, heirs to a complex tradition. Typically, thought about "natural law" in the seventeenth and eighteenth centuries — and, thus, the core of the classical education given to people bound for politics and government — melded Aristotelian with Stoic elements.[121] Al-

[118] *See* MARTHA C. NUSSBAUM, THE THERAPY OF DESIRE 359–401 (1994) (discussing the texts on the Stoic doctrine of the worthlessness of "external goods," and their related view of detachment).

[119] *See* SENECA, *supra* note 108, at 119–24. For analysis of this epistle, see Nussbaum, *Duties of Justice*, *supra* note 107, at 189–91.

[120] Even internal consistency suffered: it was difficult, or impossible, to square the denial of vulnerability with the Stoic commitment to non-domination and republicanism. Not that Stoics admitted this: but at this point their writings betray strain. *See* NUSSBAUM, THE THERAPY OF DESIRE, *supra* note 118, at 429–38 (analyzing the tensions in Seneca's *On Anger*, book III, chapters 14–15). For the relevant Latin text of *On Anger*, see SENECA, DIALOGORUM LIBRI DUODECIM 105–07 (L.D. Reynolds ed., 1977). *See also* Miriam Griffin, *Philosophy for Statesmen: Cicero and Seneca*, *in* ANTIKES DENKEN — MODERNE SCHULE 133, 140–47 (H.W. Schmidt & P. Wülfing eds., 1988); Martha C. Nussbaum, *Philosophical Norms and Political Attachments: Cicero and Seneca* (forthcoming) (on file with the Harvard Law School Library).

[121] A typical but unusually clear example (since he cites his sources far more than do most philosophers of the time) is Grotius, the Dutch philosopher whose 1625 work *On the Law of War and Peace* had enormous influence on all subsequent thought about international law. HUGO GROTIUS, DE JURE BELLI AC PACIS (Francis W. Kelsey trans., Oxford Univ. Press 1927) (1625). The section in which he defines and proves the existence of natural law, *id.* at 38–43, contains citations to Aristotle, Cicero, Seneca, Plutarch's *Life of Cato the Elder* (the Stoic hero), and Epictetus, as well as numerous Biblical texts and Christian authors. Cicero, as usual, plays a particularly prominent role. For general studies establishing that Aristotle played a role in the early modern development of natural law, alongside the more obvious Stoic sources, see Kelly Lynn Grotke, Natural Law and Eighteenth-Century Prussia (Jan. 2006) (unpublished Ph.D. dissertation, Cornell University) (on file with the Harvard Law School Library); and MANFRED RIEDEL, METAPHYSIK UND METAPOLITIK 237–53 (1975). For Lord Coke's use of Aristotelian/Stoic natural law ideas, see 7 EDWARD COKE, REPORTS (1608), *reprinted in* 1 THE SELECTED WRITINGS AND SPEECHES OF SIR EDWARD COKE 161, 195–96 (Steve Sheppard ed., 2003).

though different combinations of ideas could be made, one attractive and enduring marriage, compatible with Christian beliefs, was a combination of the Stoic idea of the equal worth of all human beings with the Aristotelian idea of human vulnerability. Despite the enduring attraction of Stoic ideas of invulnerability, Aristotle's view was strongly commended by common sense and by most people's experience of loss, age, the damages of war, and so forth. Hugo Grotius, Adam Smith, Kant, and the American founders all accepted the Stoic idea of equal dignity, while turning to Aristotle to understand the many ways in which human beings need help from the world in order to live well.[122]

B. Early American Thought: Liberty of Conscience

In England, in the wake of the civil wars, ideas of internal religious toleration were beginning to be defended as the best way to achieve a lasting peace. We associate the move toward toleration with John Locke's famous work, *A Letter Concerning Toleration*, published in 1689.[123] More than forty years earlier, however, Roger Williams, a classical and religious dissident who had by then taken refuge in the New World, published two works that, together, comprised a defense of religious liberty much more comprehensive and radical than Locke's, and of equal philosophical distinction.[124] Because Williams

[122] *See* GROTIUS, *supra* note 121, at 179–80 (discussing property); *id.* at 430–37 (discussing damages); *id.* at 203–05 (discussing acts that human life requires). He states: "Human life exists under such conditions that complete security is never guaranteed to us" — and he goes on to assert that only God can protect us from fear, a most un-Stoic sentiment. *Id.* at 184. Smith explicitly repudiates Stoic detachment in favor of a view similar to Aristotle's in the area of damages to one's family, country, and friends. *See* SMITH, THE THEORY OF MORAL SENTIMENTS, *supra* note 48, at 292–93 (arguing that the extreme degree of detachment prescribed by the Stoics leaves an insufficient basis to motivate virtuous conduct on behalf of family and country). He calls Aristotle "a philosopher who certainly knew the world." *Id.* at 258. Grotius does not explicitly quarrel with the Stoics, but simply assumes that the damages of war are real and significant. Kant modifies the doctrines of Stoicism by insisting that we have a duty to promote the happiness of others and that we are permitted to pursue our own happiness in ways that do not interfere with the happiness of others. *See* KANT, *supra* note 52, at 37–38. For the views of Madison and Paine, see *infra* section III.C.

[123] JOHN LOCKE, A LETTER CONCERNING TOLERATION (James H. Tully ed., Hackett Publ'g Co. 1983) (1689).

[124] ROGER WILLIAMS, THE BLOUDY TENENT OF PERSECUTION (1644) [herinafter WILLIAMS, BLOUDY TENET], *reprinted in* 3 THE COMPLETE WRITINGS OF ROGER WILLIAMS (Russell & Russell, Inc. 1963); ROGER WILLIAMS, THE BLOODY TENENT YET MORE BLOODY (1652) [hereinafter WILLIAMS, YET MORE BLOODY], *reprinted in* 4 THE COMPLETE WRITINGS OF ROGER WILLIAMS, *supra*. Both these works were published in England to considerable controversy, and because Williams's first job after his university education was as chaplain at the same noble house, Otes in Essex, where Locke later wrote his *Letter*, it seems likely that Locke knew Williams's work and used it as a source. *See* MARTHA C. NUSSBAUM, LIBERTY OF CONSCIENCE: IN DEFENSE OF AMERICA'S TRADITION OF RELIGIOUS EQUALITY (forthcoming 2008) (manuscript at ch. 2, on file with the Harvard Law School Library) [hereinafter NUSSBAUM, LIBERTY].

was setting up the colony of Rhode Island at the same time that he was writing his two massive works on religious liberty, his ideas achieved lasting fame and influence.[125]

Williams's ideas were shaped by classical sources. His excellence as a young classical scholar led to his becoming the protégé of Sir Edward Coke, whose own work uses natural law ideas that both were ubiquitous during this period and found their origins in the works of Aristotle and the Stoics.[126] Williams's central concept is "conscience," and he defines it in almost exactly the way the Stoics defined the power of moral choice. Although, given his topic, he focuses on its religious employment, he also makes it clear that conscience is a general faculty of searching and choosing that directs the whole conduct of life.[127] For Williams, as for the Stoics, this faculty is in all human beings and is infinitely precious and worthy of respect.[128] Although some people use it well and others use it badly, we are all equal in possessing the faculty, and on this account deserve *equal respect* and impartial treatment from one another.[129]

As we saw, the Stoics held that equal respect requires little from the world of laws and institutions, since the power of choice is invulnerable. Williams, with the more Aristotelian side of the natural law tradition, denies this. A highly rhetorical writer, he obsessively repeats two images to illustrate the ways in which all existing governments

---

125 *See* NUSSBAUM, LIBERTY, *supra* note 124 (manuscript at ch. 2). People in the colonies who did not know his writings knew the bold political experiment in which his ideas were embodied (and the extensive correspondence with political leaders in New England in which versions of the ideas are contained). For Williams's letters, see the two volumes of THE CORRESPONDENCE OF ROGER WILLIAMS (Glenn La Fantasie ed., 1988) [hereinafter WILLIAMS CORRESPONDENCE]. Among good biographical studies of Williams, see EDWIN S. GAUSTAD, LIBERTY OF CONSCIENCE: ROGER WILLIAMS IN AMERICA (1991); W. CLARK GILPIN, THE MILLENARIAN PIETY OF ROGER WILLIAMS (1979); TIMOTHY L. HALL, SEPARATING CHURCH AND STATE: ROGER WILLIAMS AND RELIGIOUS LIBERTY 17–39 (1998); PERRY MILLER, ROGER WILLIAMS (1953).

126 *See* R.H. Helmholz, Bonham's Case, Judicial Review and the Law of Nature (July 2006) (unpublished manuscript, on file with the Harvard Law School Library) (discussing Coke's use of natural law argumentation in this famous case). One striking example of Coke's use of natural law argumentation is in Calvin's Case (1608), where he cites both Aristotle and Cicero (whom he calls by his middle name Tully) as sources for his natural law doctrine. COKE, *supra* note 121, at 195–96.

127 *See, e.g.*, WILLIAMS, YET MORE BLOODY, *supra* note 124, at 440; Letter from Roger Williams to Governor John Endicott (1651), *in* 1 WILLIAMS CORRESPONDENCE, *supra* note 125, at 337, 339–40; Letter from Roger Williams to John Whipple, Jr. (July 8, 1669), *in* 2 WILLIAMS CORRESPONDENCE, *supra* note 125, at 586, 586.

128 *See* Letter from Roger Williams to Governor John Endicott, *supra* note 127, at 339 (it is "holy *Light*"); *id.* at 340 (it is "in all mankinde," including "*Jewes*, *Turkes*, *Papists*, *Protestants*, *Pagans*, etc.").

129 The theme of impartiality is a huge one in Willams's writings. *See, e.g.*, WILLIAMS, BLOUDY TENENT, *supra* note 124, at 401–02; WILLIAMS, YET MORE BLOODY, *supra* note 124, at 33, 113, 290.

have abused the human conscience: imprisonment and "soul rape."[130] Consciences are imprisoned when they are prevented from worshiping in their own ways; they are more profoundly damaged, or violated, when governments attempt to force people to worship or utter statements of belief against their consciences. Most often, governments favor the religion of the dominant group; they grant ample liberty to this group and they pretend to be in favor of liberty in general, but they do not acknowledge that in this way they are treating human beings with gross partiality. As Williams wrote in a 1670 letter to the governors of Massachusetts and Connecticut, both of which had coercive Puritan orthodoxies, "Your Selvs praetend Libertie of Conscience, but alas, it is but selfe (the great God Selfe) only to Your Selves."[131] Liberty of conscience, for Williams, is grounded in our possession of basic human dignity, and is an entitlement for those in religious error as much as for those who have (what the ruling group takes to be) the correct religion.

Williams understood that governments were necessary for the protection of liberty of conscience. His own experience setting up a colony showed him that constant watchfulness and good laws were required lest people interfere with the worship and beliefs of others. It is not enough that government itself does not interfere: people must really be free to worship in their own way, and this takes an aggressive public policy of toleration and laws that promote it. In a move that shocked the English, Williams insisted that the protection of liberty of conscience be written into the colony's charter (as well as a related protection for the freedom of action of the Indians and a defense of their property rights).[132] Protecting consciences from both rape and imprisonment meant not only the zealous protection of all groups from interference by others (Rhode Island welcomed Jews, Baptists, Quakers, Catholics, and all sorts of unaffiliated "seekers," and Williams's writings defend liberty for Muslims and atheists as well), it also meant making sure that the state itself was religiously neutral. Williams is more radical than Locke and is a precursor of Madison, in that he sees

---

130 *See e.g.*, Letter from Roger Williams to Governor John Endicott, *supra* note 127, at 338 (invoking imprisonment); WILLIAMS, BLOUDY TENENT, *supra* note 124, at 182, 219 (invoking soul rape); WILLIAMS, YET MORE BLOODY, *supra* note 124, at 495 (same).

131 Letter from Roger Williams to Major John Mason and Governor Thomas Prence (June 22, 1670), *in* 2 WILLIAMS CORRESPONDENCE, *supra* note 125, at 609, 616.

132 *See* THE CHARTER (1663), *reprinted in* 2 RECORDS OF THE COLONY OF RHODE ISLAND AND PROVIDENCE PLANTATIONS IN NEW ENGLAND 3 (John Russell Bartlett ed., 1857); Letter from Roger Williams to the Town of Providence (1654), *in* 2 WILLIAMS CORRESPONDENCE, *supra* note 125, at 423.

all religious establishments as threats to both the liberty and equality of citizens.[133]

For Williams, the capability of conscience requires protection of the widest possible space that is compatible with the safety and survival of the state. In his writings he insists that only the strongest possible government interest, namely an interest in safety and survival, could possibly justify any diminution of the space within which conscience exercises itself.[134] He strongly suggests that the space that ought to be protected includes a freedom to disobey at least some laws of general applicability if they burden one's conscience: thus he seems to have forged the concept of free exercise accommodation, an idea that soon became widespread in the colonies.[135]

Williams sees that protection and support for the capability of searching for the meaning of life in one's own way is no small matter: it requires careful protective action on the part of the State, and it requires, as well, an enforceable ban on all religious establishments, as enemies of the capabilities of citizens. Nonestablishment was a very new idea, which would not crop up automatically: it had to be put in place by deliberate, and extensive, legal policies. All of this machinery is required if citizens are to be protected from the rape and imprisonment of their basic human powers, or, to put it in another way, if all human beings are to breathe the air. In all these ways, Williams draws inspiration from both the Stoic idea of equal human dignity and the Aristotelian idea of human vulnerability.

In one respect, however, Williams breaks away from the Stoic/Aristotelian tradition, and it is a break of decisive importance for our contemporary attempt to build a nation that is fair to citizens with different religious convictions. Aristotle and the Stoics thought that there was just one correct account of the overall good life for a human being and that politicians could learn that account (for example, by going to Aristotle's lectures!). So, even though their respect for choice prevented them from forcing everyone to function in the desired way, they felt that they knew the goal whose preconditions they were distributing. Where religion was concerned, this made their task very easy: Aristotle is mainly concerned that citizens should have enough money to participate in the state's established religion. The Stoics believe that people always have the ability to choose the correct view,

133 Rhode Island under his leadership not only had no religious orthodoxy, it also avoided having Sunday laws, which Williams (who had his own doubts about the correct day for worship) saw as burdensome.

134 *See* Letter from Roger Williams to the Town of Providence, *supra* note 132, at 423–24.

135 *See* Michael W. McConnell, *The Origins and Historical Understanding of Free Exercise of Religion*, 103 HARV. L. REV. 1409 (1990) (discussing "peace and safety" overrides in state constitutions); *see also* NUSSBAUM, LIBERTY, *supra* note 124, (manuscript at chs. 2 and 4).

that is, Stoicism. Williams, by contrast, seeing the diversity of religions in society, reasons that law must not only protect ample space for all citizens to pursue a search for life's meaning in their own way, but it must also prescind from announcing or celebrating anything in religious matters. All orthodoxies are threats to the human capability of conscience.

Williams insists that, nonetheless, politics and public life can and do have a moral character, because there is an ethical space we can share as citizens who differ about ultimate religious matters. Addressing his Massachusetts opponents, who insisted that the character of a person's Christian convictions was highly relevant to his selection as a political leader, Williams declares that what is relevant to political office is a particular set of moral virtues, but that these virtues are separable from religious convictions.[136] Good moral principles are routinely found, he says, in people who have a religion that one may take to be in error. What politics should be doing, then, is operating within that shared moral space, making sure that it does not get hijacked by any particular doctrine, in such a way as to jeopardize both liberty and equality.[137]

Williams's ideas were not universally accepted. Many people felt that the interest in homogeneity outweighed an interest in ample and state-supported liberty. There came to be increasing agreement, however, that the question of establishment implicated a fundamental human capability: individual liberty and the quality of that liberty. James Madison's *Memorial and Remonstrance*, a major document concerning religious establishment that reappears frequently in modern constitutional analysis, stressed, like Williams, that establishments were a threat to individual conscience.[138] Madison, indeed, went further than Williams, seeing in any taxation for the support of an established church, even with strong guarantees of liberty, an implicit threat to liberty and equal liberty.[139]

---

[136] *See* NUSSBAUM, LIBERTY, *supra* note 124, (manuscript at ch. 2); *see also* WILLIAMS, BLOUDY TENENT, *supra* note 124, at 398–99.

[137] *See* NUSSBAUM, LIBERTY, *supra* note 124, (manuscript at ch. 2); *see also* WILLIAMS, BLOUDY TENANT, *supra* note 124, at 398–99.

[138] JAMES MADISON, MEMORIAL AND REMONSTRANCE AGAINST RELIGIOUS ASSESSMENTS (1785), *reprinted in* MICHAEL W. MCCONNELL ET AL., RELIGION AND THE CONSTITUTION 49, 50–51 (2d ed. 2006).

[139] All citizens, writes Madison, should enter the polity "on equal conditions," *id.* at 50; a tax for religious purposes, even one that is extremely benign, threatens that equality in standing and also, ultimately, threatens liberty itself, *see id.* at 49.

C. The Eighteenth Century: Smith on Education, Paine on Social Security

The eighteenth century saw a widespread fascination with Stoic ideas of equal dignity, which influenced the ideas of republican thinkers on both sides of the Atlantic. Most often, however, these ideas were borrowed in combination with an Aristotelian understanding of human vulnerability. The task of government thus came to be understood as that of protecting certain core human abilities so that they might develop and become effective. One could write the entire history of political philosophy in this period as a set of variations on these two themes of dignity and vulnerability. For our purposes, however, two key texts will suffice, significant in their own right and also highly influential in the American founding. The first is Adam Smith's *The Wealth of Nations*.[140] The second is Thomas Paine's *Rights of Man*.[141]

The philosophers of the Scottish Enlightenment formed the core of James Madison's education in political theory at Princeton University, a largely Presbyterian university. In 1783, asked to draw up a reading list for the Congress, Madison favored Scottish authors throughout, and prominently recommended Smith's *The Wealth of Nations* under the section entitled "Politics."[142] So we can assume that not only Madison but also his colleagues in Congress, provided that they did their homework, were familiar with Smith's by-then extremely famous book. Madison alludes to Smith's ideas several times in the

[140] SMITH, THE WEALTH OF NATIONS, *supra* note 1. Smith was already famous for his *Theory of Moral Sentiments*. I discuss the ideas of this section in MARTHA C. NUSSBAUM, *"Mutilated and Deformed": Adam Smith on the Material Basis of Human Dignity* [hereinafter NUSSBAUM, *"Mutilated and Deformed"*], *in* THE COSMOPOLITAN TRADITION, *supra* note 113 (manuscript at ch. 4); this chapter was presented as a keynote address at the Hume Society conference in July 2005 and was posted on their website prior to that meeting. For other relevant scholarship on Smith in the spirit of these remarks, see SAMUEL FLEISCHACKER, A THIRD CONCEPT OF LIBERTY: JUDGMENT AND FREEDOM IN KANT AND ADAM SMITH (1999); SAMUEL FLEISCHACKER, ON ADAM SMITH'S *WEALTH OF NATIONS* (2005); JERRY Z. MULLER, ADAM SMITH IN HIS TIME AND OURS (1993); and EMMA ROTHSCHILD, ECONOMIC SENTIMENTS (2001).

[141] THOMAS PAINE, RIGHTS OF MAN (1791–1792), *reprinted in* RIGHTS OF MAN, COMMON SENSE, AND OTHER POLITICAL WRITINGS 83 (Mark Philp ed., 1995). *Rights of Man* was published relatively late in Paine's career, but its thought about equal natural rights is fully consistent with Paine's earlier writings. *See* Mark Philp, *Introduction* to *id.* at vii, xvii. On Paine's wide influence (some believed that he wrote the Declaration of Independence), see *id.* at xxv. Philp nicely remarks: "[W]hat Paine brought to these principles [that is, those of the Declaration] was first-hand experience of struggle and failure in a society divided by birth and title; what he read in them was an invitation to citizenship in a classless (and racially equal) society." *Id.* at xxv; *cf.* PAINE, *supra*, at 271 ("It is to my advantage that I have served an apprenticeship to life.").

[142] Roy Branson, *James Madison and the Scottish Enlightenment*, 40 J. HIST. IDEAS 235, 236 (1979).

Federalist Papers.[143] On topics ranging from trade to religious non-establishment, there are strong signs of Smith's influence.[144] There is also a great deal of evidence for the work's importance among other leading participants in the Founding, including Thomas Jefferson and Noah Webster. It figured several times in constitutional debates.[145]

Adam Smith's writings are suffused with Stoicism; he turns to Aristotle, however, for a correct understanding of the worth of family, friends, and many of the material conditions of human flourishing.[146]

Admittedly, some of the impediments to human capabilities that Smith sees in the England of his time consist in wrong-headed and intrusive legal restrictions, such as restriction on trade and the free movement of labor.[147] In such cases, Smith urges deregulation, and he has thus become a favorite source for libertarian minimalists. It is clear, however, that a minimalist reading of Smith is inadequate.[148] His touchstone is always the question: what form of action by government permits human abilities to develop and human equality to be respected? Smith favors less government action when such action inhibits the development of human capabilities, and he understands quite well that it will take law to unmake law. Thus he supports the abolition of apprenticeship, and laws against monopolies and restrictions on lobbying by powerful financial interests, which, in his view, make citizens' influence on the political process grossly unequal, and guarantee that government will be held hostage to what he calls a

---

143 *See* Samuel Fleischacker, *Adam Smith's Reception Among the American Founders, 1776–1790*, 59 WM. & MARY Q. 897, 908–15 (2002).

144 *See id.* at 905–15.

145 *See id.* at 901–03.

146 *See* Nussbaum, *Duties of Justice*, *supra* note 107, at 179. Smith's ideas on this topic appear to change over time and are by no means absolutely consistent. The later editions of *The Theory of Moral Sentiments*, written near the end of his life, at times appear to defend the invulnerability thesis in a modified form. *See* NUSSBAUM, *"Mutilated and Deformed"*, *supra* note 140, at pt. VI. The earlier and more political *The Wealth of Nations*, however, insists strongly on the importance of government action in defense of human capabilities.

147 *See* 1 SMITH, THE WEALTH OF NATIONS, *supra* note 1, at 452–98 (discussing trade restrictions); *id.* at 135–40 (attacking mandatory apprenticeship laws that impeded the movement of labor).

148 ROTHSCHILD, *supra* note 140 (demolishing the minimalist reading).

"standing army" of wealthy elites.[149] These proposals are supported by considerations of justice as well as efficiency.[150]

Among Smith's most radical arguments in favor of government intervention is a set of arguments late in *The Wealth of Nations*, calling for government provision of free compulsory public education. The context of the discussion is a set of Aristotelian observations concerning the waste of human abilities among the working classes. Early in the work, Smith emphasizes the fact that habit and education play a profound role in shaping human abilities: the philosopher and the street porter differ in education, not by nature, although the "vanity" of the former supposes otherwise.[151] Much of *The Wealth of Nations* is accordingly dedicated to documenting the many factors that can cause key human abilities to fail to develop. Some of these factors are straightforwardly physical. Poverty is unfavorable to life and health.[152] "[P]overty, though it does not prevent the generation, is extremely unfavourable to the rearing of children. The tender plant is produced, but in so cold a soil and so severe a climate, soon withers and dies."[153] Elsewhere, Smith generalizes the point. Any class that cannot support itself from wages will be afflicted with "[w]ant, famine, and mortality."[154]

These passages show Smith breaking with the Stoics and developing an Aristotelian account of the human being and of basic needs. He reminds his reader that human dignity is a "tender plant" that will wither if it encounters a cold soil and a severe climate. This means that we cannot take the view that the distribution of material goods is irrelevant to human dignity, for dignity requires, at the very least, life, and the lives of children are in the hands of these material arrangements.

---

149 1 SMITH, THE WEALTH OF NATIONS, *supra* note 1, at 471–72; *see also id.* at 84, 157–58. He also favors the abolition of the slave trade, and indeed he campaigned on behalf of this cause. *See id.* at 387–88 (arguing that slave labor is unproductive and uneconomical in many circumstances); *see also* Adam Smith, Report of 1766, *in* LECTURES ON JURISPRUDENCE 452 (R.L. Meek et al. eds., 1978) (describing the "tyranic disposition" to enslave). He shows at least some sympathy with wage regulations that favor workmen. *See* 1 SMITH, THE WEALTH OF NATIONS, *supra* note 1, at 90–91. He is especially concerned that all workmen should be guaranteed that "lowest rate that is consistent with common humanity." *Id.* at 91.

150 *See* 1 SMITH, THE WEALTH OF NATIONS, *supra* note 1, at 138, 157. Smith's concern for equal respect also extends outside national boundaries: he strenuously opposes colonization, on the grounds that it is a way of exploiting the colonized people, who lose both political autonomy and economic control. *See* 2 *id.* at 564–641.

151 1 *id.* at 28–29.

152 Some nations are so poor that they are forced to practice infanticide, and to leave the elderly and sick "to be devoured by wild beasts." *Id.* at 10. Even in Britain, however, Smith insists, high child mortality is characteristic of the working, and not the more prosperous, classes. *Id.* at 97.

153 *Id.* Whether deliberately or not, Smith uses the comparison that I have cited in my epigraph from Pindar.

154 *Id.* at 91 (discussing unemployment produced by general economic decline).

But it is in his lengthy discussion of education that Smith develops most fully his ideas about the fragility of human dignity. The question he faces is whether the state ought to take responsibility for the education of its people and, if so, in what way. He observes that the newly fashionable division of labor, combined with a lack of general education, has a very pernicious effect on human abilities:

> The man whose whole life is spent in performing a few simple operations . . . has no occasion to exert his understanding . . . . He naturally loses, therefore, the habit of such exertion, and generally becomes as stupid and ignorant as it is possible for a human creature to become. . . . Of the great and extensive interests of his country, he is altogether incapable of judging . . . . But in every improved and civilized society this is the state into which the labouring poor, that is, the great body of the people, must necessarily fall, unless government takes some pains to prevent it.[155]

The danger, Smith continues, is not great for those who are not poor because they have the time and resources to obtain an adequate education before they begin work.[156] The common people have no such luxury.[157] Without education, a person "is as much mutilated and deformed in his mind, as another is in his body, who is either deprived of some of its most essential members, or has lost the use of them."[158] Even if educating the common people does not lead to the nation's overall enrichment, "it would still deserve its attention that they should not be altogether uninstructed."[159]

Smith argues, however, that such a calamity is not inevitable. No state, he believes, can guarantee all citizens as extensive an education as the rich currently receive at their parents' expense. But it can (as Scotland typically did) provide all with "the most essential parts of education," by requiring them to learn reading, writing, and accounting before they are permitted to take on paid employment.[160]

Smith attains here an insight that lies at the heart of the CA. Human abilities come into the world in a nascent or undeveloped form and require support from the environment — including support for physical health and especially, here, for mental development — if they are to mature in a way that is worthy of human dignity. Smith clearly

---

155 2 *id.* at 782.

156 *Id.* at 784.

157 *Id.* at 784–85.

158 *Id.* at 787.

159 *Id.* at 788.

160 *Id.* at 785. He describes a scheme for low-cost compulsory education in parish schools, in which useful subjects, such as geometry and mechanics, would replace frivolous subjects, such as Latin. *See id.* Smith does not advocate free education, because Smith thinks that if the salary of teachers were paid entirely by the state there would be too little parental oversight. Instead, he suggests a fee "so moderate, that even a common labourer may afford it," combined with government support. *Id.*

believes that all normal human beings are capable of developing the more mature or advanced capabilities that would make their lives fully human, not "mutilated and deformed." His discussion of the philosopher and the street porter has already made the point that the differences among men that bulk large in society are the work of habit. We simply do not have a full human life if we stunt the powers of mind in which humanness so largely resides.[161]

Like Adam Smith's anticipated audience in Britain, Americans in the mid-eighteenth century were steeped in the texts of ancient Greek, and especially Roman, philosophy (besides being steeped in Smith's own works). For the American founders, as for the modern thinkers whom they read (including Rousseau, Smith, and Kant), Roman political philosophy was of enormous importance, and, above all, the philosophical ideas of Roman Stoicism, together with the Stoics' eclectic fellow-traveler Cicero. As Gordon Wood puts it, "[P]eople could not read enough about Cato [the Stoics' stock example of virtue[162]] and Cicero."[163] Not only philosophically inclined writers such as Thomas Paine, but also the general educated public, shared this passion.[164] No doubt, on the eve of the Revolution, Americans were fascinated by the fact that philosophy was not just an academic pursuit in ancient Rome; it was also a political movement.[165] Even more gripping, however, was the specific content of the Roman ideas, which, once again, Americans interpreted by focusing on the idea of equal human dignity and equal entitlement, rather than on the unpromising idea of human invulnerability. They understood all too well that government could block human capabilities, because they had experienced the hand of tyranny. They also understood that a full set of human capabilities could not be secured in a vacuum: government had a job to do. As our Declaration of Independence states this ubiquitous idea:

> We hold these truths to be self-evident, that all men are created equal, that they are endowed by their Creator with certain unalienable Rights, that among these are Life, Liberty and the pursuit of Happiness. That to se-

---

161 *See* Smith, Report of 1766, *supra* note 149, at 539 ("[W]hen a person's whole attention is bestowed on the 17th part of a pin," it is unsurprising that "people are exceedingly stupid."). Smith contrasts England, where boys are sent to work at age six or seven, with Scotland, where "even the meanest porter can read and write." *Id.* at 540.

162 *See, e.g.*, SENECA, DIALOGORUM LIBRI DUODECIM, *supra* note 120.

163 GORDON S. WOOD, THE RADICALISM OF THE AMERICAN REVOLUTION 103 (1992).

164 *See id.*

165 People lived and died for philosophical ideas. The conspiracy to assassinate Julius Caesar, in 44 B.C.E., was philosophical in inspiration. *See* Sedley, *supra* note 116. Both Cicero and Seneca, like Brutus, died violent deaths, fighting for republican institutions. *See* Nussbaum, *Philosophical Norms and Political Attachments: Cicero and Seneca*, *supra* note 120 (discussing the deep tension between these lives and the Stoic idea of detachment). All this by itself was enough to move well-read and thoughtful Americans who were about to embark upon a perilous political course.

cure these rights, Governments are instituted among Men, deriving their just powers from the consent of the governed . . . .[166]

And of course the document goes on to argue that any government that does not deliver on that task may be altered or abolished. Moreover, one of the Declaration's central complaints against George III is his *inaction*: "He has refused his Assent to Laws, the most wholesome and necessary for the public good."[167]

Thus, the idea that the Framers favored "negative liberty" is extremely misleading. The Framers were not libertarians. Like Smith, they knew what they did not like: tyrannical government, bilking average citizens for the benefit of selfish elites, while neglecting the welfare of working people. But a dislike of bad government was not a dislike of government per se. One striking example of the way in which a combination of Stoic equality with Aristotelian need worked its way into the Framers' conception of government is Thomas Paine's *Rights of Man*.

Like other intellectuals at the time of the Founding, Paine dislikes a lot of the government action that he sees. Government is founded on the natural rights of human beings;[168] its proper goal is "the good of all, as well individually as collectively."[169] Existing governments, however, do not pursue this goal. Instead, they operate "to create and encrease wretchedness"[170] in the poorer parts of society. In the long chapter entitled "Ways and Means of Improving the Condition of Europe," Paine argues for a complete overhaul of government action and especially of taxation. Taxation should cease to be regressive and become progressive. The poor-rates should be entirely abolished, and the power of elites to divert taxes away from themselves should be curtailed. (Paine mordantly describes "what is called the crown" as "a nominal office of a million sterling a year, the business of which consists in receiving the money."[171]) A detailed scheme of progressive taxation is proposed, starting at a rate of three pence per pound and ascending, in rather short order, to a rate of twenty shillings per pound, that is, one hundred percent![172] (Paine is way ahead of Sweden at its most draconian.)

The revenue thus gained would be used to support human capabilities, in three areas above all: youth, age, and unemployment. Like

---

166 THE DECLARATION OF INDEPENDENCE para. 2 (U.S. 1776).

167 *Id.* at para. 3; *see also id.* at paras. 4–5.

168 *See, e.g.*, PAINE, *supra* note 141, at 248.

169 *Id.* at 251; *cf. id.* at 263 ("Whatever the form or constitution of government may be, it ought to have no other object than the *general* happiness.").

170 *Id.* at 263.

171 *Id.* at 282.

172 *Id.* at 304–06.

Smith, Paine favors state-subsidized compulsory primary education.[173] He notes that young people often take to crime because they have never had an education that would open employment opportunities for them, and he concludes that government inaction is to blame:

> When, in countries that are called civilized, we see age going to the workhouse and youth to the gallows, something must be wrong in the system of government. . . .
>
> Civil government does not consist in executions; but in making that provision for the instruction of youth, and the support of age, as to exclude, as much as possible, profligacy from the one, and despair from the other. Instead of this, the resources of a country are lavished upon kings, upon courts, upon hirelings, imposters, and prostitutes . . . .[174]

Calculating that a large proportion of England's poor are either children or people over the age of sixty,[175] he proposes a cash subsidy to poor families, out of surplus tax revenue, of four pounds per year for each child attending school.[176] He notes that in this way "the poverty of the parents will be relieved, . . . ignorance will be banished from the rising generation, and the number of poor will hereafter become less, because their abilities, by the aid of education, will be greater."[177] They will thereby gain employment opportunities. For families somewhat less poor, a per-child school subsidy is proposed, including money for school supplies.[178]

As to the "aged," Paine holds, on the basis of observation and experience (he is fifty-four when he writes), that people in their fifties are typically sound of mind (indeed their judgment is better than ever), but are beginning to flag in bodily strength and endurance. After sixty, he writes, people become unfit for work.[179] He therefore proposes a scheme of cash subsidy for all but the well-off, six pounds per year in one's fifties and ten pounds per year thereafter.[180] "This support," he repeatedly stresses, "is not of the nature of a charity, but of a right."[181] It is part of the general task of government to support the life cycle of citizens.[182]

---

173 "A nation under a well regulated government, should permit none to remain uninstructed. It is monarchical and aristocratical government only that requires ignorance for its support." *Id.* at 297.

174 *Id.* at 271.

175 *See id.* at 293–94.

176 *Id.* at 294.

177 *Id.*

178 *Id.* at 297.

179 *Id.* at 294–95.

180 *Id.* at 295–96.

181 *Id.* at 296; *see also id.* at 295 ("[It is] not as a matter of grace and favour, but of right . . . .").

182 "It is painful to see old age working itself to death, in what are called civilized countries, for daily bread." *Id.* at 295.

Beyond this, Paine is aware that, particularly in cities, there are many people who temporarily cannot find work for one reason or another.[183] Here he makes one of his boldest proposals: a government-financed scheme of guaranteed temporary employment in a government facility where people will find a wide range of tasks available.[184] People are to be received with no nosy inquiries; the only condition is that they work.[185] In proportion to their work, they receive nutritious food, warm lodging, and cash savings to take with them when they depart. In this way, people afflicted by temporary distress can regroup, and be on the lookout for employment later. This is not exactly the WPA, and Paine has thought too little about how the dignity and autonomy of poor people could be respected in such a residential institution; but his proposal is in the spirit of the New Deal. Paine wants a lot more government action supporting basic human welfare, a lot less supporting elite self-enrichment.

Paine's ideas find a striking echo in James Madison's idea that government should combat factionalism:

> 1. By establishing a political equality among all. 2. By withholding *unnecessary* opportunities from a few, to increase the inequality of property, by an immoderate, and especially an unmerited, accumulation of riches. 3. By the silent operation of laws, which, without violating the rights of property, reduce extreme wealth towards a state of mediocrity, and raise extreme indigence towards a state of comfort.[186]

Repeatedly, Paine gives his reader the likely costs of his proposals. His point is that one may honor the entitlements of poor people while remaining decently minimalist in the sense of opposing burdensome taxation, particularly for the poor and the middle classes. Supporting social security is not costly; it is the narcissism of the wealthy that drives up costs.

D. Nineteenth and Twentieth Centuries: The Capabilities Approach Opposes Utilitarianism and Libertarianism

Far from being suited only to pre-industrial societies, the CA has seen some of its most striking political applications in the modern era, in which industrial development has given rise to new threats to the capabilities of both children (sent to labor in factories at an early age) and adults (laboring under unsafe and burdensome conditions, without the leverage to contract for a better arrangement). At the same time,

---

[183] *See id.* at 298–99.

[184] *See id.* at 299 ("[T]o have in each of these places as many kinds of employment as can be contrived, so that every person who shall come may find something which he or she can do.").

[185] *Id.*

[186] James Madison, *Parties*, NAT'L GAZETTE, Jan. 23, 1792, *reprinted in* 14 THE PAPERS OF JAMES MADISON 197, 197 (Robert A. Rutland et al. eds., 1983).

the modern era has seen a new awareness of the obstacles to human development imposed by traditional discrimination on the basis of race, sex, and disability, all of which have proved to be focal points for recent CA-style analysis. Post-industrial societies need the CA more than ever: both to remedy entrenched discrimination whose evils are by now evident and to combat new obstacles to human development deriving from post-industrial conditions. In such circumstances, applying the CA takes an unusual degree of historical understanding and practical imagination, since it is crucial to assess the obstacles to human freedom and choice inherent in situations of many types, in the workplace, in the public square, and in the family, some of them quite new.[187]

Nineteenth-century Britain saw striking and influential anticipations of contemporary American discussions about human capability.[188] One influential source of such arguments is John Stuart Mill, who clarified the relationship of political liberty to human self-development[189] and demonstrated the harm done by discrimination to the opportunities and capacities of women.[190] For example, Mill compared the restrictions imposed by the discriminatory legal regime governing marriage to slavery.[191] Mill's influence on American ideas of freedom has been large;[192] his ideas on gender, neglected in Britain in his lifetime, have been formative for women's movements in many na-

[187] It is not surprising that the social novel reached its peak during the Industrial Revolution, since members of the more prosperous classes urgently needed the type of understanding of the situation of the laboring poor that novels made possible. The novel has also proven a major vehicle of understanding where the struggles of traditionally deprived groups are at issue. *See generally* NUSSBAUM, POETIC JUSTICE, *supra* note 48. Dickens, for example, in *Hard Times*, refers to the surprise with which Louisa Gradgrind confronts the individual lives of workers whom she has previously known only "in crowds passing to and from their nests, like ants or beetles." CHARLES DICKENS, HARD TIMES 159 (Terry Eagleton ed., Methuen 1987) (1854).

[188] *See* Nussbaum, *Mill Between Aristotle and Bentham*, *supra* note 20 (discussing Mill's relationship to Aristotelian ideas); Martha C. Nussbaum, *Millean Liberty and Sexual Orientation*, 21 LAW & PHIL. 317, 325–27 (2002) (discussing the influence of Mill's ideas on state constitution making in the United States).

[189] *See* MILL, ON LIBERTY, *supra* note 14, at 56–74.

[190] *See* JOHN STUART MILL, THE SUBJECTION OF WOMEN (Susan Moller Okin ed., Hackett Publ'g Co. 1988) (1869) (arguing for equal educational and political rights for women). More than most, Mill lived consistently with his ideals. He went to jail in his youth for distributing contraceptive information in London and later, as a member of Parliament, introduced the first bill for female suffrage. *See* MICHAEL ST. JOHN PACKE, THE LIFE OF JOHN STUART MILL 56–59, 492 (1954).

[191] *See* MILL, THE SUBJECTION OF WOMEN, *supra* note 190, at 15–16, 33 (comparing archaic social norms of female behavior and women's vulnerability to rape within marriage to slavery).

[192] *See, e.g.*, Nussbaum, *Millean Liberty and Sexual Orientation*, *supra* note 188, at 325–30 (discussing the influence of *On Liberty* on several state constitutions).

tions.[193] After Mill's death, T.H. Green, a professor of philosophy and advisor to the British Liberal Party, used Aristotelian ideas to repudiate both the influential utilitarianism and libertarian minimalism of the day.[194] He influentially supported a variety of social legislation initiatives[195] and defended their limitations on freedom of contract with an appeal to "that general freedom of [society's] members to make the best of themselves, which it is the object of civil society to secure."[196] Green's disciple, Ernest Barker, a distinguished scholar of ancient Greek at Cambridge University,[197] sowed the seeds of the CA globally, since at that time Cambridge drew graduate students from many nations. British legislative developments were well known in the United States and anticipated many of the programs of the New Deal and Great Society, including legislation protecting workers' rights, establishing compulsory education, fostering the education of poor children, and, ultimately, protecting vulnerable minorities from discrimination.

Today, the CA has assumed a renewed prominence as an approach to the ethical foundations of global development. The work of Nobel Prize–winning economist Amartya Sen has made the idea of capabilities, as an alternative to the utilitarian focus on wealth maximization, central to discussions about the goals of development.[198] This "Human Development Approach," exemplified in the annual *Human Development Reports* of the United Nations Development Programme,[199]

---

193 At the Fourth World Conference on Women, a conference on women's equality in Beijing in June 1995, for example, Chinese feminists spoke of the formative influence of the Chinese translation of *The Subjection of Women* on their movement.

194 *See* Paul Harris & John Morrow, *Introduction* to T.H. GREEN: LECTURES ON THE PRINCIPLES OF POLITICAL OBLIGATION AND OTHER WRITINGS 1 (1986) (discussing Green's career); John Deigh, *Liberalism and Freedom*, *in* SOCIAL AND POLITICAL PHILOSOPHY 151, 151–65 (James P. Sterba ed., 2001) (discussing Green's use of an Aristotelian idea of human capability).

195 The legislation Green supported included bills for free compulsory education, workplace safety regulations, a limitation on working hours, a ban on child labor, and limitations on contracting between landlords and tenant farmers.

196 T.H. Green, Lecture on "Liberal Legislation and Freedom of Contract," *in* T.H. GREEN: LECTURES ON THE PRINCIPLES OF POLITICAL OBLIGATION AND OTHER WRITINGS, *supra* note 194, at 194, 201. This lecture was given to a Liberal Party gathering in 1881, and issued as a pamphlet shortly thereafter.

197 Barker made the Aristotelian pedigree of his ideas very clear. *See, e.g.*, ERNEST BARKER, THE POLITICAL THOUGHT OF PLATO AND ARISTOTLE 1–16, 520–22 (Dover Publ'ns 1959) (1906).

198 *See, e.g.*, SEN, DEVELOPMENT AS FREEDOM, *supra* note 7 (discussing the essentials of his approach); Amartya Sen, *Equality of What?*, *in* 1 TANNER LECTURES ON HUMAN VALUES 195, 217–19 (Sterling M. McMurrin ed., 1980) (applying this approach to disability). A fine set of analyses of the implications of this work for gender issues, together with Sen's own most prominent writings on gender, is in CAPABILITIES, FREEDOM, AND EQUALITY: AMARTYA SEN'S WORK FROM A GENDER PERSPECTIVE (Bina Agarwal, Jane Humphries & Ingrid Robeyns eds., 2006).

199 The reports, published annually since 1990, are available at http://hdr.undp.org/reports.

has begun to have significant influence by affecting the way nations report, understand, and evaluate their achievements.[200]

IV. THE CAPABILITIES APPROACH IN AMERICAN CONSTITUTIONAL LAW

The CA is an approach to basic political principles. It does not tell us how these principles are to be implemented. It does, however, suggest that many of the most central human capabilities, given their enormous importance to basic social justice, should be placed beyond majority whim through constitutionally protected status.[201] History shows us that legislative majorities are susceptible to panic and polarization; they can easily be led to demonize unpopular minorities and to seek restrictions of their rights. If rights of the most fundamental type can be removed as the result of a hasty popular judgment, minorities will enjoy less security and a nation's citizens will, hence, enjoy less equality.[202]

The special status of fundamental entitlements need not be guaranteed through a written constitution, but that is one common way of protecting them and ensuring that they are not held hostage to the vicissitudes of politics; the popularity of this approach speaks in its favor. A nation that chooses to protect human capabilities through a written constitution will require an independent judiciary and judicial review of legislation to make constitutional guarantees more than words on paper.[203] Minority rights are always at risk in a majority-driven world; an independent judiciary is a crucial part of a structure

---

200 The Human Development and Capability Association, founded in 2004, now has about seven hundred members from seventy countries, all of whom study the further development and implementation of the approach from a variety of disciplinary perspectives. *See generally* Human Development and Capability Association, http://www.capabilityapproach.com (last visited Oct. 6, 2007).

201 *See* Nussbaum, *Capabilities as Fundamental Entitlements*, *supra* note 7 (arguing in favor of defining a specific set of capabilities as the most important to protect).

202 *See* NUSSBAUM, LIBERTY, *supra* note 124 (manuscript at ch. 5) (arguing that the tradition of constitutionally protected free exercise rights provided an important bulwark against the persecution of Jehovah's Witnesses and Roman Catholics). A contrasting case, supporting the same conclusion, is India, where, during the Emergency of 1975–77, Indira Gandhi succeeded in convincing her parliamentary majority to suspend a large group of "Fundamental Rights" in order that she could clamp down on her political enemies. In the wake of that disastrous epoch, the Supreme Court of India declared that a group of essential features of the Constitution could not be amended. *See* NUSSBAUM, THE CLASH WITHIN: DEMOCRACY, RELIGIOUS VIOLENCE, AND INDIA'S FUTURE 122–51 (2007).

203 The scope of judicial review is a topic too large for this Foreword, but again, the case of India is instructive. Indian citizens can approach the Supreme Court directly by petition, and the Court has utter discretion regarding which petitions it hears; this provision of the constitution gives the Court wide quasi-legislative powers.

that protects, on a basis of equality, the rights of those who lack power in majoritarian politics.

The precise demarcation between legislative and judicial functions and a detailed account of the judicial role are not part of the CA as such. People who sympathize with its general goals can differ about institutional allocation, and to some extent different nations may reasonably do things differently, depending on their own particular traditions and problems.[204] In all cases, however, a political scheme will not realize the goals of the CA unless it identifies a core group of entitlements that deserve to be protected stably, regardless of majority whim, and then asks carefully whether people face unequal obstacles to the enjoyment of their basic entitlements, devoting particular attention to traditionally disadvantaged groups.

On the whole, our constitutional tradition has done very well protecting some capabilities — namely, those enumerated in the Bill of Rights — although even here, interpretation has fluctuated between an analysis that focuses on capabilities or substantial freedoms and a more minimalist analysis. The tradition of heightened scrutiny under the Equal Protection Clause and, on occasion, the recognition of fundamental rights under the Due Process Clause have also led to a focus on substantive opportunities — what people are actually able to do and to be. Equal Protection Clause jurisprudence, like the modern uses of the CA in the areas of gender, race, and disability, has focused on areas affected by traditional discrimination.[205] Our tradition, however, has been far more reluctant than many to offer constitutional protection, through judicial interpretation, to human capabilities in the areas covered by social and economic rights, although a beginning was made in the late 1960s and 1970s.[206] This job has largely been left to legislative action, as in the New Deal, and the protections are thus vulnerable to changes in public opinion, as the Reagan Revolution has shown. Protection of basic material entitlements clearly involves an active legislative role, since many welfare rights require the appropria-

[204] For example, nations will need to ask how the likely candidates for judicial appointments are placed relative to the average citizen. In a nation with a low literacy rate, judges, of necessity highly educated, are likely to be very distant from the average citizen in life experience, and might not understand well the concerns of the average citizen. In such a nation there could be a strong argument for a narrower understanding of judicial competence than would be appropriate to a nation in which educational opportunity is more broadly distributed. In a nation riven by religious conflict, by contrast, a judiciary appointed for life might prove usefully resistant to sectarian animosities, providing a powerful protection for citizens' rights. Such a situation would give rise to a plausible argument for a somewhat broader judicial role.

[205] *See, e.g.*, City of Cleburne v. Cleburne Living Ctr., Inc., 473 U.S. 432, 450 (1985) (determining that a municipality's denial of a permit to a home for people with mental disabilities did not survive rational basis review); *see also infra* pp. 71–72 (discussing Mills v. Bd. of Educ., 348 F. Supp. 866 (D.D.C. 1972)).

[206] *See* CASS R. SUNSTEIN, THE SECOND BILL OF RIGHTS, *supra* note 5, at 149–71.

tion of funds, a task beyond the power of courts. Even in such cases, however, courts still play a major role in interpreting statutory provisions,[207] and they also play a role in determining when cost-cutting measures pursued by legislatures are violative of fundamental rights.[208] In recent years, courts in other nations have frequently pursued a more ambitious program in the area of welfare rights, working in partnership with legislatures in order to ensure that the fundamental rights of citizens are safeguarded.[209] The CA can thus help us to see what we have done right so far and what we might do much better, if we want to be a decent society.

One thing the CA can offer constitutional law, then, is an account of the incompleteness of the U.S. Constitution. That, however, is not its only role: it can also supply, in those many cases in which our tradition has not been neglectful, a benchmark for adequate reasoning about the Constitution we actually have. The Constitution identifies a range of fundamental rights; these entitlements, however, exist only as words on paper until they are interpreted. The CA offers a distinctive set of suggestions for such interpretation. Its suggestions correspond to one strong tradition within our history of judicial interpretation, although this tradition has not always been dominant.

How, according to the CA, should judges reason when interpreting basic entitlements? As I have said, they cannot put things into constitutions that are not there. Judges must reason within the limitations of text and tradition;[210] if they like the idea of a housing right, they must simply wait until such a right is added to the Constitution by the usual process, unless they have a persuasive argument that it inheres in some other enumerated right.

The CA, however, does offer guidance for judicial reasoning in areas that are touched on by text and precedent. The first and most crucial suggestion is that the judge ought to think about the rights as capabilities, asking: are people really able to enjoy this right, or are there subtle impediments that stand between them and the full or equal access to the right? Judges should attend closely to history and social context, eschewing lofty formalism in favor of perception. A second and closely related suggestion is that judges should consider the equality of access to a right as part of the right itself and should be aware

---

207 *See infra* section V.A, pp. 74–77.

208 *See infra* pp. 60–62.

209 *See generally* Mark Tushnet, *State Action, Social Welfare Rights, and the Judicial Role: Some Comparative Observations*, 3 CHI. J. INT'L L. 435 (2002).

210 Those limits, naturally, are understood differently by different theories of constitutional interpretation, but all such theories agree that a constitutional text and its associated tradition of precedent supply constraints of some type on judicial reasoning. Textualists and their critics typically differ over how to find the meaning of the constitutional text, not over its relevance.

that history and social circumstance frequently affect that access. Equality should be understood not in a distanced way, as mere formal symmetry, but in terms of people's actual abilities to do or be. The CA's third suggestion is that judges should be aware that many entitlements that do not appear to be welfare rights may yet have material necessary conditions, and they should make sure that a given right is not rendered off limits to a group of people by the absence of such conditions.

These principles, abstract though they seem, correspond to some distinctive features of our tradition of constitutional interpretation — features that are in contention, often, with other styles of interpretation, and are more prominent in some areas and times than in others. The CA illuminates what is rightly done in some cases, and what is a falling-off — often, toward libertarian minimalism, lofty formalism, or both.

Where, in the U.S. Constitution, are human capabilities protected? An obvious partial answer is: "In the Bill of Rights." The Bill of Rights does indeed identify a list of fundamental entitlements, setting these beyond majority whim. The items listed are, obviously, plural and noncommensurable, and all of them are to be protected for all citizens, no matter what a concern for overall welfare would suggest. Thus the Constitution commits us to a politics that is, at least in this sense, nonutilitarian. Even the largest gain in overall welfare or satisfaction is off limits if it is purchased at the price of even one of these freedoms.[211]

Beyond this small list, basic entitlements are implicit in the Due Process and Equal Protection Clauses of the Fourteenth Amendment. A set of illustrations shows that the reach of the CA in American constitutional law is wide, despite the large gaps that exist in the areas of health and basic welfare. I begin with a relatively obvious example, showing how the CA would direct judges in interpreting a right that has been explicitly recognized in the Constitution and has nothing to do with the welfare rights with which the CA is often associated. I argue that this style of interpretation is amply attested in our legal tradition. Next, I turn to cases involving the idea of equality, showing how the CA has informed (and rightly) a series of decisions involving "separate but equal" facilities. Finally, I turn to a more contentious area,

[211] Of course, consequential overrides are sometimes built into the more detailed account of a fundamental entitlement, as they have been with both the Religion and Speech Clauses of the First Amendment. *See, e.g.*, Brandenburg v. Ohio, 395 U.S. 444, 447–49 (1969) (asserting that the freedom of speech may be limited in situations in which speech threatens to produce imminent lawless action); Sherbert v. Verner, 374 U.S. 398, 402–03 (1963) (stating that religious freedom may be limited by a compelling state interest).

that of education, where the CA shows its presence, but has not always prevailed.

A. The Religion Clauses

I have said that not just any list of rights will count as a fulfillment of the CA: those rights have to be understood in the sense of real opportunities for choice and activity on a basis of equality. Consider the First Amendment's Free Exercise Clause.[212] The tradition of interpretation prior to *Employment Division v. Smith*[213] was an exemplary fulfillment of the CA. In cases such as *Sherbert v. Verner*[214] and *Wisconsin v. Yoder*,[215] the Court asked about the unequal burdens that are faced by members of minority religions in a majority world. If those burdens are substantial, then the state may not impose them without a truly compelling interest. Adell Sherbert, a long-term employee in a South Carolina textile factory, and a Seventh-Day Adventist, was fired for refusing to work on Saturdays.[216] Any employee of the textile factory would have been fired for that reason, but Mrs. Sherbert had a special difficulty, because she was unable to find comparable work compatible with her religious commitments.[217] She was denied unemployment compensation from the state of South Carolina, on the grounds that she had refused "suitable work."[218] We might say that South Carolina was following Wechsler here, applying a formalistic rule from a lofty distance without asking what "suitable" really meant for Mrs. Sherbert, given her minority religion.

The Supreme Court, however, was not satisfied by this formal analysis. It asked: what was really at stake for Mrs. Sherbert, and what were her real opportunities? The answer was that they were clearly unequal to those of majority worshippers: members of the majority religion could go to church as their conscience commanded with no loss of employment, and she, on account of her minority religion, could not.[219] The substantial burden on her religious choice was not justified by any compelling state interest.[220] That inquiry into what is really at stake for people — asking whether they are *really* able to avail themselves of their basic rights on terms of equality with others — is a good paradigm of what the CA requires. The very concept of

---

[212] *See* NUSSBAUM, LIBERTY, *supra* note 124 (manuscript at ch. 4).

[213] 494 U.S. 872 (1990).

[214] 374 U.S. 398 (1963).

[215] 406 U.S. 205 (1972) (holding that the Free Exercise Clause required an exception to public school attendance for the Amish, with respect to the last two years of mandatory attendance).

[216] *Sherbert*, 374 U.S. at 399.

[217] *Id.* at 399 & n.2.

[218] *Id.* at 401 (quoting S.C. CODE ANN. § 68-114 (1962)).

[219] *Id.* at 399–404.

[220] *Id.* at 406–09.

"substantial burden" asks for CA-style reasoning: a judge dealing with such a case must ask what the plaintiff's religious commitments are, and what the precise circumstances of the complaint are, in order to take the measure of the burden that is, or is not, imposed. The very concept of free exercise accommodation goes against lofty formalism and embodies the spirit of the CA, for it is basically the idea that a generally applicable law needs to contain exceptions for people whose conscientious commitments it burdens. It therefore directs the interpreter to understand the nature of the minority person's struggle for liberty, asking what that person is actually able to do and be, rather than imposing an exceptionless rule on everyone.

Notice that, while the Free Exercise Clause protects a major liberty, it is also seen to protect the equality of that liberty. The *Sherbert* majority considered the burden on Mrs. Sherbert extremely unfair: "[T]o condition the availability of benefits upon this appellant's willingness to violate a cardinal principle of her religious faith effectively penalizes the free exercise of her constitutional liberties."[221] The *Sherbert* Court might well have interpreted the Free Exercise Clause to mean that ample liberty is sufficient, and equality with respect to that liberty is unimportant. But in insisting on nondiscriminatory liberty, *Sherbert* shows the role of judicial interpretation relative to the goals of the CA at its very best: taking a vaguely specified right, the Court interpreted it by asking searching questions about people's actual abilities and possibilities in a world where minorities often labor under special burdens.

Sherbert also shows why a strong judicial role is an important part of realizing the CA in some areas. Legislators are often fond of formal rules driven by majority preferences, and are often insufficiently sensitive to the burdens faced by small minority groups who may also be unpopular. Judges have time to hear the entirety of a minority person's story, and their job is understood as involving the careful consideration of it in all its particularity. The individualized nature of the judicial process prompts a CA-style inquiry.

Smith, which drastically curtailed the judicial role in free exercise accommodations, was, in that sense, a falling away from the CA, leaving the question of accommodation for reasons of conscience to the vicissitudes of the political process.[222] The majority conceded that the decision to refuse judicially mandated accommodations "place[d] at a relative disadvantage those religious practices that are not widely engaged in," but this is called an "unavoidable consequence of democ-

---

[221] *Id.* at 406.

[222] In *Employment Division v. Smith*, 494 U.S. 872 (1990), the Court held that the Free Exercise Clause did not prohibit the application of Oregon drug laws to the religious use of peyote by Native Americans. *Id.* at 890.

ratic government."[223] The majority emphasized the idea that law must be exceptionless; the alternative would be "courting anarchy."[224] The opinion repudiated a *Sherbert*-style attempt to examine closely the burdens faced by practitioners of Native American religions, or to ask how judicial action might protect the rights of Native American religious practitioners on a basis of equality with members of other religions. The defense of exceptionless rules is reminiscent of Wechsler's lofty formalism. The formalism of the majority was all the more striking in that, while *Sherbert* and *Yoder* were not technically overruled, they were read in a surprisingly narrow way.[225]

Of course, *Smith* does not repudiate the goals of the CA: legislative accommodations are still permissible. Nonetheless, the Court emphasized that they are not to be relied on, given the power of majorities, and the opinion simply dismissed the idea that in such cases the goals of the Constitution must be fulfilled through a judicial role that vindicates the rights of religious minorities on a basis of equality.[226] Given the Court's very plausible view of the way in which democratic majorities behave, its conception of the judicial role represents, in effect, a decision not to protect the equality of minority religious rights where majorities have not already done so. *Smith* shows clearly what is at stake in giving an independent judiciary a strong role in interpreting fundamental constitutional guarantees, and why judges should not hold too narrow, or too formalistic, a conception of their role.

In the wake of *Smith* (and the demise of the Religious Freedom Restoration Act of 1993[227] (RFRA) in *City of Boerne v. Flores*,[228] at least as applied to the states), cases such as *Church of the Lukumi Babalu Aye, Inc. v. City of Hialeah*[229] still ask searching questions about fairness to minorities and the unequal burden of hostility they may face on the way to exercising their religious rights. Moreover, given

223 *Id.*

224 *Id.* at 888.

225 Thus, *Sherbert* was understood to support accommodation only in unemployment compensation cases, and *Yoder* was understood to support accommodation only for cases involving mixed rights claims (not just free exercise, but also the rights of parents, were at stake). *See id.* at 881–83.

226 *See id.* at 888–90.

227 Pub. L. No. 103-141, 107 Stat. 1488 (codified as amended at 42 U.S.C. §§ 2000bb-1 to 2000bb-4 (2000)), *invalidated in part by* City of Boerne v. Flores, 521 U.S. 507 (1997).

228 521 U.S. 507. RFRA had attempted to reintroduce the more protective *Sherbert* standard through legislation; it was invalidated as applied to the states in *Boerne*. *See id.* at 529–36. Congress's attempt to accomplish through legislation what *Sherbert* previously achieved was thus held to exceed Congress's power. However, the Religious Land Use and Institutionalized Persons Act of 2000 (RLUIPA), 42 U.S.C. §§ 2000cc to 2000cc-5 (2000), attempted to reinstate at least a part of RFRA's protections. The Court upheld RLUIPA in *Cutter v. Wilkinson*, 544 U.S. 709 (2005).

229 508 U.S. 520 (1993) (holding that city ordinances dealing with the ritual slaughter of animals were not neutral, nor of general applicability, and not justified by governmental interests).

that RFRA is still intact as applied to acts of the federal government,[230] small religions may still be protected comprehensively in some domains.[231] In *Gonzales v. O Centro Espirita Beneficente Uniao do Vegetal*,[232] Chief Justice Roberts emphasized that a judicial role in connection with protecting minorities is built into RFRA itself: "RFRA . . . plainly contemplates that *courts* would recognize exceptions — that is how the law works. . . . RFRA makes clear that it is the obligation of the courts to consider whether exceptions are required . . . ."[233] Recent free exercise jurisprudence thus continues to contain elements of the CA.

Meanwhile, Establishment Clause jurisprudence also provides useful examples of contextual imagining in the service of protecting human capabilities.[234] Ever since Roger Williams, and, very prominently, Madison's *Memorial and Remonstrance Against Religious Assessments*, it has been understood that religious establishments threaten the equality of citizens' standing in the public realm.[235] They threaten, first, the equality of liberty, holding open a permanent possibility of unequal curtailment.[236] But even when they do not threaten liberty, establishments make a statement: some citizens are the preferred group, and others the dispreferred.[237] A major strand in recent Establishment Clause jurisprudence, associated with Justice O'Connor and the Madisonian "endorsement test," has focused on that issue. For Justice O'Connor (and, often, with her a majority of the Court), the right question to ask when considering a putative Establishment Clause violation was: would an objective observer, acquainted with all the historical and contextual facts of the case, judge that the governmental policy in question makes a statement that creates a favored

230 This had remained in dispute for some time, but is made clear in *Gonzales v. O Centro Espirita Beneficente Uniao do Vegetal*, 126 S. Ct. 1211, 1220 (2006).

231 *O Centro* concerned a Brazilian sect with only 130 members that wished to use a hallucinogen called *hoasca*, illegal under the Controlled Substances Act, in its sacred ceremony. *See id.* at 1217. The Act had already been amended to permit the sacramental use of peyote by Native Americans (the right in question in *Smith*), but the small group in the present case lacked the political clout of the Native Americans. *See id.* at 1222.

232 126 S. Ct. 1211.

233 *Id.* at 1222 (citing provisions of RFRA).

234 *E.g.*, County of Allegheny v. ACLU, Greater Pittsburgh Chapter, 492 U.S. 573 (1989); Lynch v. Donnelly, 465 U.S. 668 (1984).

235 *See* MADISON, *supra* note 138, at 49, 50–51.

236 *See id.* at 50 (stating that "it is proper to take alarm at the first experiment on our liberties").

237 *Id.* ("[T]he Bill violates that equality which ought to be the basis of every law . . . . [A]ll men are to be considered as entering into Society on equal conditions . . . . Above all are they to be considered as retaining an '*equal* title to the free exercise of Religion according to the dictates of conscience.' . . . As the Bill violates equality by subjecting some to peculiar burdens; so it violates the same principle, by granting to others peculiar exemptions.").

class of citizens, an in-group, and a disfavored class, an out-group?[238] That question is really a CA question *par excellence*, because it requires us to ask what people are actually able to do and to be in society: Are they able to enter the public square "on equal conditions,"[239] as Madison said? Or are they in some subtle way stigmatized by the act of government and made into an out-group? Moreover, the jurisprudence of the endorsement test has the hallmarks of detailed contextual reasoning that we have understood to be so closely linked to the implementation of the CA. In cases such as *Lynch v. Donnelly*,[240] *County of Allegheny v. ACLU, Greater Pittsburgh Chapter*,[241] *McCreary County v. ACLU of Kentucky*,[242] and *Van Orden v. Perry*,[243] the Court searchingly examined the whole history and context of the public displays in question for signs of the statement that government was making through its sponsorship. What can seem messy or unduly fussy in the Court's recent Establishment Clause jurisprudence looks, therefore, like wise Aristotelian practical reasoning, posing the right questions about what citizens are able to be.[244]

B. Separate but Equal

The U.S. Constitution protects human capabilities in a variety of ways. Explicit enumeration is one way, but the Fourteenth Amendment allows a marked expansion of the list of protected items. Through the Due Process Clause and the Privileges and Immunities Clause, fundamental rights such as the right to vote, the right to appeal a criminal conviction, and the right to travel between states have been seen as implicit in the notion of ordered liberty.[245] Equally significant is the protection afforded some important human capabilities through the Equal Protection Clause. Minorities often face unusual obstacles and burdens, and equality (often with particular reference to

---

238 *See Lynch*, 465 U.S. at 691–94 (O'Connor, J., concurring). The test is then applied by Justice Blackmun in *Allegheny*, 492 U.S at 594–597 (opinion of Blackmun, J.). The expanded version of the test, referring to the objective observer, is introduced in *Wallace v. Jaffree*, 472 U.S. 38, 69, 76 (1985) (O'Connor, J., concurring in judgment).

239 MADISON, *supra* note 138, at 50.

240 465 U.S. 668.

241 492 U.S. 573 (1989).

242 125 S. Ct. 2722 (2005).

243 125 S. Ct. 2854 (2005).

244 The fact that the approach asks the right questions does not entail that all its answers are correct: we could agree that the right questions have been posed while disagreeing about the result.

245 United States v. Guest, 383 U.S. 745 (1966) (regarding the right to travel); Reynolds v. Sims, 377 U.S. 533 (1964) (regarding the right to vote); Griffin v. Illinois, 351 U.S. 12 (1956) (regarding the right to appeal); *see also* Shapiro v. Thompson, 394 U.S. 618 (1969) (regarding the right to travel). A list of these and related instances is given in Justice Marshall's dissent in *San Antonio Independent School District v. Rodriguez*, 411 U.S. 1, 99–100 (1973) (Marshall, J., dissenting).

minorities) often enters into the interpretation of a basic freedom, as with both of the religion clauses, where the equal liberty of minorities has been a persistent concern. The Equal Protection Clause, however, has allowed the protection of capabilities to extend more widely, as arrangements that seemed to treat all parties similarly were found unconstitutional in a range of cases because they did not promote substantively equal freedoms. Both our civil rights tradition and our tradition of pursuing sex equality pose, centrally, the question: what are these people actually able to do and to be? It was through that searching question that the formal symmetry of "separate but equal" arrangements was unmasked as a device for the perpetuation of hierarchy.

In *Brown*, the existence of separate arrangements that looked equal on paper was not the end of the matter for the Court. Insisting emphatically on the vital importance of education for personal development and opportunity,[246] the Justices pressed the question about the human capabilities of students: How have they been enabled to learn and to function? "Does segregation of children in public schools solely on the basis of race . . . deprive the children of the minority group of equal educational opportunities?"[247] The answer is that there is a great inequality at the level of capability: the stigma of segregation was itself a burden that put unequal obstacles in the way of minority students. Segregation "generates a feeling of inferiority as to their status in the community that may affect their hearts and minds in a way unlikely ever to be undone."[248] Separation is seen as discriminatory as the result of a thought process that is not lofty and formalistic (like Wechsler's, in his critique of the reasoning in the case), but immersed in history and context.

Similarly, in *Loving v. Virginia*,[249] the laws of Virginia offered a simulacrum of equality in the form of formal symmetry: blacks could not marry whites, whites could not marry blacks. The State argued that this symmetry meant that the laws did "not constitute an invidious discrimination based upon race."[250] The Supreme Court, however, looked beneath the formal symmetry, asking about the meaning of the prohibition on miscegenation for what people were really able to do and be. The prohibition, the Court concluded, was not truly symmetrical, since it was part of the enforcement of "White Supremacy": it carried a stigma that made the civil rights of blacks systematically un-

246 Brown v. Bd. of Educ., 347 U.S. 483, 493 (1954) ("[I]t is doubtful that any child may reasonably be expected to succeed in life if he is denied the opportunity of an education.").

247 *Id.*

248 *Id.* at 494.

249 388 U.S. 1 (1967).

250 *Id.* at 8.

equal, and was explained by "invidious racial discrimination" alone.[251] Not being able to marry a white person meant being unequal in general, whereas (for a white) not being able to marry a black person, while at times inconvenient, did not systematically affect the entirety of one's social standing. Once again, the Court was willing to think concretely about the meaning of enforced separation for both parties. In this way, a pertinent anti-subordination principle was articulated, and this principle is both fully rational (not, in Wechsler's sense, an exercise of "naked power") and far more pertinent than Wechsler's bare associational principle.

But perhaps the most resonant equal protection case, as far as the CA is concerned, is *United States v. Virginia*,[252] the case that opened the doors of the Virginia Military Institute (VMI) to women. Sex-based classifications, Justice Ginsburg's majority opinion observed, summarizing a group of precedents, may be used to compensate women for economic disabilities they have suffered, to promote equal employment opportunity, and "to advance full development of the talent and capacities of our Nation's people."[253] The idea of developing the capacities of citizens is of course the idea at the very heart of the CA. Equally significant is the observation that some affirmative measures may be justified in the name of truly equal opportunity, a corollary of the CA to which its proponents have frequently drawn attention: the traditionally disadvantaged may need more state support if they are to end at a position of similar capability. "State actors controlling gates to opportunity," however, "may not exclude qualified individuals based on 'fixed notions concerning roles and abilities of males and females.'"[254] Such pre-fixing and, thus, limiting of human development is what proponents of the CA, from Aristotle to Smith to Mill and Green, have struggled against.

Equally striking is the majority's analysis of the purportedly "separate but equal" remedial alternative, the program at Mary Baldwin College called Virginia Women's Institute for Leadership (VWIL). A remedy, the majority wrote, "must closely fit the constitutional violation; it must be shaped to place persons unconstitutionally denied an opportunity or advantage in 'the position they would have occupied in

---

251 *Id.* at 11.

252 518 U.S. 515 (1996).

253 *Id.* at 533–34.

254 *Id.* at 541 (quoting Miss. Univ. for Women v. Hogan, 458 U.S. 718, 725 (1982)). Striking examples of the ways in which gender-based stereotypes have been used in our judicial history to limit the strivings of women are enumerated throughout the opinion. This part of the opinion bears a strong resemblance to J.S. Mill's attack on gender-based stereotypes as forms of "enslave[ment]" for women. *See* MILL, THE SUBJECTION OF WOMEN, *supra* note 190, at 15.

the absence of [discrimination].'"[255] Here we have a clear statement of our notion of combined capability: the people must be in the same total position, where opportunity is concerned. The Mary Baldwin program, by contrast, was "different in kind from VMI and unequal in tangible and intangible facilities."[256] The analysis asked what hypothetical graduates from that program would actually be able to do and to be (thus arriving at an account of capabilities through experienced practical imagination).[257] The VWIL student, it was argued, lacked many opportunities characteristic of the VMI graduate. She was taught by an inferior faculty, with fewer Ph.D.s.[258] Her curriculum was a "pale shadow"[259] of VMI, and her institution had grossly unequal financial reserves. She did not enjoy the full benefits of VMI's alumni network.[260] So, she simply lacked many opportunities that the average VMI graduate had. The remedy, however attractive it may have appeared at first glance, did not pass the test of promoting truly equal capabilities.

The opinion thus reads the situation of women in a way that brings obstacles to fully equal opportunity to light, exhibiting the very type of historically precise and contextually attuned analysis that Wechsler's lofty formalism repudiates.

C. *Poverty and Due Process*

Unlike many nations, the U.S. has never embraced the idea of constitutionally guaranteed welfare rights. India and South Africa, for example, have done much more judicially to put a minimum floor under living conditions, health, and housing. Like the Britain of Green's time, which focused on legislative enactment, the United States, during the New Deal, pursued its ambitious social program through the legislature, only to face the hostility of the courts. During the late sixties and early seventies, however, existing constitutional materials were mined for an approach to basic welfare very much in the spirit of the CA. As Frank Michelman argued in his 1969 *Foreword* in the *Harvard Law Review*, the aim of the liberal jurisprudence of this period was not equalization, it was (as in the CA) the provision of a decent social minimum.[261]

---

255 *United States v. Virginia*, 518 U.S. at 547 (alteration in original) (quoting Milliken v. Bradley, 433 U.S. 267, 280 (1977)).

256 *Id.* at 517.

257 For a discussion of the differences between the programs, see *id.* at 526, 552–53.

258 *Id.* at 526.

259 *Id.* at 553 (quoting United States v. Virginia, 44 F.3d 1229, 1250 (4th Cir. 1995) (Phillips, J., dissenting)) (internal quotation marks omitted).

260 *Id.* at 552.

261 Frank I. Michelman, *The Supreme Court, 1968 Term—Foreword: On Protecting the Poor Through the Fourteenth Amendment*, 83 HARV. L. REV. 7, 9 (1969). I would argue, however, that

A case that neatly captures the era's approach to basic welfare is *Goldberg v. Kelly*.[262] This was a procedural due process case, involving the termination of welfare benefits without an evidentiary hearing.[263] It did not, then, raise the question whether welfare was itself constitutionally required. Justice Brennan's famous opinion, however, did focus on the unequal burden faced by extremely poor people in the situation under review: they had a right to be heard "at a meaningful time and in a meaningful manner,"[264] but they were made to wait until after benefits were terminated before the hearing, during which time they may have had nothing at all on which to live. The extremely poor person's situation thus "bec[ame] immediately desperate,"[265] and the ensuing focus on daily subsistence was likely to undermine his ability to claim welfare benefits.

Invoking *Sherbert*, Justice Brennan argued that the fact that welfare was not itself constitutionally required did not remove the constitutional obligation to administer it, once it was legislatively enacted, in an even-handed and non-exclusionary way.[266] Just as South Carolina was at liberty to cancel all unemployment compensation, but not at liberty to withhold it unequally from Mrs. Sherbert on account of her conscientious scruples, so New York, while free to terminate welfare, was not free to offer it in ways that discriminated against the extremely poor.

This was as far as Justice Brennan could go, so far as constitutional interpretation is concerned, given the materials at his disposal. Arguing that an evidentiary hearing served important government interests, however, he added a famous set of reflections on the purpose of government, emphasizing the importance of social welfare programs, relative to both dignity and equality:

> From its founding the Nation's basic commitment has been to foster the dignity and well-being of all persons within its borders. We have come to recognize that forces not within the control of the poor contribute to their poverty. . . . Welfare, by meeting the basic demands of subsistence, can help bring within the reach of the poor the same opportunities that are available to others to participate meaningfully in the life of the community. . . . Public assistance, then, is not mere charity, but a means to "pro-

Michelman is too much influenced by utilitarian thought, then in its (pre-Rawls) heyday as the progressive philosophy: he understands the goal as that of a minimum level of "desire satisfaction," whereas what the record actually shows (fortunately, since, as I have argued, desire satisfaction is a very unreliable idea and one that biases policy in favor of the status quo) is attention to basic human capabilities or opportunities.

262 397 U.S. 254 (1970).

263 *See id.* at 255.

264 *Id.* at 267 (quoting Armstrong v. Manzo, 380 U.S. 545, 552 (1965)) (internal quotation marks omitted).

265 *Id.* at 264.

266 *See id.* at 262.

mote the general Welfare, and secure the Blessings of Liberty to ourselves and our Posterity."[267]

As one can see, Justice Brennan's account of the purpose of government focuses not on the satisfaction of desire, but on human capabilities.[268] The nation's founding idea, as set forth in the Preamble to the Constitution, is interpreted (correctly, I believe) as that of securing a set of basic opportunities for meaningful participation or activity: that is what is meant, said Justice Brennan, by "promote the general Welfare" and "secure the Blessings of Liberty."

D. Education

Education has always been central to proponents of the CA. One cannot have combined capabilities without first having internal capabilities, those developed capacities of mind and body that prepare a citizen to pursue personal achievement and to play a meaningful role in the community. It was in this area that the clash between libertarian minimalism and the CA was at its most intense, in the times of both Smith and Green. Consequently, it is not surprising that education has been the focus of some of the most contested Fourteenth Amendment cases, such as *Brown* and *United States v. Virginia*.

No proponent of the CA holds that everyone must have the same education. But if education is to have the role of enabling young people to develop their human potential, then the minimum offered must be ample enough, and at least that minimum amount must be delivered in a way that respects the equal entitlement of all people within the jurisdiction of the states.

Plyler v. Doe[269] is a landmark case in this regard. Addressing a challenge to a Texas statute that excluded the children of illegal immigrants from the public schools, the Court emphasized that the Equal Protection Clause applies to "*any person within* [*a state's*] *jurisdiction*,"[270] and held that the children of illegal immigrants are plainly included within the clause's meaning, just as they are also subject to the criminal law. Although precedent made it clear that education, unlike voting, does not have the status of a fundamental right for Fourteenth Amendment purposes, the majority opinion (authored, again, by Justice Brennan) emphasized that it does have a special status in Ameri-

---

267 *Id.* at 264–65 (quoting U.S. CONST. pmbl.).

268 His phrasing bears a striking resemblance to that of T.H. Green in his lecture on "Liberal Legislation and the Freedom of Contract," *see* Green, *supra* note 196, although the connection is probably indirect. (Justice Brennan majored in Economics at the Wharton School of the University of Pennsylvania, and thus probably had little if any formal contact with philosophy.)

269 457 U.S. 202 (1982).

270 *Id.* at 210 (quoting U.S. CONST. amend. XIV, § 1 (emphasis added)).

can life.[271] The analysis used ideas of capability and opportunity that have deep roots in the history of the CA.

The discussion of education begins with a fundamental assertion of the equality of persons: "The Equal Protection Clause was intended to work nothing less than the abolition of all caste-based and invidious class-based legislation."[272] Public education, the majority wrote, plays a "pivotal role" in "maintaining the fabric of our society" and in "sustaining our political and cultural heritage."[273] Education is "necessary to prepare citizens to participate effectively and intelligently in our open political system if we are to preserve freedom and independence."[274] It is also crucial to individual opportunity and self-development:

> Illiteracy is an enduring disability. The inability to read and write will handicap the individual deprived of a basic education each and every day of his life. The inestimable toll of that deprivation on the social, economic, intellectual, and psychological well-being of the individual, and the obstacle it poses to individual achievement, make it most difficult to reconcile the cost or the principle of a status-based denial of basic education with the framework of equality embodied in the Equal Protection Clause.[275]

Again, the denial of education denies "them the ability to live within the structure of our civic institutions, and foreclose[s] any realistic possibility that they will contribute in even the smallest way to the progress of our Nation."[276] In effect, the opinion sees the equal right to educational benefits as inherent in the equal dignity of persons, given the pivotal role of education in securing human capabilities.[277]

The question of what *equal* entitlement really means has been a difficult one, particularly in the light of the Court's refusal to deem education a fundamental right. In *San Antonio Independent School District v. Rodriguez*,[278] nine years before *Plyler v. Doe*, the majority acknowledged the special status of education as a necessary condition of the meaningful exercise of other constitutional rights, including the freedom of speech and the right to vote, but denied that education was

---

271 *Id.* at 221.

272 *Id.* at 213.

273 *Id.* at 221.

274 *Id.* (quoting Wisconsin v. Yoder, 406 U.S. 205, 221 (1972)) (internal quotation mark omitted).

275 *Id.* at 222.

276 *Id.* at 223.

277 Compare the case in India that gave rise to the addition of primary and secondary education to the list of constitutionally protected entitlements, *Unni Krishnan v. State of Andhra Pradesh*, A.I.R. 1993 S.C. 2178. The court held that the right to education flows from the right to life and is related to the dignity of the individual. *Id.* at 2231–32.

278 411 U.S. 1 (1973).

(like the right to travel) a right implicit in the Constitution. Moreover, even if a right to "some identifiable quantum of education" could possibly be seen as implicit in other constitutional rights, the Court held that there was no evidence that the Texas system's very large inequalities of funding pushed some people below this minimum.[279] The provision of "basic minimal skills" is the most that might even arguably enjoy constitutional protection, and Texas appeared to provide this.[280]

In his famous dissent, Justice Marshall argued that the "gross disparities in . . . the Texas financing scheme" were enough to "deprive[] children in their earliest years of the chance to reach their full potential as citizens."[281] While precise numerical equality in the distribution of benefits is not constitutionally required, he argued, gross discrimination in distribution is not constitutionally excusable under the Equal Protection Clause.[282] Citing other instances (the right to vote, the right to travel) in which the Court had recognized a fundamental right despite the absence of explicit wording to that effect,[283] he urged that education, because of its immense importance for citizenship, deserves that status. Education "directly affects the ability of a child to exercise his First Amendment rights" of free speech and association.[284] It "provide[s] the tools necessary for political discourse and debate."[285] It thus involves a governmental interest of the highest order.

Justice Marshall's dissent marks the limit of the forward march of the CA in American law, at least where social and economic rights are concerned (although the opinion correctly refuses to separate these rights from the political and civil rights that they undergird). Subsequent cases, including *Plyler v. Doe*, tread cautiously, refusing to give education the status urged by Justice Marshall. Nevertheless, education does continue to enjoy some sort of special status, as the *San Antonio* and *Plyler* majorities acknowledge.

Such ideas of equal entitlement and of the fundamental importance of education, while they did not generate further case law in the area of unequal expenditure, were not utterly infertile. In two important cases, courts used these core ideas to extend free, suitable public education to children with mental and physical disabilities. In 1972, in *Mills v. Board of Education*,[286] the U.S. District Court for the District of Columbia ruled in favor of a group of children with mental disabili-

---

279 *Id.* at 36–37.
280 *Id.* at 37.
281 *Id.* at 71 & n.2 (Marshall, J., dissenting).
282 *Id.* at 88–89.
283 *Id.* at 99–101.
284 *Id.* at 112.
285 *Id.* at 113.
286 348 F. Supp. 866 (D.D.C. 1972).

ties who challenged their exclusions from the District of Columbia public schools. In an analysis that self-consciously set out to apply *Brown v. Board of Education*, the court held that the denial of free suitable public education to the mentally disabled is an equal protection violation.[287] (Notice that the opinion understood *Brown* to be about the difference between exclusion and inclusion, not about a ban on special affirmative remedies: indeed, it understood the *Brown* framework to suggest, very strongly, the need for such affirmative remedies.[288] Children with disabilities, the court held, need special support in order to be fully integrated into the public schools.[289]) Moreover, very important for our purposes, the court held that this equal protection violation could not be reasoned away by saying that the system had insufficient funds and these children were unusually expensive to include. "The inadequacies of the District of Columbia Public School System whether occasioned by insufficient funding or administrative inefficiency, certainly cannot be permitted to bear more heavily on the 'exceptional' or handicapped child than on the normal child," the opinion argued.[290] Significantly, the court cited *Goldberg v. Kelly* to make the point that the state's interest in the welfare of its citizens "clearly outweighs" its "competing concern to prevent any increase in its fiscal and administrative burdens."[291] Similarly, reasoned the court, "the District of Columbia's interest in educating the excluded children clearly must outweigh its interest in preserving its financial resources."[292] Like *Goldberg v. Kelly*, the opinion emphasizes that the inclusion is not a matter of charity, but one of entitlement and basic justice.

The United States lags behind some other nations in recognizing the importance of guaranteeing some key social and economic entitlements to all and placing these beyond the vicissitudes of majority politics. Nonetheless, the CA constitutes at least one prominent strand in our thinking about what it means to protect a fundamental entitlement for all. Where an entitlement has been constitutionally recognized, the CA provides a normative benchmark for interpreting that right in a way that recognizes the equality of all citizens. This normative understanding corresponds to some prominent aspects of our legal tradition.

---

287 *Id.* at 874–75. Technically, because of the legally anomalous situation of the District of Columbia, the court held that such a denial was a due process violation under the Fifth Amendment and that the Equal Protection Clause in its application to education is "a component of due process binding on the District." *Id.* at 875 (quoting Hobson v. Hansen, 269 F. Supp. 401, 493 (D.D.C. 1967)).

288 *See id.* at 874–76.

289 *See id.* at 878–80 (specifying measures to be taken).

290 *Id.* at 876.

291 *Id.* (quoting Goldberg v. Kelly, 397 U.S. 254, 266 (1970)).

292 *Id.*

It also provides, in this connection, an attractive account of judicial reasoning that is sometimes the dominant approach to interpretation, although lofty formalism has also had great influence.

V. THE CAPABILITIES APPROACH IN THE 2006 TERM: FAILURES OF "PERCEPTION"

When cases involving central human entitlements come before the Supreme Court, many factors are rightly involved; a court cannot and should not apply a normative philosophical program, even one that seems very attractive. Due respect must be shown to text, precedent, and other legal constraints. Nonetheless, the fact that a case is before the Court frequently means that it is a hard case, in which these other factors do not determine a clear solution. In thinking about such cases, philosophical argument can be helpful in identifying and clarifying features of our constitutional tradition, in illuminating general goals and values that are clearly at issue, and in providing a related account of pertinent features of judicial reasoning.

The 2006 Term contained a number of difficult and disputed cases, where the weighting of relevant factors must necessarily be complex. In such cases, judges need to call on their sense of history and context, and their understanding of the human meaning of the concepts implicit in the relevant statute or constitutional text. As I argue above, that kind of experienced imagination of particulars, which Aristotle calls "perception," proves especially crucial, and has been especially prominent, in cases dealing with the equal rights of groups subject to historical discrimination. A good judge must have a keen sense of what stands between members of such groups and the opportunity to function as fully equal citizens. Despite being a normative theory whose goals can be characterized, to some extent, in general terms, the CA consistently emphasizes the need for confrontation with the real and complex situations within which people are trying to function as equals. In that way, it is closely associated with ideals of context sensitive reasoning embedded in the common law tradition.

When assessed against the normative and methodological benchmark supplied by the CA, the 2006 Term shows some notable forward strides. It also, however, contains some ominous signs for the future. In a group of deeply disputed cases, we find a marked turning away from the realistic sort of imagining in which a judge grapples seriously with all the facts in their historical, material, and social context. In its place we find an obtuse though competent legal formalism of a type highly reminiscent of Wechsler; sometimes we also find ideological fantasy. Meanwhile, some eloquent dissents give us examples of CA-style reasoning as striking as any since Justice Brennan's opinions in a previous era.

A. Good News on Environment and Education

The 2006 Term includes two decisions that markedly enlarge support for human capabilities. *Massachusetts v. EPA*[293] affirmed that states have standing to challenge the failure of the EPA to regulate greenhouse gas emissions, thus recognizing a carefully limited right of citizens to shape the kind of relationship they have with the surrounding environment.[294]

More closely connected to the issues I have pursued in this Foreword, however, is *Winkelman v. Parma City School District*,[295] which held that the Individuals with Disabilities Education Act[296] (IDEA) gives rights not only to disabled children, but also to their parents, permitting parents to represent themselves in court when challenging their child's Individualized Education Program (IEP).[297] The case turned on the interpretation of a rather clearly written statute, so the 7–2 decision is perhaps unsurprising. The whole history of the issue, however, illustrates a fruitful partnership between judicial and legislative action in the furtherance of human capabilities.[298]

Concern for the entitlements of people with disabilities has been a hallmark of the modern development of the CA, both as an issue of importance in its own right and as a test that indicates the superiority of the CA to other approaches. In his first articulation of the CA, in the 1980 article *Equality of What?*, Amartya Sen argued that a formalistic approach favoring giving all citizens an identical quantity of all-purpose resources would fail to grapple well with the special needs of people with disabilities. A person using a wheelchair, he argued, will need more expenditure in order to come up to the same level of mobility than a person with "normal" mobility, given that society has been designed with the needs of the "normal" in mind.[299] He argued that the social aim should instead be to produce a certain level of capability in all citizens.[300] In *Frontiers of Justice*, I argue that the equal dignity

[293] 127 S. Ct. 1438 (2007).

[294] *Id.* at 1458; *see supra* note 15 (noting the capability of living with concern for and in relation to other species and the world of nature). For an elaboration of the implications of the CA for environmental thought, see Breena Holland, Environment and Capability: A New Normative Framework for Environmental Policy Analysis (August 2005) (unpublished Ph.D. dissertation, University of Chicago) (on file with the Harvard Law School Library).

[295] 127 S. Ct. 1994 (2007).

[296] 20 U.S.C. §§ 1400–1482 (2000 & Supp. IV 2004).

[297] *Winkelman*, 127 S. Ct. at 2006.

[298] *See* NUSSBAUM, FRONTIERS OF JUSTICE, *supra* note 7, at 155–223 (discussing the history of disability issues and their relationship to the CA).

[299] *See* Sen, *Equality of What?*, *supra* note 198, at 203–04. Sen actually treats this case as one of straightforward natural difference, failing to note that the reasons why the person in a wheelchair is less mobile are thoroughly social: absence of ramps, wheelchair accessible buses, etc.

[300] *Id.* at 218–19.

of people with mental and physical disabilities gives us a major reason to prefer the CA to alternative approaches, as a source of more helpful political principles to deal with these cases. The principles involved in the cases leading up to IDEA figure in my argument as examples of the helpful recognition that equal protection requires special measures to ensure that children with disabilities really have full and equal access to education.[301]

As I discussed in Part IV, *Mills v. Board of Education* held that children with a wide range of mental and physical disabilities have enforceable rights to inclusion, on a basis of equality, in the public schools of the District of Columbia.[302] A year before, the federal district court in *Pennsylvania Ass'n for Retarded Children v. Pennsylvania*[303] issued a consent decree compelling Pennsylvania public schools to provide access to "appropriate" education and training programs to children with mental disabilities.[304] Because absence of adequate local funding was clearly an obstacle to the fulfillment of these judicially mandated obligations, a national debate ensued, leading to a major legislative initiative. In 1975, Congress passed the Education for All Handicapped Children Act,[305] which turned the *Mills* decision into federal law, giving a wide range of mentally disabled children enforceable rights to free suitable public education and making funds available to the states to help them meet their constitutional obligations. This law was slightly modified and elaborated in 1997 in the form of IDEA.

The guiding principle of IDEA is that children with disabilities are individuals, equal in dignity to "normal" children, and that, in consequence, education should be based on a careful, individualized consideration of a child's educational needs. The central vehicle of this idea is the IEP, "a written statement for each child with a disability that is developed, reviewed, and revised."[306] IDEA requires that states affirmatively undertake to identify and locate all children with disabilities whose needs have not been addressed.[307] It also requires that districts establish extensive procedural safeguards to give parents input in decisions regarding the evaluation and placement of their children, as well as access to records and rights to participation in due process

301 NUSSBAUM, FRONTIERS OF JUSTICE, *supra* note 7, at 200–05.

302 Mills v. Bd. of Educ., 348 F. Supp. 866, 874–76 (D.D.C. 1972).

303 334 F. Supp. 1257 (E.D. Pa. 1971).

304 *Id.* at 1258.

305 Pub. L. No. 94-142, 89 Stat. 773 (1975) (codified as amended at 20 U.S.C. §§ 1405–1406, 1415–1420 (2000 & Supp. IV 2004)).

306 20 U.S.C. § 1414(d)(1)(A)(i).

307 *Id.* § 1412(a)(3)(A).

hearings and judicial review.[308] In general, IDEA obligates states to educate children with disabilities in the "[l]east restrictive environment" appropriate to meet their needs.[309] It thus urges "mainstreaming" of these children. But the underlying recognition of individuality is paramount; thus, if a child will profit more from special education than from mainstreaming, the state is obligated to support a special placement, which sometimes will have to be in a tuition-charging private school.

The Act has noble aspirations, and yet its implementation has been fraught with difficulty. For one thing, the funds were not appropriated for a long time, and even now the funding is not complete.[310] Another major problem is the IEP process, in which parents must negotiate with school committees that are not always well educated about the child's specific disability and that often try to save money, even at the cost of not supporting a special placement for a child who clearly needs one. Autism spectrum disorders (the type of disability at issue in *Winkelman*) often pose particular problems, making mainstreaming difficult.[311] A whole range of human capabilities, from citizenship to intellectual and emotional development, are at stake in the IEP process, making adequate representation crucial.

Many poor parents, however, cannot afford to hire a lawyer. If they are denied the right to represent themselves, the already striking inequities of IDEA, which clearly favors educated and articulate parents, become yet more striking. When discussions with the Parma, Ohio, school district led to an impasse, the Winkelmans followed IDEA's administrative review procedures, and when they lost, filed a complaint in federal court, followed by an appeal to the Sixth Circuit.[312] The Sixth Circuit had recently held that IDEA does not grant parents independent rights,[313] and accordingly, it ruled that the Winkelmans could not proceed unless they hired a lawyer.[314] The Supreme Court reversed.[315] As I have said, the statute, carefully read, is not ambiguous, and thus the parents' victory breaks no new legal ground. It does, however, illustrate an ongoing dialogue and partnership between legislative and judicial action that has resulted in the

---

308 *See* Winkelman v. Parma City Sch. Dist., 127 S. Ct. 1994, 2000–02 (2007) (discussing provisions of IDEA).

309 20 U.S.C. § 1412(a)(5).

310 *See* NUSSBAUM, FRONTIERS OF JUSTICE, *supra* note 7, at 208–11 (discussing funding and other difficulties in the law's implementation).

311 *See id.* at 206–07 (discussing difficulties with "mainstreaming" for autism spectrum children).

312 *Winkelman*, 127 S. Ct. at 1998–99.

313 *See* Cavanaugh v. Cardinal Local Sch. Dist., 409 F.3d 753, 757 (6th Cir. 2005).

314 *Winkelman*, 127 S. Ct. at 1999.

315 *Id.* at 2007.

protection of human capabilities for many of our most vulnerable young citizens.

In a sense, this victory for the CA is indicative of its current weakness, for it was in a statutory case, in which the statute was clearly written, that the Court protected the capabilities of a vulnerable minority. The Court did not need to engage in detailed historical and contextual imagining (although the opinion did say some useful things about the relationship between IDEA and children's capabilities[316]); they only needed to read the statute. Other groups, as we shall see, were less fortunate.

B. Women's Health and Employment: Paternalism and Obtuseness

The equality of women is both a key topic for the theorists of the CA and (as in the case of disability) a test for its adequacy, showing its superiority to utilitarian and minimalist approaches.[317] Women are often unable to enjoy the fruits of a nation's or a region's general prosperity, on account of unequal impediments of many kinds, in areas including education, employment, bodily integrity, health, and the ability to direct their own destiny. Confronting utilitarian approaches with the facts of women's lives therefore shows a weak point in such approaches. Similarly, the minimalist's reluctance to involve the state in the protection of a wide range of human capabilities leaves women particularly vulnerable to violence, ill health, illiteracy, and discrimination and harassment in the workplace, and pointing to these facts helps us to make a powerful case against libertarian minimalism. Women's issues show us, as well, the danger in relying on any abstract and formal approach to decisionmaking: we need to take stock of what actually impedes women's full social and political equality, and this requires a detailed understanding of individual workplace and family situations.

What is always important in considering women's equality (argues the proponent of the CA) is to ask what they are actually able to do and to be, and to look closely at subtle or hidden impediments to those abilities. One cannot assume that a situation that appears fair on the surface is fair in fact, since many of the obstacles to women's equality lie concealed beneath an attractive veneer of symmetry or al-

---

[316] *See id.* at 2000–01 (elucidating the concepts of "free appropriate public education" and the role of the IEP); *id.* at 2003 (clarifying the Act's commitment to an idea of equal opportunity that entails special efforts on behalf of children with disabilities).

[317] *See* CAPABILITIES, FREEDOM, AND EQUALITY: AMARTYA SEN'S WORK FROM A GENDER PERSPECTIVE, *supra* note 198; NUSSBAUM, WOMEN AND HUMAN DEVELOPMENT, *supra* note 7; Amartya Sen, *Gender Inequality and Theories of Justice*, *in* WOMEN, CULTURE, AND DEVELOPMENT: A STUDY OF HUMAN CAPABILITIES 259 (Martha C. Nussbaum & Jonathan Glover eds., 1995).

leged fairness. A good judge in such cases must be able to imagine the real obstacles women face. This sort of imagining informed *United States v. Virginia*, as it has informed the landmark decisions on sexual harassment.[318]

Ledbetter v. Goodyear Tire & Rubber Co.[319] is a case in which perception, the informed and realistic understanding of a complex situation in all its historical particularity, makes all the difference. Perception, however, is in short supply in the majority's competent and closely reasoned opinion. As a matter of law, the case boils down to an exercise in analogical reasoning. We have the case to be decided, Lilly Ledbetter's claim of sex discrimination in pay. The question before the Court was whether she could sue, given that the pay decisions that took place within the statutory 180-day filing period were not *in and of themselves* (i.e., in isolation from their history) discriminatory decisions.[320] On one hand, in *United Air Lines, Inc. v. Evans*,[321] *Delaware State College v. Ricks*,[322] and *Lorance v. AT&T Technologies, Inc.*,[323] the Court found that the plaintiff could not sue for events that took place outside the 180-day period. On the other hand, in *Bazemore v. Friday*[324] and *National Railroad Passenger Corp. v. Morgan*,[325] the Court suggested that, in cases of incremental or cumulative discrimination, each new act was itself a new offense, and thus occasion to bring suit, because it formed part of a discriminatory historical pattern; the history infects the current acts. Justice Alito attempted to show that Ledbetter's case was more like *Evans* and its siblings and to distinguish *Bazemore* (and the relevant portions of *Morgan*); in dissent, Justice Ginsburg attempted to distinguish *Evans* and its siblings, and to show that Ledbetter's case is rightly seen as linked to *Bazemore* and in light of the contrast announced in *Morgan*.

Because the entire case turns, and rightly turns, on these contrasting exercises in analogical reasoning, there is no substitute for coming

---

318 *See* NUSSBAUM, POETIC JUSTICE, *supra* note 48, at 104–11 (analyzing Carr v. Allison Gas Turbine Division, 32 F.3d 1007 (7th Cir. 1994), and arguing that the detailed account of the way in which an asymmetry of power infected the whole workplace environment was crucial to both the analysis and the result).

319 127 S. Ct. 2162 (2007).

320 *See id.* at 2166.

321 431 U.S. 553 (1977).

322 449 U.S. 250 (1980).

323 490 U.S. 900 (1989).

324 478 U.S. 385 (1986) (holding that the defendant employer did have a duty to eliminate race-based salary discrepancies that originated before Title VII was enacted and that the plaintiffs could introduce statistical analyses that reflected these pre–Title VII disparities).

325 536 U.S. 101 (2002) (holding that in cases charging hostile work environment, plaintiffs may present evidence of acts that would be time-barred as the basis of an independent lawsuit if those acts constituted part of the same actionable hostile work employment practice and an actionable act falls within the statutory time period).

up with a nuanced human understanding of the case. No mechanical formula will tell us from on high which features are the most salient in making comparisons. Perception of which factors are salient and which are not requires judgment based on history, context, and a general familiarity with the conditions of human life. In *Ledbetter*, what is required is a sympathetic and realistic understanding of the reality of women's all too common experiences in the workplace. In the light of that understanding, certain features of earlier decisions will naturally assume salience and others will not.

Perception of this type would seem to be a necessary part of good judicial interpretation, especially regarding a statute like Title VII,[326] which addresses a host of issues. Congress was painting on a large canvas, and it seems implausible that they could resolve all contested issues in advance. Here, the perception of judges plays a natural and indeed an ineliminable role.

Lilly Ledbetter was a supervisor at Goodyear from 1979 until her retirement in 1998.[327] For most of that time, she worked as an area manager; most other area managers were men.[328] At first, Ledbetter's salary was in line with that of men performing similar work.[329] Over time, however, her pay declined by comparison to the males in the same job.[330] By 1997, even though Ledbetter had considerable seniority, her pay was $3727 per month; males in the same position made between $4286 and $5236 per month.[331] Ledbetter was able to prove at trial that a pattern of discrimination at her plant, not bad performance on her part, accounted for the pay differential, and that during the 180-day filing period her pay was substantially less than that of a man doing the same work.[332] What makes her case a complicated one is that much of the evidence of discriminatory intent came from a period outside the 180-day period.[333] The majority argued that she would have had to file charges year by year, each time Goodyear failed to give her salary increases similar to those received by men;[334] in other words, she could bring suit only for pay decisions made within the 180-day period, during which time there was slight evidence of discriminatory intent.[335]

---

326 Civil Rights Act of 1964, tit. VII, 42 U.S.C. §§ 2000e to 2000e-17 (2000).

327 Ledbetter v. Goodyear Tire & Rubber Co., 127 S. Ct. 2162, 2178 (Ginsburg, J., dissenting).

328 *Id.*

329 *Id.*

330 *Id.*

331 *Id.*

332 *Id.*

333 *See id.* at 2165–66 (majority opinion).

334 *See id.* at 2169.

335 *See id.* (stating that "Ledbetter . . . makes no claim that intentionally discriminatory conduct occurred during the charging period").

This approach, insisting that a wronged employee immediately contest her pay discrimination, "overlooks common characteristics of pay discrimination," as the dissent correctly argued.[336] Pay discrimination is often incremental, and it can take a while to see that discrimination is at work: only the pattern over time shows this clearly. "Small initial discrepancies may not be seen as meet for a federal case, particularly when the employee, trying to succeed in a nontraditional environment, is averse to making waves."[337] Moreover, comparative pay information is often hidden, and it was hidden in this case, since Goodyear kept salaries confidential.[338] It is only when the discrepancy becomes "apparent and sizable" that we could expect the employee to understand the nature of her situation.[339] The Court's decision thus makes it impossible for many victims of discriminatory pay policies to avail themselves of Title VII.

That is the reality. What of the law? The majority pointed to a group of cases in which the Court held that a suit must be filed within the 180-day period.[340] The opinion treated these cases as analogous to Ledbetter's.[341] The dissent argued, however, that they had a feature that rendered them importantly distinct: they all involved a "one-time discrete act"[342] that was "immediately identifiable."[343] In *Evans* and *Ricks*, the act was a termination of employment;[344] although the basis of the suit in *Lorance* was an ongoing, discriminatory system of seniority, that system was nevertheless introduced and publicly announced at a single time.[345] Unlike Ledbetter, then, the plaintiffs in these three cases were well aware of the act that was at issue, and the act was a single thing, rather than an incremental pattern unfolding over time. Pay discrimination, however, *does* unfold over time, and it is thus significantly unlike discriminatory firing. The dissent's foregrounding of this difference was underwritten by common sense and imaginative perception of the situation of a female employee under such circumstances. The majority's failure to consider it salient appears to result from a rather obtuse formalism, or perhaps from a consciousness that was focused solely on the consequences of the case for employers, rather than for the victims of discrimination.

336 *Id.* at 2178 (Ginsburg, J., dissenting).
337 *Id.* at 2179.
338 *Id.* at 2182.
339 *Id.* at 2179.
340 *See id.* at 2169 (majority opinion).
341 *See id.* at 2169–70.
342 *Id.* at 2183 (Ginsburg, J., dissenting).
343 *Id.* at 2182.
344 *See* Del. State Coll. v. Ricks, 449 U.S. 250, 252 (1980); United Air Lines, Inc. v. Evans, 431 U.S. 553, 554 (1977).
345 *See* Lorance v. AT&T Techs., Inc., 490 U.S. 900, 902 (1989).

On the other side, the dissent argued that *Bazemore*, a race discrimination case, sufficiently supported the conclusion that in incremental pay-differential cases, once the pay scale had been "infected by gender-based (or race-based) discrimination,"[346] *each new paycheck* constituted a new act of discrimination "whenever a paycheck delivers less to a woman than to a similarly situated man."[347] Thus, the actions that occurred outside the 180-day period were not themselves actionable, but they were relevant to determining whether a system is "infected" by discrimination, and thus to assessing the lawfulness of the conduct within that period. (The dissent also made use of *Morgan*'s characterization of the incremental nature of hostile-environment discrimination.[348]) The relevance of *Bazemore* is evident when viewed through experienced perception of the nature of incremental pay discrimination. In other words, if one looks at Ledbetter's case in the light of context and experience, it looks relevantly like *Bazemore*, whereas, if one neglects the real obstacles that stand between women and the vindication of their rights, one can make a formal move that distinguishes it.[349]

What the majority's reasoning really entailed was that women will often be unable to sue for pay discrimination. They have rights on paper, but are virtually unable (in this very common type of case) to exercise them. If the statute and the precedents allowed only a single reading, then one might conclude that the Court had done its job well and fully, but that a statutory remedy was urgently required. It is clear, however, that the analysis of the precedents can go in either direction, and that there is a large and salient (salient in the context of real life) distinction between the cases on which the majority relied and Ledbetter's case. Therefore one must conclude, more critically, that the majority used analogical reasoning obtusely, in a way that utterly neglected the actual capabilities of women in Ledbetter's position, showing concern only for the situation of employers.[350]

---

346 *Ledbetter*, 127 S. Ct. at 2179 (Ginsburg, J., dissenting).

347 *Id.*

348 *See id.* at 2180.

349 The Court's reasoning in *Bowles v. Russell*, 127 S. Ct. 2360 (2007), seemed similarly formalistic, in that it once again placed extraordinary obstacles between a person and the real exercise of his rights. In *Bowles*, a criminal defendant's appeal was blocked because he missed the filing deadline, even though he was following instructions given him by the district court, which had incorrectly advised him that the extension period was seventeen days rather than fourteen days. *See id.* at 2363, 2367. The four dissenters protested: "It is intolerable for the judicial system to treat people this way . . . ." *Id.* at 2367 (Souter, J., dissenting). The dissent invoked the (Aristotelian) notion of equity, *see* ARISTOTLE, ETHICA NICOMACHEA, *supra* note 13, at 1143a19–20, concluding, "[w]e have the authority to recognize an equitable exception to the 14-day limit, and we should do that here." *Bowles*, 127 S. Ct. at 2370 (Souter, J., dissenting).

350 Here, in addition to lofty formalism, a link to libertarianism is suggested, since libertarians typically oppose antidiscrimination laws as unjustified infringements of employer freedom, *see*

The difference between the majority and the dissent is nicely captured in a difference of intellectual styles. The majority opinion is utterly impersonal, crisp and focused on formal analysis; in essence a very well-done example of lofty formalism. Despite the proficiency of the majority's technical analysis, the opinion made no attempt to come to grips with Ledbetter's situation, which faded utterly into the background.[351] In the dissent, by contrast, Ledbetter's story was presented at length, and the common nature of the problem it raised (incremental pay discrepancies) was analyzed as a problem that very often affects women in the workplace.[352] The majority did not mention the fact that Goodyear kept employees' pay secret; the dissent emphasized this fact, a key feature of the case.[353] The majority never alluded to the general purpose of Title VII; the dissent focused on the importance of interpreting the statute "with fidelity to [its] core purpose,"[354] charging the majority with a "cramped interpretation . . . incompatible with the statute's broad remedial purpose."[355] Here we do see something like the contrast between Wechslerian formalism and Aristotelian perception — though without Wechsler's pained acknowledgment of the difficulty of the issue and the urgency of the social task ahead.

The Court showed a similar lack of perception in its approach to abortion in the 2006 Term. Abortion is a difficult issue for the CA, as

---

EPSTEIN, *supra* note 33; if such laws exist, the libertarian will want to construe them as narrowly as possible. Two other cases with libertarian links, both highly technical in the issues they raise, are *Bell Atlantic Corp. v. Twombly*, 127 S. Ct. 1955 (2007), and *Leegin Creative Leather Products, Inc. v. PSKS, Inc.*, 127 S. Ct. 2705 (2007). In *Bell Atlantic*, the Court appeared to adopt a stricter view of the pleading requirement for the plaintiff in an antitrust case, *see Bell Atlantic Corp.*, 127 S. Ct. at 1974 (requiring the plaintiff to plead facts that make the claim "plausible" rather than merely possible); in *Leegin*, the Court overruled a precedent almost one hundred years old, *Dr. Miles Medical Co. v. John D. Park & Sons Co.*, 220 U.S. 373 (1911), and held that it was no longer per se illegal under the Sherman Act for a manufacturer to agree with a distributor to set a minimum resale price; from now on, courts should use a "rule of reason" instead. *Leegin*, 127 S. Ct. at 2725. In both cases the Court, in highly disputed technical contexts, favored business and disfavored consumers. *Leegin*, however, is particularly surprising because it overrules a long-standing precedent on grounds that, as the dissenting opinion notes, appear not to conform to factors previously found relevant, particularly in statutory cases. *Id.* at 2734–37 (Breyer, J., dissenting). *Leegin* is also fascinating from the point of view of the CA and its interest in perception. Indeed, its holding that a per se rule will be replaced by a context-sensitive rule of reason should in general please the supporter of the CA. The dissent, however, argues that the per se rule was adopted because of the unusual likelihood of harms and the difficulty of separating harmful from beneficial price-fixing. *Id.* at 2729–31, 2734. In such a case, the Aristotelian would agree that there is good reason to favor a per se rule because it is unlikely a judge would have the knowledge and experience to make perception possible, a necessity for individualized judgment. *See supra* section II.C, pp. 24–33.

351 *See Ledbetter*, 127 S. Ct. at 2170–72 & n.4.

352 *See id.* at 2179, 2181–82 (Ginsburg, J., dissenting).

353 *See id.*

354 *Id.* at 2187.

355 *Id.* at 2188.

it is for our society. On the one side, the CA will acknowledge that the state has a legitimate interest, up to a point, in the protection of fetal life; on the other side, the state also has a very urgent commitment to protect a wide range of capabilities that are often at issue in the decision to have an abortion: a woman's life and health, her ability to avail herself of society's opportunities on an equal basis, and her decisional freedom. Indeed, the CA provides a way of seeing how one might bring together two approaches to the abortion issue that have often been seen as antithetical: the privacy-based approach (focusing on the need to protect intimate choices from government interference) and the equality-based approach (focusing on the importance of ensuring that women are not second-class citizens). What the privacy-based approach gets right (albeit using an unclear concept[356]) is the importance of a woman's decisional freedom, with regard particularly to her own health, but also with regard to the overall shaping of her life. What the equality approach[357] gets right is the fact that such basic liberties are not adequately granted unless they are granted in a way that respects women's full equality as citizens. In order to assess whether that is the case, any adequate approach must be aware of the history of hierarchy and discrimination under which women have labored. The CA marries the privacy and equality concerns, asking what these groups are actually able to do and, as a result, be in society. In doing so, the CA asks the decisionmaker to focus on the protection of spheres of choice, but to do so in a way that takes stock of the special obstacles and burdens some groups in society face.

In *Planned Parenthood of Southeastern Pennsylvania v. Casey*,[358] the Court's majority asked these questions, emerging with an analysis that gave due weight to both competing interests.[359] The Court also recognized that the issue of choice with respect to abortion has both a privacy aspect (it involves "the most intimate and personal choices a person may make in a lifetime, choices central to personal dignity and autonomy"[360]) and an equality aspect (it affects "[t]he ability of women to participate equally in the economic and social life of the Nation"[361]).

356 *See generally* Martha C. Nussbaum, *Sex Equality, Liberty, and Privacy: A Comparative Approach to the Feminist Critique*, *in* INDIA'S LIVING CONSTITUTION 242, 242–45, 254–74 (Zoya Hasan et al. eds., 2002) (arguing that the concept of privacy is confused and confusing, and that it would be better to enumerate specific decisional liberties that deserve protection).

357 *See generally* CASS R. SUNSTEIN, THE PARTIAL CONSTITUTION 257–61, 270–85 (1993) (outlining the equality-based approach to women's sexuality and arguing that restrictions on abortion are problematic because they co-opt women's bodies in a way the law never co-opts men's).

358 505 U.S. 833 (1992).

359 *Id.* at 857 ("[O]ur cases since *Roe* [*v. Wade*, 410 U.S. 113 (1973),] accord with *Roe*'s view that a State's interest in the protection of life falls short of justifying any plenary override of individual liberty claims.").

360 *Id.* at 851.

361 *Id.* at 856.

In *Gonzales v. Carhart*,[362] a case dealing with the constitutionality of legislation banning "partial-birth abortion," the Court appeared to turn toward a different approach, in a case whose actual holding is narrow, but whose greater implications for the future of sex equality are ominous.

Carhart upheld the constitutionality of the Partial-Birth Abortion Ban Act of 2003,[363] holding that the Act did not on its face impose unconstitutional substantial obstacles on women seeking late-term, but previability, abortions. *Carhart* shares the key failing of *Ledbetter*: a failure to recognize fully a major impediment to women's equal possibilities.[364] The opinion's reading of *Casey* and *Stenberg v. Carhart*[365] was bizarrely narrow. The majority made no persuasive argument as to why the failure to allow an exception for a woman's health is not a fatal defect.[366] Nor did the opinion offer a cogent analysis[367] of the notion of "undue burden,"[368] which might show whether the statute in question did in fact "place a substantial obstacle in the [woman's path]."[369] Surprisingly, the majority failed to make a distinction between previability and postviability abortions, a distinction that was crucial to the *Casey* framework. Moreover, the allusions to the state's respect for fetal life[370] spin like an idle wheel, given that the holding does not actually protect fetal lives, in that it permits a range of alternative techniques for late-term abortion. Finally, in place of the sober formalism of *Ledbetter*, which was simply devoid of real-world understanding, we find a fanciful ideology of gender that treats women (without the slightest evidence) as frail creatures who cannot be expected to know their own minds or to make their own choices.

At issue, as *Casey* made clear, are a wide range of capabilities in women's lives. As the *Carhart* dissent summarized, the decision whether to bear a child is vital "to a woman's 'dignity and autonomy,' her 'personhood' and 'destiny,' her 'conception of . . . her place in society,'"[371] her right "to participate equally in the economic and social

---

[362] 127 S. Ct. 1610 (2007).

[363] 18 U.S.C. § 1531 (Supp. III 2003).

[364] It has, however, a number of other failings as well; it is not, like *Ledbetter*, a tightly argued piece of legal reasoning.

[365] 530 U.S. 914 (2000).

[366] *See Carhart*, 127 S. Ct. at 1635–38.

[367] *See id.* at 1629–35.

[368] Planned Parenthood of Se. Pa. v. Casey, 505 U.S. 833, 878 (1992) (joint opinion of O'Connor, Kennedy, and Souter, JJ.).

[369] *Id.*

[370] *See, e.g.*, *Carhart*, 127 S. Ct. at 1626 (asserting that "the government has a legitimate and substantial interest in preserving and promoting fetal life").

[371] *Id.* at 1640 (Ginsburg, J., dissenting) (omission in original) (quoting *Casey*, 505 U.S. at 851–52).

life of the Nation,"[372] and her "ability to realize [her] full potential."[373] At stake is not "some generalized notion of privacy," but, rather, "a woman's autonomy to determine her life's course."[374] *Casey* emphasized that "the health of the woman" was of particular importance, *even after viability*.[375] The State was not permitted to subject a woman to health risks even in the sense of making her choose a less safe mode of abortion. As the *Carhart* dissent emphasized, *Casey* also drew attention (as did *United States v. Virginia*) to the capability damage created by myths about women that often hold them back from the full and equal exercise of their legal rights.[376]

In the *Carhart* majority opinion, the risks to women's health were dismissed by a tendentious reading of the medical evidence. It is clear that the vast preponderance of the responsible medical evidence supported the conclusion that the banned procedure is sometimes necessary to preserve a woman's health. The congressional findings, as the dissent noted, "do not withstand inspection, as the lower courts have determined and this Court is obliged to concede."[377] In *Stenberg*, moreover, the Court parsed the phrase "necessary, in appropriate medical judgment,"[378] making it clear that this phrase could not "require unanimity of medical opinion."[379] The *Carhart* majority offered no account at all of its abrupt departure from this sensible analysis, and from the established principle that the presence of disagreement "signals the presence of risk, not its absence."[380] Instead, we find vague references to "[r]espect for human life,"[381] without any attempt to show that a single life would be saved by forcing women into an alternative abortion procedure; suggestions of an open possibility for individuals to challenge the law in a specific case,[382] without any attempt to show that a woman awaiting an abortion would ever be able to avail herself of such a remedy; and, above all, pious and condescending remarks about women that are classic examples of the sort of attitude that has impeded women's equality in the past.[383]

---

372 *Id.* at 1641 (quoting *Casey*, 505 U.S. at 856) (internal quotation marks omitted).

373 *Id.*

374 *Id.*

375 *Casey*, 505 U.S. at 846.

376 *Carhart*, 127 S. Ct. at 1641 (Ginsburg, J., dissenting) (citing *Casey*, 505 U.S. at 856).

377 *Id.* at 1643.

378 Stenberg v. Carhart, 530 U.S. 914, 937 (2000) (quoting *Casey*, 505 U.S. at 879 (joint opinion of O'Connor, Kennedy, and Souter, JJ.) (quoting Roe v. Wade, 410 U.S. 113, 165 (1973))) (internal quotation mark omitted).

379 *Id.*

380 *Id.*

381 *Carhart*, 127 S. Ct. at 1634.

382 *See id.* at 1638–39.

383 *See, e.g.*, *id.* at 1634.

The majority asserted that "[r]espect for human life finds an ultimate expression in the bond of love the mother has for her child."[384] It is difficult to attach any precise meaning to this sentence. (How is love supposed to be an example of respect? Some people love their spouses or their children or their pets without respecting them in the least. Respect is closely linked to autonomy, love, all too often, to paternalistic control.) Moreover, in its context, discussing the ban on partial-birth abortions, the sentence clearly expresses the unsubstantiated view that women have a deep bond of love with their fetuses, even at a relatively early stage. Is there any evidence for this? The majority then went on to repeat a stock piece of anti-abortion propaganda, namely, that women who have abortions come to regret their decisions, in ways that damage their mental health: "While we find no reliable data to measure the phenomenon, it seems unexceptionable to conclude some women come to regret their choice to abort the infant life they once created and sustained."[385] If "some" means "not none," then no doubt some cases may be found; but reliable evidence for the Court would have to be more substantial than this. In particular, it would have to compare the regrets and impediments faced by women who are *prevented from* aborting, or who are forced to choose less safe procedures because of legal restrictions, with those women who do undergo abortions.[386]

The paragraph is all the more disturbing given that it had no justificatory purpose. Ostensibly, its purpose was to point out that women need full information and may not always get it. This problem, however, would naturally lead to a conclusion that the Court would be prepared to uphold a law mandating full information, not to the actual holding in the case, which had nothing to do with giving better information. What, then, might its purpose have been? It appears that the majority, having nothing at all to say in defense of its decision to ignore dangers to a woman's health, was trying in a backhanded way to create the impression of caring about women's health by representing itself as protecting poor, fragile women from the health-impairing consequences of their own freedom. As the dissent said, "[t]his way of thinking reflects ancient notions about women's place in the family and under the Constitution — ideas that have long since been discredited."[387] "Discredited," however, does not, unfortunately, indicate a lack of social power. The endorsement of these ideas by the Court itself constitutes a new barrier to women's equal capabilities.

384 *Id.*

385 *Id.*

386 The dissent did a good job of showing the range of relevant psychological research as it currently exists. *See id.* at 1648 n.7 (Ginsburg, J., dissenting).

387 *Id.* at 1649.

C. *Bad News on Education: Curtailing Race-Based Remedies*

From its inception, the CA has been linked to a limited and principled defense of affirmative action. As discussed in section V.A, Sen's *Equality of What?* used the example of aid to people with disabilities to show that the simple formula of formally similar treatment is inadequate. His argument suggests the thought that if we give the same amount of resources to a "normally" mobile person and a person who uses a wheelchair, the latter will probably not attain the same level of actual ability to move around in society. To produce equal capabilities, we will need to provide more resources to the latter than to the former. Although Sen does not emphasize the remedial character of this extra expenditure, one should do so: the reason that a person in a wheelchair has such difficulty getting around in "normal" settings is that such settings were long designed without taking his or her situation into account. There is a history of discrimination and neglect, and it has informed the construction of buildings, the design of buses and trains, the shape of the pavement, and so forth. The proponent of the CA, then, sees a focus on equal capability as a way of choosing policies that remedy past injustice and that do so in a principled and limited way and with a specific goal always in view: people should be truly equal with respect to their basic political and social entitlements. In a similar way, the CA has advocated spending more on the education of girls in societies where they face unequal historical obstacles to becoming fully equal participants — not for reasons of naked favoritism, but because additional spending is required to meet the objective of equal empowerment and capability.

Attempts at affirmative action have several elements, which were clearly set forth in Justice Breyer's dissent in *Parents Involved in Community Schools v. Seattle School District No. 1*.[388] First, they contain a "historical and remedial element"[389]: special attention is given to minority status in order to set right an unjust situation that existed previously. Second, they contain an "educational element"[390]: that is, they focus on the educational benefits of an integrated setting. Finally, they contain a "democratic element: an interest in producing an educational environment that reflects the 'pluralistic society' in which our children will live."[391] Whether the remedies concern disability, race, or gender, they typically have all three of these elements.

The CA's approach to affirmative action makes it abundantly clear that there is a salient asymmetry between measures that aim to include

---

388 127 S. Ct. 2738 (2007).

389 *Id.* at 2820 (Breyer, J., dissenting).

390 *Id.*

391 *Id.* at 2821 (quoting Swann v. Charlotte-Mecklenburg Bd. of Educ., 402 U.S. 1, 16 (1971)).

a previously excluded or disadvantaged group and measures that prefer one group because they aim to exclude or stigmatize another: for the goal is fully equal capability (or, in some cases, a high threshold level of capability for all), and measures of the first kind may promote it, while measures of the second kind never do. We have seen how an analysis of this sort was at work in a whole range of Fourteenth Amendment cases, prominently including *Brown*, *Loving*, and *United States v. Virginia*, in order to defeat the contention that formally symmetrical remedies are all that the equal protection of the law requires.[392] In all these cases, the Court was concerned with the actual abilities of the minorities affected by the arrangements in question: what were they actually able to do and to be? The answer, in each case, was that despite the formal symmetry of the arrangements, they were grossly unequal in what they enabled people to do and to be. They could not, then, survive an equal protection challenge. In each case, the Court adopted something like the CA's account of what true equality means: not just "fine words on paper," as Justice Breyer wrote of *Brown* in *Parents Involved*,[393] but equality "as a matter of everyday life in the Nation's cities and schools. . . . [O]ne law . . . not simply as a matter of legal principle but in terms of how we actually live."[394]

These cases concerned legal permissibility: they held that states were not permitted to maintain the separate but (putatively) equal arrangements in question. Subsequently, where education and race were concerned, the Court allowed states to work hard to come up with workable measures of various sorts that aimed at ending the baneful legacy of segregation.[395] As a result of *Parents Involved*, most of these race-conscious remedies would now appear to be violations of the Equal Protection Clause.

The long and intricate opinions in *Parents Involved* reach a result that can be simply described: for Chief Justice Roberts and Justice Thomas, special attempts to aid minorities, looking at race as one salient factor, are no longer permitted. Three characteristics of the prevailing opinion are striking in the light of our legal history: the astonishing use of *Brown* in defense of an analysis that is utterly unlike *Brown* in spirit and result; the failure to confront with perception the history and current reality of racial segregation in the United States; and the obtuse formalism, as an array of technical distinctions are mobilized to avoid confronting historical reality.

Both Chief Justice Roberts and Justice Thomas invoke *Brown* as if it stood for the proposition that race must never be taken into account

392 *See supra* section IV.B, pp. 64–67.

393 *Parents Involved*, 127 S. Ct. at 2836 (Breyer, J., dissenting).

394 *Id.*

395 *See id.* at 2800–02.

in education, no matter whether the reason for doing so is to include or exclude.[396] Of course *Brown* stood for no such thing: indeed, the very measures that were struck down in *Brown* and in *Loving* were in a sense race-neutral measures — at least superficially — and they were struck down because they failed to consider how the reality of race infects the entire experience of participants in the allegedly symmetrical institutions in question. *Brown* stood for the idea that one should not rest content with obtuse formalism: one must ask what children are actually able to do and to be. Justice Stevens rightly spoke of a "cruel irony"[397] in the Chief Justice's invocation of *Brown*, saying that it reminded him of Anatole France's observation, "[T]he majestic equality of the la[w], forbid[s] rich and poor alike to sleep under bridges, to beg in the streets, and to steal their bread."[398] Justice Breyer, similarly, showing in detail how the school measures in question were attempts to "bring about the kind of racially integrated education that *Brown v. Board of Education* long ago promised,"[399] denounced the prevailing opinion's neglect of the distinction between "exclusionary and inclusive use of race-conscious criteria in the context of the Equal Protection Clause."[400] Chief Justice Roberts appears to reduce the meaning of *Brown* to little more than what I have named lofty formalism: in reality, *Brown* was the unmasking of just such formalism, in the name of a practical concern for substantive equality. It is, Justice Breyer concluded, "a cruel distortion of history to compare Topeka, Kansas, in the 1950's to Louisville and Seattle in the modern day."[401]

A related characteristic of Chief Justice Roberts's opinion is its lack of attention to history. In order to assess the equal protection issue, we need to know what children have actually been able to do and be in schools with different plans, and to do this we need to confront the history of the school districts' attempts to achieve integration in all their detail. What we see when we do this is that both Seattle and Louisville had histories in which segregation was a legal or governmentally fostered reality, and both have grappled in good faith, over time, with a variety of remedies for that history.[402] The present use of race-based criteria is the result of the failure of plans that relied to a *greater* extent on race as a criterion, particularly plans involving busing. The districts have attempted over time to give children more,

---

[396] *See id.* at 2767 (opinion of Roberts, C.J.); *id.* at 2786 (Thomas, J., concurring).

[397] *Id.* at 2797 (Stevens, J., dissenting).

[398] *Id.* at 2798 (alterations in original) (quoting ANATOLE FRANCE, THE RED LILY 95 (Winifred Stephens trans., 6th ed., 1922) (1894)) (internal quotation marks omitted).

[399] *Id.* at 2800 (Breyer, J. dissenting) (citation omitted).

[400] *Id.* at 2835.

[401] *Id.* at 2836.

[402] *See id.* at 2802–09.

rather than fewer, opportunities to be educated in the schools closest to their homes. Nor, as Justice Breyer convincingly argued, do the historical facts suggest that any less race-conscious solution could solve the problem of ongoing segregation.[403] Looking at the history, we must see these efforts as decent if far from perfect continuations of the legacy and promise of *Brown*, and not as race-based measures that stigmatize and exclude. Chief Justice Roberts's rosy picture of an available "non-racial" way of educating children[404] is simply unrealistic in the light of history and current realities.

The conclusion of the prevailing opinion, which removes from local school boards an area of discretion they had long enjoyed, is shocking in light of the history of equal protection jurisprudence. It is defended not only by adherence to a specious symmetry but also by attachment to certain formal distinctions, in particular the distinction between de jure and de facto segregation, and the distinction between dictum and holding. Concerning the first distinction, Justice Breyer showed very convincingly that the Court never limited the use of race-based remedies to cases where a court had already ordered compliance.[405] In fact, many districts, both in the South and elsewhere, voluntarily adopted pro-integration measures without a court order. Relying particularly on *Swann v. Charlotte-Mecklenburg Board of Education*,[406] he clearly demonstrated that "the government may voluntarily adopt race-conscious measures to improve conditions of race even when it is not under a constitutional obligation to do so."[407] Concerning the second distinction, as Justice Breyer argued, Chief Justice Roberts's opinion then downplayed the significance of *Swann* and related cases "by frequently describing their relevant statements as 'dicta.'"[408] Justice Breyer plausibly contended that this distinction, like the de jure/de facto distinction, is not hard and fast, and, in light of the nation's long reliance on the challenged statements, he objected to the Court's "overly theoretical approach to case law, an approach that emphasize[d] rigid distinctions between holdings and dicta in a way that serve[d] to mask the radical nature of today's decision."[409] Although the CA is a theoretical approach, the proponent of the CA heartily agrees with Justice Breyer's statement. Unlike its utilitarian and minimalist rivals, the CA directs judges to consider the case in light of history and context, thinking clearly about what people are able to do

---

403 *See id.* at 2802.
404 *See id.* at 2768 (opinion of Roberts, C.J.).
405 *See id.* at 2816 (Breyer, J., dissenting).
406 402 U.S. 1 (1971).
407 *Parents Involved*, 127 S. Ct. at 2814 (Breyer, J., dissenting).
408 *Id.* at 2816.
409 *Id.*

in their actual circumstances. The CA is theoretical, in that it offers an overall view about what one should consider salient and seek to promote. It is also, however, quite anti-theoretical when it confronts excessively abstract uses of theory that neglect human realities. Indeed, from its inception in ancient Greece to the present day, its role has persistently been to defend experienced human perception against the oversimplifications proposed by other theoretical approaches.

I have suggested that several of the 2006 Term's major cases are characterized by a Wechslerian lofty formalism: they stand so far back from the history and experience of the parties that crucial facts cannot be seen. The prevailing opinion in *Parents Involved* is, of all the past Term's opinions, the most clearly Wechslerian. Exactly like Wechsler, the prevailing opinion purported to be balanced and fair-minded — that is what the allusion to the legacy of *Brown* clearly expresses. Nonetheless, like Wechsler, the Court ignored the asymmetry between exclusion and inclusion, which is among the most striking features of the history of race relations in the United States. Neglecting this, Chief Justice Roberts's argument can be neither accurate nor fully fair. The focus on formal analysis (the persistent use of the dictum/holding distinction, for example) obscures a failure to grapple with the historical problem. Only from a Wechslerian distance could the conclusion be reached that "[t]he way to stop discrimination on the basis of race is to stop discriminating on the basis of race"[410] — a statement whose verbal and intellectual fluency markedly contrasts with its failure to attend to the human salience of the distinction between exclusion and inclusion. The statement's balanced use of words conceals this important distinction. With this formalistic approach one may contrast Justice Breyer's insistence that "[t]he historical and factual context in which these cases arise is critical,"[411] along with his detailed analysis of those facts.[412] With the prevailing opinion's emphasis on merely formal symmetry one may contrast Justice Breyer's determination to look for an equality that is not merely a matter of "fine words on paper," but, instead, a matter of "how we actually live."[413]

The legacy of the civil rights movement consists, above all, in a certain quality of imagination, in which the experience of exclusion is understood, in which the measure of its pain and indignity is taken, and in which it is strongly distinguished from governmental approaches that seek to include and remedy. For the libertarian minimalist, the two actions of government look similar: both represent exactly the sort of governmental engineering that the libertarian dislikes.

---

410 *Id.* at 2768 (opinion of Roberts, C.J.).

411 *Id.* at 2801 (Breyer, J., dissenting).

412 *See id.* at 2801–11.

413 *Id.* at 2836.

Although the prevailing opinion's lofty formalism is not a clear example of libertarianism (Wechsler, after all, was no libertarian), the aversion to governmental action that it expresses has underlying links with libertarianism, as well as with Wechslerian formalism. For the libertarian, as for Chief Justice Roberts, the way to end the evil of discrimination is simply to stop government intervention of all sorts on the basis of race. In human experience, however, and in the assessment of human possibilities, exclusionary and inclusionary government measures are utterly dissimilar. The CA registers this dissimilarity; Chief Justice Roberts and Justice Thomas deny it.[414] The link between lofty formalism and libertarianism, here, consists in an unwillingness to confront the more unpleasant aspects of our history and the motives that gave rise to them, and the need to use law to address these problems. (In that regard libertarianism, like lofty formalism, would seem to be a willfully naïve approach to human life.)

In one sense, then, Chief Justice Roberts's opinion was libertarian: it instructed governments to stop discriminating. It is important to bear in mind, however, that in another way it was not in the least libertarian: the opinion argued that the strong power of the federal government should be used to stop local communities from making choices informed by their own sense of their history.

What can be said of Justice Kennedy's concurrence, which, as the narrower holding, controls? Unlike the Chief Justice's opinion, it at least emphasized the importance of the nation's historical struggle to establish racial justice, and it understood that racism has not been fully overcome. In consequence, Justice Kennedy concluded that race-based remedies may in some instances be used,[415] while identifying some real defects in the plans under review.[416] Apart from these virtues, however, the opinion exhibited many of the characteristics of Justice Kennedy's majority opinion in *Gonzales v. Carhart*: loose reasoning, lack of definitional clarity, and a marked preference for fantasy over reality. Justice Kennedy argued that race-conscious measures may sometimes have to be used to remedy historical discrimination, but his main objection to the Seattle plan was that it used racial typing.[417] However, he never offered any clear account of how, in the context of elementary education, one could be race-conscious without

---

[414] Justice Thomas's concurrence has a strong link to libertarianism, in its aversion to governmental remedies for social problems. *See id.* at 2768–88 (Thomas, J., concurring).

[415] *See id.* at 2797 (Kennedy, J., concurring in part and concurring in the judgment).

[416] *See id.* at 2790. Particularly troubling is the binary division into "white" and "non-white" in the Seattle plan, which causes difficulty for remedial treatment of African Americans as the Asian population rises. *Id.* at 2790–91.

[417] *See id.* at 2792.

using racial typing. He cited *Grutter v. Bollinger*[418] as an example of how racial criteria may be used along with other criteria, but this is where the opinion veers off course, for there is no relevant similarity between a law school admissions program and a program of assigning children to primary schools. In the former case, the applicants are planning to live away from home, so the main problem in the latter case, distance between home and school, simply does not exist. In the former case there is a dossier on a candidate that contains many factors, since by the age of law school application the candidate has been and done many relevant things. Little children can have no such admissions dossier, from which other factors relevant to admission might be drawn. This all-important opinion is a cipher: it did not announce a set of workable criteria that might possibly substitute for the Seattle criteria, which Justice Kennedy rejected on utterly unclear grounds.[419]

D. *Religion and Standing: Mere Words on Paper?*

Since the seventeenth century, it has been well understood that establishments of religion threaten individual liberty of conscience.[420] This threat was a central theme of James Madison's *Memorial and Remonstrance*, which focused on the evil of taxing citizens for the sup-

---

418 539 U.S. 306 (2003) (holding that the narrowly tailored use of race in law school admissions decisions is not prohibited by the Equal Protection Clause).

419 Another case involving students' capabilities in the area of education is *Morse v. Frederick*, 127 S. Ct. 2618 (2007), which dealt with a student who held up a banner stating "BONG HiTS 4 JESUS." This case is complicated because, as the CA insists and as the Court's precedents state, the entitlements of minors are not the same as those of adults: to produce adult abilities, we sometimes need to curtail young people's freedoms, as the very idea of compulsory education acknowledges. In *Bethel School District No. 403 v. Fraser*, 478 U.S. 675 (1986), the Court noted that "the constitutional rights of students in public school are not automatically coextensive with the rights of adults in other settings." *Id.* at 682. Moreover, the Court in *Bethel* held that certain restrictions on speech were essential to protect an atmosphere of civility within which students learn skills of citizenship. *Id.* at 683. The CA agrees, and thus the capabilities question is clearly two-sided. In *Morse*, then, it is not surprising to find arguments referring to capabilities on both sides. The majority, citing *Tinker v. Des Moines Independent Community School District*, 393 U.S. 503 (1969), which held that student expression may be limited only if school authorities reasonably believe that it will "materially and substantially disrupt the work and discipline of the school," *id.* at 513, emphasized the disrupting effect that the promotion of drug use can have on the climate of learning, following the general line of argument in *Bethel*. *See Morse*, 127 S. Ct. at 2628. The dissent is concerned that the silliness and vagueness of the sign's reference to drugs may license a wide-ranging set of restrictions on student speech. *Id.* at 2650 (Stevens, J., dissenting). Both sides have strong capability-type arguments, and thus the case is a difficult one. One might well think *Bethel* wrongly decided, because the student speech that caused so much alarm was incredibly silly and sophomoric and not particularly disruptive; once that case is a precedent, however, Morse's silly sign seems no less, if no more, disruptive. Finally, both *Bethel* and *Morse* show a certain failure of imagination, in the sense that someone who lives (sympathetically) around adolescents or can imagine what it is like to be one would probably not be as shocked by the utterances in question as some of the Justices appear to be.

420 *See supra* section III.B, pp. 41–45.

port of the established church. In its 1968 *Flast v. Cohen*[421] decision, the Court, citing Madison, adopted an unusually broad account of standing in the context of Establishment Clause challenges. In support of this view, the Court stated that:

> The concern of Madison and his supporters was quite clearly that religious liberty ultimately would be the victim if government could employ its taxing and spending powers to aid one religion over another or to aid religion in general. The Establishment Clause was designed as a specific bulwark against such potential abuses of governmental power, and that clause of the First Amendment operates as a specific constitutional limitation upon the exercise by Congress of the taxing and spending power . . . .[422]

Flast concerned a specific appropriation, and thus did not address the question of spending for religious purposes that derives from general discretionary funds. The use of such funds by the Executive to hold conferences in connection with the President's Faith-Based and Community Initiatives was challenged by a citizen group in *Freedom from Religion Foundation, Inc. v. Chao*.[423] In 2006, a three-judge panel of the Seventh Circuit, in an opinion by Judge Posner, held that the group did have standing under *Flast* to challenge the appropriations for these conferences.[424] In *Hein v. Freedom from Religion Foundation, Inc.*,[425] the Supreme Court reversed. The opinion written by Justice Alito and joined by Chief Justice Roberts and Justice Kennedy held that the Seventh Circuit interpreted *Flast* too broadly. The proper interpretation, in Justice Alito's eyes, was that *Flast* protects taxpayer standing only in the case of specific congressional appropriations.[426] Justices Scalia and Thomas, concurring in the judgment, favored overruling *Flast* altogether.[427] Justice Souter's dissenting opinion, joined by Justices Stevens, Ginsburg, and Breyer, agreed with the Seventh Circuit.[428]

Hein, even more than *Ledbetter*, was a difficult case from the legal point of view, in that both the prevailing opinion and the dissent had good legal arguments. Inevitably, therefore, a judge's sense of the nature of the problem and its history played a larger than usual part. Judge Posner did indeed defend a broad reading of *Flast* that is not absolutely entailed by the text (although his powerful argument was buttressed by his use of *Bowen v. Kendrick*[429]). Nonetheless, when one

---

421 392 U.S. 83 (1968).
422 *Id.* at 103–04 (footnotes omitted).
423 433 F.3d 989 (7th Cir. 2006).
424 *Id.* at 996–97.
425 127 S. Ct. 2553 (2007).
426 *Id.* at 2568 (plurality opinion).
427 *Id.* at 2584 (Scalia, J., concurring in the judgment).
428 *Id.* at 2587–88 (Souter, J., dissenting).
429 487 U.S. 589 (1988).

considers the importance of the underlying issue at stake, it is difficult not to be alarmed by Justice Alito's indifference to the problem of minority conscience, a central issue in our political tradition since long before the Founding. The problem Judge Posner raised is a large one: if *Flast* were not read broadly, the Executive would be permitted to erect a national mosque using taxpayer money.[430] Judge Posner chose his example hypothetically, preserving a polite detachment from political reality. The reality, however, would of course be the use of taxpayer money to create a national Christian church, or in countless other ways to sponsor programs that put the official stamp of approval on Christianity and implicitly disendorse and marginalize other religions. (The taxpayer group's challenge used the language of endorsement and disendorsement, familiar from Justice O'Connor's reformulation of Madison's *Memorial and Remonstrance*, to express what they found troubling about the President's choices.)

In a case where the law is to some extent indeterminate, perception often plays the deciding role. In *Hein*, the dissenters were rightly worried about the threat to equal liberty of conscience posed by the use of taxpayer money for religious purposes. By contrast, Justice Alito's opinion, written as if the burden of an imagined flood of litigation were the major problem presented by the case, exhibited a startling indifference to an issue that is so deeply implicated in the whole history of our nation. Equal liberty of conscience, as Madison made clear, lies at the root of more or less all of our capabilities as citizens, since it affects our ability to enter the public square "on equal conditions."[431]

VI. CONCLUSION: CAPABILITIES AND THE 2006 TERM

From its inception, our nation has made a commitment to the protection of human capabilities, on a basis of equality for all. Some of these capabilities receive explicit protection in the constitutional text; others have been recognized as fundamental rights through the jurisprudence of the Fourteenth Amendment. Still others have never been securely recognized as *constitutional* rights, and have been pursued primarily through legislative action. (Nonetheless, such capabilities still raise constitutional issues in some contexts: education often raises issues of equality, while welfare rights raise procedural due process issues.) The Court, then, has a significant role to play in protecting human capabilities through its interpretive role. Much hangs on its orientation to that task. Do the Court's opinions attempt to understand the particular struggles of historically disadvantaged groups with de-

430 Freedom from Religion Found., Inc. v. Chao, 433 F.3d 989, 994 (7th Cir. 2006).

431 MADISON, *supra* note 138.

tail and realism, or do they stand so far above history that these struggles can barely be seen? Do they ask about the obstacles real people face on the way to exercising their legal rights, or do they ignore such realities in favor of a lofty formalism?

The CA has always been but one strand in our tradition of constitutional jurisprudence. It has never been unopposed, and one could easily find cases in previous Terms that exemplify the features that I have criticized in some of the 2006 Term's cases.[432] A group of highly contested cases, however, signal a possible change of course, a shift away from the CA toward a different type of jurisprudence altogether. It is hard to characterize this new type. The opinions studied here contain few clear elements of utilitarianism. They do contain some signs of libertarian minimalism in their tendency to restrict the scope of ameliorative government action. Above all, however, what is particularly striking about these opinions is, as I have said, their lofty Wechslerian formalism, and the sense they convey that history and people's actual situations do not matter. At the very least one can see an increasing trend toward formalist victories; we also see, in that connection, an increasing willingness on the part of the Court either to overrule precedents that were not decided in a formalist spirit or to read them very narrowly.

The cases I have discussed, however, are difficult cases, in which formalism does not actually lead to a decisive result. The appearance of clarity is frequently purchased through an omission of history. In some cases, moreover, the very concepts involved — the concept of equal protection most conspicuously — are best understood to invite the judge to ask questions about what people are actually able to do and to be. The formalist approach, in such a case, is not just incomplete, it is an evasion of the best understanding of the constitutional text.

Where does this lofty formalism come from, and what does it mean? In the history of "separate but equal" facilities, from *Brown* to *Loving* to *United States v. Virginia*, opinions that focused on formal symmetry were clearly masks for something worse: a determination to defend entrenched power against the demands of the powerless. Who could possibly say that laws against miscegenation impose equal disabilities on both black and white? Only someone who stands so far away from real life that the suffering of exclusion cannot be seen. And why might someone stand so far away from real life? Perhaps because of inexperience (although there would usually be some further reason

[432] One of the most obvious such cases is *Plessy v. Ferguson*, 163 U.S. 537 (1896). I argue above, for example, that *Employment Division v. Smith*, 494 U.S. 872 (1990), embodies some of the features of "lofty formalism." One could easily read *Bowers v. Hardwick*, 478 U.S. 186 (1986), along similar lines.

why an educated adult would remain so inexperienced). Perhaps because of a fear of upsetting the social applecart: if one really looks at the excluded, they make demands, and these demands are often very unsettling. Or perhaps out of a fear of political contestation: if only one could resolve difficult cases involving competing groups through some abstract formal device, then (so it might be thought) peace could be more easily preserved. Perhaps out of an asymmetrical cultivation of sympathy: the powerful are more familiar, more like one's friends, and the powerless just do not look as big or as significant. The CA says: Don't be like that. Get some experience. Learn about the world. Use your imagination.

One hesitates to compare the work of the current Court to the most obviously flawed judgments of the Court's (and the nation's) past. And yet, one can at least observe that the refusal of realistic imagination involved in so many of these disturbing cases, and, with it, the concealing and comforting embrace of an obtuse formalism, have the result of entrenching power and privilege, and of marginalizing the weak. If they do not have that purpose, at least they have that effect.

Such an approach is dangerous for our nation, so admirable in its purposes, so deficient, often, in delivering real opportunities to real people.

[8]

Constitutions and Capabilities: A (Necessarily) Pragmatic Approach

Diane P. Wood*

I. INTRODUCTION

Professor Nussbaum has thrown down the gauntlet in her Foreword:[1] do countries have a moral obligation to develop and abide by constitutional principles that will lead to the full development of all human beings? Or is it either necessary or appropriate to take a more laissez-faire approach to the nurturing of human potential, perhaps because of the risk that governments might be too intrusive, or because of a concern about diverting enough resources from private control to governmental control to get the job done?

There is a great deal to admire in Professor Nussbaum's Capabilities Approach (CA). Human beings are fundamentally social creatures. Before it is anything else, human history is the tale of groups of people and how they have chosen to live together and to interact with other groups. As the Foreword notes, the Founders of the United States drew on a rich intellectual history when they wrote the federal Constitution.[2] Someone reading the Constitution for the first time, however, is not likely to think immediately of the CA. That suggests two questions: First, is Professor Nussbaum right when she argues that a society's constitution *ought* to include provisions designed to develop human capabilities? And second, even if this is a worthy goal, is there anything useful that judges can or should do to further that goal?

---

* Circuit Judge, US Court of Appeals for the Seventh Circuit, and Senior Lecturer in Law, The University of Chicago.

1 Martha C. Nussbaum, *Foreword: Constitutions and Capabilities: "Perception" Against Lofty Formalism*, 121 Harv L Rev 4, 56–59 (Nov 2007).

2 Id at 40–41.

II. Capabilities and Their Place in Law

A. Generally

It is helpful to begin with a quick review of the CA. In footnote 15 of the Foreword, Professor Nussbaum sets out the specific capabilities that she has identified (in the Foreword as well as in other work) as "necessary conditions of a life worthy of human dignity."[3] Here is the list:

1. Life
2. Bodily Health
3. Bodily Integrity
4. Senses, Imagination, and Thought
5. Emotions
6. Practical Reason
7. Affiliation (both with respect to associations with others and with respect to one's personal dignity with worth equal to that of others)
8. Respect for Other Species
9. Play
10. Control over One's Environment[4]

Law intersects with these capabilities in numerous ways—even more ways than Professor Nussbaum identifies in the Foreword. At a very practical level, law authorizes the employment of police, who must assure public safety and security and restrain those who do not respect the rights and autonomy of others. It protects freedoms to speak, to associate, and to choose and follow a religion. It forces those who might pollute the environment to internalize the costs they are imposing on all around them. It provides for mechanisms through which things like health care and education are delivered.

But law is capable of doing more than this. One can see a glimpse of that potential in the two great international covenants on human rights: the International Covenant on Civil and Political Rights (ICCPR), to which the United States is one of 165 states parties,[5] and the International Covenant on Economic, Social and Cultural Rights (ICESCR), to which the United States is

---

3 Id at 15 n 15; see also Martha C. Nussbaum, *Frontiers of Justice: Disability, Nationality, Species Membership* 76–78 (Harvard 2006); Martha C. Nussbaum, *Women and Human Development: The Capabilities Approach* 78–80 (Cambridge 2000).

4 Nussbaum, 121 Harv L Rev at 15 n 15 (cited in note 1).

5 International Covenant on Civil and Political Rights ("ICCPR") , 999 UN Treaty Ser 171 (Dec 16, 1966, entered into force Mar 23, 1976); UN, *Status of Multilateral Treaties Deposited With The Secretary General: International Covenant on Civil and Political Rights*, online at http://treaties.un.org/Pages/ViewDetails.aspx?src=TREATY&mtdsg_no=IV-4&chapter=4&lang=en (visited Nov 21, 2009).

not among the 160 states parties.[6] The two covenants entered into force in 1976.[7] They are expressly designed to operate together (in spite of the fact that nations may subscribe to one but not the other, as the United States has). Thus, the third paragraph of the ICCPR recognizes "that, in accordance with the Universal Declaration of Human Rights, the ideal of free human beings enjoying civil and political freedom and freedom from fear and want can only be achieved if conditions are created whereby everyone may enjoy his civil and political rights, as well as his economic, social and cultural rights."[8] The ICESCR says exactly the same thing, just reversing the final two phrases.[9]

The ICCPR calls on states parties to refrain from discriminating on a variety of grounds, including "race, colour, sex, language, religion, political or other opinion, national or social origin, property, birth, or other status."[10] It specifically requires states to ensure equality between men and women;[11] it guarantees a right to life;[12] it prohibits slavery of all kinds;[13] it assures the right to "liberty and security of person" and a variety of criminal procedure rights;[14] it assures liberty of movement;[15] it forbids arbitrary or unlawful interference with "privacy, family, or correspondence" and "unlawful attacks on . . . honor and reputation";[16] and it provides for "freedom of thought, conscience and religion," and the right to marry and found a family.[17] In short, the ICCPR spells out in even more detail than the Bill of Rights in the US Constitution a comprehensive set of civil rights. Most, if not all, of the rights recognized in the ICCPR are negative in character, which is to say that they describe areas into which government may not intrude, or actions that government may not take.

---

6 International Covenant on Economic, Social and Cultural Rights ("ICESCR"), 993 UN Treaty Ser 3 (Dec 16, 1966, entered into force Jan 3, 1976); UN, *Status of Multilateral Treaties Deposited With The Secretary General: International Covenant on Economic, Social and Cultural Rights*, online at http://treaties.un.org/Pages/ViewDetails.aspx?src=TREATY&mtdsg_no=IV-3&chapter=4&lang=en (visited Nov 21, 2009).

7 ICCPR, 999 UN Treaty Ser 171 (cited in note 5), ICESCR, 993 UN Treaty Ser 3 (cited in note 6).

8 ICCPR, Preamble, ¶ 3 (cited in note 5).

9 ICESCR, Preamble, ¶ 3 (cited in note 6).

10 ICCPR, Art 2.1 (cited in note 5).

11 Id at Art 3.

12 Id at Art 6.

13 Id at Art 8.

14 ICCPR, Arts 9, 10, 14, 15 (cited in note 5).

15 Id at Art 12.

16 Id at Art 17.

17 Id at Arts 18, 23.

The ICESCR, in contrast, picks up the theme of affirmative rights—areas in which governments must act. Many of its provisions look as if they came straight out of Professor Nussbaum's CA. The ICESCR recognizes that states (particularly developing countries) may not have the resources to achieve full compliance with its terms immediately, but it requires each state "to take steps . . . to the maximum of its available resources, with a view to achieving progressively the full realization of the rights recognized in" the Covenant.[18] Thus, the ICESCR recognizes not only the right to work, but also the right to "technical and vocational guidance and training programmes, policies and techniques."[19] Not only that, but it requires states to ensure fair wages, equal pay for equal work, the ability to earn "[a] decent living for [workers] and their families," safe and healthy working conditions, equal chances for promotion, and adequate rest and limitation of working hours.[20] The ICESCR also recognizes "the right of everyone to social security, including social insurance."[21] Articles 11, 12, 13, and 14 are especially notable in their congruence with the CA.[22] Article 11 acknowledges "the right of everyone to an adequate standard of living for himself and his family, including adequate food, clothing, and housing."[23] Article 12 recognizes "the right of everyone to the enjoyment of the highest attainable standard of physical and mental health."[24] Articles 13 and 14 address the right to education.[25] Article 13.1 flatly says, "The States Parties to the present Covenant recognize the right of everyone to education. They agree that education shall be directed to the full development of the human personality and the sense of its dignity, and shall strengthen the respect for human rights and fundamental freedoms."[26] The ICESCR calls for free and compulsory primary education and the progressive introduction of free secondary education "in its different forms, including technical and vocational" education.[27] Finally, it recognizes the right of all persons to participate in cultural life.[28]

---

18 ICESCR, Art 2.1 (cited in note 6).

19 Id at Art 6.

20 Id at Art 7.

21 Id at Art 9.

22 ICESCR, Arts 11–14 (cited in note 6).

23 Id at Art 11.

24 Id at Art 12.

25 Id at Arts 13–14.

26 ICESCR, Art 13.1 (cited in note 6).

27 Id at Art 13.2(a)–(b).

28 Id at Art 15.1(a).

The US Constitution recognizes treaties, along with the Constitution and the laws of the United States, as part of the "supreme Law of the Land."[29] Before turning directly to the Constitution, it is therefore fair to ask what impact the ICCPR has on US law, given the fact that the United States is a party to that Covenant. The answer is more complex than one might imagine. As Professor Louis Henkin has pointed out, the United States has regularly attached to its ratifications of the major human rights treaties "a 'package' of reservations, understandings and declarations (RUDs),"[30] designed to ensure that the treaty in question will not be understood as creating individually enforceable rights and to underscore the Senate's understanding that the treaty does not require any changes to existing US law.

A set of RUDs to this effect was appended to the Senate's consent to ratification of the ICCPR.[31] It is noteworthy that Section II, Paragraph 5 of the RUDs explicitly states that the power to implement the ICCPR lies primarily in the hands of the federal government; that is to say, the Covenant is not self-executing and does not create any new domestic rights of its own force.[32] By so providing, the Senate ensured that no possible argument could be made under *Missouri v Holland*,[33] to the effect that the treaty conferred rights that went beyond those that Congress could have embodied in legislation, and it also gave notice that the United States did not regard its adherence to the Covenant as requiring any changes in existing US law or practice.

The ICCPR remains important for US law insofar as one is talking about congressional action and executive branch policy. But, as a result of the RUDs, it cannot be invoked directly in court as a source of rights. *A fortiori*, the ICESCR does not have the force of law in the United States, because the United States is not a party to that Covenant. The net result is that neither treaty provides a solid basis for someone seeking to find legal support for the CA in US law. For that, it is necessary to turn directly to domestic law and to see whether, or to what extent, there is a basis from which one could develop a more self-conscious CA.

---

29 US Const, Art VI, ¶ 2.

30 Louis Henkin, *U.S. Ratification of Human Rights Conventions: The Ghost of Senator Bricker*, 89 Am J Intl L 341, 341 (1995).

31 US Senate Resolution of Advice and Consent to Ratification of the International Covenant on Civil and Political Rights, Ex Cal 17, 102d Cong 2d Sess in 138 Cong Rec S 4781 (Apr 2, 1992) (Listing the reservations, declarations, and understanding to accompany US ratification of the ICCPR).

32 Id; see also *Buell v Mitchell*, 274 F3d 337, 372 (6th Cir 2001) (recognizing that the ICCPR is not self-executing and citing other cases to the same effect).

33 252 US 416, 432–33 (1920) (holding the constitutional limitations on the legislative power of the federal government do not apply when the national government ratifies a self-executing treaty).

B. Constitutional Recognition

As Professor Nussbaum notes, many countries with more recently written constitutions, including places like India and South Africa, have included in their constitutions provisions that explicitly adopt or reflect the CA.[34] (Many of these countries wrote their constitutions well after the entry into force of the ICCPR and the ICESCR; it is thus not surprising to see the principles of the covenants reflected in them.)[35] These constitutions guarantee such benefits as access to health care, adequate housing, and a basic education to all persons in the country.[36]

Provisions addressing these topics are not unknown in the United States, but they do not appear at the federal constitutional level. State constitutions, to a degree, are a different matter. Because, under the original constitutional design, the states retained sovereignty over everything that was not delegated to the federal government, the states were (and in some ways still are) the governing entities of last resort in the United States. States remain responsible for some of the most fundamental government tasks, such as the creation of relationships between people (marriage, adoption, inheritance), education, the definition and enforcement of property rights, and the law of contract. While federal criminal law exists and is growing, the states remain the primary actors in the criminal arena.

It is beyond the scope of this Article to provide details about all of those fields, but since education figures so centrally in the CA, a look at the education provisions in several state constitutions helps to illustrate the potential importance of the states for someone committed to the CA. Some state constitutions firmly establish a right to an education. Thus, the constitution of Arizona states, "The legislature shall enact such laws as shall provide for the establishment and maintenance of a general and uniform public school system."[37] The constitution of Massachusetts goes on at rather flowery length about the importance of education:

> Wisdom, and knowledge, as well as virtue, diffused generally among the body of the people, being necessary for the preservation of their rights and liberties; and as these depend on spreading the opportunities and advantages

34 Nussbaum, 121 Harv L Rev at 67 (cited in note 1).

35 See, for example, India Const, Art 38 (enacted in 1978 and providing for the promotion of "the welfare of the people by securing and protecting . . . a social order in which justice, social, economic and political, shall inform all the institutions of the national life"); South Africa Const, Arts 26–27, 29 (enacted in 1996 and providing a right to basic education, adequate housing, and access to health care services).

36 India Const, Arts 21A, 38; South Africa Const, Arts 26–27, 29.

37 Ariz Const, Art XI, § 1.

> of education in the various parts of the country, and among the different orders of the people, it shall be the duty of legislatures and magistrates, in all future periods of this commonwealth, to cherish the interests of literature and the sciences, and all seminaries of them; especially the university at Cambridge, public schools and grammar schools in the towns; to encourage private societies and public institutions, rewards and immunities, for the promotion of agriculture, arts, sciences, commerce, trades, manufactures, and a natural history of the country; to countenance and inculcate the principles of humanity and general benevolence, public and private charity, industry and frugality, honesty and punctuality in their dealings; sincerity, good humor, and all social affections, and generous sentiments among the people.[38]

Kentucky takes a more terse approach; its constitution says only, "The General Assembly shall, by appropriate legislation, provide for an efficient system of common schools throughout the State."[39] And the constitution of Alabama, while acknowledging the policy of the state "to foster and promote the education of its citizens in a manner and extent consistent with its available resources," cautions that nothing in the constitution should be understood as creating any right to an education or training at public expense.[40] Illinois's constitution proclaims that "[a] fundamental goal of the People of the State is the educational development of all persons to the limits of their capacities," and it requires the state to provide for "an efficient system of high quality public educational institutions and services," that is free through the secondary level.[41] It appears, therefore, that many if not most of the states are already convinced of the central importance of education to a fully functioning community.

Matters are different at the federal level, although part of the reason for this has to do with the kind of federal structure the Framers of the Constitution chose to adopt. As is well known, the 1787 text of the Constitution was devoted almost entirely to the machinery of government. James Madison and Alexander Hamilton, in the essays that were later published as *The Federalist Papers*, argued that a properly organized government will deliver justice to all, will contain within itself all that is necessary to defeat factionalism, and basic rights will be protected by legislatures.[42] The people of the several states, however, were unwilling to place all their trust in this indirect protection of basic rights, and so they insisted that a Bill of Rights be added to the Constitution—as it was, in

---

38 Mass Const, Pt 2, Ch V, § 2.

39 Ky Const, § 183.

40 Ala Const, Amend 111, § 256.

41 Ill Const, Art X, § 1.

42 The Honorable Diane P. Wood, *Madison Lecture: Our 18th Century Constitution in the 21st Century World*, 80 NYU L Rev 1079, 1087–1088 (2005) (arguing, among other things, that the Framers did not intend for the Constitution to contain a complete list of protected individual rights).

1791. The Bill of Rights addresses a few of the prerequisites to a CA, but, as Professor Nussbaum's Foreword demonstrates, far from all.[43] To the extent that the US Constitution has made room for a CA at the constitutional level, it has been through devices such as incorporation of many parts of the Bill of Rights through Section 1 of the Fourteenth Amendment (thus ensuring, for example, that the states, to the same degree as the federal government, are forbidden from establishing a religion, or from imposing prior restraints on speech, or from conducting unreasonable searches and seizures), or the doctrine of "substantive due process," through which the law protects certain aspects of the dignity and inviolability of the individual.[44]

Nevertheless, some clauses in the federal Constitution—though not as many as Professor Nussbaum might prefer—might be seen as guides to the two democratically elected branches of government, Congress and the President, telling them what kind of legislation ought to be passed, and in what spirit that legislation ought to be enforced. The Preamble to the Constitution can be read as just that kind of instruction. Its familiar language announces that the Constitution is being created in order (among other things) to "promote the general Welfare and secure the Blessings of Liberty to ourselves and our Posterity."[45] These purposes presumably inform the understanding of all that follows. Article I, Section 8, Clause 18, known as the Necessary and Proper Clause, gives Congress the power to "make all Laws which shall be necessary and proper for carrying into Execution the foregoing Powers and all other Powers vested by this Constitution in the Government of the United States."[46] Article I, Section 9, Clause 8, the Titles of Nobility Clause, forbids all such distinctions among people.[47] It can fairly be seen as an early expression of the equality principle. Finally, Article VI, Paragraph 3, anticipates the Religion Clauses of the First Amendment in its command that "no religious Test shall ever be required as a Qualification to any Office or public Trust under the United States."[48] Clauses like these, including the Republican Form of Government clause of Article IV, Section 4, have not typically been recognized as giving rise to individual rights enforceable in courts.[49] But it would be a great fallacy to think that a part of the Constitution that is addressed to the Legislative or Executive Branch is somehow unimportant. The contrary is true. Indeed, for

---

43 See Nussbaum, 121 Harv L Rev at 56–59 (cited in note 1).

44 US Const, Amend XIV, § 1.

45 Id at Preamble.

46 Id at Art I, § 8, Clause 18.

47 Id at Art I, § 9, Clause 8.

48 US Const, Art VI, ¶ 3.

49 Id at Art IV, § 4.

someone committed to the CA, these clauses may be just as important (if not more so) than the more conventional judicially enforceable constitutional rules.

III. The CA as an Interpretative Guide

As one comes closer to a strong version of the CA that could actually be enforced in domestic courts by individual litigants (as is the case in some other countries around the world), it becomes more difficult to imagine how one might implement Professor Nussbaum's ideas. Before turning to domestic applications, it is worth noting that the position of international courts like the International Court of Justice (ICJ) is different. The ICJ hears only cases between states, and Article 38 of the court's Statute explicitly recognizes international conventions as a source of law.[50] But a decision of the ICJ interpreting either the ICCPR or the ICESCR would be binding on a particular country only if it had consented to the court's jurisdiction, and the United States has not done so for disputes relating to the ICCPR. In parts of her Foreword, however, Professor Nussbaum points the way to an intriguing possibility: that is, using the CA as a canon of constitutional and statutory interpretation.[51]

A. The Charming Betsy

Returning to the topic of domestic US law, there are some useful analogies to be drawn between the CA and other areas the courts have encountered. In many ways, the CA calls to mind a very old Supreme Court decision known as *Murray v Schooner Charming Betsy*,[52] where the Court addressed the similarly knotty question of how customary international law is to be treated in US courts. Its conclusion in *Charming Betsy* is now practically Holy Writ among international lawyers: "[A]n act of Congress ought never to be construed to violate the law of nations if any other possible construction remains."[53] Substitute "the capabilities approach" for "the law of nations," and one would have something close to what Professor Nussbaum's Foreword advocates.

In some ways, the CA is quite similar to customary international law. The American Law Institute's Restatement (Third) of the Law of Foreign Relations, in discussing the sources of international law, begins with the statement that "[a] rule of international law is one that has been accepted as such by the

---

50 See Statute of the International Court of Justice, Art 38(1)(a), 59 Stat 1055, Treaty Serial No 993 (1945).

51 See Nussbaum, 121 Harv L Rev at 56–60 (cited in note 1).

52 6 US (2 Cranch) 64 (1804) (stating that "an act of Congress ought never to be construed to violate the law of nations if any other possible construction remains").

53 Id at 118.

international community of states (a) in the form of customary law."[54] It then describes "customary international law" as law that "results from a general and consistent practice of states followed by them from a sense of legal obligation."[55] This is plainly a far cry from a statute that one can find in black and white in a book, or a provision of a written constitution, although it has some kinship with the common law. Because it is more difficult to ascertain the precise content of customary international law, and there are times when it seems to be honored in the breach, some people are not sure if it ought to be called "law" at all. Others, including the authors of the Restatement (Third), take the position that there is indeed a difference between the rules of customary international law and day-to-day government policy.[56]

It is well beyond the scope of this Article to take and defend a position on this longstanding debate. Rather, it is enough to point out that the CA's position in the legal order is similarly difficult to pinpoint: is there really a legally enforceable right to an education? Do people really have a right to state-supported development of their capabilities? What happens if the state falls down on the job? A presumption like that of the *Charming Betsy* works only if it is fair to assume that this is the tiebreaker that Congress (or any other legislature) wants—that is, to comply with customary international law, or to advance the CA. Although it is difficult to point to concrete evidence showing that Congress is committed to a CA approach, it may be even more difficult to support the position that Congress is hostile to it. If, therefore, in case of doubt a court is compelled to make one or the other assumption (that is, should the law be read in a way consistent with the CA, or inconsistent with it) sources from the Preamble to the Constitution to the statements of purpose in statutes might, in many contexts, support a default assumption that reflects the CA.

B. Context Versus Plain Meaning

Another way of looking at the CA is as a method of interpretation, rather than some kind of canon. This is particularly useful if the case at hand requires careful attention to the details of a person's condition, rather than the "lofty formalism" that Professor Nussbaum condemns. None of the methods of interpretation that are currently the subject of debate among the Justices on the Supreme Court is a perfect fit for the CA, but some may be more compatible with it than others. One school of thought is "originalism," which Justice Scalia has advocated strongly; in his view, this is the only legitimate approach to

54 Restatement (Third) of the Foreign Relations Law of the United States § 102(1)(a) (1987).

55 Id at § 102(2).

56 Id at §§ 101–103.

constitutional interpretation. While there are now several strands of originalism, Justice Scalia's version favors strict adherence to the plain meaning of the words in the Constitution, as they would have been understood at the time the relevant section was written.[57] Thus, in *District of Columbia v Heller,*[58] Justice Scalia's opinion turns to eighteenth century dictionaries and to phrases elsewhere in the Constitution in order to interpret the Second Amendment.[59] He also consults other written documents of the founding period to see how the phrase "keep arms" was used by the authors of the Amendment.[60] What he did *not* find relevant was the context of the right to bear arms in the modern world, or the reasons why the people of the District of Columbia might have been concerned about gun violence, or even Mr. Heller's need for a gun.

Justice Breyer, in a number of debates with Justice Scalia, has urged a different kind of contextual approach—one in which courts defer to the judgments of the democratically elected branches of government unless there is reason to fear the kind of tyranny of the majority that Madison decried.[61] Although there is no guarantee that this "active liberty" approach, as Justice Breyer calls it, will coincide perfectly with the CA, in practice there appears to be significant overlap. By focusing on factors like congressional intent, the purpose of a law, the problem that the law was designed to address, and the question whether the law as applied in the particular case will further or frustrate those purposes, someone following Justice Breyer's approach will acquire a rich understanding of the human dimensions of the case before the court. The law itself does not change, of course, but the factual matrix to which the law is applied is likely to be more complex. Professor Nussbaum predicts that greater nuance will be fostered by a deeper understanding of the facts, and that this in turn is likely to produce decisions that are relatively more consistent with the CA than decisions that restrict the range of relevant information to the "plain meaning" or "original intent" of the law.[62]

---

57 Consider Justice Antonin Scalia, *Foreword*, 31 Harv J L & Pub Pol 871 (2008) (summarizing Justice Scalia's view of originalism); see also Steven G. Calabresi, *A Critical Introduction to the Originalism Debate*, 31 Harv J L & Pub Pol 875, 883 (2008) (providing an introduction to the debate over originalism and some of the varying strands).

58 128 S Ct 2783 (2008) (holding that the Second Amendment protects an individual right to bear arms for self-defense).

59 Id at 2791–94.

60 Id at 2791–92.

61 *A Conversation on the Constitution: Perspectives from Active Liberty and A Matter of Interpretation*, American Constitution Society debate between Justice Scalia and Justice Breyer (Dec 5 2006), online at http://www.acslaw.org/node/3909 (visited Nov 21, 2009).

62 Nussbaum, 121 Harv L Rev at 78–79 (cited in note 1).

The Court is split, as Professor Nussbaum's Foreword shows, between Justices who think it important first to look at the entire background and purpose of a statute or constitutional provision and then to ask how it ought to apply to the particular person before it, on the one hand, and those who favor a more formalistic approach, on the other.[63] Those who are attracted to the image of Lady Justice with the blindfold on her eyes will tend to favor the Scalia approach—individual differences do not and cannot matter, else overall justice will not be done. Those who prefer Portia as their model and want their justice tempered with mercy and tailored to the particulars of a case are likely to try harder to understand the purpose of the law and how it will affect those to whom it applies. To the extent that the law is flexible enough to permit this inquiry, the outcomes are more likely to be consistent with the CA.

IV. The CA as a Source of Individually Enforceable Rights

The most difficult application of the CA for courts in the United States—or, more starkly put, the least likely application—is as a source of individual rights that can be directly enforced in a court.[64] Here it is important to recall the various elements of the CA that Professor Nussbaum has described. A recent example from the Seventh Circuit shows how difficult it would be to introduce CA-based rights directly into American jurisprudence. The case was called *Sandage v Board of Commissioners of Vanderburgh County*.[65] The plaintiffs were relatives of three people who had been murdered by a man named Moore while Moore was on work-release from a four-year prison sentence he was serving for robbery.[66] One of the victims, Sheena Sandage-Shofner, had contacted the

63 Id at 82.

64 It is worth noting that courts in countries whose constitutions reflect the principles of both the ICCPR and the ICESCR, and which are parties to both Covenants, may be less constrained in this respect. Article 2 of the new Optional Protocol to the ICESCR, adopted in late 2008, offers individuals within the jurisdiction of a State party a new avenue to seek enforcement of the rights enshrined in the ICESCR. See *Optional Protocol to the International Covenant on Economic, Social, and Cultural Rights, Resolution A/RES/63/117*, UN General Assembly, 63d Sess (Dec 10, 2008), UN Doc A/RES/63/117. Consider Michael J. Dennis and David P. Stewart, *Justiciability of Economic, Social, and Cultural Rights: Should There Be an International Complaints Mechanism to Adjudicate the Rights to Food, Water, Housing and Health?*, 98 Am J Intl L 462 (2004). As Dennis and Stewart point out, it is very difficult to draft provisions that at the same time confer individually enforceable rights and yet take a realistic approach to the ability of any given State to find the resources to comply with those rights.

65 548 F3d 595 (7th Cir 2008) (noting that as "the Constitution is a charter of negative liberties," there is no federal constitutional right to be protected against private violence that the government is not complicit in).

66 Id at 596.

sheriff's department twice to complain that Moore was harassing her, but the authorities failed to respond until it was too late.[67] The plaintiffs' effort to hold the sheriff responsible did not succeed.[68] Some of the language in Judge Richard Posner's opinion for the court throws light on the difficulties that one would encounter in trying to implement the CA in this most immediate way:

> We assume, given the procedural posture, that the defendants were reckless in failing to act on the complaint of harassment . . . . There is no federal constitutional right to be protected by the government against private violence in which the government is not complicit. So the Supreme Court held in *DeShaney v. Winnebago County Dept. of Social Services*, 489 U.S. 189 [1989] . . . . In *Bowers v. DeVito*, 686 F.2d 616, 618 (7th Cir. 1982) . . . we had said that while "there is a constitutional right not to be murdered by a state officer, for the state violates the Fourteenth Amendment when its officer, acting under color of state law, deprives a person of life without due process of law, . . . there is no constitutional right to be protected by the state against being murdered by criminals or madmen . . . . The Constitution is a charter of negative liberties; it tells the state to let people alone; it does not require the federal government or the state to provide services, even so elementary a service as maintaining law and order." . . . There is a moral right to such services—protection against violence is the single most important function of government—and a government that fails in this duty invites well-deserved political retribution. But there is no enforceable federal constitutional right.
>
> Such a right would be impractical. The federal courts would have to decide how much money each state and every local community would be required to allocate to protection of life, limb, and property. They would have to decide how much money must be appropriated for police and prosecutors and prisons, how police resources should be deployed across neighborhoods, the minimum length of state prison sentences, when if ever probation or parole should be substituted for imprisonment or a prison sentence suspended, and which state prisoners should be allowed to serve part or all of their sentences in halfway houses, at home, or on work release. The federal courts would fix the speed limits on state highways, prescribe the lighting on state streets, regulate fire departments, public hospitals, and paramedic services.[69]

The *DeShaney* case to which Judge Posner alluded had equally horrifying facts. There, child welfare workers repeatedly visited the home of little Joshua

[67] Id.

[68] Id at 600.

[69] *Sandage*, 548 F3d at 596.

DeShaney, observed that he was being abused by his father, and did nothing.[70] The father eventually beat Joshua so severely that he suffered permanent brain damage and was rendered profoundly retarded.[71] When the family sued, however, the Supreme Court of the United States held that the family failed to state a legal claim against the county department of social services. Once again, indifference—even reckless indifference—on the part of the county was not something that the law reached.[72]

These two cases may well have come out the other way, if the CA were a judicially enforceable part of US law. But the concerns that Judge Posner raised are not fanciful. Judges are ill-equipped to decide whether a sheriff's department should immediately dispatch a deputy after a call, or if a wait-and-see approach is acceptable; or to decide on funding levels for social service departments; or to decide whether a 25-to-1 student-to-teacher ratio is low enough to permit effective learning.

Before the CA could be adopted in this final robust form, it would be necessary to find principled ways in which to draw these kinds of lines. Ideally, those lines would be drawn by the legislature, in implementing legislation. Without such an anchor, judges would be hard-pressed to explain the sources of law on which they were relying. Although it may be tempting to draw the line between public liability and non-liability based on the severity of the harm to which the inaction led (death in *Sandage,* profound mental retardation in *DeShaney*), there is a troublesome *ex post* quality to such a rule. Another possibility might be to draw sharp lines between individual liability and government liability, but it is worth noting that both *DeShaney* and *Sandage* were primarily against institutions rather than individual officers. One might look at the right that the state is failing to deliver—health care is a good example for the millions of uninsured people in the United States—and ask what kind of remedy a judge could give that might change things for them.

I confess that I find it difficult to imagine how a federal court could implement the most ambitious parts of the CA, other than by the more modest interpretative conventions noted earlier. Judges in countries with specially designated constitutional courts have also had more freedom to act, since the

---

70 *DeShaney v Winnebago County Department of Social Services*, 489 US 189, 191–93 (1989) (holding that "nothing in the Due Process Clause itself requires the State to protect the life, liberty, and property of its citizens against invasion by private actors").

71 Id at 193.

72 Id at 195–203.

citizens of those countries have openly opted for this degree of judicial review.[73] One technique that has worked elsewhere has been to understand CA-based constitutional provisions as setting goals that must be realized progressively by legislatures. This, after all, is the approach to which much of the international community is committed, through its adherence to the ICESCR.

One can only hope that Professor Nussbaum will tackle this final problem in her future scholarly work. There is much to admire in her explication of the CA and how it relates to constitutions, not least the fact that she has made it impossible to pretend that formal equality of position will automatically lead to equality of outcomes, or to forget that (to borrow a phrase from a former governor of Texas, Ann Richards) some people are born on third base and think that they hit a triple. Our society can and should do better. The first step is to identify what a full human existence requires, and then it is possible to begin anew to work on ways to achieve it, through all of the institutions and legal mechanisms available.

---

73 See, for example, South Africa Const, Ch 8, Art 167, ¶ 5 (stating that "[t]he Constitutional Court makes the final decision whether an Act of Parliament, a provincial Act or conduct of the President is constitutional").

Part IV
The Family

[9]

The Problem with Polygamy

Thom Brooks
University of Newcastle

Polygamy is a hotly contested practice and open to widespread misunderstandings. This practice is defined as a relationship between either one husband and multiple wives or one wife and multiple husbands. Today, "polygamy" almost exclusively takes the form of one husband with multiple wives. In this article, my focus will center on limited defenses of polygamy offered recently by Chesire Calhoun and Martha Nussbaum. I will argue that these defenses are unconvincing. The problem with polygamy is primarily that it is a structurally inegalitarian practice in both theory and fact. Polygamy should be opposed for this reason.

I

Polygamy is a hotly contested practice and open to widespread misunderstandings. This practice is defined as a relationship between either one husband and multiple wives or one wife and multiple husbands. Today, "polygamy" almost exclusively takes the form of polygyny: one husband with multiple wives.[1] Polygamy is neither exclusively Western nor non-Western: it has been practiced by some Hindus, Mormons, Muslims, and other cultural and religious groups.[2] Furthermore, the Christian Bible notes several polygamous marriages, beginning with Adam and

Eve's grandson, Lamech (who was also the father of Noah), and including several important biblical figures, such as Abraham, David, and Solomon.[3] Nevertheless, the number of polygamous marriages is "relatively minuscule" despite the cross-cultural presence of polygamy (Gher 2008, 561).

The standard of debate over the permissibility of polygamy has been characteristically poor. Thus, for example, some proponents of polygamy argue that it is acceptable, in part, on the grounds that many in Western societies also cohabit with multiple partners, such as married men forming relationships with mistresses.[4] Proponents argue that such persons form relationships that involve "emotional commitments" that are "not easily terminated," not unlike polygamy. Therefore, in essence, a married man and his mistress are engaged in a polygamous relationship, and this does not appear to generate much hostility in the West.[5]

However, it is disingenuous to claim that because a not insignificant number of married men pursue extramarital affairs that these affairs are then unproblematic. There are a number of reasons why this view does not stand up to scrutiny. For example, these affairs are often seen as acts of betrayal. A polygamous marriage may be one where wives recognize each other as wives, but a monogamous marriage may often be one where wives do not recognize mistresses as having equal status. This view is also found in law where mistresses are normally not recognized as having any rights to inheritance from a deceased married lover unless explicitly noted in a will. Furthermore, adultery may no longer be illegal in Western societies and perhaps even widely practised, but adulterous affairs are most often performed secretly and hidden from the public's gaze whereas polygamous marriages are publicly recognized. Thus, polygamy and extramarital affairs are not the same, even if both involve multiple partners. Finally, an additional problem is that this defense of polygamy reduces marriage to only a sexual relationship. On the contrary, the institution of marriage encompasses far more than sexual relations, but extends to a host of other functions, such as property rights, family alliances, and the raising of children. Not only is it a mistake to view polygamy and extramarital affairs as the same, but it is also a mistake to view marriage in terms of sexual relations alone.[6]

Opponents of polygamy offer similarly unconvincing arguments. One example is the 1878 case of *Reynolds v. United States* where the U.S. Supreme Court denied Mormons an exemption from laws criminalizing polygamy because of their religious conviction.[7] First, *Reynolds* claims that polygamy is practised exclusively by "Asiatic" and "African" people: polygamy is thus "odious" and foreign to Western civilization.[8] Mormons are then wrong to attempt to introduce a non-Western practice into American society. This claim fails as polygamy is far from alien in Western culture, not least its practice by major biblical figures.[9] Secondly, *Reynolds* argues that polygamy was "injurious to public morals."[10] The problem with this argument is that the Court does not specify any supporting evidence and, instead, falsely takes the damage to public morals to be obvious.

Thirdly, the Court argues in *Reynolds* that sanctioning polygamy would be akin to legalizing acts such as "human sacrifice" or even *sati*, where wives are burned alive on the funeral pyres of their dead husbands.[11] However, the victims of human sacrifice do not consent to their murder, whereas polygamous partners normally do consent to their marriage. Human sacrifice is then unlike polygamy. Likewise, *sati* has long been illegal in India largely on the grounds that the consent of women is lacking (Nussbaum 2008, 195). Thus, both human sacrifice and *sati* are fundamentally unlike polygamy as only the latter involves consent. If we did sanction polygamy, then there is no reason to believe that it would lead to our sanctioning human sacrifice, *sati*, or similar practices.

In this article, my focus will center on powerful new limited defenses of polygamy recently offered by Chesire Calhoun and Martha Nussbaum. I will argue that these defenses are unconvincing because polygamy is a structurally inegalitarian practice in both theory and fact. I will conclude that, while Calhoun and Nussbaum provide an important new series of arguments in favor of a limited defense of polygamy, this defense is not ultimately successful. Polygamy should be opposed.

The article is structured as follows. Section 2 presents evidence from several studies of polygamy that women in polygamous marriages are at a greater risk of harmful effects. I then explain Calhoun's and Nussbaum's limited defense of polygamy in section 3. In the following section 4, I offer further arguments against their defenses arising from problems associated with the contemporary practice of polygamy. Finally, section 5 will focus on further worries with polygamy even if the practical problems in the preceding sections did not obtain.

II

One argument against polygamy is that it is more likely to present harmful effects, especially toward women and children, than monogamy. There are several studies that appear to support this position.[12] For example, women in polygamous marriages are at higher risk of low self-esteem, as well as depression, than women in nonpolygamous relationships (Al-Krenawi et al. 2002; Slonim-Nevo and Al-Krenawi 2006). Other studies show that these women also enjoy less marital satisfaction and more problematic mother-child relationships (Al-Krenawi and Slonim-Nevo 2008). In addition, further studies demonstrate that women in polygamous marriages are especially vulnerable to depression after becoming pregnant, as their husbands become more likely to turn their attention to their other wives (Fatoye et al. 2004; Ho-Yen et al. 2007). Women in polygamous marriages are typically subservient to their husbands who hold their wives primarily responsible for childbearing (Gher 2008, 584). These women are often unable to exercise any control over the addition of new wives by their husbands, contributing to feelings of powerlessness and emotional abuse (Cook 2007; Hassouneh-Phillips 2001). Women may also lack control over their ability to seek employment, as several studies have found that only a small fraction of women in polygamous marriages work outside the home (Al-Krenawi 2000; Elbedour et al. 2002, 257; Peterson 1999).

Furthermore, women in polygamous marriages have also been found to be at a greater risk of sexual diseases, including AIDS. For example, one study of 1,153 Nigerian men and women found that not only were men with three or more wives more likely to engage in extramarital sex but they also were at greater risk of contracting sexual diseases and infecting their wives than men with one or two wives. Thus, women were at greater risk from men with three or more wives, both as their wives and as extramarital sexual partners, than from men with one or two wives (Mitsunaga et al. 2005).

Studies have also found that children from polygamous families may be at a greater risk of several harmful effects. For example, there is "[c]onsiderable research that children of polygamous families experience a higher incidence of marital conflict, family violence, and family disruptions than do children of monogamous families" (Elbedour et al. 2002). Moreover, children from polygamous marriages are at a greater risk of both behavioral and developmental problems (Elbedour et al. 2003). There is also some evidence that young women from polygamous families perform less well in school than those in monogamous families (Elbedour et al. 2000). In addition, the Utah Supreme Court has recently stated that polygamy "often coincides with crimes targeting women and children[, including] incest, sexual assault, statutory rape, and failure to pay child support" (Strasser 2008, 88–89).[13]

Polygamy has also been linked to several negative effects regarding men. For example, some studies have shown that men are more likely to suffer from alcoholism which is thought, in turn, to perhaps arise from psychological problems with men from polygamous families (Olley 2004). Additionally, men in polygamous marriages are also more likely to fall below men in monogamous marriages in terms of educational attainment (Al-Krenawi and Lightman 2000).

This body of evidence makes clear that there is at least a *prima facie* case to believe that polygamy is linked to an increased likelihood of several harmful effects. These effects impact upon all members of a polygamous family, although women are at the greatest risk. This is not to conclude that women only face such effects in polygamous marriages. Rather, it is clear that women may suffer from these harmful effects in other social contexts as well (Calhoun 2005, 1040). Instead, my purpose here is only to argue that women face a greater risk in polygamous marriages than in monogamous marriages. Thus, polygamy is a structurally inegalitarian practice in fact given what we have learned from several studies because polygamy subjects women to greater risks of harmful effects than men, even if men suffer an additional risk of harm, too.[14]

III

The standard argument against polygamy is that it subordinates women and fails to treat women as equals with men (Okin 1999).[15] For example, John Rawls argues that the state generally should take no interest on "fully voluntary" family arrangements for fear that taking an interest would illegitimately endorse one comprehensive doctrine over others as long as these family arrangements did "not result from or lead to injustice."[16] For Rawls, an unjust family arrangement would be one that undermined "the equality of women" and failed to recognize that "wives are equally citizens with their husbands" with "the same basic rights, liberties, and opportunities as their husbands."[17] Polygamy should then be forbidden by the state insofar as it fails to treat wives as equals with their husbands, denying women the same rights, liberties, and opportunities available to men. Therefore, polygamy represents an unjustified asymmetry of power between men and women: polygamy should be banned.[18]

Chesire Calhoun and Martha Nussbaum are highly sympathetic with this view. For example, Nussbaum argues that polygamy is "a structurally unequal practice" (1999, 98). This inequality lies in the fact that polygamy as practised today normally permits only men to marry multiple wives and it does not normally permit women to marry more than one husband. In fact, Nussbaum argues that "the most convincing" argument against polygamy is that "men are permitted plural marriages, and women are not" (2008, 197). This asymmetry of power is unacceptable. In addition, structural inequality informs Nussbaum's concerns with other issues affecting women. She argues that an "[a]symmetry of power plays a crucial role in the law of sexual harassment" (1999, 407 n. 4). Indeed, one of her arguments against female genital cutting is that it is "unambiguously linked to customs of male domination" (1999, 124). Likewise, polygamy also represents an asymmetry of power between men and women that appears similarly linked to male domination of women.

These arguments do not then lead Nussbaum to reject polygamy in all circumstances. Instead, these reservations against polygamy are conditional upon polygamy justifying the unequal status of women. If women shared equal opportunities to marry more than one husband, then the asymmetry of power between men and women might be broken. Thus, "if there were a sex-equal polygamy" that respected the consent of men and women equally, then such a polygamy would be justified (2008, 197).[19]

Similarly, Calhoun agrees that while there may be structural asymmetries in the practice of polygamy, the unequal status of women is not necessarily essential to the practice of polygamy. She would accept that polygamy is not justified if it were only polygyny in fact. However, polygamy would become justified if either a man or a woman could marry multiple partners. Polygamous marriages then need not entail an unequal status for women and polygamy can be justified (Calhoun 2005, 1038–40).

Polygamy might also be justified on the grounds of consent.[20] For example, when all parties consent to form a polygamous marriage, Nussbaum believes that polygamy is justified so long as there is no asymmetry of power present that would prevent women from choosing multiple partners (2000, 229; 2008, 129). Thus, for Nussbaum, polygamy is only objectionable when it is reserved only for men and where consent is lacking (2000, 229).[21] Polygamy is therefore not entirely unjustified, in principle.

Likewise, Calhoun agrees. She argues that contemporary liberal society does not tolerate any form of civil marriage that fails to assign "equal importance to the consent to all spouses, and which did not offer the exit option of divorce to all spouses" (Calhoun 2005, 1040). The implication of this view is that we should not oppose forms of civil marriage where the consent of all spouses is granted equal importance. Polygamy may offer the opportunity for such consent and, if so, it would be justified.

Neither Calhoun nor Nussbaum argues that polygamy cannot be objectionable. Both demand that polygamous marriages must recognize the equal status of women. Therefore, both men and women should be able to form polygamous marriages with multiple partners: it would be unacceptable to permit only men to marry multiple wives without permitting women to marry multiple husbands. Where such equal opportunities are lacking, polygamy is not justified. Furthermore, it is important that all persons in a polygamous marriage consent to the relationship. Where such consent is lacking, polygamy is not justified on this ground either. Thus, both Calhoun and Nussbaum offer a defense of polygamy within clearly defined parameters.[22]

IV

I believe that Calhoun's and Nussbaum's limited defenses of polygamy fail for several reasons. These reasons are independent of whether there are higher risks of harmful effects associated with polygamy, as discussed in section 2. Both Calhoun and Nussbaum argue that polygamy is unjustified if women are unable to marry multiple husbands. The first problem with this view is that contemporary polygamy is almost exclusively polygyny in fact (Parekh 2006, 290). Polyandry—where one woman has multiple husbands—is exceedingly rare.[23] Part of the reason is that many cultural and religious justifications for polygamy permit only men to marry multiple partners (Rehman 2007). Thus, even if equal opportunities were permissible by law for men and women to marry multiple partners, men and women would not be equal in terms of their actual functionings.[24] This is because the law may permit equal opportunities for polygyny or polyandry, but polygyny and polyandry would not be equal in fact. Consequences matter.[25] When we defend polygamy, our defense may justify both polygyny and polyandry in theory, but only polygyny in actual practice.[26] Our defense of polygamy then is far more likely to legitimize the subordination of women rather than the equal treatment of women. Therefore, polygamy is unjustified (Parekh 2006, 285).

Of course, this objection to polygamy is conditional. If the consequence of permitting polygamy did not lead to polygynous marriages alone, but also to a significant number of polyandrous marriages, then this objection to polygamy would no longer hold (Parekh 2006, 292). Calhoun and Nussbaum may then reply that, if this picture is correct, we have only demonstrated that polygamy is unjustified as practised: we have not successfully argued that polygamy cannot be justified. In section 5, I will address whether polygamy is theoretically sound, even if it should remain problematic in practice.

However, in addition, Calhoun argues that "gender inequality is a contingent, not a conceptual, feature of polygamy" (2005, 1039). As we have already seen, one reason is that polygamy need not be gender inegalitarian if it permits both polygyny and polyandry. Here a second reason is that whether there is gender inequality may also be historically contingent. For example, it was the case that Mormon women in polygamous marriages in Utah enjoyed various rights and privileges unavailable to New England women in monogamous marriages in nineteenth-century America, such as rights to own property and the greater ability to divorce (Calhoun 2005, 1038).

The problem with this argument is twofold. First, it is unclear whether the benefits enjoyed by these women in Utah were the result of living in a polygamous marriage rather than a product of the unique social history of Mormonism. For example, these benefits have not arisen similarly for women in polygamous marriages living elsewhere at any other time. There is no clear evidence that polygamy helped engender these benefits above other competing factors.

Secondly, the argument that gender inequality is historically contingent cuts both ways. For example, Javaid Rehman argues:

> Given the changes in the social, political and legal environment, the continuation of the practice of polygamy demands a substantial explanation. Many of its historic reasons within the Islamic world for justifying polygamous marriages (for example, the surplus of women and loss of men through battles and armed conflict) are no longer tenable. (2007, 115)

While gender inequalities may change over time due to evolving circumstances, changes do take place. If the current circumstances are such that gender inequality is far more likely to be the result of supporting polygamy, then perhaps polygamy becomes a practice that is both currently gender inegalitarian and unlikely to change for the foreseeable future given current conditions. Therefore, polygamy faces substantial justificatory hurdles even if we can imagine the possibility of its permissibility. Nevertheless, polygamy as practised is unlikely to allow for a situation where different consequences would obtain and where the equal standing of women would not be undermined (Parekh 2006, 292).

V

Now let us suppose that polygamy was equally available for men and women in practice without any harmful effects. Furthermore, let us also assume that all persons in these polygamous marriages freely consent to these relationships. Both Calhoun and Nussbaum argue that polygamy may be justified where both conditions hold. In this section, I will argue that polygamy is problematic on the grounds that it threatens the equality between polygamous partners and it discriminates against nonheterosexuals. Each will be taken in turn.

In the previous section, I have argued that polygamy almost exclusively takes the form of polygyny where one man has several wives in fact. Thus, polygamy as a practice is normally a relationship among one man and multiple women. However, polygamy does not only threaten the equality between men and women, but also the equality among polygamous partners. For example, there is the problem with the asymmetrical ability to leave a polygamous marriage. Thus, a husband can divorce any (or all) of the other partners; a wife may only divorce him.[27] Only the husband can choose who will join or leave the relationship through either marriage or divorce. The wives can only choose to marry or divorce their husband, but they cannot choose who else might join or leave the polygamous marriage beyond their husband.[28]

There is then an asymmetry between the opportunities available for a husband versus any of his wives within a polygamous marriage.[29] Let us suppose that a husband has three wives: A, B, and C. While each wife may have consented to each person entering into a polygamous marriage with a shared husband, this is where her consent ends. Each wife may only either agree to all fellow polygamous partners or divorce her husband and leave behind his other wives. Instead, only the husband alone may agree to marry or divorce each wife. As a result, the husband may choose to divorce wife A or rather both wives B and C.

This asymmetry exists whether a polygamous marriage is polygynous or polyandrous. Both polygamous forms entail either one man or woman with multiple partners of the opposite sex. The multiple partners similarly enjoy fewer asymmetrical opportunities than the single husband in a polygynous marriage or a wife in a polyandrous marriage. Therefore, polygamy may not only threaten the equality between men and women in practice (sections 2 and 4), but polygamy also threatens the equality between polygamous partners. If we argue that we should "assign equal importance to the consent to all spouses" including "the exit option of divorce to all spouses" (Calhoun 2005, 1040), then polygamy is unjustified because spouses lack equal options to divorce.[30]

Polygamy also discriminates against nonheterosexuals. Polygamy takes the form of either polygyny (one man with multiple wives) or polyandry (one woman with multiple husbands). Both polygyny and polyandry exclude non-heterosexuals. All forms of polygamy then presuppose that polygamous marriages are heterosexual marriages. If we defend polygamy, then we would have to make available opportunities that would include heterosexuals and exclude nonheterosexuals. Polygamy should then be opposed.

It is not clear that Calhoun and Nussbaum should disagree. For example, Calhoun argues that same-sex marriage advocates may find support in the history of polygamy (2005). While this may remain true, it is also the case that polygamous marriage problematically excludes same-sex marriages with multiple partners. Nussbaum argues that all human beings must be able to exercise several capabilities, including the capability to affiliation. However, this capability forbids discrimination on the basis of sexual orientation (Nussbaum 2000, 79). Thus, polygamy violates the capability to affiliation as it discriminates on the basis of sexual orientation in excluding nonheterosexuals.

One nonmonogamous family structure that may appear more preferable is polyamorous relationships, sometimes referred to as "the postmodern polygamy" (Gher 2008, 572; Sheff 2005). "Polyamory" is a relationship of multiple men and women. These relationships may take the form of one man with several female partners, but they may also take the form of two men and several female partners or even several women with no men.[31]

Polyamory may have several advantages over polygamy. For example, polygamy engenders an asymmetrical power relationship among a man and his wives: he may divorce any or all his wives, but his wives are free only to divorce him and unable to divorce other wives. A polyamorous relationship offers more equal opportunities for divorce than polygamy as all have an equal voice in how the relationship develops. Furthermore, only polyamorous relationships offer more equal opportunities for marriage as only polyamory is inclusive of nonheterosexuals. In fact, a polyamorous relationship may consist only of nonheterosexuals. If our concern is with symmetrical power relationships where all parties freely consent, then polyamory may appear to be more acceptable than polygamy.[32]

The promise of polyamory may be found in its greater inclusiveness, permitting both heterosexuals and nonheterosexuals opportunities to form relationships with multiple partners. However, the primary problem with polyamory is not unlike what we have seen with polygamy. Virtually all polygamous marriages are polygynous in fact. There is no evidence that polyamorous relationships are less likely to lead to polygyny similarly.[33] Thus, polyamory remains problematic for much the same reasons that the current practice of polygamy is problematic. Polyamory is not a clearly preferable alternative to polygamy.

In this section, I have assumed that polygamy need not be structurally inegalitarian in practice whether because there is evidence that women in polygamous marriages are at greater risk of suffering harmful effects (section 2) or because polygamy is almost always polygyny in fact (section 4). Nevertheless, polygamy has been found to be structurally inegalitarian in theory even if practical problems did not obtain. This is grounded in inequalities concerning participation in a polygamous marriage. Whether or not the marriage is polygynous or polyandrous, the multiple married partners always lack equal opportunities to exit. Moreover, all forms of polygamy discriminate against nonheterosexuals as they are excluded from opportunities to form polygamous marriages and nor are polyamorous relationships less problematic. Thus, polygamy is structurally inegalitarian in unavoidable respects even if we bracket the structural asymmetries associated with the current practice of polygamy.

VI

In this article, I have focused on Calhoun's and Nussbaum's limited defenses of polygamy. I argued that these defenses are unconvincing on at least two grounds. The first ground is that polygamy is a structurally inegalitarian practice in fact. I have provided at least *prima facie* evidence that polygamous marriages subject women to a greater risk of harmful effects. Furthermore, I have argued that polygamous marriages are most often polygynous marriages in fact. Therefore, women lack the equal opportunity of men to form polygamous marriages with multiple partners of the opposite sex in practice.

The second ground is that polygamy is a structurally inegalitarian practice in theory. I have argued that polygamy not only threatens the equality of men and women in fact, but also the equality of polygamous marriage partners as the latter have asymmetrical opportunities to divorce. Finally, I have argued that polygamy is further structurally inegalitarian insofar as it discriminates against nonheterosexuals.

Therefore, while recent work by both Calhoun and Nussbaum provide an important new series of arguments in favor of a limited defense of polygamy, this defense is not ultimately successful. Polygamy is a structurally inegalitarian practice in theory and fact that should be opposed.

ACKNOWLEDGMENTS

This paper was presented at the Global Gender Justice Workshop held at the University of Oslo. My sincere thanks to Brooke Ackerley, Linda Martin Alcoff, Corwin Aragon, Gillian Brock, Ann Ferguson, Fabian Freyenhagen, Christel Fricke, Peter Jones, Eva Kittay, Ruth Macklin, Patrick O'Donnell, Vandana Shiva, Rachel Silvey, Cynthia Stark, an anonymous referee for this journal, and, most especially, Alison Jaggar for tremendously helpful advice on previous drafts.

NOTES

1. Polyandry—where one wife is married to multiple husbands—can be found in sparsely populated rural areas, such as Bhutan, Mongolia, and Tibet. Polyandrous marriages form a significantly small number of polygamous marriages.
2. The widespread practice of polygamy across the globe by different cultural and religious groups suggests that arguments against, or in favor of, the practice need not necessarily serve as an endorsement of any one cultural or religious group over another.
3. See Genesis 4:19, 23, 25:1–2; 1 Samuel 25:43–4; and 1 Kings 7:8.
4. Proponents also argue that husbands are more faithful to their wives in polygamous, rather than monogamous, marriages although this assertion remains unproven (Mitsunaga et al. 2005).
5. For further criticism of these views, see Parekh 2006, 283.
6. I am very grateful to Alison Jaggar for pushing me on this point.
7. *Reynolds v. United States,* 98 U.S. 145 (1878). See *Braunfeld v. Brown,* 366 U.S. 599, 605 (1961); *Davis v. Beason,* 133 U.S. 333 (1890); and also Ariz. Const., Art. XX, par. 2; Idaho Const., Art. I, §4; N.M. Const., Art. XXI, §1; Okla. Const., Art. I, §2; and Utah Const., Art. III. §1. My criticisms of *Reynolds* are in agreement with Nussbaum's analysis (see Nussbaum 2008, 191–98).
8. See *Reynolds v. United States,* 98 U.S. 145, 164 (1878) and Nussbaum 2008, 195.
9. See footnote 3 above. Additionally, there is nothing intrinsically wrong with a practice solely in virtue of its being alien.
10. *Musser v. State of Utah,* 333 U.S. 95, 103 (1948).
11. See *Reynolds v. United States,* 98 U.S. 145, 166 (1878) and Nussbaum 2008, 195.
12. I cannot hope to offer an extensive examination of the full scientific literature on polygamy and any related harmful effects. Instead, I will only highlight some key studies with the aim of presenting at least a *prima facie* case that there is reason to believe that there are higher risks of harmful effects resulting from polygamous marriages than found in monogamous marriages. This is not to claim that monogamous marriages lack these effects.
13. *State v. Green,* 99 P.3d 820, 830 (Utah 2004).
14. I do not deny that there is pervasive gender inequality that may also arise in monogamous marriages. Instead, my argument is that the inequalities and related harms discussed in this section are less in monogamous marriages than with polygamous marriages.
15. See Fichte 2000, 274: "Polygamy is predicated on men's belief that women are not rational beings like men, but only tools for the man, lacking a will or rights of their own."
16. Rawls 1999a, 587, 599; 1999b, 147, 161; and see 2001, 163.
17. See Rawls 1999a: 587, 587 n. 38, 596 n. 60, 597; 1999b: 147, 147 n. 38, 157 n. 60, 159; and 2001, 10, 166–67.
18. This is not to say that men and women otherwise lack an asymmetry of power. Instead, my argument is that the unjustified asymmetry is *more* with polygamy.
19. It is worth noting that, while she attempts to defend America's views on religious freedom in *Liberty of Conscience* (2008), Nussbaum may find that the United Kingdom scores better than the United States on the issue of polygamy. While polygamy remains illegal, UK courts have recognized polygamous marriages enacted elsewhere for several decades. Thus, for example, Lord Justice Salmon argues that: "it is plain from the authorities to which I have referred that there are purposes for which a polygamous marriage will be recognised as a valid marriage in this country, and also that in some statutes the word 'wife' may be construed as covering a polygamously married wife" (*Iman Din v. National Assistance Board,* [1967] 2 Q.B. 213, 220). (See *Hussain (Aliya) v. Hussain (Shahid),* [1983] Fam. 26.)
20. See Kautilya, *Arthà-Shàstra,* in Radhakrishnan and Moore 1957, 203: "Any kind of marriage is approvable, provided it pleases all those that are concerned in it."
21. See Nussbaum 2008, 186: "the concept of consent could be hazy" and women were often pressured to accept their husbands' demands for further wives. Nussbaum also notes that *The Book of Mormon* is not unambiguous in its promotion of polygamy (2008, 184–85).

22. One objection to this section is that Calhoun and Nussbaum defend polygamy only insofar as it should be legally permissible. The objection lies in the fact that bad practices may remain legally permissible: we can argue for permissibility even for bad practices. The problem with this objection is that they argue for more than legal permissibility. For example, Calhoun argues that the "legal recognition of polygamous marriage is incompatible with a liberal, democratic, and egalitarian society" (2005, 1027). Not only should polygamous marriages be granted legal recognition, but the history of popular opposition to these marriages may helpfully inform how we might overcome opposition to the legal recognition of same-sex marriage. Nussbaum primarily focuses on the right to free religious expression guaranteed by the U.S. Constitution and polygamous marriage (see 2008, 184–98). Both Calhoun and Nussbaum do argue for the legal recognition of polygamy on specific conditions. However, neither argues that polygamy may be no more than legally tolerated because it cannot be morally or politically justified. Therefore, this objection fails.
23. Perhaps the most well-known polyandrous marriage was Draupadì's marriage to five Pàndava brothers (see *The Mahàbhàrata* 1975).
24. By using "actual functionings," I refer to a range of functions that marriage may satisfy in addition to the function of a sexual relationship.
25. See Sen 1999, 66: "To ignore consequences in general, including the freedoms that people get—or do not get—to exercise, can hardly be an adequate basis for an acceptable evaluative system."
26. Not everyone agrees with this conclusion. For example, see Carens and Williams 1998 and a critique of their views in Barry 2001, 396 n. 96.
27. This leads Barry to argue that "[t]he whole idea of egalitarian polygamy is manifest nonsense" (Barry 2001, 369–70 n. 96).
28. I am most grateful for very helpful comments on this section by Alison Jaggar and an anonymous referee.
29. This asymmetry extends beyond one's sexual partners in a relationship to include one's partners in raising children, holding property rights, and other functions that marriage may satisfy.
30. One objection might be that all partners appear to have equality with respect to divorce. Thus, the husband can divorce all those that he is married to (e.g., his wives) and each wife can divorce all those that she is married to (e.g., the shared husband). This is true. However, it is also true that a polygamous marriage should not be viewed as a relationship between only two people. Instead, the wives may only be married to a shared husband, but together they do form a larger nuclear family. Only the husband is able to choose who is a married member of his nuclear family. His wives are each a member of a polygamous marriage where they have unequal exit options concerning their nuclear family as a polygamous family than their shared husband. This remains the case even if each wife is married only to a shared husband and any other wife.
31. On polyamory, see Leith 2006. It is worth noting that there does not appear to be any movement in favor of, nor against, polyamorous marriage. Thus, I refer to polyamory in terms of "relationships" and not "marriage."
32. See *Sweatt v. Painter,* 339 U.S. 629, 635 (1950): "[e]qual protection of the laws is not achieved through indiscriminate imposition of inequalities." See also *Romer v. Evans,* 517 U.S. 620, 633 (1996).
33. For criticisms of polyamory, see Klesse 2006.

BIBLIOGRAPHY

Al-Krenawi, Alean. 2001. "Women from Polygamous and Monogamous Marriages in an Out-Patient Psychiatric Clinic." *Transcultural Psychiatry* 38: 187–99.

Al-Krenawi, Alean, J. R. Graham, and Vered Slonim-Nevo. 2002. "Mental Health Aspects of Arab-Israeli Adolescents from Polygamous versus Monogamous Families." *Journal of Social Psychology* 142: 446–60.

Al-Krenawi, Alean, and E. S. Lightman. 2000. "Learning Achievement, Social Adjustment, and Family

Conflict among Bedouin-Arab Children from Polygamous and Monogamous Families." *Journal of Social Psychology* 140: 345–56.
Al-Krenawi, Alean, and Vered Slonim-Nevo. 2008. "The Psychosocial Profile of Bedouin Arab Women Living in Polygamous and Monogamous Marriages." *Families in Society* 89: 139–49.
Barry, Brian. 2001. *Culture and Equality*. Cambridge: Polity.
Brooks, Thom (ed.). 2008. *The Global Justice Reader*. Oxford: Blackwell.
Calhoun, Chesire. 2005. "Who's Afraid of Polygamous Marriage? Lessons for Same-Sex Marriage Advocacy from the History of Polygamy." *San Diego Law Review* 42: 1023–42.
Carens, Joseph H., and Melissa S. Williams. 1998. "Muslim Minorities in Liberal Democracies: The Politics of Misrecognition." In *Secularism and Its Critics*, ed. Rajeev Bhargava, 137–73. Delhi: Oxford University Press.
Cook, Cynthia T. 2007. "Polygyny—Did the Africans Get It Right?" *Journal of Black Studies* 38: 232—50.
Dowding, Keith. 2006. "Can Capabilities Reconcile Freedom and Equality?" *Journal of Political Philosophy* 14: 323–36.
Elbedour, Salman, W. M. Bart, and J. M. Hektner. 2000. "Scholastic Achievement and Family Marital Structure: Bedouin-Arab Adolescents from Monogamous and Polygamous Families in Israel." *Journal of Social Psychology* 140: 503–14.
Elbedour, Salman, Anthony J. Onwuegbuzie, and M. Alatamin. 2003. "Behavioral Problems and Scholastic Adjustment among Bedouin-Arab Children from Polygamous and Monogamous Marital Family Structures: Some Developmental Considerations." *Genetic, Social, and General Psychology Monographs* 129: 213–37.
Elbedour, Salman, Anthony J. Onwuegbuzie, Corin Cardidine, and Hasan Abu-Saad. 2002. "The Effect of Polygamous Marital Structure on Behavioral, Emotional, and Academic Adjustment in Children: A Comprehensive Review of the Literature." *Clinical Child and Family Psychology Review* 5: 255–71.
Fatoye, F. O., A. B. Adeyemi, and B. Y. Oladimeji. 2004. "Emotional Distress and Its Correlates among Nigerian Women in Late Pregnancy." *Journal of Obstetrics and Gynaecology* 24: 504–9.
Fichte, Johann Gottlieb. 2000. *Foundations of Natural Right*, ed. Frederick Neuhouser, trans. Michael Bauer. Cambridge: Cambridge University Press.
Gher, Jaime M. 2008. "Polygamy and Same-Sex Marriage—Allies or Adversaries within the Same-Sex Movement?" *William and Mary Journal of Women and the Law* 14: 559–603.
Hassouneth-Phillips, Dena. 2001. "Polygamy and Wife Abuse: A Qualitative Study of Muslim Women in America." *Health Care for Women International* 22: 735–48.
Ho-Yen, Signe Dörheim, Gunnar Tschudi Bondevik, Malin Eberhard-Gran, and Björn Bjorvatn. 2007. "Factors Associated with Depressive Symptoms among Postnatal Women in Nepal." *Acta Obstetricia et Gynecologica Scandinavica* 86: 291–97.
Jacubowski, Nadja 2008. "Marriage Is Not a Safe Place: Heterosexual Marriage and HIV-related Vulnerability in Indonesia." *Culture, Health & Sexuality* 10: 87–97.
Klesse, Christian 2006. "Polyamory and Its 'Others': Contesting the Terms of Non-Monogamy." *Sexualities* 9: 565–83.
Leith, William. 2006. "Welcome to the World of Polyamory." *Observer* July 9.
The Mahâbhârata. 1975. 2 vols., trans. J. A. B. van Buitenen. Chicago: University of Chicago Press.
Mitsunaga, Tisha M., Antonia M. Powell, Nathan J. Heard, and Ulla M. Larsen. 2005. "Extramarital Sex among Nigerian Men—Polygyny and Other Risk Factors." *JAIDS—Journal of Acquired Immune Deficiency* 39: 478–88.
Nussbaum, Martha C. 1993. "Capabilities as Fundamental Entitlements: Sen and Social Justice." *Feminist Economics* 9: 33–50, reprinted in Brooks 2008, 598–614.
Nussbaum, Martha C. 1997. "Capabilities and Human Rights." *Fordham Law Review* 66: 273–300.
Nussbaum, Martha C. 1999. *Sex and Social Justice*. Oxford: Oxford University Press.
Nussbaum, Martha C. 2000. *Women and Human Development: The Capabilities Approach*. Cambridge: Cambridge University Press.
Nussbaum, Martha C. 2008. *Liberty of Conscience: In Defense of America's Tradition of Religious Equality*. New York: Basic Books.
Nussbaum, Martha C., and Amartya Sen (eds.). 1993. *The Quality of Life*. Oxford: Oxford University Press.
Okin, Susan Moller. 1999. "Is Multiculturalism Bad for Women?" In *Is Multiculturalism Bad for*

Women? ed. Joshua Cohen, Matthew Howard, and Martha C. Nussbaum, 587–97. Princeton, N.J.: Princeton University Press, reprinted in Brooks 2008.

Olley, B. O. 2004. "Predictors of Hazardous and Harmful Alcohol Use among Nigerian Freshmen." *African Journal of Medical Science* 33: 327–33.

Parekh, Bhikhu. 2006. *Rethinking Multiculturalism: Cultural Diversity and Political Theory*, 2nd ed. Basingstoke: Palgrave Macmillan.

Peterson, S. A. 1999. "Marriage Structure and Contraception in Niger." *Journal of Biosocial Science* 31: 93–104.

Phillips, Anne. 2001). "Feminism and Liberalism Revisited: Has Martha Nussbaum Got It Right?" *Constellations* 8: 249–66.

Radhakrishnan, Sarvepalli, and Charles A. Moore (eds.). 1957. *A Sourcebook in Indian Philosophy*. Princeton, N.J.: Princeton University Press.

Rawls, John. 1999a. "The Idea of Public Reason Revisited." In *Collected Papers*, ed. Samuel Freeman, 573–615. Cambridge, Mass.: Harvard University Press, 1999.

Rawls, John. 1999b. *The Law of Peoples*. Cambridge, Mass.: Harvard University Press.

Rawls, John. 2001. *Justice as Fairness: A Restatement*, ed. Erin Kelly. Cambridge, Mass.: Harvard University Press.

Rehman, Javaid. 2007. "The Sharia, Islamic Family Laws and International Human Rights Law: Examining the Theory and Practice of Polygamy and Talaq." *International Journal of Law, Policy, and the Family* 21: 108–27.

Robeyns, Ingrid. 2003. "Sen's Capability Approach and Gender Inequality: Selecting Relevant Capabilities." *Feminist Economics* 9: 61–92.

Sen, Amartya. 1984. *Resources, Values, and Development*. Oxford: Blackwell.

Sen, Amartya. 1985. "Well-being, Agency, and Freedom: The Dewey Lectures 1984." *Journal of Philosophy* 82: 169–221.

Sen, Amartya. 1987. *Commodities and Capabilities*. Oxford: Oxford University Press.

Sen, Amartya. 1992. *Inequality Reexamined*. Oxford: Clarendon Press.

Sen Amartya. 1999. *Development as Freedom*. Oxford: Oxford University Press.

Sheff, E. 2005. "Polyamorous Women, Sexual Subjectivity and Power." *Journal of Contemporary Ethnography* 34: 251–83.

Slonim-Nevo, Vered, and Alean Al-Krenawi. 2006. "Success and Failure among Polygamous Families: The Experience of Wives, Husbands, and Children." *Family Process* 45: 311–30.

Strasser, Mark. 2008. "Marriage, Free Exercise, and the Constitution." *Law and Inequality* 26: 59–108.

Winslow, Wendy Wilkins, and Gladys Honein. 2007. "Bridges and Barriers to Health: Her Story—Emirati Women's Health Needs." *Heath Care Women International* 28: 285–308.

[10]

WHO SECURES WOMEN'S CAPABILITIES IN MARTHA NUSSBAUM'S QUEST FOR SOCIAL JUSTICE?

AMRITA BASU*

Among the many issues that feminists have debated, three stand out for their urgency and significance: the relationship of theory to practice, universalism to particularism, and the transnational to the local and national. Feminism as theory continues to have a complicated and vexed relationship to women's activism. Even women who engage in struggles that observers might term feminist do not necessarily share feminist identities or participate in women's movements. Similarly, feminists continue to be troubled by universalism. Although certain forms of universalism are integral to most feminisms, Western feminist universalism has been presumptuous in condemning non-Western practices with scant understanding of the cultural and historical contexts which give them meaning. Feminist movements in the global South have sometimes been undermined by Western funded projects which have narrowed the agendas and constituencies of women's movements and by hegemonic Western feminists' appropriation of local discourses. As I elaborate below, I believe that debates about global feminisms have influenced Nussbaum's work and its reception.

I begin by describing the key tenets of the human capabilities approach and show how it represents an advance over human rights. I then place capabilities in the context of women's movements transnationally. I assess the different ways in which national states and transnational

---

* Paino Professor of Political Science and Women's and Gender Studies, Amherst College. Representative works include *Two Faces of Protest: Contrasting Modes of Women's Activism In India* (1992), *Appropriating Gender: Women's Activism and Politicized Religion in South Asia* (Amrita Basu & Patricia Jeffery, eds., 1998); *Localizing Knowledge in a Globalizing World* (Amrita Basu ed., 2002); and *Women's Movements in the Global Era: The Power of Local Feminisms* (Amrita Basu ed., 2010).

The author would like to express her gratitude to Kristin Bumiller, Cynthia Enloe, Joan Cocks, Mary Katzenstein, Mark Kesselman, Eileen McDonough, Melissa McEllin, Uday Mehta, Martha Saxton, Molly Shanley, Sayres Rudy, and Elisabeth Wood, for very helpful comments on a draft of this paper. Martha Nussbaum inspired this paper and her comments helped greatly improve it.

organizations impede and support the recognition of capabilities. I argue that social movements have a critical role to play in determining and realizing capabilities.

Capabilities represent a clear and deliberate advance over human rights in addressing relations between universalism and particularism, theory and practice, and transnationalism and nationalism.[1] Human rights advocates primarily focus on civil and political rights and have traditionally neglected rights within the private domain of the family. By contrast, Nussbaum rejects the view that civil, political, economic, and social rights should be attained sequentially and argues that capabilities are interdependent: the recognition of one of them requires the recognition of others. In *Frontiers of Justice* she states,

> [C]apabilities cover the terrain occupied by both the so-called first-generation rights (political and civil liberties) and the so-called second generation rights (economic and social rights). And they play a similar role, providing an account of extremely important fundamental entitlements that can be used as a basis both for constitutional thought within a nation and for thinking about universal justice. [2]

Nussbaum identifies ten basic capabilities which, if realized, would enable people to achieve human dignity. They include literacy, liberty of conscience, political participation, freedom from physical violence, engaging in economic transactions, and developing the senses and practical reason.[3] She argues that justice demands that all citizens should achieve the thresholds that the capabilities approach specifies.

Human rights advocates have tended to ignore the role of the state in addressing socio-economic inequalities. By contrast, Nussbaum identifies a key role for the nation-state in realizing capabilities and recognizes the futility of rights and of equality of opportunity when people lack the resources to make meaningful choices. She develops an outcome-oriented approach which supports substantial freedoms. She argues that the radical

---

[1] MARTHA C. NUSSBAUM, WOMEN AND HUMAN DEVELOPMENT: THE CAPABILITIES APPROACH (2000) [hereinafter NUSSBAUM, WOMEN AND HUMAN DEVELOPMENT].

[2] MARTHA C. NUSSBAUM, FRONTIERS OF JUSTICE: DISABILITY, NATIONALITY, SPECIES MEMBERSHIP 284 (2006) [hereinafter NUSSBAUM, FRONTIERS OF JUSTICE].

[3] MARTHA C. NUSSBAUM, SEX AND SOCIAL JUSTICE 41–42 (1999) [hereinafter NUSSBAUM, SEX AND SOCIAL JUSTICE].

potential of liberalism lies in forging links between individual freedom and state responsibility.

In contrast to traditional human rights perspectives, feminism influences Nussbaum's conception of key capabilities. "Senses, Imagination, and Thought," encompass" Being able to use the senses; being able to imagine, to think and to reason . . . [and]to use the imagination and thought in connection with experiencing and producing expressive works and events of one's own choice, (religious, literary, musical, etc)."[4] "Emotions" concern the ability "to have attachments to things and persons outside ourselves. . . ."[5] Another capability entails "Being able to laugh, to play, to enjoy recreational activities."[6] Feminism expresses a consciousness of and resistance to gender inequality which can be manifest in everyday life as well as in episodic fashion, in culture and the arts, and in the private and public domains. What Mary Katzenstein terms the "discursive dimensions" of feminism are integral to capabilities.[7] As I elaborate below, feminism figures more in Nussbaum's conception than in her discussion of the enactment of capabilities.

The most controversial aspect of Nussbaum's approach is her unabashed universalism. She argues that the capabilities approach is designed for each and every citizen, in each and every nation.[8] In her words,

> The body that labors is in a sense the same body all over the world, and its needs for food and nutrition and health care are the same. . . . Similarly the body that gets beaten is in a sense the same all over the world, concrete though the circumstances of domestic violence are in each society.[9]

Nussbaum argues that individuals and governments have moral obligations to promote justice for people outside their own borders, and thus feminist philosophy should increasingly focus on the urgent needs of

---

[4] *Id.* at 41.

[5] *Id.*

[6] *Id. at* 42.

[7] MARY FAINSOD KATZENSTEIN, FAITHFUL AND FEARLESS, MOVING FEMINIST PROTEST INSIDE THE CHURCH AND THE MILITARY (1998).

[8] *Id.* at 6.

[9] NUSSBAUM, WOMEN AND HUMAN DEVELOPMENT, *supra* note 1, at 22–23.

women in developing countries.[10] Her universalism is linked to her rejection of double standards towards gender inequality in the global North and South. She forcefully denies that privacy is or should be less valued in India than in the United States where matters of gender inequality are at stake.[11] Nussbaum's universalism also leads her to set a high standard for states in creating the conditions under which capabilities can be recognized.

The value of universalism, however, cannot be determined simply by evaluating its philosophical premises. As Pratap Bhanu Mehta points out, universalism embodies the historical project of imperialism.[12] It has tended to presume rather than to demonstrate a commonality of interests, needs, and ideas. Its claim to special authority has exempted it from scrutiny and contestation. This is not to say, Mehta notes, that universalism is inevitably ethnocentric, but rather that it has been associated historically with one set of cultural practices.[13] The challenge that confronts universalist approaches then is to engage the political. Placing the capabilities approach within the context of social movements illuminates how political actors have deliberated, debated, rejected, and embraced capabilities.

The difficult questions concerning capabilities emerge in translating abstract philosophical conceptions into the messy world of politics. Are all capabilities equally important in all societies? Do they mean the same thing everywhere? Do different groups understand a particular capability the same way within a single society? Take, for example, the question of education as a central capability. There are enormous differences cross-nationally about what it means to be an educated person. Does it refer to being literate or well educated? To reading a newspaper, reading a third grade textbook, or exercising citizenship rights? How do the illiterate and uneducated regard education and what form of education do they value? As these questions suggest, exploring who will enforce capabilities inevitably necessitates reconsidering the very meaning and importance of capabilities in particular contexts.

---

[10] *Id.* at 7.

[11] Martha C. Nussbaum, *Sex Equality, Liberty and Privacy, A Comparative Approach to the Feminist Critique*, *in* INDIA'S LIVING CONSTITUTION, IDEAS, PRACTICES, CONTROVERSIES 242 (E. Sridharan et al., eds., 2002) [hereinafter Nussbaum, *Sex Equality, Liberty and Privacy*].

[12] Pratap Bhanu Mehta, *Cosmopolitanism and the Circle of Reason*," 28 POL. THEORY 619, 622 (2000).

[13] *Id.* at 622

I argue that social movements give concrete meaning to capabilities. Social movements often give voice to those who are formally voiceless. They express conceptions of capabilities that states neglect and deny. The social movements in which women have participated can be capabilities in and of themselves, catalysts for women's appreciating capabilities, or pressure groups on the state to recognize capabilities. Women's movements often seek to influence constitutional provisions for equality with respect to gender and sexual orientation, force states to deliver capabilities, make universal capabilities contextually meaningful, develop local arenas in which capabilities can be realized, and create possibilities for self-realization and dignity outside and beyond state control. Even conservative social movements which oppose gender equality, as many do, deliberate with their own constituencies and with the larger society and negotiate with the state. Such contestation and deliberation are indispensable both to formulating and implementing capabilities.

Attention to social movements helps to name the processes by which states are galvanized into recognizing capabilities. Social movements have often made states support capabilities and influenced their decisions about which capabilities to recognize. Authoritarian states are unlikely to support capabilities precisely because they repress social movements. Differences in the character of states call for different social movement strategies in interpreting and enforcing capabilities. All of these questions bear on the issue of universalism.

I. THE CONTEXT

Nussbaum published her influential book *Sex and Social Justice* in 1999[14] and *Women and Human Development* the following year,[15] on the heels of some critical developments in women's movements transnationally. Major international conferences on human rights (Vienna in 1993), reproductive rights (Cairo in 1994), and women's rights (Beijing in 1995) witnessed increased agreement and support for gender equality among governments and between governments and non-governmental organizations. Transnational women's advocacy organizations grew dramatically during this period.[16]

---

[14] *See generally* NUSSBAUM, SEX AND SOCIAL JUSTICE, *supra* note 3.

[15] *See* NUSSBAUM, WOMEN AND HUMAN DEVELOPMENT, *supra* note 1.

[16] On the growth of transnational advocacy networks and movements, see VALENTINE MOGHADAM, GLOBALIZING WOMEN: TRANSNATIONAL FEMINIST NETWORKS (2005); CATHERINE ESCHLE, GLOBAL DEMOCRACY MOVEMENTS, SOCIAL MOVEMENTS AND

The bitter North-South conflicts among women which were evident at the international women's conference in Mexico City in 1975, had abated by the Nairobi conference in 1985 and further dissipated in Beijing a decade later. Women's movements in the global South had dramatically grown and come to command the attention of their national governments. They had arguably become stronger and more effective in this respect than their counterparts in the global North. Many women's movements in the South were grappling simultaneously with political representation, property rights, violence against women, reproductive rights, and a host of other issues. The growth of human rights activism and the increasing inter-twining of women's and human rights movements and discourses created new ways of addressing violence against women.[17]

This is the complex terrain in which Nussbaum made an important but contested contribution. In her years at the WIDER Institute in Helsinki and in her travels to India, she became increasingly attentive to gender inequality, especially in poorer countries. Nussbaum positioned herself as both a theorist and a practitioner through her work with the UNDP, particularly on the Human Development Reports, which measure the quality of life by examining capabilities. Together with Amartya Sen, she founded the Human Development and Capability Association in 2003.[18] Her work reflected and contributed to the increasingly international character of feminism.

Nussbaum's position is controversial, however, because growing internationalism generates new debates as it puts others to rest.[19] Many feminists are wary of universalism of any kind, particularly when it is prescriptive. They worry that transnational feminism will simply reflect geo-political inequalities in a world in which the U.S. government has

---

FEMINISM (2001); MAXINE MOLYNEUX, WOMEN'S MOVEMENTS IN INTERNATIONAL PERSPECTIVE · (2001); and GLOBAL FEMINISM: TRANSNATIONAL WOMEN'S ACTIVISM, ORGANIZING AND HUMAN RIGHTS (Myra Max Feree & Aili Marie Tripp eds., 2006).

[17] *See* MARTHA E. KECK & KATHRYN SIKKINK, ACTIVISTS BEYOND BORDERS: ADVOCACY NETWORKS IN INTERNATIONAL POLITICS (1998); JULIE PETERS & ANDREA WOLPERT WOMEN'S RIGHTS, HUMAN RIGHTS: INTERNATIONAL FEMINIST PERSPECTIVES (1995), *and* WOMEN, GENDER AND HUMAN RIGHTS: A GLOBAL PERSPECTIVE (Marjorie Argosin ed., 2001)

[18] *See* Human Development and Capability Association, Home Page, http://www.capabilityapproach.com (last visited Feb. 1, 2010).

[19] Some of these contending positions are expressed in the volume edited by Maxine Molyneux and Shahra Razavi, GENDER, JUSTICE, DEVELOPMENT AND RIGHTS, (Maxine Molyneux & Shahra Razavi eds., 2002)

justified militarist foreign policies, toward Afghanistan, for example, on feminist grounds. They fear that the growth of human rights discourses is linked to the hegemony of neo-liberalism and the concomitant demise of radical ideologies which advocate equality rather than rights. Some feminists believe that liberal discourses obscure the importance of community-based identities and that individual rights undermine the rights of minorities and indigenous communities. For example, Rosalva Aida Hernandez Castillo argues that mainstream women's movements in Latin America have undermined and neglected the concerns of indigenous women. [20] Some are concerned that the growing institutionalization of women's movements—both through their closer relations with states and with international organizations—has dissipated their radicalism. Sangeeta Kamat describes the NGO-ization of grassroots movements in India and Sonia Alvarez describes a similar phenomenon in Latin America. [21]

II. THE NATIONAL, TRANSNATIONAL, AND THE LOCAL

Nussbaum holds nation-states responsible for providing citizens with the resources necessary to make meaningful choices. She recognizes that "even a highly moralized globalism" needs nation-states because transnational structures are not sufficiently accountable to citizens and do not adequately represent them.[22] She argues that external powers should not force sovereign governments to make decisions unless they have committed the gravest abuses.[23] Thus, Nussbaum accords a secondary role to multilateral organizations and to transnational and domestic non-governmental organizations.

Nussbaum rightly avoids the excessive importance that some feminist scholars have accorded to transnational institutions—which they regard as having supplanted national institutions and movements. As significant as the growth of transnational organizations may be, feminists

---

[20] Rosalva Aida Hernandez Castillo, *Towards A Culturally Situated Women's Rights Agenda: Reflections from Mexico, in* WOMEN'S MOVEMENTS IN THE GLOBAL ERA (Amrita Basu ed., 2010) [hereinafter WOMEN'S MOVEMENTS IN THE GLOBAL ERA].

[21] *See* Sangeeta Kamat, DEVELOPMENT HEGEMONY: NGOS AND THE STATE IN INDIA, (2002), Sonia E. Alvarez, *Translating the Global: Effects of Transnational Organizing on Local Feminist Discourses and Practices in Latin America,* 1 MERIDIANS: FEMINISM, RACE, TRANSNATIONALISM 29–67 (2000)

[22] NUSSBAUM, WOMEN AND HUMAN DEVELOPMENT, *supra* note 1, at 105.

[23] *Id.*

continue to confront powerful states and nationalist forces within the domestic context. The transnational feminist organizations which have intervened most effectively to support gender equality are organizations like Women Living Under Muslim Laws (WLUML), which have worked simultaneously locally, nationally and transnationally.[24]

Many national women's movements view the growing influence of transnational networks and funding as mixed blessings. The resources that help sustain women's organizations often have strings attached. While many donors support the creation of women's policy bureaus, fewer support organizations that radically challenge economic inequality. And women's bureaus are far less likely than women's movements to promote women's agency. Some conservative states have fiercely resisted international attempts to monitor and change their policies on gender and the family. International support for women's rights may ultimately increase women's vulnerability as a result of the misogynist backlash it triggers.

A further question is whether non-democratic states will support human capabilities. Although the Indian state can be encouraged to recognize capabilities, it is not typical of post-colonial states. India is characterized by extensive poverty and gender inequality, as well as by strong courts, a vibrant civil society and a free press. India's Constitution contains extensive directive principles which encourage the state to pursue social justice. Unlike the U.S. Constitution, it provides for non-discrimination on grounds of sex.[25] It is a living, changing document which has frequently been amended. Thus, while activists may sometimes appeal to international human rights norms and laws, they have generally not asked international agencies to influence the Indian state. But think of numerous countries in which gender inequality is pervasive and democracies and constitutional protections are absent or weak. In these countries there are fewer prospects of state recognition of capabilities and to the extent they exist, they are created by women's movements,

Nussbaum is most compelling when she grounds her arguments in particular contexts. In *Women and Human Development*, she focuses on India and appreciates the diversity within it. As she points out, while patriarchy constrains the choices all women make, their lives are also influenced by their caste and class backgrounds, the regions they inhabit,

---

[24] *See* Women Living Under Muslim Laws, http://www.wluml.org/ (last visited Feb. 1, 2010).

[25] India Const., art. 14 (Equality Before the Law) & art. 15 (The Prohibition of Discrimination on Grounds of Religion, Race, Caste, Place, Sex or Place of Birth).

their relationships with their families, and their incomes.[26] She opens and closes with the experiences of two women, Vasanti and Jayamma.[27] Whereas Vasanti is a lower middle class Rajput living in Ahmadabad and working with the non-governmental organization (NGO) Self Employed Women's Association (SEWA), Jayamma is a poor lower caste Ezha from Kerala who has no sources of income or support from her family.[28] In these examples, Nussbaum differentiates normative ideals of womanhood from women's lived experiences and explores economic and political influences on cultural practices. She thereby dispels essentialist assumptions about the fixed, homogenous, quarantined character of cultural identities and their rootedness in religion.

Nussbaum's understanding of Indian politics enables her to appreciate the vexed status of laws governing the family.[29] In principle, uniform secular law provides greater rights to women within the family than the current system of religious laws for India's five major religious communities. However, Nussbaum supports maintaining religious laws with the provision of exit options alongside the creation of a comprehensive secular code of civil law.[30] Indian feminists increasingly support this option to avoid making Muslim minority women choose between their community and gender identities. They have ceased to demand a uniform civil code to distance themselves from the Bharatiya Janata Party (BJP) which has supported it. Nussbaum's position reflects her respect for pluralism and religious freedom. The challenge for Nussbaum is to think about rights contextually when discussing capabilities in the abstract.

Nussbaum praises the Indian women's movement,[31] but none of her books devote much attention to its role in debating, enhancing, and implementing capabilities. She accords more importance to NGOs among

---

[26] NUSSBAUM, WOMEN AND HUMAN DEVELOPMENT, *supra* note 1.

[27] *Id.* at 15–23, 106–09.

[28] *Id.* at 16–17.

[29] *See generally* Nussbaum, *Sex Equality, Liberty and Privacy*, *supra* note 11.

[30] NUSSBAUM, WOMEN AND HUMAN DEVELOPMENT, *supra* note 1, ch. 3 (discussing the dilemmas that religion creates)

[31] MARTHA C. NUSSBAUM, THE CLASH WITHIN: DEMOCRACY, RELIGIOUS VIOLENCE AND INDIA'S FUTURE (2008) [hereinafter NUSSBAUM, THE CLASH WITHIN].

poor rural women.[32] However, NGOs are less likely than social movements to support capabilities. Most NGOs are confined to localities and do not have a national impact. They tend to be highly specialized and narrowly concerned with particular issues which they have been funded. They generally consider themselves non-political. One of the most shocking instances of NGO failure was during the Gujarat violence in 2002, the main focus of Nussbaum's *The Clash Within.* Gujarat has among the largest number of NGOS of any state in India.[33] However, most NGOs, including the Self Employed Women's Association (SEWA), which Nussbaum praises in *Women and Human Development,* were silent during the pogrom. Although SEWA stated that it did not want to jeopardize the safety of its members by taking a stance, nor, clearly, did it want to risk state sanction.[34]

We come full circle to the relative importance of national as opposed to international forces and of social movements as opposed to NGOs in implementing capabilities. Nussbaum argues, "[A] good idea is just that, a good idea. . . . But in all implementation a fundamental role remains for the nation state."[35] The question is often not whether rights are good or bad in the abstract but, rather, who is proposing them? Why? And who will implement them? What underlies resistance to these ideas? As important as the nation should be in enacting capabilities, it often is not. Ultimately, international actors may assume greater importance than Nussbaum would advocate precisely because of geopolitical realities and global inequalities. Ideas cannot be evaluated outside of the contexts in which they exist. This does not mean that good ideas should be discarded, but what remains unspecified is how to ensure that ideas refining the meaning of capabilities, can be shared, understood, debated, and adapted.

I turn to the many ways in which social movements are vital in addressing capabilities.

---

[32] NUSSBAUM, WOMEN AND HUMAN DEVELOPMENT, *supra* note 1, at 17, 23, 40, 106–11 (discussing the strides of SEWA and other NGOs in the areas of literacy and economic independence for rural women).

[33] Amrita Basu, *The Long March From Ayodhya: Violence and Democracy in India, in,* IMPLEMENTING PLURALISM AND DEMOCRACY IN INDIA, (Wendy Doniger & Martha Nussbaum eds., forthcoming 2010) [hereinafter Basu, *The Long March From Ayodhya*].

[34] Interview with Mirai Chatterjee, SEWA member, Ahmedabad, Jan 13, 2007.

[35] NUSSBAUM, THE CLASH WITHIN, *supra* note 31, at 103.

III. SOCIAL MOVEMENTS

A. Movements as Capabilities

Social movements might be viewed as capabilities when they are committed to social justice and engage in deliberation. The Indian women's movement has enabled women to achieve access to credit, land rights and political representation. It also affords activists opportunities to develop friendships, exercise freedom, and engage in creative self-expression. Since movements are dynamic entities, they may become capabilities as activists attain agency, dignity, and freedom.

B. Deliberating capabilities

Most social movements are informed by activists' knowledge, reflection, and communication about structural and systemic sources of inequality. Deliberation also takes place within movements. Because activists generally disagree with one another, they routinely compare the importance of key capabilities. For example, feminists have long debated the attention they should accord to poverty, illiteracy, reproductive freedom and violence against women.

C. Appreciating the inter-linkages among capabilities

Because movements are dynamic and continually changing, activists who begin by addressing one set of issues often take up others that they had not anticipated. Women's movements have frequently grown out of other social movements—nationalist, revolutionary, democratic—which have both supported and reneged on their commitments to women's rights. In numerous peasant struggles originally targeting land rights, for example, women activists have come to challenge men's excessive alcohol consumption and domestic violence.[36] Women's movements have explored the linkages among capabilities by examining the connections between women's subjection to domestic violence and their lack of education, income, and property.

---

[36] I discuss this in my book. AMRITA BASU, TWO FACES OF PROTEST: CONTRASTING MODES OF WOMEN'S ACTIVISM IN INDIA (1992).

D. Influencing Constitutions

In Zimbabwe,[37] Poland,[38] Iran[39], and Pakistan[40], among other countries, women's movements have played critical roles in placing pressure on states to recognize capabilities. The experience of the women's movement in Zimbabwe provides an excellent example of the dialectic between the women's movement and the state. As a result of women's activism in the nationalist movement in the 1960s and 1970s, the state adopted legislation that would improve women's position, particularly within the family. Women's organizations felt empowered to demand constitutional change. They forged alliances with other groups and organized meetings throughout the country around a Women's Charter. When the state failed to respond, the women's movement organized sufficient support to defeat a state-sponsored referendum. Although the state responded with repression, the women's movement has allied with other civil society organizations and is at the forefront of the struggle for democracy and gender equality.[41]

E. Pressuring the state to realize capabilities

In India, movements organized by the lowest castes and by women have pressured the state to implement constitutional commitments to promote gender and caste equality. A comparative analysis of women's movements reveals that states are most apt to adopt policies and legislation supporting gender equality when women's movements compel them to do so.[42] In a study of thirty-six countries, Laurel Weldon finds that the most

---

[37] Shereen Essof, *Ramagwana Rakajeka/The Future Will Be Better The Next Time: Opportunities and Challenges of the Zimbabwean Women's Movement, in* WOMEN'S MOVEMENTS IN THE GLOBAL ERA, *supra* note 20.

[38] Elzbieta Matynia, *Polish Feminism Between the Local and the Global: A Task of Translation, in* WOMEN'S MOVEMENTS IN THE GLOBAL ERA, *supra* note 20.

[39] Nayereh Tohidi, *The Women's Movement and Feminism in Iran: A Glocal Perspective, in* WOMEN'S MOVEMENTS IN THE GLOBAL ERA, *supra* note 20.

[40] Farida Shaheed, The *Women's Movement in Pakistan: Challenges and Achievements, in* WOMEN'S MOVEMENTS IN THE GLOBAL ERA, *supra* note 20.

[41] Shireen Essof & *Ramagwana Rakajeka, The Future Will Be Better The Next Time: Opportunities and Challenges of the Zimbabwean Women's Movement, in* WOMEN'S MOVEMENTS IN THE GLOBAL ERA, *supra* note 20.

[42] LAUREL WELDON, PROTEST, POLICY AND THE PROBLEM OF VIOLENCE AGAINST WOMEN (2002).

important determinant of improved government responsiveness to violence against women is the existence of strong autonomous women's movements.[43] Women's policy bureaus, in the absence of such movements, have been unable to promote government action on violence against women. One reason, Weldon notes, is that movements advance moral and political arguments to create public support for their claims.[44] Strong women's movements not only create a groundswell of support for public policies that promote gender equality but also increase the legitimacy of democratic governments.

F. Thinking strategically about the respective roles of the state, international bodies, and NGOs

Social activists often shift course depending on the conditions they confront in particular contexts, at particular moments in time. Thus movements which refuse to work with state agencies at certain moments might do so at other times. They thereby demonstrate the need for proponents of capabilities to think strategically about the role of key actors, particularly the state, in supporting capabilities. The women's organizations which have benefited most from transnational ties have had strong national foundations and can use transnational resources without being controlled by them. Strong women's movements have often sought to selectively accept foreign funding and work with the state, while maintaining some autonomy. They have also attempted to forge transnational alliances which do not entail accepting funding in order to avoid state scrutiny.

G. Realizing such capabilities as affiliation, play, the use of the senses, imagination, and thought

Social movements provide an incubator for cultivating citizenship based on affiliation, imagination, and practical reason. In *The Clash Within,* Nussbaum argues that Gandhi provided a spiritual and philosophical basis for Indian democracy by calling all Indians to a higher vision of themselves and by getting people to perceive the dignity of each human being.[45] She explains that Gandhi understood *swaraj,* self-rule, not only as a means of achieving independence but also of freeing the inner self. Gandhi knew that

---

[43] *Id.* at 187.

[44] *Id.*

[45] NUSSBAUM, THE CLASH WITHIN, *supra* note 33, at 105–06.

for democracy to flourish it had to cultivate the inner world of human beings, equipping each citizen to contend against the passion for domination and accept the reality, and the equality, of others.[46] She rightly praises Gandhi's non-instrumental, ethical form of political engagement.[47] I would add that Gandhi's commitment to self-transformation was associated with a deep skepticism towards centralized state power and appreciation of decentralized, democratic struggle. Today, social movements of diverse ideological persuasions continue to appeal to Gandhian ideals.

Nussbaum also deeply values the cultivation of imagination, the arts, and self expression in the creation of democratic citizenship. She writes admiringly of Bengali writer and Nobel laureate, Rabrindranath Tagore, who viewed freedom as rational, emotional, and imaginative.[48] In 1901, Tagore founded Shantiniketan, a school in what is now West Bengal, to provide the kind of education that is essential to democratic citizenship.[49] It emphasized studying Bengali and learning about Bengali culture, inculcating habits of questioning, critical reasoning, and deliberation, learning about cultural differences at home and abroad, and nourishing the imagination through immersion in literature and the arts.[50] As Ashish Nandy notes, Tagore, like Gandhi, rejected reliance on the state and valued popular struggles for political justice and cultural dignity.[51] He placed self-self over self-other dialogue.

Nussbaum directs us to the importance of identifying culturally specific ways of elaborating ethical concepts.[52] The state can certainly create conditions under which capabilities are squelched or strengthened, but, as Nussbaum demonstrates so well, these capabilities often flourish in arenas free from state control. Shantiniketan's autonomy from public institutions enabled it to avoid the rote learning that deadens creativity.[53]

---

[46] *Id.* at 16, 99–100.

[47] *Id.* at 101, 105.

[48] *Id.* at 87.

[49] *Id.* at 86.

[50] *Id.* at 86–88.

[51] ASHISH NANDY, THE ILLEGITIMACY OF NATIONALISM: RABINDRANATH TAGORE AND THE POLITICS OF SELF 2–3 (1994).

[52] *Id.* at 89–90.

[53] *Id.* at 85, 284–85.

Though he was a critic of patriotism, Tagore sought inspiration from his own cultural traditions.[54] The implementation of capabilities must entail promoting rich forms of practical reason, affiliation, and aesthetic expression.

Women's movements have visualized how practical reason, affiliation, and aesthetic expression can be realized outside the state. They have negotiated the relationship between private and public and individual and self, both when democracy exists in the formal political arena but not the family, and when democracy is absent in both domains. The slogan of the women's movement in Chile during the struggle against the Pinochet dictatorship was "Democracy in the country and in the home."[55] This aspect of movements is especially important to cultivating a respect for human dignity which Nussbaum believes is vital to democratic citizenship.

The Indian women's movement offers many examples of realizing capabilities through play, imagination, and practical reason. One such event occurred in the days following the symposium to honor Nussbaum. On February 9, 2009, the Ram Sena, (Army of Lord Ram) a right wing Hindu organization, attacked a group of women who were drinking and dancing in a bar in Mangalore.[56] A group of women who described themselves as a "Consortium of Pub-Going, Loose, and Forward Women" organized a creative and well-planned protest against this and other incidents of sexual harassment by the Hindu right. Their most notable act was to organize women to send "pink chaddis" (underwear) to the office of the Ram Sena on Valentine's Day. A web site and extensive media coverage documented 47,738 pairs of pink underwear being delivered to the Ram Sena office.[57] The pink underwear was a spoof on the deadly seriousness with which the Rashtriya Swayamsevak Sangh has donned khaki shorts as symbols of brotherhood. The organizers also encouraged women to head for the nearest bars on Valentine's Day.

The "pink chaddi" campaign is a wonderful illustration of how creative forms of activism are linked to capabilities. This protest entailed women using imagination and reason to laugh, play, and enjoy themselves.

---

[54] *Id.* at 90–92.

[55] Alicia Frohmann & Teresa Valdes, *Democracy in the Country and in the Home, in* THE CHALLENGE OF LOCAL FEMINISMS: WOMEN'S MOVEMENTS IN GLOBAL PERSPECTIVE, (Amrita Basu ed., 1995).

[56] *See* The Pink Chaddi Campaign, Homepage, http://thepinkchaddicampaign.blogspot.com (last visited Feb 1, 2010)

[57] *Id.*

The campaign asserted women's rights to live in an environment which was free from physical violence and insisted on the state's responsibility to ensure this. The state government was pressured into arresting Pramod Muthalik and other Ram Sena members to prevent them from harassing women on Valentine's Day.[58] Rejecting the allegation that they were westernized, the activists asserted the universal right of women to engage in self-expression. The protest promoted public deliberation and debate about women's freedom.

IV. CONCLUSION

I pose questions about how human capabilities can be secured with some trepidation. Nussbaum has already developed an approach to philosophy which is explicitly normative and grounded in women's material lives. She is unabashedly normative, feminist, and humanist. Her commitment to sympathetic understanding is evident in all aspects of her work. She takes an especially strong stand in addressing the needs of women who have suffered the most extreme deprivation and violations. Hasn't Nussbaum contributed enough to the formulation of gender justice? Is it fair to ask for more?

It is fair, because Nussbaum is concerned with how capabilities can be enacted. She challenges the value of separating theory from action and identifies the many ways in which theory creates a road map for change. She states that she intends to go beyond a negative conception of rights and an unqualified defense of freedom. She embraces a positive conception of social justice, both because of the magnitude of suffering and because she believes that capabilities can be realized—that is, they are not simply utopian. "The capabilities approach is not remote and impractical but urgently practical when it urges us to rethink our ideas of social cooperation," she argues.[59] Moreover, she claims that capabilities are only effective when the means of securing them exist. Effective measures must be created to enable people to exercise rights.[60]

Is it possible that Nussbaum does not delve too deeply into the question of implementation because doing so would open to scrutiny the troubled question of how widely capabilities are held? Deliberation might lead not to a consensus but to a questioning or prioritizing of capabilities.

---

[58] *Police Crackdown on Muthalik*, TIMES OF INDIA, Feb. 14, 2009.

[59] NUSSBAUM, FRONTIERS OF JUSTICE, *supra* note 2, at 306.

[60] *Id.* at 287.

The adoption of capabilities may only be possible if we suspend community-based democratic decision making. It would be ironic if the attainment of capabilities rested on the whims of the state, to the detriment of democratic deliberation. However, I do not believe that Nussbaum wants to evade deliberation for she contends that the realization of capabilities rests on their public acceptance. She states, "The threshold level of each of the central capabilities will need more precise determination, as citizens work towards a consensus for political purposes."[61] What she does not adequately explore is how citizens can seek this consensus.

Missing from Nussbaum's account is an appreciation of the place of communities in engaging in deliberation. Her emphasis on individuals and institutions ignores the potentially vital role of groups within civil society. Even mechanisms to detect and prevent corruption often fail to secure social justice in the absence of popular consent and mobilization from below. Some scholars suggest that deliberation can develop standards for protecting people from cruel, inhuman and degrading treatment and thereby promote more positive forms of well-being. Abdullahi An Naim proposes inter-community cross-cultural dialogue.[62] Sally Merry suggests that the deliberation of rights within the local context may result in their vernacularization, or adaptation to the material, cultural and political circumstances of people's lives.[63] Whatever forms deliberation takes, it is difficult to imagine capabilities being justified, let alone implemented, in its absence.

Social movements have assumed a variety of forms, including some which have opposed gender equality and capabilities. However, social justice movements are attuned to the contexts in which universal capabilities can be realized. In this respect, they engage in the search for the kind of precision that Nussbaum calls for. Moreover social movements represent deliberation in action. They are dynamic, strategic entities which are responsive to the changing political environment. Women's movements contend routinely with tensions between the universal and the particular—women's shared and specific interests based on their identities and location. As strategic actors, movements often engage in a variety of approaches to fostering change.

---

[61] NUSSBAUM, WOMEN AND HUMAN DEVELOPMENT, *supra* note 1, at 77.

[62] ABDULLAHI AN NAIM, HUMAN RIGHTS IN CROSS-CULTURAL PERSPECTIVES: A QUEST FOR CONSENSUS (1995).

[63] SALLY ENGLE MERRY, HUMAN RIGHTS AND GENDER VIOLENCE: TRANSLATING INTERNATIONAL LAW INTO LOCAL JUSTICE (2006).

Part V
Cosmopolitanism and Global Justice

[11]

ASSESSING GLOBAL POVERTY AND INEQUALITY: INCOME, RESOURCES, AND CAPABILITIES

INGRID ROBEYNS

Abstract: Are global poverty and inequality on the rise or are they declining? And is the quality of life of the world's poorest people getting worse or better? These questions are often given conflicting answers by economists, the World Bank, and social activists. One reason for this is that assessments of quality of life can be made in terms of people's income, their resources, or their functionings and capabilities. This essay discusses the pros and cons of these evaluative approaches, and it argues that all approaches have complementary strengths and should therefore in principle all be considered. Moreover, being aware that assessments of poverty and inequality can be made using these different frameworks helps us to understand the conflicting claims.

Keywords: capabilities, global justice, income, inequality, poverty, primary goods, resources, social activists, World Bank.

1. Introduction

Are there fewer people living in poverty today than there were ten or twenty years ago? Is inequality between the poor and the rich countries decreasing? Do people in poor countries benefit from economic globalization? Have they become better off thanks to the policies of the International Monetary Fund (IMF) and the World Bank? Will their children face a better future and live happier lives, or does the available evidence suggest otherwise?

The answers that are typically given to these questions differ dramatically. Scholars, politicians, and social activists on the left of the political spectrum tend to answer the questions in the negative. Barbara Ehrenreich and Arlie Russell Hochschild, for example, write that "over the last thirty years, as the rich countries have grown much richer, the poor countries have become—in both absolute and relative terms—poorer" (2002, 8). The activists' collective Notes from Nowhere claims that "the central fact of our time is the upwards transfer of power and wealth—never have so many been governed by so few" (2003, 25). Similarly, Sarah Anderson, John Cavanagh, and Tea Lee assert that "wherever globalization impinges, inequality deepens. From Mexico to Japan, the rich are getting richer while the poor are becoming more desperate and numerous" (2000, x).

Most mainstream economists, scholars and politicians on the right, and spokespeople of the World Bank and the IMF answer these questions in the affirmative, giving much more upbeat assessments of current levels and trends in global poverty and inequality. Recently, the World Bank argued that between 1981 and 2001 the number of people below the poverty line of one dollar a day had halved (World Bank 2004a, b). According to David Dollar and Aart Kraay, "the best evidence available shows . . . [that] the current wave of globalization, which started around 1980, has actually promoted economic equality and reduced poverty" (2002, 120). However, Branko Milanovic (2002), who was at the time working at the World Bank, calculated on the basis of improved data for the period 1988–1993 that world income inequality is not only very high but has also been rapidly increasing.

Those who claim that global capitalism is a force for good for the world's poorest people, and that inequality in the world is decreasing, often argue that those who think otherwise are ignorant at best and despite their good intentions may even damage the causes they defend. *The Economist* (2004), for example, writes that both global poverty and inequality are decreasing, and that social activists and global-justice scholars are doing "nothing but harm" to the world's most destitute people by opposing global capitalism.

In this essay I will discuss three evaluative approaches that can be used to assess well-being, poverty, and inequality in the context of globalization and global justice. By spelling out these three approaches, and by looking at their differences and their respective weaknesses and strengths, I will try to shed some light on the different languages and conflicting claims made by advocates and critics of global capitalism regarding the current levels and trends in global inequality and poverty. These three frameworks are income metrics, resourcism, and the capability approach. Sections 2 to 4 discuss each of the three evaluative frameworks in turn. Section 5 clarifies an obscurity in the debate between resourcism and the capability approach. Section 6 analyzes a core difference between Rawlsian resources and the capability approach: the question of whether conceptualizations of inequality and social justice should account for naturally caused inequalities. Section 7 then takes up the core question of this essay: What are the advantages and disadvantages of each of these evaluative frameworks for the assessment of global poverty and inequality? I will defend the claim that these frameworks can best be seen as complementary, rather than purely rival alternatives. Section 8 analyzes Thomas Pogge's claim that capability metrics, and the Human Development Index in particular, conceal global inequality.

2. Income Measures

Most statistics and assessments of world poverty and inequality are constructed using money metrics, that is, using income as the variable of comparison. In economic theory, it is standard knowledge that income can only serve as a proxy for individual welfare under specific assumptions (for example, the absence of negative externalities, such as environmental damage), and at the cost of neglecting production in the nonmarket economy. Income, despite its limitations in fully registering individual welfare, let alone well-being or the quality of life, is widely used because there is no consensus on a better alternative, and income is one-dimensional and thus allows for precise calculations and estimates.

Comparisons between countries, especially between poor countries and affluent ones, only complicate such calculations. As Robert Wade (2003) notes, these complications include the fact that these comparisons can be made using exchange rates, general-consumption purchasing-power parities, or purchasing-power parities that are based only on the goods typically consumed by the poor. The income data for some countries (including very large countries, such as China) is also unreliable. For the poverty statistics, there are problems caused by the fact that the income distribution is very flat at its lower end, implying that choosing a slightly higher poverty line could lead to a large increase in the number of officially poor. With respect to inequality statistics, it is generally acknowledged in welfare economics that they are sensitive to the measure chosen (Sen 1973).

What, then, are the results derived from the empirical studies of income trends? Some economists claim that the number of extremely poor people worldwide is declining and that the global gap between rich and poor is getting smaller (Chen and Ravallion 2004; Dollar and Kraay 2002; *The Economist* 2004; World Bank 2004b).[1] Other researchers have either used other data which suggest that income inequality is increasing rapidly (Milanovic 2002) or have criticized the World Bank poverty estimates, arguing that these conclusions are unwarranted and that the number of poor may even be increasing (Pogge and Reddy 2003; Reddy and Pogge 2003; Wade 2003).

At present the World Bank is the only producer of global poverty statistics. For the past few years, the World Bank has published annual estimates of global poverty, announcing any trends in the data with press releases that are then widely cited. In April 2004, the World Bank (2004a) announced in a press release that global poverty had halved since 1981. The number of poor people in developing countries, defined as those

[1] However, Chen and Ravallion's estimates (2004) also show that the 400 million fewer people living below the $1 a day line are almost entirely situated in China, and that the number of the poor under the $2 a day line increased between 1981 and 2001.

living on less than $1 a day, had dropped from 1.5 billion in 1981 to 1.1 billion in 2001. In percentages, this amounts to a reduction of extreme poverty from 40 percent to 21 percent of the total population in the developing countries.

We should note, first of all, that this press statement is inaccurate and misleading, as it tells us that the extremely poor people are those who have to live on less than a dollar a day. For many readers in affluent societies, this probably sounds like a plausible poverty line. Such readers are likely to believe that in Malawi or Bangladesh $1 must buy a local person quite a lot, as everything is assumed to be cheap. But this is not what these poverty statistics really measure: in fact, "a dollar a day" is shorthand for "the purchasing-power parity of $1.08 in the United States in 1993." In other words, a person is poor if he or she has to get by with fewer commodities than one could have bought with $1.08 in the United States in 1993. Such misleading press releases conceal the fact that the World Bank's poverty line is very low, which drastically reduces the poverty incidence, thereby downplaying the catastrophic nature of the current global poverty levels.[2] Indeed, according to the latest estimates by top economists of the poverty unit of the World Bank, the global poverty count went up over the same period if one uses the "two dollars a day" poverty line (Chen and Ravallion 2004). The fact that a global poverty estimate is so sensitive to its poverty line should make us cautious about the significance that can be attached to these estimates, and about how readily they are presented to the public as uncontested facts. After all, which newspaper reader has any comprehension of the difference between getting by on the purchasing-power equivalent of $2 rather than $2?

There are thus two problems with this debate: the wider public is not likely to comprehend fully the significance (or insignificance) of the 1$ a day poverty line, and the World Bank does not sufficiently highlight the contested nature of its poverty estimates, as this would jeopardize its own policy agenda.

In addition, Sanjay Reddy and Thomas Pogge have formulated a crushing critique of the World Bank's poverty statistics (Pogge and Reddy 2003; Reddy and Pogge 2003). They argue that the $1 a day poverty measure is arbitrary and lacks any conceptual foundations. The World Bank's poverty counts are not based on how we think of poverty, as people being undernourished or without shelter, or lacking other basic necessities. Instead, the global poverty line is chosen as the median of the lowest domestic poverty lines for the countries in the World Bank's data set (Reddy and Pogge 2003, 5–6; Ravallion 2003, 4). The World Bank's

[2] For a more profound critique of how the international discourse on global poverty tries to conceal the catastrophic situation of extreme poverty, in the context of the first U.N. Millennium Development Goal (which is based on the same World Bank poverty statistics), see Pogge forthcoming.

calculations also use purchasing-power parities that take into account the price levels of *all* goods and services in proportion to their share in the international consumption expenditure. In this calculation, the prices of basic necessities play a minor role, whereas they play a huge role in the consumption of the poor. Services in developing countries are relatively cheap in comparison with the consumption prices of basic necessities, which make up the consumption of the poor. Finally, Pogge and Reddy also show that the World Bank's method is internally inconsistent, and that a change of base year can have significant effects on the poverty estimates. They conclude that at this moment we do not know how many people in the world are poor, but that the biases in the current methodology most likely lead to an underestimation of the incidence of global poverty.

Reddy and Pogge do not suggest that we give up monitoring global poverty. Instead, they offer the outline of an alternative methodology, whereby an international poverty line would be developed starting from some basic capabilities or needs, which should be selected through an international deliberative process, and using the amount of money that would be needed to meet such needs to make international poverty comparisons:

> The serious flaws in the [World] Bank's method have a common root and are avoidable through a straightforward innovation: the definition of severe income poverty must be more appropriately focused on what being poor consists in: on what people generally need to achieve a set of elementary capabilities, rather than on arbitrary dollar amounts. (Reddy and Pogge 2003, 12)

It is remarkable that in his reply to Pogge and Reddy World Bank economist Martin Ravallion (2003) does not address this foundational critique. He argues that he would be surprised if consensus were possible on a fixed bundle of goods, as people consume different things in different countries, whereas there is consensus on the $1 a day concept. Angus Deaton (2003) uses the same argument that the $1 a day concept can rely on a consensus and has proven its value because it is widely used.

This strikes me as a poor argument in favor of the $1 a day concept. First, it is not clear that this supposed consensus actually exists. *All* simple statistics produced by international agencies are widely used (especially in the media), and this reflects less about their quality than about their availability and the authority of the institutions that produce and circulate them. Second, while the consensus on the $1 a day concept might be a consensus in Washington or among the supporters of World Bank methodologies and policies, it is certainly not a consensus among other people concerned with poverty and destitution. Social activists might well ask how on earth one should be able to survive on what $1 could have bought in the United States in the 1990s. But more important, applying Pogge's and Reddy's method would not, as Ravallion claims, require a consensus on specific commodities (such as rice or bread); rather, it would require a consensus on certain valuable states of being, such as being well nourished and minimally dressed and having access to some basic shelter. The poverty line would be defined as the money needed to buy the cheapest possible bundle of commodities that would deliver minimum levels of those crucial dimensions of well-being.

3. Classifying Resources

A second approach to global poverty and inequality assessments is resourcism. It is possible to identify at least five different accounts of resources that might be used in such assessments.

Type 1: GNP per capita. Gross national product (GNP) is the total income generated through market production in a particular country, after deduction of the cost for the inputs in this production. An increase in GNP per capita is economic growth, which is a crucial goal of macroeconomic policies. GNP per capita is a rough indicator of economic production, and its use as a proxy for well-being or the quality of life is dubious. Environmentalists have argued that GNP ignores whether economic production and the basic institutions in society are damaging or protecting our environmental resources. Feminists have argued that it ignores unpaid nonmarket production, like domestic production, and especially the vital activities of caring. More generally, GNP per capita values economic production in terms of its market value-added (that is, price minus the total costs), even if it concerns weapons production that will subsequently be used to oppress or kill people. Because it has been one of the few statistics available for each country, however, it has been widely used in research on global poverty and inequality.

Type 2: Individual disposable income. Welfare and development economists who work on the microeconomic aspects of development focus on individual disposable income, or in case one is looking at people who live partly in a subsistence economy, on consumption directly. These measures were discussed in the previous section.

Type 3: Individual entitlement of material goods. This notion extends individual disposable income by including an estimate for nonmarket production and the provision of public goods, and thus it gives us a more extended account of resources than does individual disposable income. This type of resource is used in more fine-grained micro studies in welfare economics but hardly ever in discussions about global poverty and inequality.

Type 4: Dworkinian resources. Dworkin's (1981) philosophical theory of equality distinguishes between two types of resources, impersonal resources and personal resources. Dworkin's impersonal resources are equivalent to individual entitlement to material goods. Personal resources in Dworkin's account are personal bodily and mental resources, like intelligence, physical and mental abilities and disabilities, and so forth.

Type 5: Rawlsian social primary goods. These resources are the goods that a rational person is presumed to want regardless of whatever else she may want. Social primary goods include income, wealth, liberties, opportunities, and the social basis of self-respect (Rawls 1999; 1982; 2001, 57–61). Thus, Rawlsian social primary goods are a combination of individual disposable income (type 2) and some civil and political human rights, opportunities, and the social basis of self-respect. Note that Rawls does not include the Dworkinian personal resources. I will discuss the implications of this in section 6.

4. Functionings and Capabilities

A third and final approach to assessing global inequality and poverty is the capability approach (Sen 1980; 1985; 1992; 1993; 1999).

As I pointed out earlier, welfare economics generally focuses on the means to achieve a good life, which are consumer goods and services, or the resources needed to generate them. Sen's core claim is that goods are important not in themselves but in what their characteristics enable people to do and to be, that is, in the capabilities that a person can generate from these goods and services. The extent to which a person can generate capabilities from goods and services depends on the factors that determine how smoothly this conversion can be made.

Three different types of conversion factors can be distinguished: social, environmental, and personal. The social conversion factors are determined by a number of societal aspects, such as social institutions (for example, the educational system, the political system, the family, and so on), social norms (including gender norms, religious norms, cultural norms, and moral norms), traditions, and the behavior of others in society (for example, stereotyping, prejudiced behavior, racism, sexism, homophobic behavior, and so forth). The environmental conversion factors are determined by the environment in which a person lives—for example, whether deforestation has caused erosion and flooding that threaten the stability of one's shelter. The personal conversion factors are determined by one's mental and physical aspects; these personal characteristics, such as disabilities or bodily vulnerabilities, affect the type and degree of capabilities one can generate with resources. Note that not all capabilities require some good or service as an input; for example, being respected by your peers often only requires respectful behavior from other people. A person's capability set, which comprises all the capabilities of a person, represents her freedom to achieve well-being and agency—and this is the dimension that Sen proposes as the informational basis for assessments of inequality, poverty, justice, and development. However, as a person's capabilities are her real and genuine opportunities to do what she wants to do and be the person she wants to be, these capabilities obviously are difficult to observe. Instead, what we can observe are those capabilities she has chosen to act upon, the capabilities she has chosen to realize. These realized capabilities are called her achieved functionings.

An important aspect of the capability approach, but one that is extremely hard to measure, is people's agency. The capability approach refuses to see people as patients, who can be helped by being given a handout or a cure that they can take or leave, but sees them rather as agents, who can and should be given the power and the necessary conditions to take their lives into their own hands. While agency may be relatively less important in the discussion of the capability approach as an approach to the *assessment* of inequality and poverty than it is in debates on policy design and public action, it has some bearing on the debate on global justice, as I will try to argue toward the end of the essay.

5. Capabilities versus Resources: A Clarification

Capability theorists and resourcists have formulated arguments for or against a particular type of resource for a specific purpose, such as the conceptualization of social justice or measurement of the quality of life. Sometimes the conclusion of these arguments have subsequently been used in another debate, without sufficiently acknowledging that some arguments in favor of (or against) one type of resource are convincing for some purposes but not for others.

For example, in his comparison of capability and Rawlsian resourcist accounts of social justice, Pogge argues that the feminist critique formulated by capability theorists is orthogonal to the comparison between resourcist and capability approaches (Pogge 2002a, 183–84). Capability theorists have criticized resourcist accounts of types 1, 2, and 3 by arguing that these resourcist accounts conceal inequalities between men and women. But Pogge reads this critique as if it were formulated as a comparison between the capability approach and resources of type 5—that is, social primary goods. While Pogge may perhaps be right that feminist arguments are orthogonal to the contrast between the capability approach and Rawlsian social primary goods, they are certainly not orthogonal to the contrast between the capability approach and resources as GNP per capita, individual disposable income, or individual entitlement to material goods. There are some structural reasons why income measures are unsuited to a nonreductionist account of gender inequality, including the fact that they cannot account for intrahousehold inequalities and also do not allow for the fact that while women may be worse off in most areas of life, men might be worse off in some other areas (Robeyns 2002; 2003).

Sen's writings have also sometimes failed to distinguish between different strands of resourcism. By discussing real income, Dworkinian resources, and Rawlsian social primary goods simultaneously, and by insufficiently explaining and stressing the differences between different types of resources, Sen has contributed to the belief that objections against one type of resourcist account can be generalized to others. For example, in *Development as Freedom,* in a section entitled "Incomes, Resources and Freedoms," Sen discusses real income, Rawlsian social primary goods, and the critique by Mahbub Ul Haq (1995) and the United Nations Development Program (UNDP) on the dominance of GDP. In that section, Sen also downplays the differences between social primary goods and resources understood as individual entitlement to goods when he writes:

> The broadening of the informational focus from incomes to primary goods is not, however, adequate to deal with all the relevant variations in the relationship between income and resources, on the one hand, and well-being and freedom, on the other. Indeed, primary goods themselves are mainly various types of general resources, and the use of these resources to generate the ability to do valuable things is subject to as much the same list of variations ... in the context of reviewing the relationship between income and well-being: personal heterogeneities, environmental diversities, variations in social climate, differences in relational perspectives and distribution within the family. (1999, 72–73)

Sen is suggesting here that Rawlsian social primary goods boil down to material impersonal resources. This seems to me an unwarranted reduction of social primary goods, since liberties and opportunities and especially the social basis of self-respect go well beyond individual entitlements to material goods. Thus, Sen's capability critique of real income cannot automatically be extended to social primary goods. In conclusion, the debate between the capability theorists and resourcists can only be properly conducted if we distinguish more carefully between different types of resources.

6. Are Natural Endowments Morally Relevant?

Pogge (2002a) argues that the real difference between Rawlsian resourcists and capability theorists is whether they hold that natural endowments, such as disabilities, should give rise to compensatory claims of justice. I do not have the space here to make a full and detailed analysis of how the capability approach and Rawslian social primary goods deal with issues of disability and other natural endowments in theories of social justice, as this sort of analysis would require us to discuss other aspects of theories of justice as well, such as the Rawlsian social contract, the Rawlsian idea of the original position, and the underspecification of the capability approach (but see Brighouse 2001; 2004; Kittay 1999; Robeyns 2004). Instead, I will limit my analysis here to the question of whether *in the context of global inequalities and poverty* the evaluative metric should be sensitive to natural endowments.

Let us first take the case of international aggregate comparisons of poverty and inequality, that is, the comparison of countries. If the natural endowments that are negatively affecting the conversion of resources into functionings are randomly distributed among those countries, then the differences in poverty or average welfare levels between different countries will not be very much affected by whether we use a social primary goods or a functionings metric. To put it somewhat more precisely, the ranking of countries in terms of poverty count or average welfare level will not be affected. However, if the natural endowments are not randomly distributed in the world—that is, when some countries have many more disabled people than other countries—then international comparisons will be affected by the choice between a disability-sensitive versus a disability-insensitive metric. For example, income metrics, or social primary goods metrics, are unable to register the HIV/AIDS pandemic when making international comparisons, as these metrics are sensitive only to the indirect effects of HIV/AIDS on the distribution of primary goods and income, whereas the effects on functionings are much more devastating.

If we want to make microcomparisons of poverty and inequality, the case for moving beyond social primary goods and income to include deprivations in functioning because of handicaps is even stronger. If any of the resourcist approaches want to be able to make a claim that social institutions should be designed so as to limit the loss in quality of life caused by a disability, then they need to appeal implicitly or explicitly to a metric of well-being that must take into account how different resources affect functioning (Brighouse 2004). Pogge is concerned that acknowledging natural endowments in the capability approach leads to a stigma on the disabled. However, it is not at all clear that acknowledging a disability and providing the necessary financial compensation for additional medical and nonmedical expenditures would create any stigma. I submit that so long as a natural endowment significantly affects some core functionings, there is no inherent and unavoidable stigma in compensation for any additional costs needed to try to enhance these functionings. The difficulty for a government is how to demarcate those natural endowments and functionings that are a legitimate concern for government intervention, such as being paralyzed and unable to hold a job or move around, from those that are not, such as being sufficiently handsome to attract a sexual partner. The capability approach definitely needs to do more work in spelling out such distinctions, but I subscribe to its principle that we should not ignore all effects of natural endowments on people's functionings.

It seems to me that most people would—rightly—see the lack of compensation for the additional costs of trying to expand one's capabilities that are affected by a disability as an injustice, whereas Pogge holds that this falls outside the scope of justice:

> Even if there are some of us who have special needs and disabilities that the rest of us have no duties *of justice* to alleviate—because we did not contribute to their emergence and do not benefit from their existence—we may nonetheless have other quite stringent moral reasons individually or collectively to engage in such alleviation: duties of humanity towards all human beings, for example, or duties of solidarity towards those with whom we share a common political life. (2002a, 189–90, italics in original)

As Kittay (1999), Brighouse (2001), and others have pointed out, it is remarkable that the social primary goods approach sees our duties toward the disabled as lying outside the scope of justice—especially since Rawls regards justice as the first virtue of society. I fail to see how this disagreement about the scope of justice can be solved with rational arguments. However, it does make a difference for measurements of poverty and inequality: if these measurements are to correspond to a notion of justice, the social primary goods approach will be unable to pick up the negative effects of disabilities on a person's quality of life, in contrast to the capability approach.

7. Comparing Assessments Based on Income, Resources, and Functionings

Income metrics, resources metrics, and capability metrics are based on different theoretical conceptualizations of the quality of life. Income and resources metrics focus on the means of the quality of life, while capability metrics focus on the constitutive elements of the quality of life.

The consequence of the different conceptual foundations between income metrics, primary goods metrics, and functionings/capability metrics is that the last are able to process information that the former two cannot, information that may change the overall assessment of inequality or poverty. Let us look at two examples. First, take the case of Filipino women who leave their families to work as nannies in North America and Europe. Most of these Filipinas have children of their own, whom they leave in the care of their own mothers, their sisters, or a nanny back home. In financial terms, this "international care chain" is undoubtedly a positive process, as the Filipinas earn significantly more than they could in the Philippines, and they might create an income-generating opportunity for someone back home. An evaluation in terms of social primary goods would lead to the same conclusion. The remittances they send home feed, clothe, and shelter their own children and also provide an income for the women who are taking care of these children. Sometimes another family member, like the father, is able to start a small business, although sometimes the money sent home may also be spent on alcohol. According to Rhacel Salazar Parreñas (2002, 41), remittances constitute the largest source of foreign currency in the Philippines, totaling almost $7 billion in 1999. Such capital flows surely have a tempering effect on global poverty and inequality measurements of the type discussed in section 2.

However, if we do not assess this type of care worker's emigration in terms of income or resources but rather make assessments based on achieved functionings, the situation looks different. Several authors argue that while the financial evaluation may be positive, there are also nonfinancial effects that are negative (Ehrenreich and Hochschild 2002; Hochschild 2002; Parreñas 2002). It is estimated that 30 percent of Filipino children grow up in a household where at least one parent is working oversees (Hochschild 2002, 22), and that these children suffer "inevitable trauma" (Ehrenreich and Hochschild 2002, 13). The children endure emotional hardship, and older siblings are often forced to take on the role of substitute parents. Parreñas's (2002) study shows that these children suffer the loss of family intimacy and feel that they are denied time with their parents, and they all say that they would never leave their own children to take jobs as migrant workers. As one child in her study puts it, "Time together is something that money can neither buy nor replace" (Parreñas 2002, 51). The mothers, too, suffer emotional hardship, as they badly miss their children. While most mothers try to keep in touch with their children through letters, phone calls, and the odd visit back home, it is very doubtful that they can develop a profound emotional and social relationship with their children. As a result, some of these mothers are abandoned by their adult children later in life. In sum, the capability approach has the theoretical tools to pick up this morally relevant information that is overlooked by income metrics or resourcist approaches that are broader, such as social primary goods.

A second example illustrating this claim is Sabina Alkire's (2002) fieldwork in Pakistan, in which she evaluated three different poverty-reduction programs. Alkire (2002, 233–96) found that one project had a much greater positive effect on the inner peace of people and on their social relations. When these nontangible effects and the monetary effects go in opposite directions, the overall evaluation explicitly needs to address the trade-offs between monetary and nonmonetary effects. Suppose global poverty is decreasing, as the World Bank wants us to believe. If this comes at the expense of nonmonetary capabilities, such as democratic agency, respect, emotional well-being, and social cohesion, the overall evaluation is not automatically positive but would ultimately depend on what one values most. Mainstream economists tend to value only income, while social activists often value democratic agency and social relations very highly. A capability evaluation can make full theoretical sense of this. A social primary goods evaluation can make some theoretical sense of it, but not what concerns emotional and social-relation capabilities, except if one stretches the notion of social primary goods way beyond Rawls's original definition. An income evaluation is unable to capture these trade-offs at all.

The example of Filipino immigrant workers and their love-deprived children does, however, also indicate the main limitation of the capability approach: that it is difficult to operationalize and has structural limitations in measurement, because there are many morally relevant functionings and because many nonmaterial functionings, such as the quality of parental relationships, are very hard to measure. Economists generally hold that parsimony is a virtue; the capability approach obviously does not share that view. Achieved functioning levels can be measured, as the empirical survey in Kuklys and Robeyns (2004) shows. But often a capability assessment will be imprecise. Capability theorists are not bothered too much by this, since they hold that an ambiguous and complex phenomenon should not be assessed with measurement tools that are designed for precise phenomena. But obviously it will be hard to make inequality comparisons among more than 150 countries based on a multidimensional selection of fuzzy functionings. As the literature mentioned in section 2 makes abundantly clear, it is already hard enough to try to measure global poverty and inequality one-dimensionally. This would thus suggest that income, resources, and functionings based assessments should be seen as complementary to one another. However, Christian Barry (2003) has argued that these measurement problems will also be encountered by the more plausible resourcists views, such as Rawlsian social primary goods. In terms of measurability, there seems to be a continuum, with the most simple income metrics at one end and the most complex version of the capability approach at the other.

Apart from this complementarity, we could also ask whether income metrics, social primary goods, and capabilities correspond to a macro-micro continuum. A micro assessment allows for an abundance of data and a subtle weighting of all the different dimensions, but these often get lost in macro assessments. Of course, this is not to claim that income is unimportant at the microlevel, or that functioning achievements have no information to add at a macrolevel. Good counterexamples of the latter are the data on the numbers of girls and women "missing" from the aggregate population statistics, caused by female infanticide and sex-selective abortion (Sen 1990; Klasen and Wink 2003). These statistics, which could be understood both as a social primary good (the liberty to live) or as a capability (the capability to live) but which would never be captured by an income metric, do tell us something important about international differences in this dimension of gender inequality.

As we've seen from the discussion in this section, both capabilities and the different types of resources have strengths and weaknesses. I would therefore suggest that we start from the general assumption that both informational bases have advantages, and that either one of them, or both, might be appropriate to use, depending on the concrete kind of inequality or poverty analysis under consideration. Thus, I would suggest that the basic point of departure should be to consider *both* approaches, and to ask which one should be used for the assessment of local and global inequalities and poverty.

8. Does the Human Development Index Conceal Global Inequalities?

The Human Development Reports (HDRs) (UNDP 1990–2004) and in particular the widely used Human Development Index (HDI) are based on the capability approach, although it is fair to say that they are not the most refined applications of the capability approach. In his elaborate critique of the capability approach, Pogge also criticizes the HDI, arguing that it conceals global inequalities:

> Among economists, these issues—how global inequality is steadily increasing and how global institutional arrangements are exacerbating poverty and inequality—are taboo. In fact, the UNDP took heavy flak for printing [that inequality increased at a 3.04 average percentage during the 1990–97 post-cold-war globalization period]. By comparing countries in terms of their HDI scores, the UNDP now avoids such unpleasantness. Its tables of countries and their HDI scores (ranging from Norway's 0.942 to Sierra Leone's 0.275) are of merely ordinal significance and thus provide no information about inequality or inequality trends. HDI scores convey no sense of what life is like for the majority of people in a poor country. And they encourage the thought that each country is solely responsible for its own development. (Pogge 2002a, 216)

And a few paragraphs further on, Pogge concludes:

> [T]he large increase in global inequality and the consequent persistence of massive severe poverty in the developing world have contributed to the stunning success of the capability approach in international organizations as well as in popular and academic discourse. Capability metrics tend to conceal the enormous and still rising economic inequalities which resource metrics make quite blatant. (217)

There is some truth in this statement about the limited usefulness of the HDI if one wants to focus on global inequality. Indeed, Mahbub ul Haq (1995), who founded the Human Development Reports, has been quite clear in his writings that he believes that developing countries have primary responsibility for their own development, which clearly contrasts with Pogge's (2002b) focus on the responsibility of rich countries for the current state of affairs in the poor countries. Based on my present knowledge of the causal evidence, it seems to me that one needs both arguments, though I am sympathetic to Pogge's view that we must become more aware and analyze in more depth the degree to which the current international global structures create an injustice for which the rich countries are primarily responsible. If that is our goal, I agree that the HDI is not the appropriate assessment tool.

However, at least four arguments can be developed in defense of the HDI and the capability approach. First, the HDRs offer a much broader discussion of poverty and inequality in human development than the HDI only. Every HDR contains some narratives of best practice and failed strategies and adds much more detail and qualitative assessment than the HDI alone can capture. Thus, while the HDI might conceal the pervasiveness of poverty and inequality, the full reports do pay more attention to these issues.

Second, it is possible that the selection of capabilities in the HDI is so limited that it downplays global inequalities. If that is the case, then Pogge's critique of the UNDP is in fact a critique of the *selection* of the capabilities in the HDI, not of measuring inequality and development in capabilities per se. For example, advocates of the virtues of global capitalism often argue that the outsourcing of jobs to the South creates jobs for local people there, who accordingly improve their net disposable income, which will also be picked up by the income, poverty, and inequality measures of the World Bank. But these jobs vary enormously in their quality and thus can lead to drastically different effects on people's capabilities, such as being treated with dignity, having control over one's time-allocation, reproductive freedoms (as young women are often fired or not hired if they are pregnant), sexual safety and bodily integrity, occupational health, and so forth. These capabilities are obviously not captured by the HDI.

Third, insofar as the HDI conceals inequalities, we should ask to what extent this is due to its ordinal character, rather than the fact that it goes beyond GDP per capita to include some proxies of functionings. Pogge does not disentangle these two effects in his critique.

Fourth and finally, there is nothing that prevents us from using the HDI and income metrics simultaneously. To get a clear picture of trends and levels of inequalities, Pogge is right that global income inequality statistics remain vital. But they will not tell us the full story, perhaps not even half the story, of the current trends in local and global inequalities. I see no reasons why they could not be used simultaneously, given that they shed a different light on the subject matter.

It is somewhat ironic that Thomas Pogge himself, in two papers written with Sanjay Reddy, can be interpreted as providing a strong case for the capability approach as the basis of global poverty assessments. But while it is ironic, it need not be inconsistent. Pogge (2002a) *only* analyzes the capability approach as the basis of a theory of social justice, whereas the capability approach is also used in a range of areas that do rely on a capability-related notion of well-being without addressing issues of justice per se, such as poverty measurement, cost-benefit analysis, efficiency evaluations, and inequality evaluations. Pogge might thus hold the internally consistent view that the capability approach is useful for poverty measurement, but not as the foundation for a theory of social justice.

As explained in section 2, Reddy and Pogge advocate a capability-based global poverty assessment as an alternative for the $1 per day poverty line used by the World Bank to monitor trends and levels of severe poverty (Pogge and Reddy 2003; Reddy and Pogge 2003). In my view, their work provides a very good illustration of one way in which the complementariness between resources and capabilities could work. Recall that their proposal is that "the definition of severe income poverty must be more appropriately focused on what being poor consists in: on what people generally need to achieve a set of elementary capabilities, rather than on arbitrary dollar amounts." Pogge and Reddy's proposal shows that while the philosophical foundation of a poverty assessment could be in terms of achieved functioning levels, poverty could be translated into a monetary value so that the statistical comparison will be expressed in an income metric. Thus one is able to have a poverty measure that has a sound conceptual meaning and can be translated back to the income dimension in order not to compromise its measurability.

Pogge may not have conceived of his proposal in terms of capabilities, but in my understanding this is a capability metric (more precisely, an achieved-functionings metric), not a resource metric. It is a capability metric that defines the poverty line as the monetary value of the bundle of social primary goods needed to achieve the thresholds of the selected functionings. However, if Pogge and Reddy's conceptualization of poverty is interpreted as a functionings measure, then it should be noted that it does not account for each individual conversion factor. It will not, for example, account for differences in metabolic rates. As discussed in section 7, only measures at the microlevel allow for these fine-grained dimensions of the capability approach, whereas capability measures at the macrolevel, such as the global poverty statistic, will always have to make some simplifications.

9. Conclusion

In the past decade, issues of global poverty and inequality have regained renewed interest. In large part this is due to political activism of the global social movement (see, e.g., Fisher and Poniah 2003, Hertz 2002, Notes from Nowhere 2003, Roy 2001). These social activists are often reproached for ignoring the "fact" that inequality and poverty are decreasing, thereby doing more harm than good to the global poor through their anticapitalist activism.

My analysis of the literature suggests a different understanding. It suggests that so far as monetary assessments are concerned, there is substantial disagreement about the actual size and especially the trend of global income poverty and inequality. The confident rhetoric in the World Bank's press releases, along with the often insulting and arrogant tone in the articles by those who think that poverty and inequality are decreasing, may convince the broader public, but it does not get us any closer to the truth.

Moreover, another reason why social activists' views are so strongly at odds with those of their opponents might be that they use a very different evaluative framework. In this essay I have spelled out three main evaluative frameworks. Social activists are closer to a capability account (with particular attention to democratic capabilities) than to resourcist or income-based evaluations. I have provided arguments for why additional considerations should be taken into account when addressing whether the poorest people are better off and global inequality is less severe than before. If we endorse the conceptual arguments of the capability approach to well-being assessment, we would need to look at a wider range of issues, among them those that include people's agency. A person can live with a fixed amount of financial resources, but in one scenario she has relative economic security and control over her own labor, while in another she is vulnerable to the whims of the global capitalist markets and the bosses of the international corporations and their local subcontractors. Social activists would say that the purely income-based poverty and inequality measures cannot give us any information on people's democratic capabilities, that is, the extent to which they have a fair political decision-making power over things that matter to them. Activists generally have a comprehensive view of what poverty and inequality mean, not a view that first reduces poverty and inequality to economic poverty and economic inequality and then reduces them even further to income inequality.

People's agency to take their lives into their own hands and to make collective decisions about how to organize their communities and manage their commons can be as important for them as to secure minimal material or financial welfare. While the quantifiable functionings and capabilities may well be limited in capturing these dimensions, the overall framework of the capability approach gives a clear rationale for why we should pay due attention to nonmaterial dimensions, such as family time together, emotional well-being, and democratic agency. And it is precisely on those latter dimensions of agency and democracy that many of the social activists focus, dimensions that the purely income-based indicators of poverty and inequality are unable to capture.

University of Amsterdam
Department of Political Science
Oudezijds Achterburgwal 237
1012 DL Amsterdam
The Netherlands
i.robeyns@uva.nl

Acknowledgments

An earlier version of this essay was written while I was a visiting scholar in the Department of Philosophy at Columbia University, New York, and was presented at the University of Maryland and Bryn Mawr College. For comments and discussions, I am grateful to Christian Barry, Harry Brighouse, David Crocker, Thomas Pogge, Roland Pierik, and Sanjay Reddy. The financial support of the Dutch Organization for Scientific Research, NWO, is also gratefully acknowledged.

Bibliography

Alkire, Sabina. 2002. *Valuing Freedoms: Sen's Capability Approach and Poverty Reduction*. New York: Oxford University Press.

Anderson, Sarah, John Cavanagh, and Thea Lea. 2000. *Field Guide to the Global Economy*. New York: New Press.

Barry, Christian. 2003. "Education and Standards of Living." In *A Companion to the Philosophy of Education*, edited by Currren Randall, 456–70. Oxford: Blackwell.

Brighouse, Harry. 2001. "Can Justice as Fairness Accommodate the Disabled?" *Social Theory and Practice* 27, no. 4:537–60.

———. 2004. "Primary Goods, Capabilities, and the Problem of the Public Criterion of Justice." Paper presented at the Annual Meetings of the American Political Science Association, Chicago, September 5–7.

Chen, Shaohua, and Martin Ravallion. 2004. "How Have the World's Poorest Fared since the Early 1980s?" *World Bank Research Observer* 19, no. 2:141–69.

Deaton, Angus 2003. "How to Monitor Poverty for the Millennium Development Goals." *Journal of Human Development* 4, no. 3:353–78.

Dollar, David, and Aart Kraay. 2002. "Spreading the Wealth." *Foreign Affairs* 81, no. 1:120–33.

Dworkin, Ronald. 1981. "What Is Equality? Part 2: Equality of Resources." *Philosophy and Public Affairs* 10:283–45.

EhrenreichBarbara, Barbara, and Arlie Russell Hochschild. 2002. In *Global Woman: Nannies, Maids and Sex Workers in the New Economy*, edited by Barbara Ehrenreich and Arlie Russell Hochschild, 1–13. London: Granta Books.

Fisher, William, and Thomas Ponniah, eds. 2003. *Another World Is Possible*. London: Zed Books.

Hertz, Noreena. 2002. *The Silent Takeover: Global Capitalism and the Death of Democracy*. London: Arrow. First published in 2001.

Hochschild, Arlie Russell. 2002. "Love and Gold." In *Global Woman: Nannies, Maids and Sex Workers in the New Economy*, edited by Barbara Ehrenreich and Arlie Russell Hochschild, 15–30. London: Granta Books.

Kittay, Eva Feder. 1999. *Love's Labor: Essays on Women, Equality, and Dependence*. New York: Routledge.

Klasen, Stephan, and Claudia Wink. 2003. "'Missing Women': Revisiting the Debate." *Feminist Economics* 9, nos. 2–3:263–99.
Kuklys, Wiebke, and Ingrid Robeyns. 2004. "Sen's Capability Approach to Welfare Economics." Cambridge Working Papers in Economics no. 0415. University of Cambridge. Available at http://www.econ.cam.ac.uk/dae/repec/cam/pdf/cwpe0415.pdf.
Milanovic, Branko. 2002. "True World Income Distribution, 1988 and 1993: First Calculations Based on Household Surveys Alone." *Economic Journal* 112 (January):51–92.
Notes from Nowhere. 2003. "Emergence: An Irresistible Global Uprising." In *We Are Everywhere: The Irresistible Rise of Global Anticapitalism*, edited by Notes from Nowhere, 19–29. London: Verso.
Parreñas, Rhacel Salazar. 2002. "The Care Crisis in the Philippines: Children and Transnational Families in the New Global Economy." In *Global Woman: Nannies, Maids and Sex Workers in the New Economy*, edited by Barbara Ehrenreich and Arlie Russell Hochschild, 39–54. London: Granta Books.
Pogge, Thomas. 2002a. "Can the Capability Approach Be Justified?" *Philosophical Topics* 30, no. 2:167–228.
———. 2002b. *World Poverty and Human Rights*. Cambridge: Polity Press.
———. Forthcoming. "The First UN Millennium Development Goal: A Cause for Celebration?" *Journal of Human Development*.
Pogge, Thomas, and Sanjay Reddy. 2003. "Unkown: The Extent, Distribution, and Trend of Global Income Poverty." Mimeo, Columbia University, New York.
Ravallion, Martin. 2003. "How *Not* to Count the Poor? A Reply to Reddy and Pogge." Mimeo, World Bank, Washington, DC.
Rawls, John. 1999. *A Theory of Justice*. Revised edition. Oxford: Oxford University Press. Original published in 1971.
———. 1982. "Social Unity and Primary Goods." In *Utilitarianism and Beyond*, edited by Amartya Sen and Bernard Williams, 159–86. Cambridge: Cambridge University Press.
———. 2001. *Justice as Fairness: A Restatement*. Edited by Erin Kelly. Cambridge, Mass.: Harvard University Press.
Reddy, Sanjay, and Thomas Pogge. 2003. "How *Not* to Count the Poor." Version 4.5. Mimeo, Columbia University, New York.
Robeyns, Ingrid. 2002. "Gender Inequality: A Capability Perspective." Unpublished Ph.D. disseration, University of Cambridge.
———. 2003. "Sen's Capability Approach and Gender Inequality: Selecting Relevant Capabilities." *Feminist Economics* 9, nos. 2–3:61–92.
———. 2004. "Justice as Fairness and the Capability Approach." Paper presented at the Annual Meetings of the American Political Science Association, Chicago, September 5–7.

Roy, Arundhati. 2001. *Power Politics*. Second edition. Cambridge, Mass.: South End Press.

Sen, Amartya. 1973. *On Economic Inequality*. Oxford: Clarendon Press.

———. 1980. "Equality of What?" In *The Tanner Lectures on Human Values*, edited by S. McMurrin, 195–220. Salt Lake City: University of Utah Press.

———. 1985. *Commodities and Capabilities*. Amsterdam: North Holland.

———. 1990. "More Than 100 Million Women Are Missing." *New York Review of Books*. December 20.

———. 1992. *Inequality Re-examined*. Oxford: Clarendon Press.

———. 1993. "Capability and Well-Being." In *The Quality of Life*, edited by Martha Nussbaum and Amartya Sen, 30–53. Oxford: Clarendon Press.

———. 1999. *Development as Freedom*. New York: Knopf.

The Economist. 2004. "Special Report: Global Economic Inequality." 13 March, 69–71.

Ul Haq, Mahbub. 1995. *Reflections on Human Development*. New York: Oxford University Press.

UNDP. 1990–2004. *Human Development Report*. New York: Oxford University Press.

Wade, Robert Hunter. 2003. "The Disturbing Rise in Poverty and Inequality: Is It All a 'Big Lie'?" In *Taming Globalization*, edited by D. Held and M. Koenig-Archibugi, 18–46. Cambridge: Polity Press.

World Bank. 2004a. "Global Poverty Down By Half Since 1981 But Progress Uneven As Economic Growth Eludes Many Countries." News Release 2004/309/S. 23 April.

World Bank. 2004b. *World Development Indicators*. New York: Oxford University Press.

[12]

Cosmopolitan Law?

Noah Feldman

INTRODUCTION

We have ethical and moral responsibilities to citizens of other countries who live far away and whose lives barely interact with ours. But do we have *legal* duties to those people? Do we have legal duties, that is, to people who do not personally belong to any political association to which we belong and whose governments and ours do not both belong to relevant legal or political associations? If so, are the duties reciprocal? Can we also make legal demands and impose legal liabilities on people with whom we are not joined in any meaningful form of political association?

These questions are of the utmost practical importance. In one form or another, they have haunted several of the most important decisions to face our courts and our government in recent years. What legal duties have we toward persons captured outside the United States—in Afghanistan and elsewhere—and then held outside the United States—in Guantánamo and beyond?[1] Are there some people in some places whose treatment falls entirely outside any legal order or regime? What kinds of legal claims—if any—are cognizable in U.S. courts regarding events that took place outside the United States and may not even have involved any U.S. citizens?[2]

In the realm of partisan politics, these questions have generated a range of cross-cutting answers, not all of which are internally consistent. Many on the left of the political spectrum believe that war criminals such as former Chilean dictator Augusto Pinochet should be tried by courts wherever they may be found under a theory of universal jurisdiction; yet many of these same people oppose the idea that Osama bin Laden's driver, one Salim Ahmed Hamdan, can be put on trial by the United States in Guantánamo. Meanwhile, on the right, many who embrace the Guantánamo military tribunals reject out of hand the notion of universal jurisdiction for heads of state and strongly oppose entrance by the United States into the treaty creating the International Criminal Court.

Within the U.S. government, answers to these pressing questions have been proffered by courts striving to determine and specify the law of the United States; by officials seeking to guide the executive branch with

---

1. *See, e.g.*, Hamdan v. Rumsfeld, 126 S. Ct. 2749 (2006); Hamdi v. Rumsfeld, 542 U.S. 507 (2004); Rasul v. Bush, 542 U.S. 466 (2004).

2. *See, e.g.*, Sosa v. Alvarez-Machain, 542 U.S. 692 (2004) (considering the liability of one noncitizen to another noncitizen for events taking place outside the United States under the Alien Tort Statute and the Federal Tort Claims Act).

predictions of what courts might do in future cases;[3] and by legislators considering the best way to design U.S. law to accord with American values and interests. These government actors have tackled the issues from different perspectives corresponding to their different institutional roles. Although they have not always acknowledged it, each of their inquiries implicates a fundamental problem in legal theory: is political association a necessary condition for law?

Traditional liberal conceptions of law tend to hold that law, properly so called, can only exist and justifiably coerce people when it emanates from some political association such as a state, a treaty regime, or the international community (conceived as a meaningful political association). In what follows, I set out to explore the possibility that law may arise, and coercion to comply with it may be justified, even when the law does not issue from a political association. Doubtless political associations have the capacity to make law and to justify legal coercion. And any institution that applies law will probably have to be some sort of political association. But perhaps there are other ways for binding law to come into existence.

To see what these might be, I draw on the difficult, contested, but nonetheless important concept of cosmopolitanism. In particular, I consider two recent, powerful attempts—by Martha Nussbaum[4] and Kwame Anthony Appiah[5]—to make cosmopolitanism useful for political theory, and I reflect on the legal implications of these undertakings. The reason for this turn to cosmopolitanism is that, while much liberal theory treats political association as a necessary condition for law, cosmopolitanism generally directs our attention away from political associations like states as relevant makers of moral categories. By treating the individual as primary, and his or her political associations as secondary, cosmopolitanism can clear the way to imagining not only moral and ethical but also legal duties justifiably arising outside the bounds of state or other political power.

It is no coincidence, I suggest, that modern legal and political theory treats the state (or some comparable association) as the necessary source of legal

---

3. Many such internal government memoranda appear in THE TORTURE PAPERS: THE ROAD TO ABU GHRAIB (Karen J. Greenberg & Joshua L. Dratel eds., 2005). For my view on their character, see Noah Feldman, *Ugly Americans*, *in* THE TORTURE DEBATE IN AMERICA 267 (Karen J. Greenberg ed., 2006).

4. MARTHA C. NUSSBAUM, FRONTIERS OF JUSTICE: DISABILITY, NATIONALITY, SPECIES MEMBERSHIP (2006).

5. KWAME ANTHONY APPIAH, COSMOPOLITANISM: ETHICS IN A WORLD OF STRANGERS (2006) [hereinafter APPIAH, COSMOPOLITANISM]; KWAME ANTHONY APPIAH, THE ETHICS OF IDENTITY (2005) [hereinafter APPIAH, ETHICS OF IDENTITY].

obligation: these theories developed to justify the coercion characteristic of the modern state and its claim to monopolize violence. But there was law before there were modern states—law that claimed to derive its binding authority not from political association but from other sources and that was applied by institutions of very limited and certainly nonexclusive power. That law may have been capable of having the moral authority to bind through coercion—and it still may, whether it is found in failed states, where no one has a monopoly on violence, or in the international sphere, where there are many laws whose authority cannot so easily be said to derive from political association.

My argument proceeds in three steps. First, I consider briefly what is meant by cosmopolitanism itself. I then consider Nussbaum's and Appiah's arguments and investigate their implications for the question of law on which I focus. Finally, I offer three possible approaches to the problem of cosmopolitanism and law.

I. WHAT IS COSMOPOLITANISM?

A. *Political Theory and the Citizen of the World*

In today's English, a "cosmopolitan" is the kind of person who knows where to find the good tapas bars in Barcelona, the graphic artists in Osaka, the most interesting khat-fueled salon conversation in Aden.[6] A cosmopolitan judge (the standard is lower) wears English suits, speaks French or Swedish, and is not averse to citing international legal materials he or she picked up while summering in Salzburg with judges from other countries. "Cosmopolitan" is, of course, also the name of a mid-market magazine and, more tellingly, of a pinkish vodka drink (now thankfully passé) that somehow was thought to capture the glamour of the pre-9/11 cultural moment in New York.

The evident triviality of these contemporary uses of the term bears some consideration in the light of its historical origins. Its inventor seems to have been Diogenes the Cynic (d. 323 B.C.E.), who, when asked where he came

6. *Cf.* Jeremy Waldron, *Minority Cultures and the Cosmopolitan Alternative*, 25 U. MICH. J.L. REFORM 751, 754 (1992). Waldron revisits some of these ideas in Jeremy Waldron, *What Is Cosmopolitan?*, 8 J. POL. PHIL. 227, 231-34, 243 (2000).

from, replied, "I am a citizen of the world [*kosmopolites*]."[7] Diogenes was himself an exile from his native Sinope.[8] Like his contemporary Aristotle, though unlike Socrates and Plato, he was a stranger in Athens, not a citizen. His answer, then, captured both his own sense of unrootedness and a more profound suggestion about the pointlessness of citizenship. To be a citizen of the world, Diogenes implied, is to feel at once common affective bonds with the whole world and—in the absence of any imaginable world state—to acknowledge political bonds with no one at all.

As with most comments attributed to Diogenes, we have this cryptic statement only by secondhand report and without much context. But it is fair to say that, as in many of his recorded remarks, Diogenes intended some complicated combination of superficial parody and foundational depth. His suggestion would have been deeply subversive of contemporary Greek ideals of the virtue of participatory citizenship.[9] Indeed, Diogenes's whole career may be read as a sort of critical send-up of the familiar Athenian virtues of action and contemplation. Asked what sort of a man he considered himself to be, he replied, "A Socrates gone mad."[10]

Diogenes, then, was not a theorist of the polis, but a gadfly. His coinage was meant to call into question the centrality of political allegiance as a category of self-construction. So it is intriguing that today, political theorists in particular use the term "cosmopolitan" in a serious, distinctive, and developed way.

It was not always thus. As its name implies, political theory is primarily directed toward the relations formed within and around the polis. The polis has been, in its day, a city, a kingdom, and even, for some theorists, a religious community like St. Augustine's City of God[11] or the *umma* of the Muslims.[12] In

7. 2 DIOGENES LAERTIUS, LIVES OF EMINENT PHILOSOPHERS bk. VI, para. 63, at 65 (Jeffrey Henderson ed., R.D. Hicks trans., Harvard Univ. Press 2005) [hereinafter DIOGENES LAERTIUS].

8. *Id.* bk. V, para. 20, at 23. "[W]hen some one reminded [Diogenes] that the people of Sinope had sentenced him to exile, 'and I them,' said he, 'to home-staying.'" *Id.* bk. VI, para. 49, at 51.

9. *See, e.g.*, ARISTOTLE, NICOMACHEAN ETHICS bk. IV, at 15-16 (G.P. Goold ed., H. Rackham trans., Harvard Univ. Press rev. ed. 1934) (c. 384-322 B.C.E.) (discussing the active life of politics).

10. DIOGENES LAERTIUS, *supra* note 7, bk. V, para. 54, at 55.

11. *See* AUGUSTINE, THE CITY OF GOD (Marcus Dods trans., Modern Library 1950) (426).

12. For works treating the *umma* as a polis see, for example, AVERROES ON PLATO'S *REPUBLIC* (Ralph Lerner trans., Cornell Univ. Press 2005); and IBN KHALDÛN, THE MUQADDIMAH: AN INTRODUCTION TO HISTORY (Franz Rosenthal trans., Princeton Univ. Press 1967).

the modern era, however, the polis par excellence has been the state. Consequently, political theory since Thomas Hobbes's *Leviathan*[13] has focused largely on the functioning of states. With its three epochal wars among states,[14] the twentieth century seemed to confirm the value of this state-centered focus. The most influential work of political theory written during the third—or "cold"—war of the century was John Rawls's *A Theory of Justice*,[15] which focused mainly on evaluating the distributive arrangements adopted internally by states.[16]

The end of the twentieth century, however, led to some reconsideration of political theory's focus on the polis. The rise of the European Union and the end of the Cold War combined to make states seem both less necessary and (after the collapse of the Soviet Union and Yugoslavia) less durable than before. Political theorists gradually started to focus on other levels of communal organization and to ask questions about the relationship between those organizations and the state. One direction taken, under the rubric of multiculturalism, was to focus on cultural or ethnic groupings that typically operated at the sub-state level.[17] Another was to focus on identities, groupings, and organizations that might operate above and outside the state.[18] This latter conversation, closely related to the topic of multiculturalism, has proceeded under the heading of cosmopolitanism.

For contemporary political theorists, cosmopolitanism as citizenship of the world also implies a critique of ordinary theories of political obligation, with

---

13. THOMAS HOBBES, LEVIATHAN (Richard Tuck ed., Cambridge Univ. Press 1991) (1651).

14. *See generally* PHILIP BOBBITT, THE SHIELD OF ACHILLES: WAR, PEACE, AND THE COURSE OF HISTORY (2002) (describing a single long war in the twentieth century made up of the two world wars and the Cold War).

15. JOHN RAWLS, A THEORY OF JUSTICE (1971).

16. Robert Nozick's famous contemporary work *Anarchy, State, and Utopia* also related primarily to the distributive consequences of the author's account of the justifiable state structure. ROBERT NOZICK, ANARCHY, STATE, AND UTOPIA (1974). Rawls did of course touch on international issues in *A Theory of Justice*, *see* RAWLS, *supra* note 15, at 377-79, but the book's overall focus was on justice at the state level.

17. *See, e.g.*, WILL KYMLICKA, MULTICULTURAL CITIZENSHIP: A LIBERAL THEORY OF MINORITY RIGHTS (1995); THE RIGHTS OF MINORITY CULTURES (Will Kymlicka ed., 1995).

18. *See, e.g.*, CHARLES R. BEITZ, POLITICAL THEORY AND INTERNATIONAL RELATIONS (1979) [hereinafter BEITZ, POLITICAL THEORY]; THOMAS W. POGGE, REALIZING RAWLS (1989) [hereinafter POGGE, REALIZING RAWLS]. Also useful are shorter works by these authors, such as Charles R. Beitz, *Bounded Morality: Justice and the State in World Politics*, 33 INT'L ORG. 405 (1979), and Thomas Pogge, *Rawls and Global Justice*, 18 CAN. J. PHIL. 227 (1988). Although both Beitz and Pogge have been important in the subsequent cosmopolitanism debates, neither by himself sparked the degree of attention to problems of international justice that followed the end of the Cold War.

their tendency to focus on our duties to fellow citizens, not to people elsewhere. The ultimate literal expression of cosmopolitanism would of course be a single world government with corresponding global citizenship. Today, such an aspiration is almost unheard of in serious circles, notwithstanding the imaginings of the Michigan Militia and their paranoid brethren everywhere.[19] Nevertheless, there is a type of contemporary cosmopolitanism with origins before the end of the Cold War that seeks to include everyone in the world in a single global web of mutual obligations. This approach took Rawls's influential theory and expanded it to the international plane.[20] Rawls had famously proposed that, in the original position, behind the veil of ignorance, the members of a society would rationally agree to a system of redistribution that would leave the worst-off person at least as comfortable as he would have been under conditions of strict egalitarian redistribution. The global approach – call it contractarian cosmopolitanism[21] – took this Rawlsian redistribution to the world level.

At a theoretical level, this expansion may be accomplished either by treating states (or the peoples composing them) as members of a redistributive social contract that follows an initial social contract within states,[22] or by treating individual people, wherever they live, as the participants in a single, one-stage hypothetical social contract.[23] Whatever its theoretical appeal, however, at a practical level there is something unsatisfying about contractarian cosmopolitanism. Though not as utopian as world government, it is plagued by the mismatch between the theory of a global contract and the reality of the power and persistence of the state system in the face of the weakness and unenforceability of international agreements. A theorist of contractarian cosmopolitanism could find it "astonishing" that Rawls himself appeared to accept familiar, state-centered principles of international law.[24] But in making

19. *See* Jack Goldsmith, *Liberal Democracy and Cosmopolitan Duty*, 55 STAN. L. REV. 1667, 1691-92 (2003) (summarizing the primary objections to world government and noting that "[c]osmopolitan theorists are usually quick to deny any desire for [one]"). This was not true a century ago, when world government was the rage among a certain group of utopian thinkers. *See* John Fabian Witt, *Crystal Eastman and the Internationalist Beginnings of American Civil Liberties*, 54 DUKE L.J. 705 (2004).

20. *See* BEITZ, POLITICAL THEORY, *supra* note 18, at 136-43 (describing a Rawls-inspired principle of cross-border natural resource redistribution); POGGE, REALIZING RAWLS, *supra* note 18, at 240-73 (arguing for globalized contractarianism).

21. *Cf.* POGGE, REALIZING RAWLS, *supra* note 18, at 240 (referring to Rawls's vision as "cosmopolitan").

22. *See, e.g.*, BEITZ, POLITICAL THEORY, *supra* note 18, at 136-43.

23. *See, e.g.*, POGGE, REALIZING RAWLS, *supra* note 18, at 243-44.

24. *Id.* at 243.

the social contract first a phenomenon of individual peoples and only second and more weakly a global phenomenon, Rawls was in effect acknowledging the reality of the preeminence of states and the weakness of international institutions.[25]

The practical limitations of contractarian cosmopolitanism opened the door to another trend in political theory: the attempt to bring something of the ideals of cosmopolitanism into relation with existing duties of citizenship. It is not easy to epitomize the content of such an approach or to explain exactly what is cosmopolitan about it. Contractarian cosmopolitanism at least has the advantage of being obviously cosmopolitan, in that it confers rights and duties on people everywhere as though they were citizens of the same world entity. More subtle, complex kinds of cosmopolitanism, however, insist on a balance between thinking of oneself as a citizen of an actual state and imagining oneself in terms of global obligation. Balancing makes for good political theory, of course, but it does not always make for clarity or ease of exposition. Nonetheless it deserves our attention, now more than ever.

B. *Prelude to Complex Cosmopolitanism*

One step in the development of the political theory of complex cosmopolitanism took place in 1994, when Martha Nussbaum published an essay under the title *Patriotism and Cosmopolitanism*.[26] In the essay, Nussbaum, who is not only a philosopher but also a classicist, introduced cosmopolitanism through its Stoic origins. The Stoics, she argued, transformed Diogenes's *bon mot* into a more fully formed theory. For them, the aspiration to be a citizen not of a particular polis but of the world meant "that we should give our first allegiance to no mere form of government, no temporal power, but to the moral community made up by the humanity of all human beings."[27] Nussbaum hastened to note that the Stoics were not seeking "the abolition of local and

25. *See id.* at 241 (noting that Rawls conceived of justice as a property of institutions that, "by hypothesis, are absent on the global plane"); *see also* RAWLS, *supra* note 15, at 8 (asserting that the "significance" of considering justice within a particular society "is obvious and needs no explanation").

26. The essay appeared in the *Boston Review* together with a number of responses by important philosophical and legal figures. Martha C. Nussbaum, *Patriotism and Cosmopolitanism*, BOSTON REV., Oct.-Nov. 1994, at 3. It was later collected and expanded into a short book alongside those and other responses. Martha C. Nussbaum, *Patriotism and Cosmopolitanism*, *in* FOR LOVE OF COUNTRY: DEBATING THE LIMITS OF PATRIOTISM 2 (Joshua Cohen ed., 1996) [hereinafter Nussbaum, *Patriotism and Cosmopolitanism*].

27. Nussbaum, *Patriotism and Cosmopolitanism*, *supra* note 26, at 7.

national forms of political organization and the creation of a world state."[28] They had in mind something else altogether—a shift in one's internal perspective away from the "local origins and group memberships, so central to the self-image of the conventional Greek male."[29]

In presenting Stoic cosmopolitanism, Nussbaum emphasized the participatory aspects of the view over its self-alienating aspect. The choice reflected her goal of making cosmopolitanism into a useful tool for political theory. As she well knew, the Stoics embraced the notion of exile in a deep sense.[30] They were fully capable of seeing the cosmopolitan—even one who lived as a citizen in the place where he was born—as a kind of internal exile, a lonely man who by embracing a universal perspective weakened his affective bonds to the existing political community around him.[31] This notion has a long subsequent philosophical history. From Avempace (d. 1138) in *The Governance of the Solitary*[32] to Joseph Soloveitchik (d. 1993) in *The Lonely Man of Faith*,[33] there have always been thinkers who emphasized the obligation of the reflective individual to separate himself inwardly from the society in which he is enmeshed. But this particular philosophical tendency, embraced by at least some ancient thinkers who could be called cosmopolitans, is in tension with

28. *Id.*

29. *Id.* at 6-7.

30. *Cf.* PLUTARCH, *On Exile* (c. 90-110), *in* 7 PLUTARCH'S MORALIA 513, 527 (Phillip H. de Lacy & Benedict Einarson trans., Harvard Univ. Press 1959) ("For by nature there is no such thing as a native land, any more than there is by nature a house or farm or forge or surgery . . . ."); *id.* at 533 ("For nature leaves us free and untrammeled; it is we who bind ourselves, confine ourselves, immure ourselves, herd ourselves into cramped and sordid quarters."); *id.* at 537 ("Indeed, if you lay aside unfounded opinion and consider the truth, the man who has a single city is a stranger and an alien to all the rest . . . ."); *id.* at 545, 547 ("Zeno indeed, when he learned that his only remaining ship had been engulfed with its cargo by the sea, exclaimed: 'Well done, Fortune! thus to confine me to a threadbare cloak' and a philosopher's life . . . ."). In at least one subsequent work, Nussbaum has explicitly addressed the tension between Stoic cosmopolitanism's participatory and self-alienating aspects. Martha C. Nussbaum, *Kant and Stoic Cosmopolitanism*, 5 J. POL. PHIL. 1 (1997).

31. Nussbaum herself has acknowledged as much. *See* Martha C. Nussbaum, *Compassion and Terror*, DAEDALUS, Winter 2003, at 10, 22 (noting that for Marcus Aurelius, achieving evenhanded concern for humans required the extirpation of personal attachments, creating a world "strangely lonely and hollow").

32. ABU BAKR MUHAMMAD IBN BAJJAH [AVEMPACE], TADBIR AL-MUTAWAHHID (Ma'an Ziade ed., 1978) (c. 1095-1138). For excerpts in English, see Avempace, *The Governance of the Solitary*, *in* MEDIEVAL POLITICAL PHILOSOPHY 122 (Ralph Lerner & Muhsin Mahdi eds., Lawrence Berman trans., Cornell Univ. Press 1963).

33. Joseph B. Soloveitchik, *The Lonely Man of Faith*, TRADITION, Summer 1965, at 5, *reprinted as* JOSEPH B. SOLOVEITCHIK, THE LONELY MAN OF FAITH (1992).

the alternative impulse to make the philosophical content of political theory useful to state governance in the real world.

In a parallel sense, Nussbaum deemphasized the world government theme that arguably can be found in Roman Stoicism. If a world state were unimaginable to Diogenes at Athens, and if the Greek Stoics speaking of citizenship were "picturing, as it were, a dream or image of the philosopher's well regulated society,"[34] the same was hardly the case for the citizens of the Roman Empire at its world-dominating height. One leading Stoic, Marcus Aurelius, was actually the emperor. For him, and perhaps for other Roman Stoics, the notion of citizenship of the world may have corresponded to citizenship of the Empire. This cosmopolitan interest in at least the possibility of world government would have been inappropriate for Nussbaum's purposes, given the unpopularity and great unlikelihood of world government today, not to mention the discrediting of the Roman Empire itself.

By injecting cosmopolitanism into practical prescriptions for political theory and insisting on a cosmopolitanism with room for local, "patriotic" attachments, Nussbaum foreshadowed what would become a characteristic and often difficult feature of complex cosmopolitanism. For cosmopolitanism to contribute to political theory—not to mention policy debate—it must necessarily abjure some of the radicalism that may be found in its ancient origins, and indeed beyond. It must move away from Diogenes the Cynic's hint that civic duty is a bit pointless. To be useful in the real world, cosmopolitanism must be understood to engage actual political duties, not to demonstrate their evanescence and unimportance. It must deemphasize the side of Stoicism that commands internal alienation and focus on the side that commends political activity to help people everywhere. To some degree, complex cosmopolitanism must also steer away from the universalist one-worldism arguably present in some of its forms. A political cosmopolitanism must be modified, regulated, and controlled so as to engage the realities of the modern state and the system in which it operates.

Such a reining-in of cosmopolitanism was visible in the response to Nussbaum's essay written by the philosopher and cultural theorist Kwame Anthony Appiah.[35] This essay, entitled *Cosmopolitan Patriots*, took as its starting

34. Plutarch, *On the Fortune of Alexander* (c. 46-120), *in* 1 THE HELLENISTIC PHILOSOPHERS 67a (A.A. Long & D. Sedleyt eds., 1987). For a discussion of this passage, see Sandrine Berges, *Loneliness and Belonging: Is Stoic Cosmopolitanism Still Defensible?*, 11 RES PUBLICA: J. LEGAL & SOC. PHIL. 3, 6-9 (2005).

35. Like Nussbaum's essay, Appiah's essay first appeared in the *Boston Review*. Kwame Anthony Appiah, *Loyalty to Humanity*, BOSTON REV., Oct.-Nov. 1994, at 10. It was then reprinted in

point two different statements by Appiah's father: a newspaper article arguing that Ghana (his home country) was worth dying for, and an ethical will to his children reminding them that, as both Ghanaians and Englishmen, they should "[r]emember that [they] are citizens of the world."[36] Appiah reconciled the two "sentiments"[37] of cosmopolitanism and patriotism by asserting that cosmopolitanism, far from demanding a universal form of identity, "celebrates the fact that there are different local human ways of being."[38] At the same time, Appiah went on to suggest that the state itself is a morally significant (and desirable) structure, insofar as "living in political communities narrower than the species is better for us than would be our engulfment in a single world-state."[39]

Appiah's formulation of two balanced sentiments was well drawn to contribute to political theory. It eschewed the alienation and extreme universalism of radical cosmopolitanism. It was also well timed. As Appiah explicitly noted, the "current preoccupation" within political theory was coming to center on the question of how to extend Rawls's political theory to the international realm, where Rawls himself had not (yet) taken it.[40] As it turned out, Nussbaum and Appiah were to become two of the major figures in the conversation about complex cosmopolitanism. In 2006, more than a decade after their essays appeared, they both published books addressing the issues first raised therein. It is to these works that we now turn.

II. MORALS BEYOND BORDERS

A. *What's Wrong with the Social Contract?*

Although Nussbaum's *Frontiers of Justice* takes the form of a sustained criticism of Rawls, by her own account Nussbaum is after even bigger game.

---

expanded form. Kwame Anthony Appiah, *Cosmopolitan Patriots*, *in* FOR LOVE OF COUNTRY, *supra* note 26, at 21 [hereinafter Appiah, *Cosmopolitan Patriots*].

36. Appiah, *Cosmopolitan Patriots*, *supra* note 35, at 21.

37. *Id.* at 23.

38. *Id.* at 25.

39. *Id.* at 29.

40. *Id.* at 24. In 1993, Rawls gave a lecture entitled *The Law of Peoples*. John Rawls, The Law of Peoples (1993), *in* ON HUMAN RIGHTS: THE OXFORD AMNESTY LECTURES 41 (Stephen Shute & Susan Hurley eds., 1993). That same year, he also published *Political Liberalism*, and in 1999, *The Law of Peoples*. These works took up the challenge of considering, in Rawls's formulation, "how reasonable citizens and peoples might live together peacefully in a just world." JOHN RAWLS, THE LAW OF PEOPLES, at vi (1999).

She sets out to criticize and supplement the basic idea of the social contract, which has dominated political theory since Hobbes. One important tool she uses to accomplish this task is a species of complex cosmopolitanism. It rests on the insight that social contract theories correspond so closely to the design of states that they cannot really tell us how to do justice to those who fall outside the basic requirements of equal citizenship.

The argument of the book is involved, but Nussbaum's challenge to liberal social contract theory[41] can be summarized with only limited damage to its structure.[42] It begins with the "Circumstances of Justice" (always capitalized in the book), which are, approximately, the conditions under which justice can be said to apply as a relevant criterion. The locus classicus for an account of these conditions is the work of David Hume, who argued that the facts of human selfishness, limited generosity, and the comparative scarcity of the material stuff we need to sustain ourselves were the circumstances that created a need for cooperation through a system of laws.[43] Rawls drew on Hume's account, emphasizing that the possibility and need for cooperation arise when individuals coexist in the same territory; are "roughly similar in physical and mental powers" so that none alone can dominate the others; live subject to conditions of "moderate scarcity"; and have differing life plans alongside their complementary interests in cooperation.[44]

Nussbaum argues that social contract theories usually rely on something like the circumstances of justice to explain why the contract would be desirable for individuals to enter. This worries her, for two reasons. First, she focuses on Rawls's suggestion that the parties suitable for social cooperation must be free, equal, and independent.[45] What troubles Nussbaum are the cases in which these conditions cannot be said to apply. Most important for our purposes, she argues that nation-states cannot be imagined as rough equals, given that they differ so widely in size, power, and resources.[46] This would appear to preclude

---

41. Nussbaum restricts her critique to liberal (i.e., non-Rousseauian) social contract theories. *See* NUSSBAUM, *supra* note 4, at 25.

42. For ease of exposition, the order of the argument presented here differs slightly from Nussbaum's own.

43. Hume's discussion may be found in DAVID HUME, A TREATISE OF HUMAN NATURE bk. 3, pt. 2, § 2, at 311-22 (David Fate Norton & Mary J. Norton eds., 2000) (1737-1740).

44. RAWLS, *supra* note 15, at 126 & n.3, 127.

45. *See* NUSSBAUM, *supra* note 4, at 28.

46. *Id.* at 32. The severely disabled, Nussbaum says, also cannot be imagined as roughly equal for social contract purposes. *See id.* at 31-32. Neither can nonhuman animals, who moreover are not free. *See id.* Important as these subjects are, they are not directly relevant to the topic of cosmopolitanism, and I therefore do not address them here.

states from having the right incentives to enter into a redistributive social contract of their own, which in turn means that the citizens of those states may end up living under conditions of great inequality in which some are barely surviving or are not surviving at all. Bracketing the possibility that the social contract should exist among all persons regardless of their states,[47] Nussbaum considers this result to reflect a major problem for social contractarianism.

Nussbaum's second worry about the conditions for the social contract has to do with the idea that human selfishness provides the motivation that explains why people would (either actually or hypothetically) enter into an agreement for mutual advantage.[48] Hobbes managed this problem by pointing out that although our natural passions put us at odds with one another, the fact that humans are by nature roughly equal in physical and mental capacities means they have an incentive to enter into the social contract.[49] Without fully embracing Hobbes's anthropology, Locke likewise thought that mutual advantage was a source for the social contract, and, says Nussbaum, even "Kant seems to hold that it is . . . advantageous . . . for all persons to join the contract."[50]

Nussbaum finds this starting assumption about mutual advantage problematic. What happens when we cannot find a mutual advantage for cooperation in a given situation in which some people—such as those living in other countries—are nevertheless in dire need? Can it really be the case that justice as a category does not apply under these circumstances? For Nussbaum, this limitation of social contract theory gives us a reason to seek an alternative account of political justice.[51]

The place to start looking, Nussbaum suggests, is Hugo Grotius's account of the "basic principles of international relations," which have domestic uses as well.[52] The core of these principles, she says, derived from the ancient Stoics (also, recall, the inventors of cosmopolitanism), who believed that humans had both an inherent dignity and an inherent bent toward sociability.[53] Emphasizing these features—rather than equality or selfishness—led Grotius to reject a theory of mutual advantage: "Grotius argues explicitly that we must *not*

47. Nussbaum points out that Rawls in his later work did imagine that the social contract ideal might be applied among peoples organized into states. *See id.* at 238-55.

48. *See id.* at 34.

49. *See id.* at 30 (citing HOBBES, *supra* note 13, ch. 13, at 86-87).

50. *Id.* at 51.

51. *See id.* at 25.

52. *Id.* at 36.

53. *Id.*

attempt to derive our fundamental principles from an idea of mutual advantage alone; human sociability indicates that advantage is not the only reason for which human beings act justly."[54]

The avowedly Grotian alternative Nussbaum proposes grounds justice in the idea of what she calls central human capabilities.[55] These are universal capacities of everyone everywhere, without which one cannot live a life "worthy of human dignity."[56] Nussbaum explains that her theory shares with Rawls's theory (and with liberalism generally) the core ideas of human dignity and the inviolability of the person.[57] It differs, though, by explicitly rejecting the procedural fairness model in favor of particular outcomes. Indeed, says Nussbaum, the capabilities approach is outcome-driven and consequentialist: it begins with the basic human capabilities, then works backward to develop an account of justice that assures that people everywhere will be entitled to exercise those capabilities.

Taken on its own terms, the capabilities approach would seem to represent a basic challenge to contractarianism: if the social contract cannot provide justice to all who deserve it, this would seem to call into question its value as the basis for a theory of justice. Nussbaum modestly prefers to say "not that we should reject Rawls's theory or any other contractarian theory, but that we should keep working on alternative theories, which may possibly enhance our understanding of justice and enable us to extend those very theories."[58] Elsewhere she states that the capabilities approach may be seen as "an extension of or complement to Rawls's theory, with . . . new problems in focus."[59] She also explains that she does not wish to reject the contractarian cosmopolitanism of Thomas Pogge or Charles Beitz,[60] and her main criticisms of them relate to their vagueness.[61] Given Nussbaum's professedly consequentialist view with respect to capabilities, however, and her observation

54. *Id.* at 37.

55. *See id.* at 76-78. Nussbaum has developed the capabilities idea in her earlier work. *See, e.g.*, MARTHA C. NUSSBAUM, WOMEN AND HUMAN DEVELOPMENT: THE CAPABILITIES APPROACH (2000).

56. NUSSBAUM, *supra* note 4, at 78.

57. *Id.* at 75.

58. *Id.* at 25.

59. *Id.* at 69; *see also id.* at 95 (describing contractarian theories as "close allies of the capabilities approach").

60. *See supra* notes 18-24 and accompanying text.

61. *See* NUSSBAUM, *supra* note 4, at 264-70.

that her project is "urgently practical,"[62] one might wonder whether her unwillingness to jettison contractarianism might stem from similarly consequentialist motives.

Cosmopolitanism is not explicitly invoked in *Frontiers of Justice*—in fact, the term does not even appear in the book's index. Nonetheless its relevance to the capabilities approach is clear, and not only from the Stoic origins that Nussbaum assigns to Grotius. Nussbaum says that her argument grew out of her thinking about international development policy,[63] the area from which Amartya Sen's cognate work on capabilities also sprung.[64] As she acknowledges, the capabilities approach was originally born as a way to replace the utilitarian economic reasoning so prevalent in this field,[65] but of course utilitarianism is not the only target of the progressive movement in international development. Still more fundamental an enemy is the view that certain moral duties do not run across borders, to people in faraway places.[66] Nussbaum's concern that an adequate theory of justice must apply to all persons everywhere flows naturally from her cosmopolitan view that national boundaries are morally arbitrary.

B. The Social Contract and the State

It is, I think, significant that Nussbaum's cosmopolitan skepticism, which dates back at least to her 1994 essay, has now led her to question social contract theory. Her outcome-oriented approach grows from the problem that social contract theory does not do an adequate job of accounting for justice to persons outside the state. The historical context in which social contract theory developed helps illuminate why this should be so: born and reared alongside the modern state, social contract theory gets into difficulties when it must confront either premodern or postmodern challenges of the kinds raised by cosmopolitan theory.

---

62. *Id.* at 306.

63. *See id.* at 71-72.

64. For the comparison, see *id.* at 70, 284-87, 315-16. For Sen's work on capabilities, see, for example, AMARTYA SEN, COMMODITIES AND CAPABILITIES (1985); AMARTYA SEN, DEVELOPMENT AS FREEDOM (1999); and AMARTYA SEN, INEQUALITY REEXAMINED (1992).

65. NUSSBAUM, *supra* note 4, at 71.

66. Thus, in one important essay, Nussbaum defends Cicero's "cosmopolitan" view that duties of justice run to all humans, while rejecting his (corresponding) view that duties of material aid run in the first instance to one's own fellow citizens. Martha C. Nussbaum, *Duties of Justice, Duties of Material Aid: Cicero's Problematic Legacy*, 8 J. POL. PHIL. 176 (2000).

Social contract theory is the archetypal liberal solution to the question of the justifiability of the modern state. It does its strongest work in making sense of the state's structures and the duties and obligations of citizens living within it, and in justifying the coercive legal apparatus that the state deploys to accomplish its goals. If we begin with assumptions about the autonomy of individuals, we need some theory to explain why the state might be justified in coercing those rights-bearing individuals against their wills to do the things that the state deems necessary.

Social contract theory traditionally answered this question by the controversial mechanism of consent. We may justifiably be coerced either because we have agreed to be coerced (actual consent) or because we would have agreed to be coerced were we rational and given the choice (hypothetical consent). Because we have agreed—or ought to have agreed—we are not really being coerced at all, and (in principle at least) our autonomy remains intact. If the state wishes to do something to us that we would not have agreed to have done, then in fact this cannot be justified. Our inalienable rights are protected, and through them our dignity and inviolability as humans.

Notice that in its classical, Lockean form, social contract theory mostly accounted for rights held against the state, while authorizing coercion that did not violate those rights.[67] This function corresponded to the legal structures of the eighteenth century, which protected negative liberties (rights against the state) rather than positive liberties (rights to opportunities or resources). Rawls saved social contract theory from oblivion by using it to justify the redistributive structure of the modern welfare state. Had it not been able to explain the emergence of a positive right to share in the overall wealth of society, social contract theory would have seemed irretrievably irrelevant to the existing political order.

In the process, Rawls also sought to shift the function of consent in contractarianism. Instead of following the traditional view that hypothetical consent to certain principles authorizes coercion, he proposed that the heuristic device of the hypothetical agreement of reasonable people offers a reason for believing that there is a natural duty to comply with the state's just demands. Rawls's historical importance thus derives from his extraordinary accomplishment of grafting a Kantian-inspired moral theory onto a familiar—yet modified—discourse of social contract and then using the resulting product to justify the Western welfare state, and thus welfare capitalism itself.

---

67. *See generally* JOHN LOCKE, TWO TREATISES OF GOVERNMENT (Peter Laslett ed., Cambridge Univ. Press 1988) (1690). On positive and negative liberty, see ISAIAH BERLIN, *Two Concepts of Liberty*, *in* FOUR ESSAYS ON LIBERTY 118 (1969).

COSMOPOLITAN LAW?

In Rawls's work, then, as in that of his predecessors, social contract theory corresponded to the legal structures of the state, which now through taxation appropriated wealth and redistributed it in the form of property. It is no coincidence that *A Theory of Justice* (1971) was roughly contemporaneous with *Goldberg v. Kelly* (1970),[68] in which the constitutional-legal character of the redistributive welfare state came closest to being acknowledged by the Supreme Court. According to the logic of *Goldberg*'s holding, welfare entitlements were not just government largesse; they were actual entitlements due to citizens and held by them in some version of familiar property terms.[69] The state, on this view, was redistributing wealth as a matter of the citizen's right—and contractarian political theory explained why this was justified.

So we should not be especially surprised if, as cosmopolitanism moves political theory beyond the level of the state itself, social contract theory begins to look inadequate to the task. Through Rawls, one may see the astonishing flexibility and durability of social contract theory. Hobbes's contractarianism could justify despotism; Rousseau's contractarianism could, if necessary, be made to justify a dictatorship of the proletariat; Locke's, a property-protecting slave republic; Rawls's, the welfare state. Indeed, one could be forgiven for thinking that social contract theory, properly tinkered with, could justify any internal state structure.

But this flexibility depended, crucially, on the metaphor of cooperation among politically associated people trying to preserve mutual advantage, and that metaphor was closely conjoined to the structure of the state. The force of Nussbaum's complex cosmopolitanism is to urge us to move our attention away from the state, to persons far away—and when we do so, the power of the contract metaphor begins to melt away. Nussbaum is quite right that we cannot easily be imagined to have entered into a mutually advantageous agreement with all the people in the world, much less all the beings. Similarly, we would not find it easy to imagine joining others everywhere in being governed by a common law—not unless we were to postulate a world-governing God for whom distance is as nothing and the nations of the world are as a drop from the bucket.

---

68. 397 U.S. 254 (1970).

69. *See id.* at 262 n.8 (quoting Charles A. Reich, *Individual Rights and Social Welfare: The Emerging Legal Issues*, 74 YALE L.J. 1245, 1255 (1965)) (citing Charles A. Reich, *The New Property*, 73 YALE L.J. 733 (1964)).

C. *Law and the Consequences of Capabilities*

What actual, legal obligations or institutions would arise if we were to adopt Nussbaum's capabilities approach as our own? The specter of world government and the need to avoid it haunt Nussbaum's concrete proposals for implementing the capabilities approach. She wants everyone everywhere to be entitled to all the capabilities on her list. She wants rich nations to transfer wealth to poor ones, and she wants multinational corporations to promote capabilities wherever they do business.[70] But she also wants state sovereignty to be protected, because the state is a morally meaningful "expression of human choice and autonomy"[71] and because of the risks of tyranny, unaccountability, and the erosion of diversity.[72] So when it comes to establishing international institutions to facilitate the transfer of wealth necessary to deliver on the capabilities approach, Nussbaum calls for only a "thin system of global governance" with limited coercive powers.[73] On further investigation, this system turns out to resemble closely the international order we have now, albeit with certain improvements. Here are, in essence, a World Bank, an International Monetary Fund, a General Agreement on Trade and Tariffs, a World Health Organization, and other usual suspects; to these Nussbaum would add "world environmental regulations with enforcement mechanisms," enhanced "global labor standards for both the formal and the informal sector," and "some limited forms" of globally redistributive taxation.[74]

This recommendation is perfectly reasonable, and it successfully represses the threat of world government. But in so doing it runs into the other horn of the dilemma created by a chastened and constrained cosmopolitanism: will it matter, in legal terms? States are not so different from individuals when it comes to doing the right thing: laziness, self-interest, and collective action problems all stand in the way of universal voluntary compliance with improving the status of people elsewhere. If we are not to have a world government, who is going to make sovereign states comply with their duties under the capabilities approach by actually funding international institutions and transferring wealth to poorer countries?[75]

70. *See* NUSSBAUM, *supra* note 4, at 316-18.

71. *Id.* at 262. Nussbaum does not expand on this point except to insist that, unlike Rawls, she attributes no agency to "peoples." *Id.*

72. *See id.* at 313-14.

73. *Id.* at 319.

74. *Id.* at 319-20.

75. For Nussbaum's own expression of this concern, see *id.* at 315-20.

COSMOPOLITAN LAW?

I suggest later in this Review that it may be possible to envision legal duties without a unified government or treaty regime at the back of them,[76] but for now it suffices to raise the question of how we should give practical effect to the cosmopolitanism of capabilities. Of course states inspired by the capabilities approach could pass their own laws directing their governments to promote capabilities of persons elsewhere. But these would not amount to the creation of legal relations between the citizens of the donor states and the recipients of their Nussbaum-inspired redistribution. A worldwide treaty promising to deliver the key capabilities to all persons everywhere might do the trick. It would certainly create international legal duties between the signatory states and maybe, by association, between signatory states and the individuals to whom duties are owed. But on closer examination such a treaty looks like contractual cosmopolitanism, a position Nussbaum does not, in this work, adopt. Her reasons for this restraint are plausible ones, to be sure – namely, the difficulty of imagining such an arrangement working in theory or in practice.

It emerges that the capabilities approach differs from the contractarian in that it does perhaps a better job of telling us what people outside the contract are owed morally – but it does not tell us why or even if we would be justified in coercing other people to give them their due. Nussbaum acknowledges as much when she says that the allocation of responsibility for capabilities-promotion to various international institutions is "aspirational" and lacks any "coercive structure over the whole that would enforce on any given part a definite set of tasks."[77] Indeed, says Nussbaum, referring back to Grotius and his Stoic predecessors, her approach "is a version of the old natural law approach: the requirements at the world level are moral requirements, not captured fully in any set of coercive political structures."[78]

In principle, the capabilities approach could justify coercion regarding, say, the transfer of property without recourse to a global social contract. The state may be justified in taking my property through force or threat of force because someone else needs it more than I do and, indeed, cannot live a life of human dignity without it. The location of that other person is morally irrelevant. According to this avowedly non-contractarian view, it does not matter that I myself might not consent (hypothetically or otherwise) to a system of government that takes my property for the purpose of raising to decency the standard of living of people on another continent. Those people are owed such a basic standard as a matter of morality, and it is my bad luck if I object.

76. *See infra* Part IV.

77. NUSSBAUM, *supra* note 4, at 315.

78. *Id.*

Nussbaum does not take this tack,[79] perhaps because she does not wish to compromise the ideal of autonomy in order to effectuate the ideal of universal dignity—a tradeoff that sounds in the tradition of Marx's 1844 *Manuscripts*,[80] with their classic formulation of the notion of a "truly human functioning."[81] There may be a connection between the state-centered localism of social contract theory and what is usually thought to make that theory liberal: the focus on autonomy. The ideal of autonomy underlies the mythic notion of free individuals coming together by choice to form the polis.

By encouraging a view of humans not primarily as citizens of such voluntarily constructed entities, but rather as members of a broader world, Nussbaum's version of cosmopolitanism encourages us to consider the unchosen fact of being human over what classical liberalism imagined as the chosen fact of political citizenship. In this sense, at least, cosmopolitanism creates some tension with traditional contractarian liberalism and its concern with justifying coercive law. According to classical social contract theory, our status as citizens of particular law-governed states is freely chosen and, by hypothetical consent, continuously re-chosen. None of us, however, chooses to be born into the world.

III. ETHICS AND OTHERS

A. *The Cosmopolitan Self*

Appiah would surely reject the notion that a focus on autonomy runs counter to cosmopolitanism. Indeed, in two nearly simultaneously published books, *The Ethics of Identity* and *Cosmopolitanism: Ethics in a World of Strangers*, he develops an attractive version of cosmopolitanism that derives from a Millian commitment to the construction of the self through a series of highly autonomous personal choices.[82] Both books build on the ideas Appiah first laid out in his 1994 reply to Nussbaum;[83] and if *The Ethics of Identity* is a systematic work while *Cosmopolitanism* is more of an extended philosophical meditation

79. Nussbaum does acknowledge the work of Pogge and Beitz, which seeks to move the ground of the contractarian model to the whole world. *See id.* at 264-70.

80. KARL MARX, ECONOMIC AND PHILOSOPHIC MANUSCRIPTS OF 1844 (Dirk J. Struik ed., Martin Milligan trans., Int'l Publishers 1964).

81. NUSSBAUM, *supra* note 4, at 74 (quoting Marx).

82. On Appiah's debt to John Stuart Mill, see, for example, APPIAH, ETHICS OF IDENTITY, *supra* note 5, at 1-13, 271-72.

83. *See* sources cited *supra* note 35.

on his father's two dicta,[84] both sustain an internally consistent ethical vision, according to which we must remember our obligations to people far away even as we take an interest in the peculiarities of human difference. For Appiah, taking an interest in difference means noticing the ways individuals shape their lives using the tools and materials provided by culture. This, then, is a cosmopolitanism driven precisely by liberal autonomy.

The differences between Appiah's cosmopolitanism and Nussbaum's are pronounced. Appiah's brand—which he calls both "rooted cosmopolitanism"[85] and, in a moment of candor, "wishy-washy" cosmopolitanism[86]—is more fine-grained and subtle than Nussbaum's and is also less radically demanding in the sphere of recentered consciousness. His ancient motto comes not from a philosopher wracked by the torments of self-alienation, but from Terence, the Carthaginian slave turned successful comic playwright: "I am human: nothing human is alien to me."[87]

For Appiah, the key to a defensible and manageable cosmopolitanism is that it must reconcile itself to "at least some forms of partiality."[88] (This acknowledgment goes all the way back to Appiah's 1994 response to Nussbaum and his desire to reconcile the twin sentiments of patriotism and cosmopolitanism.[89]) To justify such partiality, Appiah has recourse to Ronald Dworkin's distinction between ethics, which "includes convictions about which kinds of lives are good or bad for a person to lead," and morality, which "includes principles about how a person should treat other people."[90] Ethics is a way of talking that makes sense only within a particular community of persons who share a vision of the good life: "Ethical obligation . . . is internal to . . . identity."[91] In the ethical sphere, therefore, partiality is appropriate, and even necessary, to the extent that one is partial to the ethical community to which one belongs. Partiality, however, has no place in moral discourse, in which all persons must be treated as possessing equal worth.

---

84. *See supra* note 36 and accompanying text.

85. APPIAH, ETHICS OF IDENTITY, *supra* note 5, at 213.

86. *Id.* at 222.

87. APPIAH, COSMOPOLITANISM, *supra* note 5, at 111.

88. APPIAH, ETHICS OF IDENTITY, *supra* note 5, at 223.

89. *See supra* notes 35-39 and accompanying text.

90. APPIAH, ETHICS OF IDENTITY, *supra* note 5, at xiii, 230 (citing RONALD DWORKIN, SOVEREIGN VIRTUE: THE THEORY AND PRACTICE OF EQUALITY 485 n.1 (2000)). The distinction is developed over several pages, *see id.* at 230-37, with reference added to Hegelian *Sittlichkeit* and *Moralität*, *see id.* at 232-33.

91. *Id.* at 236.

Distinguishing partial ethics from universal morality turns out to have far-reaching effects. It leads Appiah to propose a further distinction between the state and other forms of community, ranging from the nation to "the county, the town, the street, the business, the craft, the profession," and beyond.[92] These forms of organization have *ethical* significance because they are "cared about by autonomous agents."[93] Communities like these deserve our partiality to the extent that they enable (and presumably result from) the autonomous choices of individuals to author their own lives in the Millian sense that Appiah values. The state, by contrast, is something else again. "States . . . have intrinsic *moral* value: they matter not because people care about them but because they regulate our lives through forms of coercion that will always require moral justification."[94]

What does this distinction between ethically significant communities and the morally significant state mean for rooted cosmopolitanism? Rootedness—partiality to one's community—is desirable on ethical grounds. So, too, is cosmopolitanism, understood as concern for others elsewhere and an interest in how they live. Within states, Appiah says, there can be "decrees and injunctions"[95]—in other words, laws with coercive effect that must be justified in moral terms.[96] But when the conversation is not "within but among polities,"[97] law no longer applies, so moral justification is not the issue. "We must rely on the ability to listen and to talk to people whose commitments, beliefs, and projects may seem distant from our own."[98] This is cosmopolitanism as ethical enquiry—rich and deeply valuable, but operating on a different plane than that occupied by a political theory focused on the state.

As a result of the distinction between ethically significant communities and the morally significant state, it turns out that Appiah's "rooted cosmopolitanism" applies to the realm of personal relations situated within communities but is of limited applicability at the level of the state. To speak of rooted cosmopolitanism as an approach capable of justifying binding laws would be an analytic error. Cosmopolitan ethics cannot on their own justify the

92. *Id.* at 246.

93. *Id.* at 245.

94. *Id.* (emphasis added).

95. *Id.* at 246.

96. For Appiah, state coercion is justified only when the state treats persons impartially and as possessing equal moral worth. *See id.* at 88-99, 228-30.

97. *Id.* at 246.

98. *Id.*

decrees and injunctions of coercive law—for that work of political theory we need a moral accounting, not an ethical one.

It follows, I think, that for Appiah the cosmopolitan ethical attitude is not well formed to do the work of justifying legal coercion. Rather, it will give us good ideas for how we ought to structure our lives. We may well want to adopt some of those ethical insights into positive law, but we are not going to be under a moral obligation to do so, and indeed some forms of partiality that would be ethically desirable within communities would be morally impermissible if the state were to attempt to make them into law. The justification for coercion in our system will have to come from some other source than cosmopolitan ethics.

This approach of Appiah's is wonderfully clear, and in applying it to law one can see that it is also theoretically elegant. But for our purposes, it is important to note the apparently limited applicability of Appiah's ethical cosmopolitanism to the analysis of legal duty. In its small-scale horizon, the measured, witty cosmopolitanism of Terence has little to do with the wild-eyed philosophical ideal of the Stoics or, for that matter, the relentless universalism of the contractarian cosmopolitans. Being worldly-wise is not quite the same as being a citizen of the world.

B. Neutrality, Cosmopolitanism, and Coercion

Appiah is rigorously consistent in maintaining a distinction between moral forms of argument that justify state coercion and ethical forms of argument that, at least when applied to states, amount to nonbinding (though by no means weak) normative suggestions. This leads to some surprising results in the controversial areas of lawmaking that one might expect to be informed by cosmopolitan ethical attitudes. In particular, when Appiah addresses the question of how law should engage problems of identity, his terms of reference derive from moral theory, not ethical theory.

Take as one example the problem of respect for beliefs that we might consider unreasonable. Imagine that the state adopts a law ordering blood transfusions for unconscious patients who have a medical need for them. In *The Ethics of Identity*, Appiah introduces a moral principle—"neutrality as equal respect"—according to which the state must not "disadvantage anyone in virtue of his identity."[99] He then applies this principle to blood transfusion law. Jehovah's Witnesses, he says, may object to the law on the ground that a transfusion will lead to damnation. The state must then consider whether there

99. *Id.* at 91.

is some policy that would avoid thwarting the Witnesses.[100] But there is no such policy, for "a policy requiring us to establish consent would endanger the lives of many."[101] The state may therefore justifiably adopt the law imposing transfusions on the unconscious. Even though the Witnesses (among others) will be coerced, Appiah contends, they are not being coerced because they are Witnesses but because we have made a general law that cannot tolerate exceptions without costing lives. They have therefore been given equal respect.

Of course it will not look that way to the Witnesses. They will surely feel that their concerns were rejected precisely because they were the concerns of a fringe religious minority. Appiah acknowledges that if we believed the Witnesses and agreed that transfusions lead to damnation, we would have a reason not to pass the law in the first place.[102] Indeed, says Appiah, "[w]e mostly do not think it is even reasonable to believe" that transfusions lead to damnation.[103] The key to his view that the Witnesses are nonetheless being respected equally must be that their belief is false (and irrational) – irrespective of the fact that they hold it *as* Jehovah's Witnesses. We would react the same way to the false, irrational views of nonreligious persons or indeed anyone. The moral claim to equal treatment does not entitle a group to have its partial views accepted or even treated as plausible, just not to be rejected on identitarian grounds.

Yet in *Cosmopolitanism*, Appiah offers a striking counterpoint through a discussion of theories about the causes of disease. In Ghana, he says, it is not uncommon to ascribe illness to witchcraft.[104] Appiah acknowledges that this attribution will seem mistaken to Westerners who have been reared on the germ theory, and he in fact raises the possibility that the belief in witchcraft is not merely false but "irrational,"[105] much like the Witnesses' belief that blood transfusions lead to damnation. Yet he rejects this suggestion, and on interesting grounds. He points out that when most Manhattanites encounter minor illness, they attribute the cause to viruses even when the virus cannot be treated and no tests have been done to ascertain the cause.[106] Unless they are virologists, the Manhattanites are relying on authority, not independent proof,

100. *Id.* at 93-94.

101. *Id.* at 93.

102. *Id.*

103. *Id.*

104. APPIAH, COSMOPOLITANISM, *supra* note 5, at 35.

105. *Id.* at 36.

106. *Id.* at 38.

for their theory of disease, just as the residents of Kumasi, Ghana, rely on authority in ascribing similar illnesses to witchcraft.[107]

From the undeniable fact that most people rely on authority rather than proof to explain the world around them, Appiah concludes that Ghanaians who believe in witchcraft are not being unreasonable: "What it's reasonable for you to think, faced with a particular experience, depends on what ideas you already have."[108] This recognition turns out to be an important piece of the cosmopolitan ethical picture. It clarifies that we must engage in cross-cultural conversation without necessarily expecting agreement.[109] To be a cosmopolitan does not require relativism about the truth—I am still entitled to believe that viruses affect health while witchcraft does not—but it does require a certain attitude toward reasonableness.

What is remarkable about the *Cosmopolitanism* passage on the reasonableness of witchcraft is how it differs from the passage in *The Ethics of Identity* on blood transfusions. Strictly speaking, the two passages do not contradict each other: according to Appiah, the falsehood of the Witnesses' view—not its unreasonableness—is what allows us morally to overrule it. (In this Appiah differs from Thomas Nagel, according to whom we have no need to justify the state's rational decisions in the face of irrational beliefs.[110]) But compare the attitudes in Appiah's two contemporaneous books. When it comes to making law, there are truths and falsehoods, winners and losers. The Witnesses have a moral right to be treated neutrally but not to win the argument, because (we assert) they are wrong about damnation. But when it comes to developing a cosmopolitan ethical attitude, we are urged to consider that the belief in witchcraft is no less reasonable than the (coincidentally true) belief in the germ theory of disease. The difference here depends on the distinction between the impersonal morality of the state and the deeply personalized ethic of cosmopolitanism.

This result is striking, to say the least. The respectful cosmopolitan attitude buys the minority little that is legally useful to them. Their particularity—in the sense of the ideas they "already have"[111]—is what makes their views reasonable; yet the state must ignore this particularity to fulfill its moral duty of neutrality. Even Appiah's concern to try to avoid coercing the Witnesses

---

107. *See id.* at 38-39.

108. *Id.* at 39.

109. *See id.* at 44.

110. *See* APPIAH, ETHICS OF IDENTITY, *supra* note 5, at 92-96 (discussing Thomas Nagel, *Moral Conflict and Political Legitimacy*, 16 PHIL. & PUB. AFF. 215 (1987)).

111. APPIAH, COSMOPOLITANISM, *supra* note 5, at 39.

comes not from his cosmopolitanism but from the liberal moral duty of equal respect.

Notice the difference between this outcome and the one that might be urged by an alternative cosmopolitan legal order. Beginning with Appiah's expansive cosmopolitan conception of reasonableness, we might conclude that the state should treat equally all conceptions of the world that are in this sense reasonable. If that were so, we could not so cavalierly dismiss the Witnesses' belief as false, and we could not so easily justify coercing them through the force of law. Cosmopolitanism of this sort, with legal teeth, would raise serious and difficult problems for explaining how it might ever be justified to coerce people who in practice do not accept the reigning orthodoxies of the state. It might lead us to the conclusion that the state in fact cannot coerce people who reject the grounds for coercion. That would mean that the government of a cosmopolis might be pretty weak internally when it came to certain outlying cases—but it would also be a government with very attractive and extensive respect for rights. Its affirmative responsibilities to give aid to people living elsewhere might not be very extensive, but its duty to respect the views of persons everywhere might well be rigorous.

The difficulty with applying Appiah's cosmopolitan ideas to law is also revealed when Appiah, in *Cosmopolitanism*, discusses the right regime to govern cultural patrimony. He adopts a cosmopolitan ethical standpoint,[112] one that pays attention both to local cultures and to the interest of people everywhere in being exposed directly to important art of all kinds. Appiah thinks that articles of cultural heritage should not themselves be repatriated, for they in some sense belong to humanity. But he also thinks Western museums should compensate the peoples whose artifacts they plundered by sending them world art, including Western art.[113] This is true cosmopolitanism: reasonable, worldly, and perhaps just the slightest bit utopian.

The result of this original and rather appealing analysis, however, is not a single legal or moral principle that must be applied by states. Instead we get a looser set of recommendations that states or international organizations would (by Appiah's lights) do well to consider. Laws could certainly be adopted that flow from Appiah's ethical arguments, but the justifiability of any coercion that followed would come not from the ethical character of the laws but from the moral justifiability of the entities that adopted them and their internal political procedures—no small concern in the realm of international law. The well-developed difference between the moral and the ethical in Appiah's writing

112. *See id.* at 126-27.

113. *See id.* at 122-24.

ultimately makes it difficult to think of cosmopolitanism as a source for justifying legal obligation.

IV. COSMOPOLITAN LAW

A. The Political Conception of Law

1. Political Association as a Condition of Law

To reexamine the question of cosmopolitan law, it is worthwhile to begin by reminding ourselves how we think law justifiably arises within the polis. The traditional liberal answer to why the state is justified in coercing us through law—and why we have a corresponding duty to obey the law, if we do—relies on consent. In one familiar version of the consent story, the polis itself is understood to arise out of collective agreement among autonomous individuals. Duly constituted by contractual agreement, the polis was from its very origin empowered to enact and apply coercive law subject to the limitation that it may not violate basic rights.[114] The consent could be presented as an event that actually occurred, either expressly or tacitly (the Lockean view), or it could be understood as hypothetical consent that a reasonable person would logically give (Kant's approach).[115] Either way, classical liberal theory makes entrance into political agreement a condition precedent for the imposition of justifiable legal duty.[116]

114. A related yet distinct answer, focusing on the "agency or will that is inseparable from membership in a political society," may be gleaned from Thomas Nagel, *The Problem of Global Justice*, 33 PHIL. & PUB. AFF. 113, 128 (2005). Technically, Nagel here is not justifying legal coercion in the first place but is giving an argument for why we are responsible for addressing arbitrary economic inequalities within a given political society in which coercive law already operates. In the course of so doing, however, he describes the state of membership in terms of the observation that "we are both putative joint authors of the coercively imposed system, and subject to its norms." *Id.* It is worth noting that Nagel downplays the element of consent in *entering* political society—he considers the act of membership accidental—while emphasizing the element of agency (and by implication, consent) that comes from *participating* in political society.

115. For this account of two forms of consent theory, see Leslie Green, Globalization, Disobedience, and the Rule of Law, http://www.law.nyu.edu/kingsburyb/fall06/globalization/papers/Leslie%20Green.pdf (last visited Jan. 31, 2007).

116. There are quirky cases like the legal duties of foreign visitors or residents. But it is customary (and somewhat plausible) to say that these individuals have also consented to be governed by their host country's law by being there, despite the fact that they have not entered into the political agreement that applies to citizens. *See* Jeremy Waldron, *Special Ties and Natural Duties*, 22 PHIL. & PUB. AFF. 3, 8-9 (1993).

In recent decades, skepticism about the mechanism of consent has given rise to a new set of liberal arguments designed to ground the justifiability of state coercion in some other moral framework. Such justifications grow out of doubt about whether tacit consent is meaningful and whether hypothetical consent can ever really do the work of consent at all. Aiming to avoid these problems, such theories do not rely on traditional notions of consent but rather on some other feature of membership in a political community that is thought to provide a ground for justifying coercion. Thus, for example, as part of his influential theory of law, Dworkin argues that "associative or communal obligations" provide the basis for justified state coercion.[117] When certain conditions of mutuality, concern, and respect apply, says Dworkin, people in communities have these associative obligations "whether or not they want them."[118] According to this view, the fact of associative membership is necessary to justify coercion. Absent such association, binding obligations cannot justifiably be conferred: "I would not become a citizen of Fiji if people there decided for some reason to treat me as one of them."[119]

Let us call a *political* conception of law any theory that makes either consent or some weaker form of communal association a condition of law.[120] Nussbaum seems to hold some version of this view, and something like it is also implicit in Appiah's view that legal obligation arises within states, not among them.[121] It has several important consequences for legal duties to people who are outside the polis – consequences that operate at the level of legal duties of both individuals and states.

It follows from a political conception of law that in the absence of political membership, there can be no justified legal duty.[122] According to the political

117. RONALD DWORKIN, LAW'S EMPIRE 196 (1986).

118. *Id.* at 201.

119. *Id.* at 202.

120. In *The Problem of Global Justice*, Nagel distinguishes between what he calls the political conception of justice and the cosmopolitan conception of justice. In his account, according to the political conception, justice properly speaking is a virtue of states. *See* Nagel, *supra* note 114, at 119-21. The political conception of legal duty that I am developing is a little different. It makes political agreement the condition for justified legal duty, but it admits of the possibility that this political agreement could be between states – hence the legal duties of international law could be thought to arise from the political theory of legal duty.

121. *See* APPIAH, ETHICS OF IDENTITY, *supra* note 5, at 246 ("[O]nce we are speaking not within but among polities, we cannot rely upon decrees and injunctions.").

122. Note that this view need not entail any commitment regarding whether law is best understood in positivist or interpretivist terms. The agreement that is a condition of justified legal duty according to this view is the political agreement to form or enter the polity, not an agreement about the content of law.

conception, individual legal duties justifiably arise toward individual people who live outside the polis only to the extent that such duties may be derived from legal duties that the state imposes on its own citizens, who belong to a political association and are therefore bound by its laws. Thus, the state may justifiably direct its citizens not to engage in certain harmful conduct wherever they might be and thereby create in its citizens a duty not to do certain kinds of harm even when they are outside the polis. The United States Congress may, for example, justifiably pass a law prohibiting its citizens from traveling abroad for the purpose of having sex with minors.[123] This law creates a legal duty to minors abroad—insofar as they encounter Americans.

As for the state, it may enact laws binding itself (through its own actors) from engaging in certain conduct, wherever it might be acting. A salient example in this context would be the statute recently enacted by Congress prohibiting government personnel from engaging in acts of torture anywhere.[124] This law also creates a duty that applies outside the polity insofar as Americans (in this case, government officials) are active there. A variant on this scenario is the entrance by the state into an international treaty obligation, such as the Convention Against Torture.[125] Even if the treaty is not self-executing, so that no individual legal duty arises absent the enactment of a separate statute, the state nevertheless incurs an international legal duty not to torture.[126]

---

123. *See* Prosecutorial Remedies and Other Tools To End the Exploitation of Children Today (PROTECT) Act of 2003, Pub. L. No. 108-21, 117 Stat. 650 (codified as amended in scattered sections of 18, 21, 28, and 42 U.S.C.).

124. Detainee Treatment Act of 2005, Pub. L. No. 109-148, div. A, tit. X, § 1003, 119 Stat. 2739, 2739-40 (codified at 10 U.S.C.A § 801 note and 42 U.S.C.A. §§ 2000dd to 2000dd-1 (West Supp. 2006)) ("No individual in the custody or under the physical control of the United States Government, regardless of nationality or physical location, shall be subject to cruel, inhuman, or degrading treatment or punishment.").

125. Convention Against Torture and Other Cruel, Inhuman or Degrading Treatment or Punishment, Dec. 10, 1984, S. TREATY DOC. NO. 100-20 (1988), 1465 U.N.T.S. 85.

126. One would think it obvious that this obligation applies everywhere. But astonishingly, the U.S. government has sometimes suggested otherwise. Article 2, section 1 of the Convention Against Torture states that "[e]ach State Party shall take effective legislative, administrative, judicial or other measures to prevent acts of torture in any territory under its jurisdiction," *id.* art. 2, § 1, and Article 16, section 1 adds that "[e]ach State Party shall undertake to prevent in any territory under its jurisdiction other acts of cruel, inhuman or degrading treatment or punishment which do not amount to torture," *id.* art. 16, § 1. The government has occasionally claimed that this language means the Convention does not apply to its activities outside "its jurisdiction"—i.e., the United States. *See* Letter from William E. Moschella, Assistant Attorney Gen., to Sen. Patrick J. Leahy, Ranking Minority Member, Senate Comm. on the Judiciary (Apr. 4, 2005), *available at* http://www.scotusblog.com/movabletype/archives/CAT%20Article%2016.Leahy-Feinstein-Feingold%20Letters.pdf; Marty

According to a political conception of law, however, a state could not justifiably enact or enforce laws governing the conduct of persons who have never been in political association with it. Congress, on this view, could not pass a law prohibiting just anyone from having sex with minors anywhere; it would be unjustified for the United States to enforce such a law against, say, a German citizen who had sex with a minor in Thailand. Unlike an American citizen, the German could not be said to have consented, actually or hypothetically, to be bound by U.S. law.

It is an important but easily overlooked feature of this theory that under it, logically there can be no law except where political association exists. Thus, according to the political conception of law, if the United States is under no international or domestic legal duty not to engage in certain conduct, that conduct necessarily remains unrestricted. Consider inhumane treatment that falls short of torture as defined by either positive or customary international law[127] and is outside the purview of the Eighth Amendment: if no law prohibits the U.S. government from engaging in the conduct, then according to the political theory of legal duty it remains lawful. This feature has been at the heart of the debate about recent legislation specifying U.S. obligations to detainees under the Geneva Conventions[128]: critics have argued that the legislation in effect permits (by not criminalizing) inhumane treatment that falls short of torture.[129]

Lederman, *Has Congress Prohibited "Torture Light"?*, Balkinization, May 11, 2005, http://balkin.blogspot.com/2005/05/has-congress-prohibited-torture-light.html. This seems to me a misreading.

127. The complex and important question of customary international law is beyond the scope of this Review. For our purposes it should suffice to note that just as the political conception of legal duty entails no commitment to one or another theory of the nature of domestic law, it also entails no necessary commitment to any theory about the nature or sources of international law. Customary international law could be understood as binding because state parties have actually or hypothetically consented to be bound by its norms by their entrance into the world community. *Cf.* Alvarez-Machain v. United States, 331 F.3d 604, 613 (9th Cir. 2003) (en banc), *rev'd sub nom.* Sosa v. Alvarez-Machain, 542 U.S. 692 (2004) (asserting that customary international law "derives solely from the consent of states").

128. The key pieces of legislation are the Military Commissions Act of 2006, Pub. L. No. 109-366, 2006 U.S.C.C.A.N. (120 Stat.) 2600 (to be codified in scattered sections of 10, 18, and 28 U.S.C.), which was signed on October 17, 2006, and the Detainee Treatment Act of 2005.

129. *See* Marty Lederman, *Senators Snatch Defeat from Jaws of Victory: U.S. To Be First Nation To Authorize Violations of Geneva*, Balkinization, Sept. 21, 2005, http://balkin.blogspot.com/2006/09/senators-snatch-defeat-from-jaws-of.html.

2. *The Political Conception and U.S. Law*

Does the political conception of legal duty underlie the practices of U.S. law? This is not at all clear. Consider the following formulation from section 402 of the *Restatement (Third) of the Foreign Relations Law of the United States*:

> Subject to § 403 [which prohibits jurisdiction when it would be "unreasonable" for a set of specified reasons], a state has jurisdiction to prescribe law with respect to
> (1) (a) conduct that, wholly or in substantial part, takes place within its territory;
> (b) the status of persons, or interests in things, present within its territory;
> (c) conduct outside its territory that has or is intended to have substantial effect within its territory;
> (2) the activities, interests, status, or relations of its nationals outside as well as within its territory; and
> (3) certain conduct outside its territory by persons not its nationals that is directed against the security of the state or against a limited class of other state interests.[130]

The *Restatement* is not (consciously) a book of moral philosophy. Nevertheless, this passage is intended normatively, and it makes sense only if construed as intended to give an account of where and to whom U.S. law may justifiably be applied.[131] Its logic corresponds closely to the political conception as I have presented it. The focus is first on the state's territory, the space in which the political association finds its primary expression; second on the "nationals" of the state, which is to say those who are directly implicated in the association; and third and most remotely on extraterritorial conduct by nonnationals that nevertheless directly affects the state or its (important) interests. Conduct abroad not involving the state or its citizens is putatively excluded.

Yet despite this formulation, some U.S. laws seem to go beyond a political conception of law by holding liable persons who have not entered into political association with the United States. The Alien Tort Statute (ATS) confers

130. RESTATEMENT (THIRD) OF THE FOREIGN RELATIONS LAW OF THE UNITED STATES § 402 (1987).

131. Thus if Congress were to pass a law that applied more broadly, the authors of the *Restatement* would presumably consider the law unwise and unjustified but not invalid or unconstitutional.

subject matter jurisdiction on U.S. courts to adjudicate cases in which noncitizens have violated either a U.S. treaty or "the law of nations," without regard to where that conduct has occurred.[132] Although the treaty regime or the law of nations might be said to derive from some form of international political association, at least some kinds of international law cannot be so derived. Federal law makes it a crime for anyone to kill—or even conspire to kill—Americans abroad.[133] This law embodies what is sometimes called the "passive personality principle," which might be justified under a political conception of legal duty on the ground that the state is protecting its citizens wherever they go. (Although it remains unclear why this self-protective motive justifies the imposition of duties on others.) The Torture Victim Protection Act goes further, creating civil liability in the U.S. courts against anyone who has engaged in extrajudicial torture or killing outside the United States under color of law.[134] Another U.S. law criminalizes hijacking an aircraft outside the United States.[135]

The *Restatement* provides a principle that covers such expansive exercises of extraterritorial jurisdiction:

> A state has jurisdiction to define and prescribe punishment for certain offenses recognized by the community of nations as of universal concern, such as piracy, slave trade, attacks on or hijacking of aircraft, genocide, war crimes, and perhaps certain acts of terrorism, even where none of the bases of jurisdiction indicated in § 402 is present.[136]

It seems possible that this formulation of universal jurisdiction, like the ATS that it arguably covers, does not rest on the political conception of legal duty. Persons subjected to liability under the terms of a U.S. treaty or even the law of

132. 28 U.S.C. § 1350 (2000) ("The district courts shall have original jurisdiction of any civil action by an alien for a tort only, committed in violation of the law of nations or a treaty of the United States."); *see also* U.S. CONST. art. I, § 8, cl. 10 (granting Congress the power "[t]o define and punish Piracies and Felonies committed on the high Seas, and Offences against the Law of Nations").

133. *See* 18 U.S.C. § 2332(a)-(b) (2000) (criminalizing murder of and conspiracy to murder a U.S. national outside the United States).

134. Torture Victims Protection Act of 1991, Pub. L. No. 102-256, 106 Stat. 73 (1992) (codified at 28 U.S.C. § 1350).

135. 49 U.S.C. § 46,502(b) (2000). On the history of this law and on extraterritorial enforcement more broadly, see Andreas F. Lowenfeld, *U.S. Law Enforcement Abroad: The Constitution and International Law*, 83 AM. J. INT'L L. 880 (1989).

136. RESTATEMENT (THIRD) OF THE FOREIGN RELATIONS LAW OF THE UNITED STATES § 404 (1987).

nations may never have entered into political association with the United States. It would appear that, when the crimes get serious enough, the baseline assumption of a political conception of law begins to be supplemented by something else.

Of course a political conception of legal duty *could* be at work here. International political agreements or duties arising out of the association of nations with each other ("the community of nations") might be the reason that prosecutions under universal jurisdiction are justified, and all persons might be understood to belong to such associations. But it seems at least a little far-fetched as an account of why it is justifiable to hold an individual—who, let us imagine, may be a stateless person like a pirate—liable for actions barred by a law derived from the association among states.

It is true that the U.S. legal principle of personal jurisdiction requires that a party either be in the United States or have substantial contacts with the United States before U.S. courts can apply to him laws such as the ATS.[137] One could perhaps argue, then, that the personal jurisdiction requirement incorporates the political conception of legal duty. Through its application, U.S. laws will be applied in U.S. courts only to persons who have entered into some sort of (limited) association with the state by being present therein.

The problem with this suggestion is that the ATS—like all U.S. laws—can be applied to persons who are unwillingly and even unlawfully present within the jurisdiction of the U.S. courts.[138] They might have been kidnapped ("*male captus*"), or extradited, or captured on the battlefield, or served with a subpoena while in the country on United Nations business, but in any case it is very difficult to claim that they have a political or communal association with the United States sufficient to make them subject to U.S. law. Even if such a claim could be sustained in the case of someone who kills a U.S. citizen—the doubtful theory being that by that act the killer associates himself with the community of persons subject to U.S. jurisdiction—it would not work, presumably, for a person who is abducted abroad, brought into the United States, and then subjected to jurisdiction.[139] This would surely be taking too far the theory of involuntary political association as a condition for legal duty.

---

137. *See, e.g.*, Int'l Shoe Co. v. Washington, 326 U.S. 310, 316-19 (1945).

138. This is the so-called Ker-Frisbie rule. *See* Frisbie v. Collins, 342 U.S. 519 (1952); Ker v. Illinois, 119 U.S. 436 (1886). On this rule, see Andreas F. Lowenfeld, *U.S. Law Enforcement Abroad: The Constitution and International Law, Continued*, 84 AM. J. INT'L L. 444, 460-67 (1990).

139. As was the case with, for example, the Panamanian dictator Manuel Noriega. *See generally* STEVE ALBERT, THE CASE AGAINST THE GENERAL: MANUEL NORIEGA AND THE POLITICS OF AMERICAN JUSTICE (1993) (explaining the legal proceedings against Noriega).

Furthermore, in the case of the ATS, even if the defendant enters the United States willingly, it is far from clear that by this act he associates himself with the United States in such a way as to justifiably be held liable for conduct he may have performed years before, outside the United States. In the extreme case, the conduct may have been lawful when it was performed but then became unlawful via a retrospective treaty conferring civil liability.[140] This does not look much like a political conception of law. It leaves us to wonder if some other theory might be at work.

B. *Cosmopolitan Law*

1. *Nature's Option*

How would a cosmopolitan conception of law differ from a political conception? A world government would create legal duties on all and toward all – and could do so without, in theory, violating the principle of political membership. Contractarian cosmopolitanism offers another possible version of cosmopolitan law, according to which all persons, wherever they are, are said to be sufficiently associated in the world community that the community may justifiably bind and coerce them through universal law. A world treaty arrangement might effect the same result in a less abstract manner. Its institutions could create political associations across borders sufficient to ground the conferral of legal duties on and toward all states or citizens.

But notice that these views, though undoubtedly cosmopolitan in their substance, essentially embrace the political conception of legal duty. Association is made the condition of legal duty – it is just that the association is extended globally, either through the original social contract or through some secondary contract among peoples or states. Legal coercion is said to be justified by virtue of participation in that border-transcending association.

I take it as given that political associations may, under the right conditions, justifiably make laws. I want to suggest, however, that it is possible to imagine – and subsequently to evaluate – a conception of law that is cosmopolitan in a different and arguably deeper sense. Such a conception would eschew the notion that law necessarily derives from political association, however extended. Perhaps the coercive imposition of legal duty could be justified on the basis of some other principle that would extend to people and

140. Following *Calder v. Bull*, 3 U.S. (3 Dall.) 386 (1798), retroactive civil liability has often been found not to violate the Ex Post Facto Clause or constitutional due process. *See, e.g.*, Landgraf v. USI Film Prods., 511 U.S. 244 (1994); United States v. Sperry Corp. 493 U.S. 52 (1989).

places everywhere, regardless of whether they had ever been in political association with each other; perhaps this principle would also justify a corresponding duty to obey certain laws.

What principle, then, would satisfy this cosmopolitan conception of law? One possible answer is that legal duty is justified insofar as it may be understood as a species of natural duty. It seems implausible to think that there could be a natural duty to comply with any old law promulgated by any old lawgiving entity. But perhaps some laws do rise to the level of justifiably mandating obedience as a matter of natural duty. If so, the duty to obey such a law could apply even if one had no association of any kind with the entity that brought the law into existence. The duty would apply everywhere, and to everyone. Such a conception of law would be distinctively cosmopolitan, not political in the sense I have been using of deriving from association.

What laws would fill this bill of mandating obedience as a natural duty? The most obvious and traditional answer—and one in some disrepute today—is that natural laws (laws inherent to the nature of humans and their relations) must be followed as a matter of natural duty, regardless of political association. As Nussbaum hints by pointing our attention to that great natural lawyer Grotius and then back to antiquity,[141] this would certainly have been the answer of the Stoic cosmopolitans, who were sympathetic to the notion of a universal law of nature. Another person who treats me with hostility, said Marcus Aurelius, must be met with the recognition of his common humanity. I must acknowledge that he "is from one of the same stock, and a kinsman and partner, one who knows not, however, what is according to his nature. But I know; for this reason I behave towards him according to the natural law of fellowship with benevolence and justice."[142]

This natural law deserves my obedience just because it is natural, and it certainly transcends political association. Indeed, this view of humans as belonging to a common stock tends to undercut the very notion of political duty by destabilizing the archetypal political distinction between friend and

141. *See supra* note 78 and accompanying text.

142. This is the felicitous translation of George Long, appearing in THE THOUGHTS OF THE EMPEROR MARCUS AURELIUS ANTONINUS 114 (George Long trans., Boston, Little, Brown & Co. 1891) (c. 161-180). For the Greek text, see MARCUS AURELIUS, THE COMMUNINGS WITH HIMSELF OF MARCUS AURELIUS ANTONINUS EMPEROR OF ROME bk. III, § 11, at 60 (C.R. Haines ed. & trans., Harvard Univ. Press 1916). Charles Haines translates this passage as: "while that comes from a clansman and a kinsman and a neighbour, albeit one who is ignorant of what is really in accordance with his nature. But I am not ignorant, therefore I treat him kindly and justly, in accordance with the natural law of neighbourliness . . . ." *Id.* bk. III, § 11, at 61 (emphasis omitted).

foe.[143] But Marcus Aurelius was not undermining the notion of *legal* duty. (After all, as emperor he was presiding over and contributing to the most advanced legal system the world had ever known.[144]) The reason Marcus Aurelius did not think he was weakening legal duty by weakening political duty is presumably that he did not believe the former was dependent on the latter. Rather, he likely thought that our obligation to perform legal duties, whether enacted by the emperor or otherwise, rested upon the natural law of human benevolence, not on promulgation by a political association.[145] Take the state away, and that duty would remain.

Closer to home than ancient Stoicism, the affinity between natural law theory and a cosmopolitan conception of legal duty may go some way toward explaining those elements of U.S. law that seem to rely on such a cosmopolitan conception of law. After all, the authors of the Declaration of Independence articulated a universal natural law ideal to justify what was otherwise an act of disobedience to the norms of the British Constitution. The U.S. Constitution itself studiously avoided the problem of natural law, but vestiges of natural law theory may be found in various places in our legal universe.[146] Natural law ideas have also come into play whenever complex problems of obedience to legal duty have arisen in American legal thought. Martin Luther King, Jr.'s *Letter from a Birmingham Jail*, with its dual appeal to the law of God and the laws of man, provides one of the most famous examples.[147]

Of course today it is at the very least unfashionable—and, given the great difficulty in identifying the laws of nature, very possibly irresponsible—to subscribe to the notion of natural laws. Our account of which laws mandate a natural duty of obedience will have to be more circumscribed and will have to

143. *Cf.* CARL SCHMITT, THE CONCEPT OF THE POLITICAL (George Schwab trans., Univ. of Chi. Press 1996) (1932).

144. *See* 1 THE SCRIPTORES HISTORIAE AUGUSTAE 157-63 (David Magie trans., Harvard Univ. Press 1921).

145. *See* THE THOUGHTS OF THE EMPEROR MARCUS AURELIUS ANTONINUS, *supra* note 142, at 114 (describing "the natural law of fellowship with benevolence and justice"); *id.* at 174 ("For there is one universe made up of all things, and one god who pervades all things, and one substance, and one law, [one] common reason in all intelligent animals, and one truth . . . ." (footnote omitted)).

146. *See, e.g.*, Lawrence v. Texas, 539 U.S. 558 (2003) (grounding the due process right to be free from prohibitions on consensual same-sex sexual conduct in an account of human functioning); Planned Parenthood of Se. Pa. v. Casey, 505 U.S. 833, 851 (1992) ("At the heart of liberty is the right to define one's own concept of existence, of meaning, of the universe, and of the mystery of human life.").

147. MARTIN LUTHER KING, JR., *Letter from a Birmingham Jail* (1963), *in* WHY WE CAN'T WAIT 77 (1964).

derive not from nature but from the inherent justice of those laws. Nevertheless, this possibility of a natural duty to obey at least some just laws, regardless of association with a political entity that enacted them, is not as outré as it might at first sound.

Building upon Rawls's view that the duty of justice is "a fundamental natural duty" requiring us "to support and to comply with just institutions that . . . apply to us,"[148] Jeremy Waldron has argued that "we have a *natural* duty to support the laws and institutions of a just state."[149] For Rawls, the words "apply to us" seem to capture some notion of political association. Waldron, too, acknowledges that there is something special about the duty to comply with just institutions that, in Rawls's phrase, "apply to us" in that we may be counted among the persons "in respect of whose interests a just institution is just."[150] But he extends this duty beyond borders to include what one might call the weakly cosmopolitan natural obligation not to interfere with just institutions in someone else's country, with which one has no particular political association.[151]

More important for our purposes, Waldron goes on to suggest that if an institution presents itself as capable of administering justice for some relevant range of persons and actually is capable of so doing, there may be some duty to support and comply with it, not only to refrain from interfering. He concludes that his theory of natural duty "envisages moral requirements binding us to a political organization . . . quite apart from our agreement to be so bound, and quite apart from any benefits the organization has conferred on us."[152]

What I am imagining as a cosmopolitan natural duty to comply with a just law, regardless of political association, builds upon but goes still further than Waldron's natural duty to obey the laws of a just state. For Waldron, the natural duty flows to the just state that promulgates the law, and that organization can only claim our compliance if it is actually capable of delivering on its promise of justice. It must, it seems, be a state or some other sovereign political institution to make its legal dictates binding. But the institutional pedigree of a law is not necessarily relevant to the existence of a natural duty to comply with it. In fact, I want to propose that there may be a natural duty to obey a truly just law even if it was not promulgated by a state (or states) at all.

148. RAWLS, *supra* note 15, at 115.

149. Waldron, *supra* note 116, at 3.

150. *Id.* at 19.

151. *See id.* at 13.

152. *Id.* at 20.

To see why this is so, consider why it is that Waldron makes the natural duty to obey a just law run to the state: it is because he is following Rawls's view (derived in turn from Hume[153]) that justice is the virtue of political organizations. It would, according to this view, be absurd to speak of a "just" law promulgated by anything other than a political organization. The feature of justice in a law is borrowed from the justice of the institution that gives the law life. But this view depends, I think, on the idea that laws properly so called always come into existence from the top down, from the commands of unitary sovereigns or sovereign-like entities capable of assuring cooperation. Waldron explains that assurance of cooperation is a key feature of justice, and he says that such assurance "can be provided only if the number of institutions addressing the problem . . . is limited (perhaps to one)."[154]

This need not be the case. Legal systems often come into existence piecemeal, first competing with other means of dispute resolution and of the exercise of power. The modern state may need to assert a monopoly on violence, but there can be (there were!) laws without modern states. Whether it is a medieval English king urging individuals to seek justice in his courts rather than in those of the feudal lords, or a *qadi* setting up shop to adjudicate disputes under Islamic law in the wake of the state's collapse in Somalia or Afghanistan, there are persons and institutions who do law in the absence of any political agreement—and their legal judgments are susceptible of being adjudged just or unjust.

Thus, when one initially powerless person or entity proposes some law, and many persons or states then develop the practice of complying with it, there can emerge a just norm that eventually may be enforced by a collectivity that has formed around the practice of compliance. Historically, this would be a king offering to dispense justice in a proto-state where a plurality of legal options exists, then gradually building his legal system until it eventually monopolizes justice. Today, it might be a Muslim scholar offering to decide a case between neighbors in Mogadishu where there is no functioning state at all, then finding that other scholars in similar courts did the same, until an association of such courts might make a claim to governing and reestablishing the state. Or it might be a group of countries establishing a particular dispute-resolution mechanism that eventually gains ground and comes to be seen as legally binding.

I mean to suggest that even before broad-based compliance has arisen in these cases—indeed, even if it never does arise—there are still laws in place that

153. *See* HUME, *supra* note 43, bk. 3, pt. 2, § 2, at 321-22.

154. Waldron, *supra* note 116, at 23.

may make a claim to obedience if in substance they are just. It would be a mistake, I think, to say that in any of these cases the initial proposal to do law is not susceptible of being described as just, and that only the fully developed, enforceable norm associated with a robust institution is capable of being so described. A feudal or royal court operating under conditions of legal pluralism is still doing law, even if it does not have a legal monopoly. An Islamic court is doing Islamic law even if there is no state that can enforce its judgments. A group of nations may be doing law even when there is no overarching international political association that can enforce the results reached by the court that has been created. In each of these situations, it would be strange to suggest that there is no law to consider just or unjust. A monopoly on force may be a condition of the modern state, but if I am right that there can be law without states, it is not the condition of law. In brief, a norm only modestly and incompletely enforced can be just, and it can be law.

Now if it is true that there can be just laws without states attached to them, then there could perhaps be a natural duty to obey some such laws. This natural duty would exist wholly outside of political association of any kind. In fact, such a natural duty to obey just laws may be especially salient when there is no single dominant political agreement, no effective modern state. This situation—the circumstances of justice for such laws, if you will—would obtain in failed states or quasi-anarchic situations. And it would obtain, *mutatis mutandis*, in the international sphere. Certain asserted international laws could be just, and there could be a natural duty to obey them, not because they derive from the political association of states, but simply because they are, in fact, just. These laws need not be backed by the threat of force from an overarching international association; but it might well be justifiable to enforce them through coercion.

2. *The Moral Argument for Universal Jurisdiction*

It is possible, then, to imagine a cosmopolitan conception of law that relies on a natural duty to comply with just laws. But what if we wish to avoid the difficult subject of natural duty altogether and postulate other versions of a cosmopolitan conception? One way to get at an alternative is to examine the legal doctrines that seem to rest upon such a conception and to try to uncover their theoretical roots.

Universal jurisdiction is the leading example of a legal doctrine that sits uneasily with the political conception of legal duty. The view associated with universal jurisdiction seems to be that all legitimate local legal systems ought to embrace some universal commitments to persons everywhere. But why?

It is of course possible that the laws to which universal jurisdiction applies are derived from the political association among all nations or persons—from, let us say, the international community.[155] But not everyone thinks that the international community is sufficiently powerful in associational terms to promulgate justifiably binding law in the way a state does; and on some important matters, it will be difficult to claim that a law actually has been promulgated at all. To see if it is possible to account for universal jurisdiction in such cases, it is worth asking whether there might be another explanation of the practice.

One alternative answer is to argue that legal systems must embrace certain universal commitments simply in virtue of being legitimate legal systems. To be a legitimate legal system, on this view, requires satisfying some basic moral requirements. Those requirements will add up to a moral account of what justifies the very undertaking of doing law, of coercing and demanding compliance. This account does not focus on the duty to comply with a system that satisfies these moral requirements. Instead it focuses on the justifiability of coercing people who, as a matter of luck, come into contact with the system. The justification for subjecting them to jurisdiction would derive from the cosmopolitan insight that the moral significance of persons or actions should not depend on accidents of place.[156] In other words, it would be morally arbitrary to exempt some persons from legal regulation just because of where they happened to live or where they happened to be when the system encountered them.[157]

Let me begin by sketching the claim that a legal system, to qualify as legitimate, must satisfy certain moral requirements.[158] I will not try to list all

155. This seems to be, for example, the view of the authors of *The Princeton Principles on Universal Jurisdiction*, which presents universal jurisdiction as a tool for vindicating "the fundamental interests of the international community as a whole." PRINCETON PROJECT ON UNIVERSAL JURISDICTION, *Introduction* to THE PRINCETON PRINCIPLES ON UNIVERSAL JURISDICTION 23 (2001).

156. *See id.* princ. 1.1, at 28 ("[U]niversal jurisdiction is criminal jurisdiction based solely on the nature of the crime, without regard to where the crime was committed . . . or any other connection to the state exercising jurisdiction.").

157. There could of course be pragmatic reasons for trying someone in the first instance in the jurisdiction where the crime occurred. But these concerns need not rise to the moral level, and according to the theory I am now sketching, it is the system in which the accused finds himself that must be justified.

158. I have in mind substantive requirements, not the procedural requirements described in Jeremy Waldron, The Concept and the Rule of Law, http://www.law.nyu.edu/clppt/program2006/readings/Concept%20and%20Rule%20of%20Law%20WALDRON.pdf (last visited Jan. 31, 2007).

such requirements here. But let us say that one such moral requirement is the one Appiah applies to the state: a legal system must not make morally arbitrary judgments among persons.[159] Another might be that heinous crimes—a category defined in moral terms—must not be left unpunished when the system has the capacity to punish them at reasonable cost. A third requirement might be that basic human rights must be protected.

These three moral requirements, which are only a subset of all the requirements one could imagine, should suffice to make out the basic argument I have in mind. There will no doubt be disagreement among legal systems about which distinctions among persons are arbitrary, which crimes are heinous, and what exactly counts as a basic human right. But no matter: we should be able to agree that no legal system that fails to satisfy some version of any of these three principles should be counted as a morally legitimate system.

Now consider the situation of a particular local legal system that finds itself seized of someone who has committed unquestionably heinous crimes. (The standard theory of universal jurisdiction includes piracy, hijacking, and other crimes notable mostly for occurring outside the boundaries of states; but it also includes genocide, presumably because it is thought to be so horrible.[160]) The system must not let these crimes go unpunished. It would be morally arbitrary to punish only nationals, not nonnationals, for these crimes.

Notice that this systemic approach differs subtly from the natural law view, embraced by both Grotius and Locke, that there is a natural right to punish that derives not from the state but from a prior natural right of the individual.[161] Both Grotius and Locke used natural law to explain why the state was justified in punishing foreigners who had not consented to be governed by the state's law. According to the view I am suggesting here, it is not that the state exercises its citizens' delegated right to punish, but rather that the act of establishing a legal system that exercises coercive power subjects the system itself to certain moral duties, among them the duty not to make morally arbitrary distinctions among persons.

---

159. *See* APPIAH, ETHICS OF IDENTITY, *supra* note 5, at 88-99, 228-30; *see also supra* text accompanying notes 95-98.

160. *See supra* note 136 and accompanying text (quoting the list of crimes in the *Restatement (Third) of the Foreign Relations Law of the United States* that may trigger extraterritorial jurisdiction).

161. For the parallel between Grotius and Locke, see RICHARD TUCK, NATURAL RIGHTS THEORIES: THEIR ORIGIN AND DEVELOPMENT 62-63 (1979). For the passages from Grotius's *De iure praedae*, see Benjamin Straumann, *The Right To Punish as a Just Cause of War in Hugo Grotius' Natural Law*, STUD. HIST. ETHICS, Feb. 2006, at 6-7, http://www.historyofethics.org/022006/StraumannRightToPunish.pdf. For Locke's passages, see LOCKE, *supra* note 67, bk. II, §§ 8-9, at 272-73.

If the legal system is to satisfy its requirements for moral legitimacy, it must therefore try to punish the offender, albeit without violating his basic human rights. It is not a satisfying answer to say that whether a nonnational may be tried is itself an instance of the question whether it would be morally arbitrary not to punish foreign nationals. Even if one were to concede that different moral standards are applicable to the question of the wrongfulness of the defendant's conduct or the propriety of holding him liable,[162] it still must be explained why it would not be arbitrary to punish one murderer and free another just because of the accident of where the crime was committed. The cosmopolitan would surely hold the view that the location of the crime is irrelevant: murder is as wrong here as in Persia.

The justifiability of coercive legal action in this instance does not rest primarily on the legal duty of the defendant. It is simply an accident that he has fallen into the hands of this legal system. It is his bad luck. Indeed, even if some legal wrong has been done in bringing him into custody—if he falls under the doctrine of *male captus*—this fact may also be morally arbitrary with respect to the system's duty to punish him. (This is the cosmopolitan moral insight behind the Ker-Frisbie rule, which allows a person to be subjected to jurisdiction even when he should not be in the United States.[163]) We are faced here with a case not dissimilar to the freeing of a murderer on a procedural technicality; and as we know, justifying such a decision on moral grounds will generally depend on some claim about the justice of the system. Here, the legitimacy of the system probably cannot withstand the decision to release the murderer because of his crime's accident of place.

Fully cashed out, this view would generate a cosmopolitan conception of legal duty insofar as each system would have the duty to apply its version of the set of universal laws to everyone with whom it comes into contact. According to this view, the cure for the quandary of failing to do justice to the people who fall outside a jurisdiction is simply to override the jurisdictional boundaries and do justice to all comers. The United States, accordingly, might not be warranted in enacting and then seeking to apply a traffic code purporting to govern the behavior of Germans in Thailand. But it might well be warranted in passing and applying laws that protect the universal human rights of all minors against forcible sexual exploitation. Human rights violations anywhere are the business of good persons—and good legal systems—everywhere.

162. This would be an example of what Liam Murphy calls non-monism in analysis—differentiating an institutional morality from a personal one. *See* Liam B. Murphy, *Institutions and the Demands of Justice*, 27 PHIL. & PUB. AFF. 251, 254-57 (1998).

163. *See supra* note 138 and accompanying text.

Notice that this universal jurisdiction idea, which is by no means fanciful, does not imply or require any institutions of world government. To the contrary, it leaves us with the local legal systems we have and seeks to have each of them do what is morally right. Something like this notion arguably inheres in the ATS's authorization of suits by one foreigner against another for violations of the law of nations that may have taken place outside the United States.[164]

The strongest theoretical argument against this kind of universal jurisdiction is that it conflates the moral wrongs done by human rights violators with legal wrongs and so assumes that any serious moral harm must be susceptible to legal sanction. In a sense this is a fair criticism. Nevertheless, the argument rests not on the notion that some wrongs are so grave that they must be unlawful, but rather on the proposition that actually existing legal systems must address grave wrongs that come before them if they are to justify their existence. Legality and morality are not wholly conflated. The universal moral principles enforced in various jurisdictions can be made known in advance. They will not reach all wrongs, only the most egregious. Those wrongs may be sanctioned, not because their doers have agreed to be bound but because it would be morally illegitimate for a just legal system to let them pass unpunished.

3. *Minimalist Legal Cosmopolitanism*

Although not unrealistic from the standpoint of implementation, the foregoing account of a cosmopolitan conception of legal duty derived from the theory of universal jurisdiction is nonetheless potentially quite radical in its practical reach. It could be used to expand universal jurisdiction to cover a broad range of crimes on which there is no international consensus. As a result, it is likely to be unpopular with those who fear expanding the grounds on which individuals may be subjected to the legal regimes of other countries. It could also lead to practical unworkability, with many courts attempting to try people all over the world, and odd forum-shopping distortions introduced by prosecutors, victims, and defendants alike. So it is also worth considering a more modest version of a cosmopolitan conception of legal duty.

Like the approach derived from universal jurisdiction, this approach would begin with an account of the morality of legal systems. But instead of focusing on the moral legitimacy of any one particular legal system, this approach—call it minimalist legal cosmopolitanism—would focus on the moral legitimacy of

164. *See supra* note 132 and accompanying text.

the summed set of all operating legal systems around the world. Although the point could be disputed, the suggestion here is that it is possible to consider a set of institutions taken as a whole and to deem the collective set legitimate or illegitimate. The intuition behind this claim is that frequently an institution taken in isolation does not claim to be able to satisfy the full range of conditions that would make it morally legitimate. Background conditions beyond the control of a particular institution, as well as the decisions and actions of persons outside the institution, may directly affect its moral legitimacy.[165]

The central claim of minimalist legal cosmopolitanism would be that we are justified in applying coercive law to particular persons in order to achieve the overall goal of rendering legitimate the entire global set of legal systems. The core insight behind such a minimalist cosmopolitan approach is the normative view that *some* law must apply to every person as well as to every action, either authorizing or prohibiting it. According to this view, no conduct or person should be deemed "off the grid," legally speaking, because of the morally arbitrary accident of where the person is or where the conduct occurs. The set of global legal systems would be morally illegitimate if it allowed law-free zones in which the accident of place or status meant that there was no law at all. Not all law must reach everywhere, but every place and person must be subject to some law.

It would be insufficient, according to this view, if the local law that did apply were wholly inadequate to satisfy basic substantive standards of moral legitimacy. For the summed set of legal systems to be legitimate, each person must be within the reach not just of some law, but of some morally adequate law. The argument I advanced for universal jurisdiction depended on the idea that a legal system that purports to coerce necessarily incurs certain moral obligations.[166] The argument here relies on the parallel idea that the summed set of legal institutions, taken as a whole, must satisfy some basic moral standards. The reason is not that these institutions are in any political association with one another, but simply that they coexist within the world and that their moral legitimacy cannot adequately be assessed in isolation. In this sense, minimalist legal cosmopolitanism shares with Nussbaum's capabilities approach a certain outcome orientation[167]: we can measure moral legitimacy by

165. Take, for example, a state's provision of asylum. If an asylum-seeker can get asylum in several places, the decision of a given state not to provide asylum seems to be morally unproblematic. But if no one else will provide asylum, the same policy of denial might begin to veer toward moral illegitimacy. (I am grateful to Stephen Holmes for the example.)

166. *See supra* Subsection IV.B.2.

167. *See supra* text accompanying notes 55-62.

whether individuals are being treated according to morally adequate legal standards.

This approach differs from universal jurisdiction, because in the world envisioned by minimalist legal cosmopolitanism, individual legal systems would ordinarily stick to applying their own local laws. But those local laws would be arranged and interpreted so as to avoid the anomaly of situations in which no law at all applies and in which failing to apply law would rise to the level of creating some moral illegitimacy in the set of all legal systems. If some local legal system refused to admit that its laws applied to a given (serious) situation, then other legal systems would, in a limited way, be justified in expanding their jurisdictions to fill the apparent gap. Indeed, there would exist a general moral duty that at least one legal system extend itself to fill it, provided of course that the gap be important enough that its continued existence would undercut the moral legitimacy of the whole summed set of systems. There would not need to be a single principle of universal jurisdiction, but *some* jurisdiction would apply everywhere. The result would preclude the possibility of legal vacuum—a possibility that could logically arise under the political conception of legal duty. No place on earth[168] would be treated as a law-free zone.

The Rome Statute of the International Criminal Court (ICC) arguably enacts a version of this sort of minimalist legal cosmopolitanism.[169] Although the ICC is sometimes depicted in the United States as the harbinger of universal jurisdiction, in fact its jurisdiction kicks in only when a local legal system has inadequately addressed a major and serious crime (crimes against humanity, war crimes, genocide, or aggression), by failing either to prohibit the conduct or to bring an offender to justice.[170] The ICC therefore functions as a stopgap to fill legal vacuums that are treated as morally illegitimate. It would of course be possible to have minimalist legal cosmopolitanism without an international organization stepping in to fill local gaps. The gaps could be filled locally. But it is easy to see that there is a practical benefit to a single entity's playing this role, provided it has adequate resources and performs well.

Guantánamo Bay gives us an illustrative example of what minimalist legal cosmopolitanism would look like in practice at the local level. In front of the Supreme Court, the Bush Administration maintained that Guantánamo was not governed by U.S. law, but also was not governed by Cuban law because it

---

168. International space law lies outside the bounds of this Review.

169. Rome Statute of the International Criminal Court, July 17, 1998, 2187 U.N.T.S. 90.

170. *Id.* arts. 5, 17.

was leased in perpetuity from the predecessor government of Cuba.[171] (The island of Diego Garcia, leased by the United States from the British Crown, is another example of a spot where the "off the grid" argument could be mounted;[172] there are persistent reports of secret U.S. detention facilities there.[173])

Minimalist legal cosmopolitanism would hold that it is justified and indeed obligatory for *some* law to apply in Guantánamo. It is possible to interpret the Court's decision in *Rasul v. Bush* along these lines. Although a precedent of the Court had denied that the federal habeas corpus statute applied in Guantánamo[174] (which was the reason the government had put the detainees there in the first place), the Court bent over backwards to distinguish that case, all but overruling it.[175] The Court asserted that the United States exercised effective control over Guantánamo and that the federal habeas law therefore applied there.[176]

These statements suggest that the Court did not want to accept the government's argument that Guantánamo is a place where no law applies. The Justices' motivation could have been simply that such a holding would render U.S. law morally illegitimate; but even this view suggests that the illegitimacy would be part of a broader international problem about the legitimacy of the set of all legal systems. Allowing such a gap would have invited the international community to attempt to plug it in some way.

A different version of the argument against legal gaps may be seen in *Hamdan v. Rumsfeld*.[177] This time the government maintained not that a place was off the legal grid, but that certain persons were: it asserted, inter alia, that no provision of the Geneva Conventions applied to "enemy combatants"

171. *See* Rasul v. Bush, 542 U.S. 466, 480-81 (2004).

172. *But see* R (Bancoult) v. Sec'y of State, [2001] Q.B. 1067 (U.K.) (holding that persons expelled from Diego Garcia by the Crown were entitled to redress as "belongers" to territory under the Queen's jurisdiction). *Bancoult* was decided on facts that applied before the United States leased the island.

173. *See, e.g.*, Dana Priest & Scott Higham, *At Guantanamo, a Prison Within a Prison: CIA Has Run a Secret Facility for Some Al Qaeda Detainees, Officials Say*, WASH. POST, Dec. 17, 2004, at A1.

174. *See* Johnson v. Eisentrager, 339 U.S. 763 (1950).

175. *See Rasul*, 542 U.S. at 475-79.

176. *See id.* at 480-85. In *Rasul*, it was not necessary for the Court to decide whether, in the absence of a statute, the Constitution would have applied in Guantánamo. But with Congress's subsequent enactments restricting the statutory reach of habeas to detainees held outside the United States, *see* sources cited *supra* note 128, it may still be necessary for the Court to reach this issue in a further case.

177. 126 S. Ct. 2749 (2006).

captured on the battlefield in Afghanistan.[178] Once again, the Court rejected the government's view. It held narrowly that Common Article 3 of the Geneva Conventions did apply to the detainee in question and to others similarly situated.[179]

What makes this view cosmopolitan, despite its reliance on U.S. laws implementing Common Article 3, is its normative suggestion that as a citizen of the world, I should always be protected by some law – in this case provisions of international law codified by U.S. statutes. This is not, or at least not necessarily, because I owe or am owed some political duty to the polis in that place, nor is it because some agreement unites the world. It is because law ought to protect the citizen *of* the world everywhere *in* the world.

On this view, legal duties still correspond to political boundaries. But jurisdiction is not a moral or theoretical consequence of borders; it is a practical consequence of them. To a cosmopolitan, we are only accidentally citizens of states. We are not, however, only accidentally bound by laws. Wherever we go, some law should find us and bind us.

CONCLUSION

At its irreducible core, cosmopolitanism demands that general human qualities be put ahead of particular allegiances. Notwithstanding the rooted cosmopolitanisms of Nussbaum and Appiah, it follows that, through the heuristic device of the "citizen of the world," cosmopolitanism does intend to weaken somewhat our sense of the primacy of political obligation. It is therefore intriguing that, taken on its own terms, the cosmopolitan attitude does not weaken *legal* obligation the way it does particular *political* bonds. One might imagine that given the close association between the polis and the law, weakening bonds to the one might weaken the sense of duty to the other. Yet there is no discernible antinomian thread in the cosmopolitan tradition.

Why doesn't cosmopolitanism weaken legal obligation alongside political obligation? The reason lies, I think, precisely in its stubborn insistence that the state is not the right level of analysis for making sense of our lives and obligations, even our legal obligations. For the cosmopolitan, there is no weakening of legal duty when one turns away from the state because legal duty

178. *See id.* at 2794-96; *see also* Memorandum from Jay S. Bybee, Assistant Attorney Gen., to Alberto R. Gonzales, Counsel to the President, and William J. Haynes II, Gen. Counsel, Dep't of Def. (Jan. 22, 2002), *available at* http://www.washingtonpost.com/wp-srv/nation/documents/012202bybee.pdf (articulating this argument in more detail).

179. *See Hamdan*, 126 S. Ct. at 2796-97.

does not ultimately derive from the state—nor, one might add, from fear of punishment by it.

Cosmopolitanism has always been interested in the predicament of the stranger, whether it is the expatriate who has abandoned his state to become a citizen of the world or the inwardly exiled philosopher who has weakened his affective bonds to the political community. I have argued in this Review that the emphasis on the stranger may also suggest some theories that would account for our legal duties to the stranger, and his to us.

Law, on the account I have offered, contains at once the commands of a particular community and an aspiration to the universal. Diogenes the Cynic made a characteristically barbed comment that may be read to incorporate this duality of the global and the local. "[I]t is impossible," he said, "for society to exist without law."[180] Yet at the same time, "there is no advantage in law without a city."[181] Law, in its purest and most general sense, is the condition for civilization itself. But the institutions that apply law best are in the end political ones; and without them, the best legal principles can give humans no advantage.

180. DIOGENES LAERTIUS, *supra* note 7, bk. VI, para. 72, at 75.

181. *Id.*

Name Index

FSC
www.fsc.org
MIX
Papier | Fördert gute Waldnutzung
FSC® C083411

Kolibri 360 GmbH
Ferdinand-Jühlke-Straße 7
99095 Erfurt, Deutschland
produktsicherheit@kolibri360.de